John James
Audubon
A Biography

John James Audubon
A Biography

by Alice Ford

Abbeville Press • Publishers • New York

Front cover:
John Syme
John James Audubon, 1826
Oil on canvas, 35½ × 27½ in.
The White House, Washington, D.C.

Editorial director: Walton Rawls
Editor: Amy Handy
Copy editor: Don Goddard
Art director: Howard Morris
Designer: Stephanie Bart-Horvath
Production manager: Dana Cole

Library of Congress Cataloging-in-Publication Data

Ford, Alice, 1906–
  John James Audubon: a biography / Alice Ford.
    p.   cm.
  Bibliography: p
  Includes index.
  ISBN 0-89659-744-X
  1. Audubon, John James, 1785–1851. 2. Ornithologists—
  United States—Biography. 3. Artists—United States—
  Biography. I. Title.
QL31.A9F63   1988
598.092′4—dc19
[B]   88-955
                                                    CIP

Contents

Illustrations

Acknowledgments

France

Archevêché, Archives, Nantes
Archives de la Charente-Maritime, La Rochelle
Archives de la Marine, Archives Municipales, Rochefort-sur-Mer
Archives de la Marine, Lorient
Archives Departémentales, Municipales, and La Préfecture, Nantes
Archives de la Roche-sur-Yon
Archives Nationales, Paris
Bibliothèque, Ministère de la France d'Outre-Mer, Paris
Bibliothèque Nationales, Paris
Lavigne Estate, Couëron
Musée de l'Histoire Naturelle, Paris
Service Historique de la Marine, Paris

Mademoiselle Geneviève Beauchesne
Monsieur Henri de Berranger
Mademoiselle Jacqueline Bodin
Marquise de Chasseloup Laubat
Monsieur Gabriel Debien
Mademoiselle Odette Du Puigaudeau
Monsieur Marcel de la Fosse
Abbé Joseph Jugeau
Madame Henri Lavigne
Mademoiselle Marie-Gabrielle Madier
Mademoiselle Marie-Antoinette Ménier
Madame Nicole Tourneux

Great Britain

British Museum Library and Archives, London
Chetham's Library, Manchester
Derby Public Library
Friends Library, London
Lichfield Public Archives
Linnaean Society, London
Liverpool Public Library Archives
Royal Museum, Edinburgh
Royal Society, London
Somerset House, London
University of Edinburgh, Archives
University of Liverpool, Library
University of Liverpool, Department of Fine Arts
York Public Library, Archives

S. P. Bland, Esq.
Mrs. Thomas Campbell
C. P. Finlayson, Esq.
F. Fisher, Esq.
Robert Kennedy, Esq.
Mrs. Sybil Le Brocquy
Douglas G. Lochhead, Esq.
Miss Hilda Lofthouse
Miss Ada S. MacDonald
Sir Alan Hilary Moore
Miss Dorothy Norman
Mrs. Sybil Rathbone
Mr. and Mrs. Neville Stokoe
Mrs. Yvonne Waterton
T. Wragg, Esq.

United States

Alabama State Archives, Montgomery

American Museum of Natural History, New York
American Philosophical Society, Library, Philadelphia
Audubon Memorial Museum, Henderson, Kentucky
Audubon Shrine, Audubon, Pennsylvania
Beinecke Library, Yale University, New Haven
Buffalo Museum of Natural History
Cincinnati Historical Society
Cincinnati Public Library
Filson Club, Louisville, Kentucky
Frick Art Reference Library, New York
Friends Historical Library, Swarthmore, Pennsylvania
Grey Art Gallery, New York University
Haverford College Library, Haverford, Pennsylvania
Historical Society of Pennsylvania, Philadelphia
Houghton Library of Harvard University, Cambridge
Library of Congress, Washington, D.C.
Los Angeles Athletic Association
Massachusetts Historical Society, Boston
Metropolitan Museum of Art, New York
Missouri Historical Society, St. Louis
Montgomery County Historical Society, Norristown, Pennsylvania
Munson-Williams-Proctor Institute, Utica, New York
National Archives, Washington, D.C.
National Audubon Society, Library, New York
Newberry Library, Chicago
New-York Historical Society
New York Public Library
Pierpont Morgan Library, New York
Presbyterian Historical Society, Library, Philadelphia

Princeton University, Library
Schenectady Historical Society
Smithsonian Institution, Library, Washington, D.C.
Stark Foundation, Orange, Texas
United States District Court, Philadelphia
Western Reserve University, Library, Cleveland
E. Weyhe Gallery, New York
Winterthur Museum, Library, Wilmington, Delaware

Mrs. Barbara Adams
Mr. Stanley Clisby Arthur
Mrs. Donald Bakewell
Mr. Peter Brannon
Mrs. Thomas Burgess
Mrs. Leroy Burris
Mr. Albert Bush
Mrs. Elizabeth Carroll-Horrocks
Mrs. Annie Roulhac Coffin
Mrs. Seth Dennis
Mrs. Ruth Duncan
Mr. Henry Francis du Pont
Mr. Edward Dwight
Miss Hazel Gay
Mr. Edward W. Graham
Mr. Bradley Grisson
Dr. Francis Hobart Herrick
Mrs. Gertrude Hess
Dr. William Lingelbach
Mr. Savoie Lottinville
Mr. Albert Lownes
Mrs. Blanche Manion
Mr. and Mrs. H. Bradley Martin
Miss Grace Mayer
Mrs. Margaret Edwards McCormick
Dr. Walter Muir Mitchell
Mr. J. d'Arcy Northwood
Mr. Thomas Clinton Pears III
Mr. Walton Rawls
Mrs. Helen Marbury Raymond
Mr. William Reese
Mrs. Theodore Douglas Robinson
Countess Monica de la Salle
Miss Susan Lewis Shaffer
Mr. William Bakewell Shaffer, Jr.
Mr. James P. Shyrock

Dr. Frank K. Sommer III
Miss Ruth Sparrow
Mrs. Willman Spawn
Mrs. Lutcher Stark
Mrs. Beatrice Taylor
Mr. Samuel W. Thomas

Dr. Patricia Trenton
Mr. Morris Tyler
Mr. Victor Morris Tyler
Mr. Owen Wister
Miss Marjorie Wynne

For the rejuvenation of *John James Audubon* in this new, truly comprehensive edition after more than two decades since its first appearance, Walton Rawls of Abbeville Press deserves much recognition. Discoveries that came to light during that interval might, but for his interest, never have been freed from obscurity. For her praiseworthy editorial services Amy Handy is entitled to special thanks and appreciation.

Alice Ford

John Woodhouse Audubon. John James Audubon, *c. 1843*. *Oil on canvas. Courtesy Department of Library Services, American Museum of Natural History, New York.*

PART ONE: BIRD OF PASSAGE

I. Three Worlds

L IKE AN INDIAN ON THE TRACE, the painter of birds, victim
of mischance, fled a shadow, a secret all his days, leaving
behind a trail of absurd contradictions.

How to begin, and where, and without recourse to imag-
inings and whimsical interpretation? Where, if not with the
salt of the Breton earth, or the salt air of the seafaring men of
La Vendée? Yet the affinity of John James Audubon was for
neither. His passion crossed with wild nature to create *The
Birds of America*, his "great Book."

Les Sables d'Olonne, the Seashore of d'Olonne, lies on an
arc of dunes along the Bay of Biscay. Gulls wheel and whine
above the broad gleaming phalanx of surf that rides in and
crashes on the strand. The waters fall trancelike, curl, boil,
eddy, then disappear beneath another and yet another white-
capped line. Salt marshes, small lakes, and green lowlands
reach eastward into the earldom of La Vendée.

When Les Sables d'Olonne began is time's secret. With
Basque fishermen found there by the Romans? Howsoever

that may be, it remained a simple settlement until, in the six-teenth century, fortification for civil war lent it an official air. Its fishing fleets began to grow rich on the catches of New World waters.

A decline began on a day in 1751 when a storm swept in from the Bay, battered away a part of the town, and snapped the cables of fifteen ships. The building of a walled inner basin approached by a narrow canal was not, after that, enough to protect the town from the winds of change. Even before the onset of the Revolution, blunders of the monarchy promised its downfall.

A century later, Les Sables d'Olonne became a watering place, traces of which remain visible to this day.

Brightly painted fishing boats whose oculi give the evil eye to the dangers of the deep lie at anchor or beached while nets dry on the cobblestones around the crowded market stalls. A forest of masts with reefed sails rises from boats whose stir-rings bring in the tang of the open sea. Bustling markets, at the center, nestle about the gray Renaissance bulk of Notre-Dame de l'Espérance (Our Lady of Hope), from whose high arches within hang ship model ex-votos.

Before the high altar of the church, of which an Audubon was at one time vicar, the great-grandparents of the painter were married in 1697, uniting venerable lines of marine cap-tains.[1] Pierre Audubon and Louise Tasseron were both sired by captains of the long-course fishing fleet. Their son Pierre took for his bride, in August 1737, Anne Martin, daughter of a captain who dowered her with a thousand pounds in goods and silver. The wedding drew relatives and friends from inland Luçon and also from the village of La Chaume a little down the coast. These were by no means the "humble folk" of the autobiographical sketch "Myself" by Audubon the painter, much as, for reasons of his own, he wished the world to believe it. The signatures of witnesses—town officials, doctors, notaries, and lawyers—are proof to the contrary.

Jean, son of that union, was born on October 11, 1744, after the death of two infant brothers. He was to be the father of the painter Audubon. Even before his birth he was destined to follow the family tradition. In April 1757, at thirteen, when France and England were at war for control of the Atlantic, he went with his father for the first time to fish for cod off Louisburg in the waters of Cape Breton. Homeward bound a year and a half later, at Quebec, a little before the defeat of Montcalm and his French army, they were seized along with their *Marianne* and borne off to prison in England. They had three years in which to recover from their wounds before going home.

Pierre, his health broken, had had his fill of the merchant marine. Put aside forever were thoughts of returning to the house he had bought in Les Cayes, Saint-Domingue (now Haiti) as a young fortune hunter in the Antilles. Jean, on the other hand, though weakened in one leg, hoped to visit the islands some day. Meanwhile, he signed on for three voyages to Newfoundland as an apprentice sailor. It was not until he reached young manhood that he made his first voyage to Saint-Domingue and began to think of making many more, and a decent fortune.[2]

The short, stocky, sandy-haired, gray-eyed twenty-seven-year-old Jean Audubon was bound for Les Cayes in July 1772 when his cargo ship *La Dauphine* put in to load wine at Paimboeuf, the last river port before the open Atlantic. He was impatient to finish the job and return to Les Cayes and the welcome that he could count on from the planter Gabriel Bouffard, his regular host. The quadroon daughters of his friend, a native of La Rochelle, had promised a welcome as warm as the one before.

The pause was neither as brief nor as uneventful as expected. When he returned to the helm in September he was a bridegroom.[3] It was the work of his employers, the wine exporters Coiron Frères of Nantes, up the Loire. They thought to do him a favor by urging him to call on one of their prosperous investors, the cordial widow Anne Moynet, whose husband, George Ricordel, ship carpenter and property owner, had left her the small fortune bequeathed to him by his first wife.[4] Childless, practical, and twelve years Jean Audubon's senior, she recognized the ruddy-cheeked, affable young officer as the ideal partner for the realization of her own ambitions. He reciprocated so willingly that only a search for the record of his baptism in Luçon, and the issuance of a special certificate of birth to end the suspense, delayed the wedding. Banns were published, and in August invited guests gathered for the ceremony held at the Church of Saint Opportune. Her father, the Nantes wine merchant François Moynet, and Audubon's sister, Marie-Anne-Claire of Les Sables, were present.

Wedding and grape harvest over, wine pressed and put aboard in casks, the bridegroom, without his bride, slipped away to resume his journey across the ocean.

Les Cayes, port town, reposes in an Elysium of fertile emerald valleys. It was, and is, low-lying, graceful, lethargic. To Port-au-Prince, far north and populous even then, and like some Tartar camp, it bore no resemblance. A congeries of plantations spread in all directions. The buccaneering, freebooting era of Spanish rule that followed the discovery by Columbus was long past. Many planters and merchants, who were sometimes both, belonged to the second or third generation born since Spain ceded half of the island to France.

Pride of the world ruled. Rival interests divided white society; wealth could be judged by the number of slave huts, horned cattle, mules, and horses on each plantation. Officials outranked professionals, who in turn rated higher than merchants. Because merchants were permitted by law to set prices, planters were obliged to build their own warehouses and stores if they hoped to prosper. No amount of wealth or success made a merchant the equal of the bluebloods. Audubon's friend Bouffard had discovered this not long after he and his brother Etienne left the Charente-Maritime in France to become stone masons and builders in Les Cayes in 1755.[5] Etienne had given up and returned home. Gabriel took up with a woman of color, with whom he lived openly and had a large family. He prospered as planter and merchant but remained something of a pariah. Under the law, common marriage was all that was possible; church law ruled out baptism of natural children.

Nonetheless, the family Bouffard lived in mutual love and devotion. It could be argued that there was more harmony and dignity among them than in many of the supposedly more respectable *ménages*. By 1772, Augustin, "Sanitte," Rose, Lorimée, Bonne, and Marie-Louise had been born to Françoise. Augustin was preparing to take his mistress, Marguerite Deller, and a "favorite," also named Françoise, of the Ilo Nation, to live on another plantation owned by Bouffard at Cavaillon in the highlands.[6]

"Sanitte," named either Marguerite or Catherine—no one any longer remembered which—had grown in awareness since Audubon's last visit. There was an attraction, such as was felt by many a colonist, for the alluring dusky girls in their long, full, striped or figured skirts and bright bandanas set off by brass earrings. Audubon counted himself lucky to be amongst them, enjoying their warm smiles, their grace, their delicious *calaloux* redolent of garlic and pimiento. On their heads they often bore trays of pomegranates, figs, bananas, oranges, and sweetmeats. No wonder they were anathema to the tedious creole coquettes, who never ceased to flaunt their ways, their huge, flattering straw hats, their bare feet and swing.

This time Audubon spent a year in the *casa* of Bouffard. It was located in one of a string of loosely joined settlements of Les Cayes du Fond de l'Isle à Vache, the strip of coast opposite the great reefs of the offshore island called Isle à Vache (Cow Island), eight miles out to sea. His mind set on becoming a planter and slaveholder here among his friends, Audubon was oblivious to, or at any rate undeterred by, the tensions among those of color. Blacks, or "bossals," hated their free mulatto brothers who curried favor among the whites. They dreamt of a black messiah who would lead them out of bondage and wipe away the memory of seizure and of death in the holds of slave ships. The burning brand, the whip of the auctioneer and overseer, the merciless sun on bare backs in the fields, the tearing apart of families, the flagrant corruption of black daughters and granddaughters by white overseers and planters could not go on forever. But Audubon, looking on the bright side through the eyes of the Bouffards, understood none of this yet.

Returning to Nantes and to Anne in 1773, he spent his half year there preparing for his next West Indian voyage. Anne was probably no less eager than he for the wealth that Saint-Domingue could provide, even if the cost were to be long separation. So, in the spring of 1774 he boarded the ship *Marquis de Levy* for another journey west.

At the port of St. Louis he learned of the death of Louis XV at Versailles. The ascension to the throne of the poorly educated Louis XVI inspired only gloomy prospects. No matter, Audubon did not intend to surrender his dream. He remained resolute even when informed that a new head tax on slaves could prove more defeating than the dwindling supply of slaves themselves. Importuned by the cheerful Bouffard to remain at Les Cayes, he promised to return before he made his unexpectedly swift arrangements for cargo and left for Nantes. With him he brought a slave, Elizabeth, promised to Anne.

His share in the voyage, and in his next commissioned call on the island as captain of a privateer in which he had acquired a substantial interest, enabled Audubon to reappear in Les Cayes after only seven weeks in Nantes. With his profits he bought a plantation in the settlement known as Perche, close to the Bouffards.

When he headed for Nantes in the autumn of 1775 at the helm of the ship *Les Bons Amis*, Sanitte, his housekeeper and *ménagère*, was with child.

Anne, though the daughter of a vestryman, knew how to swim with the tide. Cheerfully she invested in his next commission before her ambitious mate sailed down the Loire again, this time as captain and part owner of the *Comte d'Artois*. In the *casa* at Perche, his first-born, Marie-Madeleine, awaited him. The place of Sanitte was by now sure, and the past year and a half with Anne forgotten for a time. When he departed in February 1777, Sanitte was again with child.

News of the purchase of a plantation, a sugar refinery, and a store, all of which promised a yearly profit of ten thousand francs, apparently eased the pain of whatever rumors may have reached Anne. Her faith in his fortunes and the partnership itself had lost none of their durability.

But Audubon's cares were to grow. He was back with his island family in 1778, but unrest in France, and on Saint-Domingue, generated deep fears for the plantation. Before leaving for Nantes again in the spring of 1779, Jean sold his own interest in the ship *Comte d'Artois* to two slave-trading partners who were also exporters, friends, neighbors, and trustworthy men. He accepted their promissory note and was off again.

Audubon was well out to sea on the twelfth day of May when an English privateer approached his heavily armed, overloaded vessel. The battle was over almost before it began. He had little more than attempted to set the *Comte d'Artois* on fire when it was under tow and on its way to Portsmouth, England, and early destruction. With his frightened crew he was borne off to jail in British-occupied New York City.

After attempting to obtain indemnity for a loss that he feared he himself might have to bear, Audubon was granted amnesty under the aegis of Ambassador de la Luzerne. He strode out of prison determined to avenge himself after this second imprisonment by an old enemy. The American Revolution was about over when he joined the French fleet under the Count de Rochambeau in Philadelphia. As commander of the corvette *Queen Charlotte* he witnessed the surrender of Lord Cornwallis at Yorktown on October 19, 1781.

After the war, opportunities abounded for mariners of his experience who wished to return to France. Audubon applied to David Ross & Company of Richmond, Virginia, and was promised a share in a shipload of tobacco on the *Annette*, which he sailed to Nantes.[7] Relieved that his life had been spared when he lost the *Comte d'Artois*, that he was out of prison, and that his new American connection assured him of more commissions, Anne greeted him again with tolerance, though it is hard to imagine that word of his liaison in

Les Cayes had not reached her ears since last they met in 1778.

In Les Sables d'Olonne, Audubon went about settling the estate of his mother, who had died during his absence. He then brought his sister Marie-Anne-Claire, a spinster of thirty-seven, back to Nantes with him to be Anne's companion, and he acquired La Gerbetière, a villa nine miles down the Loire near the village of Couëron.[8] Some years earlier the Audubons had bought lots nearby on the owner's promise that he would one day sell them the villa. As their new home was being readied, orders arrived from Ross & Company for Jean to sail their ship the *Queen* back to Richmond.

The ship was near Brest, off the coast of Brittany, when an English privateer loomed up from nowhere. The *Queen*'s cannon beat off the intruder, but the narrow escape bothered Audubon less than whether he could collect from Ross, already his debtor, for the cost of repairs.

It was during Jean's next stay in France that Jean-Baptiste Le Jeune de Vaugeon, a widower[9] and father of three children—the eldest of whom was six—married Marie-Anne-Claire Audubon. The marriage, celebrated on September 18, 1783, at the church of Saint Clément in Nantes, represented a slight step downward for Le Jeune, at least from the point of view of his first wife's noble blood.[10] But class distinctions mattered a good deal less in Brittany than in the North. Only the scion of a family inherited wealth. His brothers, if any, married a fortune if they could, or, perforce, the daughter of an honorable fellow parishioner of lowly birth. With luck, she might be the daughter of a tanner, one of the bourgeoisie whose means allowed engaging in trade and, perhaps, growing rich.

The dowry of Marie-Anne-Claire reflected the modest but respectable circumstances of her late parents. Captain Audubon gave her away. The first to sign the register was his cousin Captain Louis Papineau of Les Sables d'Olonne, whose wife Elizabeth Priou had numerous cousins in Les Touches, parish of the bridegroom. Most of them were cousins or relations of Madame Audubon and her parents François Moynet and Julienne Richard. Charles Coiron, the wine exporter who had brought Audubon and Anne together, signed next. Coiron now hired Audubon to take full charge of a shipment of wine for Les Cayes and to handle his affairs on the island.

On October 23 the ship *Le Conquérant* left the Quai de la Fosse for the port of Paimboeuf and the Atlantic. Captain Jean-Louis-Antoine Lefêbvre, brother-in-law of Charles Coiron, owned a plantation in the same district as Bouffard and Audubon. At the head of the list of passengers[11] were the names of Jacques Pallon de la Bouverie—retired court lawyer of St. Louis (Les Cayes' twin port)—his wife Rose Génerès, and their daughters, aged nineteen, fifteen, and twelve, who were returning to St. Louis after five years in the province of Navarre. Accompanying them was "Jeanne Rabin, twenty-five, chambermaid, of the parish of Les Touches, the diocese of Nantes."[12] The clerk took her pronunciation of her name, "Rah-been," for feminization of Rabin, an old custom. No matter, to all she was simply Jeanne.

"Extraordinarily beautiful," Jean Audubon was to describe her. Whether he had ever laid eyes on her before that day there is no telling. That she could neither read nor write is unremarkable. Forty percent of France was illiterate, forty percent sparsely educated, and only twenty percent entered the lycée, even as late as the year 1850. Madame Audubon herself depended on Charles Coiron to relay messages to her husband in his absence.

The plantation to which she was going had a bizarre history. The estate of Génerèse, father-in-law of Pallon de la Bouverie, was settled a few years earlier by lottery. A little negress, Louise, drew ballots from a hat while notaries watched. To Rose and Pallon went the place at Les Cayes, to her brother Laurent a smaller one at nearby Torbeck. Her brothers Antoine and Joseph, and her sister Madeline, lost out entirely.[13]

Within weeks Jeanne Rabine fled her post. The Audubon plantation was not far away. Jean Audubon was one who, certainly, could help expedite her passage home. It is possible that her flight was caused by a tropical illness that left Jeanne Rabine unfit to serve. On May 21, 1784, Laurent Sanson, physician and planter, came to minister to the Audubon household. Besides the names of several slaves he wrote that of "Mademoiselle Rabin" on his statement.[14]

By the following October she was with child, and again ailing. What thoughts must have passed through the mind of one of such pious upbringing? She may have wondered whether by some merciful stroke of fortune the childless Anne, twenty-six years her senior, might not live to know what an unthinkable tragedy had befallen her. That Audubon had spent scarcely four of the past eleven years with his aging wife did not ameliorate the dread of her finding out. The presence of a black mistress was one thing, the imagined intrusion of a white woman, known by some to be the mother of her husband's expected child, quite another. Beyond doubt in despair, Jeanne perhaps prayed that she herself would not survive the months ahead.

It was not that Jeanne Rabine did not know the ways of the world. Her grandmother Marie Texier Rabine had helped a young neighbor, Pélagie Douet, in need. She had carried the infant son of the girl to his baptism in the absence of the "unknown father," then convinced the widower Guillaume Le Ray that he must accept matters and marry Pélagie.[15]

One night at the beginning of April, Sanson was summoned. Jeanne's illness did not respond to his nostrums and mineral waters. Another call of more desperate urgency two weeks later brought him in a hurry with the surgeon Guérin.[16] Labor continued for two days, until the birth of a boy on the night of April 26, 1785. Contrary to custom—Breton custom—there was no baptism. There could be none for a child born out of wedlock, born in secret.

Six days later, Sanson revisited mother and child. Six weeks after that he lanced an abscessed breast.

Island fevers and infections hastened the end for Jeanne Rabine. Christian burial was not denied her. The register of the Church of Notre-Dame de l'Assomption bears this brief notice: RABIN——On November 11, 1785, has been buried in the cemetery of this parish the body of Demoiselle Rabin, native of Nort, diocese of Nantes, who died yesterday. Aged twenty-four years.[17] She was in truth twenty-seven; it did not matter. How and when, or even whether, the Rabines were notified will remain a mystery.

Between Sanitte and Audubon matters stood as before. There is indication enough that she did not relinquish her rights in the *casa*. She charged small luxuries, along with necessities, at her father's store. His nephew Guillaume-Gabriel Bouffard, a fairly recent arrival from La Rochelle, rendered this bill, among others: "Nineteen thousand livres. Debt of Catherine Bouffard, living at Perche 5, with J. Audubon, merchant."[18] Bills for jewelry survive. Young "Gabriel the younger," as the clerk was called, had taken a fancy to his cousin Rose (Bouffard's second daughter) and accepted the dubious honor of acting as godfather to her little Pasquille in a christening that was an exception to the rule. His attachment to Rose was to be an abiding one.[19]

Sanitte's and other debts weighted heavily on Audubon. Sanson continued to dun him for yet another accouchement of Sanitte's; it occurred six months after the death of Jeanne Rabine.[20]

By spring fresh rumors of deeper unrest had reached France. Enmity between blacks and whites, as well as between blacks and all people of color, was growing in intensity by the hour. More than a few of the planters and merchants were leaving for good. It was with utmost reluctance that Jean Audubon, too, made up his mind to sell—for $69,000—all of his property except his warehouse. Once again he trusted to luck by agreeing to a down payment, one large enough for the purchase of a cargo vessel in which to sail for New York City with a load of his own sugar. The promissory note of the absentee owner was to be handled for one Elois de Janserac of Paris by his agent.[21]

Before Audubon could think of departing, there remained the question of the safety and future of his only son, Jean. To accompany the infant to France, even were it possible, would have been to do so under the cloud of scandal. Yet there was no leaving him behind while the air was charged with a black uprising sure to come. Audubon believed there was less to fear where Sanitte and their daughters were concerned. She could be sure of a welcome on her father's plantation, and of comfort and leisure where his fifty slaves cultivated his coffee and cane, and tended his large herd of cattle and flocks of sheep. Or she could join her brother in the safety of the highlands above at Cavaillon, if tensions mounted. As for her favorite sister, Rose, she and her son Pasquille and the infant "Laize" (Louise) whom Guillaume-Gabriel Bouffard had fathered, they would remain with him while he made good his intention to stay on.

At anchor off Les Cayes lay the merchant vessel *Le Duguesclin*, which, since May, had been taking on cargo. Its name did honor to a fourteenth century Breton warrior, Bernard Duguesclin, affectionally remembered for having abandoned schooling and gone to sea. Its captain, Charles Garet of Nantes, a friend of Audubon's, agreed to bear Jean Rabine off to France. On July 12, 1788, he welcomed the three-and-a-half-year-old aboard. This event occurred at a time when children were usually entrusted to the care of a cabin boy when traveling unescorted. It is more than likely that fifteen-year-old Charles Garet, the nephew and namesake of the young captain, had such an assignment when not on duty as apprentice pilot.

What transpired for the infant Jean instilled a lifelong detestation of the sea. Although used to the care and understanding of the black *bossal* who had carried him to the ship, he was under constant orders from strangers, men only, while the vessel ploughed eastward, now under burning sun, now through stormy waters.

The brief passenger list held but three names, entered in ink in a hand so fine and vague as to be almost illegible. One was a ship carpenter from the vessel *Le Lokro*, the other a passenger whose occupation and place of origin were not recorded. There is no hint of their having any role in the rather conspiratorial rescue of the child whose name was given as "Le Mr. Maison Neuve, agé de 3 ans, fils du Mr.

Audubon" (Monsieur Maison Neuve, aged 3, son of Monsieur Audubon).[22]

That such a preposterous entry bears scrutiny goes without saying. At first glance it would seem to have been a little private joke about a lad called Maison Neuve[23] (in English, Newhouse), bound for a new home. But there is too much possible crossruffing to leave it at that. The fact is that Garet was chosen, probably by Madame Audubon, once her husband had sought her agreement and gained it. During her years in Paimboeuf she knew the family of the wife of Captain Charles Garet well. The aunt of Madame Garet, born Rénée Croizet, was living directly across the Loire from the Audubon villa whose master was Captain Joseph Fouché.[24] She too had been born in Paimboeuf, and had born a son whom Napoleon I was one day to make Duke of Otrante for his notorious services as Minister of Police. Madame Garet was the godmother of a child of the Director of the Mint, Réné Maisonneuve, whose brother Jacques-Gilles was Deputy Mayor of Nantes when the *Duguesclin* dropped anchor at a quai of the city. The wife of the Deputy Mayor, Marie-Gabrielle Turpin,[25] bore the same name as a Couëron family, two of whose members were to witness the last will of Madame Audubon. As if that were not enough, by itself, to banish any idea that the name Maisonneuve was chosen at random for the boy, there is the instance of Agathe Maisonneuve, sister of Réné and Jacques-Gilles, and wife of a close friend of Captain Audubon, Jean Perchais, notary and justice of the village of St. Etienne-de-Montluc near Couëron.

That there might have been fears that the Rabines would seize the boy if they knew of his arrival may or may not have led to the use of a pseudonym. If so, it was hardly the primary reason. In such times the Rabines had cares enough. Moreover, Audubon had in mind another rescue before too late: that of his favorite and youngest daughter, Rose, and as the child of Jeanne Rabine, without the stigma of color. Risky perhaps, but there was no better way.

The young voyager would not long remember the cacophony of the galleries of the casa, the gibbering of pet monkeys, the shrilling of caged parrots, the cries of hoola birds all around, the shouts of children, the kitchen sounds and smells, the hypnotic drumming and sad songs of the blacks outside their huts, in everlasting longing for freedom and their own equatorial firesides at evening.

There was little to choose between France and Saint-Domingue when Audubon set out in the spring of 1789 for America, his white hope. A pause in Richmond to collect from Ross for repairs to the *Queen* some years earlier proved a futile exercise. On reaching New York City he left his ship in the East River, and hastened by ferry and stage to Philadelphia. There he looked for a farm with the idea of bartering with his sugar as part payment. His former acquaintance, the Quaker cabinetmaker and journeyman David Ross, who had made him a squirrel cage in July 1781, called his attention to a "for sale" poster.[26] A certain Henry Augustin Prevost, retired Swiss mercenary officer of the British Army, was offering Mill Grove, his "plantation" twenty-three miles or so northwest of the city, in Montgomery County. He had bought it after the Revolution from a former Londoner, Robert Vaux, who had called it Vaux Hill. Like Vaux he had reasons for wishing to live in England. Of the many owners of the fieldstone dormered mansion built in 1762 by James Morgan—among them Governor John Penn—Vaux had more memories of this corner of William Penn's chartered territory.[27] He had played host to Washington while the general and his ragged troops encamped one winter at Valley Forge. Bullets from a certain lead vein, rumored to be still unexploited, had helped General Sullivan win a victory for the Continentals at the ford below. Vaux, a friend, had witnessed the trampling of his estate which afforded panoramas like many in England, and he had watched trees and fences cut down by troops of both sides at his and a neighboring place later named Fatland Ford.

The potential of wealth beneath the 200 or more acres of Vaux Hill attracted Audubon, sight unseen, far more than its arable soil. He found the land much the worse for wear from careless farming by tenants. The price, $3,500, he thought a bargain, provided he could barter.[28] On April 10, 1789, he reached an initial agreement with Prevost to pay off the small mortgage held by an Albany physician, and to make payments yearly until final settlement not later than New Year's 1794. Prevost agreed to accept the sugar, worth 600 pounds sterling. After Audubon brought it down to the port of Philadelphia on the Delaware, he called for a custom-made sulky he had ordered and had it drawn into the hold.[29] His family coat-of-arms had been ciphered on the door by the coach-makers.

On Saint-Domingue, meanwhile, there had been savage fighting, although Les Cayes maintained an artificial calm. Port-au-Prince and the northern regions had suffered. Immediately upon his return, Audubon joined the newly formed National Guard, which was prepared to quell an expected uprising.

Inspired by the Declaration of the Rights of Man and the Citizens, the blacks had risen in the north against their owners and oppressors. In Paris, royal troops had failed to stop the fall of the Bastille on July 14, 1789. A powerful National Guard had been formed by order of the new popular National Assembly after the demise of the ancien régime. Providentially, the new government denied admission of Saint-Domingue's three deputies, who had sided with the mulattos against the blacks in their own country, to the fatal meeting during which the old Estates-General was overthrown.

Differences between the feeble royalist retainers and the progressive whites of Les Cayes weakened their defense against their former slaves. Colonists, who had been discreetly leaving, now began to disappear in numbers. Audubon spent six months harvesting his own sugar and buying more, then sold his ship and booked as a cargo-carrying passenger on the none-too-seaworthy schooner *La Victoire*.[30] The hesitation of the hired captain to put forth before completing needed repairs brought delays (and at least one false start) until a new captain was summoned from Bordeaux for the command. Audubon sailed in June, knowing it was for

good, and that his presence in Les Cayes would only increase the danger to his family in the event of insurrection. It
is not probable that he was on hand for the birth of Sanitte's
Louise-Françoise-Josephine, which appears to have coincided
more or less with his leavetaking from the fairly distant port
of Cap Français, on the other side of the mountains.[31]

The schooner *La Victoire* came up the Delaware with one
storm-wrecked mast on July 6, 1790. Nearly out of funds, Audubon appointed a prominent Quaker lawyer, Miers Fisher,
whose probity George Washington had once praised, to
handle a promissory agreement fuller than the first. He was
to provide a new water wheel for the mill and new fence
rails, and to pay Prevost "one ear of Indian corn each April 1,
if lawfully demanded," besides the agreed-on profit from the
sale of the sugar and the balance due. Prevost obliged him by
taking a short lease on Mill Grove at a rental of £170 a year in
order to keep William Thomas, the tenant, on the land. With
that, Prevost decided to sail with Audubon and to lend him
passage money for the balance of the journey to his destination, France.[32] At Belle Isle off Brittany, Prevost changed to a
ship bound for London.[33]

Audubon had no more than reached the Quai de la Fosse
in Nantes when he learned that a mulatto uprising in Les
Cayes had cost fifty lives. Sanitte and the children had escaped unharmed.

Republican though his sympathies, and anti-monarchist
his sentiments, Audubon was nonetheless not anxious to
jump into the fray in middle age. Imagining himself still
in control of his destiny, he sought to interest his brother
Claude, of Bayonne, in financing the purchase of a merchant
vessel, as part of a partnership for trade in places that might
still be open to it.[34] Claude, more realistic, chose to serve the
Republican Navy instead. If Claude was not yet aware of his
brother's pashalike life in the Antilles, he soon would be.

As soon as it became clear that such an alternative did not
exist, Audubon went to the Town Hall in the spring of 1791
and offered his services to the Committee of Public Safety, an
arm of the National Guard. From then on, and for the next

ten years, he was little more than titular head of the household in the rue de Crébillon, which rarely saw him.[35] His absences from the turbulent city were in the line of duty at places down the Loire. There was, however, one grave personal matter yet to be taken care of, the rescue of his daughter Rose Bonnitte, on which his heart was set.

The solution lay with his neighbor from across the river from the Audubon villa, Captain Martin Gautreau of Le Pellerin, who was about to make one last voyage to Les Cayes with cargo and to bring back a few passengers. He expected to return to Nantes not later than the third week of June. When he had not done so by July the Audubons and many others on the watch for loved ones worried that Gautreau and his ship *Le Tancrède* had been lost. News of horrors on the island reached Nantes. At Cap Français live bodies of whites were broken on racks, disemboweled, and mutilated. A mob impaled an infant and bore the body aloft like a grim standard. All of Saint-Domingue was said to be on an irreversible course of murder, burning, and destruction.

Actually, the delay of the *Tancrède* was due to the failure of the owner of two bonded servants of color to put their exit papers in proper order. They left the ship in Martinique.

First on the passenger list, and perhaps first to go ashore, was a neighbor of Augustin Bouffard of Cavaillon, the planter Victor Grandier, from whom Jean Audubon had bought sugar before sailing for America.[36] After his name came that of "Demoiselle Rose Bonnitte, aged four, natural daughter and orphan of Demoiselle Rabin, white." (Jeanne had been dead for five years, or nearly; her name served as a protective shield. Gautreau, who some years later was to be a witness to a guardianship action taken by Audubon, well knew this. The designation "blanche," for white, is without precedent in an entire shelf of colonial passenger lists in Paris and Nantes. "Noir" and "mulâtre" are common enough.) Next came the two unaccompanied children of the planter Le Prêtre; they were aged ten and seven. There were also Lieutenant de Vaisseau Esmaynard from a plantation in Torbeck; another unaccompanied child of eight; a merchant tailor; and a trader. The ship had finally left the tropics on June 24, a full two months later than expected.

Chances are that Gautreau managed to put Bonnitte ashore by dory at Port Launay. If not, he or someone else must have accompanied her up the short dramatic distance to the Audubon town house, up cobbled streets that ran past the great gray mass of the Castle of the Dukes of Brittany in the city named for Namnetes, king of the Gauls; on up the winding road to the cathedral; and a few streets west to a tall, formal house in a row of nearly identical residences. She was too young to have grasped what her half-brother—with his large, bright, hazel eyes, bronzed brown curls, entrancing smile, and already mercurial personality—was learning of local history at age six. The story of the duke who ordered his guests plunged in the castle moat to waken them for breakfast no doubt delighted him. If, at Mass, he wondered at the cavernous interior of the Cathedral of Sts. Peter and Paul, what must he have thought of the tale of the church that stood there until the Normans burned it? At its center there had been an enormous ruby that cast shafts of light from its center up into the gleaming pewter vaults.

Anne, fifty-eight, vigorous, kindhearted, ready as ever to meet life halfway and on its own terms, took Bonnitte to her heart no more hesitantly than she had accepted the—in any case—irresistible Jean Rabine. Soon it was to be as if the little girl had known and loved no other mother. Black Elizabeth, whom the captain had brought for Anne on the *Bons Amis* in May 1776, was a reasssuring presence to fugitives from the island, as were other such reminders as pet birds and monkeys from Saint-Domingue.[37]

Legal adoption of the children had to be delayed for a host of reasons. Possible interference by the Rabine family was not one of them. Jeanne's mother had died in Les Mazures while Captain Audubon was on his way to Philadelphia for the last time.[38] In the midst of all the political ferment there was hardly any need on the part of one of her kinsmen, about to become vice-president of the Nantes Republican

Administration, to interest himself. Madame Le Jeune de Vaugeon and her husband had quit Montigné and the Les Touches country when the royalist Rohans and their lands were in danger. Her sons had, however, been baptized in Les Touches and given the baffling names Anonyme I and Anonyme II, and were to be referred to as "majeur" and "mineur."[39] By the time of the arrival of her brother's natural son, Jean, his presence not far from her in the city was an old story; family ties were none the worse for the slight embarrassment. The boy's eyes, mouth, and profile made his paternity obvious enough.

The time had come for some schooling, for here was a child going on seven still unable to do more with a pencil than sketch a stuffed dove. The doting Anne was in no hurry to burden her charges with studies. They were often with her at the villa down the Loire, among its vineyards, orchards, nightingales, wagtails, and pirouetting green *fauvettes*, in a countryside favored by Duke François II very much earlier. The nearby village, Couëron, was as its name suggests the ancient ancestral region of Coiron Frères. Little Jean Rabine was by no means the first to be drawn to the natural wonders all around him. The famous ornithologist Pierre Belon had studied and drawn birds there in his youth two and a half centuries earlier. Belon was to share honors with a Swiss for having been first to create actual "portraits" of the songsters and waterfowl, an ambition which in Jean Rabine—John James Audubon—would be transcendent.

The villa was then quite close to the Loire, which has often changed course and shifted its banks. Between Couëron and Le Pellerin, which perches high like a kind of amphitheatre above the water, the broad sweep is much like that of a lake. Passing up and down were the white sails of boats, already far fewer than when Couëron was the destination of Dutch merchant ships that carried the town's luxurious millinery and much else back to Holland. Not only the old stone walls but the very roofs of the cottages were hidden by tall marsh grasses, growing along footpaths and coach lanes down to the margins of the Loire. For Jean Rabine, from the start, the lure was not that of water but of lanes, fields, swamps, and meadows, bird-filled, beckoning.

By late autumn, Nantes was the place for Anne and the children. As for schools, alternatives were few in such unpredictable and volatile times. Bonnitte was, certainly, too young to attend the eleven o'clock classes for demoiselles. Jean played truant even for drawing lessons available from "Monsieur Hussard" on the Place Bretagne. How he would fare, if ever he learned to read, at the logical school for him, the Académie Polysophique on the rue de Bossuet, was unpredictable. This strict, select choice of merchants and nobility for their young was called simply, "the School."[40] Penmanship, dancing, flute, and composition might prove no problem; but Latin, English, history, geography, and the more exacting subjects almost certainly would. His ready but undisciplined talent for music led to violin lessons. Trioche, headmaster of "the School," was so versatile that, it was said, he played the flute to theorems, danced through declensions, and did both while racing from classroom to classroom. Dance classes were mixed; in these Jean gained in grace while trying to overcome his shyness, his *mauvaise honte*. School days were not without their pangs. In a tussle with classmates he fell and cut his forehead so severely that, from then on, he had a strong aversion to physical violence.

Often he walked toward school with a small lunch basket on his arm, but then took a woodland path instead. He would return home, anon, his basket filled with plants, lichens, pebbles, and nests.

A fencing master of the town taught him, in time, how to handle foils. Grace at fencing and in the cotillion and minuet, like aptitude for appreciating books on natural history, were assets and virtues. But he lacked a zest for practical learning. The virtual disappearance of his father into the National Guard, and agitation that was sometimes violent in the city, not to mention frequent school closings for the safety of the children, were no help to regularity and discipline. All ears were open to the latest news and wild rumors from

Paris. Louis XVI had been guillotined. The Republicans were about to seize control of the nation. For seven months, beginning in May 1792, Captain Audubon, now called "Citizen Audubon," held the office of Commissioner for the "civil, moral, and political state" of the outlying communes.[41] There was fighting in the streets of the city while he was on duty at Savenay, a village twenty-five miles northwest. Trioche was called up and left "the School" for the Guard and the Tribunal.

Jean was to write, in manhood, of the first skirmish that he supposedly watched from behind shutters. In one other such twist of retrospection he wrote of having witnessed the murder of his aunt during a street battle. (Madame Le Jeune de Vaugeon died a natural death in 1815, more than twenty years later.)[42] That he ever saw actual bloodshed must be held in doubt. Much of what he heard around him, during the counterrevolution, was true, and to become part of dramatic local history. The melting down of church bells and leaden coffins into cannon by the Republicans, to drive back the royalist leader Charette, was unforgettable.

The possibility of Jean Audubon's return to Mill Grove any time soon was decidedly remote. An American sea captain conveyed Audubon's compliments to Miers Fisher, with apologies for not writing while "defending the country against the brigands."[43] Such defense was going none too well for him. Scouting with his men for needed material to be used in clashes with England, Spain, and the Netherlands was presently abandoned. Next, he was ordered to organize a guard in the vicinity of Couëron. At Le Pellerin he put a boatload of enemies to flight only to have them return to renew the fray within hours. He posted proclamations at Port Launay and, from there, went to Paimboeuf to collect rents, if he could, for a house Anne had rented to the town administrator and his staff. Feckless duties of this kind ended with his recall for coastal service as commander of the lugger *Le Cerbère* on the Bay of Biscay.[44] At Toulon a promising Corsican youth named Bonaparte was helping to turn the tide in favor of the Republicans. An order for Audubon to serve as an intermediary in a parley at Les Sables d'Olonne with

Vendean generals Westermann and Boulart effected no more than an inconclusive meeting with their agents.

The climax of his service to the Revolution came with his next engagement. His lugger was under attack by a British corsair, the *Brilliant*, for three hours. Wounded in the rump and thigh, he fought on while his marine surgeon tried to stanch the flow of blood. The doctor who dressed his damaged limb—the already frail one—praised Audubon's valiant response to the fourteen-cannon barrage.

A reign of terror began in Nantes in winter. Patriots, Audubon among them, were shocked by Robespierre's violent seizure of power in Paris, following the murder of the equally ruthless Danton. None could foresee that the dynamic little corporal Bonaparte was moving toward total domination in France, with ambitions that reached far beyond its borders.

Fugitives from the islands seldom came to Nantes by late 1793. On the eve of a renewed insurrection by blacks, the peace of America was preferable to the perils of Europe. Those who chose Nantes had cause for regret. The city and all of western Brittany were nearing their severest test.

The Bouffard men had few illusions about the risks of remaining on Saint-Domingue; still they hung on. For a year or so Gabriel "the younger" had been visiting Cavaillon, now and then, with an armed escort. He found his "mulatto cousins" ready to be "extremely good" to him and still on good terms with their white neighbors. Bitter fighting in Les Cayes occurred during one such visit. In July 1792, the Audubon plantation was vandalized; everything but the warehouse was burned. The Paris buyer had long since ceased to pay. Most of Jean's and Anne's investment was gone; only the land remained, along with some goods which were for the most part ruined. Jean may or may not have learned of the death of his firstborn, Marie-Madeleine, sixteen, in the carnage on the Plain of Jacob at Les Cayes.[45] Sanitte had taken up life anew with a successor to Jean Audubon, and it was not long after Marie-Madeleine's death that she gave birth to Rose Victorine, whose christening was witnessed by Joseph Martin, "ship captain of the merchant marine," possibly a kinsman of the Bouffards of La Rochelle and Martin cousins there.[46] Bouffard "the younger," expecting death unless fortune spared him, drew up his last will, leaving his house to Rose and "Laize." He remembered Rose Bonnitte and his godson with modest bequests. Although he was to live until September 4, 1801, he did not alter the testament, which, in its naming of Bonnitte, would not be honored by his relatives in France.[47]

On a bitter cold New Year's Day, 1794, a bloody siege gripped Nantes. Citizen Carrier, the Revolutionary agent who had come down from Paris to weed out all those who were believed to be still loyal to the lost cause of monarchy, struck terror in the hearts of the Nantais. He ordered thousands of prisoners to be set adrift in boats, fitted with traps through which they were lowered into the frigid currents of the Loire. Plague, fever, and violence brought death to nine thousand people within weeks.

The Audubons saw what havoc their own deaths would bring upon their small dependents. Unless the two were legally adopted they stood no chance of rightful inheritance under the rigid laws which denied natural children any and all bequests. The formalities of adoption had to be approached with utmost caution.[48]

The Audubons led their boy and girl through the battered streets to the Town Hall on the seventh day of March 1794. Openness about the background of Jean Rabine must be cunningly avoided, they knew. The same was true of the origin of Bonnitte. Saints' names would have to be foregone, now that the Church was outlawed along with its priests, save for the few who took the oath of loyalty to the State. The name of Fougère, meaning fern, was given Jean in the register, which declared him "the son of Jean Audubon and a woman living in America but deceased for about eight years." Rose received the name of Muguet, or lily of the valley. Their birth dates were approximated, no doubt as an added protection;

yet their ages were correctly stated. Afterward, Captain Audubon returned to the *Cerbère* with marine surgeon Julien
Beuscher, a formal witness.

In November Jean Audubon took command of the dispatch boat *L'Eveille* for more coastal duty. His brother Claude
joined him as ensign, but not for long; in the spring, a vessel
to which he was transferred disappeared on a voyage to
Spain.[49]

Before returning to the great naval base at Rochefort-sur-
Mer, where he had been in command of a training corvette,
Captain Audubon paid his family a brief visit. His scheme of
visiting Chesapeake Bay on a tour of duty had prompted him
to write to Fisher some months before and ask him to send
an account of Mill Grove affairs in care of the Republican consul, Benoit, at Norfolk, Virginia. By this time the chances of
such convenient orders had come to nothing. Fisher's appeal
to the consul for a leave that would enable Audubon to visit
his estate went begging. The Captain was to be spared knowledge of its "very suffering condition" from freshets that had
borne off fences, wrecked the dam, and damaged the race.
There was a judgment against him "for about £250" to
the "Widow Wert" of Newcastle, presumably a party to the
feckless affair of David Ross & Company of Virginia. The
five-year lease to William Thomas still went unapproved
while he farmed the plantation.[50]

When Audubon called for a tune on the violin from his
son, he was displeased to note that the strings were slack
and the case dusty. Not even the boy's sketches of birds were
finished enough to merit praise. His indifference to rudimen-
tary studies was as marked as ever. Rose Bonnitte, on the
other hand, faithful to her childhood name, played on the
spinet, to her father's delight and satisfaction. Ominously
humming a tune, the Captain told Jean to pack for the journey to Rochefort.

The next morning father and son were off by stagecoach.
While his parent read a book, Jean was left to his thoughts of

the natural world that he was leaving behind for a navy career in the family tradition.[51]

Three days later the Audubons passed through the Arsenal gates. Rochefort-sur-Mer, despite its name, lies nine miles inland. In the seventeenth century the old irregular paths of this capital of the Fourth Maritime District had given way to wide, straight streets converging on the formal Place Colbert. At the foot of the station's low, rocky hill lay the deep river harbor of the Charente, at the mouth of which batteries stood ready. Across the river a broad marshland spread in all directions. Tall training ships, coastal vessels, and other craft were continually conducted up the dangerous channel for repair. High tree-fringed ramparts, with mounted sentinels at their gates night and day, enclosed both the Arsenal and the city.

The eleven-year-old was proudly introduced. After a short tour of inspection with his father, he was sent off alone to explore the historic ropewalk and wall. There was much else to admire—a splendid new hospital, the marine guard barracks, the fine tribunals and mansions, and the artillery grounds. Nothing caught his eye quite so much as the steward's residence, still called "King's House," and its rear garden of fruit trees, bright borders, and kitchen garden that reached down to the Charente in parklike order.

The boy's adoring foster mother had reason for anxiety about him. The malarial marshlands were a well-known hazard of late summer. When the one and only town fountain— the monumental affair in the Place Colbert—went as dry as its canals, the often contaminated wells had to be relied upon. However, for far more unacceptable features of the life in Rochefort, young Jean did not have to wait long. Immediately the atmosphere of confinement left him feeling like "a prisoner of war on parole." For skipping a mathematics lesson he was hustled aboard a detention pontoon after being seized in the Secretariat gardens, and was held until the return of his father from a cruise. He was soon released, but not without a stern warning against any more caprices.

"Jean Audubon, mousse," cabin boy, first appears on the rolls in August 1796.[52] Ambidextrous, he soon mastered the knots and braids of the riggings in the shop of the Arsenal. He became a powerful swimmer, adept at fencing, good at drawing, and clever with flute and fiddle. But the moment of truth arrived on April 5, 1797, when his name was nineteenth on the list of *mousses* or "mice" aged twelve (which he became on April 26) and eighteen. They boarded the training corvette *L'Instituteur*, of which his father was in command.[53] Before they could apply for theoretical nautical knowledge they had to have six months of coastal duty; few intended to pursue a career with rank. Seasickness and low spirits ended young Jean's duty at sea. When the captain put his charges ashore and transferred them to the coastal lugger *St. Pierre*, bound for Brest and more training, Jean was not among them. Rather, he returned to Rochefort-sur-Mer, as his father sailed for Falmouth to exchange some prisoners of war. Hard though it was to rejoin two hundred or more other boys in the Arsenal at forty francs a day, young Jean was assured that his chances for better were not over. He had only to pass a test on September 20, 1797, to prepare for officer's candidacy.

When the dreaded day arrived, several names were entered on the Register of Acts at the School of Mathematics and Hydrography: "Today have appeared before the municipal deputies of the commune of Rochefort the citizens Etienne Perrade, aged 14; Jean Audubon, aged 14; Charles Deuxliards, aged 17; Joseph Armand, aged 17 and 5 months; Vincent Gressiot, aged 15. They have declared their desire to enter the School . . . and to that end they have made their declaration and been received."[54] Only Deuxliards, the eldest, passed. The rest went back to the Arsenal.

Shortly after his return from Falmouth, Captain Audubon was made *Lieutenant de Vaisseau*, one degree below full marine captain, his final rank. There could be no protest, no redress, despite his long and deserving record of service. Old wounds, and a pulmonary illness grown worse, caused him to file a mild protest in the form of a request for port detail before his approaching retirement. Throughout the winter and spring he served as head of several court martial juries at Rochefort-sur-Mer. A request to be allowed to have his wife and daughter join him there was granted.[55]

Jean, his mother, and his sister returned to Nantes in March 1800. His father soon followed, his days at sea over.

The Audubons knew that the house they had leased for five years in the rue Rubens would not be safe from the spectre of conscription. Before arrangements for long sojourns in Couëron could be made, an important but precarious step had to be taken—the baptism of Jean Rabine. Such an act would prove indispensable in the unpredictable years before him. How it was to be managed in the virtual absence of clergy recognized by Rome was the question. It was to be hoped that at least some clergyman willing to overlook a statistic or two could be found. The Concordat between Napoleon and the Holy See was still months away.

The return of Lieutenant Audubon for a brief leave in October brought a solution. The sixty-year-old former Couëron parish priest Abbé Hyacinthe Tardiveau seemed the logical choice to administer baptism. He had been reluctant to flout Rome at the start, and for this had been run out of the village after the sacking of his church and rectory. But in Nantes, pledged to the Constitution, he became the self-appointed head of the only church left open, St. Similien. Fugitive priests were now beginning to return, ready to revive the dormant parishes. Baptisms and marriages performed without the approval of Rome were about to be validated.

How the Audubons hoped to keep the long carefully guarded secret of Jeanne Rabine is suggested by their choice of Abbé Tardiveau. A native of Le Grand Fougeray, north of Les Touches and Les Mazures, and no stranger to the Audubons because of mutual acquaintances in Couëron, Tardiveau—for sympathetic treatment of a confidence—was a likely risk. While Julien Beuscher, a witness at Jean Rabine's adoption six years earlier, stood by as godfather and Rose Bonnitte as godmother, the priest wrote as directed: "Jean Jacques-Fougère, adopted son of Jean Audubon and Anne Moynet his spouse."[56] The day when the Abbé would be for-

given by Rome and become a not-too-distant neighbor at Por-
nic was near.

The Peace of Amiens in March 1802 did not halt the steady
harvest of youth. Bent on ruining English overseas trade,
Napoleon continued to call up young and old. No hearth
with fodder for guns was safe from the recruiters. The "First
Consul," as Bonaparte had called himself since 1799, aspired
to eclipse the might of Alexander the Great. Though he had
done some good by improving roads and canals and sweeping out corrupt officials, he also thirsted for universal conquest. Though he might better have devoted himself to the
study of art in Paris or Nantes, Couëron was a safer place for
young Audubon. The friendship and prestige enjoyed by his
father among the local petty officials, who were still under
the thumb of Nantes directors, served to help fend off conscription for the moment.

Nantes had not forgotten the history-making visit of
Jacques-Louis David, painter to the court of Napoleon and
radical Republican. Nor had Jean Rabine. The event had
seized his imagination until, before many years more, he was
to wish the world to believe he had been a pupil of this master. The comprehensive records of David in Paris lend no
support to the uneasy claim, made to compensate for moments of shame and insufficiency.[57] The talent of Audubon
by 1802 could have been no less modest than in 1805, when
he produced work that indicates innocence of any such training. It was that infallible teacher, nature, that took him in
hand, as he proceeded by trial and error to grope among her
mysteries and to be guided, as well, by the published delineations of various painter-naturalists. Near La Gerbetière lay
the more imposing estate La Bernardière, where his rambles
may have taken him. Grandchildren of his father's friend
François Lory were then living in the fine old house of the
sea captain on a wooded tract. A few miles north, at Le
Buron, Madame de Sévigné had summered and kept her
journal in her day. A long circuitous path led northeastward
to the favorite hunting grounds of Duke François II.

Lieutenant Audubon was not equal to visiting Les Cayes to press for rents and money due him in his tangled affairs. His agent, the planter Jean-Baptiste Blanchard, had thus far failed to negotiate for him. His island fortune of one and one-half million francs appeared to be spindrift.

A letter of April 3, 1802, from Fisher brought an abrupt end to further indecision about Mill Grove. To all that the agent had said in repeated letters for a score of years, with seemingly inexhaustible patience, and which he now reiterated fully, he was able to add one encouraging announcement. He was granting tenant William Thomas an "abatement" in rent not only for his repairs to the place, but for word of what would probably turn out to be "a very rich lead mine." He had done so under duress; Thomas was threatening to give up his lease if Audubon failed either to come himself or send some "confidential person" to form a mining partnership with him. Fisher sent a sample of the ore, thought to be plentiful. He had declined to sell the land in question to the eager Thomas: "I told him I had no authority to sell . . . but promised to inform thee thereof, and hoped thou would soon come to this country or send some person with authority to examine into the matter and make an Agreement with him." It was expedient to keep Thomas as a tenant at least while the vein had to be kept secret and until Audubon could take protective measures.

Fisher hoped that Audubon himself might come; but in any case he desired "no private benefit" to himself or to see the mine do other than "restore all losses." The supposed balance of seven or eight hundred dollars in account with Fisher had gone up the flue when Prevost's seventh bond was presented for payment. The person who presented it was the representative of soon-to-be Vice-President Aaron Burr, to whom Major Prevost had assigned it during the former's colonelcy days. Fisher's "long correspondence" with Burr's attorney Dallas proved no postponement was possible; a judgment was threatened. This left Fisher with nothing at all unless and until Thomas appeared with the rent, now three hundred dollars instead of four. At least the farm was unencumbered. "I cannot say, but were it mine, I would think it my duty to attend to it. I am not conscious of having neglected it as thine," Fisher closed, "considering the feeble powers (if powers they might be called) I had over it." Meanwhile, he awaited orders.[58]

The purchase of Louisiana by the United States in April 1803 lent itself to numerous schemes on both sides of the Atlantic. To Lieutenant Audubon it suggested the advisability of sending young Jean to Mill Grove plantation on a passport that would give Louisiana as his birthplace. Early in the summer of 1803 he sent Francis Dacosta, a Nantes acquaintance with some knowledge of mineralogy and metallurgy, to act as overseer of the mining experiment in Pennsylvania.

In August, he put his son aboard the ship of a New England friend, Captain Smith, doubtless aware that new, easier laws would simplify naturalization problems, should events compel a step in that direction. The unsuspecting French customs, vigilant in the cause of conscription, saw the youth sail away on a supposed "visit." As far as Anne Moynet Audubon was concerned, that was the very most that the absence of her beloved adoptive son must be. She was in no way resigned to losing her favorite, whimsical, and unquestionably spoiled child forever. Even the occasionally slurring remarks of his snobbish cousin, Anonyme Le Jeune de Vaugéon, in his presence, would be preferable to such a loss.

There was more than one object in sending Jean-Jacques Audubon abroad. He would slip out of range of the recruiters, learn the English language, and pick up what he could of management and farming. In his pocket was an introduction that from the moment of landing was to make him, by his own declaration, another person. He would be Jean no longer but, instead, John James Audubon. His father had made him pledge to keep his illegitimacy secret in America. Eager to be free of the shadow that his presence cast in Nantes and Couëron and inclined to despise the obfuscating name of "Jean Rabin," which he nevertheless knew full well to be the real one, he had eagerly promised.

"This will be handed to you by my son," ran the letter to,

presumably, the overseer Dacosta, "to whom I request you will render every service in your power, wishing that you should join Mr. Miers Fisher to procure him a good and healthy place where he might learn English. I come to point out to you Norristown, and look for a good and decent family in that place, to recommend him to her as your own son. This service from you will deserve my everlasting gratitude. I am, Sir, with consideration, your most obedient servant, Jean Audubon."[59]

Never had his fair command of English—a relic of prison days—so well served the Lieutenant, his son, and a grateful posterity.

Phoebe. *Plate 120 of* The Birds of America. *Engraved by Robert Havell, Jr., in 1831 after the original study drawn in New Jersey, May 1829.*

II. Mill Grove

AN EPIDEMIC OF FEVER had been bringing death to many in New York City. It accounted, more than the August heat, for the quiet of the streets. Captain John Smith took his ship a short way up the East River, above the busy harbor. The excited eighteen-year-old immigrant hurried ashore to walk to Greenwich Village and change his money.[1] He felt so unwell on his return that the Captain thought it best for him to head for Norristown, Pennsylvania, without delay. At the boardinghouse of two Quaker ladies he would be well cared for.

It was two weeks before John James Audubon rallied from the all but fatal illness. Miers Fisher brought him away in his carriage for a visit of convalescence at Ury, his country place near Fox Chase on Pine Road near Pennypack Creek.[2] The solid, self-assured Fisher so intimidated young Audubon that he longed to turn in at Mill Grove instead.

Not even for the sake of politeness could the Virginia-bred former assemblyman or his lady find it in their hearts to delight at what emerged from the baggage of their guest. The

45

sight of crayons, flute, and violin elicited no pleased exclamations from these Friends. A minuet was never heard, much
less danced, beneath their roof. Although his sons Samuel
and Redwood, both in their teens, talked enthusiastically
of hunting, Fisher suggested that the sport should be enjoyed with due restraint. Sally, the younger of the daughters,
seemed to Audubon to take an embarrassingly romantic interest in him. The plain little Philadelphian was fascinated by
his smile and his wavy mane, which had grown long during
the voyage and his illness. His use of the Quaker "thee" and
"thou" much sweetened his already charmingly broken English. Unaware that Friends do not "marry out of Meeting,"
he began to wish himself a safe distance from the girl and the
extreme propriety of the household. Still, the thick, dour
walls of Ury, which dated back to before 1700 and occupied
the site of a Swedish fort, could not have been altogether
austere. (John Adams told in his diary of a lavish dinner of
"duck, ham, chicken and beef, pig, tarts, &c., beer, porter,
punch, wine" enjoyed at the Philadelphia town house of the
Fishers at Fifth and Front Street.)

Miers Fisher needed little urging to drive the unfathom-
able son of his client back to Norristown, where the storekeeper, Morris Jones, could offer Audubon room and board.
The Reverend John Jones, a former Virginian, and principal
of Norristown Academy, agreed to tutor him in English in exchange for drawing lessons.[3]

Dacosta, who since his arrival from Nantes, had been
rooming in Philadelphia to await the spring before opening a
lead vein at Mill Grove, remained aloof. He was never to live
at Mill Grove in Audubon's day.

Audubon lost no time in walking out to the farm. With
William Thomas, a Quaker whose own farm was farther down
the road, he entered the large, reddish brownstone mansion
with classic dormers, formal portals, and huge chimneys.
But the small, close, low-ceilinged rooms—stripped of furniture—strange and interesting though they were, did not
long hold the visitor. He may be pictured taking the terrace
in a few long strides on his way down hill to the mill pond,

then into the woods and out over the sere brown bottom-lands leading to the Schuylkill's margins.

Audubon soon forsook his duties in Norristown for Mill Grove. By late autumn he was lodging with the Thomas family, shooting his first quail, and trapping his first mink to draw it in watercolors. He failed to see how a gun, snares, traps, and a good retriever were to be paid for out of his small allowance, to be handed to him quarterly by the tenant as part of the annual rent of $350 for Mill Grove land. The small store that he came upon at the crossroads a mile west of the plantation offered little in the way of temptation. It appeared unlikely that the corner would ever burgeon into a village, in accordance with the owner's hopes.[4] However, the first ride of five miles into Norristown, the county seat, was not without inspiration.

William Thomas had no horse to spare for the rides back and forth to Mill Grove, where his young charge spent his days hunting and drawing. He suggested that the English purchaser of Vaux Hill, down the road, who was expected daily, would be stocking his place and know of sales. From the word "Englishman" the understandably prejudiced Audubon recoiled a little; but while he went on with his nest-gathering and sketching, oblivious of whispers about his strange behavior, he kept the advice in mind.

Two days after the arrival of William Bakewell, his wife, two sons, and several daughters at Vaux Hill on November 9, Audubon overcame his shyness in his eagerness for advice.[5] But Bakewell, wearied by the journey from New Haven, Connecticut, referred the question to Brigadier General Andrew Porter, another caller. Porter, a gentleman farmer from near Norristown, gave some hints. Bakewell was pleased with his guests' praise of the view from the formal portico of the handsome mansion. It encompassed a twenty-mile panorama that included Valley Forge. Because early settlers called the rich acres of these farmlands "the fatlands of Egypt Road," the new owner renamed the plantation Fatland Ford. It held more promise than the unproductive farm and worthless brewery he had abandoned in New Haven.

The readying of the house, two large stone barns, a wash-house, springhouse, servant tenement, and walled garden occupied Bakewell for a week or two. Then one morning he called at Mill Grove. No expatiating by Mrs. Thomas on the rumored beauty of the daughters of this neighbor had sufficed to send Audubon back again. She explained to his visitor that he was off on one of his solitary rambles. The mild-mannered, pensive Bakewell promised to return soon with his son Thomas.

The aloofness of their French neighbor became noticeable to the Bakewells, Pawlings, Porters, and even to the Pennsylvania Germans. He made himself conspicuous by it, and no less so by his dedication to the carefree life. Not all the bustle at Fatland Ford, the herds of Merino sheep and blooded cattle that were being brought there from distant auctions, or the sight of its good saddle horses and hunting dogs could induce Audubon to return the call.

Fate, however, was not to be flouted. Soon after New Year's, Audubon, with his fine new gun and dog bought on credit, met Bakewell face to face beside the Perkiomen. Both were out after game among the firs, and they talked together as they followed their dogs along the snowy banks. The much embarrassed Audubon apologized for his rudeness. The kind gray eyes of the Englishman made it easy to forget merely historical grievances.

However, days passed before he made good his promise. His meeting with Bakewell had convinced the plain French-man that, with his makeshift education and simplicity, he was no match for the obviously wealthy, clever intellectual and his household. Much more urging by the anxious, kind-hearted Mrs. Thomas was required before he would muster courage to lift the great brass knocker at Fatland Ford, but at last he did.

A servant woman admitted him. She was one of many refugees who had lately come ashore from a ship in the Delaware River. Bakewell was to pay the captain her wages until the cost of her passage from Germany was cleared away. Wordlessly she motioned the caller into a small sitting room.

There beside a cheerful open fire sat Lucy, the eldest daughter. She looked up, surprised, from her sewing. Before her stood the handsome neighbor about whose peculiarities she had been hearing. As shy as he but too poised to show it, she apologized for the absence of her father and brother and sent a servant after them. She explained that her mother had been indisposed since their journey and was confined to bed. Then she motioned Audubon to a place opposite her by the fire. His eyes that glowed like an eagle's, his appealingly visible uneasiness, soft voice, and captivating accent soon banished her reserve. She spoke so precisely and reassuringly in her best clipped English that he could not fail to understand. He secretly hoped that her father would not show up too quickly, as, with angelic intuition, she helped him find words. He became his most disarming and witty self as they exchanged impressions of their new country. To emphasize his remarks he snapped his strong, artistic fingers and now and then half-rose in the excitement of describing his adventures. The "thee" and "thou" of the Thomas household were no doubt part of his charm, and destined to remain so.

Not once did his eyes leave Lucy's face. In two days she would be eighteen. Although her nose was a mite too long and low-bridged for beauty positively startling, her comforting gentleness, velvet voice, gray eyes, high coloring, infinitesimal waistline, and above all, her Anglo-Saxon mystery, made her somehow quite different from the French coquettes. Here was a pride, a reserve, and a feminine character unlike any he had known. She matched his account of the good Loire Valley life with an equally glowing one of her days on the Derbyshire plantation she had left behind. As she spoke of the glens and moors of her hilltop home in Crich village, he saw that her detestation of cities was no less fervent than his own. Her pianoforte in the corner and her songbooks hinted at a mutual passion for music. There was little need to stress his love of nature and drawing; she had heard about it from the neighbors and could not keep from smiling when he broached the subject. If he apologized for his long locks that reached to his shoulders, he may have remarked that Benjamin Franklin, whose maxims and *Disappointed Pendulum* Jean's father liked to quote, had adopted such a style without ill effects.

At five o'clock the Bakewells assembled for tea. Thomas, approaching seventeen, did not conceal his pleasure at meeting a neighbor fond of hunting. Beside fourteen-year-old Eliza, the family beauty, sat her charming younger sisters, Sarah and Ann. Five-year-old William listened, transfixed, to all the talk of guns. Mrs. Bakewell appeared none too pleased with her isolation on the farm, a sentiment echoed by Lucy. Between the climate and the problem of servants, she wished that the family had never left England. But William Bakewell voiced cautious satisfaction with Pennsylvania, despite the disappearance of his capital at a rate even more rapid than in England, whose taxes and burdens he had fled.

Mr. Bakewell's brother Benjamin had emigrated with his wife and infant son in 1793 in order to enter the mercantile trade in New York City. His sister-in-law Sarah White Palmer followed with her stepson, John Palmer. She was the widow of the Reverend John Palmer, who had been editorial assistant to the Republican reformer, discoverer of oxygen, and early protagonist of Unitarianism, Joseph Priestley, himself an emigrant to Pennsylvania in 1794. The younger John Palmer managed Benjamin's New York venture, in which William had a share, while Benjamin established an ale brewery in New Haven, Connecticut. Finally, after several years of pleading and one exploratory voyage to America, William agreed to join in the speculation and bring his family.

Bakewell's sister Sarah Bakewell Atterbury and her husband Job had also settled in the East with their many children.

It had been Priestley's wish that the Bakewells, Palmers, and others sympathetic to his religious and political views might settle near him in western Pennsylvania. Although Lucy's father had bought a tract in Northumberland from Priestley, he had no intention of joining the proposed colony. Audubon now began to hear the names not only of Priestley (then within weeks of death, as it happened), but also of Dr.

Erasmus Darwin, the famous botanist and grandfather of the evolutionist Charles. Darwin had at times been the Bakewell's family doctor in Derby. His *Loves of the Plants* and *Botanic Garden* were among Lucy's treasured possessions. Unsophisticated in political and scientific matters, Audubon wisely kept silent; but his parting glance for Lucy betrayed an eagerness to return to Fatland Ford.

From the day of Audubon's visit, Lucy said no more of boredom with Pennsylvania. Her admirer returned the hospitality of the Bakewells with a prompt invitation. On their way to Brigadier General Porter's place—called Selma—Lucy, Eliza, Thomas, and their parents, accompanied by their New York guests, paused at Mill Grove. Audubon rather overreached himself in his eagerness to please. He declared that the Washington portrait above the mantel in the sitting room was the gift of the general to his father, "Admiral" Audubon. Incurably indifferent to precisions of every sort, he added that the gift had been presented at the time of the "battle of Valley Forge." He was unaware that the latter was a campsite, rather than a battleground, and that his father was far removed from Mill Grove at the time. What he did know, however, was that his father did not become even *lieutenant de vaisseau* until near retirement. The Bakewells were well pleased to be able to reply that General Washington had also visited their house in flight from defeat at Chadd's Ford. For the rest, there was the language barrier to excuse obscurities; yet even the enchanted Lucy should have had her doubts about his claim of tuition under the artist David of France.

The party climbed the narrow staircase to the dormer bedroom which the avid amateur called his museum. The floor, shelves, and table were decked with stuffed birds and rodents. The honest, realistic crayons of a mink and a feathered winter resident or two showed promise. Audubon predicted that by spring the room would be festooned with eggs and skins and would hold far better sketches. The spring migrations were a heady prospect as Lucy could well see.

On another day the Bakewells came over to skate on the mill pond. The day after, Audubon joined Bakewell and

Thomas with their guns. The lessons that he and Lucy had promised to exchange—drawing and French conversation— were well under way.

Audubon had been pining to speak his own language; a chance meeting with Jean de Colmesnil, a refugee who had fled Saint-Domingue with his father and uncle, won the young man an invitation to visit Mill Grove.[6] At the neighborhood dances a rival interest in Lucy sprang up between host and guest. Audubon, in new satin finery and silver buckles, fiddled and stepped to the cotillion. By capriciousness he strove to keep the enviable charm of Colmesnil in the background. William Bakewell grew worried as he saw his daughter spellbound by these rivals and their attentions.

Not only the neighbor Pawling, but also Lucy, thought Audubon a marvel on skates. One day her brother Thomas held his cap high while the undoubted show-off passed and repassed on gleaming blades. Then, at the ring of a signal, the boy tossed the cap up for Audubon to riddle it with shot at twenty paces. William Bakewell was not amused by the report of the escapade and forbade a repetition.

One winter's day Audubon headed a line of duck hunters on skates up the Schuylkill. Suddenly an air hole tripped and engulfed him. If the current had not cashiered him to the surface a few yards onward his career might have ended that afternoon. His comrades shared their garments to replace his freezing attire before he led the shivering line back through the dusk.

The attentions of Jean de Colmesnil became so ardent by February that William Bakewell gave the boy fair warning to stay away from Lucy. But in March he dared to appear again at Fatland Ford, though only to lend a hand with planting and plowing, along with Audubon. Nevertheless, he was dismissed for the final time. Convinced that he had lost his place in Lucy's affections, even though Audubon himself declared him the more eligible, Colmesnil left Mill Grove in defeat.

Bakewell's uneasiness about Lucy did not end there. She continued her daily walks with Audubon even while her father feared he might be deceiving her in ways. Before his departure for New England on business, William Bakewell cautioned her and admitted his lack of faith in the romance. On his return in May a few weeks later, the illness of Sarah and her failure to respond to the ministrations of Dr. Benjamin Rush of Philadelphia came first.[7]

Bakewell was busy planting corn when the whispers of a hired hand sounded a new alarm. Lucy and Audubon had been seen disappearing into a sheltered rock cave above the creek.

Bakewell spent a sleepless night before deciding to question the tenant of Mill Grove. William Thomas soon told him that the grotto visits had been going on only during the nesting of "pewees" and were quite harmless. The birds had become so tame that Audubon could take the parents in his hand for study. Finally he had banded some with filaments in order to be able to recognize them in coming seasons.

Relieved that the reports were unwarranted, Lucy's father continued to regret his daughter's seriousness about the Frenchman. If she actually meant to marry him, at least his background was no handicap; Miers Fisher had vouched for the soundness of his family. But to become a good farmer was plainly not in the boy. Nature and drawing were his only apparent interests.

To make her forget about him, Lucy was sent to her Aunt Atterbury's in Baltimore for a month. Audubon continued his daily visits to help Thomas with the mowing and hope that the understanding Mrs. Bakewell would pass him a message from Lucy. These enclosures invariably addressed him as "Dear Laforest."[8] The sincere and plainspoken girl had a taste for romantic novels and sentimental verse. Her friend, who began to fancy himself an "American woodsman"—*un homme de la forêt*—responded warmly to the name "Laforest." If his imagination and eagerness to please spun out allusions to the nobililty of Les Touches, the family Laforest of La Garenne may well have been mentioned with effectiveness. While there was no lineal tie between him and these aristocrats, the extremely idealistic, aspiring, and sometimes even snobbish Lucy Green Bakewell could be beguiled by the mention, perhaps, of a royal equerry and castle, which would surely have held more magic than the image of a thatched cottage in Les Mazures.

Soon after Audubon and Tom cut ears from the rye, Lucy reappeared. She and her mother joined in the mowing, reaping, and binding, although in a separate field. She was pleased that Audubon had been allowed to visit during her absence, to help with the chores, stay for supper, and then lead the swimming in his mill pond on hot evenings.

The arrival of Ferdinand Rozier of Nantes, son of a close friend of Lieutenant Audubon, cast another shadow on the friendship. Rozier, eight years older than his host, was ludicrous and uncouth in Lucy's eyes. His incessant *"Dîtes donc!"* (You don't say!) earned him the nickname "Didon" at Fatland Ford. The Bakewells would have been happier if the cutter *Experiment* had not brought Rozier that spring; his travels as a seaman to the Cape of Good Hope, Cadiz, Tenerife, and Mauritius had given him no *savoir faire*.

The engagement of Audubon and Lucy, yet to be announced, was scoffed at by the overseer of Mill Grove. Ignored by the Bakewells, Francis Dacosta had begun to send indignant reports to Miers Fisher and to Couëron of Audubon's posing as the squire of the plantation. He himself hungered for a partnership and had been making progress in that direction. Lieutenant Audubon promised him half interest on the strength of his first attempts to locate minerals on the land. Papers were on the way, together with a power of attorney that gave the overseer a free hand. From a notice in the New York *Herald Tribune* and *Rolf's Gazette*, one might have believed the speculation full of promise: "The lead mine discovered on Perkiomen Creek . . . the property of Francis Dacosta, has been lately opened, and attended with great success."

Aubudon ignored the agent. He divided his time between Lucy and experiments with drawing, heedless of the tenant's warning that their interests were being jeopardized. Audubon had been too busy galloping to Norristown at dawn for wire to put birds in lifelike attitudes, and such matters, to notice.[9] But William Thomas refused to stand by and give Dacosta his way; he reminded the overseer that he had no right to claim discovery of a vein about which he himself had learned years earlier from its real discoverer, neighbor Gilpin. He demanded a concession of $600 in rent for information about another vein and hinted for a share in the coming speculation. Fisher advised against more than the cash allowance, which infuriated Thomas.

Gradually, Audubon and the tenant saw eye to eye. It was clear that Dacosta was scheming for full control.[10] Audubon thoroughly discussed with William Bakewell and Lucy the wisdom of going to France to expose Dacosta's suspected chicanery. In the meantime, the rollicking evenings of dance and song continued at Fatland Ford. "Noisyish," the Bakewell journal dismissed the gatherings.

Before time to gather apples and sow wheat the Bakewells drove to Philadelphia. On the September evening of their return, Audubon and Rozier, who had made a trip to France and back since his previous visit, welcomed them with lanterns. But the month ended in deep mourning on the plantation; two weeks after her return, Mrs. Bakewell was stricken with dysentery. She died on the last day of September, after only ten days of illness.[11] The next day she was buried in a small plot across the meadow from the garden. Audubon and Rozier were among those who heard a "suitable" psalm read by William Bakewell for the brief service.

Rozier, accompanied by François Gillette, a Saint-Domingue refugee and brief visitor at Mill Grove, left for Nantes. Gillette, or Gillet, was the son of a grocer on whom the elder Audubon was soon to call for a very special favor. Only the permission that John James Audubon awaited kept him from sailing with the two.

Audubon's tendency to speak of Mill Grove as part of his potential fortune was not displeasing to his prospective father-in-law. William Bakewell began to think that the mines might actually come up to expectations. Unbeknownst to him, Lieutenant Audubon's opposition to the marriage increased even as his own diminished. These sentiments were already on their way to Dacosta:

> Remember, my dear Sir, I expect that if your plan succeeds, my son will find a place in the works, which will enable him to provide for himself, in order to spare me expense which I can hardly support. . . . My son speaks to me about his marriage plans. If you will be so kind as to inform me concerning his intended, as well as about her family, their manners, conduct, means, and reason for being in that country—whether because of misfortune that drew them away from Europe, you will be doing me a signal service. And I beg of you, besides, to oppose this marriage until I may give my consent to it. Tell these good people that my son is not at all rich and that I can give him nothing if he marries in his present condition.

III. A Mission

O N THE DAY AFTER NEW YEAR'S, 1805, Francis Dacosta left
his Philadelphia rooming house in spite of the "enormous snow banks." He kept going until he reached Miers
Fisher's house beyond the city limits.[1] Now that Fisher had
become his lawyer and agent, Dacosta believed his position
to be stronger—whether for or against the Audubons remained to be seen in the months ahead.

John James Audubon, hovering between life and death
since early December at Fatland Ford, was powerless to intervene.[2] The abscess that had confined him to bed there, after a
fainting spell, brought fever, then delirium. After ten days,
however, the crisis passed. Determined to try walking on
crutches, he fell in a faint again and was confined to bed
through Christmas time and for weeks thereafter. The news
that his father had been seriously ill in France set him back
even more than did word that Dacosta planned to occupy the
Mill Grove mansion by spring.

Lucy read English novels to her patient and kept him well
informed. On Christmas Day she described a scene of excite-

ment outside the barns. Dr. James Mease,[3] an agrarian expert and authority on hydrophobia, had come from Philadelphia to observe a lively demonstration by William Bakewell and the mechanic Prentice, who had built a two-horse machine that threshed a record number of bushels of wheat.[4]

On February 6, Audubon undertook his first canter since the onset of his illness. A week later he and Tom rode to Philadelphia through the drifts. He advised Miers Fisher that he intended to go to France and warn his father of Dacosta's schemes. He then approached the culprit himself; and, after bitter words were exchanged, he obtained from Dacosta what he supposed to be a letter of credit toward passage.[5]

Having returned to his lodgings at the Thomas farm, Audubon set out on the last day of February for New York. His traveling companion, Thomas Pears of Coventry, England, a clerk in the employ of Benjamin Bakewell, had been a guest at Fatland Ford. (Thirty years later, in writing "Myself," Audubon was to recall, erroneously, having made the ninety-mile journey on foot.)

Upon presenting the supposed letter of credit to the banker Kauman in New York City, he was unnerved to hear that it merely suggested sending him back to Pennsylvania or, better still, by force to China. Mrs. Sarah Palmer, the sister of Lucy's Aunt Bakewell, restrained him from returning to Philadelphia in a homicidal rage. He wrote a reasonable plea to Dacosta, then let Fatland Ford know of his dilemma. Lucy persuaded her father to have his brother Benjamin honor his promise of repayment for advancing the sum of $150 to Audubon.[6] Meanwhile, Audubon borrowed the Bakewell gig and was thrown out, bruised but unharmed, in a runaway on Bloomingdale Road, seven miles up Broadway.

A day or so later Thomas Bakewell arrived home. His ride on his father's mare had been one of repeated detours caused by snowdrifts, and the trip had been made even worse by "very bad" indigestion from wayside fare and poor cider, and by the added hazard of sleighs and stagecoaches mired along the route. But he had finally reached Budd's Ferry, boarded his mare, and ferried the Hudson for "York."

Although no ships were due to sail for France before mid-March, the Anglo-American colony began a round of farewell activities for the young Frenchman, now at the Bakewell's, now at Mrs. Palmer's. Among those present were merchants Thomas and Arthur Kinder and Benjamin Page; all would be of future importance to Audubon. Anthony Bleecker, for whose Dutch forebears a street was named, joined in the "forfeits and blind man's buff," after showing his candle-eating trick. Kept indoors by snowfall, Audubon led Lucy's brother and cousin in lighthearted "painting bouts." But then, despite bad weather, he roamed among the ships at anchor until he booked passage on the brig *Hope* before it began to take on final cargo.[7]

Audubon and his companions heard a lecture at the young but ill-fated Cabinet of Natural History.[8] Everywhere he went the crayon portraits of a French artist, Saint-Mémin, caught his eye; he himself intended to try his hand at such "heads" of Americans some day. He joined the throngs that paid admission to see one of the most popular current attractions, a live elephant which, despite frozen ears, obeyed the haranguing of its trainer by uncorking and imbibing cider. One night he joined Tom and Benjamin Bakewell, at the sound of fire bells, in carrying water in bitter cold towards the East River; but only one of a row of warehouses was left standing.

On a wild, windy March 12 the *Hope* was ready to sail. Meanwhile, a letter from Couëron which indicated no awareness of Audubon's approach gave Dacosta positive assurance of a partnership in Mill Grove. Dacosta let Kauman know of his sudden willingness for moderation; but it was, nevertheless, the cash provided by William Bakewell that made Audubon's departure sure.

What Audubon did not know before sailing was that Dacosta had received still another letter from Lieutenant Audubon urging him to keep on good terms with their tenant, repair the roof, and open more "tunnels" in the mine. He also said that "bad advice" by those who goaded his son's "self-esteem" must be to blame for his behavior. "Perhaps he has been immature enough to boast in the house to which he

goes that his plantation ought to fall to him alone," the lieutenant suggested. He likewise told Dacosta to destroy any
such illusions and to rely on the rebuke which he was enclosing for John James and his indiscretion. He was much displeased that Meirs Fisher had written him nothing about the
scolding he should have administered, much less about the
mines. He did not wish his son to be sent back to Couëron;
his reasons for having sent him in the first place remained
unchanged. In a word, he implored Dacosta to be patient
with his charge:

> Only an instant is needed to make him change from bad to good; his
> extreme youth and petulance are his only faults—and if you have
> the goodness to give him the indispensable, he will soon feel the ne-
> cessity of making friends with you, and can be of great service if you
> use him for your own benefit. It is necessary then, my Dear Sir, that
> we try, by gentleness, to bring him round to duty. If you are indul-
> gent with him, it will be I who ought to feel every obligation toward
> you. I hope the enclosed letter will work a change with him. This is
> my only son, my heir, and I am old. When Mr. Fisher shall have
> shown my letter to the would-be father-in-law, he will see that he is
> mistaken in his calculation upon the assumed marriage of his daugh-
> ter. For, should it take place without my consent, all help on my part
> would cease from that instant. This, if you will be so kind, is what
> you may say to the would-be father-in-law, that I do not wish my son
> to marry so young.[9]

A mysterious leak off New Bedford, the home port of the
brig, forced her to put in for repairs. Although Audubon suspected that newly wed Captain John Williams merely wanted
one more rendezvous with his bride, the truth was that the
Hope was soon to be declared unseaworthy in Bordeaux. The
gales that whipped her as she set out again washed a crewman overboard to his death; yet in mid-ocean the calm was
such that schools of dead fish could be seen floating eerily
about.

After nineteen days the *Hope* entered the mouth of the
Loire, then anchored briefly off Paimboeuf.[10] The chief customs inspector took Audubon by barge to the Couëron landing. About eleven o'clock that night he was running up the
garden walk, uncertain of a warm welcome except from Anne.

Lieutenant Audubon's astonishment gave way, in spite of all, to satisfaction. There could be no doubt that an appropriate reply to another threat from Dacosta might now be undertaken, settling once and for all the unaccountable failure of the partnership papers to reach Philadelphia. Charles-Marie D'Orbigny, a friend of the Audubon family, had witnessed the action before it was dispatched in December, but Dacosta continued to doubt that it had ever been sent and suspected the Audubons of being in league to cancel the agreement.

This was no moment to allow Dacosta to bring suit in the highest court over the question of severance. Lieutenant Audubon got off a conciliatory answer which in its honesty, simplicity, and force was a veritable portrait of himself. It made no mention of the presence of his son, nor did it speak of their mutual counsel. He reminded Dacosta to keep close to the facts. If indentures that held good in France lacked validity in America, nothing could void what legally bound Frenchmen regardless of their whereabouts. The lost paper was sure to turn up momentarily. "Distance, not any negligence" was accountable, or perhaps failure on the part of the "honest and lax" Miers Fisher. Jean Audubon urged Dacosta not to be resigned to the failure of his recent attempt to collect $1,600 from David Ross & Company of Virginia, but to go after it again "with iron hooks" if need be, to finance the mining venture.

Rather than allow his son to be seen and drafted in Nantes, the lieutenant himself requested the "honor" of executing a small business commission as a favor to Benjamin Bakewell. By letter John James Audubon explained to his "dear friend and generous protector," William Bakewell, that he himself was keeping to the house as if ill, rather than venture near the "snares of the eagle" in the politically charged air of France. The collection of Loire Valley bird portraits intended for Lucy had to be undertaken with utmost caution and the cooperation of the family physician, the young Charles-Marie D'Orbigny, a naturalist whose enthusiasm for birds constantly lured him away from his practice. D'Orbigny scored Audubon's lack of scientific method in measuring and draw-

ing species until he began to see an improvement which led
to real skill at taxidermy, as well.

Confinement to La Gerbetière in May, at the peak of the
nesting season, made it impossible for its prisoner not to
think obsessively of the ship and the "good wind" that would
carry him back to Pennsylvania. Yet he felt extremely unhappy that by departing once more he would be depriving
his father of an only son and his dearest possession. He
begged his future father-in-law to believe that there was no
mere flattery in the constant questions of his parents regarding the charming Bakewells and their ways, which they in
Couëron wished to imitate. How he was to provide the Spanish donkey requested by Lucy's father for breeding mules,
and bring it with him when he returned, he refrained from
predicting. "Kiss all yours for me without forget Lucy," he
ventured to close, in his bravely groping English, "I am with
the greatest pleasure your eternal humble servant, Audubon
fils."[11] His signature was identical to that of his father, even
to the flourish beneath with its cryptic dots.

The fulminations of Dacosta continued while he refused to
resume mining until his positive, equal partnership in Mill
Grove should be verified by the arrival of the missing papers.
Again Jean Audubon reasoned with him. "You speak of my
going to that country," he said as he complained of weakened lungs and need of home care. "If such had been my intention I should have done so long since. . . . You, better
than anyone, know what my situation was at the time I sold
you a share. We must proceed in such a way as to gain our
ends—if not on a grand scale, at least the best in our power,
with reasonable expectations. For that I count on you." He
sent off an indenture to replace the lost one, promised slate
for the leaky roof at Mill Grove, and once more told Dacosta
to form a mining company to end the stalemate. But it appeared unlikely that Dacosta would wish to share the huge
profits of which he dreamed.

For the aging Anne the visit of her favorite passed far too
quickly. Proudly, one Sunday in August, she saw him take his
place beside Rose as they became the godparents of Gaston-

Édouard, Dr. D'Orbigny's second son. The infant was, like his brothers yet unborn, to become a zoologist of note in young manhood.

Audubon's furtive rambles to the outskirts of Nantes and over the countryside could not have led him as far afield as Les Touches and Les Mazures for a glimpse of his mother's old district. He could have approached without fear of recognition, now that Jeanne Rabine's father had been buried for three years. His aunt, Madame Le Jeune de Vaugeon, had long since left Montigné. Her husband was within months of his death in Nantes.[12]

On December 16, 1805, Rose "Bonnitte" was married to Gabriel-Loyen Du Puigaudeau, a Port Launay country squire sixteen years her senior. His brothers André and Joseph were seamen, and Joseph had served under Lieutenant Audubon on the *Eveille*.[13] "Mademoiselle Rose Bouffard, aged nineteen, younger daughter of the late Catherine Bouffard, native of Saint-Domingue, and adopted daughter of Monsieur Jean Audubon and his wife Anne Moynet," the register frankly disclosed. Among the signers was "John Laforest James Audubon," his name in garbled order and "Fougère" dropped in favor of "Laforest." Ferdinand Rozier, also present, sympathized with him that although he was to return with him to Mill Grove as business partner in the spring, there could be no marriage to Lucy until practical matters were untangled. Jean Perchais and his wife, a Turpin, were present. So was the wife of Jacques-Gilles Maisonneuve.

To raise cash Lieutenant Audubon had recently sold half of his remaining share in the plantation to the Roziers.[14] Claude, the elder Rozier, had agreed that the youths should come to terms with Dacosta, or, that failing, settle with him and enter commerce together in some likely place. On April 12, 1806, the partners boarded the American ship *Polly* at Saint-Nazaire, Rozier as a native of Holland, and Audubon as a native of Louisiana.

The voyage was not devoid of excitement. Two young noblemen, fugitives from conscription, dueled for the honor of rescuing the bonnet of a Virginia belle when it blew into the sea. The lady, a congressman's daughter, grieved over the death of the loser. One day a British privateer, the *Leander*, looted the *Polly*, then bore off two of her crewmen and her hogs, sheep, and wine stores. By hiding his cash in a sock beneath a cable in the bow, Audubon outwitted the brigands of the ship, which he was to refer to forever after as the *Rattlesnake*.

Thirty miles off Sandy Hook, New York, a fishing smack warned of British frigates on the prowl. The *Polly* fled to Long Island Sound, where a gale grounded her until the tide rose, allowing her to put about for Manhattan.

IV. Preludes

I MMEDIATELY UPON LANDING, on May 28, 1806, Audubon and Rozier made for the Bakewell countinghouse to announce their partnership. If they should find the sale of Mill Grove to Dacosta their best move, the advice of Benjamin Bakewell regarding ways and means of becoming merchants was to be decisive. Thomas Bakewell, by now an apprentice clerk with his uncle, took leave to accompany them to Pennsylvania and help with the reaping.

The beauty of springtime was at its height on June 4 when Lucy welcomed Audubon. But the austere, critical, dry-souled Rebecca Smith, the thirty-eight-year-old spinster from Philadelphia whom William Bakewell had married before Christmas, did not take to the excitable, witty guests.[1] As for Lucy's father, he committed his view of matters to his diary: "Don't like their being here in idleness. Mr. Audubon did not bring his father's permission to marry nor the $150 lent him. Tom seems to have applied well to business and is attentive and active."[2]

Ferdinand Rozier approached Dacosta, while Audubon

excused himself from the negotiations on the pretext of having to gather specimens for Dr. D'Orbigny without delay. He sent to New York for birdlime, needed for luring hummingbirds. He, Lucy, and Thomas swam in the mill pond daily; and Audubon demonstrated the dexterity at basket-weaving he had acquired in his Rochefort days. For the benefit of little William Bakewell, whom he sometimes took into the saddle with him, he jumped his horse over the snake rails at a gallop. The boy loved to watch his adroitness with foils and to join him and Lucy in their nature walks in the woods and fields. These exploits drew no admiration from Lucy's parents, but only the hope that the temperance and prodigious physical strength of her suitor augured something better.

The grotto above the Perkiomen was again the refuge of the "pewees" which Audubon had banded two years before. At any rate, the male, his thread anklet still visible, had returned and built a new nest. He was as amenable to human friends as before; but his new mate, successor to one killed for fish bait by the miller's son, took alarm.

Neither of the young Mill Grove partners looked forward to farming. The reaping and hauling of wheat and oats, calling for two dozen extra hands at Fatland Ford, was singularly lacking in appeal. The commotion, the incivility of the hirelings, and the unforeseen accidents turned them away from the idea. Actually, Audubon was sketching wildflowers in the woods while the last of the oats were reaped. He drew sprays of false foxglove for Lucy, then a nighthawk and a fish hawk.[3] That Lucy could not identify the false foxglove is not surprising. Scarcely six weeks before Audubon drew it a small group of scientists had founded the American Botanical Society on June 6, 1806, in Philadelphia.

Sometimes the lovers took their ease beneath a tree near the portico to watch Lucy's uncle's former clerk, Thomas Pears, cradle grain in the blazing sun. Pears had come out to study farming before his marriage to Sally Palmer in the coming autumn. He was not amused that his friends should dawdle in the shade, after weeding only "five square yards" of garden, merely to tease him. Audubon laughed that for his part, he should rather "turn merchant" in New York and take up where Pears left off at commerce. When Pears quoted him to Sally in his letters, she replied that Audubon struck her as "extremely unfit" for the smothering "confinement" of business, particularly if married to one as openly fond of "liberty" and rural living as Lucy.

Dacosta alone seemed not to experience the discontent, idleness, and indifference of the younger Frenchmen at Mill Grove. By late summer he easily persuaded his partners to withdraw, at least partially, from a stake in the place. They agreed to sell all except one hundred arable acres across the creek. The house, mills, mines, and surrounding 113 acres were to be deeded to Dacosta as soon as he could manage to pay.

But first it was important to hear from Lieutenant Audubon and Claude François Rozier of Nantes that the sale met with their approval. Moreover, John James Audubon did not wish to enter agreements subject to American law without at least token citizenship. On September 5 he went to Philadelphia and declared himself "desirous to be naturalized."[4] With studied indifference to vital statistics, he called himself older by two years than, in fact, he was. Also, in the apparent belief that it would simplify matters, he said that he had landed in the United States a year earlier than he actually had. "John Audubon, a free white person . . . born at Aux Cayes in the Island of St. Domingo sometime in the Year 1783 . . . [arrived] about August 27, 1802."

The truth was that Lieutenant Audubon could not have thwarted such swift capitulation to Dacosta even if he had wished. He saw no possibility of meeting the sum of $500 which he had long owed his partner. So desperate had his own need of cash become in Couëron that when he saw the chance to acquire some by a legal maneuver, not even pride and discretion deterred him. A report of the rumored death of Sanitte Bouffard had recently been corroborated, and in a strange manner. A man identified only as "Monsieur Ferrière" was reported to have sought guardianship of her children and control of her considerable estate. The gentleman, evidently Audubon's successor in her affections, had begun the action in New York or New Jersey. Lieutenant Audubon openly declared himself the father of the "five minors," although his adopted Rose Bonnitte was the only one whose name he could give. He called himself their "loving father," despite ignorance of their names and whereabouts, and sued to become their lawful guardian.[5] Without mentioning that Gabriel Du Puigaudeau was Bonnitte's husband, he appointed him deputy guardian. Among the sea captains who witnessed his paternity was Pierre Gautreau, the brother of the captain of the *Tancrède*, which brought Bonnitte to Nantes. The failure of Ferrière's counsel to produce Sanitte's will gained the day for the Lieutenant.

A reckoning with Dacosta could no longer be postponed. Benjamin Bakewell had promised to take John James Audubon as an apprentice clerk in September and to place Rozier with his friends, the Hurons, Philadelphia importers. This arrangement was made in order to form trade ties with Ferdinand's father in Nantes. Except for the acres across the Perkiomen, all of Mill Grove went to Dacosta for a down payment of $4,580 by bond, rather than cash, toward the sale price of $9,640.30.[6] Dacosta boasted that he would reduce the balance by eight hundred dollars within three years. He promised an additional $5,000 from the mines, as well as half the gross in time to come, although the yield of minerals and ore remained impossible to reckon.

The marriage and departure of Sally Palmer and Thomas Pears in mid-September had the expected effect on Lucy. Audubon, more resigned than eager, had already left to be initiated into the mysteries of commerce.[7]

Not long after Audubon had begun to come to grips with ledgers and bills of lading, he sent a draft of $8,000—unsealed—to a Pennsylvania bank. He invested in indigo shipments and promptly took a loss. From the first, infrequent sailings and the routing of cargo via Bordeaux made trade with Nantes a slow business. Twice between January and May, in letters to Rozier senior, young Audubon betrayed his irrepressible addiction to drawing. In faulty French he slipped an order for good pastels and crayons into a list of timber and indigo prices.

No one could have explained better than Dr. Samuel Latham Mitchill, a friend of Benjamin Bakewell, why the clerk Audubon seemed absentminded. A prominent physician, senator, and sytematic collector, Mitchill had rented the room where Audubon stuffed birds for him each evening.[8] Mitchill began to share his considerable knowledge with his helper. But he devoted most of his time to the *Medical Repository*, his brainchild, founded with Dr. Edward Miller (1760–1812). The offensive fumes of the work fostered by the future founder of the Lyceum of Natural History brought out the constable after the neighbors made angry protests. Audubon haunted the dawn markets; there, and in the fields on weekends, he found new birds deserving of the best portraits he could render. American ducks, especially, commanded his rapt attention, with results imperfect but impressive.

Late in January he availed himself of a ride to Fatland Ford to find a tenant for his acreage. Not until February 15 could he bring himself to return to New York. Once more, in April, he begged permission of Couëron to marry:

> My dear Father . . . I deed send . . . a small Box containing some very curious seeds and some useful ones. . . . I do hope they are now in thy possession. Thou have been so often disappointed that it always pains me to think that they have been Miscarried. . . . I have seen in the News Paper that a ship called the Betzey had been in Nantz. . . . There are on board of her Many Birds and a collection of seeds from America for thee. . . ; pray when thou answer to this be kind enough to mantion these little things.
>
> I am allways in Mr. Benjamin Bakewell's store where I work as much as I can and passes my days happy. . . . My Biloved Lucy . . . constantly loves me and makes me perfectly happy. I shall wait for thy Consent and the one of my good Mamma to Marry her. Could thou but see her and thou wouldst I am sure be pleased of the prudency of my choice. . . . I wish thou would wrights to me ofnor and longuely. Think by thy self how pleasing it is to read a friend's letter. . . . Kiss mamma, Rosa and Brother Pigaudeau for me.[9]

Young Audubon also said that he had sent "some Turtle fit to be eaten in soupe," and begged a lock of his father's hair, whatever sheet music Rose could spare, and a miniature of his father from a new portrait in officer's dress. "It will cost thee little and will please me much," he added. Audubon scored D'Orbigny's failure to write thanks for the curiosities sent to him. As to the prospective retail store with Ferdinand, he dropped no more than a hint of it before closing. "Good by farwell good father. Believe me for life thy most sincere friend, be well be happy, thy son, J. J. AUDUBON. *J'espere que tu poura lire—adieu—adieu.*- (I hope that you can read this—farewell—farewell.)

Audubon's lengthy and dutiful but always colorful and droll letters to the elder Rozier continued. They called for copper-studded morocco powder flasks, music boxes with "good pieces and gay music," and wax seals, some of the merchandise to be held as stock for himself and Ferdinand and to be paid for as soon as the remaining acres at Mill Grove had been sold. English language books from Paris promised "great profit," if C. F. Rozier would oblige. There was the matter, too, of books for Mrs. Bakewell by Madame de Genlis, the famous educator, and a map of the departments of France for Thomas, whom Audubon was already calling "brother-in-law." Although "Mr. B. B." marked goods but a third over cost, Audubon quipped that learning "to shave Messrs the Americans" was not beyond his own growing potentialities. On an enclosed bill of lading marked "*pour Mr. Audubon père, aussitôt que possible*" ("for Mr. Audubon, father, as soon as possible") he listed nineteen varieties of seeds and bottled creatures which he was sending. At the bottom of the note he wrote: "If thou findest in my letter to Monsieur Rozier anything which displeases thee, remember that I am thy son. Adieu! Farewell, my good friend. Thine for life."

Ill and discouraged, Claude François Rozier complained that Bakewell's remittances were far too leisurely. But Bakewell had begun to direct orders to certain Nantes competitors of Rozier, whom he had found too slow. The competitors led Rozier to express disgust and suspicion in a letter to Audubon, who replied, "Believe nothing, and be well assured that Mr. Bakewell is our friend."

Audubon's orders and replies continued quite as if the tri-
umvirate were not doomed: ". . . the extravagances of the
women equals or rather quite balances the circumspection of
the men, so that all articles for women should be beautiful,
that is to say, conspicuous." But he asked Rozier to refrain
from sending any more of the too perishable yellow and
bottle green gloves and the far too dutiable laces.[10]

Ferdinand Rozier began to talk of visiting France. The
death of one of his employers made him anxious about his
ailing father, his best adviser. But Audubon feared that his
partner might never return if he left now; indeed, he wrote
his own father that such a trip might not prove to be in their
interest. By promising Ferdinand that he would go west with
him at once, instead, he forestalled a threatened break. Louisville attracted Audubon, who had heard the tales of the professional hunters of that area. He knew that Tom Bakewell,
just back from a lively adventure in New Orleans, would
take his place in the Bakewell firm. (Tom was still recovering
from the excitement of having had his uncle's ship, the *Clyde*,
and her wine barrels seized and then surrendered to him,
the supercargo, after no end of trouble.)

Ferdinand left to Audubon the task of telling the dying
Rozier their plans. "In a short time we are leaving for a voyage upon the Ohio, the details of which you will learn [from
Ferdinand], or from my father, and which I believe will be
very advantageous to us. We hope to sell Mill Grove this autumn, which we shall do, however, only at a profit."[11] He
was sending one more shipment of live birds and seeds for
the Rozier garden and La Gerbetière. His farewell included
best wishes for his proud cousin, Anonyme Le Jeune de
Vaugèon the elder, now a merchant of Nantes.

Benjamin Bakewell, generous to a fault, accepted a note
for $3,647.29. It was for store goods to be sent down the river
from Pittsburgh, and would not fall due until April 1808,[12]
two days after the wedding of Audubon and Lucy. After settling accounts between Lieutenant Audubon and Dacosta,
the two young Frenchmen mortgaged their remaining Mill
Grove land for $10,000. On the last day of August they de-

parted from Fatland Ford for Kentucky. By way of preparing for life with Audubon among the Louisville emigrés, Lucy began to pack for New York and classes in French.

Rozier's diary tells how heavy rains slowed their coach in the Alleghenies. Sometimes it took six horses to cover the more difficult stretches, at one mile per hour or so. Bleak accommodations and food were all that the taverns offered. Tales of "wild animal hunting in the mountains" diverted Audubon at least as much as they depressed Rozier, who preferred to chat with French merchants on the way. He could find no words for the "terrible monotony, hardships and deprivations" of an Ohio flatboat. Sleeping on deck, exposed to the elements, was all the more trying when his hardy partner snored peacefully beside him. On clear nights the ark kept on course, but in storms it took refuge along some shore or wild island. Sandbars compelled all men aboard to take to the water and free the clumsy boat, to the curses of the low-born captain.

Claude François Rozier, who was never to see the chronicle kept for him by his son, died on September 7, 1807, as the partners neared Louisville. They knew that this settlement, on a plateau above the south bank of the Ohio, was the most important river port between New Orleans and New York. It had been a magnet for settlers ever since Boone blazed his trail from Tennessee. For forty years they had been coming over the Wilderness Road in wagons, on horseback, or by the river, until now there were 1,300 souls in bustling Louisville.

The main street, a half-mile-long thoroughfare lined with red brick houses and stores, had space to let. Rozier set up trade while Audubon went about the all-important task of fraternizing with the townsfolk. Nathaniel Wells Pope, their clerk, knew the woods and refused no chance to escape the routine of the store and show Audubon the bird haunts.

Local sportsmen soon discovered the inclinations of the new storekeeper. He voiced curiosity about every aspect of outdoor life. William Croghan, an Irish veteran of the American Revolution, had met Jean Audubon during the war and professed to seeing a strong resemblance between father and son. His son George became one of Audubon's hunting companions. His Titian-haired wife, Lucy Clark Croghan of Locust Grove estate, just north of Louisville, was the sister of George and William Clark, both, to Audubon, heroic American prototypes.[13] General George Rogers Clark, a paralyzed fifty-five-year-old, was a permanent guest on his sister's plantation. He willingly recounted his past campaigns against the Indian nations, his black eyes gleaming. William, the youngest brother of the red-haired "savior of Kentucky," was a thirty-seven-year-old veteran living in St. Louis as superintendent of Indian Affairs. William Clark's talk of his conquest of the Northwest Territory the year before with Meriwether Lewis kindled a like ambition in John James Audubon. The discovery that William had often sketched birds and mammals as Indian agent increased rapport with the Croghan household.

Croghan, eager to help his new friend, led Audubon to an old sycamore to watch the chimney swifts flock into its hollow at twilight. Repeated visits led them to the conclusion that no fewer than 9,000 of the birds took refuge there.

Dr. William Galt, a botanist and civic leader of Louisville, was pleased to learn of Audubon's friendship with Dr. Samuel Latham Mitchill. The prospective arrival of Lucy Bakewell delighted the Galts when they learned of her acquaintance with the late Erasmus Darwin of England. All in all, Audubon made an excellent beginning for her. The budding frontiersman from Couëron began to blossom into a full-fledged "American woodsman," quite in accordance with his ambitions. By the same token he wanted no part of the hapless "Jean Rabin, creole of Saint-Domingue."

Shippingport, the Bois de Boulogne of Louisville, welcomed Audubon. The village of wealthy French settlers beside the Falls of the Ohio was a paradise for nature lovers. Audubon returned day after day during the autumn migrations of passenger pigeons, Canada geese, and other species new to him. James Berthoud, a native of Neuchatel,[14] his wife, and their son, Nicholas, took a particular liking to him.

Berthoud, a barge builder, had sailed from Frankfurt to Philadelphia; then, quite recently, he had settled in Kentucky. He and a neighbor and former employee, the flour miller Louis Anastasius Tarascon, had built fine homes for their families. Tarascon was proud of his 1,200-foot rope walk, known to be the longest in the United States.[15] The former Marseille resident told unashamedly of downing geese with a small cannon as they flew over.

What promised at the start to be an idyllic existence was dealt a stunning blow three days before Christmas when the Embargo Act of 1807 became law and wiped out the mercantile house of Benjamin Bakewell. Trade was paralyzed, as the enterprise of Audubon and Rozier soon found out. Payment of the note due Bakewell on April 7 was more urgent, yet more difficult, than ever. Whether marriage to Lucy could be risked, or even permitted, could be decided only after a journey to Fatland Ford in the spring. Meanwhile, Audubon advised Couëron of the emergency.

V. A Wilder Range

O N THE EVE OF THE WEDDING of Audubon and Lucy a light fog lay on the horizon. A violent northwesterly wind blew rain through the night. In the gray dawn of Tuesday, April 5, 1808, clouds hung low. Only a robin and a bluebird or two hopped in the bare branches. Orchards were still tightly budded; only some bouquets of the hardy hepatica and arbutus rewarded search.

Near noon the sun began to glow a little as carriages streamed toward Fatland Ford. Friends gathered in the parlor while William Latta, minister of two Chester County churches, Charlestown and Great Valley, read the Presbyterian nuptial service.[1] By night the high, wild, prophetic winds returned.

Three days later, on a bright frosty morning, the bride and groom, accompanied by Rozier, left for Philadelphia to go from there by stagecoach to Pittsburgh. The thaw that followed snow flurries made the new turnpike beyond Lancaster hazardous. During the climb up the ridge near Chambersburg, Audubon left the coach to lighten the burden of the three struggling teams. Near the top the coach careened and upset with the frightened Lucy inside it. At an inn where she stopped to rest, her injuries proved less serious than Audubon had feared when he drew her, badly shaken and bruised, from beneath the vehicle. The memory, however, was never to fade for Lucy. It turned an old aversion for travel into a lifelong dread.

Hundreds of other emigrants shared the crude accommodations of the river flatboat from Pittsburgh.[2] The livestock, wagons, furniture, and spinning wheels of the families bound for a life on the frontier added to the crowding and turmoil. In one of but two cabins, each having a single porthole, Lucy joined the women and children. On rainy spring days the squalor, lack of privacy, and discomfort within were preferable to the decks. But Audubon, in every kind of weather, oblivious of the monotony and confusion, searched the skies and shoreline for birds.

At the Indian Queen in Louisville the facilities for washing up in the open courtyard on arrival caused the fastidious Easterner to shudder a little. To reach private quarters one passed dormitories filled with beds for commercial transients.

Except for Rozier, who was uneasy over business prospects while the embargo lasted, the newcomers began to find the happiness they had looked forward to in Kentucky. They declined to worry while everyone else was riding out the times. The refulgence of spring inspired reflections less earthbound.

Through the summer and autumn Audubon made quiet trading an excuse for spending many hours beside the Falls of the Ohio. As he canvassed the surrounding neighborhoods on horseback for business, he paused continually by the wayside. One day he let his horse stray, with a saddlebag of cash, while he pursued an unfamiliar warbler into the canebrake. Although luck was with him, it was no wonder that Kentuckians had begun to suspect him of being more the dreamer than the man of commerce.

On June 12, 1809, Victor Gifford Audubon was born at the Indian Queen.[3] The following March witnessed something even more fateful. Out of a little boat named the *Ornithologist* stepped the Scots-born Alexander Wilson, tinware peddler, penny poet, and naturalist, with a portfolio of drawings beneath his arm. Wilson's stopover on his way from Philadelphia to New Orleans, to solicit orders for a work on birds already begun and to continue through several brilliant volumes, was truly providential. It was to prove in what mold the mercurial Audubon was cast. The "Wilsons" of the world and their aspirations were not new to him. Long before he left Couëron, the American birds of Mark Catesby, as well as those of the Frenchman Vieillot—the true father of American ornithology—were well-known classics.

Wilson deposited his flute, wares, and caged parrot at the Indian Queen, then asked directions to the store of the naturalist about whom Benjamin Bakewell, now a thriving flint glass manufacturer of Pittsburgh, had told him. Audubon needed little persuasion to subscribe, once he had run through the fine colored plates that Wilson spread across the counter. Not doubting in the least that here was a notable contribution to science, he seized his pen and was about to sign when a far too audible whisper from Rozier reminded him that there was no cash available in hard times for such expendable items. Besides, added Rozier in front of the stunned visitor, Audubon had a better bird portfolio of his own.

Wilson, stung by what he overheard, withdrew, but not before his keen eyes, hooked nose, prominent cheek bones, and look of poverty that well suited the son of a Paisley weaver left their indelible impression. A generation older than Audubon, he let his fading era be guessed by his shabby short coat and gray waistcoat and trousers. Another Scottish artist of Philadelphia, Alexander Lawson, his engraver, had rescued Wilson from suicidal melancholy, then persuaded him that nature illustration could be learned—and for a better living than such odes as his long poem *The Foresters* provided. His first ornithological volume, printed in 1808, proved conclusively that his study of land, sea, and water birds would brook no rivals.

That evening the much injured guest piped moodily on his

flute at the hotel by way of refusing conversation. Not until Audubon proposed a ramble in the morning to show Wilson some rare water birds, did polite condescension take the place of silence. Three days later the doleful peddler presented Gwathmey[4] of the Indian Queen with his parrot and continued his odyssey down the river. His diary, later edited for publication by George Ord, an enemy of Audubon's, is said to have contained these megrims:

> March 19. Examined Mr. A———'s drawings in crayon—very good. Saw two new birds he had, both Motacillae [flycatchers]. . . . March 21. Went out shooting this afternoon with Mr. A. Saw a number of sandhill cranes. Pigeons numerous. . . . March 23. I bade adieu to Louisville . . . received not one act of civility . . . one subscriber . . . nor one new bird.[5]

From the day of his arrival in 1810, Wilson personified Audubon's own latent ambitions. The recognition of this rival as the foremost authority became a figurative windmill with which he was to tilt for the remainder of his days. Not even Alexander Wilson's death in 1813 would end the struggle for ascendancy. Even before the little *Ornithologist* cast off, with a new sketch or two and some notes, Audubon's fever to surpass what he had seen was rising. While Rozier brooded over trade, he himself fumed that Wilson had declined to exchange observations by letter. If ever he learned that his guest had left Scotland in 1794, under the cloud of a conviction for libelous poetry composed as blackmail against a rich textile mill owner—whose charges landed Wilson in jail—he did not use the tale to denigrate his rival.

Throughout the spring, Audubon, obsessed by birds as never before, paid little attention to Rozier's own *idée fixe*—escape from Louisville. The pleasant round among friends there and in Shippingport made uninviting the suggestion of removal to Red Banks, 125 miles down the Ohio.

In the end the obdurate Rozier had his way. After a tour of inspection, Audubon, attracted to the wilds of Henderson, agreed to the immediate opening of a log-cabin store situated between two tobacco warehouses near the river. The little place, for some years known as Red Banks but recently renamed in honor of the guarantor of the Transylvania Company, held no charms for the fastidious Lucy. But she resigned herself to the idea that if such people as Dr. Adam Rankin and his wife of Meadow Brook plantation, a mile from town, had found happiness there, so could she.

However, within a matter of months Rozier began to have his doubts about their prospects in Henderson. He proposed moving on to Ste. Genevieve, a village north of the lead-mining district not far from St. Louis. Indeed, he wished to start before winter closed the river. Again it was the prospect of taking up a free-ranging existence among the forests where Daniel Boone was still living that won Audubon over.

The problem of where Lucy and Victor should wait while the partners made a start was readily solved by Elizabeth Speed Rankin's eagerness to draw Lucy into her lively household as the tutor of her children. Such fine diction, manners, and erudition were not to be found among the rural teachers. Lucy readily accepted the friendly offer. She had often been a guest of the Speeds on the Bardstown Road near Louisville and knew of their ancestral brilliance. Captain James Speed, Mrs. Rankin's father, was a Revolutionary War hero and a descendant of England's foremost chronicler, John Speed. In 1782 he and his wife had brought their children on horseback over the Wilderness Road from Virginia. (A page of family history remained to be written; before too many years a son of Elizabeth Rankin's twin brother was to become one of Lincoln's most intimate friends, and the son of another brother was to wed the niece of the poet John Keats.)

In a heavy snowfall in December 1810, Audubon, Rozier, Pope, and two crewmen cast off in a new keel boat.[6] With four oars in the bow they could run five miles an hour with a favorable current. Above the covered stern, which held barrels of whisky, gunpowder, and sundries for sale in the Missouri Territory, there spread a sixty-foot main oar hewn from a tree trunk and carved like a dolphin's fin.

At the Cache River, six miles above the confluence of the Ohio and Mississippi, where the village of Trinity was soon to rise, weather waylaid the party. From the shore another traveler bound for Ste. Genevieve signaled for them to join him and his men. Jules de Mun, a refugee from Saint-Domingue and the grandson of a marquis, warned of ice ahead in the Mississippi.[7] They all pitched camp together in comradely fashion on Christmas Eve.

Early on Christmas Day, a band of Shawnees who were headed for their Arkansas winter hunting grounds led the campers in search of deer and bears on the promise of a knife and scissors. The Indian women paddled the canoes across the Illinois River to the Tennessee banks while their men dozed in blankets. At the end of the hunt the blowing of conchs brought the women running to gather up the mounds of wild swans and game. That night there was feasting on nut soup and bear fat. The women plucked the swans' creamy feathers, destined to deck the bon tons of Europe.

Audubon lay by the fire, his mind filled with visions of swans dipping and floating on the freezing lake. Before dawn he awakened to see a woman, delivered of twins in the night, lashing hide to bark for a cradle, then rocking it with a length of grapevine as if the birth were nothing so momentous.

The river was rumored to be open as far as Cape Girardeau. Audubon hailed a swarthy youth in a canoe from across the stream and found him willing to pilot the keel boat. The young man said that his father, the former Spanish territorial agent Lorimier who was in command at the Cape, would know what lay ahead. With stronger oars and tow ropes of bullock hide they set out at dawn. Ice floes at the mouth of the Ohio slowed them to three miles per hour. In order to warp their boat against the current, everyone but Lorimier went ashore and towed with ropes across their backs. Even so, only seven miles were put behind by nightfall.

Long before daybreak the party moved on at two miles per hour. But progress was so slow and the weather so harsh that Lorimier decided, after two more hard days, to give up and await the thaw. At the great bend of Tawapatee Bottom oars were laid up, and a log shelter was raised. The prospect of six weeks in the wilderness delighted Audubon as much as it appalled Rozier.

Osages and the last of the Shawnees bound for winter grounds led Audubon along the traces. Unlike the Shawnees, the shy, noble Osages spoke no French. But Audubon's crayons of birds and animals familiar to the Indians broke down their reserve. "When I made a tolerable likeness of one of the Indians with red chalk they cried out with astonishment and laughed excessively," he chronicled. They showed their mastery with bow and arrow. He demonstrated his marksmanship by shooting between the gleaming eyes of wolves that skulked in the shadows near the campfire. Sometimes he tossed bones to lure them nearer the light of the blazing trunk before firing.

The disappearance of Indians, the source of supply for meal, was followed by a bread shortage. Wild turkey breast buttered with bear grease, tough roast bear, and opossum caused stomachs to revolt. Audubon and Pope searched for Indians with meal. Finally succeeding, they cached a supply, marked the tree beside it, and with several loaves impaled on their gun barrels walked into camp. Crewmen went to rescue the cache and haul it back by sled.

Indians continued to drift towards the campfire. They would squat in silence with their tomahawk pipes while their women wove baskets. Sometimes the men danced tribal steps while the chortling women watched. The duets of Audubon and Pope on violin and flute left the circle spellbound.

One night in February the ice-locked currents of the Ohio and Mississipppi surged, then with a great roar broke through. The sleeping camp leaped to life, rushed to the keel boat to remove the cargo, and bound cane for a jetty to save the craft. For the voyage that could now be undertaken the party hunted until the trees around the camp resembled butcher stalls. They baited trout, pike, and catfish at ice holes. Two days later they cut the jetty away, reloaded, and went aboard. An unforgettable six-week idyll was at an end.

But the hardest navigation still lay ahead. By poling through the ice and shallows, the travelers managed to reach Cape Girardeau. The father of their patron, a little man in moccasins, a soiled dress uniform jacket with epaulets, and buckskins with iron knee buckles and Indian gaiters, greeted them. Old Lorimier, now a strutting, pathetic figure of the past, had once led Tory fighters in Ohio. He had also once escorted Daniel Boone's party. After George Rogers Clark drove him across the Mississippi, he became a commandant much respected by the Indian nations. Secure though his place had been until 1804, when Upper Louisiana became Missouri, his best days were over.

The keel boat pushed on through the ice jams, past Grand Tower Rock's swirling currents, until it reached Ste. Genevieve.

VI. Cross Currents

L UCY AUDUBON'S TWENTY-FOURTH BIRTHDAY, on January 18,
1811, could hardly have been festive. Not all the quilting
bees, sleigh rides, Yuletide balls, and social life at Meadow
Brook could make up for Audubon's absence. Under the
strain of anxiety, her natural gravity and decided likes and
dislikes deepened. Only teaching, her second love, brought
tranquillity of a kind.

One April evening Audubon hurried up the path, his
hunting dog at heel. He had tramped 125 miles in three days.
So inundated were the prairies that he had seen deer standing in inches of rainfall. But he was not at all wearied, despite
the disappointment of having found Ste. Genevieve to be
only a small squalid place. Rather than bring Lucy there, he
had abandoned his interest in the partnership. A down payment and promise had sealed the separation. Rozier had chosen, at thirty-six, to remain in Ste. Genevieve, settle down, and
marry. He chose Constance Roy, a girl of French-Canadian
descent who was half his age. With Constance, whom he
married on August 19, 1813, he proposed to found a Mis-

souri clan—an ambition that was to succeed beyond his fondest hopes.

Audubon's straitened circumstances were no secret to the Rankins. Eager to keep Lucy on as teacher, they invited the couple to remain until the new store they planned to open in Henderson showed a profit. Louisville, where Audubon went for fresh stocks, had lost its appeal. It bore little resemblance to the place he had seen four years before. Its population, including 500 slaves, was a third greater. The unsurfaced streets were lined with 250 houses, stores, and taverns. The boom in rope, rope yarn, cotton bagging, wheat, corn, rye, tobacco, hemp, flour, meal, and spirits, and the high cost of slaves at $500 each, were all one heard about there.

It was not long before Audubon was again leaving most of the drudgery of trade to the clerks. Much hunting and considerable drawing, unhampered by any frowns from the departed Rozier, staved off boredom. There were neighborhood parties and huge holiday picnics to break the monotony of existence. The Audubons often swam to the Indiana shore and back and rode horseback together.

Lucy's half-wild mustang, "Barro," was one that Audubon had first seen when its previous owner drove it roughshod into town from the Arkansas headwaters. The fellow, one Barrow, had bought it for thirty-five dollars in tools and trinkets from the Osages. It had been running for a month on a diet of prairie grass and cane, finally varied by Natchez corn, but it had reached Henderson as fresh as at the start. The stallion, of that Arabian strain introduced by the Conquistadores into the Rio Grande Valley, peered warily at Audubon through a thick forelock, switched his long tail, dilated his nostrils, and stamped his hooves. Audubon jumped him over logs, rode him through swamps, spurred him into the Ohio, then had Lucy try his paces at Meadow Brook. For fifty dollars, or about half what Louisville asked for less sturdy horses, the animal became Lucy's. Barro was to carry Audubon to a fateful encounter before too long.[1]

Toward the end of summer Thomas Bakewell, fresh from

three years of mercantile training with the Kinder Brothers of New York, turned up at Meadow Brook on his way to New Orleans. He planned to become a consignee for a Liverpool concern. He had come from Pittsburgh to Cincinnati in a skiff with one oarsman, then on to Louisville by "broad horns," and finally to Henderson by river. He was favorably impressed by the wide acquaintance of the Audubons. It occurred to Thomas that his brother-in-law's Gallic verve might prove a business asset in creole society. Lucy dared hope that New Orleans would soon be their home. Meanwhile, it was agreed that they would establish the firm of Audubon & Bakewell, with headquarters in the southern city but with Kentucky as an important part of the axis. Thomas proposed that Audubon go east at once and appeal to William Bakewell for a loan Thomas himself wished to take on. Ferdinand Rozier was one of the first to receive their printed broadside and price list.[2]

Early in November 1811, Audubon prepared to travel east on horseback with Lucy and Victor.[3] He buckled breastplates to the saddle flaps for greater safety on the rises. Victor rode in a basket secured to his father's saddle horn. Over open fires, between far-separated taverns, wild game provided ideal fare along the way. They stopped for a brief visit with the Benjamin Bakewell family in Pittsburgh; Audubon paid Lucy's uncle his share of fifty-five dollars still due him. He had already reminded Rozier to do likewise.[4] In little more than three weeks, at the rate of forty miles per day, the trio reached Fatland Ford as December began.

Rebecca, more the martinet than ever, concealed neither her reluctance to have Lucy and Victor as guests until spring nor her relief that Audubon would be off for New Orleans in a few days. He intended to return for his family after making final arrangements with Thomas, and, hopefully, settle with them in Louisiana instead of Kentucky. It annoyed Rebecca that the balance of $200 still due William Thomas for his disclosures had been left for her husband to discharge.[5] Although William Bakewell had managed to dispose of the last of Audubon's Mill Grove acres in 1810, he complained of the "great burthen" and the "trouble and anxiety" involved in realizing $8,000, less his own hard-earned discount as agent. He had been obliged to carry the cash, paid in specie, to Philadelphia by coach, where a counterfeit note was found in a bundle from the purchaser, Joseph Williams. Bakewell gave Audubon to understand that no matter how well the sum might serve his needs for the new firm, it was to go to the Kinders of New York to pay off the mortgage on the land; he agreed to lend Thomas a generous sum instead. Then he invited Audubon (still indebted to him for having paid a certain long-standing obligation in town) to pay Lucy thirty-eight dollars, the price fetched by the mare she had left behind after her marriage.

The atmosphere of the East was charged with rumors of the probable disaster to be expected from the embargo and with talk of war. A new grave in the burial ground across the meadow added a note of melancholy as winter descended on Fatland Ford. Mrs. Sarah Palmer of New York had died while on a visit to Thomas and Sally Pears at Wheat Hill and was buried beside her cousin, Lucy Green Bakewell. Audubon departed, his mission handsomely accomplished. He felt confident that fate would favor his latest venture in spite of ill omens. He consoled himself that the failure of the Mill Grove mines to live up to the expectations of the investors proved his own good fortune, Dacosta's unsettled mortgage notwithstanding. No market had been found for the disappointing yield of metal.

At an inn near Juniata Falls, between Harrisburg and Pittsburgh, Audubon fell in with a well-known New Orleans merchant named Vincent Nolte. The Leghorn-born gentleman invited him to his table beside the fire. To his suggestion that the long-haired Kentuckian in the Madras bandana must be French, "original throughout," came the reply: "Hi heem Heenglish!" So picaresque a man himself as one day to become the stuff of the popular novel *Anthony Adverse*, Nolte was not deceived. Then with a laugh Audubon gave his birthplace as La Rochelle in France and his first American residence as Louisiana. "I am somewhat cosmopolitan," he added facetiously. "I belong to every country."[6] He might have added that he possessed the Celtic fondness for tall tales.

Next morning they set out together. Near the Natural Bridge, Barro won a race proposed by Nolte. In Pittsburgh, just after New Year's, 1812, Nolte invited Audubon aboard one of his twin arks about to descend the Ohio. His young Livonian partner, Edward Hollander, followed with the horses in a second flatboat. At Maysville (then known as Limestone, Kentucky) Audubon and Nolte returned to their saddles and parted only at Lexington, where the latter turned towards Frankfort in hopes of hearing Henry Clay's oratory.

On the Kentucky barrens a distant rumbling made Barro prick his ears, whinny, lower his head, then spread his legs for support before the trembling of the earth. Brief though the violent tremor was, Audubon could not but fear for Nolte even as Nolte feared for him. At Meadow Brook and Henderson no one was harmed. But a series of earthquakes of the kind were to keep the entire region in a state of dread until spring. One winter's night after a wedding party at the plantation, the timbers rattled and the ground quaked, rousing the family and guests and causing them to flee in their nightclothes into the open barnyard. In the morning came rumors of cows in trees and islands lost from sight in the Ohio.[7]

Between apprehensive messages from Thomas Bakewell and Rozier's cautious refusal to send the thousand dollars that he owed for a final settlement, Audubon had no incentive to visit New Orleans.[8] Instead he took passage on a flatboat bound for the East in February. If one more attempt to extract final payment from Dacosta should fail, now that he himself had sold his interest in Mill Grove, it appeared best to bring Lucy nearer their future home, wherever it might be.

Again Dacosta showed himself no more willing to part with his money than the next man, particularly on what seemed the eve of war with England. When, in April, Lucy was pregnant, Audubon felt little sorrow over having to linger and abandon himself to the leafing woods, the birds, and his "art room." While he sketched a pair of wrens that were nesting outside the window, Lucy read to him from Scott and Edgeworth. To lure the male bird indoors and gently seize him in order to sketch an outline, Audubon tossed him some insects. Although wary before his release, the wren returned without fear to the nest and resumed his singing. Thereafter he kept his distance from his captor.[9]

Young William climbed to a nest high above the Perkiomen and brought a female broad-winged hawk down beneath a kerchief. Audubon perched her on a stick at his drawing table. She offered no resistance as he smoothed her ruffled feathers, but instead remained immobile. When he launched her at the window, she flew off without a sound or outcry.[10]

One day Audubon called on Alexander Wilson in Philadelphia. The impoverished painter put aside the eagle portrait that occupied him but would not speak of birds. Instead, he rose abruptly and proposed a walk to call on Rembrandt Peale, of the famous "painting Peales," to see the version of *Napoleon Crossing the Alps* he was completing.[11] Audubon took one look, then feeling unwelcome, he withdrew.

On June 18, 1812, America declared war on England. On the eve of Independence Day of the same year, Audubon became a naturalized citizen, an occasion on which he again showed indifference to dates and vital statistics. He swore allegiance in the presence of Peter Du Ponceau, lawyer and philanthropist of note. The naturalization of William Bakewell on December 28, 1809, had already made Lucy a citizen. A fortnight later the Audubons, accompanied by Lucy's brother William, were bound for Kentucky in the barge of General William Clark, who had sent word that it was at the disposal of all those anxious to start home before hostilities began.[12]

At Louisville the Berthouds' reluctance to take the Audubons to New Orleans by barge compelled their return to Meadow Brook. They set out by skiff for Henderson with two Negro crewmen. While his charges slumbered on the open deck, Audubon watched the owls streak across the hazy moonlight. On the final night of the cruise the terrified oarsmen pulled for the nearest landing as infernal shouts rose from the northern woods. The war whoops turned out to be only a camp meeting in the beeches.

Perhaps it was on this return that Audubon suffered a terrible contretemps described in after years. He found that 200 or more drawings, left in a chest for safekeeping, had been chewed by Norway rats. For three days he brooded in suicidal melancholy until it dawned on him that within a year or two he could replace the lost and damaged productions with far better. He may have recalled how once, in Louisville, he had watched a female rat dart from a Dearborn wagon newly arrived from the East, followed by her young, which were to breed a voracious tribe.[13]

In August while Audubon was painting one of three otters trapped on Long Pond across the Ohio—depicting it in a defiant post with its claw in a steel trap—Thomas Bakewell walked in.[14] He had tramped across the Indian lands to Nashville, then on to Meadow Brook to announce the failure of the firm in New Orleans. He needed little urging to remain as Audubon's local partner until peace with England.

On November 30, 1812, the day John Woodhouse Audubon, a wailing and sickly infant, was born, his father drew a butcherbird in a highly attenuated pose that reflects his agitation.[15]

Early in 1813, Audubon bought a roomy log cabin beside his store with four acres of orchard and meadow for livestock, poultry, caged wild birds, and a variety of pet rodents. Three or four slaves made an artificial pond to assure a supply of his favorite turtle soup. Thomas bought a cabin nearby, his thoughts on going east to choose a bride.

Audubon again visited Ste. Genevieve in May, but with no more success. Before setting out from Henderson he had sent word to Daniel Boone that he hoped to go hunting with him. He was disappointed when a riverboat captain brought a brief answer saying that the venerable frontiersman was leaving such pleasures to his son because of growing blindness and the infirmities of age.[16]

When Audubon returned from Missouri, the prairies were

carpeted with wild flowers. There were clouds of butterflies and bees beneath the waves of birds migrating from the southlands. At the Big Muddy River, Audubon's horse, covered with linen to protect him from the insects that were killing deer and bison, bolted into the stream. While Audubon dried his buckskins at a wayside cabin, the animal died of the stings. It was sunset and too late to continue on foot. Audubon's peaceful overnight stay with a squatter's family was the genesis of an episode, a fanciful recital of horror in his *Ornithological Biography*.[17]

Audubon arrived home to find Lucy near death of fever. Almost at once he himself fell ill. For weeks their recovery appeared doubtful.

Quite well by midsummer, however, he was returning from Louisville in his boat when the self-styled "General" José Alvarez de Toledo y Dubois hailed him. He and the soldier of fortune lashed their arks together and visited far into the night.[18] A Spanish refugee, the officer said he was bound for Mexico and needed more recruits for his army. He promised that if Audubon would become his bodyguard as colonel, he too would share in wealth from the seizure of a province ripe for revolution. For an artist who had twice left France to evade the military life, the offer lacked appeal.

The "General" bought a young Negro from Audubon, who also sent him around to the horse traders and to likely recruits in Henderson. The Spaniard presented him with a Spanish dagger and Lucy with a ring in return for overnight hospitality. Even after he continued on his way, his real identity remained unknown. A triple spy and also a fugitive from a deputy post in Santo Domingo for the National Assembly of Cadiz, he was an agent for opposing Spanish colonial factions, as well as for James Monroe.

Meanwhile, William Bakewell was losing faith in his ability to escape the disastrous effects of wartime on farming. But he intended to wait until an acceptable bid came along for his plantation.[19] His disciple, Thomas Pears of Wheat Hill, influenced by his outlook, put his own farm up for sale and it went at once. The news reached Henderson at a moment when Thomas Bakewell was persuading Audubon that they should try a grist and saw mill. In need of capital, he wrote Pears to come down and discuss joining the venture. He also suggested that the mechanic Prentice, whom William Bakewell had helped to start in business for himself in Philadelphia after he had performed some successful experiments on the farm, be brought along.

The impressions of Thomas Pears when he visited Henderson in the spring were so dismal he hesitated to write his wife of his decision to invest. He agreed to put up $4,000 if Bakewell would risk a like amount. Audubon was to assume the balance, or more than twice what his partners were investing. He would be the richest—or poorest—in the end.

The reaction of Sally, awaiting word in Pittsburgh at her Uncle Bakewell's, was one of terror of the West. She pictured the British marching on Kentucky, aided and abetted by Indian uprisings. Life bade fair to be lived among "half-savages, except for Mr. Audubon and a few others." Pears replied reassuringly that it would be quite a trick for either the English or Indians to reach Henderson. "If they do," he added humorously, "it will be a matter of great congratulation if any ever get back. Be assured that an Indian would sooner be bitten by a rattlesnake than be in sight of a Kentuckian."[20]

In August of that turbulent year 1814, Pears returned east to fetch his family and enlist Prentice. The millwright agreed to build a sixteen-horse engine, "including castings, blacksmithing, and wages for hands to set the fly-wheel in motion," all for $4,000.[21] He wanted his far too liberal terms to be kept secret. He called for the use of Thomas Bakewell's cabin and free board with the Audubons.

A farewell call by Pears at Fatland Ford caused him deep shock and sorrow. William Bakewell had suffered sunstroke in his fields. Invalided at fifty-two, he had to turn direction of the farm and household over to Rebecca. For some time it had been known that she keenly resented his affection for and financial aid to his children. Sally Palmer had heard from Eliza that Bakewell hardly dared "bestow the smallest presents" on any of them. In fact, the family beauty, Eliza Bakewell, her stepmother's scapegoat because of her failure to marry, had only lately fled to her uncle's in Pittsburgh. She had no intention of returning to the nagging Rebecca, but trusted that the Audubons would allow her to join them in Kentucky. Her brother William was leaving soon for an apprenticeship with Thomas.

The Treaty of Ghent, ending the war between Britain and the United States, was signed on Christmas Eve, 1814. But until the news crossed the seas, hostilities continued. Meanwhile, the Capitol and much of Washington were burned; the Battle of New Orleans in January was superfluous.

The benefits of peace did not soon take effect in Henderson. Audubon had bought several lots for the mill site, all of them too far from the river. Months slipped by before the partners leased a site from the township directly beside the Ohio. Prentice had arrived for duty in November, but spent the winter rigging an engine for his ark to pass the time. Nothing prevented his sailing to Pittsburgh and back in the spring—one of the earliest steam voyages on the Ohio— while deliberations about building the mill dragged on.

The crowding of the cabin that held the Audubons, including a new infant daughter, Lucy, the large Pears family, and Eliza and William Bakewell was not conducive to peaceful living.

By the time the huge bulk of the mill began to rise in the spring of 1816, Audubon was praying that his contribution of $15,000 would bring a fair return. Thomas Bakewell, mentor of the undertaking, had not considered how little lumber was called for, here where he was dreaming of a fortune. Nor did he realize that scarcely enough wheat was grown to justify the existence of a large grist mill. Prentice fumbled ahead with the machinery. Pears, already disillusioned, began to imbibe too freely and often, while Sally declared she could not rear her children in such a town. After the marriage of her cousin Eliza Bakewell to Nicholas Berthoud of Shippingport in March, she carried out her threat to leave in order to give birth to an infant at her aunt's in Pittsburgh. Benjamin and Anne Bakewell were given to understand that Audubon's inattention to business while he chased after birds would be the ruin of the venture. Pears withdrew from the company to go east and learn the flint glass trade with Sally's indulgent uncle who, when Thomas Bakewell wrote that Audubon was no more at fault than Pears, took a neutral stand.

Most disturbing to the Audubons of any of their troubles was the sudden illness of little Lucy. Unable to diagnose the malady that hung on through the summer and fall, the doctor thought it possibly a form of dropsy. Lucy, overburdened, was not comforted when Thomas returned from the East in the summer with a bride, Elizabeth Page, for whom they nonetheless made room. The daughter of Benjamin Page, an associate of Benjamin Bakewell, Elizabeth was a disappointing choice, not only to Lucy, but to the entire family.

Before Christmas, unhappy in her new surroundings and, like Sally Pears, unwilling to bear her child in Henderson, Elizabeth gave Thomas a pretext to withdraw. Bank failures in Kentucky increased his eagerness to go. He announced to Audubon that inasmuch as the town had lacked "allurements" for his bride from the first, and since her "dislike" destroyed its "inducements" for him, he would remain only until July. He preferred to lose his $4,000 or $5,000 rather than stay on, but nevertheless wished Audubon to pay him $5,500 in full by summer, or "twenty percent per annum" until that sum was realized. "I consider him to have the best of the bargain," Thomas let his parents know, "but my great desire to leave Henderson and to live in Pittsburgh was the motive by which I acted." [22]

Audubon bowed to this stinging return for his patience and hospitality. He was spared the knowledge that Thomas, finally aware of the reasons for their failure, was hoping to profit by his experience in Pittsburgh. Good local supplies, reliance on domestic buhrstones instead of imports, and on the Ohio instead of wells, and the prospect of a site near the Bakewell glassworks could hardly fail. This time Thomas intended to supervise Prentice who, he thought, would be an asset in the venture.

Neither William nor Benjamin Bakewell warmed to the

proposal. William was unimpressed by Thomas's estimated paper wealth of $10,000 and declined to lend him half that sum for which he dared hint.

The two-year-old Lucy died in the winter of 1817. Until she could be buried on the General Samuel Hopkins plantation in the spring a grave was made for her in the garden.[23]

Several Henderson men, undismayed by signs and portents, invested in some mill shares, as did Benjamin Page, Thomas's father-in-law, in the course of a visit. Even the level-headed Nicholas Berthoud of Shippingport acquired a small interest, now that credit was easing and recovery seemed near. Thomas's departure in July with Elizabeth and their infant, with his brother William, and with Prentice as partner, cleared the air no little.

VII. Aftermath

AUDUBON HIT ON THE IDEA of convincing his father that he, Anne, Rose, and Gabriel ought to come over and share in the good life that a rising fortune promised. Even before Thomas deserted him, he had been intimating to Couëron that he might soon have assets worth $50,000.[1] He was acquiring more land in Henderson on the chance of a future land boom. His father, much disenchanted and failing fast, replied that for a man of wealth France offered more positive inducements. Besides, Anne wanted her son to return. Gabriel and Rose were more than contented with the neighboring villa Les Tourterelles—the Turtle Doves—which they had taken over in Couëron in 1813, along with its extensive gardens, orchards, tenant houses, and view of the Loire. Their four-year-old Gabriel would be its next master.

The time had come for Lieutenant Audubon to ask a favor. How matters stood with him he made clear. His thoughts fixed on death—and very far from life abroad—he asked for his son's power of attorney to make Gabriel the executor of his will. Audubon went before the French notary Barband of

Henderson to do his father's bidding—to use the name "Jean Rabin." After beginning, ". . . I, John Audubon," he employed the name "Rabin" four times in succession, the last as "Jean Rabin, husband of Lucy Bakewell." This done, he signed himself "John J. Audubon."[2]

Lieutenant Audubon had his reasons, none of them a mystery to his children. In 1812 the three greedy daughters of his brother Claude of Bayonne and the son of his sister Marie-Anne-Claire Audubon Le Jeune de Vaugeon had his first will rendered null and void under the terms of a French law forbidding inheritance by "natural children."[3] In order to strengthen the chances of his son's inheritance through a second will, subterfuges—and use of the name "Rabin"— were to be avoided. He made Madame Audubon his sole beneficiary, with the proviso that her own will and testament name her adoptive children as her beneficiaries. His natural children would be secure in regard to inheritance if established as only her adoptive legal heirs. She, too, referred to her son as "Jean Rabin" in her will. Neither testament divulged his whereabouts more specifically than as "America"; neither mentioned the heirs as the children of Jean and Anne Audubon—adoptive or otherwise. Except for Anonyme the elder, the four cousins were like strangers to Audubon. Anonyme II did not then, or ever, take part in this suit. Nor does the failure of his name to turn up in available documents lend itself to explanation.

The exodus of the mill partners had its compensations. Peace returned to the Audubon cabin. Victor, six, and John, three, amused themselves with their father's pencil stubs and colors. They blew on his flute, sawed on his fiddle, and listened to the evening duets of their musical parents. Sometimes Lucy guided their fingers at the piano which had come down the river from home. It meant to her much what gun and pencil did to Audubon.

The inhabitants of the dooryard were an unfailing source of amusement and surprise. One of the Canada geese had been hatched from an egg the cook had retrieved and placed beneath a setting hen. She and the rest of her domesticated tribe, with a notable exception or two, ruled the yard. Unlike the others, she paid no heed to the honking migrants overhead. The little termagant mated with another wild captive. No less redoubtable was the trumpeter swan that chased the children and defied the slaves until the day she slipped through the unlatched gate and hopped and ran on pinioned wings toward doubtful freedom.

The pet wild turkey cock was the favorite until his sad undoing. He would fly to villagers who hailed him, but paid no attention to domesticated turkeys, preferring to roost in solitude on the roof. In the spring he disappeared for the mating season. One morning Audubon was out hunting with his dog Juno. A handsome gobbler appeared in the path, and, oddly enough, made no attempt to flee. At first the dog refused to obey, but then he padded warily up to the bird for an exchange of greetings. To protect the rescued pet from hunters Lucy put a bright red ribbon about his neck. One sad day, an unsuspecting hunter failed to recognize the warning until too late.

It was well known in Henderson that Audubon was clever with foils. When a veteran of the Napoleonic Wars came to town and began boasting that he could beat anyone at broadswords, Audubon was dared to take him on. Between the insistence of the town youths and the bragging of the "expert," he had to forget his intense dislike for brawling and, with one cunning pass, send the fellow on his way.

He took up the challenge the day a boorish farmer rode into town with the warning that the dog beside his wagon could whip any cur or coward in the place. With a stick he dealt the brute a smart blow on the muzzle that sent it slinking to safety between the wheels.

His perspicacity in regard to the genus *Homo sapiens* in no way equaled his growing knowledge of wildlife. His determination to see the good in those around him sometimes allowed him to be as easily snared as his feathered friends. Aglow with optimism and the incurable belief that providence was his friend, he applied for a federal land grant in August 1817. Jacob Gall, a bibulous settler, got wind of the application for several hundred acres of timberland near Vincennes, Indiana, beside the Wabash River.[4] He saw this situation as Audubon might have viewed a turkey through his rifle sight.

Aware that Audubon must have an endorsement for the 560 acres, Gall offered to sign in exchange for a loan of $300. As a concession, he agreed to cut and deliver 2,500 trees on the tract at one dollar per trunk. After Gall signed, Audubon left the inebriated fellow "in disgust." When Gall was jailed for disturbing the peace, Audubon bailed him out for the sum of $180. The rascal's next move was to represent the grant as his own and sell it to a local partnership for a large consideration. A lawsuit involving all concerned began. Meanwhile Audubon had already taken over the tract and hired a boatload of migratory hands to cut down trees. But they had no more than begun when they seized his oxen, tools, and axes and made off down the Ohio.

In the spring of 1818, Audubon's tribulations were augmented by news from Couëron. His father had died in a Nantes roominghouse on February 19 while on a visit to the city.[5] The family had not long to wait for the next move on the part of the Lieutenant's nieces and his nephew Le Jeune de Vaugeon who, on April 1, was to wed Cecile Vilmain, granddaughter of the man whose ship had rescued Jean Rabine. In May the voracious foursome sued again with an audacity that could be heard all the way from the high court of Savenay to Nantes, and probably in the Vendée. The piece of land which Le Jeune had acquired from his uncle at a bargain in 1815, and still another concession of the kind, had not appeased him.[6] With mock reverence for the memory of the relative whose last will he and his cousins were determined to break, he had his attorneys impugn the honor of Madame Anne Audubon. They condemned as a blot on her late husband's fair name her formal declaration that he was the father of the "illegitimates," Rose Bouffard and "Jean Rabin, creole of Saint-Domingue." They asked the court to deny her, as well as the "children of adultery," all right to inheritance—the right they wished to arrogate to themselves.

Audubon dreaded to imagine the gossip in Henderson if these scandalous proceedings should reverberate across the ocean. Tampering with the mails was a constant offense on the frontier. He put off writing his condolences lest he invite more bulletins about the lawsuit. Between Le Jeune and one of the cousins, the wife of a Nantes helmsman, there might be a move to track him down, if he did not take care.

By the month of July, Audubon could put off writing no longer. He expressed hopes of visiting France before long. Then he would give all of his news. What he might have added, but did not, was that he could risk no further correspondence with Les Tourterelles until the lawsuit subsided.[7]

His mood is reflected by his reception, that summer, of a visitor, a stringy-haired, bearded Greek named Constantine Rafinesque[8] who asked the way to "Mr. Audubon's house." Told that he was speaking to Audubon, the little foreigner began searching the pockets of his long, grimy, yellow nankeen coat and baggy waistcoat. From among plants and grasses gathered along the way he drew a sealed introduction from Tarascon of Shippingport asking that Audubon "take pity on the odd fish" and aid his search for new fauna. The ravenous tatterdemalion was accordingly led home to supper.

That night, after the household had retired, Audubon heard a commotion in the guest room. He found Rafinesque pursuing a bat with the bow of his cherished Cremona. The next morning, wanting to teach his guest a lesson in the perils of too avidly seeking fame through the naming of species, he brought out some supposedly rare drawings. With feigned magnanimity he invited Rafinesque to copy the nonexistent—and horrendous—fishes, highly unlikely "herons," and a preposterous "scarlet-headed swallow."

Before Rafinesque left Henderson with his treasured forgeries, intent on publishing them all, Audubon led him through the canebrake. When they emerged from the exhausting excursion, the Greek was fully cured of wishing to skim the cream of the region. It remained for posterity to weigh his gullibility and vanity against Audubon's mischief and form a judgment rather in the Greek's favor.

Visitors of quite another stamp arrived soon after the departure of Rafinesque. George Keats and his sixteen-year-old bride, Georgiana, had been married in England in July. This brother of the not yet famous poet John Keats had been advised by Thomas Bakewell to call on the Audubons. The couple had gone as far as Princeton, Illinois, the post office for a new settlement of refugees from the Napoleonic upheaval. Deciding that the colony of Birbeck and Flower was not for them, they turned back to see what Henderson might have to offer.

George Keats left no doubt about his aims. The twenty-one-year-old was out to win a quick American fortune and erase the memory of an impoverished boyhood. He thought that his countinghouse experience would surely turn the trick. Audubon seemed an admirable example of the successful European-born pioneer. Keats readily accepted an invitation to remain as paying guest and decide whether to settle.[9]

Clever, pretty Georgiana could hardly wait to share her experiences with her brother-in-law the poet. The unsophisticated daughter of a Fifeshire adjutant of infantry, she had promised John Keats, when the three parted in Liverpool, to write her impressions. She half wished that he had come along; but he had seen them only to the docks, then departed on a walking tour of Scotland. (She might have begged him to come had she known his tour would end in consumption.)

"You will do well in this country," Audubon told George, who had large eyes and a sensual mouth so like his brother's. "I could chop that log in ten minutes—you have taken an hour—but your persistence is worth more than experience."

Even before John Keats received his first letter, he was clamoring for "bang, smoke and feathers." He hoped that Georgiana might bear "the first American poet." But if the Americans were really "great"—which he doubted—they could never be called "sublime" as long as they lacked a bard to sing their greatness. Providence would seem to have agreed with Keats. Six months later, almost to the day, Walt Whitman was born.

VIII. Windward

L ATE IN JANUARY 1819, the legacies meant for Audubon and Rose were rendered null and void. This decision was entirely in accordance with their father's wishes. He had paved the way for the action in the event of a contest to break his final last will and testament after his death. On February 12, Anne Moynet Audubon became his sole heir.[1] But it had taken all the skill of a lawyer so well known in Brittany that for years he had signed himself simply as "Ménard of Nantes Town Hall." His success in wresting the verdict from the four cousins in the supreme court of Savenay, although rewarding enough, brought only expense and worry for Gabriel, Rose, and Madame Audubon. Gabriel thought it only fair that Audubon be made to interest himself in litigation which was sure to flare up again. To arm him against the common foe, he got off a bundle that included the joint adoption papers, the Lieutenant's final will, and the summons of Madame to Savenay, along with her forthright defense.[2] The defense claimed that by declaring both "Jean Rabin of San Domingue" and Rose the "natural children" of their father, she was doing only what he himself had done before her. Ménard reaffirmed, for Nantes and the whole of Brittany to hear, what Madame Audubon had testified as to the status of her children: "Jean Audubon married Anne Moinette. During his marriage and in the course of voyages to America and elsewhere he had two children by women other than Anne Moinette . . . the girl Bouffard and the gentleman Jean Rabin. On March 7, 1794, he adopted the two children of adultery. He made his will on March 15, 1816. He died on February 19, 1818."[3]

Nothing was settled. The suit would drag on, Gabriel predicted. He had brought Audubon up to date in April and May on how he had been obliged to borrow 1,200 francs to pay their lawyer. His 800 francs a year in rents, his sole income, could not be spared. He hinted to know whether Dacosta had ever paid in full for Mill Grove.[4] As for the old David Ross affair, he enclosed a yellowed document to refresh Audubon's memory on the score in order for him to try and collect, if he could. Madame Audubon was weathering the legal storm tolerably well, considering her years, and begged to be remembered "with all her heart" to her son, whom she "embraced." The letter closed affectionately but with frank "impatience" for a reply that would end Gabriel's "vegetating."[5]

The chorus of cousins shrilled its demands. Unaware that Audubon was caught in a farrago of his own, Gabriel continued to send him pleas for help. Incredulous at first, then inclined to suspect that some enemy was intercepting letters that he felt sure must be coming from Kentucky, he suggested that messages be carried by someone bound for New Orleans. There a certain Nantes sea captain would deliver them in person when he reached France. Gabriel confessed himself at his wit's end, now that a mysterious "Dame Ferret," one of the late Lieutenant Audubon's many debtors, was threatening them through a Nantes solicitor. Unable to understand the silence, he finally exploded, "Why have you not written? Why? I cannot bear to accuse you of negligence. . . . Frankly, I cannot believe that you, my brother, have not written to me in a year."[6]

Gabriel might have said much more. He had been trying to collect £1,400 from Dr. D'Orbigny.[7] Jean Audubon had often lent the physician enough for necessities until he moved from the village. After that, D'Orbigny remained stubbornly incommunicado. Through the engraver Chessé of La Rochelle, Gabriel had also been making discreet inquiries into the doings of Rose's octoroon cousin "Laize," a recent arrival from Haiti. Laize's mother had written to her niece, Rose Du Puigaudeau, in hopes of learning about her daughter's new position and conduct among the affluent brothers and sisters of the late Guillaume-Gabriel Bouffard in La Rochelle. The aunt with whom Laize was living, Madame Supiot, was the widow of a well-born Frenchman.[8] Guillaume's will had recently been executed, but the bequest to Rose Bonnitte Bouffard Du Puigaudeau was ignored.

Thomas Bakewell's entreaties were less easily ignored by Audubon than Gabriel's importunings. Thomas was whining to his father that he had paid "as much as $3,000" to liquidate debts of the firm.[9] He thought Audubon should be the one to return the $5,000 borrowed at Fatland Ford for Audubon & Bakewell, thus enabling the elder Bakewell to assist the Prentice and Bakewell enterprise during the current Louisville recession. William Bakewell put a stop to such hints by advising Thomas to ask a bank for help.

Having two children to support and another on the way, Thomas was bound to make Audubon shoulder more of their crushing debt. He handed over to him a worthless note for $4,250, the price of a boat he and Prentice had foolishly sold to a former Henderson business competitor, Samuel Adams Bowen & Company. If Audubon succeeded in collecting from Bowen, to whom he and Thomas happened to be in debt, the boat would be his. If he failed, he would find himself responsible for settlement with Thomas. He tried, none too happily, to see the development as a possible bonanza. He and Keats agreed that steam navigation would revolutionize river commerce. He had even convinced his protégé and guest that he ought to invest in a boat which, unbeknownst to both, lay at the bottom of the Mississippi, along with its cargo, a total loss.[10]

Bowen disappeared down the Ohio with one of his partners before Audubon could approach him. Indignant, then furious, Audubon made his skiff ready, buckled on his dagger to please Lucy, and with two slaves went in pursuit of him and the unpaid-for *Henderson*. He was soon testifying in New Orleans, under $8,000 bond, that he was the lawful owner of the craft. The sheriff failed to attach the boat because Bowen had already surrendered it to prior claimants and returned to Kentucky. Under a second bond of $8,500 Audubon charged fraud. Attempts to trace the boat outside its jurisdiction were not the concern of the court, which dismissed the case. Audubon aired his opinion of Bowen in the streets and taverns. After a week or so he sold his skiff and slaves and caught the *Paragon* for home.[11]

Old James Berthoud and Lucy's brother William, guests at the Audubon cabin, warned of Bowen's threats against him. Soon after his return he was crossing the road to the mill, his right hand in a sling because of an injury from a mill wheel. Suddenly Bowen came up from behind him with a club. Audubon stood motionless under a rain of blows, then with his quick left hand that was as efficient as the right he plunged his dagger into Bowen's chest. While he himself managed to stagger back to his cabin, Berthoud and William bore his assailant off through the gaping crowd; many were creditors of Audubon and friends of Bowen. In a few minutes the hecklers were before the Audubon gate, yelling for the murderer to come out and be horsewhipped. Lucy and her sons remained in the bedroom. Berthoud returned, seized his gun, and took his stand in the doorway. Behind him were the carpenter and some slaves armed with knives, clubs, and rifles. He spoke to the crowd, his white hair flying, gallantly insisting they go home and let the law decide.

Audubon knew his plea of not guilty of assault with a

deadly weapon, used in self-defense, to be just. The judge who conducted the hearing laughed, when it was over, that Audubon ought to have killed "the damn rascal." Bowen's wounds were not fatal, but the affair proved that Audubon's creditors sadly outnumbered his friends in Henderson. Even George Keats had turned on him and decided to move on to Louisville. The loss of the boat that he had never so much as laid eyes on coincided with news of the death of his brother Thomas Keats. He and Georgiana, who was tired of Lucy's "airs," and their infant Emily were cordially received by Thomas Bakewell. Keats left Emily there while he went abroad to help settle his brother's estate.

James Berthoud's death on July 19, 1819, during his visit, intensified Audubon's deep gloom. He began to repeat a desire, often expressed to Keats, to visit his mother. He wanted to enlist her aid as an investor in some new venture, perhaps in England. The Bowen company, hearing of this, at once charged perjury, slander, and intent to flee Kentucky. They asked $10,000 and Audubon's arrest. The town trustee, Fayette Posey, posted a $10,000 bail against a warrant for arrest. When Audubon protested that he could not win a fair hearing in his own community, the case was moved to the circuit court in Owensboro. The Bowen element failed to appear, after having obtained one postponement, and the case was dropped. Near collapse, Audubon trudged half-way to Henderson before a passing wagon offered him a lift. He had, in fact, walked from the mouth of the Ohio all the way to Shawnee Town.[12]

The loss of his store left Audubon no choice but to sell out entirely. Nicholas Berthoud stepped into the breach by taking over Audubon's interest in the mill for $14,000, but without any intention of abandoning Shippingport. This reduced the debt of $10,000 due Berthoud.[13] He also bought the house and furnishings for $7,000 and took over the timber tract certificate. Even after meeting as many debts as this sacrifice made possible, Audubon was far from solvent. He sold his prize Canada geese, sixty prairie chickens, and livestock, and prepared to leave Henderson for good.[14] By fleeing he would escape jail for a debt of $500 he owed a certain George Mittenberger.[15]

Soon after dawn on July 19, with only his gun, dog, portfolio, and the clothing on his back, he disappeared down the road. Lucy had no idea when she would see him again. She was soon to be confined and could only hope that she and the little boys would follow, wherever he might go.

This time the birds in the thickets "looked like enemies." In his thoughts of the "infernal" mill, Audubon would have done well to remember how he had watched the swallows fight the "pick-axes and shovels" to save their homes in the sandbanks when the mill was rising. It might have consoled him, had his often dependable prescience been working, to realize that in less than a century a wild blaze would light Henderson upon the burning of the mill.[16] Fire would give the sandbanks back to the swallows.

At the end of three hot, dusty days on the road, Audubon let himself be jailed for debt in Louisville. An old friend, Judge Fortunatus Cosby, had him file a petition of a kind he did not know existed. The bankruptcy action set him free, but not before Lucy heard of his arrest. When she insisted on going to her husband, Senator Isham Talbot sent his coach to take her and the children away from Henderson. Audubon may have consoled himself that only a few weeks after his last meeting with Alexander Wilson, the poor fellow was suspected of spying for Canada and thrown in jail in Haverhill, New Hampshire.

Eliza took pity on Lucy and the boys and welcomed them to her home, White House. But Berthoud and Thomas Bakewell ignored Audubon's hints to find him a clerical post on some river steamer. Thomas saw the idea as a thin pretext for him to drop out of sight along the Ohio's bird-filled margins. Actually, the sickening fear that perhaps, after all, he could not support a family by commerce—or indeed by any other means—gripped Audubon. He yearned to disappear from the scene of his tribulations and let his more provident kinsmen look after his dependents while he got his bearings.

On the parlor wall of White House hung a pair of chalk

portraits of James Berthoud and his wife, sketched by Audubon in better days. It dawned on him that perhaps his pencil and chalks could tide him over his monetary crisis. His published notice for sitters and pupils met with a response encouraging enough to enable him to rent a small place in Louisville. The birth of his daughter Rose delayed the move; the illness of Lucy and the infant during a wave of autumn fever prolonged their stay in Shippingport.

Georgiana Keats and her infant, Emily, stricken with fever in Louisville, were nursed through a crisis by the Bakewells, who had lent George the money to reach England. Thomas had not attempted to soften their opinion of Audubon. John Keats's reaction to the affair of the sunken boat arrived too late to comfort anyone but Georgiana:

> I cannot help thinking Mr. Audubon a dishonest man. Why did he make you believe that he was a man of Property? How is it his circumstances have altered so suddenly? In truth, I do not believe you fit to deal with the world, or at least the American world. But, good God!—who can avoid chances. You have done your best. Take matters as cooly a you can, and, confidently expecting help from England, act as if no help was nigh . . . be careful of those Americans. I could almost advise you to come, whenever you have the sum of 500, to England. Those Americans will, I am afraid, fleece you. . . . I know not how to advise you but by advising you to advise with yourself. In your next, tell me at large your thoughts about America . . . for it appears to me you have as yet been somehow deceived. I cannot help thinking Mr. Audubon has deceived you. I shall not like the sight of him. I shall endeavor to avoid seeing him. . . .[17]

But the ambitious George could not prove that "Mr. Audubon" was actually "a swindler." Moreover, he fell out with John on reaching England. His methods of settling the estate of their late brother earned the contempt of the poet's best friend, Haslam, who denounced George as a "scoundrel" as resoundingly as anyone had ever slandered Audubon. Haslam was even to blame him for John's death of consumption not long after.

Elizabeth Page Bakewell and Georgiana Keats had more than their British origin for a bond of friendship. An aversion for Lucy Audubon gave them a special affinity nowadays. What Georgiana thought of her, and of "American ladies" in general, she did not conceal from the poet Keats. Her candor gave him food for thought, and he replied:

> I was surprised to hear of the state of society in Louisville. It seems you are just as ridiculous there as we are here—three-penny parties, half-penny dances. The best thing I have heard of is your shooting. . . . Give my compliments to Mrs. Audubon and tell her I cannot think her either goodlooking or honest. Tell Mr. Audubon he's a fool. If the American ladies are worse than the English they must be very bad. You say you should like your Emily brought up here. You had better bring her up yourself. You know a good number of English ladies—what encomium could you give of half a dozen of them? The greater part seem to me downright American. I have known more than one Mrs. Audubon. Their affectation of fashion and politeness cannot transcend ours. Look at our Cheapside sons and daughters. . . .[18]

Of the thousands of words from Audubon's glib pen, perhaps no passage is more affecting than his description of his departure from White House:

> . . . One morning, while all of us were sadly desponding, I took you both, Victor and John, from Shippingport to Louisville. I had purchased a loaf of bread and some apples; before we reached Louisville you were all hungry, and by the riverside we sat down and ate our scanty meal. On that day the world was to me as a blank, and my heart was sorely heavy, for scarcely had I enough to keep my dear sons alive; and yet through these dark days I was being led to the development of the talents I loved. . . . I never for a day gave up listening to the songs of our birds, or watching their peculiar habits, or in delineating them in the best way I could. Nay, during my deepest troubles I frequently would wrench myself from the persons around me, and retire to some secluded part of our noble forests.[19]

Finances were more of a problem than ever. Thomas and William had asked the court for an injunction against further payments by Berthoud to their debtor, Audubon, for property transfers. Portraits at five dollars each became the artist's existence. Sometimes there were night calls to sketch the dying—and at no little distance—and under bizarre circumstances if the dying proved to be the dead.

The day came when Audubon's pad was barren of portraits and his atelier of pupils. Tarascon of Shippingport came to the rescue with news that the recently established

Western Museum of Cincinnati College needed a temporary taxidermist. They could offer $125 monthly for stuffing birds and fishes. General William Lytle and Robert Todd, influential citizens, wrote in Audubon's behalf on February 12, 1820. (Lytle and his wife were later to pose for him.) They asked the trustees to consider Audubon as professor of French and drawing, or of either, for which he was "eminently qualified." "He has nearly finished a collection of American birds and is anxious to see Wilson's *Ornithology* to ascertain whether or no there is [sic] any birds in his collection which he, Mr. Audubon, has omitted to paint." The volumes might come down on the steamer *Pike* "in a box" and would be returned by Audubon, "who ought not to be neglected, as he would be a great acquisition to your institution and to your Society."[20]

The supply of sitters had run out, it was true; but Audubon had other reasons for thinking that even taxidermy would be preferable to life in Kentucky. The intemperate land-trafficking Jacob Gall and his tricks were behind a new lawsuit in which Audubon and his "cloven hoof" were maliciously disparaged.[21] It helped little to know that the relentless barrage from Henderson and Evansville must sooner or later end in complete vindication.

The troubles in Couëron rang out in a letter from Gabriel, whom Audubon had no choice but to ignore:

> For the past year I have received no news of you. To what can I attribute this silence? What adversity has caused it? If so, let us try to devise a way to thwart this imposition that can only block our interests. What astonishes me is that since your last of July 22, 1818, none of the eight letters that I have addressed to you has arrived. . . . From this you can infer that I have not been neglecting any means to assure Madame Audubon's inheriting the estate, inasmuch as we ourselves could not do so, and as her intentions towards us are still good. . . . Madame Audubon is quite well considering her age . . . very anxious for news of you, and fearing some unpleasantness has befallen you. Like us, she cannot imagine that it should be due to forgetfulness. In the name of God, reassure us. . . . Count ever on my tender friendship even as I depend on your not denying me yours.[22]

Whooping Crane. *Plate 226 of* **The Birds of America.** *Engraved by Robert Havell, Jr., in 1834 after the original study drawn in Louisiana, November 1821.*

IX. Down the Mississippi

THE VERY LEANINGS that brought about Audubon's downfall in Henderson found encouragement in Cincinnati. The aim of Dr. Daniel Drake, the founder of the Western Museum Society, was to collect curiosities of the "Western Country" for a school of natural history yet to be founded.[1] The newly established Cincinnati College made a room or two available for the growing collection. While Drake continued to battle a clique opposed to the founding of a new medical college, he left Audubon to the curator, Robert Best.

Among the specimens in the crowded laboratory was a live rattlesnake. Its two-year hunger strike and volatile behavior earned it more than casual notice in Audubon's ledger of observations.

Best occasionally led Audubon to bird haunts across the river. The cliff swallows at Newport were not delighted by the visits. A little matriarch among them "called out the whole tribe" as he approached one day at sunset. The swallows lunged at his hat, legs, and body, flew between him and their nests, darted close to his face, and, in short, twittered "their rage and sorrow" until he withdrew.[2]

Audubon, an early riser and not one to fraternize in late, smoky communion with his fellows, seldom joined the circle of artists who spent their evenings together at Mrs. Amelung's boardinghouse. As soon as he found a small, cheap furnished house, he was joined by his family. Rose, however, was not among them; at seven months she had died and been buried in Louisville.[3]

Lucy at once grasped the truth of the Cincinnati situation. The Western Museum showed no sign of making regular salary payments. To make ends meet she advertised for private pupils and began to teach. Audubon could not imagine that Doctor Drake, whose jovial head he had sketched for posterity, would not keep his word. Meanwhile, rather than spend even three cents for a pound of beef, he shot wild partridges among the hogs that scavenged in the street or brought game from the woods.

Uncertain when Drake would pay him his wages, Audubon advertised for pupils in mid-March, at fifteen dollars per term of three months. Benjamin Powers, whose younger brother, Hiram, was one day to become a famous sculptor, had written in his *Inquisitor-Advertiser* late in February: "Mr. J. J. Audubon, a French gentleman of the most extraordinary qualifications is on a visit to Cincinnati, and contemplates opening a school . . . for lessons in Drawing and the French language."

Among his twenty-five pupils, many of whom wished only to master lettering and sign painting, was nearly thirteen-year-old Joseph Mason (1808–1842), whose parents came to Cincinnati from Baltimore in 1804. (Audubon was to call him "about 18" in his 1820 journal.) The boy had a remarkable knowledge of botany and an exceptional gift for delineating flowers. He seemed to be the assistant Audubon needed to paint botanical backgrounds for his birds. His English-born father even allowed him to accompany Audubon south later in the year. In his feverish anxiety to get on with the task of drawing species that were lacking in his portfolio, Audubon did not hesitate to delegate an important share of the work for its enhancement. But the portraits engraved on copper for *The Birds of America* pass over the name of Mason, bearing only that of Audubon.

On the last day of April, the Western Museum, out of funds, had to dismiss Audubon for the time being, but with the promise that his wages would soon be met. Audubon knew there was no turning back to Kentucky—much less to Fatland Ford or France. Only recently Rebecca Bakewell had been warning Lucy that the $200 paid to William Thomas would be "taken from Mr. Audubon's share of the estate."[4]

Despite the praise, by June 22 it was clear that the Western Museum might temporize forever. Daniel Drake hinted that five dollars was "a very considerable amount for anyone to obtain for a day's Labour" at the moment. Thanking him for his "politeness" to him and Lucy since their arrival, Audubon decided to "take the liberty" to speak "with the frankness" that he himself preferred to be shown. If, he said, he had become like a pensioner of the Museum Society on account of past (unpaid-for) services, and an "incumbrance," he would be "perfectly willing" to bring to an end an "engagement" meant to last "sometime longer." To save Drake the expense of advertising this connection, he sent Victor with the letter, which can, to this day, be read at the Cincinnati Historical Society.

A month or so earlier, Audubon chanced to meet his former partner Pears on the street in Cincinnati. He expressed hurt that Pears had never called on him and Lucy and urged him to do so. Pears, downhearted over his failure to obtain local orders for flint glass from the Bakewell works in Pittsburgh, replied stiffly that he was not sure he would come. With that he walked on, having long since decided to have nothing to do with bad memories; this he told his wife in a letter of May 7, 1820.[5]

At the opening of the museum, though Audubon was no longer employed there, Dr. Drake hailed him as "one of the excellent artists" hired by the Society. He noted that his drawings of several hundred birds included many species not given by Wilson and others in their works. Echoing Drake, Benjamin Powers pronounced the art of Audubon "unrivalled."

In his report to the Society, the Museum president, Reverend Elijah Slack, remarked that the new display cases for the birds and fishes mounted by Audubon were also "beautifully ornamented with appropriate scenery," thanks to his crayons and watercolors. The fact that Slack referred only, and gullibly, to the artist as "formerly from Paris" invites the inference that Audubon did not, perhaps, go so far as to claim his having had tutelage with Jacques-Louis David.[6]

Audubon's portfolio appeared to him, as well as to Drake and others, to be an increasingly "valuable acquisition." His only wealth, it invited unusual exertions, which, in some unforeseeable manner, might justify existence. Given several months in the South, a good assistant like Mason, and freedom from family cares, he believed that he could win out over poverty, disgrace, and failure. Lucy agreed to remain behind and support their sons by teaching and to continue trying to collect the wages the museum still owed. She and Audubon wrote separate letters to Henry Clay, Benjamin Harrison, and other luminaries to ask for letters of introduction for use in the South.

While Audubon searched for a boat captain willing to let him earn passage for himself and Joseph, another appeal arrived from Gabriel. He complained bitterly of having written "at least twenty times" to no avail: "Two years have passed without our having any news of you. What a long lapse of time, and in what anxiety we are plunged! In God's name give us some news of yourself, if it be but a word to set us at rest in regard to your condition." While the family refused to believe that Audubon was angry with them, they had nonetheless given up and gone about settling the estate without him. The heirs of Sanitte were still pressing their demands— and rather successfully—through Nantes lawyers. Bills left unpaid by Lieutenant Audubon continued to arrive. Madame Audubon, ninety years of age, had given up her dull, lonely

life at La Gerbetière for a room of her own at Les Tourterelles. "She does not cease to speak of you, and is as much
astonished as I am that we receive no news of you," Gabriel
closed, urging that a confidential letter be sent through New
Orleans for safety.[7]

On October 12, 1820, Audubon and Mason boarded the
cargo ark of the rough Captain Jacob Aumack. They were followed by Captain Samuel Cummings, a civil engineer, South
Seas veteran, and first-rate sportsman, who was about to
make a survey of the rivers. Entitled *The Western Pilot* on
publication in Cincinnati in 1825, this survey was to remain
the indispensable authority for years. Audubon doubted he
could keep a promise to Lucy to shave weekly and keep his
leather buckskins mended in such surroundings. The crew,
an uncouth, jigging, singing Irishman from Baltimore and a
grog-loving tramp of the rivers, guffawed at the idea. The
Yankee from Boston who owned the cargo, two Pennsylvania carpenters, and a paying passenger "fond of jokes and
women" made up the rest of the party. A gun, paper, and
some chalks were all that the penniless Audubon took along.

In Louisville, during a two-day stop, it was whispered that
he was a wife deserter and blackguard. Near Henderson the
boat veered away from its banks and the "infernal mill" and
turned in at Evansville, Indiana, on the opposite shore. He
deputized Mason and Cummings to go after his retriever
Dash, left behind when he fled Henderson.[8]

Southbound cranes, geese, ducks, grouse, and turkeys;
thrushes and flashing paroquets; and lone divers such as the
bald eagle and telltale godwit were overhead and along the
margins. The autumn air inspired musings, in a journal,
which hint of the opulent prose style one day to cascade
from the artist's quill: "The *Indian Summer,* that extraordinary
Phenomenon of North America is now in all its splendor.
The blood-red rising sun—and the constant *smoky* atmosphere, is undoubtedly not easily to be accounted for. It has
been often supposed that the Indians, firing the prairies of
the West, were the cause, but since we have left Cincinnati

the eastwardly winds have prevailed without diminishing, in any degree, the smoke. It is extremely bad to most eyes and particularly so to mine."

At poverty-stricken, half-empty New Madrid, reached in mid-November, Audubon considered the squatters less decent and poorer than the Indians. They killed one another as they might the "deer or racoon." The wife of the storekeeper was a husband-deserter from Ste. Genevieve and lived in a "partnership rendered agreeable by a mutual wish of nature." She welcomed Audubon, rather to his disgust, with "much of the French manners."

When his hunting clothes could await mending no longer, a woman from an ark, which for days had been drifting near, came to his rescue with her needle. To ward off melancholy he relied on his battered copy of Turton's *Linnaeus,* his flute, and above all, the drawing of birds that often occupied him until nightfall. He wrote that the wild merging of the Ohio and the Mississippi powerfully suggested a whirlpool of the "thousands of difficulties" which threatened to engulf him. He remained, however, blissfully unaware that he was repeatedly drawing birds as new species when they were merely immature. First he mistook a duck, then a loon, then a screech owl, and, once more, a bald eagle for new species. It is for such innocent errors that his work has on occasion been discounted by modern men of science who fail to take into account steady if painful progress. No artist, past or present, could feel other than stunned admiration for the force and truth of Audubon's pencil and crayons, his nomenclature and any anachronisms notwithstanding.

One Sunday late in November, while he was examining his new drawings, he turned from them to a pastel of Lucy that he invariably kept in view on the Sabbaths of his odyssey. Vague fears of death for her, for their sons, or for himself seized him as he imagined her expression had changed to one of sorrow. What he thought might well be a precognitive warning impelled him to begin a short autobiography in his journal.[9] It would be written, he began, for Victor and John.

The life sketch is marred by distortions, if not by so many as the later more prideful, self-conscious versions, one of which a rectitudinous granddaughter tampered with at will. In this account of 1820 Audubon related that his "three brothers" died in the Black Insurrection and his "extraordinarily beautiful" mother soon after. His father had "remarried in France" and chosen "that best of women," Anne Moynet. Although Audubon confided to Mason the fact of his birth on Saint-Domingue, he omitted the bitter truths of the past and present, truths Gabriel's letters prove he knew.

Audubon's premonition regarding Lucy came close to the mark. Her loneliness in Cincinnati, with its ceaseless talk of land and livestock, and her stark need were proving too much even for one of her patience. Not even the Western Museum, casual enough about its obligations, could ignore her necessities by this time. She extracted $400 from the institution and prepared to leave for Shippingport.

Early in December a poster caught Audubon's eye at the post of the Arkansas Territory. It announced an expedition survey to the Red River country, recently ceded to the United States by Spain. In the depths of discouragement after weeks of the dirt and austerities of the Aumack flatboat, he regarded the notice as something like revelation. If he were to join such an expedition to the northwest for "a couple of years," he felt he could contribute greatly to American "ornithological knowledge." As its artist he could turn out a body of work that would surpass that of Wilson and every other delineator since time began—and, with the help of the Almighty, publish in Europe to crown his success.

The lure of expeditions was nothing new. General Clark in Kentucky, Boone in Missouri, and Samuel Mitchill in New York, to say nothing of Major Stephen Harriman Long, whose party had paused in Cincinnati, had fired Audubon's brain.[10] He was not the first Frenchman to entertain such ambitions. Le Moyne of France had been first, three hundred years before, to portray the wild turkey. Vieillot had seen, drawn, and named many species before Wilson's day. Audubon wrote to Miller, the Arkansas governor, to ask his intervention, then to Lucy to say that his exploration of the wilds of Louisiana and Florida might be a mere beginning.

His luck, above Natchez on Christmas day, in acquiring a greatfooted hawk after fifteen years of vain efforts he took for a propitious sign. From the wharves, as the ark tied up beside the town, he could see countless vultures high above on the ledges. Once again he roamed among the Indian game peddlers in the shadow of the deserted fort. The hill of quicksand bore no trace of a landslide that two years before gave way and dropped houses into the muddy current. The gallows and burial ditch for slaves explained the vigilance of the vultures there, as well as along the lanes of this town of two thousand souls.

Audubon was taken aback by his sudden meeting with Nicholas Berthoud. They exchanged polite greetings, but each moved along with some embarrassment. An American artist, George Cooke (1793–1849), proved more congenial company. Sick of hack portrait painting and copying old masters, he passed two customers along to Audubon, though neither man could pay for his "head" at five dollars. Audubon's preachments on the goodness and freedom of the river life; its meals of teal, raw bacon, and biscuit; its virgin tanglewood; and its vistas removed from material cares mesmerized Cooke. He seriously considered abandoning his slight security for the harsh existence that the mellifluous tongue and imagination of Audubon rendered so Arcadian.

That night, Berthoud, snug in his hotel bed, thought of his brother-in-law shivering beneath a buffalo robe in the bitter cold of the choppy river. He sought him out in the snowy morning, insisted he share his room, and took him on his round of commercial visits. At one place a volume of Wilson that lay on a shelf sent Audubon off on a vain search of the bookshops. In the end he bought a new edition of La Fontaine to replace the battered one he knew by heart.

Berthoud declined to listen to hints for help towards the Red River scheme, which, as he was quick to see, would make him responsible for Lucy and the children. Nevertheless, he offered Audubon and Mason the hospitality of his keel boat as far as New Orleans. To Mason, a bit the worse for the rigors of Aumack's ark, the invitation was a godsend.

In the hubbub and confusion of the departure a crewman rested Audubon's portfolio of new drawings on the shore for a moment. Not until he was on his way did the artist notice his loss. Fearful of theft by some felon among the countless flatboats, he sent word to John Garnier of the Natchez hotel to advertise his loss. His dejection was such that for a day or two he ignored the birds that Mason brought him. But poverty and the captain's offer of a lucky five-dollar gold piece for a portrait shook him out of his lethargy.

At New Orleans throngs milled along the levee. Fish crows wheeled and importuned overhead on that seventh day of January, 1821. Blanketed Choctaws and Chickasaws in red flannel leggings and their beaded best roamed among the fine gentlemen from Cuba and Europe. The "citron hue of almost all" the ladies disgusted Audubon, an admirer of "rosy Yankee or English cheeks," almost as much as did the turbaned mulatto sirens. (Before many years this white half-brother of Sanitte Bouffard's children would be declaring himself against the freeing of British West Indies slaves.)

The sight of David Prentice among the crowds came as a surprise. Prentice & Bakewell had been dissolved.[11] Thomas was going it alone in the Louisville boat-building industry. Prentice showed surprising sympathy with the Red River expedition idea. Together they called on their former Kentucky friends, the Croghans, to discuss how best to interest "Washington City."

Thus far no letters had arrived from Lucy. It was therefore disconcerting to visit the post office with Berthoud and find that she had written to Nicholas and sent him gloves from her own needle for Christmas. Nothing at all came for Audubon in his quiet desperation.

At the dawn market a pickpocket made off with his wallet; and although it contained little cash, it held a small fortune in letters of introduction. Berthoud, rather to Audubon's annoyance, joked that he was quite a "green horn" in the salmagundi city. The loss of the portfolio remained the greater by far. Audubon sent Joseph to query incoming boats on the chance of its recovery, while he himself went out in a downpour after chalk-portrait jobs to keep the two of them afloat.

Competition was rife among artists. An Italian scene painter offered Audubon $100 to help finish a panorama of the kind that theatres were showing. Instead he again wrote to ask Henry Clay for help with the Red River expedition. If, before long, he had to return to the Italian, he hoped he would not be like a painter he had encountered in Natchez, John Wesley Jarvis. A successful portraitist, Jarvis had been an object of disgust, with his pink waistcoat, lace cravat, silk parasol marked 'Stolen from I,' and pet baby alligator that peered from beneath his chin. The studio of Jarvis, who ridiculed the painting of mere songsters, was lined with cages of pets that screamed and beat their wings as he fired, indoors, at a bull's-eye. Yet Audubon guessed that he was taken for "an Original, a cracked Man," also.

Finally, on January 10, 1821, Audubon broke his more than two-year silence and wrote to Gabriel and Rose. Whatever he apparently admitted of failure, and of new but unrealized ambition, left him looking so dejected that Nicholas again made him join him on his rounds. Roman Pamar, the merchant who had been Audubon's bondsman in the Bowen boat affair, pleased him with his offer of $100 for an oil portrait of his daughters. Apologizing for his ignorance of the medium, Audubon showed off a new chalk of an acquaintance of Pamar, one so lifelike as to win an order for studies of each of the three Pamar beauties. A spate of commissions at twenty-five dollars each brought Audubon sudden prosperity in New Orleans.

To Lucy went $275, along with a set of queens ware for her sister Eliza. An aging maid-of-all-work named Louisa began to tidy the shabby rooms of Audubon and Mason for ten dollars monthly. A professional hunter agreed to supply new birds for twenty-five dollars, while the habitual ransacking of the dawn markets continued. When Berthoud started north, the end of February, he carried twenty new drawings for safekeeping in Shippingport. Lucy was looking forward to his return with news.

After watching the keel boat move off with his treasure, Audubon walked back alone in gloom along the levee. A graceful, beguiling, veiled woman approached to ask whether he might be the artist sent by the French Academy to draw birds. With a smile he replied that he drew to please himself. She said that if he would consider a commission he should come to her studio in half an hour.

He browsed for a while in the bookstalls. On arriving at the intriguing address, he was ushered by a black servant into the presence of the lady. To her question, whether he had ever painted the undraped figure, he nodded yes. But about his willingness to undertake such a likeness he seemed in doubt. He asked for time to walk out and think the matter over. He returned and, behind bolted doors, began the first of several sessions for the "fair incognito." The lady called the indifferent results her "folly." Madame André, as she finally introduced herself, took up the pastels and with a few deft strokes decidedly improved the study. The blushing Audubon cursed himself for having squandered enough time on this thankless task for a few dozen more conventional chalk portraits. None of the sitters would have wounded his vanity as this woman had done by cunningly concealing her abilities. Madame André then signed her own name to the work, after Audubon had placed his, faintly, in folds of the foreground drapery, and framed the picture in gold. She told him to choose the finest gun in New Orleans as a souvenir, then asked him to have her sentiments engraved on his $125-selection: *"Ne refuse pas ce don d'une amie qui t'est reconnaissante, puisse qu'il t'égaler en bonté."* (Refuse not this gift of a friend who is grateful to thee. May it equal thyself in goodness.) Audubon himself cut on the ramrod: "Property of Laforest Audubon, February 22, 1821."

He went to the swamps with Joseph to try out the gift of the "extraordinary femelle" (present-day historians think her a certain demimondaine) whose parting words were, "Be happy—think of me sometimes as you rest on your gun—

keep my name secret forever." Then Audubon sat down and
wrote out the whole adventure as an episode entitled "A Remarkable Femelle" for Lucy. He closed it with an admission
of the lady's refusal to see him when he called to study his
drawing for one last time. "This," he wrote across the apochryphal composition, "is forwarded to my only friend"—
Lucy—"and I wish her to be careful about participating any
part. If thy brother William should tell thee he will keep it
snugg, show it him—no one else for some years." [12] His flirtation was a dangerous lark, but nothing to hide. He emerged
none the worse for it.

One week before Audubon received his gift gun, Lucy was
pursuing some old business with her pen. "Sir," she addressed Dr. Drake, "after an unpleasant voyage owing to the
rain we arrived at Shippingport and found all our friends
well. . . . Relying upon your politeness and consideration
for me I trust the demand I make will be as speedily attended
to as possible, but as the paper of Cincinnati is nothing in
value here I shall make all the use of it I can in your place—
and wish to accommodate you as much as possible in the arrangement. I returned shears and shall therefore deduct
three dollars from my account. Give kind remembrances to
Mrs. Drake and wishes for your success in your numerous
enterprizes. I am, Sir, yours, obliged, L. Audubon—in haste
Feby 15, 1821." [13] She referred to a balance still due. Six
weeks later she was informing Euphemia Gifford of Audubon's intention to publish "a large work on Ornithology"
in Europe where he planned to take it.

A notice in the Natchez *Mississippi Republican* finally brought
the lost portfolio to light. Alexander Gordon, to whose father
Thomas Bakewell had once been apprenticed and who had
taken a liking to Audubon, wrote from New Orleans to have
his agent send it there by boat. Only one plate was missing.

When John Vanderlyn, a leading historical painter of the
day, arrived in New Orleans, Gordon advised that a letter
of endorsement from such a man might help the expedition cause, if not so much as the direct appeal to the President and Congress that he advocated. That failing, Gordon
thought Audubon could do worse than test his drawings in

England for possible publication. He himself often traveled to Britain; he spoke of the transcendence of natural history in the kingdom. But the Pacific wilderness was what Audubon wanted above all else at this juncture. The thought of approaching Vanderlyn, a man perhaps as obnoxious as Jarvis, put him off. "My life has been strewed with many thorns. But could I see myself and the fruits of my labor safe, with my beloved family *all well* on a return from such an expedition," he wrote in his journal, "how grateful would I feel to my country, and thankful of the greatness of my Author."

Vanderlyn kept Audubon waiting in an anteroom so long that all diffidence was forgotten. He sweated in his wrath. By the time he was admitted, he cast his portfolio down, flung it open, then wandered away from Vanderlyn and a guest. He walked from portrait to portrait on the wall, thinking that some of the undraped figures would hardly pass muster with the critical Madame André.

"Handsome!" he heard Vanderlyn say of the drawings of birds. Audubon departed, with a very good endorsement, in the company of the caller, an officer willing to sit for him instead of for the unsuspecting Vanderlyn.

Still no word came from Lucy with her views on the expedition plans. Audubon sent suiting for Victor and John, some stockings and linen, and a sidesaddle with which he said he was "saddled" in lieu of cash for a portrait. Chalk commissions and bird sketches fully occupied him in his Barrack Street quarters. One night a rat made off with a vireo skin before he could paint it.

Two letters from Lucy, received almost together and equally despairing, had an untoward effect. She stressed that Nicholas would have nothing to do with the Red River idea and its implicit demands. Chronic toothache and painful extractions had undermined her resistance but hurt far less than the possibility of being forsaken for so long. Her silence she explained in still other ways. On March 6 her father had died at Fatland Ford. Thomas was trying to keep her from sharing in the will because of all the money Audubon owed him and the estate.[14] "I, and I doubt not, Lucy, will also relinquish all pretensions to any claim . . . until the debts by the

firm of Audubon and Bakewell be fully discharged," Thomas
assured Rebecca, whose favorite he remained.[15] As for Rebecca, she was clinging to the farm for the time being. Thomas
was at least frank about the $40,000 debt that he and Prentice
had piled up in Louisville. Now, however, he had begun to
prosper. His feigned magnanimity betrayed no sympathy for
Lucy, marooned with the Berthouds, but only smug confidence that his proper share would find its way to him.

Rebecca Smith Bakewell's eccentricities grew more conspicuous. She ignored the behest to sell the farm at once. Instead, she rented part of the house and all but one pasture to
a tenant who agreed to let half the land lie fallow. She asked
$600 a year for the parlor, bedroom, garret, cellars, and all
but the one horse and two donkeys that he promised to keep
in hay and fodder for her. He was to cut and haul wood to
heat her quarters, pay taxes, sow clover, mend fences, and
be liable for damage.[16]

Weeks passed without further word from Lucy, weeks of
merciless heat that made time stand still. But then a bitterly
discouraged and discouraging reply to his own admission of
despair over her silence reached him as he was about to put a
draft for one hundred dollars aboard the *Commerce* for her.
The letter, which has not survived, evidently warned that
Lucy could not carry on much longer while he continued to
talk of the Pacific and England as if forgetting that he must
help educate Victor. His answer reveals also that John was
not an easy youth to rear without a father. Yet she preferred
to see Audubon go anywhere rather than return to Kentucky
penniless. She had grown thin and felt too run down even to
find solace in her piano. Indeed she might, she said, never
play again. News of the death of Joseph Mason's father in
Cincinnati prompted her to suggest that the boy might easily
become a permanent burden. It is an extraordinary sign of
his confidence in Lucy's abiding love for him that Audubon
had every intention of enclosing his episode of Madame
André, unlikely though it was to lift her spirits.

In what may be the longest letter to Lucy ever to come
from the pen of Audubon, he began, on the twenty-fourth of
May, 1821, an expression of his doubts, hopes and fears,

which she fully shared. Here, for the first time, the long-separated parts of that outpouring of his begin, and end, as one. "Dearest Friend, I have just now sent thee a letter to the steamboat Napoleon, although my intention was to give it to a Mr. Lovelace with whom I came down from Cincinnati, but could not find him." He admitted that her message of June 10 had caused him some melancholy but that her invariable care to include something "soothing" relieved his sorrow. For his part he thought it "natural and necessary" to speak "with freedom" for the "continuance of strong attachments." Her "intentions" were what mattered, not the effect of her words on his "rather desponding spirits."

Lucy had evidently referred to Prentice as possibly useful to her need of "Celia," one of the slaves that the Audubons had owned before their loss of the mill and their home to Berthoud. Prentice had witnessed the whole fiasco. Without such help her housekeeping had to suffer, in one of the dependencies at White House, owned by Nicholas and made available to her. Audubon dismissed the idea of Prentice with, "I judge of men by their actions." What follows suggests that this was a question of the same Cecilia whom Lucy was later to reclaim. "I would have, on my own account, desired thy remaining at Cincinnati, had it been thy pleasure, and as to the Cursed Slaves, they will forever be begrudged thee by some of thy family, *rely on that.*"

"We never will have children more. Our boys soon will be further [along] in the world, for I am determined they shall be assured, as soon as possible, that the greatest blessing we can enjoy in Life is Independence. Then, my Lucy, we will travel by ourselves and try to keep clear of obligations. . . . The kindnesses of the family Berthoud are to be thanked for, but *somehow* I do not like this appearance of [their] helping [us], like *Mendicants.* Believe me, Lucy, poverty can be better born when *quite free.*"

With that he turned to the subject of his "extensive plan, the Pacific Project," about which he could only say that they must wait "for an answer."

"Then my Poor Birds come next," he continued. "Or will they ever come? I see yet that thou hast no faith in them. I cannot say I am much encouraged about them, but it seems my *Genius* (if I have any) was intended that way, for during all my Life I have felt a great Propensity toward following what I am now at. That they will pay my time, I cannot know. Sometimes I think well of them; at other moments, [I] look at them as Daubs and wish they never had existed. I never have yet attempted anything toward their Publication, and my Hopes may all be blasted when I present them to the High Judges of Europe, and yet can I give them up? Indeed, My Lucy, I cannot."

So already, and sooner than posterity has heretofore supposed, Audubon was thinking in terms of fame for the reward of his "genius" by Europeans qualified to pronounce his drawings worthy. "I myself *hear* that they never can be published with any Hope of meeting the public approbation before I abandon them. At present they seem to please the public eye." They were continually drawing praise around him which he discounted as "all talk and no broth." He believed that "they must be shewn in Europe and receive Inducements."

He regretted having to report that he had finished but thirty-six since he left Lucy, even though "Mr. Gordon" considered that "a good number." But, had he been free "to hunt and draw every day," he would have one hundred.

"I would like very much to be able to go up to thee to *finish, retouch*, recopy, &c., all that I have. . . . The Governor thinks they would probably meet great success in Philadelphia but I cannot think so. Willson's [*sic*] superior writing, better *understood* by our Countrymen than the shapes, coloring or attitudes of his gaudy plates will not advance mine in the [eyes of] the Public of America until actually *Engraved*. My hopes are that if, in Europe, they are called *Good*, their coming before the Public unaware they will surprise and please at once and have what, as a Painter, *I Call a good Effect*."

He did not mind admitting that although there were talented men there, who could "draw and paint beautifully," his own work was preferred. "And when I tell thee that I receive two dollars per hour per pupil it gives me some curious thoughts, either of my *superiority* or of their want of judgment." A little "shew of vanity" was essential to self-respect, to the belief that he deserved what praise was paid him.

As for portraits, he declared himself "the maker of the very best." But he wished that they were done in oil. "I am now assured that black chalk injures my eyes that are always sore, and yet I [would] regret [abandoning] that beautiful style, more particularly as I have, I believe, *Not* one adversary in America." (The French exponent, St. Mémin, would have been among such rivals had he not departed.)

"Since I have been in this city I have lived the retired life I am fond of, My thoughts about thy concern are filled every hour that my pencil has been in play. I have seen all in New Orleans that deserves the attention of a traveller, [a] stranger, to its *uncommon* habits. The extreme kindness of Mr. [Roman] Pamar, on which I can now express myself sufficiently, has rendered my séjour here more bearable than otherwise it would have been—and the company of a few pupils of mine has contributed to keep my spirits d'accord." One of these, Mrs. Heermann, the wife of the physician, was "well of figure and graced with acquirements." A sister of hers had "had the politeness" to write a note of thanks for the gift of a drawing. He admired her husband, "a man of good education" (if perhaps a mite "hasty" on occasion) and, moreover, "an excellent man of a good heart." Audubon considered a gentleman from New York City, who was taking lessons in landscape painting, possessed of "astonishing talent for that art"; "he says my coloring is superior to anything his English teacher has shewn him."

But then he wrote that he was "going on" (running on) as if to paint and varnish a "quite shining picture" of himself. "But I speak to My Beloved Lucy and feel very easy."

Nevertheless, he changed the subject to his two visits to the theatre with Joseph. They were both more interested in the painted scenery than in the actresses whose ways suited "the spirit of the day." He thought the French actors "fops" and the "dancers indifferent," although "the *house*" was "better than would be expected."

"We now and then of *Moon shining* evenings ramble to

what is called the Museum Coffee house." It cost nothing to listen to the musicians and indulge their taste to be "critics" of the "poor collection of Paintings, &c., that fill the Gallery." They could look on at the roulette table, and watch the shows of temper and the feverish concentration.

"Musquitoes are at this season so troublesome that we seldom can sit in our room after dark. We fix ourselves about the middle of the street until bed time, piping [on] the flageolet or blowing the flute." Occasionally, a painter joined them to talk art.

> We cannot be epicures. Our purse is that that suits best strong appetites. We generaly have a ham on the nail, and convenience makes us cook it by slices when hungry. During cooler weather we had cheese but the heat that disperses and sends off one part of the inhabitants of this place brings on myriads of others called maggots, with which we are not Englishmen enough to desire very close acquaintance. Salt makerels are good, for they are very cheap. We suffer the want of pure cool water; this cannot be purchased by us. The vegetable market is as good as in any part of America, and very early in the season. Fresh meat we never taste. We see it hanging in the market house and that satisfies us compleatly. Our rent, washing, cooks wages amount about one dollar and fifty cents per day. Now, My Lucy, I will proceed by thy letter.
>
> Thou are not, it seems, daring as I am about leaving one place to go to another without the means. I am sorry for that. I never now will fear want as long as I am well, and God will grant me that, as I have received from nature my little talents. I would dare go to England without one cent, one single letter of introduction to anyone, and on landing would make shillings or pence if I could not make more, but no doubt I would make enough. Prejudices and habits carry many, *I think*, too far, but I am thinking that I can raise the means. I intend to try.
>
> If I do not go to England in the course of a twelve-month we will send Victor to Lexington College. Hope, my dearest friend, that our sweet Woodhouse will lose the habits that makes thee at present fear he has not the natural gifts about him. I think his eyes are extremely intelligent; he is quick of movement; there are indications of natural sense. But he is yet a boy and has not had the opportunities of Victor to improve. The latter was thy only attention for some years before John required any. I will agree with thee that the educating of children is perplexing, but how sweet the recompense, to the parents— when brought up by themselves, only, it is rendered two-fold.

Thy liability to toothaching is very dreadful, and it is as painful for me to know thou hast had it as the drawing of those [that are] unsound can be to thee. I hope thee and our children, our real Friends, my Lucy, are now quite well. If my Lucy would try to amuse herself and have good spirits she would soon recover and have her flesh again.

Dear girl, how much I wish to press thee to my bosom. . . . I would like to hear that Victor did the marketing. The stock of cash is small, I daresay, but I hope to keep it sufficiently good. I daresay the gentlemen of the [Western] Museum found it hard to send thee anything. Mr. Best, who tells *no lies* says he has not received $10 since I left. This I doubt.

Beguilingly he thanked Lucy for a gift of new suspenders: "Thou does not say that they are from thy hands. I hope they are; I am so much of a lover, yet, that every time I will touch them I [shall] think and bless the maker. Thank thee, sweet girl, for them."

To agree that Joseph Mason was a millstone at the very time when the boy seemed touched with genius was inadmissible! "Now sweet girl, to the next question of thy letter, 'What will I do with Joseph Mason?' As long at least as I travel I shall keep him with me. I have a great pleasure in affording that good young man the means of becoming able to do well. His talent for painting, if I am a judge, is fine, his expenses very moderate, and his company quite indispensable." Having heard of the death of the father of the boy he felt still "more attached" to him. "Thou knowest I do not flatter young artists much. I never said this to him but I think so, and, to show his performance, will bring me as many people as I can attend to anywhere."

Lucy's news of the marriage of a brother of the curator Robert Best elicited this: "I know scarce a man that forms *strong, constant* attachments. Most all are connexions of interest or of ease to themselves, and perhaps it is the best way. Now, with thee I say, 'How is, or what has become of, the *Fair Incognito* who bestowed the gun?' That wonderful being has been seen only once since. Then I only looked at her, and as her conduct has been so extraordinary towards me I give thee here the affair nearly word for word, as true as surprising." The enclosed episode was more than explanation enough of his meaning.

He found it "quite impossible" to say where he might be by winter. "Migratory birds or beasts follow the mast." Were he to remain in New Orleans, he hoped to have her blessed company. He was pleased that she had declined an invitation from her brother Thomas, whose ways and doubts had so disappointed her. "We are poor but not beggars, I assure thee." The reluctance of Berthoud to help him land a job with the Red River survey (because, allegedly, he had "*fooled away what he had*" in Henderson) "gagged" him. But if he had only her own "good wishes" that he was "intent on deserving," well and good.

His feckless situation changed overnight upon his receiving some heartening news from the plantation of a pupil. On May 24 he added:

> I give lessons to a young lady here . . . daughter of a rich widow . . . her name is Eliza Pirrie. She resides near Bayou Sarah during the summer heat. Yesterday I begged to hear her sing and play on the piano. I played with her on a flute and made the mother stare. She was much surprised to hear me sing the notes. This lady asked me if I would go with them and teach her daughter (about sixteen, an interesting age), until next winter. I am to think of the terms and give an answer. This I have already formed in my mind. She must pay me $100 per month in advance, furnish *us*, Joseph and I, with one room, our board and washing, and I will devote one half of each day for her daughter. It is very high but I will not go unless I get it. If she accedes, I will have a very excellent opportunity of forwarding my collection, being able to draw every day.

The orange myrtle and cape jessamine plants that Lucy wanted for Eliza he intended to do his best to find and send. And as for Nicholas, he thought that she might as well not prod him in his behalf as to the Pacific. "No commissions will come from that quarter. . . . My future plans are, and will ever be, to do all in my power to enable thee to live with comfort and satisfaction, wherever I may chance to be carried by circumstances. Believe it, my Lucy, and I shall be ever happy and comfortable." If she herself would be happier and "not quite so hard on the world" it would help, "there being, still, a few good hearts in it." He thanked her for her latest letter, "written as if to a Beloved Friend." If it were not, then he would rather "be deceived in that way forever." At last, he signed himself, "Farewell, thy true devoted friend, J. J. Audubon."

However, before he waxed and sealed the heavy missive there came a much more alarming admonition, from Lucy, not to return to Kentucky in a state of want and to send her money so desperately needed. On May 31 Audubon countered with something like a spirit of recrimination. "Wert thou not to give me hints about money I should be sorry, as I know it is as necessary for the support of *thy life* as thy affection is to comfort of mine." He rejected her refusal to have him beside her in failure as well as security, and to risk joining him if he should call her. The reported illness of Eliza and Lucy's indispensability at White House did not seem to him excuse enough. He was protesting at a moment when the heat so affected his "faculties" as to make drawing "almost impossible" while the sweat poured from him.

> I am very sorry that thou art so intent on my *not* returning to thee. If that country we live in cannot feed us, *why not* fly from it? I am sorry thy beloved friend Eliza has been so ill. If Mr. Berthoud has wrote me it is more than I know of yet. Why, Lucy, do you not cling to your better friend, your husband? Not to boast of my *intentions* any more toward thy happiness, I will merely say that I am afraid *for thee*. We would be better, much better, happier. If you have not wrote to your Uncle Bakewell, *do not*. I want no one's help but those who are not *quite* so engaged about their business. Your great desire that I should stay away is, I must acknowledge, very unexpected. If you can bear to have me go on a voyage of at least three years, without wishing to see me, before, I cannot help thinking that Lucy probably would be better pleased should I never return. And so it may be.
>
> Kiss my dear young friends for me, pray. For life, your really devoted Audubon.
>
> P.S. I can scarce hope now to go to the Pacific. My plans, my wishes, will forever be abortive. However, I now enclose what I have written for the President. You may send it or not, as you may think best fit. But I assure you that I shall ever remember Clark's expedition. *And feel my love for you.*

But he had not yet finished this long letter. In transverse writing he said that he was sending leghorn hats for the boys. On another page (also crosswise) he penned, as if intending to safehand the thirty drawings to Lucy, a request that she have his friend the painter William Basterop open up the well packed shipment on "some fine dry day." He said that she should "look over the whole, one by one without rubbing them," and, if they were thought "worth anything, or a great deal," to inform him of the "situation." In the end he did not run such a risk.

Before posting the letter he waited to hear from Mrs. Pirrie. But, despairing, he closed apologetically, without more delay: "My Dearest Girl, I am sorry for the last part I wrote yesterday, but I then felt miserable. I hope thou wilt look on it as a momentary incident. I love thee so dearly, feel it so powerfully, that I cannot bear anything from thee that has the appearance of coolness. Write me always care of Mr. Pamar. I will leave in a few days. Know not where for. Thomas W. Bakewell has wrote me quite a positive and *brotherly* letter that I shall never answer. God bless thee, thine forever."[17]

The words "know not where for" meant more than Audubon intimated. If Mrs. Pirrie (who was not, by the way, a widow) changed her mind, he would have to find some other escape from New Orleans. Dr. Heermann had dismissed him without paying two hundred dollars for six weeks' tuition. Gossip said that a flirtation was the cause. For once the use of flattery to win needed pupils had played him false. The flirtation, harmless enough, verged on an open scandal sure to spread.

Audubon could not, even if savings warranted, retreat to Florida, or Cuba, or the Bay of Honduras to hunt and draw. The nesting season was over in the tropics. He was about to disappear into some wild corner of West Feliciana when the Pirrie offer gained the day—not with the hoped-for one hundred dollars but a mere sixty, plus food and lodgings for himself and Joseph.

X. On a Desperate Rock

A T BAYOU SARA LANDING, 125 miles northwest of New Orleans, Audubon and Mason walked uphill in the mid-June heat to the twin village of St. Francisville.[1] Oakley, the Pirrie plantation, an Eden of magnolia, holly, beech, and poplar, of tangled woodland and shadowy bayous, lay three and one-half miles northeast.[2] Warblers sang overhead and darted among the flowers and shrubs as the travel-stained artists approached the porticoed mansion.

The days passed idyllically in West Feliciana. Eliza Pirrie delighted as much in the companionship of her teacher as in his dancing, drawing, and hair-braid jewelry lessons. She often watched him and Joseph at their tasks. So absorbing did she find his portrait of a huge, freshly killed rattlesnake attacking some nesting mockingbirds that she herself tried sketching the reptile. For sixteen hours Audubon drew, measured, and made notes in the broiling heat.

After dark, and often until daybreak, he prowled the swampy lake in search of timid ibis and anhingas. Relieved that her husband was a wage earner at last, Lucy took pleasure in his reports of the beauty of the parish and its value to his art. The comforts and peace of Oakley agreed equally well with Joseph. Between his flower painting and Audubon's delineations, the portraits of birds took on a new, classical virtuosity. The hawks breathed ferocity, the whippoorwills came to pulsing life on paper. A pet sparrow hawk of Oakley was an inspiration for both the notebook of observations and the box of crayons.

But Eliza took more pleasure in the company of her teacher than was thought good by her solicitous, infatuated doctor. Toward summer's end the servants and house guests and even the neighbors began to spread talk about Eliza's rapport with her thirty-six-year-old drawing master. Mrs. Pirrie had lost five of her children, indeed all but the frail Eliza, to seasonal epidemics. She heeded Dr. Ira Smith, as fever time approached, and curtailed the lessons.

In October the mistress of Oakley dismissed Audubon altogether. For the sake of his portfolio he begged ten days' sufferance, which she reluctantly granted. Her bibulous husband, James, pitying the artist, took his part and deplored her refusal to pay for lessons not taken. He gave his word that the balance would be forwarded to New Orleans. Only for Mason did Mrs. Pirrie indicate sympathy. But Audubon ordered Joseph to refuse as beneath the dignity of his position her offer of a suit that had belonged to a son of hers not long dead.

The moment came to brave the farewell rounds of the family and guests in the upper parlor. The ineffectual Pirrie, sorry to see the artists go, lent Audubon and Mason horses for the ride to Bayou Sara.

In New Orleans there were those who pretended not to know Audubon in his worn nankeens. "Good God," he philosophized as he placed himself in the hands of a barber and tailor, "that forty dollars should be enough to make a gentleman cherished, nay admired!" He was attached to the image of himself with long, shaggy curls caught back with a silver buckle. Bare of funds after repairs to his person, and after sending $100 to Lucy with a command to come at once to

Louisiana, he had to turn to his only true friends, the Pamars and Dmitris. They thought his Oakley birds incomparably his best and were eager for their daughters to resume their lessons in his method.

If the Kentucky agent to whom the draft for Lucy was sent had not temporized, she would have been only too willing to set out. Audubon, confident that she would soon appear and help him show the gossips their mistake, met boat after boat. Her failure to arrive after weeks of waiting caused nearly chronic headache and hypochondria. The public indifference to his exhibition of drawings and his rejection by schools and institutions to which he applied for work intensified his depression. His campaign for private pupils stirred enmity in the Museum Coffee Shop coterie. One artist called him a hack, fake, and imposter from "no one knows whence." The accuser did not take up an invitation to call at Dauphine Street and repeat the insult, however.

Rather than face the forbidding headmistress of his private pupil, Eusophrine Pamar, at her boarding school twice weekly, Audubon took whatever he could find to do—a copy of a print of Vanderlyn's *Ariadne,* and the like. The medium of oils served other professionals so well that he ordered canvas. Meanwhile, he began a full-length watercolor of the colorful, seditious priest Don Antonio de Sedella, which he planned to repeat in oils.[3] To attract new pupils he also drew a hare in his most brilliant style. It induced William Brand, a friend of the Bakewells of Louisville and Pittsburgh, to enroll his child bride and his son from a previous marriage at three dollars a lesson. This move by the rich Brand, who had been among the guests at Oakley, prompted Audubon to buy a splendid frame for the hare that had brought him luck.

While Audubon was sailing away from the Oakley country, Anne Moynet Audubon was buried in Couëron. Years were to pass before he learned of her death and its repercussions. Her children's last chance to inherit was put to the test. The fourth and last will called for an equal share in her estate for her adoptives, "Rose Bouffard and brother Jean Rabin called Audubon."[4] Although she was ninety-two years of age by October 18, 1821, when she added the proviso that she be allowed the privacy and freedom of rooms set aside for her by Rose, Anne did not know that death was only weeks in the offing.

Three days after the death in Couëron, Rebecca Bakewell died while on a visit to Thomas in Kentucky. Her presence had increased Lucy's eagerness to leave. Audubon heard the news in a chance street-corner conversation. What he had yet to learn was that the only beneficiaries of his "constant enemy" were two grandsons named for her late husband and the still unwed Sarah and Ann. They fared better than Rebecca's Carlisle nieces, Esther Steel and Mary Foulke, whom she remembered only with a gold watch and a ciphered teapot.[5]

As November moved on with no sign of Lucy, Audubon grieved in his journal: "Very low of spirits; wished myself off this miserable stage." In France, on that day, he was again branded a "natural son," this time in the legal inventory of Anne's possessions. Even then, Gabriel was renewing his attempts to trace him. Du Puigaudeau had approached two Nantes merchants for help towards "possible information as to the whereabouts and activities of Mr. John Audubon, who ought to be living in Henderson, state of Kentucky." He was advised to write the "New Orleans merchant," John Garnier.[6] Actually, the émigré Garnier was the Natchez hotelkeeper who had helped find the lost portfolio and who had often talked birds with Audubon. He still had relatives at La Gascherie, one of the noblest chateaux of the Nantes region. All the Garniers were kin to the planter and philanthropist, Julien Poydras de la Lande of Pointe Coupée, Louisiana.[7]

Sore eyes—more headache—did not stand in the way of the old dream. "My Birds, my Beloved Birds of America feel [sic] all my time and, nearly, my thoughts. I do not wish to see any other perspective than the last Specimen of them Drawed." A green-winged teal held Audubon's attention to brilliant advantage, then a wild goose and a merganser. The neck of a swan posed a problem. To draw the bird in natural size within the confines of his paper, Audubon arched its neck backward as if the swan were about to take a fluttering insect. "Where does Comfort keep herself now," he asked himself amid these etiolating sessions and the grind of teaching, "on a desperate rock, unwilling to cast even a look on our wretched species?"

A chance visitor reported that Lucy was on her way. The week before Christmas the little *Rocket* steamed up the levee and discharged the family. Audubon brought them to dine with the Pamars, then took them home to Dauphine Street.

Lucy had brought all the old drawings. Next morning while cathedral bells tolled a requiem for Napoleon, who had died in May on St. Helena island, Audubon scrutinized his birds. The new drawings seemed to him closer to nature, as well as more dramatic and daring. A happy accident explained the advance, in part. A drop of water on a portrait of Lucy had responded to the rubbing of chalk, even improving the effect. Crayon over watercolor was to work wonders with the plumage of owls, whippoorwills, and chuck-wills.

On Christmas Eve, Ferdinand Rozier appeared with a drawing of a "wood grouse" from Fatland Ford days, left behind in Ste. Genevieve. It was while Rozier and the Audubons sat talking, of Nantes and the past, that Gabriel happened to be seeking Audubon through none other than John Garnier of Natchez. His letter stressed that "family business" necessitated the search.[8] If ever it reached Garnier, there is no reason to believe that he intervened.

Christmas Day and the holiday season were no exception to an intensive teaching schedule that kept the Audubons alive. Too poor to buy an 1822 diary at New Year's, the artist nonetheless made a resolution—to finish ninety-five birds in the same number of days with the cooperation of his hunter, Gilbert. One bitter morning while scanning the early morning markets for rarities, he ran across an aged friend from Kentucky wandering among the stalls. He took the "famous flutist," who had played many a concert and for many Louisville dances and weddings, home for rest and care.

The announcement that Mrs. Brand must abandon her lessons for motherhood was a blow to the economy more severe than any reverse since Cincinnati. The Brands, aware of the crisis and eager to enable Audubon to try his luck in less competitive Natchez, hired Lucy as companion. She was invited to remain until the birth of the child, or until Audubon could send for her and the boys.

In mid-March he sailed with Joseph on the *Eclat*. An explosion of gunpowder in his chest of drawings plunged him into apathy that lasted for most of the eight-day voyage. The shocking damage to his collection, while not so great as that of the classic onslaught of rats in Henderson, drained him. Again necessity compelled a response to a bid by the captain and others for chalk portraits.

Apart from the daughter of a former Majorcan merchant, Natchez afforded nothing in the way of pupils. There was little demand for portraits. At a loss, Audubon let the spring air lure him up to the post of the Arkansas to see what might be gleaned about the expedition. He soon returned with a fine drawing of a chuck-will but barren of hopes regarding the Pacific. Levin Wailes invited him for some weeks of hunting on his plantation, then had him appointed to Elizabeth Academy in neighboring Washington, Mississippi. He rented a room for himself and Joseph in Natchez and walked daily to work and back in the miserable heat. Mason began to speak of homesickness for Ohio, but his precious help could not be dispensed with just yet.

When fever struck Audubon that summer his resistance was low, owing to the confinement of the classroom. Lucy could not come to him; at the moment Mrs. Brand was delivered and near death and could not be abandoned. Indeed, as soon as Audubon recovered under the care of his young friend, Dr. William Provan, Lucy sent Victor and John to him in Natchez. Provan put them in school and met their expenses while their father rallied.

Not even to support the family could Audubon bear to go back to the humdrum of teaching. To turn commercial artist and abandon his portfolio was the alternative. He handed Joseph his old double-barreled gun of Mill Grove memories and the materials to work his way back to Cincinnati.

Audubon's first attempt at a quick sale was a large water-color copy of Trumbull's *Death of Montgomery at Quebec*.[9] Provan doubted that it would fetch the $280 asked; to dispose of it he organized a raffle that succeeded in fantastic fashion. The ten-dollar chance that he placed on it for Audubon won back the picture, along with the prize of $300. This windfall sped the artist back to painting birds.

In August, the death of the Brand infant ended Lucy's service. Audubon found her a governess post in Natchez with the family of a clergyman, who, however, soon proved unable to meet her wages. Audubon had to surrender to teaching duty at Brevost Academy where his sons were enrolled. He thought this at least preferable to taking up an offer to manage a paper mill in Mexico. Mississippi and the entire nation were plagued by the hard times that narrowed his choice.

The idea of commercial art was not dismissed. Audubon took heed of the vogue for scenic "views." One day in November, while he was sketching Natchez from across the Mississippi, an English tourist named Leacock paused to watch. As they talked, Audubon invited the visitor to meet Lucy and inspect the bird portfolio. Publication in England might very well be accomplished, Leacock suggested, if Audubon would polish his style still more, and learn to paint in oils for prestige and a surer living. The shrewd Lucy doubted his belief that it would take four or five years of residence there to win a following. In fact the few reservations that the visitor expressed brought her inner convictions about the justifiability of her husband's lofty aims into new, sharp focus. Challenged by the opinions of the encouraging yet conservative visitor, she reminded Audubon that letters from friends such as Clay, Harrison, and others would lower the barriers. As for oil painting, she failed to see why it could not be easily mastered by one so gifted.

John Steen, an itinerant limner from Washington, Pennsylvania, agreed to teach the use of oils.[10] Under his tutelage Audubon copied the watercolor of an otter in a trap. Then came his unevenly finished but undeniably appealing portraits of his sons. He and Steen began a copy of the study of Don Antonio. Altogether, matters were proceeding so satisfactorily that they formed a partnership to solicit portrait commissions by Dearborn wagon among the planters—Steen in oils, Audubon with chalk. It was decided that Victor should go along as an apprentice. What Lucy should do, meanwhile, had been most effectively worked out by Dr. Provan. His fiancée's mother had been in search of a teacher for the neighborhood school on her plantation, Beech Woods, in West Feliciana. Jane Middlemist Percy, the widow of Robert Percy, a British Royal Navy lieutenant and power of the short-lived West Florida republic of 1810, liked what she had heard about Lucy. She could promise her a thousand dollars or more a year, and a combined cottage and schoolhouse for herself and John if she would teach the four Percy daughters and their friends.

Audubon found Lucy in complete harmony with her surroundings when he called at Beech Woods for Victor in March. Mrs. Percy was charmed by his banter. So fond had his captive doves in Natchez become of him, he told her, that he had to chase them to the woods at his departure.[11] Her London brother, the artist Charles Middlemist, was expected soon for a winter of flower painting. She hoped they might meet.

The wagon of the itinerants had not rolled very far into Mississippi before differences arose. Steen objected to stopping by the wayside while Audubon went after each flash of color. The two artists soon parted ways.

If the glories of Beech Woods welcomed Audubon back, Mrs. Percy did not. Eliza Pirrie, no longer of Oakley but mistress of Greenwood, made no secret of Audubon's rift with her mother. When he learned of Eliza's nearness and her bereavement, he paid her a call. Her bridegroom, a cousin, and not the jealous Dr. Ira Smith after all, died of pneumonia soon after he carried her across a stream the night of their elopement. Eliza, most cordial, wished to hear all about Audubon's life since Oakley days.[12]

Uncertain where to turn, but sure he must not linger on at

Top: Victor Gifford Audubon, *1823. Bottom:* John Woodhouse Audubon, *1823. Oil on canvas. Tyler Collection, John James Audubon Museum, Audubon State Park, Henderson, Kentucky.*

Beech Woods, Audubon began to paint his own portrait in oils with the aid of a mirror. As Mrs. Percy kept an eye on the moody likeness she took pity and proposed that he try painting Sarah and another of her daughters. He caught their resemblances well in outline, but when he began to lay on the oils, the girls' mother protested the "jaundiced" color of their cheeks. In an uncontrollable burst of temper the artist talked back to the lady—and so frankly, from the depths of his injured feelings, that when Lucy overheard she declined to take his part.

Ordered to depart, Audubon lost no time in doing so. But his own wrath was not to carry him far. Three days later he returrned under cover of night to beg forgiveness of Lucy. A slave saw him, and Mrs. Percy herself later surprised the couple in their bed. He was told to be off and went back to Bayou Sara bitter and unchastened. True to his promise, he sent for Victor and they caught a boat for Natchez.

The scene Audubon had been painting in watercolor the day Leacock interrupted him on the banks of the city was shown to a prospective buyer, who ordered a copy in oil. So the green bluffs, fort, spire, vultures, buildings, and figures were transferred to a huge canvas in joyous anticipation of $300. Just as the work was finished the client died; and her heirs refused to pay. A storekeeper was persuaded to hang it on a wall for a chance bid; there it was to stay until long after its creator had lost track of its existence. It was eventually to find a place of pride at Melrose Plantation, near Natchez.[13]

The disenchanted Audubon willingly took up an invitation from George Duncan of Towers plantation for some weeks of hunting. There both he and Victor fell ill of yellow fever. Dr. Provan summoned Lucy, who drove alone in a one-horse carriage and nursed them back from near death. Their recovery, doubtful at first, dragged on until Mrs. Percy sent word for Lucy to return and bring both convalescents.

Audubon did not propose to count on such capricious hospitality. As he gained strength he began to speak of going north to try commerce again. Lucy would not countenance the idea. She did, however, agree that a search for an American publisher in Philadelphia might be worthwhile. Once it had been decided that he should take Victor to Kentucky to apprentice to Nicholas Berthoud, he prepared for what promised to be a lengthy absence.

Father and son boarded Thomas Bakewell's *Magnet* in October 1823. At Trinity, where Audubon and Rozier had pitched their winter camp on the way to Ste. Genevieve years before, drought waylaid them. The passengers disembarked but could find no vehicles for hire. Audubon cooked fish on shore, left the baggage to those who would send it on with the rising of the waters, and turned to Victor to ask, with doubt, if he felt equal to the walk. The thirteen-year-old, still weak from fever, scoffed at the notion that he could not tramp 250 miles onward.

Before they set out up the dry riverbed with two other stranded passengers the next day, Audubon wrote an introduction to Ferdinand Rozier for a chance acquaintance. The man, one Bienvenu, was bound for Ste. Genevieve "to recover some land on the St. Francis River," but knew no one in the region. "I am yet, my dear Rozier, on the wing," Audubon confessed to his old partner, "and God only knows how long I may yet remain so. I am now bound to Shippingport to see if I can, through my *former* friends there, bring about some changes in my situation. I am now rather wearied of the world. I have, I believe, seen too much of it." He apologized for his gloom with wistful, self-pitying words: "But I must not cool your happy feelings in the center of your family and affluent means by giving you only an idea of my dull prospects. May Heaven preserve you a long run of comfort in this life and one of perfect blessings in the next . . . with sincerest friendship. . . ."[14]

One of their companions on the walk, a braggart, set the pace while the other gladly fell behind with Victor. Over trails and fields they moved, under clouds of southbound robins, until evening. After a night or two of rest on hard cabin floors unconducive to sleep, Victor collapsed by the wayside. The sudden cackle of a wild turkey brought him back to consciousness while his father bathed his temples.

Beyond Smith's Ferry the other wayfarers had had enough of Audubon's brisk pace.

A hundred miles below Louisville a hired wagoner carried the travelers on, until blinding rain made the driver slacken the reins for his team to find shelter. Out of a new log cabin in a clearing came Willy Speed, a nephew of the Rankins, who provided supper and a bed, quite as if he knew nothing of the Bowen lawsuit in which his uncle had taken part against Audubon. By the time Audubon and Victor reached Shippingport only thirteen dollars of the money put up by Lucy remained, enough to rent a room before going to call on Nicholas and Eliza.

Old Madame Marie-Anne-Julia Berthoud, as delighted as ever to see Audubon, chatted away with him in French and teased him as always about his "Bourbon" features. Such affability was rare in Kentucky, now that so many former friends had left or turned on the "ne'er-do-well." Seeing that no portraits were wanted, Audubon had no choice but to turn to shop signs, steamboat decorations, and lettering for a temporary living. A mural of the Falls of the Ohio, daubed for a steamboat in drydock, made Audubon wonder whether he ought not to attempt a hundred American views in oil.[15]

One January morning Middleton, the doctor, galloped toward White House. "What a void in the world for me—thinking, thinking, learning, weighing," Audubon wrote sorrowfully in his journal after the death of Madame Berthoud.[16] He had lost a friend who valued him for what he was and, no doubt, would remain—a dreamer, romantic, free spirit, child of nature.

XI. Adrift Again

A S SOON AS STEAMERS WERE RUNNING to Pittsburgh in March, Audubon left Louisville. From his meager savings he planned to replace his shabby clothing with new in Philadelphia. The thought of facing the proud, formidable, intellectual stronghold left him apprehensive after an absence of ten years.

There was no doubt in his mind, once he had donned a new black suit in imitation of his hero, Franklin, about which of the city's protean personalities he should first approach. To keep the "American woodsman" role that it pleased him to play, he did not sacrifice the mane that somewhat resembled Franklin's. Dr. James Mease, whom he and Lucy thought the best person to see because of the many visits he had made to Fatland Ford to watch Bakewell's agricultural experiments, prided himself on his international acquaintances. The one-time favorite of the eminent Dr. Rush knew not only Audubon's preceptor of 1806, Dr. Samuel Latham Mitchill of the New York Lyceum, but he actually corresponded with Baron Cuvier of Paris, founder of comparative anatomy. Mease was, besides, curator of the American Philosophical Society.

The reception was cordial. Mease, fourteen years Audubon's senior, ventured to suggest that a visit to the barber might not be amiss before they went about in his caller's interest. But the artist replied, good-naturedly, that he would dislike to be parted from his frontiersman's hallmark.

Thomas Sully (1783–1872), a portrait painter of English birth and ever-widening prestige, admired the audacity of his caller in seeking scientific support of publication despite his informal training.[1] He spoke glowingly of the portfolio and cheerfully accepted Audubon's defense of his ambition, albeit on two actually parlous counts. Audubon, encouraged, dared to boast that he preferred his own academic shortcomings and unsurpassed field observations to any "closet" ornithologist's dry lucubrations. Moreover, he named that French master of masters, Jacques-Louis David, as his past teacher of art.[2] Sully might have taken exception to David's evident failure to teach his pupil the laws of perspective and the handling of oils. Instead, he himself offered to give Audubon some free lessons in the medium if he would show his daughter Sarah how to manage pastels and watercolor. The sociable, musical Sullys drew Audubon into their genial circle.

Mease took Audubon to call on the youngest, most colorful personality of the city's science arena, Charles-Lucien-Jules-Laurent Bonaparte (1803–57), Prince of Canino and Musignano by dint of his Uncle Napoleon's conquests, but, like his Uncle Joseph, an *émigré* in America. The small, set, black-eyed nephew of twenty-three bore a startling, if oddly cherubic, resemblance to the late Emperor. He was the eldest son of the second marriage of Lucien Bonaparte. Hard at work on a supplement to the Alexander Wilson classic, he was spending more time in the city than with his cousin-bride, Princess Zenaïde, at her father Joseph's Bordentown country place, Point Breeze. The couple had been living there since their recent marriage.

For Bonaparte to inquire politely which district of France

Audubon came from was only to be expected. The artist explained, perhaps with confusion, that his father brought him to the United States while serving as "admiral" under Count d'Estaing. When he spoke of his studies under Jacques-Louis David, painter by appointment to His Imperial Highness Napoleon Bonaparte, he was on perilous ground. Luckily, the Prince changed the subject to natural history and its delineation. Audubon recalled having met his illustrator, Titian Ramsay Peale of the painting Peales, when the Long Expedition passed through Cincinnati. After a mannerly if not stony silence, he admitted indifference to Peale's stiff, conventional profiles done in the eighteenth-century manner that he found uninspired and uninspiring.

Peale had every reason to fear he might lose Bonaparte's patronage. His brother, Rembrandt Peale, was the only member of the distinguished family of artists to drop a word of praise for Audubon's delineations when he saw them.

Bonaparte took his engaging new fellow naturalist to a meeting of the Academy of Natural Sciences. Audubon invited the members to examine his portfolio. One of them, George Ord, was then finishing an edition of the great work of his deceased protégé, Alexander Wilson.[3] It was he who had completed Wilson's work with a ninth posthumous volume. The pedantic, jealous aspirant to primacy did not intend that an untutored backwoodsman should surpass either Wilson or himself. The heir of an English chandler and ropemaker, Ord had benefited by an education of which he could be proud. His octavo edition, due in 1828, would enable him to bask forever in the reflected glory of Wilson; unless, of course, Audubon or someone else attempted to seize his laurels and those of the "father of ornithology." He examined the sketches by Audubon; then, to rule them out of the way of his private ambitions, he belittled what he called absurd, unnatural attitudinizing of birds in habitats too fancy and pretentious.

One personality, the brilliant French painter-naturalist Charles-Alexandre Lesueur, begged to differ with Ord. Lesueur, then illustrating part of Thomas Say's pioneering *Ameri-*

can Entomology, recognized Audubon's genius.[4] He whispered that France might favor publication, should America fail him, then wrote him an introduction to the immortal painter of roses, Pierre-Joseph Redouté (1759–1840) of Paris, just in case.[5] (The Academy president, William Maclure, had brought Lesueur from the West Indies not long after the artist had survived shipwreck in the South Pacific on a voyage with the celebrated explorer Piron.)

Young Richard Harlan, a Quaker doctor and zoologist, also took exception to the whispering campaign begun by Ord, Peale, and the engraver Lawson.[6] After Ord squelched Audubon's nomination for Academy membership, Harlan continued overtures for an exchange of information and specimens useful to his own pursuit of fame. He hoped his travail on various subjects—actually, much barefaced codifying of the work of others in poor, hasty fashion—would find acclaim.

Until the Prince could be certain of the expediency of an alliance of some kind with Audubon, he intended to steer a shrewd middle course. He did not wish to purchase any drawings without the blessings of his highly opinioned engraver Lawson, of whom Wilson had been a pupil. As he approached Lawson's house with Audubon one morning, Bonaparte could plainly see the hopes his interest aroused in his new acquaintance, hungering at thirty-nine for recognition. The big, raw-boned Scotsman was routed from bed by his daughter and seemed disgruntled at being disturbed to meet a stranger whose effrontery George Ord had already described.

Ready to defy any disparagement of Alexander Wilson, whose art was in a sense his responsibility and pride, Lawson listened to what his callers had to say about engraving Audubon's sketches. He took one up and grumpily declared it "too soft, too much like oil painting" for engraving. Bonaparte, used to Lawson's bluntness, ranged one of Wilson's birds alongside that of Audubon. This was too much for the man who had rescued Wilson from suicide and turned him into a painter-naturalist of note. (Lawson was one day to accuse Audubon, whom he had detested on sight, of having instructed his own engraver to reverse and enlarge Wilson's horned owl and publish it as "drawn from nature.") He turned to Bonaparte and, pointing scornfully at the portfolio, said to him, "You may buy them, but I will not engrave them. . . . Ornithology requires truth and correct lines— here are neither!"[7]

The Prince thought another professional opinion should be sought—that of engraver Gideon Fairman, a partner of Cephas G. Childs, and recently returned from a period of work in England, who suggested that London might be the place for Audubon. He himself lacked the men for the task but said that the supply of copper and qualified engravers and colorers was plentiful abroad, particularly for a work of the magnitude Audubon envisioned.

Lawson had not yet seen the last of his morning callers. Nothing daunted, they returned to ask him to try engraving a boat-tailed grackle. Bonaparte, meanwhile, had paid Audu-bon twenty-five dollars for his pencil and watercolor drawing of a pair of boat-tailed grackles for his own publication. He was to illustrate the species as the "Great Crow Blackbird," a name that would not stand. Lawson scrutinized the drawing, found fault with the feathers, bill, and legs, and disparaged the size of the outline. To his insistence on corrections, Au-dubon replied that all points were perfectly true to nature. "Then it is a species of crow I never saw," snapped Lawson. "I think your work extraordinary for one self-taught, but we in Philadelphia are used to seeing very correct drawing."

Audubon's impulsive retort—that he had studied for years under the greatest of French teachers, David—drew a sniff of contempt and: "Then you made some bad use of your time!" Audubon clenched his fists but stood silent. He dared not admit the imprudence of claiming David as his master, even though Charles Bonaparte might some day query David about him. If it had been truth, rather than lucid folly under fire, he might have put the claim to more effective use in 1821 when he met John Vanderlyn, a bona fide pupil of David. Lawson doubted the story, along with the Louisiana birth of this spu-

rious "backwoodsman," whom he believed a liar and imposter. Audubon, still much exercised, accepted a sum in
payment and departed, never dreaming that he would be
sharing credit for the plate with the Swiss artist Alexander
Rider. To keep Lawson happy the Prince capitulated, but not
without insisting that the name of Audubon appear on the
engraving as author of the female figure. Biding his time before telling Audubon how all this came to be, he wrote in
his description of the bird: "With these views we now give
a faithful representation of both sexes of the Great Crow-
Blackbird, drawn by the zealous observer of nature and skil-
ful artist Mr. John J. Audubon, and hope hereby to remove
all doubt relative to this interesting species."[8]

Bonaparte seemed willing to discuss a joint publication
with Audubon, on the condition that the text be by himself,
with the illustrations by Audubon. But Audubon had no
intention of surrendering his field lore—so palpably interesting and valuable—to young Bonaparte. Changing the subject, he sounded him out about supporting publication of the
portfolio, without text, in Paris, but got nowhere. Capital
was scarce among the exiled Bonapartes these days. The mu-
tually stubborn though friendly talks availed nothing.

To meet expenses after his funds ran out Audubon thought
of teaching or accepting some workaday commissions. Sully
persuaded him that his services would yield half what New
Orleans paid. An exhibition of his bird portraits for a small
admission was less than a success. Still, the situation of the
prospering Ferdinand Rozier, who arrived in Philadelphia
on business, seemed unenviably dull. Audubon continued
his lessons in oil with Sully between trips to the countryside
to watch the spring migrations.

He chose to imagine that Joseph Robert Mason, happily
employed as an artist at the botanical gardens at sixty dollars
monthly, would be pleased to see him. Behind Mason's inclination to speak of other things when the idea of his accompanying Audubon to Europe was broached lay deep resentment. He had been watching the local maneuvers of his
former employer and did not mind letting his enmity become

known to Philadelphians. George Ord was pleased to learn from Mason that Audubon's earlier promise to him of recognition for painting many of the flowers and insects in the bird portraits had thus far been denied. Mason failed to return the visit, which Audubon obliviously recorded as "delightful."

Titian Ramsay Peale was another who steadfastly kept his distance. He refused to lend species frankly coveted by his rival. The time had come for Audubon to give up and try New York. He went to have a last talk with Fairman, who by chance hired him to draw a "grous" to embellish a New Jersey bank note.[9] This brought a brief postponement of departure. Fairman showed the sketch to Edward Harris, a young gentleman farmer and naturalist of nearby Moorestown, New Jersey, who asked to meet the delineator because of his own drawing of birds and love of nature.[10] Harris took a great liking to Audubon, invited him to go snipe-shooting in the marshes, and reveled in the prospect of a lasting friendship. He gained the distinct impression that Audubon's father came to America with Count Rochambeau but that he quit the French Navy to fight alongside the American Continentals. The hero had "fought at Valley Forge" and in other battles, and "died an admiral" at the age of more than ninety. The battles, the mention of Rochambeau, the high rank, and the age of ninety were all spawned by John James Audubon's fear of failure. Yet he did not conceal his own desperate financial state from Harris, fourteen years his junior and extraordinarily sympathetic. The friend-in-need promptly bought some bird portraits that could be spared or readily replaced.

"I would have kissed him but that it is not the custom in this icy city," wrote Audubon of the favor. He showed gratitude by promising skins of cowbirds, rails, and partridges that Harris lacked for his collection.

On the day of their parting, Harris, perhaps sorry he had had to turn down the oil of the *Falls of the Ohio* as unworthy of Audubon's talents, pressed a $100 bill into his palm. "Mr. Audubon, accept this from me," he said simply. "Men like you ought not to want for money." In return, the artist gave Harris the 200 birds drawn for Lucy at Couëron in 1805.

On August 1, after Audubon had collected letters of introduction and settled for his rent at Fifth and Minor Streets, Reuben Haines, a Quaker friend of Harlan, Mease, and the Prince, proposed a "sentimental journey" to Mill Grove.[11] As the carriage rolled along the graceful winding avenue toward the mansion, Audubon turned to Haines and said he would rejoin him and his wife after a visit to his old haunt, the grotto. He jumped out and ran down to the place above the Perkiomen, but found it eroded and the bank scarred by fallen rocks. In a nostalgic mood, and skeptical of what lay ahead, he entrusted his self-portrait to Haines with the request that it be copied for Lucy, should he never be able to return from his uncertain mission.

August was not a propitious time for a New York visit. Most of those whom Audubon wanted to consult had fled the heat or else did not interest themselves in his tribulations. Vanderlyn was on hand but too full of his own importance to do more than display his trophies and the medal given him by Napoleon. However, the celebrity suddenly noticed the resemblance of Audubon's lean frame to that of Andrew Jackson. He had him pose for the figure of a portrait, for which the head of the hero had been finished in the South. The taste of posterity fully confirmed what Audubon was thinking as he posed—that Vanderlyn was less than great at his art. What no generation and no observer until now has discerned regarding this heroic portrait is that the face of the handsome orderly in a shako with pompon, just behind Jackson, happens to be that of John James Audubon.

On the day that his old friend Mitchill, the moving spirit of the Lyceum of Natural History, introduced Audubon and his "elegant performances" at a meeting of the members, there was more than hated pedantry to dread. Ord and Lawson had seen to it that their Manhattan friends heard about Joseph Robert Mason's charges against Audubon. Confronted with the ugly hint, Audubon said that as teacher of the boy he had virtually redrawn each of his studies. Nomination to

Lyceum membership depended on whether he would write for its *Annals*.[12] Determined not to die the nonentity that Philadelphia wished him to remain, he drafted a paper on the swallow with the help of rising mammalogist Dr. James E. De Kay. Its appearance in print was to mark his debut as an author.

Indifference among the publishers was as pointed as it was among the savants. The former refused to invest a penny in the grandiose idea. Audubon was strolling along Battery Park, thinking that if it were not for a letter of introduction which he was awaiting from Sully, to use in Albany, he would leave, when along came the Bonapartes—Charles; Princess Zenaïde; her sister, Princess Charlotte; and Joseph, the erstwhile King of Spain. The Prince extracted a promise of memoranda on the wild turkey as well as some skins of Louisiana birds.

Sully's recommendation proved well worth waiting for. Audubon interrupted portraits of his landlady and her child to read its praises: "I have seen in Europe drawings of birds by the first masters, but I do not hesitate to declare that those of Mr. Audubon, for strength, expression, and exquisite resemblance far exceeds them all. No eulogy of mine could, however, express their merits. . . . Introduce him to our brotherhood."

Lafayette's approach on a triumphal tour of America extinguished the last spark of interest in the portfolio and its cause. But as Audubon sat down to write thanks to Sully and a farewell to "little Diggory" and the other Sullys, he did not intend the extent of his latest failure to be realized by his friend. His New York reception he described as warmer than that of Philadelphia. He said to tell Ord he did not think of him as an enemy, in spite of all.

Audubon thought the most colorful of the passengers on the Hudson River steamer bound for Albany were twenty-three emissaries of six Indian nations, homeward bound from "Washington City."

Audubon found none of those he hoped to see in Albany. Governor De Witt Clinton was attending the reception and festivities for Lafayette in New York. (Actually he had just served as governor and would do so again a year later.) Rather than face Boston without introductions, the artist moved toward Niagara Falls to try painting one of his contemplated "hundred views" of America.[13]

At Rochester he sketched the Genesee Falls. He recalled how Wilson had visited Niagara and celebrated its grandeur with his well-known poem, "The Foresters." When he himself reached the inn at the Falls in an unkempt and weary state, he scribbled these sardonic lines in the register with his rival in mind: "J. J. Audubon, who, like Wilson, will ramble, but never, like that great man, under the lash of a bookseller." The bitter taste of Philadelphia and New York was still on his tongue. He remembered that publishers and their ways had allegedly been the death of Wilson.

A glimpse of the magnificent cliffs of water convinced him that he could never catch its sublimity, least of all in oils. Over his twelve-cent supper of bread and milk he thought of Franklin eating his roll in the streets of Philadelphia and of Goldsmith depending on music to fend off starvation. But he swore to win over poverty and anonymity by persevering in his turn. It was disheartening, meanwhile, to have to go back penniless to Lucy and rechart his course.

He started for Pittsburgh and a descent of the rivers. At Buffalo he found crowds of Indians, under Chief Red Jacket and Chief Devil's Ramrod, in town to collect annuities. The place had been burned out in the War of 1812, but at least 200 new homes had risen. Audubon paid a dollar and a half for deck passage on a lake schooner bound for Erie, Pennsylvania. He decided he would rather roll up in his buffalo robe, unwashed and unshaven, than accept the captain's offer of a berth in his cabin. During the night as he lay with his gun and knife beside him and his tin box of drawings and colors buckled to his shoulder, a gale forced the boat into Presque Isle harbor. He feared for his drawings as he was rowed to shore through the wild billows, but a gig landed him and his treasure safely on the Erie shore.

He and an itinerant painter joined forces at portrait-taking in the town, until they had seven and one-half dollars between them. Five of these they handed over to a carter to carry them on to Meadville.[14] Halfway there, the three stopped for the night. They were fast asleep in the dormitory's sea of beds when three giggling girls climbed under the covers nearby and whispered audibly for a while. They were not to be seen when Audubon arose at dawn to hunt, but he had not forgotten how longingly they had talked of wanting their pictures painted. When they appeared, dressed in their best, at the breakfast table, he sketched each pretty face. Before he left he gave a little concert on his flute for the gaping household.

By way of evergreen-, pine-, and spruce-wooded roads the travelers continued on their way. In Meadville, Audubon was taken for a missionary at the inn because of his long hair and shaggy beard, and was invited to ask a blessing at the table. After the noonday dinner he showed the storekeeper, a Dutchman named Huidekoper, his portrait of Lucy and a bird or two. In the garret above the shop, amid hogsheads of oats, piles of fur caps, toys, musical instruments, and a tumbling and mewing basket of kittens, he was put to work at sketching a boy while a small crowd gathered to watch. Huidekoper thought so well of his skill that he also posed for him, then took him home for flute and fiddle music. His itinerant companion had also found a customer or two. They forwarded their belongings to Pittsburgh and returned to the road on foot.

Low waters and low funds forced a delay of weeks in Pittsburgh. Audubon felt in no hurry to call at Maple Grove, the Benjamin Bakewell place. When he did so, however, the cordiality surprised him. The family had been hearing of his doings in Philadelphia and wished above all to learn about the Bonapartes. Thomas Pears, by this time an official in the nationally known Bakewell flint-glass works, showed plainly that the Henderson mill affair still rankled. To avoid seeing anything more of his wife's relations Audubon kept away from the Unitarian and Presbyterian services. Reverend John Henry Hopkins, whose Episcopal sermons he found agreeably free of "sham and show," became his devoted friend.

A landscape painter of Swiss-German lineage, George Lehman of Lancaster County, Pennsylvania, looked like the ideal successor to Mason, if ever Audubon could afford another assistant. But the quest for pupils and a livelihood occupied him for the moment. Hand-to-mouth existence led him to a female seminary where a forceful Irish woman, Mrs. Charles Basham, held forth as headmistress. She had been looking for a new teacher for her daughter Harriet, already a flower painter of ability. She dropped her staff teacher, James Reid Lambdin, as the girl's tutor and put Audubon in his place.[15]

Audubon was often among the favored of the city at the hospitable salons of Mrs. Basham and her English husband. As soon as he had saved a little, he wrote to Harris and proposed that they spend a week or two on the shores of Champlain and Ontario during the migrations. Harris sent regrets that illness in the family prevented.

Audubon went alone. It was during this solitary fortnight that he began to picture *The Birds of America* in the bold form it would take. Several massive volumes of life-size portraits arranged in three different classes—land, water, and shore birds—loomed in his imagination. How he should overcome the problems of scientific system and nomenclature he did not know—any more than whether England, France, or any another country would see his dream. He managed to buy a skiff and on October 24, 1824, when the waters were rising, he called on the Bashams to say good-by. To Harriet, his favorite pupil, he gave a sketchbook of watercolor studies of moths, beetles, insects, flowers, and jewel-like reptiles, and to her mother a manuscript of his episode, "Meadville."[16]

XII. Immense Ocean

A FTER FIVE NIGHTS OF RAIN AND COLD on the Ohio, the little party that had joined forces in Pittsburgh disbanded. At Wheeling, the Irish oarsman deserted. So did a fellow artist. An émigré physician named La Motte, oblivious of the death by fever in store for him in Mexico, excused himself for seeking speedier, more comfortable transportation. With no one left to share expenses, Audubon had to take a job peddling penny portraits of the touring hero Lafayette.[1] He sold his skiff and took passage on a keel boat.

He knew better than to approach Thomas Bakewell, head of a new boat foundry in Cincinnati with Alexander Gordon as an absentee partner. Gordon, the recent bridegroom of Lucy's sister Ann, had joined those disenchanted about the cause of the family artist. That the defunct Audubon & Bakewell establishment was being sued anew by Bowen of Henderson increased the undesirability of asking Thomas for a loan. Audubon was hurrying along towards other, more likely Cincinnati benefactors when two art-goods dealers spotted him and demanded payment of old bills. At a loss, as

157

his unkempt appearance proved, he walked on to the house of Keating & Bell to ask for fifteen dollars. Succeeding, he hurried back to the river and found a boat headed for Louisville. With a heap of shavings for a pillow he slept on deck in the raw night air.

It was late November when Audubon strode past the glaring pedestrians of Louisville towards Shippingport. He marveled at his own humility as he moved along in battered moccasins and shabby buckskins, his beard coarse and his long locks flying, his heart sure that destiny was with him. The gossips could whisper and echo the murmurs of kith and kin against his "lunatic assurance," but he would ignore them all.[2]

Nicholas Berthoud praised Victor's excellent application to business, as if to embarrass their unexpected caller. Berthoud declined to thaw when he learned that a letter he handed Audubon contained an introduction from Andrew Jackson to the governor of the Floridas. He paid even less attention to talk of a possible mission to England. Two or three days of his tepid hospitality more than sufficed.

At Beech Woods, Audubon let it be sensed that this time, though he must linger a while, he would not overstay his welcome. He would remain only long enough to earn passage abroad by teaching art, French, and dancing. There was the example of Lucy's $1,000 savings to give him hope. The cause of *The Birds of America* rapidly became such a familiar one that Mrs. Percy's brother, Charles Middlemist of London, began to think of turning his own visit into the creation of an American flower portfolio.

In the hotel at Woodville, fifteen miles away, Audubon dressed for the first of his Friday and Saturday dance assemblies as carefully as had the young *beau idéal* of Mill Grove. He greeted his sixty pupils and their chaperones in the public ballroom. Then he waved his bow for the ladies to follow him in a set of the cotillion. Partners approached to form a line and join in while he fiddled briskly to applause from along the wall. The more awkward beginners felt the mock blows of his bow—until it snapped in two, much to everyone's amusement. At last, with a borrowed bow and a grace that belied his forty years, Audubon danced a solo to his own fiddle and voice for the grand finale.

In spite of his popular tuition parties in Woodville, followed by others at Waverly and Beech Woods, he was sharply criticized for devoting too much time to hunting and drawing—leaving Lucy at the grindstone. Only Augustin Bourgeat of Bush Hill and Nathaniel Wells Pope, now a doctor of St. Francisville, understood Audubon. They helped to fill kegs of rum with lizards, snakes, and baby alligators for his learned correspondents in Philadelphia. They boxed plants for Haines and Bonaparte. Johnny prepared 200 insects for Thomas Say; the entomologist was about to sail for New Harmony, the Indiana socialist paradise. To Edward Harris went a variety of shrubs and fruits. Dr. De Kay of New York had more than earned a blacksnake, two water moccasins, and a rattler that was kept alive for half a day in a tub of whisky until its rattling and violent contortions subsided. Lucy was not amused to learn that the latter had sprung from the tub and tried to strike everything, even the hearth, before its recapture.[3]

A warning arrived in the midst of all this worthy activity. Charles Lesueur reported Bonaparte much annoyed over Audubon's failure to send promised memoranda for publication by the Prince. An immediate apology was sent, with assurances that the notes had been mailed before Audubon left New York but that in any case a replacement would follow. There was obsequiousness in these explanations to one whose influence was needed. Audubon pleaded for an exchange of works, that he might acquire a "gem of value." He promised skins of squirrels, including a new one, and asked permission to draw a bird especially for Princess Zenaïde. Bonaparte was given to understand that drawing was no longer a merely pleasurable pursuit, but a task never begun without ruler and compass for *The Birds of America*. "I have drawed much since I saw you, for Posterity," he declared, in April 1825, choosing as always to address Bonaparte in English. Yet there was no denying to himself that the "black-

headed titmouses" and "thousands of hummingbirds fluttering in the jessamine" and other familiar species could not
compare with what Titian Peale was probably drawing for
Bonaparte in Florida at the moment.[4] Evidently he thought
better of repeating a rash announcement made a few months
earlier in a letter to Reuben Haines with an air of hubris that
hardly concealed his state of mixed self-doubt and flagging
resolve. "My intention is to leave the United States for Russia
next January. My ideas have been much altered by some
letters that I received from that country while I was in New
York."[5] Never again did he allude to the apochryphal letters.
But it would not be long before what he had heard in Manhattan—about the passion of Russia's emperor for books on
natural history—would be confirmed.

A letter of March 15, 1825, was still on its way to him from
Bonaparte. Part could have, or perhaps should have, given
him pause but not the "annoyance" of the Prince that Lesueur
had tattled, mistakenly, about Audubon's supposed failure
to send him some needed notes and observations. Rather, he
suggested, their go-between, the "Barkeep of City Hall," was
the culprit, and asked Audubon for the name of that person
if he chanced to know it. But even if the observations concerning the "Swallow and the Great Grackle" had arrived he
could not have used them, he admitted; because, already, it
was too late. He trusted that his forthcoming volume would
be of "good use" to Audubon.

> Lawson is already engraving your drawing. I trust you will like it.
> We were obliged to make a few little changes in the superb individu-
> als that I have just received from Georgia. The females were all con-
> siderably smaller and the males larger than in the drawing. Accord-
> ingly, Lawson had to conform to my measurements in order that the
> descriptions would agree with the plates, etc. It will be one of the
> best in the work if Rider (the colorist) can manage to render the ad-
> mirable softness of your drawing.
>   . . . I hope you wish to continue our correspondence . . . useful
> to both of us and perhaps, in a way, to the amiable science which we
> cultivate. If I can be useful to you in some way or other, feel free to
> ask. Your very affectionate and obliged, Charles L. Bonaparte.[6]

On sweltering afternoons Audubon and Lucy taught the Percy girls to swim in the springhouse. Audubon's success as fencing master to the sons of Judge Peter Randolph caused an awkward incident one day in Woodville. A rival fencing teacher, a creole named Muscarville, started a rumor that the lazy husband of the schoolmistress of Beech Woods was a philanderer. The slander was intended to bring on a duel that could cause Audubon embarrassment. But a crazy rumor that the painter of birds could drop a covey of partridges with one shot was warning enough for the creole to remove himself from Woodville without testing his skill at swords.

Muscarville was not so wide of the mark. Audubon's soulful eyes, glossy curls, and sinewy frame caused many a heart to flutter. The wife of his former Henderson clerk, Mrs. Pope of St. Francisville, thought him the handsomest of men. She did not question his account of his birth in a cottage among orange groves beside the Mississippi. Lucy's intimate, she well knew the sad Kentucky chapter; Audubon could at last joke with impunity about it: "I mean to get me a coach-and-six, and ride through the streets of Louisville yet!" Mrs. Pope would not listen to the charges of neglect made by his critics. She herself had heard him lament that Lucy, his dearest friend, was aging "like a beautiful tobacco plant cut at the stem, and hung to wither."

From everywhere rumors were drifting south concerning Robert Owen's New Harmony "paradise" in Indiana. Lesueur, Say, and others were joining Maclure, president of the Philadelphia Academy, on his "boatload of knowledge." Thomas and Sarah Pears had cast their lot with the "co-operative society." Benjamin Bakewell regarded it so highly that he was thinking of trying one out in Pittsburgh if Owen's succeeded. The Pears family had stopped off in Wheeling to see Sarah Bakewell Anderson and her three sons before going on to Shippingport. First reports from Indiana admitted to great disappointment. "We are cramped in houseroom," wrote Pears. Sally felt "out of Humanity's reach forever."[7] Thomas's weakness for spirits led him from the countinghouse downward to a wool-sorting job. Audubon was too absorbed in preparations for England to pay attention to "that crazy man" Owen and his latest doings.

Harlan's pleas for an alligator sent Audubon and Bourgeat to the lake. Two Negroes poled their canoe through the beard moss, brush, and cane to a hole swarming with the reptiles.[8] It was quite safe to wade among them in their torpid state. Startled snake birds, wood ducks, ibis, and cranes flew off at the report of a gun aimed at a fine alligator on a log. The vultures circled as the reptile was roped and brought to the Bourgeat plantation. From the veranda the ladies came down to marvel at its grimace, produced by the propping open of its jaws. Somehow at that moment the alligator managed to thrash its tail and its jaws snapped shut. Finally, hoisted from a branch, it gave up, to be lowered into a hogshead of rum for the journey north.

Audubon was hoping that with the help of Bourgeat and Pope he could bring experiments with the smelling powers of the turkey buzzard to a satisfactory conclusion. He was of the opinion that it depended more on sight to detect carrion.[9] They watched a vulture alight on a stuffed deerskin. Another, however, found a carcass all but hidden from view. Sight, nevertheless, seemed to the three observers to be the telling factor. Audubon intended that Philadelphia should accept his authority in the matter.

The day of the arrival of the Bonaparte's first volume of *American Ornithology* turned to one of sorrow when Audubon saw what a trick had been played on him. Later on, after much brooding, he scrawled some angry marginalia, by no means the only ones to give the work both its due and damnation. "My drawing has been so shamefully [caricatured] by an unknown individual that to see my name at the corner of the Plate might make me wish to abandon the great Labours I have been at to represent nature as it is." Opposite a sentence about the respective size of the sexes of the grackle, he wrote, "Erroneous." Beside the author's mention of George Ord, he wrote, "I am rather surprised that a man of such sense as Charles should even mention the name." As to the

Wild Turkey. *Plate* 1 *of* The Birds of America. *Engraved by William Home Lizars in* 1827 *after the original study,* "*Great American Cock," drawn in* 1825 *in West Feliciana Parish, Louisiana.*

Wild Turkey Hen and Eight Chicks, *undated. Pencil drawing, 9¾ × 13¾ in. Museum of Comparative Zoology, Harvard University, Cambridge, Massachusetts. Study for plate 6 of* The Birds of America.

bird's call, he said, "The chuck of our species is shriller." Of Figure 1 on Plate V, the female grackle, he declared, "A pretty good figure of a male that has had his tail pulled three weeks before the Drawing was made." Most startling of all is his attestation, in defense of remarks concerning non-North American birds: "J. A. born in Santo Domingo." Finally, or perhaps straightaway, he struck out his name on the plate, and also deleted what Bonaparte had, sycophantically, written about "a faithful representation of both sexes of the Great Crow Blackbird, drawn by . . . Mr. John J. Audubon, and hope thereby to remove all doubt relative to this interesting species." As for the marginalia, they exist to this day at the Audubon Memorial Museum in Henderson, Kentucky.

Upon hearing from Reuben Haines of Audubon's fury and disappointment, Bonaparte made haste to apologize for what had happened, lest their friendship die aborning. From Saratoga Springs, where he and his Princess were vacationing, he wrote, in French, this casuistic excuse for having, admittedly, behaved so shabbily:

> I have been very troubled by the plate of the Grackles and on account of my part in it. A little explanation relative to the use of your name, which I hope does not disturb you, will be necessary—use of which may have been mistaken, and about which I consulted friends of yours, not having had time to consult you personally, and which there is still time to rectify if you so desire, a thing that I am still ready to do, although reluctantly. I had never compared the fine drawing with nature, which you made for me, and the text of my work was in print before I noticed that my description (made from nature), as to the measurements of my own specimens, did not mesh with those of your drawing. We must attribute this ill-luck to the negligence of the *barkeeper* of the City-Hotel, because if I had had the notes that should have accompanied the drawing I would have quickly perceived the difference, although it may be that it was not impossible to present a figure that contrasts manifestly with what is in the text of my work, since it must serve to clarify it; and moreover, when in fact the drawing was made to conform with the text it was still too large for the copperplate, something that I did not wish to believe, inasmuch as you had taken the exact measurements. But the engraver convinced me, after one glance, and of which you can convince yourself upon comparing your drawing with my plate. It then became necessary to place the male figure, which occupied the full

Right, top: *Alexander Rider.* Boat-Tailed Grackle, *1824. Pencil drawing. Library, The Academy of Natural Sciences of Philadelphia. Study for the "Great Crow Black-bird" in* American Ornithology, *by Charles Lucien Bonaparte, who rejected a study of the species by Audubon. Rider's study bears the forged signature of Audubon.*

Right, center: *Alexander Lawson. Uncolored engraving of Rider's* Boat-Tailed Grackle. *Library, The Academy of Natural Sciences of Philadelphia.*

Above: A Pair of Boat-Tailed Grackles. *Watercolor drawing,* 10½ ×
14 *in. Private collection. This long-lost work, which came to light in 1987,
is the original study Bonaparte had commissioned from Audubon but
rejected for publication. Audubon was outraged when the engraving of the
plate was credited in part to him.*

Opposite, below: Boat-Tailed Grackle, *1832. Pencil and watercolor
drawing. Courtesy The New-York Historical Society, New York. Original
Audubon study for plate 187 of* The Birds of America; *engraved by
Robert Havell, Jr., in 1834.*

length of the plate, in another position, despite the fact that your figure was also as large as my individual. That completely upset the composition. Mr. Lawson wished to undertake engraving it, but apart from being incapable, there was your positive reluctance to allow changing anything about your work, and that led me to resolve the problem by having a new drawing made, while not wanting to hire Mr. [Titian Ramsay] Peale for the work. (I hope that you may appreciate this step.) It was Mr. Rider, an artist well-known and well thought of by everyone who, having nature and your work to turn to, drew the outline and did the coloring, again with the guidance of nature. Mr. Lawson engraved the plate which, it strikes me, is one of the best in the work. Albeit Mr. Rider made an entirely new drawing, it had to take a great deal from yours. After my having consulted your friends, and particularly the good, modest Lesueur, we decided that the two names—Audubon and Rider—should be joined on the plate. That is often done, above all in Paris, among artists, and you both would often have seen the names of Prêtre, Huet, Redouté, Lesueur and others placed as collaborators on the same work. I hope that the excellence of the plate may keep you from considering my action a bad one; it permitted me to render the deserved tribute that I paid you in the text, an ability for which I tried even more to find an occasion to proclaim in a way that contrasted with the efforts of some individuals to obscure, (and whose numerous errors I have been busy correcting). I am therefore hoping you will approve of my conduct and that it will not be necesary to include errata in my work, since that would lessen public confidence. . . . and since Mr. Rider is satisfied, and as I do not doubt that you may be also. I have had to go into all these details out of fear that you may be astonished to see your name on a plate so different from your drawing. I repeat that if you wish it, an explanation will be found in my second volume.[10]

Bonaparte closed, "We often speak of you with Messrs. Mease, Lesueur, Haines, Lukens and your other friends at the Academy of Natural Sciences. We are in the majority!"

On October 1 Audubon responded in English to the July letter so filled with obsequious but dubious assurances and received only two days earlier. If he wondered what had become of his own drawing, so superior to the one of a grackle drawn in the South in 1821 but which had sufficed to draw him into Bonaparte's scheme of things, he did not ask. Actually, Bonaparte had deserted the luckless study, left it to Rider who in turn eventually handed it over to George Ord.

Broad-Winged Hawk. *Plate 91 of* **The Birds of America.** *Engraved by Robert Havell, Jr., in 1830 after the original study drawn in 1825 in West Feliciana Parish, Louisiana.*

Audubon declared himself "as much surprised as pleased" to have his "kind letter." At long last he was acknowledging the gift of the Prince's first volume: "Believe me, my Dear Sir, I very seldom in my life felt a greater Pleasure." He expressed satisfaction that the notes he had sent about the Wild Turkey had proven helpful. Lest he lose touch with one who might still advance his cause, and particularly so if Dr. James E. De Kay of the New York Lyceum would do the same on seeing the name "Audubon" in print, he proceeded with care. (Thus far the latter had remained silent.) But to swallow his bitterness entirely was not possible. His pen aimed a few darts at cabinet zoologists, while not naming Bonaparte but also not excluding him. He did not mind boasting a bit of his own direct observations in the field:

> It would be strange indeed if a man who spends fully three fourths of his time in the forests, in pursuit of those feathery inhabitants, was not apt to see much of their manners, and *that* so repeatedly as to retain the principal outlines of those habits. . . . I have often laughed at the *Conclusions* brought forward by those who knew me still less than they knew themselves when, at the expiration of a few weeks sight of me, tried to dispel the favorable opinion created in the minds of others by saying that *Mergansers* could never have been fed on corn!!!

At this point Audubon lapsed into French for a moment: *Mon cher Monsieur, Le temps découvre la Verité*—! But only for a moment. By this time, thanks to the patient coaching of his cultivated, quite literary wife Lucy Bakewell his command of English far surpassed both the feeble written and oral French of his boyhood. "Except," he continued, "when indeed the influenced, ignorant never leave the walks of the city where nature is much more contaminated, altered, than the flesh of the Merganser fed on corn." Then he came to what he most wanted to declare. "I am sorry you should have felt so much anxiety about the Producing of the *Graculas;* either from my drawing or that of any other person whatever. Yet I can vouch [for] the size of the *Birds Drawn by me* as correct, and that I call *Gracula B.* . . . Whatever you have done or wrote employing my name is received thankfully by me—as soon as I receive your Volume I shall write you so. I have no doubt that your journey to the Falls of Niagara has been very agreeable, and if you have rambled as I did in the Oneida swamps your ornithological collection has no doubt been much augmented." De Kay still having failed to write as promised, Audubon announced that he would leave for England in the spring, exhibit his drawings there and, "if not successful in London, go to the Continent, perhaps through Brussels, and proceed to that Capital where I fervently wish the Great Napoleon was still existing—Paris." Then he hinted for introductions from Bonaparte to the prestigious, before a lengthy closing:

> My work proceeds as fast as can be under the Efforts of an humble citizen destitute, in a very great degree, of many advantages denied by others better situated. But my courage is not the least abated and every bird increases my Collection with the progressive pleasure that cannot fail following a man impelled, by natural disposition, to study and to try to imitate those beauties of nature. I will send you by the first safe conveyance a Drawing for your Lady. Her acceptance of it is the highest prize ever bestowed on them. It is probable it shall be accompanied by a few skins of birds. . . . I killed some *Snake Birds* but the weather was so hot that I could not bear the odour of their flesh and gave up skinning them. . . . I would have wrote to you sometime since, but having no acknowledgment from you of my letters I became fearful of being importunate. With particular Respects to Lesueur, a man I shall ever esteem, and the other friends of nature. . . .JJ.[11]

It was reckless of Audubon to have chosen the talkative but neutral Haines for a confidant and still worse to have given free reign to his feelings in a letter that the impartial Quaker passed on to the Prince who, apparently, destroyed it. It sufficed to make Bonaparte turn to William Cooper of the New York Lyceum with complaints about Audubon's virtuperation, "the harshest, most selfish censure," which Haines had had the "kindness, not to say simplicity" to share. He made it clear that in the event of a controversy over the affair of the Grackle plate he would be counting on Cooper (who detested Audubon) to defend him and his first volume:

> Bad as it may be, it does not deserve such a treatment. . . . He does not even grant me the honor of my errors. I have been *misled, betrayed*, says he, and if I had confided in him instead of having my

pretended work written by Mr. [Thomas] Say (who, after all, says he, is but a *man of wit*) he would have stamped his hand upon it, whilst now it is altogether in contradiction with it! I have one part of his remarks which I read yesterday to several members of the Academy.

Say, recent publisher of the first book on his subject, *American Entomology*, was innocent enough. Bonaparte rejoiced to Cooper that Richard Harlan, a diligent compiler it was true, and on whom Audubon had lavished praise, should be the target of critics for his published errors. "Indeed," he said, "I cannot help laughing when I see people thinking that a work is of great importance to science because it is well printed, and well finished outside. Thus do many think that my reputation . . . is to rest on the description of fifteen (!) species of birds!" But then he decided to spare Cooper "more nonsenses."[12]

Audubon continued to find fault with the writings of Bonaparte while currying favor for the days ahead in England. His self-assurance was doing nicely enough that he began to minimize the achievement of Bartram, along with that of Wilson. His reckless pen was dashing off barbs at the expense of those who had hailed his efforts in Philadelphia and New York, as well as at that of his adversaries.

On his forty-first birthday, April 26, 1826, he rode off on one of the Percy horses toward Bayou Sara landing.[13] The slave boy Toby followed with baggage and more than 400 drawings. In the painter's wallet was $1,600, of which $300 was from Lucy for the good watch and piano that she expected. She had given him letters to Ann Bakewell Gordon, to be delivered at the Liverpool house just leased for a year by Alexander Gordon. Lucy agreed to clear away debts left behind for necessities.

That night Audubon stayed with the Popes in St. Francisville, then caught the *Red River* at Bayou Sara in the morning. Among eastbound vessels the *Delos* under Captain Joseph Hatch of Kennebunkport was the choice. Audubon put down $100 and was told to return in a week or so. This left time to catch the *Red River* back, for a second farewell. He borrowed a horse at Bayou Sara and surprised Lucy at three o'clock in the morning. "The moments spent afterwards full repaid me," he wrote in his journal. A neighborhood wedding and its festivities enhanced the two-day rendezvous. Before he sailed, they had a last breakfast with the Bourgeats, then he rode halfway back again with Lucy.

There was plenty of time to select a cushion for Lucy's piano stool, crayons for Johnny, and some good pen knives for Victor. He put these and some plants aboard the *Red River* as it left New Orleans for Bayou Sara. At the roominghouse of his friend Napoléon Costé he wrote a farewell to Charles Bonaparte, not to do himself out of essential favors abroad. He approached the Governor of Louisiana, and came away with an open letter that described him as "a naturalized citizen."[14] (Either a descendant or the painter himself later rubbed out but did not quite efface the word *naturalized*.)

Vincent Nolte's wealth had long discouraged Audubon from getting in touch with the merchant whose horse he and Barro had raced at Juniata Falls, that long-past winter of the earthquakes. (Once he had met Nolte's partner, Hollander, on the streets of New Orleans and made embarrassed excuses.) Nolte had been enjoying much reflected glory through Lafayette; he had financed the famous tour while a leisurely Congress voted the hero some land and money. More important to Audubon, he had recently helped the first English importers of American baled cotton, the Rathbones of Liverpool, head off a wildcat market. An introduction to these friends of his could be of value. Audubon called on Nolte and acquired letters to the Rathbones and their partner and cousin, Adam Hodgson. The good-natured Nolte pretended to forget that Audubon had once introduced himself as a native of La Rochelle, although he was to enter this myth in his memoirs. "Mr. A.," said the letter obligingly, "is a native of the U.S.A." But the second one one alluded to his "European birth" and "respectability" and his aim of publishing some handsome "*tableaux de famille*" of the bird domain. Or the work might, he said, go to some wealthy collector willing to finance more such painting, or else be sold to a museum."[15]

On May 27, Audubon bought a baby alligator for a dollar and boarded the *Delos*. For ten hours a tow boat drew her toward the Gulf before setting her free, then turned back with several farewells for Lucy.

An old enemy, *mal de mer*, made the first week at sea a nightmare, but after that Audubon was able to sketch, write, and journalize a little. During calms there was fine swimming alongside the *Delos*. On June 23, as the ship entered the Atlantic, a curious thought crept into the journal that was to be kept exclusively for Lucy. For the second time Audubon was passing south of the Equator—"really south of the line." He or someone else later effaced several lines that followed. But these reflections survive: "What ideas it conveys to me, of my birth, of the expectations of my younger days."[16] On July 4, the day Jefferson died at *Monticello*, Audubon spoke of his presentiments of evil. It took a passing brig and a visit from its captain, with praises for the portfolio, to banish the omen.

One day a hawk circled above, then plunged toward a warbler perched on the yards. Audubon dropped it in time to save its prey. When the last frigate bird and "rice bunting" had been left behind, he put away his spyglass to bury himself in the poems of Byron and *The Seasons* of James Thomson. The captain of a passing brig interrupted him with a request to stuff a petrel, promised to the Academy of Natural Sciences in Philadelphia.

Unendurable boredom set in. Audubon's cabin mate, John Swift of St. Francisville, convinced him that a tankard of porter might help. Swift was carrying eleven gallons to Ireland. The secret hope of the teetotaler exposed to temptation was that drink would allay his fears of England. The experiment was tried, and its effects were reeled off in the journal in the form of bad puns, maudlin pathos, melancholy, and some coarse and vitriolic humor: "Few memorable events (if I dare call any of them memorable) have not been recalled to memory . . . until the whole of my life has been surveyed with scrutiny. Oh England, renowned isle, how shall I enter thee? . . . I will drink the residue of my glass and write perhaps again tomorrow. . . . When I first saw thee, dearest Lucy, frequently I was asked if this passion of mine would be of lasting duration. Help, I am now entering on a sacred subject."

Land birds streaked across the sunrise off the Irish coast on July 18. Audubon rushed up to the deck, then back again to his cabin. "We have had Irish fishermen alongside," he penned excitedly. "I would call them beggars, but as they are much like me, *brothers in blood*, I would be shocked to say so, although they acted, *through a current of actual misfortunes*, as if they had been conceived and formed of inferior materials to *men American*." Brothers in blood—with these words Audubon, perhaps for the only time, openly acknowledged his Breton blood. Celts settled Armorica (Brittany) in the fifth century after their flight from the hostile Angles and Saxons in Britain. Today much of that peninsula remains, by its own declaration, curiously apart from the rest of France in peasant language, customs, and outlook; to this day Celtic is commonly heard in Brittany. Audubon described in detail the visit of the Irish fishermen who had come to barter fresh fish, potatoes, and eggs for beef, bread, tobacco, whisky, and porter. "When I compared these starved beggars with Irish gentlemen I could hardly conceive of them as of the same race. My God, why are they not independent, and able to scorn this miserable way of attaining a pittance. Oh!"

The next day Audubon resumed his train of thought. An Irish paper from shore had, by its unmistakable sympathy with the oppressive tactics of the ruling Anglo-Irish, afforded him much fresh food for thought. "The newspapers given to us by the first fishing smack that boarded us speak of Irish ways of electioneering. I have now to regret that I am *by oath* no politician, or I might or would have argued over the contents." The Irish "Liberator," Daniel O'Connell, a witness of the French Revolution in his student days, was a friend of freedom, but also the confirmed enemy of anarchy and revolutionary methods involving bloodshed.

The sailors irked Audubon with their misnaming of warblers and other birds, as the *Delos* cruised along near land. He thought them no better than that "perfect academician," George Ord of Philadelphia, who had scoffed at the assertion

that turkeys could swim. Swift passed the carafe to tran-
quilize him, then let him go back to his journal. "My dear
friend," he addressed Lucy in its pages, "oh it is thee that
concerns me. It is our dear children that fill my thoughts,
and the immense ocean that divides us, and the time that
must be spent far from thee. I cannot write—oh, may God
preserve you and bless you all!!"[17]

Two days later he looked on the low green hills of England. He was reminded of the delicate landscapes of his
favorite artist, Claude-Joseph Vernet (1714–89). The *Delos*
moved up the Mersey and anchored beside the Liverpool
docks. He went below to close his chronicle of the voyage: "I
see the dear country that gave thee birth, and I love it, because I love thee!!! . . . Now my dearest friend, I am in England. With what success? I shall go through with my undertaking. I shall be sure to inform thee. . . . God bless thee,
good night!"

PART THREE: SEA CHANGE

XIII. First Flight

WITH COAL SMOKE IN THEIR EYES and the clatter of wooden shoes on cobblestones in their ears, Audubon and Swift walked up to the Commercial Inn. There was not a moment to lose. Audubon went straight from his room to Alexander Gordon's office. How he would be received was a question; at least the letters from Lucy were a wedge. It was long since he had faced his one-time friend Alexander. At first Gordon, taken aback, pretended not to recognize his caller. Then, almost grudgingly, he went with him to the Customs to help clear the portfolios. Not until the artist put down tuppence on each drawing did Gordon so much as offer his card with a home address.

A first attempt to see Ann failed, along with his efforts to establish contact elsewhere. An engulfing homesickness was intensified by the singing of a caged lark in a window across from the Commercial Inn. To pass the time, Audubon began a portrait of that human "fox"—that "hawk"—that "contrary wind," John Swift. Again his companion recommended porter for low spirits. On Sunday afternoon Audubon yielded to the temptation. Afterward, to clear his head, he took a walk along the river and began soliloquizing: "Must I put thee, religion, aside again, when thou art the leader of all and every one of my movements, either mental or physical, vertical or horizontal? Either Sterne or some other merry-inclined gentleman of his age wrote that horizontal patterns were most congenial for all descriptions of feelings whatsoever. . . . Indeed it becomes important for persons conceived. . . . May God bless the merry or the learned Sterne, ah Sterne!"[1] Pousse-café in the salon failed to clear his head of nonsense. But he slept soundly, this habitual dawn riser, and not until 10:00 A.M. did he lift his head. Then he came to with a start, dressed hurriedly, took up his sword cane, and rushed toward Duke Street.

Richard Rathbone had already gone to his countinghouse. Audubon followed him there, handed over the Nolte letter, but then had to content himself with a hasty invitation to return to Duke Street at teatime. Again he tried to see Ann, only to be turned away at the door by a servant.

That afternoon, while he waited in the Rathbone drawing room he felt an overwhelming shyness, his old childhood "*mauvaise honte.*" How he regretted that no one had "thrashed" it out of him in boyhood!

The opinion of Richard and William Rathbone could make all the difference. Audubon hoped they shared their "good and great" father's penchant for natural history. Their great-grandfather had founded the family fortune in a rise from sawyer to merchant. Their grandfather was a famous foe of the slave trade—so vehement a one that he was nearly disowned by the Society of Friends. Their father, also an outstanding Quaker abolitionist and civic reformer, had felt such sympathy with the natural world that he built a splendid library of ornithological books for Green Bank, his country place on the outskirts of the city.

Richard and his lady turned out to be an ingratiating "Philemon and Baucis," their young children pure delight. By her soft voice, manner, learning, and interest in the arts, Mrs. Richard Rathbone charmed Audubon. Her burgeoning lit-

erary ambitions were indeed impressive. Later, Rathbone
showed Audubon the paintings at the Exchange building.
From its dome they enjoyed the view of the Mersey and
the green Welsh hills beyond. That evening the couple insisted on his seeing the current panorama attraction, *Holyrood Chapel*. They promised a full family gathering—a very
appreciative one—for a look at his drawings.

This social triumph seemed, to Swift, to call for a hearty
toast. There was the added incentive of his own departure
for Dublin in the morning.

Next day, Audubon headed for Bedford Street with his
100-pound portfolio hoisted on his shoulder. People eyed his
long hair heavily groomed with bear's grease, his rustically
full pantaloons, plain black frock coat and bafflingly foreign
look. His thoughts were too fixed on the test, both craved and
dreaded, for him to notice. He had every intention of mentioning Jacques-Louis David, James Mease, Joseph Priestley,
Erasmus Darwin, and Charles Lucien Bonaparte. Such associations would help to offset his academic shortcomings.

The kindly, gracious, sixty-five-year-old family matriarch,
Mrs. William Rathbone the elder, at once took him for a
charming original, a probable genius. She was the daughter
of Richard Reynolds of Bristol, noted Quaker philanthropist;
her salons attracted the learned of England and the Continent. Audubon saw before him a statuesque figure with an
open face, radiant blue eyes of transparent goodness, and
short-cropped, lace-capped white hair. She had managed to
have her late husband's disownment by the Friends for un-
pacific and republican views set aside. But the marriage of
her son William to Elizabeth Greg, the daughter of a staunchly
Unitarian and also republican cotton miller of Manchester
had, regrettably, earned disownment not so easily revoked
by the Quaker Meeting of Liverpool. Neither William nor
Richard enjoyed quite the public recognition of their more
brilliant father. Yet William's courage and generosity offset
his well-known temper and dyspeptic turn of mind. The day
he had stood, his head still covered, after a heckler had tried
to knock his wide-brimmed Quaker hat off during his eulogy

of the late George III would not soon be forgotten by the city.

The Nolte letters had the desired effect. The children crowded about Audubon as he threw open the big portfolio, to his own excited praise of the American wilderness. "Simple, intelligent," he overheard William whisper of him. Hannah Mary Rathbone, the beautiful sister, studied him with her shy, dark eyes and thought his speech and dress romantic—intriguing, really. The offer of the "Queen Bee"—his affectionate name for the matriarch—to arrange important introductions sent him into paroxysms of joy. The conviction that he had already made a notable beginning bore him along as if on air to Roskell, the jeweller. To celebrate his conquest he put £340, or almost a third of what was left in his wallet on landing, into gold watches, chains, and seals for himself and Lucy.

Green Bank, three miles from the city, was even more delightful than the Rathbone house on Bedford Street. The family had bought the place with its gentle terraces, languid streamlets, and gliding swans in 1787 as a summer retreat for their worrisomely frail infant William. Mrs. Rathbone had remodeled the house in "strawberry gothic revival" style. Her distinguished neighbor, the poet, author, and abolitionist William Roscoe (1755–1831), leader of the Athenaeum, had much in common with Audubon. Already famous for his lives of Pope Leo X and Lorenzo de' Medici, the foremost English historian of his day was writing on the Monandrian plants and trying to be his own botanical draftsman for the task. Once wealthy, he had failed as a banker. Mrs. Rathbone and other faithful friends had acquired his rare library and art collection for his brainchild, the Athenaeum. They continued to see that he and his daughter Jane wished for nothing until Roscoe's son, Edward, could take care of them.

Roscoe exclaimed over the beauty of the drawings in Audubon's collection while the pretty Jane, an aspiring poet and painter, fairly "anatomized" the artist. A Swiss entomologist, André Melly, soon to marry Ellen Greg, the younger William Rathbone's sister-in-law, and forsake science for business, took a lively part in the conversation. Two orphan boys, permanent guests at Green Bank, were about the age of Victor and John. These wards of the "Queen Bee's" cousin, Dr. John Rutter, founder of the Athenaeum, were magnetized by the artist in Audubon rather than by the naturalist. One, Henry Fothergill Chorley (1808–71), played the piano while the "woodsman" sketched his head in chalk before a fascinated audience. He was to become a music critic of note and a friend of Mendelssohn, Dickens, and other notables. John Rutter Chorley (1807–67), possessed of more protean intellect and charm than poetic talent despite his aspirations, was to become an intimate of Carlyle, Martineau, Mitford, and their circle.

Others called at Green Bank to meet the much discussed stranger. The London banker Barclay joined the chorus of praise. The well-known traveler and writer, Captain Basil Hall, was amused to find that he had been aboard the *Leander* when it had chased the *Polly* and passengers including Audubon and Rozier, toward Long Island Sound. The egotistical, mannered, social lion Hall at once hinted for introductions for his approaching North American journey. He was the son of the geologist Sir James Hall, and he had been commander of the *Lyra*, which carried Lord Amherst to China in 1816. A fit subject for the madness one day to overtake him, he had written books on the Far East, South America, and Mexico.

The zoologist, professor, and writer for the *Encyclopaedia Britannica*, Dr. Thomas Stewart Traill (1781–1862), agreed with the Rathbones that Audubon deserved all possible recognition and help with publication. His only regret was that there should be no text of descriptions to enhance its value. Traill noted his "unaffected urbanity" as Audubon held up the *American Ornithology* of Bonaparte for inspection. Actually, the gesture was shrewdly motivated. Audubon knew his own life-size portraits to be far more beautiful and animated than those by Wilson, Peale, and Rider. This done, he declared his unpublished notes and observations to be more penetrating, expansive, and vivid than those of his rivals. Anyone in doubt could turn to Bonaparte's biography of the turkey, based almost entirely on what Audubon had given him in writing. Or they had only to wait for Audubon's paper on the swallow, in the *Annals* of New York's Lyceum, to be convinced. He conceded that the day might come when he must, indeed, formally record his unsurpassed observations of wildlife.

A public exhibition was in order. The Rathbones and Traill saw to it that the Royal Institution made a gallery available within a fortnight. On July 31, 1826, a showing of 250 selections from the portfolio was opened to the public, admission free. In the first two hours more than 400 visitors passed through. Audubon, nervous and elated during the morning, was utterly spent by late afternoon. Adam Hodgson, partner of the Rathbones to whom Nolte had also written, invited him to spend a quiet night at his country house. In his anxious, emotional state Audubon made a slip of the tongue that the notably forthright and tolerant Hodgson let pass. Perhaps it was Hodgson's honesty that prompted Audubon to describe himself as "Haitian, of European parentage" rather than, as Nolte had already written to Hodgson, "European by birth."

Instead of feeling jubilant about finding such an impressive following overnight, Audubon felt skeptical of his sudden success. He needed the calming presence of Lucy and her cool judgment of events. The sight of the devoted Hodgsons leading "their little flock" in night prayers after he returned from a lone, restless walk through the grounds increased his homesick mood. "I thought of an evening when we were walking gently arm-in-arm together towards the waters of Bayou Sara," he wrote Lucy in his journal. "And I watched thee bathe thy gentle form in its current . . .—ah, my dearest friend."

The call of a blackbird awakened Audubon at three o'clock in the morning. He dressed, descended the stairs in stockinged feet, and donned boots on the veranda. Then he was off through the fields as far as the seashore, to return only hours later for breakfast. The Hodgson pony cart came around to take him into Liverpool once more.

Suggestions and praises overwhelmed Audubon. Jean Sismondi, an eminent Swiss historian and friend of the Rathbones, wrote him an introduction to Baron Alexander von Humboldt to use if ever he found himself near that titan of science. With the Rathbones, Roscoe, and their circle, Audubon discussed the possible wisdom of asking an admission of one shilling to view the birds. Actually, it was Roscoe who proposed the idea. At first William Rathbone sympathized with the artist's reluctance to turn two-penny showman and jeopardize the title given him by Clay and Clinton—"J. J. Audubon, naturalist."

The question began to detract painfully from the pleasure of those first days. It was accompanied by a sudden, unreasoning fear that some "great misfortune" had befallen Lucy, whom he had never needed as he did now. The possibility that their reunion might never come about provoked nocturnal fits of weeping. As he walked toward the Gordon's for dinner on Sunday, he resolved that Ann, despite her comforting "kind of likeness" to Lucy, should not discern his distress. Her new "Scotch stiffness" fell away beneath his brotherly embrace. Alexander, proud and practical still but friendlier again, thought no idea of Roscoe's should be taken lightly.[2] He, too, favored an admission charge. The Gordons listened closely to what Audubon could tell of Liverpool society. Gentility had also made room for them, if on a more prosaic level. Their attractive house guest "Miss Donathan" was visibly enthralled. The artist returned her gaze but saw her as no possible "snake in the way of fidelity." While the four walked together in the Botanic Garden after dinner, Audubon noticed even more excitement over what he could tell them of the Bonapartes.

After all agreed at Green Bank that a shilling's admission should be charged, William Rathbone drew up a notice for the papers. Just how much the outspoken Kentucky portrait painter Chester Harding, a recent arrival, contributed to Rathbone's realization of Audubon's limited resources can only be conjectured. His close friend, the architect J. G. Austin, had become well acquainted with Audubon.

The fee did nothing to lessen the popularity of the exhibition. The public and press continued to respond. But until some news could come from Lucy to quiet his prescient fears for her, Audubon felt unable to rejoice wholeheartedly in his good fortune. He poured his apprehension into his journal or bolted erratically in Ann's direction for sisterly attention. He longed to turn to "lovely and lively" Jane Roscoe, who was busy at a sonnet in his honor, or to the limpid-eyed Hannah Mary Rathbone who stirred feelings that might, he thought, "puzzle" all but Lucy.[3] Instead, he confided his loneliness to the intuitive Mrs. Richard Rathbone of Woodcroft cottage, beside Green Bank. While she guided her young ones at their lessons he watched as he had often done with Lucy and their sons.

Audubon wandered in the August drizzle, away from the excessive adulation. Where, he wondered, would it lead? At a loss to imagine the sequel, he bought colors and paper to sketch the sooty little sparrows and drive off melancholy. It occurred to him that he had not sketched one bird since landing.

The prospect of being received by Lord Stanley, the fourteenth Earl of Derby, a noted sportsman, Parliamentarian, and translator of the *Iliad*, was one more of dread than elation. But the reception could not to be put off. Adam Hodgson, a cousin of the peer by marriage, drove Audubon in his pony cart to Knowsley Hall. The occasion, though immensely successful, unnerved him. Later at Green Bank he accepted his first pinch ever of soothing snuff from the insistent André Melly, then entered his impressions in his journal before they faded:

> I looked on the hares, the partridges and other game with a thought of apprehension that the apparent freedom and security they enjoyed was very transient. I thought it more cruel to permit them to grow gentle, nay quite tame, and suddenly, and by tricks, murder them by thousands, than to give them the fair play that our game has with us in our forests, of being free—oh yes, free—and as wild as Nature made them, to excite the active, healthful pursuer to search after them, and pay for them through the pleasure of hunting them down against all difficulties.

He let Shippingport know, through an effusive account to Victor, how his titled host had knelt to admire the bird portraits spread out on his gleaming parquet. "I am in miniature what Lafayette was with us on our great scale." He added a line to ask Berthoud to see that his son drew regularly in his style (from which he wished a certain inference to be drawn that one day perseverance at painting would rescue Victor from the mediocrity of commerce).

The incessant social rounds and the English penchant for the fabulous began to pall. Audubon had heard enough about the snake-conquering, caymon-straddling Charles Waterton (1782–1865) of Wakefield, whose *Wanderings* and South American adventures were a favorite topic. He stirred cruel memories of their meeting in Philadelphia two years earlier. The yarns concerning this eccentric drew ridicule from the artist in his journal, which, unluckily for him, would be facetiously quoted among the Rathbones: "I never was troubled in the woods by any animals larger than ticks and mosquitoes, and that is quite enough. . . . I would like to have rode a few hundred miles on a wild elk or a unicorn—or an alligator." He was even weary of repeating his own "wonderful tales," and of mimicking the calls of birds, the whooping of Indians, and the howling of prairie wolves. Although the zoologist Waterton distinctly remembered having met Audubon in 1824, the artist now denied all recollection of any such occasion.

Attendance at the exhibition took a drop as September began. The lull occasioned some regret on Audubon's part that he had not remained in America two years longer to draw his birds "on a handsomer plan." He could have made them the "best in existence," indeed of all time. He also regretted not having brought Victor along as his assistant. As matters stood, he could not promise Lucy when he might be able to send for her and the boys. He chose rather to remind her that John must take his lessons with Middlemist earnestly and turn out sketches for backgrounds sure to be needed in London. He wanted eggs and skins of every kind. Not a line had he received from Lucy, Victor, or John, he complained.

Rather than mislead Lucy, Audubon chose to put off telling her in round numbers how much his Liverpool show brought him. Instead, he mentioned the circuit of Great Britain that some advisers predicted might bring him a fortune. Whatever the means, he hoped to win enough with such a traveling exhibition to begin his publication by spring. But "a solid place" in the service of the Royal Institution of Liverpool or some other such august body would do. As its official painter-naturalist he could afford to forget his dream of private patronage by some Croesus.[4]

Traill recommended that the birds be shown next in Manchester, forty miles east. He offered to let the Royal Institution curator, Munro, dismantle and help reinstall the exhibition. Audubon hesitated. His general indecision, while he painted a fine *Wild Turkey Cock* in oils, led Richard Rathbone to propose his coming as a house guest to remain for however long a heroic-size landscape with game birds might take. Rathbone said artisans could grind colors to expedite the masterpiece and relieve the painter of a task he hated. Embarrassed by a challenge for which he felt himself far from ready, Audubon murmured excuses about lack of time. Instead, he began a fresh rendering of an old standby, *Otter in a Trap*, for Mrs. Richard Rathbone. The plight of the otter with the bared teeth revolted the lady. She was tempted to decline the picture; however, her husband composed a stilted acceptance. Its tone hurt and bewildered Audubon.

Other tokens of friendship were in order. Audubon gave sketches of birds to the "Queen Bee," Henry Chorley, André Melly, and William Roscoe. For Austin he sketched Green Bank. To William Rathbone he gave a New Jersey bank note on which his "American grous" appeared. His most sentimental remembrance went to Hannah Mary—a dashing, three-quarter profile of himself inscribed "Audubon almost happy!" Lady Isabelle Douglas, invalid sister of the former Canadian governor, had her wish, as the Rathbones' guest, to see some of the bird portraits. Audubon brought a selection for her, and drew a bird from start to finish at her request.

Mrs. Richard Rathbone and Mrs. Edward Roscoe, both ac-

complished artists, begged last-minute lessons. (Mrs. Rathbone was later to paint jewel-like vignettes of birds for a book
of favorite poems.[5] Mrs. Roscoe's exquisite studies for a folio
of aquatints, *Floral Illustrations of the Seasons,* were to gain for
her a permanent niche in botanical art.)

The Rathbone family members, in three carriages, accompanied their protégé to the closing of the exhibition. Everyone appeared to sense its historic importance.

On his farewell rounds Audubon went to kiss Ann good-
bye. She offered him wine and rather injured him by displaying a letter from Lucy when he himself had none. He returned to the gallery so dejected that, when he found Munro
had not yet begun to take down the show, he wrote him a
harsh rebuke, for which he apologized next day.

Fatigue and doubt were telling on Audubon. He decided
to try Manchester next. But whether London and Paris ought
to follow he had no idea. The thought of returning "with
trembling steps" to his "venerable mother," of whose death
he knew nothing, left him in dread, much as he longed to see
her again.

On September 10, he and Munro crossed the Mersey.
Urchins ran and somersaulted beside the stagecoach, begging pennies. Parting from the Rathbones was almost as
painful as the desire for the tidings from Lucy that did not
come. As the coach rolled over the bridge, above the ships at
anchor, Audubon wondered whether one might hold a precious letter.

Pileated Woodpecker. *Plate 111 of* The
Birds of America. *Engraved by Robert
Havell, Jr., after the original study drawn in
1825 in West Feliciana Parish, Louisiana.*

XIV. Manchester

IN A ROOM RENTED from the science academy Audubon opened his showing of birds in Manchester. Then grouse and partridge shooting in the congenial company of Lord Stamford brought an invitation to exhibit, rent free, at the Royal Institution. The offer of two Italians to play background music suited to this display elicited the droll assurance that if Audubon himself had failed to make his birds seem to sing, no strings or flute could create the illusion.

A few ladies braved the seemingly endless rain, ostensibly to look at the birds, rather than the profile and "undulating locks" of the "American woodsman," who, nonetheless, held their gaze.[1] So negligible were receipts that he debated placing some drawings in shop windows with a placard inviting subscribers to support his forthcoming book. Instead, he chose the bolder method of approaching likely signers. Before he could get around to the wealthy Touchets, the family drew up before the exhibition in a body. Terrified, he hid until he heard their chaise roll away.

A banquet in his honor at the home of the American consul, with Yankee corn-on-the-cob the *pièce de résistance,* led to more invitations. "The best American illustrations of birds ever transmitted to posterity" held less interest for the banker Thomas Loyd after his five-hour banquet than his own exotic hothouse.

Saturday night dinner at Claremont, the Heywood estate, was off to an unpropitious start. Audubon was seen by the banker's spinster sister taking the five-bar gate at a leap on his arrival. The gabble about the "alligator jockey Waterton," insects, the Battle of New Orleans, and the amateurish drawings of Miss Heywood made the walk back to town through a thunderstorm a positive pleasure. Morning put the visit in no kindlier perspective. With his carafe open beside him, Audubon summed it up: "My lady's hams, if *cured well,* would turn out the more extraordinary bacon, and the maid of *Claremont* has set seventy springs aside—not counting those that creak vehemently in her corset."

An evening of music turned out no better. The grandly turbaned ladies at the concert kept their lorgnettes trained on his head, until Audubon hid his Roman nose between his fingers to escape them. At the strains of "God Save the King" he dashed up the aisle for air, clutching his watch for its protection. As he rushed through the dark streets, his head pounding, the "abandoned females" forced him "off the pavement" until he asked a watchman to walk beside him to discourage their blandishments.

Only Samuel Greg of Quarry Bank, the father of William Rathbone's wife, Elizabeth (who was Greg's thirteenth child), seemed deserving of thanks when the three feckless weeks drew to a close.[2] As Audubon prepared to return to Liverpool to discuss the printing of a prospectus with Roscoe and Traill, he felt grateful for the Gregs' kindness. One day Samuel and his son-in-law Melly had padded the exhibition till by several pounds sterling. Greg had repeatedly received Audubon at his ivy-clad Georgian mansion. The handsome structure seemed to grow out of the side of his mill, which looked like a long wing of the house, incongruous but charming. To reach the wooded valley fringed by the wide green fields of Quarry Bank, Audubon traveled on foot.

One afternoon at tea he sketched a dog with black chalk for the ladies, then used burnt cork to show his audience a trick of shading. Without such genteel femininity around him he felt, as he later confided to Hannah Mary, "like a herring on a griddle." However, the gentlemen lured him off to their discussion club for him to speak informally to them on "birds, alligators and Indians."

He brought tears to Greg's eyes by his description of Lafayette's reception in America. The family was enthralled by his account of Clay's duel with "crazy Randolph." But the "imperfect" impressions of America to which he had to listen irked him severely. For Elizabeth Greg Rathbone he sketched a portrait of her father. The tours of Manchester's charitable institutions and its mills, led by the Gregs, turned him irrevocably against the industrial city.

May and June letters that finally arrived from Lucy contained none of the needed consolation. One warned that he must not count on the hospitality of Beech Woods, should he return. Immediately he replied: "I shall take thy advice, I assure thee, and go to my good friend Bourgeat's with great pleasure, without trespassing one foot north of his line." He took with an icy calm Lucy's insistence that he call on her father's rich Derby cousin, Euphemia Gifford, and on the Gordons. If he met Miss Gifford, it would most likely occur through the Duke of Devonshire—not, he emphasized, the other way about.

His "constant" social obligations made catering to the Gordons quite out of the question. (He refrained from mentioning Alexander's failure to provide introductions for Manchester and help head off the futility of the visit.) Mrs. Percy's unwillingness to have him return was the thrust that unleashed his pen. He said Lucy might better leave her post when her term was finished and go to the Berthouds' or else New York City to await his call. She could count on him to support her, one way or another, if she should decide to quit Beech Woods. Until then he wished her to see that John practiced on the piano, a valuable social asset, and that he drew everything in nature as if his whole future depended on it. That future could be London or Paris. Audubon might bid them to come before she knew it. A guardian agreed to take charge of the exhibition for a fortnight, until Audubon's return to Manchester.

Even in the rain Liverpool lightened his heart as he left the stagecoach. He found the "Queen Bee" at her carpet loom. Her daughter-in-law Elizabeth was charting the constellations for a charity bazaar. Hannah Mary rushed in to greet him. William put down the book of poems by Roscoe that he had been reading to the others. After an exchange of greetings he again took it up, as Audubon settled contentedly between the ladies.

At Lodge Lane next morning he deferred to Roscoe's view that it would be foolish to publish a prospectus until the way opened. Twenty-four hours later it became evident that his return to Liverpool was providential.

Dr. Traill arranged for a meeting between Audubon and one of London's more successful book dealers, Henry G. Bohn, whose shrewdness at his trade had made him rich. It was therefore all the more gratifying to hear him call the portfolio "so very superior" that publication could not fail, if cleverly handled.[3] He said that London and Paris costs should be compared, scientific societies cultivated for prestige, and exhibiting stopped. Audubon was cool to a tentative suggestion that Bohn handle matters, to abandoning his exhibitions, and to advice against reproducing his birds life size. He did, however, listen intently to the declaration that no matter where his work might be engraved, it ought to be a "genuine English production" in appearance. Even a French production that bore an English title page and imprint and verisimilitude stood a better chance of succeeding, according to the Bohn theory, which the Rathbones, Roscoe, and Traill thought sound.

For the "ultimate good" of his family and the sake of his art Audubon agreed that a text of observations must soon be begun. He fully intended to follow much of Bohn's advice. The momentous decision overwhelmed him with weariness, once he had reached it. Headache and coughing besieged him while he began to fear that now that the realization of his dream seemed at hand, death might overtake him. To do as Bohn said would require him to become a "man of business" again. This he admitted with a sigh to Lucy. To help repay important favors from every quarter he asked that she be "at some trouble and expense" to obtain an alligator skeleton for Lord Stamford. John, Bourgeat, and Pope could assist. He also wanted several six-foot segments of firm-barked magnolia, poplar, beech, sycamore, oak, and sassafras, all labeled in oil across the grain and shipped by river boat to a New Orleans schooner. The Rathbones would welcome some Louisiana plants for their garden. The deserving "Queen Bee" had offered to drive him back to Manchester and through the region of Lucy's childhood. From there he would advance on Edinburgh with his portfolio.

A few last errands detained Audubon. He took his album around for friends to write their effusions, revisited his *Wild Turkey* oil at the Royal Institution, consulted with William Rathbone, and dined with the sagacious Dr. Traill.

The "Queen Bee" asked for a tiny pencil sketch of his *Turkey* to take to the jeweler Roskell for a seal adorned with his motto, "America, My Country."[4] In twenty-three minutes Audubon outlined the bird on a pebble for the intaglio. John Chorley presented him with a silver snuffbox engraved with a pheasant, and Hannah Mary gave him a cherished penknife.

Adam Hodgson's sister Mary expressed a Quaker concern that Audubon should inspect the city jail which Friends were quietly striving to reform. The "infamous treadmill" reminded him of nothing so much as a circular squirrel cage. He did not doubt that this "laborious engine of shame," conceived for the betterment of the prisoners, would throw them back upon "the vile world" worse than they had left it. Friends' belief that trades should be taught to put an end to "the mere grinding of flour" by the "poor, miserable beings" he angrily seconded. By treading the paddles they expended the same energy that climbing hills for four to six hours would call for. "I know a quick, short step is more fatiguing than a long one, and soon destroys," he wrote. "The sallow, withered, emaciated visages prove this . . . as well as my calculation of thirty uphill steps of two-and-ahalf feet to a rotation . . . or 4,500 per hour . . . 45,000 per day. . . . Both body and mind suffer. I would write more but I am not William Roscoe."

André Melly, the "Intelligent Swiss," had earned special thanks for conspiring with Samuel Greg to pad the till in Manchester. Audubon rose at dawn, tiptoed down to put on his boots at the door, and strode into town. His insistent ringing at Melly's boardinghouse roused the household. "*Eh bien, Papa,*" Melly yawned, rising on an elbow. He rubbed his head while Audubon perched on the side of his bed to deliver a speech of gratitude. There the unconventional interview ended. When the children came down at seven they found Audubon reclining on the hall sofa. They kissed him, as always, then ran out to their special garden to cut bouquets.

Another day or so and Audubon was on his way to Manchester in the family chaise with the "Queen Bee." Hannah Mary looked lovelier than ever. A maidservant held a picnic hamper for their luncheon en route. The postilion rode ahead. Their carriage was followed by one filled with the Rathbone children, off for a visit with their cousins, the Dockrays. Abigail Dockray was a popular Friends minister.

Audubon found his exhibition guardian in his cups. Receipts were as disappointing as at the start. Bohn, a chance visitor in Manchester, advised against going to London just yet. Audubon decided to give his birds a few more days in the industrial city, then see what Edinburgh might afford.

Mrs. Rathbone took Audubon to see the paintings of Reynolds and Vernet owned by Robert Greg, cousin of Samuel. Again and again she attended his exhibition. For her last glimpse of it she left a sovereign at the door. Before joining the Rathbones on an excursion to Bakewell, Audubon distributed souvenirs of gratitude among the Gregs—drawings of a chaffinch, an egret, and a wild turkey.

In the cathedral grounds at Bakewell, where he roamed

with Hannah Mary, Audubon fancied he saw the childhood wraith of Lucy running before him. The party went on to neighboring Haddon Hall, then to Matlock's wild streams and glens where Erasmus Darwin, who had trotted Lucy on his knee at her home nearby, once gathered botanical treasure. At Buxton, Audubon sketched two views in his journal for Lucy. He drew a vale for Hannah Mary, then rowed the ladies on the Derwent River to his lusty singing.

The only serious blight on the carefree outing was the disappearance of Hannah Mary's gift penknife. Audubon was in dread lest this enchanting girl, for whom he felt only platonic devotion, think him careless and ungrateful. When they reached Manchester again he tried to rectify matters by allowing them to share his journal. Each had her turn at the leatherbound tome, in spite of his vow to Lucy. He wished them to absorb his allusions to his "old master David," to Darwin, and to Priestley. These would banish any doubts raised by his loss of the knife and by his garrulousness on the ride. The lost penknife still had the power to cut away that "simplicity" his English friends prized, and to expose his timorous pride.

Hours of tramping around Manchester for introductions to Scottish savants put a strain on his correct behavior; he tossed a coin to decide whether to go back to the dear but proper Gregs and Rathbones or join a blithe acquaintance for some music. He chose the much needed light-hearted way.

At midnight, rather than rouse his volatile landlady, he went to the small, full house of the museum curator, William Horton Bentley, taxidermist and dealer in rare skins, and climbed into bed beside him. He apologized for praying aloud. Bidding Lucy an audible good night, he fell asleep. "What Bentley thought of this I do not know," he mused the next morning. Evidently the curator took everything in good part; he gave his uninvited guest a seventy-four-gun ship model for Johnny in return for a promise of nuts, seeds, and acorns from Louisiana.

At Quarry Bank his apologies were graciously accepted. A spate of farewell presents came forth for him—pin cushions, books, and more penknives. The children brought plants to press in his journal. A downpour prevented a last stroll alone with "his" Hannah Mary, but he plucked a rose for her that she wore until it faded. For the first two miles of his walk into town next morning he had the company not only of his beautiful, innnocent admirer but also that of her cousin, Agnes Greg.

Bentley gave him a second breakfast and helped prepare the portfolio for an evening departure by stage for Edinburgh. But the many errands that remained undone and a racking cough held Audubon back for a day or two. Much as he disliked to desert his needy landlady and child, he accepted the hospitality of the Dockrays who found a bed for him by crowding their nine young ones in together.

On October 24 at five o'clock in the morning Audubon arrived at the stagecoach corners. Over the furious objections of the clerk he stowed his portfolio aloft before taking his place inside. He congratulated himself, as he rolled on towards his next *champs de bataille,* that he had not left a certain chore undone. He had written to Bonaparte to ask permission to include him and his Uncle Joseph in the prospectus as subscribers. This would not commit them to purchasing the costly *Birds of America* unless, as he was careful to explain, they wished; the prestige to be gained from their good will was all he had in mind.

Except for his near arrest on suspicion of harboring a cadaver, Audubon had a peaceable enough journey. A filthy oaf seated near his trunk got off at Preston, and Audubon, for one, was vindicated. The coach wound among the hills of ragged shepherds and Cheviot sheep. Audubon discussed America, slavery, the corn laws, and English poverty with Granville Pattison, a genial Scottish doctor bound home from Cornwall with his son. Pattison induced him to sip some pure Scotch whiskey—a drink too harsh and powerful for Audubon's taste. The author of medical books seemed willing, and even determined, to oblige in the matter of introductions and guidance for the Franco-American whose adopted country he had visited and admired.

XV. False Start

AUDUBON REACHED THE BLACK BULL in Edinburgh near midnight but he was obliged to move on with his trappings to the Star, where the Pattisons were stopping. The laughter, whistling, and coughing that his foreign appearance provoked at breakfast drove him out to look for other lodgings.

The *tout ensemble* of Edinburgh at once won him over, with its dignified grays and greens, abrupt hills, broad streets, bridges, and markets, all picturesque and friendly. Only the startling contrast between poverty and riches gave him pause. At 2 George Street he found a bedchamber and parlor with buffet, bedstead, and armchairs. On the mantel, graced with marble cherubs, stood a brace of pheasants and pots of geraniums. Above hung a large print, *Charity Among the Free Masons*, a theme by no means alien to himself, "a brother Mason" since 1820 or before.[1] The porter who helped him move refused the counterfeit coin Audubon innocently slipped him.

As he went about with his introductory letters in this "multitude of learned," he was almost relieved to find the first three people on his list absent. However, Dr. Robert Knox, a descendant of the sixteenth-century religious reformer John Knox, received him in a surgeon's gown, and, with his one good eye, scanned the Traill letter.[2] Excusing himself, he merely promised to call on Audubon.

After a long walking tour of the city Audubon returned to his room. He opened up his portfolio and looked at his "Birds . . . with pleasure and yet with a considerable degree of fear that they never would be published." He felt, suddenly, intensely "alone," in need of Lucy. "I thought of the country that I have left behind and of thee," he addressed her in his journal. "Some dark thoughts came across my mind. I feared thee sick, perhaps lost forever to me, and felt deathly sick. My dinner was there, cooling, fast, whilst each particle I swallowed went down slowly as if choking me. I felt tears . . . and I forced myself out of the room to destroy this painful gloom that I dread at all times and that sometimes I fear may do more." If this was his first bout of suicidal self-doubt it would not be his last.

That Robert Jameson, a mineralogist, was the city's most influential science professor, and that he had his own journal, made his importance clear.[3] Innocent of Jameson's ties with the foremost British ornithologists, Jardine and Selby,[4] Audubon set his cap for his favor. Confident, he handed Jameson his note from the banker Heywood as he took note of the scientist's triple-parted hair. Jameson read it with indifference and barely glanced at the portfolio. To a suggestion that he might arrange a meeting with Sir Walter Scott, he replied curtly that the celebrity was too busy on a life of Napoleon for interruptions.

Audubon soon left, but as he walked down the street he swore, "Not see Walter Scott—by Washington, I shall, if I have to crawl on all fours for a mile." How often in this "crank-sided world" had he been obliged to bow to the insults of its Jamesons! If it had not been for the few like the Rathbones and for faith in "posterity," he might have begun to doubt his own worth. Past him wandered the vendors with burdens on their backs and straps across their foreheads, just as did the Indians at home. Until Audubon turned in at Holyrood, a well-dressed prostitute followed. A guide conducted him through the castle, then left him alone in the marriage and murder chambers to peer into the mirrors for a ghostly trace of Mary of Scotland.

When he reached his lodgings he studied his own reflection; and as he did so he felt drawn into the past—away from the future and its bleak uncertainty. "I saw in it not only my own face but such a powerful resemblance to my venerable father that I almost imagined it was him that I saw. The thought of my mother flew about me. My sister was also present, my young days. . . ."[5]

Pattison brought friends almost daily between ten o'clock and noon. The news spread quickly. The "delicious actress" Miss Stephens of the success *Rob Roy* called with her brother. One day the praise of his "method" became so heady that when the company had gone, Audubon soared into the public garden before its closing. He had to call for the winsome keeper to come and let him out. "Handsome stranger," she whispered.

Dr. Knox, true to his word and curious about how the drawings compared with Selby's, dropped by to see them. His verdict—that they were "the finest in the world"—he emphasized with the prediction that they would win an invitation to join the select Wernerians, the University's learned society.

One Wernerian, however, a printer and zoologist named Patrick Neill, turned the artist away at the door of his shop with the advice to return by appointment only. When next they met, Neill needed only a glance at the drawings to lead Audubon to the best engraver in the city, William Home Lizars (1788–1859). Lizars put aside the work he was doing for Selby to go and inspect the portfolio. When it was thrown open on the floor for him, the engraver—who was one of the founders of the Royal Scottish Academy—gasped: "My God, I never saw anything like this before!" He said that Selby and Jardine must see the American masterpieces.

The next day Lizars returned, bringing with him the much

Turkey Vulture. *Plate 151 of* The Birds of
America. *Engraved by Robert Havell, Jr.,
in 1832 after the original study drawn in
1825 in West Feliciana Parish, Louisiana.*

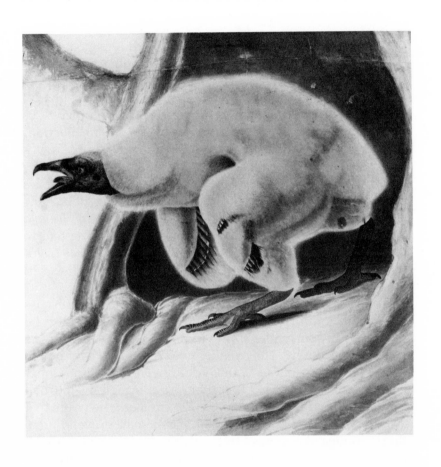

Young of the Turkey Buzzard, *undated.*
Pencil and watercolor drawing. Courtesy The
New-York Historical Society, New York.

chastened Professor Jameson, who glibly promised that he
himself would hail the birds in his *Edinburgh New Philosophical Journal*. Jameson's recent behavior caused Audubon to direct most of his remarks to Lizars, whom he was finding
wholly different from the "brute" Lawson, the Philadelphia
engraver.

A return to the Lizars shop to see the drawings of Selby,
Jardine, and Selby's brother-in-law, Captain Mitford, dis-
pelled Audubon's doubts that he could surpass their productions. "Johnny," he grunted to his journal, "could do as good."
The studies, little known, seldom seen, are surpassing.

That afternoon, while Lizars continued his inspection,
Audubon received a stream of callers, learned and aristocratic. The larger drawings he held high, the smaller ones
low and within the range of the "delicate, beautiful noses" of
the ladies. They and their husbands exclaimed over his "new
and different style." At the sight of the *Wild Turkey Hen and
Young* and the *Whooping Crane*, Lizars reacted as he had to
the *Mockingbird*. But the grandeur of the daring *Great-Footed
Hawk* left him mute. He motioned for Audubon to lower it,
then declared, *"I will engrave and publish this!"*

As artist and engraver walked out to dine and discuss
the possible future Audubon hid his elation. Whether he
could actually surrender supervision of his beloved originals
heaven alone knew. The friendly house presided over by the
lively Mrs. Lizars of the "Van Dyck brown eyes" stirred long-
ings for Lucy. He agreed to a trial engraving. In his journal,
his head swimming from wine and excitement, he wrote that
at last "the needful" was in sight, and maybe even "ame-
thysts, rubies, diamonds" from "Dames Fame and Fortune."
His careering pen conceived of recognition as a bird—its
range the wide world and its call his name. "Then Fame, ex-
pand thy universal pinions, and far, far, and high, high, soar
away! Yet smoothly circle about me wherever I go. Call out
with musical mellowness the name of this child of Nature,
her humble but true admirer. Call out, call out, call out—and
loud, loud, loud, 'AUDUBON!!!!'" The fine *Views of Edinburgh*, with which Lizars had sent him off, he stowed be-

neath his pillow like a child "at Christmas." He fell asleep wondering when Roscoe's prediction might come true—that the King of England would see the birds. His Majesty should have a copy! And the King of France—and the Emperor of Russia! Adams, Clay, and Jackson would not be forgotten.

Patrick Neill took Audubon to dine at his "little hermitage" near the city and to meet interested friends. Gulls, herons, cormorants, and gannets circled and cried above the little lake and garden when Neill appeared.[6] His bantams, pigeons, and watch dog greeted him, and even the sparrows chattered loudly in the ivy. Neill told about a "scorie" that he had raised. For years it returned to his grounds from the north, until a stray bullet ended the rare association. The portrait painter John Syme (1795–1861) asked Audubon to allow him to do his portrait for Lizars to engrave.[7] The editor David Bridges promised favorable notices in his paper for the exhibition the artist was planning. The noted phrenologist George Combe (1788–1856) likened Audubon's head to Napoleon's and Molière's.

Seldom did Audubon appear at his exhibition of "139 land and 70 water birds," opened the middle of November in a rent-free room given by the Royal Institution. He did not fancy being stared at as "The Great Unknown," much less eavesdropping among the addlepated. (Someone had asked at the entrance whether the show was worth the shilling. Overhearing, Audubon replied that it was not, and he had to smile when an idler begged to differ.)

For sixteen days from the opening date he kept to his rooms, painting a second oil of his *Wild Turkey*, one with a cock, hen, and brood of nine little ones. More ambitious than the previous one, and intended for the Royal Institution after hanging as the *pièce de resistance* of the exhibition, it held the artist during the brief hours of daylight. He had concluded that if oils were of the essence he must produce some sterling examples. However imperfect in brushwork and finish, they would lack none of that animation, that almost narrative *elán*, for which he was known.

He paid no attention to the fascinated callers. Lizars brought an artist, Joseph Bartholomew Kidd, to paint a sky behind a study of English *Wood Pigeons* so that Audubon might profit by a new kind of background for these and for figures yet to come. He repeated his trusty *Otter in a Trap*. He thought he might finish a canvas of two cats fighting over a dead squirrel, to please Daniel Lizars. (The engraver's brother thought the subject sure to win attention.) The landlady's son helped extinguish the life of the cats and wire them for combat.[8] Such oils were intended to help pay for the doorkeeper, card bearer, porter, and the cost of living while Lizars experimented. His method was to incise his tracing of the model into copper, rather than steel, engraving the figures of the birds, but etching the habitat with nitric acid in such a way as to achieve an effect of varying dark washes—like watercolor. He or his foreman then hand-colored a pattern proof for his artisans to copy for an edition.

They were no worse, he mistakenly believed, than the animal paintings of the old Dutch masters Snyders and Wouvermans in the galleries. But portraiture in oils he left gladly to Syme, for whom he posed in a hunting shirt and his wolfskin coat. The attire suited his taste too well for him to mind the attention it drew. He himself was aware of his resemblance— and his father's as well—to one of his wild models. His eyes, he thought as he viewed the wet canvas, were "more like those of an enraged eagle." (Little did he know how many oil portraits were to be attributed to him in time, with signatures forged on not a few, despite his abandonment of such attempts after studying with Sully in 1824.)

He reached a turning point in his lonely, beleaguered career on November 20, 1826. At dawn he began his "letterpress," a text of ornithological observations eventually to be published as *Ornithological Biography*. He kept a draft on the habits of the wild turkey until it was ready—or so he hoped—to place beneath his new oil of the bird on exhibition. As he reached the end his friend David Bridges came by, looked the effort over, and tactfully suggested that John Wilson of *Blackwood's* magazine might help see it through.

Still too engrossed to think about breakfast, Audubon set

out for Wilson's house down the street without changing
from lounging dress and slippers. A servant of the popular
"Christopher North," as Wilson signed himself, announced
"Mr. Audubon from America." Intrigued by such simple
effrontery, Wilson received him, read the paper, promised
help, and watched him depart rejoicing. Audubon had not
the faintest suspicion that Wilson was a confidante and crony
of the "Ord of Edinburgh," Professor Jameson.

By the close of that memorable day he held in his hands
the first finished fragment of *The Birds of America*, a superbly
engraved and colored aquatint. He decided to go ahead,
even if the undertaking were to run to sixteen years for completion. Lizars agreed to finish the first number so that Audubon might, as he was soon writing William Rathbone,
travel with it beneath his arm and beg his way in search of
"300 good substantial names of persons, or bodies or institutions," while undergoing "many sad perplexities" and perhaps never again seeing his "beloved America." He thought
two guineas a fair price for each "number" of five portraits
"the size of life." "I must acknowledge it renders it rather
bulky," he conceded to Rathbone, "but my heart was always
bent on it, and I cannot refrain from attempting it so. I shall
publish the letter-press text in a separate work." Within six
days the proofs of the first five engravings hung beside the
original studies at the Institution. Dr. Meikleham of Trinidad
stepped forward to subscribe with an eagerness that belied
his later failure to pay. In vain he tried to interest Audubon
in painting the West Indies birds that he wished to publish.

Audubon's attempt to do justice to the "miracle" in a letter
to Lucy succeeded only after four abortive attempts that
went into the fire. In his fifth letter, however, he predicted
that his "monument" to the birds would stand forever. The
artist's inevitable reaction to victory was tedium. The long,
sumptuous dinners that he had to attend, impeccably at-
tired, made him long for "roast ibis or sun perch on Flat Lake
with Bourgeat," or "jellied venison," Kentucky style.

His phenomenal endurance began to be sorely overtaxed.
Wondering, as he had done "a thousand times," why he had

received no letters from Lucy, he placed his painting of wood pigeons on the floor to study its "power and effect." Still thinking of her, he stood on a chair, brush in hand, when suddenly he fell in a faint of utter exhaustion. Sometime later he awoke in a sweat. When Lizars and his wife walked in, he was resting; seeing his state, they took him home with them for roast sheep's head.

On his return he found his landlady waiting up to hand him a letter she hoped might be from Lucy. It was an introduction from De Witt Clinton to General Lafayette for the artist's problematical descent on Paris. "Quite mad of disappointment," he poured complaints of headache and malaise into his journal: "I thought I walked beside thy lovely figure, kissed thee, pressed thee to my bosom, heard—I thought— thy sweet voice. But good God, when I looked around me, found myself in Edinburgh, alone, quite alone—without one soul to whom I could open my heart, my head became dizzy, and I must have fallen to the floor." Nor could "all the doctors in Christendom" take the place of her "kind care" if illness were to steal upon him and seek to destroy him and his life's mission. He could not believe that only a year had passed since their reunions after his Woodville classes: "I could kiss thee, gaze on thy features . . . run down with thee to the bayou, or to a celebrated room where many of my Birds of America had been looked at before they 'flew' to this mighty land of learning and science."

Once he began to sense that his paper on the turkey should never have gone to Wilson of *Blackwood's*, lest Jameson get hold of it and attack its authority, he knew no peace. Neill and Lizars persuaded him to attend a formal Antiquarian Society dinner by promising that he would be seated between them. The banquet of "old-fashioned messes of marrow bones, codfish heads stuffed with oat meal and garlic, black puddings, sheep's heads and tracheas, and grouse," ended with a toast to the King.

A toast to Audubon followed—a positive "panegyric" that made him tremble visibly. He felt his hands bead and the sweat course down his legs as he thanked the "large assembly." Feeling like "a speechless fool," he managed to say, "Gentlemen, my powers of voice are as humble as those of the Birds now hanging on the walls of the Institution. I am truly obliged for your favor. Permit me to say 'May God bless you all, and may the Society prosper.'" Lizars passed him wine with a whispered "Bravo!—take this." All eyes turned toward the next speaker, about to begin his popular impersonation of a bumblebee chaser.

A few evenings later, at a special dinner, Dr. Knox repeated that Audubon deserved nomination to the Wernerian Society. To show his gratitude, Audubon attended Knox's medical lecture next morning. But he only half-listened to the talk of "larynxes, clavicles and charnel." His mind was on Jameson, the founder of the Wernerian Society, whose vote could wipe out his gains in Edinburgh. Nothing that Bridges might have said about the coming encomiums in *Blackwood's* from John Wilson's pen could mitigate the dread.

He decided to confront Jameson directly with the fact of his powerful ballot. For a pretext he took along a paper he had just been writing on the buzzard. He intended to ask Jameson to use it instead of the one on the turkey in case the latter should be passed on by Bridges or Wilson. To his astonishment he found Jameson genial and receptive. Without examining the buzzard paper he invited Audubon to take it to his coeditor, David Brewster. He sent him off with the prediction that the University would be among the first to subscribe to *The Birds of America*.

To approach Brewster, the authority on polarization of light, genuine courage was needed. The physicist led Audubon into his study in such a hospitable manner that he took heart and began to read aloud as politely requested. A "cold sweat" stole over him, that he, an ordinary man, should be reading "his puny efforts" on something that "none but an Almighty Creator" could fathom seemed "ridiculously absurd." For he had "never looked into an English grammar, and very seldom, and unfortunately, into a French or Spanish one." He was more accustomed to solitude, "with his thoughts" in the bosom of "Nature" than to meetings that made him "awkward and shy." Brewster declared the paper "very good and interesting," if in need of some routine editing. He said that he himself would be glad to attend to this little formality.

Audubon still faced the problem of a "prospectus." He drafted one and sent it to Liverpool for approval. Weeks passed without answer. He began to fear that the crudities of his speech and his "want of knowledge" might have struck the intellectual Roscoe as laughable. After what seemed an endless wait Rathbone replied that Audubon's plan seemed overly ambitious to him and Roscoe. A son of Greg in the university medical school had been keeping them posted. Samuel expressed doubt to his daughter, Mrs. Rathbone: "What can be done about his *Birds?* It is said they will be more than £210—which will hardly do for individuals, except there could be wheels within wheels and joint stock companies formed."[9]

A curious incident marred the dignity of the exhibition. Just before the disappearance of the lovely *Black Poll Warbler*, the guardian noticed a suspicious youth in a long cloak hanging about. The culprit was found and he denied his guilt until a beggar whom he had bribed to return the stolen painting gave him away. Captain Basil Hall came forward and declared the boy his ward and the illegitimate son of the late Sir Henry Raeburn, the painter. The much embarrassed Hall presented Audubon with his book on South America and invited him to dinner to make amends.

Another of the dire hallucinations about Lucy occurred in December. Audubon fancied he saw her looking pale and ill. A flood of letters, all posted in August, ended his suspense. Eagerly he broke the seals, kissed her signature "a hundred times," and read that she was well and enjoying an occasional canter under the magnolias. He thought how puzzled she was going to be by his recent admission that although he dared not invite her to cross the Atlantic just yet, she could chance it if she wished. But he had been obliged to add that he could only promise to try to support the family if she came unbidden and of her own volition. In no frame of mind for disappointments or excuses, Lucy asked that he attend to a shamefully neglected matter—the payment of thirty dollars to Mrs. Middlemist entrusted to him on his departure. His not yet having gone to London did not excuse his failure that painfully embarrassed her. She spared him the news of a sharp falling out with Mrs. Percy all because of it, and said nothing of her intention to leave Beech Woods after Christmas.

Absorption in his own affairs and ignorance of how to send the sum to London were the sincere excuses Audubon gave before hurrying out to learn the means and do the necessary. His own pressing concerns recaptured his attention.

Charles Bonaparte had landed in Liverpool on his way to the Continent. The surgeon John Stokoe, Joseph Bonaparte's European agent and pensioner, called to convey the Prince's greetings. Stokoe, no stranger to Audubon, had been in Philadelphia during his exploratory visit in 1824. His court-martial for sympathy with Napoleon while attending him on St. Helena Island had more or less thrust him upon the good graces of the Bonapartes. He came to say that the Prince had heard of the new plans for *The Birds of America*, but felt inclined to agree with the view that they were possibly too ambitious. The only explanation that the astonished Audubon could think of was that Bonaparte had talked with William Rathbone and seconded his opinion. Rathbone's letter, incidentally, had politely requested that no bird be named for his mother, the "Queen Bee."[10] Actually, Bonaparte's reaction was independent. Moreover, it had pleased him to discover that Audubon had shown his *American Ornithology* to the Rathbones and their company.[11] Stokoe said nothing of the two subscriptions Audubon had requested. Audubon's *amour propre* smarted a little. "Since Napoleon became, from the ranks an emperor," he asked himself, "why should not Audubon be able to leave the woods of America a while, and publish and sell *a book?* No, no, I will try by heavens until each and every hair about me will have dropped from my body, dead, gray, from old age!!"

The Wernerians were expecting him. He put a freshly

killed pigeon, a hammer, and some wires in a box, then summoned a coach, congratulating himself the while that he
could leave the oral reading of the buzzard paper to Patrick
Neill. He himself had only to put up his portrait of an unpre-
possessing vulture and explain his drawing method. Jameson
praised the realism of the likeness and called the method remarkable and "inconceivably ingenious," but he had little to
say about the buzzard paper. It was Jameson who nominated
Audubon for honorary membership—to be put to a vote at
the next meeting. After a day or two Brewster led him into
the long, scarlet-papered hall of the Royal Academy of Arts,
past rows of dignified members seated in hair-cloth chairs. A
dreary philologist's report, then a paper on the mammoth
preceded a sign from the president on his red moroccan
perch at the dias for Audubon to show his work. Jardine and
Selby had come from their country estates to share the lime-
light. Selby's unqualified admiration of the portfolio made
the ornithologist seem "a man of genius not in the least re-
sembling the venomous tallow candler of Philadelphia,"
George Ord—"that possessor of three Greek words and
seven of Latin, and describer of objects yet unknown to the
Almighty." Audubon was confident that Selby would not behave like that enemy who had told "a large meeting" in
Philadelphia that he would be damned before voting for an
ignoramous. But, as the two collaborators took the floor, he
disappeared and did not hear his election by thunderous
acclamation.

On his way to breakfast with Selby and Jardine next morning, he was stopped by the pleas of a barefooted urchin. He
thought better of bringing the beggar along, and instead led
him through the wintry sunshine to his rooms for a supply
of old clothing and five shillings, besides one already given.

Selby proved the more apt and enthusiastic pupil of Audubon's method. He resolved to fill his Belford country house
with quadrupeds painted from wired models. Audubon
wondered at the failure of the men to invite him to become
their partner. To let them take note of his scientific soundness he unfolded his buzzard paper and began to read. But

he had not gone far when he made the "quite sickening" discovery that Brewster had "destroyed the matter" of the paper by making many changes. His audible reaction and shock may explain the departure of his pupils from Edinburgh without a second lesson. Selby sent him three beautiful pheasants with a polite farewell and a warm bid to visit Twizell House on his way to London.

Bewildered, Audubon took up the fine birds and felt suddenly inspired to attempt his most exacting oil thus far. *Sauve Qui Peut*, or *Devil Take the Hindmost*, he would call this masterpiece intended to show the world of Selbys and Jardines. He pounced the outline of the first pheasant, finally to be shown with a covey of fourteen, then he sketched a fox. Behind them there was to be a dense thicket, with sky above. A canvas of heroic size—nearly five feet by eight feet—he thought none too grand for the composition. On December 23, the closing day of his exhibition, he began to paint at 9:00 A.M. with the first winter daylight. He all but ignored the "complete levee" of well-wishers who filed in and out as he sat in nightcap, nightshirt, and slippers, without a coat or robe, driving his brushes until nightfall.

Never had the medium of oil baffled and harassed Audubon as now. He detested the tedium of grinding his colors and the much slower tempo. Yet he faced even more technical difficulty when it came to the stage called "finish." Had the old masters achieved their marvelous transparency by means of three clear, bright coats as much as by the glaze itself, he wondered. And had not the oils of Reynolds already begun to fade from too much glazing? Whatever the answer, he knew that at his age he need not expect to rival those who had spent a lifetime of experiment and labor in the medium. His draftsmanship he stressed as the equal of any. But, disappointed in himself, he took comfort in belittling the old-master oils of animals—Hondekoeter's among them—and the much respected and more than promising work of young Edwin Henry Landseer. Challenged at a gathering of phrenologists on how to form colors, he flushed and answered testily that if they knew the meaning of "bumps" on skulls, he knew "prismatic composition." Yet the supposed pupil of Jacques-Louis David was within days of inadvertently revealing that he had never had a lesson in perspective.

Exhibition proceeds of nearly $800 from admissions and more than 1,000 catalogues burned Audubon's pocket. He joined the Christmas shoppers long enough to select a brooch for Lucy in celebration.[12]

He hesitated to transfer the exhibition to Glasgow while Lizars was still printing the first set of birds. While awaiting light for work on *Sauve Qui Peut* he began papers on the alligator, passenger pigeon, and rattlesnake for the Wernerians.[13] Thoughts of Berthoud's "strange and painful" silence made him feel he must vent his displeasure in a letter. Not a line, he complained, had he received from Victor, although he himself found time to write because he was "no more lazy" than in Kentucky: "I do regularly with four hours sleep, and hope yet to see my family derive the benefit of my labors." He then made sport of himself as the "Mr. Audubon of the wonderful locks that hang in full abundance."

In softening tones he hinted that Nicholas ought to send birds and fossils so that he might qualify for corresponding membership in one of the Edinburgh learned societies. Then, turning to thank Sully for various introductions, he promised to post the first of the birds to be engraved, for him to present to the American Philosophical Society with the reminder that "humble talents ought to be fostered first in one's own country."

Until dusk on Christmas Eve and on the feast itself he grappled with *Sauve Qui Peut*. Headache and frustration made him throw his brush down and set out to Lizars's house for dinner. The engraver, whom he had now begun to think of as his *"bon cheval de bataille"* and whose wife he thought of as "Lady Number One," did not mind his dozing on the sofa during coffee and light after-dinner music. Mrs. Lizars and her sister cut linen that he had brought for them to replace the fraying shirts from Lucy's needle.

On November 4 he apologized to Roscoe for his silence and reported:

My Dear Good Sir . . . My Great work is at last under way, but how long it will be able to bear itself up is a matter of much doubt and concern to me. It is publishing, however, here by Mr. W. H. Lizars an eminent artist and a man of most excellent caracter [sic] and great personal amiability. It will come out in its best dress only, i.e. all colored and in the very handsomest style—that is promising a good deal in a few words and perhaps presumptuously speaking, but as it is really my *Wish* and *intention* that it should *prove* so, I have some hopes that I shall not disappoint either my friends or the world at large.

My prospectus is a very humble one and I send it you now in its nakedness that you may clothe it (if you please) as you may best think fit—to tell all my feelings would be quite impossible—my head can scarcely be said to be on my shoulders—I never before felt so wild and at a loss to speak or act, as I do now.[14]

He asked Roscoe to share the letter with William Rathbone to whom, four days before Christmas, he himself wrote rather cryptically: "Twenty times at least . . . has my heart been on the eve of opening itself entire to you all and [letting] you enter into secrets that would make you look at me with astonishment, but sensations that I cannot describe did keep me silent and I cannot now confide to paper what I regret I have not said to you on the subject I now allude to." The subject, perhaps, was his birth.

Bald Eagle. *Plate 31 of* The Birds of America. *Engraved by Robert Havell, Jr., in 1831 after the original study drawn in midwinter 1821 as "White-Headed Eagle."*

XVI.
The Monster, London

O N THE DAY AFTER CHRISTMAS the sumptuous coach of the Earl of Morton, the former Great Chamberlain to the late Queen Charlotte, turned into George Street to bear Audubon eight miles out to Dalmahoy. The decrepit but still lucid peer wished to see the birds and also a certain aquarelle, *The Death of Montgomery*, which dated back to Natchez days. The beautiful Countess, a generation younger than her husband, was waiting at the turreted neo-Gothic lion-flanked portal through which her guest passed.

The Earl, seated in his castored armchair and hardly the awesome figure Audubon had envisaged, tottered up to him like a "new hatched partridge." The miniaturelike view of Edinburgh from one of the drawing room windows impressed the artist almost as much as the array of Van Dycks, Claude Lorrains, Rembrandts, and Titians. He opened his "Book of Nature" for his host, whose platitudes—a kind of praise that bored and wearied—made him more ready to be shown upstairs.

He found his nightshirt and cap warming by the fire and

his bag unpacked in the yellow guestchamber. He tried the sofa at the foot of the crown-crested bedstead. The desk held "everything superfluous to writing." A "bathing room" beyond also had its plethora of nonessentials. He dressed quickly and declined to labor over his cravat "as a hangman does his knot." He regarded too fussy a toilet as "a vile loss of time."

Dressed in a red turban and white satin gown the Countess led her several guests to the dining salon. One elaborate course followed on another as servants in white wigs and red liveries moved about beneath the gaze of a steward in black. Audubon, in the extreme boredom of the occasion, was struck as never before by the emptiness of wealth. But whether any of it could be snared for *The Birds of America* looked doubtful.

Next morning before breakfast, his mind on a subscription, he visited the stable of Abyssinian horses, saw grazing deer, and admired the hanging gardens and winter-blooming roses. He was in the midst of a lesson in his "method," one begged by the Countess, when her falconer arrived with a belled and hooded hawk on his wrist.

At long last the coquette, while hinting for a watercolor of the *Catbirds*, signed for the Folio. She also promised letters for London and fresh pheasants needed as models for *Sauve Qui Peut*. What she dared not say, but intended to communicate through her antiquarian and Hall, was that Audubon must part with his curls and buy more conventional clothes for London. He would have to forsake his wolfskin coat, fur cap, and pantaloons.

Another test of endurance lay ahead as the year ended. Captain Hall invited Audubon to a New Year's Eve dinner party. He knew that a leading critic for the *Edinburgh Review*, Francis Jeffrey, would be present. Audubon had yet to meet the man who had ignored his calling card as well as a pass to his exhibition. At the moment of introduction by Hall the critic murmured apologies for his neglect but evoked no response. Audubon excused himself as early as he dared and started home.

The watch had been doubled to regulate the New Year's

celebrants in the streets; with great strides Audubon hurried by them. He was outlining a pheasant when his landlady coaxed him downstairs to toast the New Year at midnight with an American lady lodger. After closing his journal for 1826 he tossed through the night, his brain afire.

Sometime long after Audubon's death someone eased drawings out of the 1826 journal; Maria Rebecca Audubon gave them away, here and there. On the back of one brought to light after publication of the manuscript in 1967—a pencil sketch of a blithe crewman—this long lost final journal entry appears:

Edinburgh, December 30, 1826.

Sunday Night 12 o'clock—
and Now My Dear book, must I part with thee? back in America and fed in England and Scotland and at sea—go to My Best Friend, To My Wife, to my Beloved Lucy—yes go back return to thy own native soil and give her pleasure a while—*She* will be glad to hold conference with thee now—for she will look on thy sheets as the reflectors of my daily Life. Simple, either in times of Nothing or of wonderous events, and whilst she reads them, she will observe my very gradual advancement into a World yet unknown and dangerous to be known. A World wherein I may prosper but wherein it is the easiest thing to sink into compleat oblivion. When I open thy sheets again where will *we* be? God only knows, and how happy or miserable shall *I* be—I will not pretend at present to Investigate—or torment My brain about—for this simple reason, that God being my Supreme commander I am and for ever will be contented to act, to enjoy, to suffer or feel whatever in his Wisdom he may think best fit for me—and so well aware do I think him right in all he does, that happy or Miserable, I will enjoy or suffer perfectly satisfied that it is all for the best at Last. Go, that My Wife read this, Let my Children read it—Let the World know these My heartfelt sentiments, and believe me, my Dear Book, for ever Thy most obliged, yes truly obliged Friend. John J. AUDUBON—Citizen of the United States of North America

The aggravations caused by *Sauve Qui Peut* continued. Audubon wired a fox before dawn but could not decide where to place it or how to introduce more light into the thicket to lessen contrast with the sky. "The blue devils" forced him out in search of a coal porter to go with him to the outskirts and find stones for an accent of light in the foreground. On

January 14 he set his "miserable daub" aside until he could acquire a white pheasant as the ideal keystone of light.

Patrick Neill had been asking for five minutes to make a plaster cast of his head. This proved less of a trial than his appearance before the Society of Arts, on election, when he "shook so" he feared he would collapse in the excitement.

An invitation from Syme to exhibit with the Academy artists was incentive for another massive oil. *Black Cocks*, with its moor and Loch Lomond, was nothing so ambitious as the fox and pheasants. While Bridges watched he urged Audubon to investigate a new small prism instrument called a camera lucida, through which one had only to peer in order to arrive at correct outlines in true perspective, thanks to an English genius, William Hyde Wollaston.

The longed-for interview with Sir Walter Scott was finally arranged. Neither Brewster nor Wilson had had any luck, as neighbors of the novelist, in bringing it about. It remained for Basil Hall to obtain the appointment, the mere thought of which intoxicated Audubon: "Hundreds of times have I said quite aloud, 'Oh Walter Scott, where art thou? Wilt thou not come to my country to wrestle with mankind . . . stop their increasing ravages on Nature, and describe her for future ages . . . ? When I am presented to thee . . . I shall be mute . . . perhaps not even my eyes will dare turn towards thee, Great man. . . . "

A wigged servant ushered Audubon and Hall into Scott's study where the "great man" was standing in a purple robe, his manuscript on Napoleon's life scattered about. "No dash or glimmer or shine about him," the discerning writer judged this apparently least Gallic of Frenchmen, "but great simplicity of manners . . . slight . . . plainly dressed . . . his countenance acute, handsome and interesting, but still, simplicity is the predominant characteristic. . . . I wish I had gone to see his drawings; but I heard so much about them that I resolved not to see them—a crazy way of mine."[1]

After a day or so Audubon returned with drawings that Scott praised only halfheartedly. His plain but brilliant and much embarrassed daughter Anne tried to make amends.

Audubon, enthralled, merely took his coolness for reserve. He accepted in good faith a letter of introduction for use in London, along with an apologetic admission of ignorance of ornithology. He had not the least suspicion that Scott actually thought the birds suffered from labored and "extreme correctness."

When it came to Basil Hall's contention that the passenger pigeon paper, about to appear in Jameson's *Journal*, was anthropological nonsense, Audubon took umbrage. The jibe decidedly lowered Captain Hall in his esteem. He thought this a small reward, indeed, for labor so gruelling and so passionately sincere that his ears had been filled with "the noise of wings." "Utterly alone," he walked ten miles to shake off his gloom. The effort fatigued him more than those forty-mile sprints of his youth.

Writing had become a burden, a snare. His paper on the alligator, which he read to the Wernerians, had had a warm reception at the January meeting. They made him a "foreign member." On February 20 he was expected to speak learnedly on the rattlesnake. Dispirited by the failure of the Royal Society to elect him thus far and deeply fatigued, he nonetheless rose to speak. Of this hastily prepared treatise, from a hodgepodge of notes and impressions, he was never to hear the last.[2]

He attributed habits of the blacksnake to the rattler and had his outlandish reptile chase a squirrel into a tree, spring from limb to limb in pursuit, then kill its victim by constriction. The more conventional, not to say effective, use of venomous fangs which his *Mockingbird* and its vicious snake dramatized did not, unfortunately, figure in the chase. Whether the climbing propensities of the rattlesnake or its method of killing would wring the last or the loudest outcry from his enemies not even Audubon would live long enough to discover. His Scottish listeners were most attentive and none the wiser. After he finished, Jardine and Selby were asked to show the plates of the first volume of their new ornithology. Audubon turned, seized his *Mockingbird*, and disappeared.

The appearance on the scene of the clever nineteen-year-old painter Joseph Bartholomew Kidd gave Audubon a brilliant idea. He offered the youth free meals for lessons in "perspective," and three guineas for a copy of one of the bird portraits in oil. If the results pleased, he might offer a contract of £100 sterling, he said, for 100 oil copies. But he hesitated to tell Kidd that he was planning a universal exhibition at a thumping profit, or that his need of some such plan was critical in the extreme. Privately, he concluded that his traveling show of oils might support the *Birds* publication, his family, and himself, and provide a splendid nest egg anon.

In mid-January he accepted an invitation to visit Twizell House. Having been called a great naturalist and an artist of extraordinary gifts, he decided to bring along a few of his drawings in case of an introduction to the Duke of Northumberland. He had been gaining confidence daily in Edinburgh, particularly due to his election to the Wernerian and Antiquarian Societies and to the siege of visitors who came to his room to watch him paint and to marvel. He was sure of election to the Royal Society at his next meeting, an honor that would fortify him for the descent on London. His large new canvas depicting pheasants flushed by a fox, just finished, he looked on as a magnet to attract the eye of the nobility in that formidable city.

The Birds of America remained the driving force of Audubon's existence. He was already sure that in fifty years the Folio would command "immense prices." Confirmed in the belief, he began to distribute his prospectus on March 17, 1827. The long-desired election to the Royal Society whetted his zeal for the task.

The first American subscription came from a fashionable New York heiress and Edinburgh society favorite, Miss Harriet Douglas (1790–1872). Her nationality impelled Audubon to confide his preference for his chosen country above all others. He also, unwisely, mentioned his distrust of Jameson. Miss Douglas was glad that he had taken the advice of Hall and the Countess of Morton and got a haircut. Although she thought it made him look "like other people," he himself felt that in letting his "chevelures" be "guillotined" he was permitting God's will to be "usurped by the wishes of man." Miss Douglas rejoiced that the wolfskin coat was soon to be replaced by an English greatcoat.

The Countess of Morton felt confident that because her wishes regarding the hair and coat had been respected, the genius son of "the late French Admiral Audubon" would not find London too recalcitrant. She wondered whether her friendly designs might not cause King George himself to become the "rich patron" so ardently desired.

A March blizzard that paralyzed travel out of Edinburgh for a fortnight thwarted Audubon's anxiety to meet the "monster" London head on. Meanwhile, the smothering attentions of socialite matrons continued.

Three letters arrived from Lucy just before the storm. She announced her new situation with the agreeable William Garrett Johnson family of Beech Grove plantation, West Feliciana. She implied, but did not say directly, that the final break with Mrs. Percy had been caused by the affair of Mrs. Middlemist's money and Audubon's delay. Displeased, he answered at once that Middlemist, "a mere worm on the hearth," was out of his "books" for good. If his tour of Britain succeeded, he would send for her and the boys "without the *least hesitation*." He estimated the chances as very good, seeing that he now knew "personally, all the great men of England." He asked her to picture him in a sedan chair on his way to hear Sydney Smith deliver one of his famous sermons. "What a curious interesting book a Biographer—well acquainted with my Life could write," he reflected. "It is still more wonderful and extraordinary than that of my father!"

Less sublime was his request for facts, through some planter, on cotton cultivation and for measurements of birds, from their "guts" outward, along with sketches from Johnny. Whether his sons should "rise to eminence" depended on their application. He invited Lucy to judge for herself how far he had come from the canebrakes as he closed, "A kiss on thy lips . . . forever." [3]

On April 5, 1827, Audubon left Scotland by stagecoach for England, pausing after eleven hours at Twizell House, near Belford, Northumberland. Mrs. Selby and her visiting brother, Captain Mitford, both clever artists and assistants to Selby and Jardine, had him draw chaffinches and lapwings in his method. On his way south he prowled the turrets and bastions of Alnwick, the huge castle of the Dukes of Northumberland, with Mitford, who afterward left him near Morpeth.

At Newcastle-on-Tyne, in a cottage on a hillside, he found the famed engraver on wood, Thomas Bewick (1751–1828). The aged creator of classics on British birds and quadrupeds received him jovially. He put aside a scene of a small dog lost in a forest to see the portfolio. His hearty enthusiasm was tempered with warnings against the wiles of the book and art worlds, and particularly of the dealers and publishers, of whom he spoke contemptuously. While tea was made, he had his son play the bagpipes. Later he took up his woodblock and cut away as he confided that if he were young he, too, would try America. Within three days Bewick helped win eight subscriptions and two memberships in learned societies. He sent Audubon off with his *Birds* and *Quadrupeds* for Johnny.

The sight of lapwings wheeling and tumbling above Newcastle as he left filled him not with spring's exaltation, but with the fear of death. If only Victor and John were of an age and able to carry on, he felt he would have less apprehension about premonitions.

The Philosophical Society of York subscribed. Its officer, the ecologist Thomas Allis, head of The Retreat, a modern Quaker mental asylum, was sympathetic. (Allis was the discoverer of sclerotic bones in birds.) One member, however, Charles Waterton of nearby Wakefield, ignored a note sent to him in behalf of his too outspoken critic, Audubon.

Leeds produced five signers. The Quaker ornithologist John Backhouse seemed the most "true blue" naturalist he had met. Before leaving, Audubon walked as far as Kirkstall Abbey to sketch the ruins for Lucy on the anniversary of their parting and to swim in the icy Ayre. He had answered her latest letter: "I am uncommonly pleased that Mr. Johnson's family is agreeable to thee, and that if I wanted to go to bed to thee there I would not be sent back fifteen miles on foot to Bayou Sara instead!!! . . . Do write *why* thou left Mrs. Percy. I thought thou wert so attached to her that nothing would make you part." She had asked for a fine turban, which he cheerfully promised, but with a plea for no more questions about the latest coiffures. It puzzled him that her watch and brooch had not yet arrived.

Manchester, revisited, redeemed its previous record by adding eighteen names to the list. It also brought an order for the *Doves* in watercolor.

In Liverpool a letter from Lucy dashed Audubon's composure. She strongly desired to come over by summer, but said she must first collect a certain tuition debt of $500. Obliged to discourage her coming he sat down to urge her to sue if need be. "Thou art quite comfortable, I know, in Louisiana. Therefore wait there with a little patience." He said they must be prudent until he could better judge the future, but that she must surely know how eager he was to bring her to him. If the project foundered he would return to her, forget the *Birds*, and they would go on "together arm in arm" under the magnolias. "If I fail, America is still my country, and thou I will still find my friend."

It was painful to have to put another barrier in her way by confessing that he might have to return for more species before she could join him abroad. And it was embarrassing to have to ask her to refrain from mentioning money matters in her letters. The fact was that Hannah Mary and her mother liked to read her interesting remarks. They fairly begged for a peep into his "sacred journal."

Audubon turned to write Shippingport again and censure the year-long silence. A contrite but mildly reproachful letter was at last on its way from Victor. The boy was doing well as a clerk. He dutifully enclosed a table of Mississippi navigation data requested by his father. His uncle Nicholas, the new postmaster of Louisville, was thinking of opening a mercantile branch at Trinity village. Victor found the accolades of the English press heartening, but thought it sad that the *Birds* seemed likely to consume so many years before it rewarded either of his parents. "Mamma says you no longer speak of our going to Europe—or of your return to us. . . . "[4]

Bentley of Manchester joined Audubon on his way to London. In fact he led him about like "an ox to the slaughter." While a tailor recommended by Hall for the raven black suit that was *de rigueur* for the siege made haste, the artist went about rather self-consciously in old-fashioned pantaloons. His appearance proved immaterial to the admiring John George Children, retiring secretary of the London Royal Society, respected librarian of the British Museum's department of antiquities, and former editor of two scientific journals. The Bohn description of the ideal advocate was one Children fitted to the letter, except of course, for his lack of means. (He depended heavily on the good will of the Museum's patron and mentor, Sir Joseph Banks, through its forceful servant, Joseph Edward Gray.)

Children invited Audubon to show the portfolio to the Linnaean and Royal Societies but refrained from mentioning how little he liked to see it borne aloft on the artist's shoulders. (The loss of the drawings on the Mississippi banks had turned Audubon against porters and their remissness.) The "dull and heavy" proceedings were followed by a stimulating, if inconclusive, interview with Albert Gallatin (1761–1849), the American Minister. The aged Swiss-born diplomat assured Audubon that he could only help him reach the peevish, gouty, whist-mad King George IV by trying to slip him into one of the rare royal levees. Gallatin himself had had to wait six weeks to present his credentials. Sympathetic with scientists, he later specialized in North American ethnology. John Children queried the King's oculist, Sir J. Walthen Waller, on how to obtain this most coveted of subscriptions.[5] When the promised reply arrived it contained the expensive suggestion that *Sauve Qui Peut* be presented to the monarch.

Sir Thomas Lawrence, (1761–1830), distinguished portraitist and friend of Sully, disagreed with Sir Walthen. The "pale and pensive" Lawrence's first response to Audubon was to ask him not to call again at an ungodly half-past eight in the morning. But in the course of an orderly appointment he volunteered that the big oil might fetch 300 guineas on the market, rather than the mere perfunctory thanks of the king. Lawrence, who had made a conquest of the famous actress Mrs. Siddons, and who was at present mesmerizing her niece, the Shakesperarean player Fanny Kemble, with his "melancholy charm," thought the birds "very clever indeed." He invited Audubon to come and watch him paint and glaze; but more important, he helped find buyers for a spate of pot-boilers in oil—otters, partridges, ducks, rabbits, and common domestic fowl—which Audubon began to turn out in genuine desperation. From those he was to turn to water-color copies of small birds in his Folio, and so brilliantly as to surpass even the beauty of the originals.

A bulletin of June 16 from Lizars was the impetus for these oils, dashed off in rapid succession. They brought a negligible but at least life-sustaining $100. The letter contained the stunning announcement that the colorers, lately on strike, were still idle. "I am sorry that I cannot yet say that the coloring is recommenced," he wrote. That they would resume work at the price offered appeared unl'kely. "The high price which they have been in the habit of receiving for Mr. Selby's work has poisoned their ideas completely—one of them has gained at that work, this week, no less than £3/10/0, which is a gross imposition both upon Mr. Selby and me, and it must be remedied. Seeing that they have been in the habit of making their money so easily, and in such quantity, at that Book, it makes them reluctant at their employment, an *honest* time, in order to gain twenty or twenty-one shillings per week which is as much as they ought to have." Meanwhile, Lizars had been sending work to the colorist Graves of Peckham, but without response. "Write me," he continued to Audubon, "whether you have heard of any others in London and what are their terms, for it is best to be in possession of all the information possible on this matter."

In his dilemma Lizars had been taking art pupils—young ladies—four of whom had been worth keeping but at least ten of them so much too young and ungifted as to be dismissed. "I shall write you again . . . when I hope to give good accounts," he closed. "This has been, and yet continues to be, a most distressing business, and the more so as I cannot as yet inform you how it is to turn out."[6]

In a long, introspective message to Lucy, soon after hearing from Lizars, Audubon chose to postpone any mention of his crisis. He merely intimated that her own lot was "comparatively speaking . . . full of comforts," which included the company of their affectionate Johnny, while he himself toiled along in solitude. He did not doubt that she would have no part of his lack of like "comfort" or of his admitted insecurity. Aware of all that these lines concealed from her of his actual terror of imminent failure, he continued broodingly: "It is probable that many blame me much in America for the appearance of carelessness and absence from my family, and the same doubtless think and say that I am pleasuring whilst thou art slaving thy life away; but can they know my situation, my intentions, my wishes, or my exertions to do well and for the best? I am sure they cannot, for they do not know me a jot. Yet I have to bear the blame and hear of these things by various channels, much to the loss of my peace." He had now reached the age when he could follow his own judgment and pay no mind to unwanted "advices." In fact, he might decide to remain in England for good, if he chose. "Or accidents may send me to America once more."[7] What he meant by "accidents" he left to imagination, unmindful of the pain it would cause.

Finally, when convinced that Lizars faced defeat, Audubon sent orders, carried by Kidd, a chance visitor, to ship him a selection of both plain and colored engravings without delay. On their arrival he rushed with them to a Newman Street artist engraver, Robert Havell, whose shop he had often passed on the way to his Great Russell Street rooms. Havell, well known for his *Views of the Thames* and *Noblemen's Country Seats*, also dealt in birdskins and shells. He protested that his fifty-eight years ruled out embarking on a task almost certain to take fourteen, and offered instead to introduce Audubon to a friendly competitor, Colnaghi.

Colnaghi listened attentively to his callers. Then he brought

out a proof impression of a superlatively engraved landscape, the work of Havell's thirty-four-year-old son Robert
(1793–1878), who had fled London, years before, rather than
follow one of the professions as his father wished. Young
Havell, in town from Monmouthshire, leaped at the chance
to show his skill by rendering Audubon's *Prothonotary Warbler* beautifully on copper. Audubon did a two-step for joy,
chanting the very opposite of what he meant, "Ah, ze jeeg is
up, ze jeeg is up!"

In such a way did the firm of R. Havell & Son come into
being. Havell senior was to take charge of the coloring by a
staff eventually to number fifty men and women at the peak
of work on the gargantuan *The Birds of America*. The son was
to engrave from the original Audubon studies, with the assistance from time to time of extremely able exponents of the
art of aquatint. The "patterns," colored by the elder Havell
and assistants, would be under the surveillance of Audubon
himself. The terms—just under £115 per number of five
prints each—were one quarter less than what Lizars had
been asking for transferring the drawings onto great copper
sheets that measured up to six square feet. (Lizars had already engraved and colored more than fifty of each of the
plates for numbers 1–2.) The incomparable portraits, of
double-elephant folio magnitude—thirty-nine and one-half
by twenty-nine and one-half inches—would no longer wait
in jeopardy in Edinburgh.

To keep peace in Scotland, where Lizars could do harm
if antagonized, Audubon did not point out that his prices
angled for undue profit. Instead he appointed the engraver's
brother, Daniel Lizars, agent for the city. He also promised
to pay in full by the end of the year for labor completed, and
he said nothing about the quality of the work, which Havell
himself had granted to be poor enough to warrant certain
complaints already received. He also ordered the completion
of the remaining stock on hand without reference to the
doubtful future.

On August 6, Audubon broke his silence and let Lucy
know about his publication plans, but only in a few words

that gave no hint of the seriousness of his temporary shattering setback and precarious recovery. He changed the subject
to the "superfluity of refinement" in London and other such
matters. He reiterated his determination to have her with
him, a joy to be realized, perhaps, by his managing to circle
Great Britain two or three times yearly. He hoped, should
she come on her own, that she would bring him some "natural curiosities" for friends. If she had shipped the tree segments, seeds, and shrubs, they had not arrived, any more
than had the $200 sent in care of Alexander Gordon for a
piano that she needed, or for his use if he ran short.

Scientific enmities and rivalries had schooled the sensitive
Children. He saw to it that Audubon was kept abreast of the
latest gossip. Sometimes he quoted the powerful, conten-
tious, unpredictable Nicholas Vigors[8] or the influential Sir
Robert Inglis of the East India Company. He was too busy to
become involved, but not too busy to receive Charles Bonaparte, who invariably reminded him of similar feuding in
Philadelphia.

The Prince, more debonair than ever beneath his new
mustache and goatee, called with two distinguished friends.
His willingness to name "upwards of fifty" birds that Havell
was ready to engrave with the needed proper nomenclature
led the irrepressible Audubon to hint once more for collaboration. But it stood to reason that a fallen puppet whose valet
was still required to address him as "Your Royal Highess"
would hardly countenance an alliance with an "original,"
much less one as difficult to classify as John James Audubon.
To make up for his deafness to the plea he praised the new
drawings and insisted that the Zoological Society ought to
recognize birds claimed by Audubon as his own bona fide
discoveries.[9] He made a sincere promise to send needed
skins on his return to Rome. But collaboration was tacitly another matter—an association quite out of the question for a
"prince."

XVII. Against the Wind

H IS MAJESTY GEORGE IV signed for the *Birds* with his "particular Patronage, Protection and Approbation," in the words of his courtier Sir J. Walthen Waller, who had managed at long last to catch his ear. Sir Walthen even reported that the King had devoted some little time to examining the drawings.[1]

Audubon felt tempted to send for Lucy; instead, and until more such coups warranted that action, he shared the news calmly. As usual he asked that Johnny be kept at his "chalks and fiddle" and encouraged him to take a leaf from the nine-year-olds performing like maestros in Regents Park for a living. To the "unfair" Victor he said he was sending a flageolet, however undeserved.

He took a large canvas along on his "grand tour" of the North late in August. But 800 miles of stagecoach travel left little time for the "flock of wild turkeys" in oil, intended for the King instead of *Sauve Qui Peut* with its disappointing fox.

By late November it was not sovereign favor that obsessed Audubon but the need of five hundred—not three hun-

dred—signers to offset cancellations. Scotland's "tight dealers who with great concern untie their purses," extended a
cautious welcome. Lizars freely admitted that Havell's work-
manship was superior. He confessed to a desire to try again
as he accepted the £175 handed over to him.

The reality of Lucy's anxiety to be kept more fully informed was borne in on Audubon when he reached Liverpool. She was expecting a full account of his activities by
year's end. He asked her again to delay coming until May. By
then, with luck, he would have five or six thousand dollars a
year. But he was not such an "enthusiast" as to predict this
without reservations. Were his predictions to fail, he would,
he again insisted, dispose of his original sketches, sell his
subscription list and plates to "some bookseller for a good
sum," and give up the game. He made a point of confessing
that his oils fell short of genuine "correctness" and would
contribute little increment or prestige. (*"Man,* particularly
thy husband, cannot easily be outdone," he seemed to smile
wryly.) But Audubon did not expect to fail in the long run. A
request to Lucy for his hunting paraphernalia and Indian
trappings so that he might give them to an institution made
this clear enough.

Again he felt obliged to discourage further reference in
letters to their "pecuniary standing." He found it expedient
for the Rathbones to think him "well off, or at least independent." He had fallen more than ever into the habit of sharing
her letters with the ladies. Until he became what they chose
to imagine, Lucy must desist: "Until then, *Mum.*"[2] The recent failure of the Rathbone agency amounting to £300,000
did not mitigate his fears. He mercifully refrained from repeating a gentle protest regarding John's possible coming. "I
never dreamed of such a thing, and I love the dear boy too
much ever to part him from thee." (He had quite forgotten
that the idea had been his.)[3]

Something, perhaps the shadow of the closing year on his
conscience, impelled him to write Lucy repeatedly in December. He begged forgiveness for having assured her of his
admiration for her native country before telling Victor of his

dislike.[4] Only "blues with a vengeance" and the trials that "raised and lowered" morale could cause him to "commit these errors." Nevertheless, he was not taking the blame for all of it. He suspected, and granted, that Lucy's fear of "suffering *as much*" as he did kept her from coming. Prudence could not silence his deprecation of her attitude which, like a "lover, faithful husband," he deplored "every day, every moment." Yet she was not to imagine that he failed to pray for her each night.[5]

The tone of the letter lightened a trifle as he told her to expect the lace caps she had asked for. He had entrusted them to a brig captain, who had too much to say about the race between Clay and Jackson when he himself could think of little but 500 subscribers and a "fortune." She would be interested to know the bearer of this letter, which closed with hearty holiday wishes to her pupils, whom he called his "young ladies."[6] It was to be posted in New York by "that crazy man, Mr. Owen," who had bought the town of New Harmony, Indiana, from their "old friend" Rapp and become a "singular" architect of socialism.[7]

News from Sully dealt a blow to concentration. George Ord, Titian Peale, and their clique were excoriating the papers on the buzzard, alligator, pigeon, and, above all, the climbing rattlesnake with the unlikely fangs. They called him a liar, Münchhausen, trifler with facts. Ord had ridiculed the snake in the *Mockingbird* portrait and denied that such double-recurved fangs existed. Audubon exhorted Sully not to be hoodwinked, but instead to pass this word along.

I am not much astonished that in Philadelphia remarks such as you allude to should have been made . . . but I grieved at it. The greatest portion of my life has been devotedly spent in the active investigation of Nature. . . . For more than twenty years I have been in the regular habit of writing down every day all the incidents of which I have been an eye-witness. . . . Could I suffer myself (in relating *Tales of Wonder* which, if untrue, would load me with disgrace, ruin my family, nay prove me devoid of all honor) to be so blinded at the very moment when I am engaged in the publication of a work of unparalleled magnitude, of which the *greatest naturalists and best judges* both in America and Europe have given the fullest praise and firmest support, and from which my very means of pecuniary comfort are to be drawn . . . ? I hope I am not so devoid of common sense. . . . "*Le temps découvrira la vérité.*"[8]

Bonaparte had no direct part in the conspiracy. But these sardonic words of William Cooper of New York were in his ears even before Ord's damning innuendoes, as he sailed for Italy: "Audubon is become quite an oracle in Edinburgh, though in Philadelphia you would not receive him into the Academy. I suspect he is not to be implicitly trusted—I mean, for accuracy in his observation."[9]

Something prompted Audubon to name his true birthplace and age at the time when Ord and others were calling him a liar. Ten days before his vindictive reply to Sully he said he was born "in Santo Domingo forty-three years ago" in a letter "*To Whom it May Concern.*"[10]

He roamed the Yuletide markets bright with holly and fantastic bouquets carved from turnips and carrots; read the *Life of Tasso*, or the *Travels* of the Marquis de Chastellux; sketched a little; drew a wren for Hannah Mary and "all the parts of a duck-billed platypus" for a Greg lecture.[11] He found the play *The Hypocrite* too imitative of *Tartuffe*. He spent Christmas Eve with his bachelor subscriber, a moving spirit of the Botanic Garden and the Athenaeum, Dr. John Rutter. After attending the beautiful Church of the Blind Asylum service, he dined with Munro of the Royal Institution, then joined John Chorley. But his thoughts were of Louisiana and past celebrations.

Year-end inventory in London for a report to Lucy proved his worth—£777—twice what it was on landing.[12] It included unsold oils and ten unsold "numbers" of the *Birds,* his gold watch, and various credits. But a feverish cold and toothache and a New Year's resolution to quit snuff were not improved by the discovery that he had paid Lizars for fifty sets—250 portraits—too many. The arrival of four Edinburgh cancellations seemed a poor reward for having kept orderly accounts for the first time ever. Seizing his pen, he warned Daniel Lizars to surrender ledgers and cash and tell his brother William to remit.[13] In a matter of weeks the impecunious Kidd was appointed Edinburgh agent.[14]

John Children warned Audubon to profit by the American uproar and write for *The Birds of America* alone. He also came out once more against hoisting the portfolio across his shoulder when porters were for hire.

A conscious lack of scientific authority, the nerve-wracking supervision of flawless prints for Congress, the sad trickle of cancellations, and the raw January air brought on homesickness and bouts of insomnia. In the middle of the night Audubon rose to walk in Regents Park among the trees and the wild ducks. Not until a flock of starlings flew over at daylight did he return to down his bowl of bread and milk before withdrawing again into his art.

Bentley's arrival from Manchester with an unexpected subscription cheered him. They rode an elephant at the Cross Menagerie; called on the famous taxidermist Leadbetter; saw a play at Drury Lane that Audubon thought vulgar; and walked and talked in the Zoological Garden. But after Bentley left, Audubon turned "dull as a beetle." Even his *White-Headed Eagle*, of which he had been so proud, displeased his jaundiced eye. He took away its feast of goose and placed a catfish before it, then strove for more harmony between sky and shore.[15] The power of enmity and envy to obstruct, and of wealth to open the way for the deserving if it but would, were bitter food for thought.

Wealth soon appeared in an unexpected guise. At a dinner given by Colonial Under Secretary Robert W. Hay, kin to the Dalmahoy antiquarian W. H. Hay, Audubon thought he had found the perfect sponsor. The latter informed his brother on March 15, 1827: "Mr. Audubon is son of the late French Admiral Audubon, but he himself has lived from his cradle in the U.S., having been born in one of the French colonies."[16] Hay then wrote to a certain Eubank of Valenciennes that "this son of a Vice-Admiral" doubtless belonged to a "superior class" and could be assured of a good reception on the Continent, owing to his "great attainments as a Naturalist." He added that "26 years" of endeavor figured toward issuing descriptions for a letterpress to accompany his Folio of *Birds*.[17] To Edward Vernon he said much the same, adding that the wife of the "Vice-Admiral" was still alive "at a very advanced age in France," although in fact she was dead.[18]

The Marquis of Lansdowne, president of the Zoological Society, kept his distance both before and after Audubon's election to that body and nomination by the Linnaeans. His self-esteem much increased by that honor, Audubon paid Selby the dubious compliment of being Britain's best bird delineator—up to the moment. Envious of both, Nicholas Vigors encouraged their rivalry by confiding that British species had been but superficially treated. Presently, more than money prevented his taking up that challenge. A war crisis loomed; the failure of the British Museum to show interest in *The Birds of America* did its share of harm. Sir Thomas Lawrence, whose opinion counted, was rumored to be calling the aquatints "bad" and the portfolio "so-so." The impertinent young Earl of Kinnoul told Audubon to his face that his birds were all alike and a swindle. Only by dint of stubborn courage did Audubon pack for Cambridge in March. As he was leaving, a cage of larks arrived from Yorkshire; although he would have preferred to set them free, he left them with Robert Sully, a brother of the painter.

The scarcity of doorpulls and numerals—removed by student pranksters—ended a search for rooms. He found the Blue Boar Inn, and thanks to letters he was well received in the candlelit Gothic banquet hall by the gowned, white-haired vice-chancellor, as well as by the dons. In Trinity Chapel he did not permit the large wig that blocked his view as he prayed among the "Very Reverend, Deans," and white-robed collegians to interfere with his supplications, albeit it would have made a "capital bed for an Osage."

Back in London with five new subscriptions, he wrote Lucy that if fifty more subscribers could be gained they could retire, "perfectly independent," within ten years. He was sending her French kerchiefs, gloves, and enough cambric for half a dozen gowns. Now that her draft for $200 had arrived, she could also look for her piano, which a musician would help select.[19]

A ride on top of the stagecoach to Oxford, against buffeting winds, was redeemed by far less cordiality. Inferior work sent earlier by Daniel Lizars was held accountable for the fact that only Radcliffe Library and the School of Anatomy—and not a single one of the twenty-two colleges—subscribed. The bugling of anthems by a fellow passenger in uniform on the bitter ride back to the city cheered Audubon somewhat. And the plight of a couple trudging barefoot along the road made his own lot tolerable.

A letter from the new natural history magazine *Loudon's* awaited him. With flattering insistence John Claudius Loudon offered a tempting eight guineas for a series of articles. Afraid of the perils of authorship, Audubon agreed to surrender only his *Notes on the Bird of Washington,* a short piece, and this only because he was promised a glowing review by the zoologist William Swainson.[20] Swainson was to illustrate his remarks with line drawings after the *Birds;* Traill had once praised him to Audubon. He was engaged on an important study of American fauna with John Richardson of London.

However, still hopeful of involving Bonaparte in his endeavors, Audubon did not intend to replace him with Swainson, although he meant to do so if he must. Without such help he knew that he would have to think "strongly of returning to America" in defeat by summer. And defeat it would be, where neither Clay nor Adams had acknowledged his gift to Congress, and where De Witt Clinton was no longer alive to intervene. Instead of offering Swainson the desired first "numbers" of the *Birds* at cost in return for a good review, Audubon asked him to accept a gift of needed notes on the American shrike. He excused his refusal with the explanation that the actual cost to him of the prints remained twice what a nominal charge for help would come to. Yet he did not deny that his gamble in England had reached the critical stage.

Again he sounded out his brotherly confessor, the Prince, for whom he said he would do "anything" in his power, Bonaparte having hired an illustrator other than himself notwithstanding. If, as the estimable Temminck thought he should, he would associate himself with Audubon for a study of British birds, the "crafty booksellers could not best them." Audubon did not know that, for a year or longer, "numbers" sent to the Prince via the New York Customs had been idling undelivered in Manhattan. Bonaparte had asked Cooper to get after the "accursed" officials, and also, for expediency, to see that Audubon received his own second volume of *American Ornithology*. "He writes to me that he is delighted at the success of his vast enterprise," he confided to Cooper. "A few will patronize poor Audubon in America."[21]

Audubon's sycophantic letter was on its way just as a petulant one arrived from Italy about the missing aquatints. He got off his apologies and begged to have an unsparing critique as soon as the bird portraits reached Bonaparte:

> My lot, I believe, is that I should spend my life for the benefit of science in a very humble way, unknown, neglected, but happy still in the knowledge that I am at least trying to do good. I have been always very proud to be able to say that you have used me as a friend; and to forward science in your wake is an honor worthy the attention of every man. It would give me great pleasure and courage . . . could I ever deserve your attentions. I am desirous of having every portion of your *Ornithology* and labors, and will most heartily thank you for a copy. I do not know how I would have engaged in the nomenclature of our birds, had I not had your valuable observations on the nomenclature of Wilson's *Ornithology*.[22]

The Prince's reply came bathed in vinegar to rid it of Italian plague germs. He declined to change his mind and repeated his intention to abandon American studies.

Audubon protested: "So much remains to be done . . . that it is now with a sore heart that I must relinquish the ardent wish I had—to see, before my death, the natural history of that fine country fairly investigated!" He dramatized his own strivings: "Many besides yourself expected my work would fall through, but I have industry, perseverance and honesty on my side." The Prince was not to worry about the prints, because they would be replaced by a man not disposed to cheat, no matter how often cheated. The original drawings from which they came he said he would burn before he would see the booksellers traffic with them:

. . . as I never expect to be remembered, I shall not be disappointed and blame no one. On the contrary, had I trusted to others, I should *most likely have been ruined*, and should have censured all concerned. . . . You say that I ought to make a great deal of noise. Ah my dear Sir, I am not the man for this. Accustomed to a solitary life since my youth, forever bent on admiring the calmness of Nature in her more primitive state, I shun my species and live retired, almost unknown in London, and so neglected that many in my situation would die of a broken heart. . . . When I am *thrusted* into company I act as if a grizzly bear, and wish myself alone from the very moment that I enter a fashionable circle until I return to my lonely room.[23]

The spate of letters might have ended there if Bonaparte had not been enraged to find his name far down on the list in the new prospectus. Gratified though Audubon may have been by this inverted compliment, he put himself out to make amends. To flatter the Prince he hinted for a full-length engraved portrait of Napoleon Bonaparte, whose nephew, "a superior man," he wished always in his own simplicity to regard as a preceptor.[24]

Swainson's review in *Loundon's Magazine* was ecstatic. It lifted Audubon to such euphoria that he did not even take alarm when one of Havell's colorers, whom he had rebuked for his "miserable daubing," led a threatened walkout.

"How you have raised my talents . . . inflamed my passions with the desire to reach the degree of eminence you have been pleased to say I possess!" Audubon wrote Swainson, saying besides:

Ah, my dear Sir, that I could return to the woods of our vast western Continent, supported by a patron of wealth of such taste and knowledge as yours. Then indeed would my pencil be eager to portray the delicate and elegant contours of the feathered tribes . . . the flowers, too . . . ! How happy should I die when assured that science, by my feeble efforts, had advanced one step in its progress. . . . You, my dear Mr. Swainson, have proved without ever having seen me, that you knew my feelings, sentiments and wishes. You have made my birds fairly prattle [in your illustrations] . . . I saw doves both coy and cooing—I felt as if I must tread lightly and with care to avoid the venomous rattler. . . . Anxious as I am that your kindnesses should not fall short of their intentions, I have . . . sent to the editor of the *Times*, a copy of your agreeable review. . . . I will visit you in a few days. . . . Then, my dear Sir, it will be that congenial spirits meet!![25]

Late in May, after delays caused by work and weather, Audubon reached the Swainson farm, a modest place near London. He had warned the family to look for "an extremely plain man" anxious never to intrude.[26]

He made his peace with the discovery that Swainson and Ord had been corresponding for at least four years. Feigning resignation, he showed Swainson how he himself would wire a chaffinch. He captivated the Swainson children by his banter and expressed his appreciation of Mrs. Swainson's musical talents. The absence of his family he explained as largely due to Lucy's horror of ocean travel.

Audubon had no oil good enough for the great annual spring competition; but paint his way into it—and perhaps into Windsor Castle—he knew he must. He took out a rough sketch brought from the United States and decided to work it up into an arresting picture. In mid-June he sent this requisition to Swainson in order to begin:

> Have you in your neighborhood a young lamb . . . pure white . . . to be sacrificed for the purpose of becoming immortalized on canvas by J. J. A., F. A., S. E., etc., etc.? If you have . . . pray pay for it and send it . . . alive in a basket . . . and when you come next to town you will see him, mouth open, nostrils expanded, his eyes swollen . . . panting and vainly trying to escape the fiery Golden Eagle that has come to seize it . . . *merely* to feed his young. . . . I shall hope to see the gentle thing tomorrow or next day.[27]

Swainson sent the lamb. Cross, of the menagerie in King's Mews, supplied the golden eagle. "It went to our hearts to send you the poor little lamb for slaughtering," wrote Swainson, "but I must be content to purchase immortality with life."

Sir Walthen Waller saw the oil entitled *Eagle and Lamb* as soon as it left the easel. Pleased that he thought it good enough to offer Queen Adelaide, Audubon elected instead to keep it as a spot of honey. In a suite of the Havell building at 79 Newman Street he began to paint a fresh stream of potboilers on canvas.

Vigors tried, unsuccessfully, to persuade Audubon to write for the Zoological Society *Journal* at an attractive rate.[28] His intuition dictated a refusal that some imagined "jibes" in *Blackwood's* for June made easy.[29]

Extremely vulnerable by August because of his struggle to master oils, he gave Lucy a taste of his bitterness. He wrote that he doubted five rooms at 100 pounds a year, or a possible income of 500 would content her.[30] She had better, he said, postpone coming with John until after New Year's. His message was only a few days out to sea when a shocking ultimatum arrived. Lucy, in turn, was tired of his evasions, weary of the impositions of her employers, and bent on finding a happier situation. A loan from her brother William had enabled her to send John north to the Bardstown school near Louisville. Once he was out again and apprenticed to William, she hoped she might save enough to live near her own people. Certainly if her husband offered nothing but vague promises she would follow her lights. As for the aquatints he had sent for her to dispose of, this had not been easy.

Suicidally despondent, Audubon grieved to Swainson that Lucy was insisting he return to their "humble" and "happier" life and jettison his ambitions. It was well he had no "instrument" of self-destruction handy, or a "woeful sin" might be committed.[31] "Would you go to Paris with me?" he asked, returning to their idea of a joint mission for separate but sympathetic ends.

Having lost all heart for work he consented to pose in a green frock coat for the artist C. R. Parker, whom he had known since Natchez days.[32] His eyes lacked their usual gleam, but his jaw was more forceful than in his lugubrious self-portrait of five years earlier.

The Swainsons agreed to the Paris sojourn. Parker also caught the fever. Audubon rushed about to learn rates and routes and obtain visas. It would have taken more than Bonaparte's niggling reaction to the aquatints to dampen his spirits. The Prince was challenging his right to name the Yellowthroat for Roscoe when it belonged to Vieillot.[33] But more important, he disputed with smoldering resentment— and quite justly—the naming of the Stanley Hawk, which his friend Cooper had already published as Cooper's Hawk.

Erroneously, however, he claimed that Audubon's Louisiana Water Thrush did not originate with him but with Alexander Wilson.

Audubon refrained from arguing over the hawk he had named in honor of Lord Stanley. The matter had sowed dissension never to end between him and Cooper. He merely admitted, philosophically, that his lack of "a classical education" was a hindrance.[34] But he believed, and said so, that the accuracy of his drawing, based as it was on keen observation, made up for his academic deficiencies.

Bonaparte wrote, still more forthrightly, to Cooper to say that only thirty-six of forty-five species claimed by Audubon were bona fide. Yet he pronounced the *Mockingbird* a "really wonderful picture," regardless of the prominence of the rattlesnake in the composition.[35] Exactly how prominent the snake happened to be, Bonaparte, Cooper, Audubon, and plenty of others were soon to find out.

XVIII. Paris

AUDUBON, SPORTING A TAILED FUR CAP, left Charing Cross at 8:00 A.M. on September 1, 1828, with the Swainsons and Parker. Eight persons, among them a French trapeze artist with a balancing pole, his wife and child, and a girl whose starched blue ribbons stiffly rode the breeze, scrambled on top of the stage for places amid the clutter. Audubon teased that Mrs. Swainson need have no dread of the overnight pause at Dover. He and Parker would spread their cloaks on the beach for her like Raleigh for the Queen.[1] Nor need the party fear that the rumored "undue advantages" taken of the foreigner in Paris would affect them while he was in charge. He and his jolly party hoped to return to London via Holland.

At the end of the rough, three-and-one-half hour crossing of the Channel they boarded a wretched diligence driven by a fellow in gaudy livery. A plodding seven and one-half miles an hour for a day and a night made even the green loveliness of Normandy, its hedgeless fields, and sheer poplar windbreaks monotonous. But a pause at Amiens Cathedral offered one memorable interlude along the way before the lumbering vehicle deposited its stiff, weary passengers at the Messagerie Royale.

Audubon registered at the Hotel de France near the Louvre. He and Parker went with Swainson directly to the Jardin des Plantes to see Cuvier. The tall, swarthy, beaked Georges Léopold Chrétien Frédéric Dagobert Cuvier enjoyed the prestige of a latter-day Aristotle or Linnaeus. The noted zoologist of the Duke of Orléans's Museum of Natural History knew Swainson's name from published papers. But he had never heard of Audubon. The artist quickly informed him that he had named a wren in his honor. From then on Cuvier's gray eyes remained on his fellow Frenchman; the two spoke too rapidly for Swainson to follow.

Audubon was braver than he knew. Eighty-year-old Louis-Jean-Pierre Viellot, born near Le Havre and now near death, knew from bitter experience the dangers to be faced among the lions in the French arena of science. He too had reluctantly divided his life between business and the study of birds, first in Paris, then on Saint-Domingue from 1790 until his flight from conscription in 1798, when he spent about eight months among the southern birds of the United States. His *Histoire des Oiseaux de l'Amérique Septentrionale* (1807)— interrupted by the death of his collaborator, the painter Audubert, after two volumes of 131 plates—meets with as much respect among modern ornithologists, despite certain inevitable limitations, as it did with inexplicable indifference in his time. Leclerc, Buffon, and Cuvier virtually ignored him. Yet the contribution of Vieillot is said to rival that of Alexander Wilson in some respects, on account of his detailed descriptions and delineations, and his early recognition of immature plumage. Much of his naming of genera and species remains in good standing.

When Cuvier introduced his visitors at the French Royal Academy of Sciences, Audubon occupied the place of honor. After someone's dry lecture on the mole, Cuvier rose and introduced him as a native of Louisiana and a former pupil of David. (Visiting Linnaeans from London thought of him rather as a native of Santo Domingo.) Calling attention to the *Birds* that lay on the table in a splendid portfolio rented for

their French debut, Cuvier granted a long-standing preference for Alexander Wilson among the North American de-
lineators. But he quickly added that the bird portraits by
Audubon were the equal of any ever published in Europe or
abroad. Indeed, he conceived of them as "the greatest monument yet erected by Art to Nature," surpassing "in magnificence" anything of the kind ever likely to be painted.

Audubon was content, yet he thought Cuvier's remarks,
published in the *Mémoires* of the Academy, less "feelingly
written" than Swainson's had been for *Loudon's*. He chafed
to put them into his printed prospectus. Some days later the
prestigious journal *Le Moniteur Universel* carried a long impressive tribute by Cuvier to Audubon and his bold, beautiful undertaking.

The Prince of Massena, sports-loving son of a marshal of
Napoleon, had heard from Charles Bonaparte about "the
man of the woods" and his "wonderful drawings," sometimes facetiously called by Audubon his "pamphlet." With a
flourish the grandee put his name beneath that of the Duke
of Rutland, but he warned against expecting much of impoverished France. The engraver Duménil,[2] to whom the Prince
sent Audubon, repeated the warning. The scarcity of copper
and colorers in Paris discouraged all thought of shifting the
work to France.

There were as many exclamations over the price of the
Birds as on its size and beauty when it was shown for a second time at the Academy. One typically indifferent banker
granted that all he knew of birds was the usefulness of their
quills for posting ledgers.

Swainson resented the neglect of his own publications in
the furor over Audubon's work. He cringed whenever Audubon proclaimed himself "the first ornithological painter
and the first practical naturalist in America."[3] The room that
was given them for study at the Museum held no charms for
Audubon, whose time was taken up with calls, art galleries,
and strolls about the city. Swainson persuaded him to inter-
pret for him in the birdskin markets a time or two. He went
with Mrs. Swainson to the Louvre, but his fur cap caused
them to be turned away at the main entrance. By this time

rapport between the Swainsons and Audubon had reached the vanishing point, or nearly; and the couple were running so short of francs that they had to cut their visit short and return to England.

Parker remained to paint portraits of Cuvier, Redouté, and others through Audubon's intervention. His introduction to Pierre Joseph Redouté was the one given Audubon by Charles-Alexandre Lesueur in 1824 in Philadelphia. Redouté, "the Audubon of roses," whose floral art Audubon himself declared "incomparably better" than any other on earth, readily agreed to an exchange of works. He sent the American artist to the Duke of Orléans, future king.[4] Redouté was drawing master to the daughters of the Duke, a startlingly handsome cleft-chinned former exile with a manner far from lordly.

The Duke helped to open the portfolio, gazed enraptured at the *Baltimore Oriole,* and spouted, half in French, half in English, "This surpasses all I have seen, and I am not astonished now at the eulogiums of Monsieur Redouté!" He asked to be allowed to keep the samples as part of his subscription. Instead, Audubon promised him, in addition to other things, his oil of *Black Grouse,* then hinted for a letter to the Viscount Martignac, minister of the interior, in charge of the Royal Libraries. The Duke obliged and also promised lines of introduction to various monarchs.

It was the scientist Valençiennes who led Audubon to one of the dazzling late *soirées* of François Gérard (1770–1837), celebrated portrait painter. Gérard had studied under David years before the "woodsman" could have done so. "Welcome, brother in the arts!" he greeted Audubon. The *Paroquet* and *Mockingbird* so transported him that he seized his guest's hand and declared, "Mr. Audubon, you are the king of ornithological painters—we are all children in France and Europe! Who would have expected such things from the woods of America?"[5] The elegant company that had deserted their card games to look on politely echoed his compliments but again fell to gaming without any sign of that economic austerity of which Audubon had been warned.

Day after day he waited to hear from the ministers of state. To pass the time he roamed through the Louvre, the Panthéon, the King's Library, and the Institute of France. He went to hear *La Muette* and *Semiramis,* saw *Fiésque,* and looked in on the casinos and billiard rooms. He and Paker rode out to St. Cloud to watch 50,000 celebrants at a fête, with its musicians, jugglers, dancers, and lively concessions. They also toured the palace at Versailles.

Long since weaned away from the faith of his baptism, Audubon nevertheless heard Mass at Notre Dame de Paris one Sunday and was stirred by the organ music. At the *Champs de Mars* he watched a Mameluke fly around the course on a wild Arabian mare in an unforgettably exciting race. On another day he perched on a wall above the Plains of Issy to witness a review of the militia by pale, stooped, ugly old Charles X, whose feathered tricorn and blue shoulder sash were almost near enough to touch. He ignored the smiles and stares at his fur cap. His mind was rather on the ease with which King Charles could—if he chose—jog his ministers into subscribing without more delay!

Of all his memories of these peripatetic, none too happy days, Audubon's eight or nine meetings with Cuvier were most cherished. The Baron suggested that he appoint a Paris dealer, Pitois of Leverault, Pitois et Cie, as his French agent.

His ordeal of waiting not yet over, he idled in the King's Garden early in October. A one-eared, toeless veteran of Napoleon's march on Moscow (which he himself had so adroitly missed) declined a coin. A lively Punch and Judy traded blows in their tall, narrow box. Shuttlecocks flew, and children scrambled for chestnuts under nearly barren trees. It seemed to Audubon, as he wandered, that the four names signed on the Continent for *The Birds of America* hardly warranted a festive return to Couëron after an absence of more than twenty years. It would take a good thirty-four hours by the public diligence to reach his childhood home. Besides that, the zoologist René-Primavère Lesson had yet to be approached.

Rapport with Lesson was disturbingly swift. Not only was

he born in Rochefort (a signal for caution), but his discovery that Audubon came from Couëron prompted him to send at once for his protégé, Charles-Henry-Marie D'Orbigny. A medical student with an affinity for natural history so marked that he was about to dedicate his life to its pursuit, D'Orbigny was the son of the Audubon family doctor who in 1807 had left Couëron for Noirmoutier Island down the coast. From there he had moved to La Rochelle to become chief physician at the naval base, a post he still occupied. His cottage, near there, was filled with shells and birds that were to form the nucleus of the La Rochelle natural history museum, the nursery of the family genius.

Audubon at once mistook this son for his godchild, the one for whom he and Rose had been sponsors—Gaston— actually born a year before the younger Charles-Henry. A third son, Alçide, a disciple of Cuvier, was away in the Canaries and South America for studies. The twenty-one-year-old needed no reminder from the astounded, badly shaken Audubon that his father had once been his "most intimate friend" or that he had called him "Fifi," a pet name for birds and bird idolators.

It so happened that the elder D'Orbigny had borrowed heavily in his last distressed year in Couëron, sometimes for bare necessities with his wife's Paimboeuf property as security. His debt to Lieutenant Audubon had reached $800, and there it still stood. Attempts to collect had failed. Gabriel and the mayor of Esnandes had exchanged notes about D'Orbigny, no friend of the official. In 1819 Gabriel had entreated the doctor to pay Madame Audubon, whose hands were "full of notes" and who could "be patient" no longer. Two years later he was accusing him: "Not a single word from you. . . . Why do you abandon us in this way? By this notice I invite you to give us what you owe us; circumstances force us to ask. I am convinced you mean well. . . ."[6]

Here, before Audubon, stood a son of D'Orbigny, sure to have known all about the unhappy proceedings, but—more important—certain also to know that the self-styled "American woodsman" was in reality "Jean Rabin, creole of Saint-Domingue," once better known as Jean-Jacques-Fougère Audubon. D'Orbigny, senior, had witnessed both names in Gabriel's power-of-attorney, notarized in Henderson, Kentucky. More than the breach made the D'Orbignys anathema to Audubon at this moment. From 1803 until 1817 his octoroon half-cousin, Louise Bouffard, unwed daughter of Rose and Gabriel Bouffard (the younger), had lived with the latter's sister, the widow Supiot. She had arrived, at twenty-six, under the stigma of color; her mother, still in Haiti, had asked Gabriel and Rose to find out why she no longer heard from Louise ("Laize").[7]

Young D'Orbigny's sympathetic remarks in regard to Anne Moynet's passing came as a thunderbolt to Audubon, who did not know that for seven years his foster mother had been in her grave.

Audubon's sad, inescapable conclusion was that the lawsuit of the grasping relations and their vilification of him and Rose Bonnitte could not but have reverberated to the D'Orbignys. They knew the ugly ramifications, and, for that matter, more than did he himself, by now, about his father's tangled affairs. Troubles had been aired too often and too long for much of anything to be hidden.

That night he poured his torment into his diary. Only a bowdlerized "copy" survives.[8] His granddaughters, zealous to protect their grandfather's secret rather than preserve it "for daws to peck at," burned the original. The three spinsters, at odds with reality, made use of such lines as these to foster the "little lost dauphin" legend around the romantic figure of Audubon:

> . . . Oh how much I wish that I could go to Nantes, but alas!—I can not. Thou, only, my Lucy, knowest the reasons. The cloud that still hangs over my birth requires silence.—I must change the subject, my heart is ready to burst. . . . A singular incident took place today while with Monsieur Lesson. . . . Lucy, my blood congealed in my veins—but what am I about, oh my book, I dare not relate. . . .

Daylight brought no composure, but only the stark dread that Cuvier and the rest would learn the truth. Would young D'Orbigny speak out? If he chose to, the scandal would drift to England and thence across the ocean to enemies enough.

A day later, still in the grip of the nightmare, Audubon supposedly wrote on:

I felt as if to remain in France and to be known as I now must shortly be known to be in France, was dreadful, and made me tremble. . . . As I was going to the minister I thought of my birth, of my curious life, and of the strange incidents that have brought me to what I am *now* known to be. I felt more than once as if now was the moment to dispel the cloud and again I reflected on the consequences, wiped the stream of water that ran cold over my forehead, and concluded to carry my extraordinary secret to the grave. . . . Oh, how cruelly situated I am—and yet perhaps it is best that it should be so. . . . Lesson was in Rochefort at the time my father commanded the post, but too young, he said, to remember him. Had I told him that my father was—stop, here I am again to fly the track—peace, peace, Audubon. Good night, my Lucy, for myself I shall not close my eyes.

In the morning he allegedly continued as follows, while finding no consolation in his pen:

Oh my Lucy, what a night I have had. Oh, that I could see my father's mortal shape and obtain from his goodness the removing of the oath. . . . I turned over and over in my sweated bed until wearied (not by remorse) by sorrow. I was glad to see glimpses of daylight to change the scene. How much of my father's life I passed over would fill my book, and the strange scenes attached to my own early life so stared me in the face that I saw naught but spectres before me, Santo Domingo, France, and my beloved country all had their turn. How dreadful.—I have heard of men's hair and beard turning white on unexpected extraordinary incidences, but I was truly shocked at seeing myself in the glass whilst shaving, and yet I am perfectly innocent and so was my dear Father. . . . Lucy, I am quite wild, when young I was easily taught to keep silence and thought nothing of it, but now that I have children myself, children that at one word of mine would rise to eminence and would be— stop thy pen, or forever be damned, Audubon. I see my father before me with his proud eagle's eye frowning as if I had leaped over the abyss. But no.—No, never. Oh my Lucy, how I regret this journey, it has opened all my wounds afresh. . . . I must try to bury the dreadful past in oblivion. . . . I understand now why my father demanded of me a most solemn oath . . . I could have had no legitimate heir . . . cruel, cruel, but who may foresee the future.[9]

Audubon recovered sufficiently to go forth—indeed, to dance attendance on the ministers. Their procrastination, while he saw waves of finches migrating overhead, made him long to sail away and be lost and forgotten in the woods of the New World. Baron de la Brouillerie, the King's representative, finally handed him several subscriptions, bringing his list to fourteen—subscriptions which were to prove less real than apparent.[10]

Audubon boarded the diligence for Calais with his drawings, two fine Angora cats, Redouté's *Belles Fleurs*, and a pair of new boots. He also carried two small engravings, one a portrait of Cuvier, the other a fanciful *Phidias and the Thorn*. Two nuns who rode beside him to Boulogne "stirred not, spoke not, saw not," and turned a deaf ear to his "few remarks." At Calais his boots and cats disappeared, but the Channel that he longed to recross lay before him. He wondered when or whether his old friend D'Orbigny would reply to a friendly letter that he sent to him from Paris.

Gadwall, *1821*. *Pencil, ink, and watercolor
drawing. Courtesy The New-York Historical
Society, New York. Original study for plate
348 of* The Birds of America.

XIX. Strange Ultimatum

S WAINSON KEPT TO HIMSELF at Tyttenhanger Green. He did
not confide to his erstwhile companion details of a contract of his own with Robert Havell.

One night, his sleep troubled, Audubon "got up, struck a
light," and began to search his journal. He thought he might
come across "errors" responsible for his nightmare. "I am
not, I believe, superstitious," he told Swainson as he described a dream in which they stood face to face as "violent
enemies," sword in hand. "Yet I felt extremely uneasy."[1]

Swainson answered that dreams "must always be inter-
preted *contrawise*."[2] He took advantage of Audubon's obviously worried and solicitous state to ask for a loan of fifty
pounds, but did not explain that it was to go to Havell for
engraving his new *Zoological Illustrations*. Audubon then tried
proposing an exchange of works and offered also to have
Johnny send Swainson skins and to jog Jardine for more. He
congratulated Swainson on the favorable notice given his
Paris visit in the latest issue of *Loudon's*. He insisted Swainson ought not to imagine that certain French scientists meant

any offense by neglecting to ask for an exchange of studies. But, true to form, he did not fail to predict that Mrs. Swainson would be titillated by the latest *Winter's Wreath* piece on his long past January idyll on the Mississippi with Rozier. He expressed satisfaction with his own French mission and the fact that the Roman press had copied Cuvier's review.

Audubon dared not lose Swainson. To fortify himself against the eventuality he took Vigors, with whom Swainson happened to be feuding, into his confidence about the possible need for technical help. The volatile, whimsical, and selfish Vigors was unresponsive.

Audubon, therefore, wrote one more exploratory letter to Bonaparte. Hopeful that the Prince had read of his triumph in Paris, he said it was sad that the Philadelphians had "considerably lessened" the chances of their collaboration by labeling with "*a scoundrel*" when first they met. He added that, were the die cast, he must never more "push" for favors from any man but rely on industry alone to see himself through—perhaps eventually with luck as far as the South Seas for untold discoveries.[3] Convinced that this would bring Bonaparte around, he ventured to tell Swainson that collaboration with Prince Charles was a foregone conclusion.

Bravura also crept into his tone with Lucy. Where, first, he had written on his return to London that his weariness of separation made him "sick at heart," and yet that he feared she would not be content with his "means," he began to demand that she come or else face divorce. His "144 subscribers" would assure them a comfortable £600 a year, or enough for their mutual keep in a simple way of life. This he asked her to reject or accept along with him. If the piano was so disappointing and the gowns were saltwater damaged he would send no more.

Soon after posting this message Audubon reconsidered and began again remorsefully: "I think that it is thy wish to come over to me, and I am truly happy at the thought. Although I have not accumulated the wanted fortune . . . I think we might live together tolerably comfortable. . . . Should thou determine on coming, *thou wilt be welcome,* and thy husband will do his very best to render thy days and nights comfortable. To have thee willingly with me will add to my industry. . . . Never mind the piano . . . thou wilt have a good one here." But if she should be "discontented" after coming his "faculties" would desert him.[4]

Not one to underestimate the importance of Victor's approval, he sent Shippingport an ecstatic account of Paris and spoke of Gérard and Redouté as his "school mates." (The former was fifteen years his senior, the latter a full generation.) He begged Victor to see how the *Birds* might consume fourteen more years, and why he could send only for Lucy. "Your Mamma alone is all that I may expect to see, and she is not willing to come over until I have acquired a great fortune. How long, then, I may be without her is quite unknown, and I feel perplexed the oftener I think of it. . . . I assure you it always gives me pain to write her with so little hope of meeting her desires."[5]

A falling out with the elder Havell dashed the long-since forced mutual confidence, the insouciance. Robert the younger took over the contract in all its details. On him alone *The Birds of America* began to depend. Audubon's progress would thenceforth hang by the delicate thread of harmony with the son. The argument—failure to sell the remaining oils, and doubt that Kidd could work fast enough to bring the "perpetual exhibition" about in time—radically changed Audubon's tune. Were it not for his "extraordinary" undertaking he would leave England, he confessed to Lucy. "Dreadfully fatigued" of their separation, he said he would finish up, "dispose of plates, copyright and so forth," and thus have ample means for them to settle in America near their "dear children." Many nights were "sleepless" from the fear that he and she might "never meet again."[6]

Only to Swainson did he reveal the depths of his despair. "I have the *blues* completely," he admitted to his puzzling friend in terms that dissolved his wonted reserve—or, at any rate, for the Yuletide. "I would lay ten shillings," replied Swainson, "that old Havell has been disappointing you as he has done me. He is, in matters of business, a complete *daudle*—an old woman, and I have done with him. His son I think better of; he has a good idea of punctuality in business." That Havell senior was a "daudle" Audubon agreed. *"Je lui ai donné son congé pour toujours!"* he promptly announced, determined to confine his business to the son's shop two doors beyond the paternal establishment, which he had given its "walking papers."[7]

On Christmas Day, Sir Thomas Lawrence sought to make up for his remissness. But Audubon was dining at the house of the merchant George Goddard, nephew of a Philadelphia friend of Mease and Harlan. The presence of his "amiable pupil Miss Hudson" and her mother, cousins of his host, made the occasion particularly delightful. The charming, well-chaperoned girl had shown gratifying talent for, as Audubon expressed it, turning some of his drawings of the birds into "pictures."[8] Mrs. Heermann, the phantomlike Madame André of New Orleans, Eliza Pirrie of *Oakley*, and even the adoring Hannah Mary Rathbone and Jane Roscoe had posed no real threat to his equilibrium in the absence of his beloved Lucy; nor did Miss Hudson.

While they sat among the guests of Goddard, Sir Thomas, who was then at the opposite end of London, followed Havell upstairs to choose from among Audubon's canvasses for the Burlington House spring exhibition. "Admirable," he pronounced the *Otter.* "Fine!" he said of the *Eagle and Lamb.*[9] But *Sauve Qui Peut*—the white hope—elicited no comment whatever. Lawrence withdrew merely with the promise that he would make his choice after the meeting of the Royal Academy of Fine Arts, over which he would preside.

It was reasonable to assume that the voice of the highest officer would have weight. Audubon's confidence grew, momentarily. But no canvas of his was to be shown under such auspices in competition by spring or ever. His painful excursions into the forbidding province of oils were near an end. In a matter of weeks the Duke of Orléans would be telling a secretary to decline the pictures promised him in Paris.[10]

Audubon's doubts of Lucy's coming turned to rage. So did the ennui of London. A growing conviction that he should go home for a year to draw new species and redraw others reached its climax after New Year's. On January 20, 1829, he booked passage for the first of April and announced his plans to Lucy. "I had no wish to go there so soon, although I have often repeated to thee, I always intended to go on account of my work; but I have decided on doing so *now* with a hope that I can persuade thee to come over here with me and under my care and charge . . . never to part again."

He could not, at first, go as far south as Louisville, but proposed meeting her there—if she wished—after the migrations and nesting were over. His spring and summer would have to be spent in the northeastern states. She was not to fret about the progress of his "stupendous work" in London; John Children had agreed to serve as agent and to look in on the engraving at frequent intervals. The reliable Miss Hudson and her mother would be the custodians of his drawings and dole them out to Havell as needed. Miss Hudson would also keep a weather eye on the work itself. Lucy would find him "of the same sound heart," if much altered in manners, and, oddly enough, a full inch taller. "But we will talk of that when again our lips will meet."[11]

Again and again he had named his birds for friends. (Why, he still asked himself, did the "Queen Bee" decline the honor finally conferred, instead, on Charles Bonaparte?) Thus far, none bore Lucy's name—Lucy's Warbler. This would not do. To name a bird Bakewell's warbler would be to honor her undeserving kinsmen. The alternative was to omit her name and pay tribute in another way. Possibly in order to be able to say, when they met, that she would yet see herself immortalized among her "rivals," the birds, Audubon wrote on the margin of his study of the Swamp Sparrow: "Mr. Havell will please have Lucy Audubon name on this plate instead of mine." The May apple twig in the drawing suggests Joseph Mason's hand. Nevertheless, Havell incised on the margin, "Drawn from Nature by Lucy Audubon."[12] Could Lucy have indeed drawn the bird? Her attempts at art began and ended with the fleeting Mill Grove lessons, at least on the evidence. The pianoforte was her medium of expression, although Audubon sometimes urged her to turn to drawing again.

Audubon had thought of traveling incognito as "Mr. John

James" to keep his departure from confusing his subscribers. But Children convinced him that there need be no loss of interest on account of his absence for such valid reasons.

Mrs. Swainson found a place for his servant. The Havells stored his possessions. Pessimistic talk of a brewing European crisis he dismissed as "fudge and deception." Nor did he permit himself to look too closely at the poor start Swainson was making with his new publication that had drawn a paltry ten orders. Upon having fifty of the Havell prints placed in a splendid binding, to show the Americans, Audubon did permit himself to speculate a little about what resistance there might be to the price of some $700 for the finished work. At least his nest egg of £132 plus $200 deposited with William Rathbone for future emergencies and the £150 in his pocket as he boarded the packet *Columbia* at Portsmouth lent the indispensable illusion of continuity, security.[13]

With him sailed the landscape painter Henry Havell, a brother of the engraver intent on settling in America, and Henry Ward, the son of a leading London taxidermist. Ward had been commissioned by the ornithological painter Gould and also by Swainson to seek needed species. His brother Frederick of Philadelphia often worked for Cooper. Audubon had promised to keep the unpredictable Henry out of mischief. His landlady's son completed the party that dropped their baggage in a huge cabin for thirty-six. By far the greater number of curtained berths had been assigned to an English exporter of "cloth and twine enough to fly kites the world over." Early hope that this gentleman, Benjamin Smith, would subscribe before disembarking with his wife, children, eight servants, and five dogs was not misplaced.

Among Audubon's effects was the first volume of *Floral Illustrations*, engraved by Havell from drawings by his friend Mrs. Edward Roscoe of Liverpool, and given for him to test abroad. He had a little spaniel, Dash, of the King Charles breed, for Johnny. The dog was related to Havell's Foxy, the evident model for the dog that had replaced the fox in *Sauve Qui Peut*. The "Queen Bee" had complied with a request to return his journals by sending them to her son William in

Bedford Street with a note that sheds light on her personality and her rapport with Audubon:

My Dear William,

    I send, with this, Mr. Audubon's Journals, which have not been seen even by myself, since he mentioned a part that he wished to be sacred. Hannah, and I, had been reading in the last Volume before; but I then sealed them; perhaps at some future day, when he has taken out the part he wishes should *not* be seen,—he will indulge us with looking at them again. I hope he has received my grateful acknowledgments, and that he has, or will, assure Mrs. Audubon of my best wishes for his happy meeting with her, and their dear children, and for all their health, and prosperity, and also that Mr. A. has said for me how much I am obliged to Mrs. Audubon both for her letter, and the Box of Roots and seeds. I would write to her, but I feel an unconquerable difficulty in writing to a stranger. I am much in debt to Mr. Audubon, but I did hope the silver paper, which I troubled him to get for me, would have been charged with the next Number of *Birds*. Adieu, in haste, for the messenger is waiting. Ever thy affectionate Mother, H. M. R.[14]

On the very day of Audubon's decision to sail, Lucy went about obeying his November ultimatum. She chose to conceal her mental reservations about the wisdom of his move. "If I come," she capitulated, "I give you myself, my endeavors to increase your happiness, and my heart. Nothing more have I."[15] That they would not separate was sure. She explained how hard, and futilely, she had tried to collect the $500 in tuition still due her. But she had managed to repay William for John's schooling. She was budgeting expenses, to be able to come to the rescue if the *Birds* should founder.

Lucy spoke more ingenuously to Victor. She made a clean breast of her disappointment that the report from Paris should have mentioned so few new subscriptions. It said nothing at all about the expected visit to Couëron. The promised dresses and bangles had not come. But she had decided to make the best of everything: "Do not," she cautioned Victor, "write to your Papa anything about it." She intended to take John away from his new position as clerk with William and sail with him for England by spring of 1830.

Red-Tailed Hawk. *Plate 86 of* The Birds of America. *Audubon named this hawk "Black Warrior* harlani" *for Dr. Richard Harlan.*

XX. Wander Year

O N MAY 5, 1829, the "deep gray wall" of Sandy Hook, thirty-five miles from New York, streaked the horizon. Audubon, once more in "perfect health," scribbled Lucy an excited note as his ship neared land. Captain Joseph Delano had promised him two places on the *Columbia* for late autumn.[1]

The Jackson letter that he flashed in front of the inspectors sped him through Customs in minutes. He hurried to the Lyceum of Natural History, apparently unaware that New York and Philadelphia had been reading about him lately. Some months before he landed, the Philadelphia *Franklin Journal* had published a criticism of his rattlesnake paper. "The Romance of the Rattlesnake," by one Dr. Thomas P. Jones in probable league with George Ord and Peale, pointed out that the reptile which chased Audubon's squirrel aloft and swallowed it was a blacksnake.[2]

William Cooper gave Audubon a pointedly tepid reception. His old advocate, Dr. Samuel Mitchill, drowning in hopeless alcoholic addiction, was not on hand to help. However, as a Lyceum member, Audubon could exhibit his aquatints if he wished. While he put them on the wall he had to listen to innuendoes from Cooper about the stupidity of having discarded the birdskins that were the models for his art. It was the question of Audubon's Stanley Hawk versus the Cooper's Hawk that rankled; only lately Cooper had been repeating to Bonaparte that his "English blood" would not permit Lord Stanley to "carry off honors" meant for himself.[3] As for Bonaparte, about the same time Cooper was bristling before the artist the Prince was telling Swainson why he had consistently avoided collaboration with Audubon: "I understand how difficult it would be to speak or even admit queries, on the mere authority of his drawings. Would to God he had at least the skins of his birds! This was the reason I refused taking . . . his drawings when he first showed them to me in the United States."[4]

No one subscribed for *The Birds of America* at the Lyceum of Natural History exhibition. The painters Trumbull and Hone, and Major Long of the Long Expedition, were among those who came by. The polite judgment of the Lyceum Committee was that "the splendid work of Mr. Audubon" did him credit. Only *Silliman's Journal* came out with unstinting praise.[5]

News of the Jones article made a visit to Philadelphia an unenviable prospect. In a bitter mood Audubon wrote Lucy again before starting out. Although he said he wished to offer her himself, his "stock, wares, and chattels" and his "enthusiastic" spark, he could do so only if she promised to go to Europe with him. "If a *no* comes, I *never* will put the question again, and we probably never will meet again."[6] But if she agreed he could finish all he must do by October, meet her on the Ohio, and bear her off to London.

Henry Ward went along to Philadelphia but soon made excuses to return to New York. Audubon remained only long enough, before crossing the river to Camden for some birding, to get off a smoldering letter to Cooper.[7] It criticized his failure to censure American indifference to men like Alexander Wilson and himself.

For days Audubon observed a family of vireos at his window in Camden.[8] Sometimes he followed the pair into the fields to watch them carry grasses for their nests. When the young vireos were fledged he found a ride to Great Egg Harbor with a caravan of professional sportsmen. As he jogged along the sandy roads toward the Jersey coast, Dash beside him, his bitterness faded. At nightfall he and his driver went ahead in the dusk without the others until the unexpected thunder of runaway hooves urged them off the road toward safety.

A fisherman's cottage at Somers Point offered board and room for three dollars a week.[9] The artist watched the white-breasted fish hawk, the curlew, the meadow lark, marsh hen, and the gull, collecting 300 species in all. Yet by the Fourth of July, when he departed for Philadelphia, none of his thirteen new drawings was of an unfamiliar or unnamed species.[10] He yearned to advise Cooper that he was scrupulously preserving every birdskin. He intended to let his critic hear that those who failed to take advantage of signing soon for his *Birds* would lose out entirely, seeing that he meant to destroy the copper plates to insure the rarity of the Folio.

He was astounded and troubled to find no answer to the three letters he had written to Lucy since landing. Several solicitous, very nearly tender letters awaited him from Anne Hudson. The first, sent from Cornhill, contained a full copy of a plea from Lord Auckland to Lord Stanley for birds to be brought from America. "You had not been gone five minutes when we received the letter," wrote Anne. "Your dear little bird is on the table and will not let me write. He does nothing but nibble my pen and peck at my fingers. God bless you, accept our united best wishes and believe me your sincere friend."

A fortnight later she caught a ride to town and borrowed a pen in her cousin George Goddard's office to write Audubon in peace: "Since you left I have not touched a brush or pencil, I have felt so at a loss without my *Master*, but as soon as I leave New Cross I shall set to work and make up for lost

time." She planned to copy Parker's portrait of Audubon belonging to W. H. Bentley: "It grows more like you every day
in the opinion of your friends." She implied that for him to
teach her portraiture he, too, should practice it: "So I think
on your return you must devote a little more time to Portrait
Painting and surprise the folks with that as well as other
things. . . . You have the *Old Girl's* warmest wishes for health,
happiness and a safe return. Need I express the same for myself? . . . Adieu, God bless you, my dear friend. Say anything friendly for me to Mrs. Audubon who I shall be delighted to welcome to England, and now farewell! A. M.
Hudson."

Audubon had forgotten a little painting of birds, intended
as a gift for Victor. But in a June letter Anne promised to send
it, along with a new one of "indigo birds," before departing
for a summer in Gravesend. She had tried copying Audubon's
Thrasher and *Loggerhead Shrike* but found she could not "get
on" in painting without his guidance. She regarded John
Children as a "very particular" supervisor; he had asked an
artist to judge the output, rather than trust his own judgment. She was faithfully sharing Audubon's letters with the
Goddards. Bentley had not yet sent down the promised portrait. "It will give me much pleasure to copy it if a good likeness and if it has that peculiar air, etc.," she said, not quite
trusting the first impression she had gained before the portrait escaped her.[11]

Furious though he was at Lucy, Audubon managed to
compose a calm greeting to Victor, after which he threw himself into work for Havell.[12] He hired George Lehman, the
German Swiss of Lancaster whom he had met in Pittsburgh
in 1824, to paint habitats for his New Jersey birds. Lehman
was not of the temperament to object to receiving hardly
more recognition than had been granted Mason for his strik-
ing contribution.[13] The Pennsylvania Academy of Fine Arts
had been exhibiting Lehman's landscapes since 1825.

Until mid-July Aubudon held his tongue before rebuking
Lucy. "I have thousands of things to say to thee. Indeed I
long much to be assured that I have a wife in this world," he

remonstrated.[14] With that he challenged Victor: "Have you abandoned the idea of ever answering my letters?" If Lucy had found him oblivious "*of her situation*" in regard to cash she had never said so. He proposed that Victor or John bring their mother north, a little later, with the funds he would send for a meeting at Wheeling or Pittsburgh. But for him to face Louisville and be torn to "peacemeals" was more than he could bear at present. With Bakewell and Berthoud in mind, he added: "*I paddle my own canoe* in the face of the storm and against contrary winds, but no matter. . . . Upon my word, it is wonderful to live a long life and see the movements, thoughts and different actions of our poor degenerated species—good only through interest; forgetful; envious, or hateful, through the same medium. Well, my dear boy, so goes the world and with it we must move the best way we can."[15]

Lucy flatly refused to join Audubon anywhere before December. He answered with a volley of sentimental pleas that she cease to imagine he preferred the birds to her, and that she not fear to travel alone at least as far as Louisville. If he had to, he would meet her there by the end of summer.[16]

At four o'clock on the afternoon of August 1, Audubon took the stagecoach for Mauch Chunk, eighty-five miles west. But its "extraordinary scarcity of birds" sent him on, in a hired cart, to the Great Pine Swamp. A sudden cloudburst on the way failed to turn him back. He and his driver rumbled on over the trails until they reached the cabin of Jediah Irish, a millwright and lumberjack who offered hospitality of a simplicity to Audubon's liking. Venison, bear, and trout were the daily fare.

Whenever Irish could desert the business of stripping the hills he led the search for birds. The hemlock warbler was one of the most desired. A pair of them darted so frantically about his head that Audubon left their "three naked young" behind him on a log, but he had to confiscate their "cradle" for art's sake.[17] That night, while Audubon drew the warbler, Irish read aloud to him from Burns and told logging yarns.

Henry Ward did not keep his promise to meet Audubon in

Camden. He had squandered the money paid him in advance, by Swainson and Gould, on a marriage. To Audubon's dismay the lad had chosen a Londoner of the "lowest cast" in New York City, then began working for Harlan, until Harlan saw through his duplicity.

"If I have done wrong," Audubon apologized to Swainson as if responsible for Ward's dereliction, "*blame me*. But I hope that by writing this to you I may serve you." He did not mind admitting that he and Swainson were much out of favor in Philadelphia, unacceptable though this news might be to the Englishman, again a father and so hard up as to be painting flowers for Havell. "Mr. Isaac Lea speaks bad of your work. Therefore that, and the *very little talk* belonging to the Philadelphians, generally go against you as against me. *You* are, as well as I, accused of publishing species as new that are *long since* described, &c. Not only this, but Mr. Lea published a work along your plan, and that is saying enough."[18] Lea, an expert on mussels, was one of Wilson's publishers. But to cheer Swainson, Audubon promised him shells from the Ohio and observations on the waxwing.

The allegiance of Dr. Richard Harlan, "a very rash young man," was of doubtful value.[19] He had been severely criticized for his hasty, too ambitious writings. His fellow Quaker, Reuben Haines, seemed faithful to Audubon despite a penchant for spreading tittle-tattle. Both men had lost standing in the Society of Friends during a schism and were at odds with each other. It was Audubon's misfortune to have his prints shown to the Academy of Natural Sciences by Harlan while Haines was corresponding secretary. The Academy declined to subscribe. Harlan's offer to raise a private subscription among friends was unacceptable to Audubon.

The "Book" was much admired. But the cost of The Birds of America discouraged institutions, as Harlan rightly explained to Swainson. Indeed, he feared that Audubon was going to be "mortified at this species of illiberality" everywhere.[20]

Before he buried himself in his drawing again, Audubon took the measure of the Philadelphians. He scored their ignorance of the Great Pine Swamp, their smoothing of bow ties and their "full dress." His essay was to become part of a bosky published episode, an idyll of western Pennsylvania.[21]

By late September he had finished forty-two bird portraits in Camden with Lehman's help. A short walk and sleep were the only interruptions day after day. At the end of October he shipped portraits of ninety-five species and drawings of sixty kinds of eggs to London, as well as thousands of insects for Children.

As he made ready to start westward with his dog he took for granted that Lucy was preparing herself for the London hegira. In reality, she was thinking that it might be foolhardy to abandon her independence for doubtful security in England, particularly while Victor and John might still need her assistance. It was not that she doubted *The Birds of America* and its worth, but only its tangible rewards.

Half a day in Pittsburgh with the Bakewells was more than sufficient for Audubon. In Cincinnati he made no attempt to see Thomas Bakewell; he did, however, call on the Western Museum.

In his eagerness to see Victor he promptly forgot his resentment. He found him so changed that if the boy had not rushed up to him, in William Bakewell's countinghouse, he would hardly have known him. He pulled out the splendid gold watch that he had brought him. Then, with his *Birds* volume for a breastplate, he braved White House in Shippingport. After a day or two he left Dash to Johnny and sailed.

It was near midnight on November 17 when his steamer docked at Bayou Sara. Audubon still had fifteen miles to go. His eerie half-hour in St. Francisville and his reunion with Lucy after more than three and one-half years he himself described:

> I was aware yellow fever was still raging at St. Francisville, but walked thither to procure a horse. . . . I soon reached it and entered the open door of a house I knew to be an inn; all was dark and silent. I called and knocked in vain. It was the abode of Death alone! The air was putrid. I went to another house—another—and another . . . doors and windows were all open, but the living had fled. Finally, I

reached the home of Mr. Nübling whom I knew. He welcomed me and lent me his horse, and I went off at a gallop. It was so dark that I soon lost my way, but I cared not; I was about to rejoin my wife. I was in the woods—the woods of Louisiana—my heart was bursting with joy!

The first glimpse of dawn set me on my road. At six o'clock I was at Mr. Johnson's house. A servant took the horse. I went at once to my wife's apartment; her door was ajar. Already she was dressed and sitting by her piano, on which a young lady was playing. I pronounced her name gently—she saw me—and the next moment I held her in my arms. Her emotion was so great I feared I had acted rashly. But tears relieved our hearts, once more we were together.[22]

None of the three letters that the anxious Anne Hudson wrote to Audubon in July reached him in his peregrinations. Her message of August 2, from Gravesend, finally found him at Beech Grove. Although she had received his news of July 7 and its plaint of her failure to write, she felt it her turn to lecture: "You have written but a few lines and have only told me that you are *in the Woods*. Not one word do you say of home, or of Mrs. Audubon, or even that you are going there. Nothing but *woods, woods, woods,* till we are almost tempted to believe that you are turned *Wood Cutter* and mean to bring back a fine cargo of timber. I only wish you may arrive with it in October, but that is now impossible. October will come, but not Mr. Audubon, and yet if you thought as much as I do of the bad weather you will have to encounter later . . . and with your wife too, you surely would not delay so long."

Anne did not hesitate to importune: "You will say that I am very urgent for your return. Indeed my good friend it is more on your account than my own (though I have great reason to be interested, for I cannot get on without your instruction) but I know that your work requires your presence." She stated her concerns, and with none of the cloying civilities of most women of her time: "Mr. Havell is a very dilatory Man. In a letter I wrote six weeks ago I mentioned that from what I could learn they were a month behind hand in the delivery of *Number 12*. How they go on I have no opportunity of knowing, and when in town they seemed to regard me as a spy, and Mr. H. was particularly guarded."

It seemed to Anne Hudson quite callous of Havell not to have taken down Audubon's *Eagle and Lamb* and his other oils, along with her own, until four or five days after the close of a commercial exhibition in Suffolk Street. "The frame of the Eagle was much damaged," she informed Audubon. Not only the Goddards but one Captain D—n sent their regards. "The captain spent two days with us last week and is now a most *attentive beau*," came the hint Lucy must have read with relief. "You gentlemen are very singular beings," added Miss Hudson.

She and her mother were thinking of moving to Greenwich until Audubon's return, after which they intended to live near him, if possible, for resumption of her lessons. "So pray don't stay long . . . Mamma bids me say that she hopes to give you many a beating at whist before Christmas. . . . I am busily employed in knitting you a smart purse. Is not the old one worn out? I think I shall not send you any more letters after September. They will not reach you in America. . . . God bless you, my dear friend . . . best and warmest wishes . . . believe me very truly, Yours."[23]

Audubon worked with a zest that belied his failure to have won as much as a single subscription since landing in the United States. He refused to take seriously Lucy's doubts about the wisdom of resigning at Beech Grove. The plaintive letters from London, with their reports of the rise in cancellations and snarled accounts like that of Bonaparte, not to mention the recalcitrance of the Paris agent Pitois, ruffled him very little. He faced the fact, however, that Havell must not be left alone much longer. John Children had been too ill to be of real help as an adviser. The death of Havell's infant son, Robert Audubon, intensified the engraver's gloom.

Audubon sent condolences, and also an offer from Lucy's employer to Havell's sister-in-law. If Miss Edington would come over and teach ten or twelve young persons in the gentle arts, she could be sure of $1,000 yearly.[24]

The "discovery" of two birds meant more, perhaps, than anything else that had happened since May. He found a wren that he named for Bewick. A "new" hawk he named

"Black Warrior *harlani*" for Harlan. It had been seen and collected by others but Audubon was the first to describe it.

Sure of its uniqueness, and elated, he sent an extravagant announcement to Harlan. He said to advertise his luck and tell all Philadelphia—including "George Ord, Esqr Fellow of all the Societies Imaginable"—that Mr. Audubon sent greetings.[25] (Ord, visiting his artist son in Paris, would not receive the message.)

Because Swainson had been good enough to let Havell put the prospectus inside each copy of his *Zoological Illustrations,* Audubon shipped him 1,150 saplings.[26] For Alexander Gordon he caged a wild turkey, for Selby some squirrels, and for the London Zoo, fourteen opossums. Kentucky could supply passenger pigeons and blue jays to ship when he passed through.

On January 7, after a few days with the Brands in New Orleans, the Audubons sailed to join their sons in Louisville and attend to important matters. The boys were living with William Bakewell and his bride of a year, Alicia Matthews. On the way up the river Audubon skinned twenty Carolina parrots, two ivory-billed and four pileated woodpeckers, as well as many other accessions for England.

Lucy did not intend that her sons should be in want. She entrusted part of her savings to William for any emergency. Audubon drew up a testamentary letter, witnessed by Bakewell and Berthoud, leaving all his possessions to Lucy, except for half of his holdings in France and England, which his sons were to divide. The fate of *The Birds of America* would be up to Lucy if he died; the work was to be carried forward by their sons or sold, according to her wisdom.

It may have been this will that prompted Audubon to write Harlan that, if he prospered, so would this friend: "Should *I* become so, you shall have it from a Friend! . . . What the Devil is the use of Cash, Cash, Cash!—We cannot eat it or drink it, and worst of all when we 'Kick the Bucket' it always remains behind at the Mercy—generally speaking— of Fools who convert the mass into decease and corruption of decease! There's a train of thought for you."

He also told Harlan that Children was eager to correspond with him, and quoted the latest from Swainson: "They do not know how to appreciate you [Audubon and Harlan] in America. There is hardly one for whom I have not thorough contempt." Except for Cooper and Harlan there was no one "worthy of holding a candle" to Audubon's drawings in Swainson's opinion. Audubon was in no mood to deprecate the tribute, let alone defend his adopted country. "Where are our Washingtons, Franklins . . . nay, even Jeffersons?" he demanded of Harlan. "'No taste in America.' That is a severe judgment indeed—and yet what can we say to the contrary. For my part, was I not an American I might wish to belong to any other portion of the Globe. But America and my Enthusiasm go together, and I hope for brighter hours to come. . . . [27]

Before leaving Louisville, Audubon painted a large oil, a still life of dead game, for William. From there the Audubons went on to Cincinnati to visit the Thomas Bakewell family, and then, as March began, to see Lucy's sister Sarah in Wheeling. After that came the advance on Washington City.

"With great kindness" President Jackson first received Audubon, then Lucy.[28] The person who voiced the most ecstatic appreciation of the aquatints was Congressman Edward Everett of Massachusetts.[29] The former publisher was kind enough to have them shown in the Chambers. He led the House of Representatives in signing as a body for the Folio and expressed chagrin that Audubon should have aroused so little interest in the United States. In that spirit he handed him a letter of introduction. But the perfidious Russian envoy Krüdener and his glib promises were another story.

Baltimore was worth but three subscriptions this trip, and Philadelphia none.[30] Again the Academy resisted. The city availed nothing but the gift of a live screech owl that Audubon carried in his pocket to the *Pacific*, waiting in New York harbor. In another pocket lay a letter that had finally caught up with him. Its author, Dr. D'Orbigny, began "My dear Audubon," but closed "my dear Fifi" quite as if their old, "very sincere attachment" still held. But even a stranger to both could have noted the absence of real affection, though the doctor declared his joy over Audubon's Paris letter with its assurances that he was a "happy father, happy spouse, in a position agreeable and honorable, and still far from abandoning the sciences." For his tardy reply he pleaded illness but rejoiced that he was not forgotten. He was entrusting the letter to Paul Lecoq, a brandy merchant bound for London; he frankly and fervently hoped this good friend might benefit by Audubon's connections.

The likelihood of two subscriptions to the "beautiful work" on the birds as described in the prospectus which D'Orbigny had shown to friends, seemed, by inference, a strong hint that Audubon should help Lecoq. D'Orbigny's own "pecuniary state" did not permit him to be among the fortunate signers. He suggested that if the work were at hand, in La Rochelle, he could consult and show it to advantage. He in turn was sending Audubon a prospectus or two regarding his own scientific writings, much in need of subscribers. He begged that Lucy be informed, on behalf of himself and family, of their joy upon learning of her marriage to their old friend. "Your godson Gaston [Édouard] embraces you with all his heart and will not despair of seeing him in France or in England." Now that Audubon had let him know that he was actually in London, the doctor said that he would get off a better reply to the many questions in the Paris letter of 1828. By then he would be feeling well enough to write more fully and make up for the gap of twenty-five years. Obviously, he would have much to relate concerning his brilliant sons. "Like your own," he granted, "my ménage has been free from clouds"; his children had given him only satisfaction while he continued his earnest studies.[31] Nothing did he say of his debt to Madame Audubon or her long since discouraged heirs in Couëron.

XXI. A Return

ONLY THE SQUIRRELS AND A FEW BLUE JAYS survived the three and one-half weeks at sea. The saplings and opossums and the remainder of the birds died on the voyage.

As soon as the *Pacific* docked at Liverpool on April 2, 1830, Lucy made a beeline for the Gordon home on Chatham Street. She found Ann so gravely ill that to leave her seemed out of the question. Audubon left for Manchester and London without her next morning.

Havell was more than relieved to see his employer. To celebrate Audubon's nomination to London Royal Society membership by Children and Lord Stanley, he made a life mask of the artist's features.[1] But it would be difficult to raise fifty pounds for the honor of being handed a diploma on May 5. Audubon began a spate of oils on canvas which would have to find their way without Sir Thomas Lawrence, for, about the time the Audubons had passed Henderson on the Ohio, Lawrence's bier was moving toward St. Paul's before the King's coach.[2]

In excellent fettle, Audubon wrote Swainson a letter that

the zoologist thought an impertinence from start to finish. Swainson replied in the harshest tones:

> You think that I do not know that you are F.R.S., Fellow of the Royal Society. You are mistaken. . . . I have been fighting your battles against a rising opposition which originated among some of your *Ornithological friends* (at least so I strongly suspect) for the purpose of your name being *blackballed*. . . .
>
> The whole of your bundle of young trees reached me as withered sticks. . . .
>
> So you are going to write a book 'tis a thing of little moment for one who is not known, because they have no reputation to loose. But much will be expected from *you*, and you must, therefore . . . *put your best leg foremost*. . . .
>
> Dr. Richardson's and my own volume on the Arctic Birds, is now in press. Not being able to refer to your plates, I have not had the power to quote your work, you know how repeatedly I have applied . . . both to you and Mr. Havell in vain.
>
> I am sick of the world and of mankind, and but for my family would end my days in my beloved forests of Brazil.
>
> So Mr. Lea did not settle my account with you? . . . He is also one of your *friends* who would, if he could, cut your throat. Another *friend* of yours has been in England, Mr. Ord and has been doing you all the good he can: if these are samples of American naturalists, defend me from ever coming in contact with any of their whole race.[3]

It was to Swainson's credit that he resisted the temptation to add that Audubon, before the Royal Society balloting, had been called by the opposition "scarcely worthy" and a "mere pretender." That Ord had been "doing all the good" mischief he could was no exaggeration. He had become fast friends with the curmudgeon Waterton, visited him at Walton Hall, and learned, to his delight, that the squire also loathed Audubon. To Peale's bulletin that Audubon's American pilgrimage was quite a fiasco, Ord replied in his usual sardonic style:

> You speak of that worthy personage Audubon. Pray, what took him to America? Did he really expect to have his monstrous book encouraged, by subscriptions, in the United States? He surely knew that Wilson's charming and instructive work did not pay the cost of publication, and that Bonaparte's, as beautiful as it is, went heavily along. No. no! 'The most scientific and the greatest ornithologist in the world,' as I have heard this man termed, has mistaken the ex-

travagant and silly compliments which have been lavished upon him in Europe as proofs of merit; and time, if it does not unseal his own eyes, at least will open those of his patrons. He spoke to you of Waterton, you say. This gentleman was so disgusted with the fellow's impudence and importunity that he desired a friend [Greg] who wished to pay a visit, with Audubon, at *Walton Hall*, to abstain from so doing, as he did not wish to cultivate an acquaintance with the man.[4]

Audubon's thoughts were too taken up with his Manchester losses and how to recoup them to worry about Ord or to try to appease Swainson. He went north to adjust things if he could, first going to visit Lucy and the Gordons for a day. Bad weather and the races compelled him to close his exhibition after five days and return to London. But he blamed Havell, quite as much, for the failure in the North. Many imperfectly finished aquatints had brought complaints.

A call on the awesome Royal Society could no longer be put off. Lord Stanley greeted Audubon, feigned interest in buying his originals, and even hinted that he might need a painter for his collection of fauna at Knowsley—a post soon destined, actually, for young Edward Lear (1812–88). Captain Basil Hall demurred when Audubon began to extoll the former British colony, then he seized his hat and rushed for the door. He had seen the "woodsman" only briefly after he and Mrs. Hall returned from America late in the summer of 1828. Thanks to Audubon's notes, the Halls had dined with the Berthouds and William Bakewell in Kentucky and Benjamin Bakewell in Pittsburgh, and they had also greeted Henry Clay, "a hearty fellow." Dr. Drake had treated Hall's small daughter in Cincinnati. Harlan was also "most attentive."[5] What Hall did not report was a remark made by his imperious lady, as their steamer passed the deserted mill at Henderson, that it appeared to have been "a bad speculation—as anything Audubon undertook in the way of business would probably prove."

Weeks passed before Hall set matters aright—less from altruism than in the interest of his published *Travels:* "I trust when you have read my book you will find that it is not such a horrid production as some of your countrymen may have led you to suppose. At all events, as I value your friendship very highly, I shall be truly grieved if there be anything in it to make you think less kindly of me. We may differ in opinion on various points—but I trust you will give me credit for sincerity—and also for the truest good will to your country—let who will say to the contrary."[6]

Not to be ignored in the North, Audubon advanced on Birmingham in June with 400 printed invitations for his exhibition at the Society of Arts. The death of the King, public mourning, turmoil across the Channel, and the effects of some poorly lettered, unevenly colored prints (received earlier in the vicinity) stood in the way. For the latter, Audubon again scored Havell:

> Your letter engraver must be dismissed, or correct his past errors. When I return, *you and I* must have a regular and complete overhauling of the coppers, and see what can be done to redeem the character of a work of this magnitude . . . which you cannot but conceive of importance to your own standing as a good engraver and a good man. . . . Should I find the same complaints as I proceed . . . I must candidly tell you that I will abandon the publication and return to my own woods until I leave this world for a better one. I have fully made up my mind to that effect, and I hope you now know me too well not to believe every word of it as if I were now on my way to America. I feel sorry and mortified . . . on both your account and on mine, but depend on it, my Dear Sir, something must be done or the work will be abandoned. . . . my industry will stand any test, but if repaid only by reproaches not altogether due to me, my feelings cannot bear it long, and I would rather live in peace in the woods than tormented here when I do all in my power to please.[7]

Havell, although "extremely hurt," did not reply in kind. He felt sure that "many of the London subscribers" were "very good judges." Not one had complained to him. "I always have, and be assured, shall continue to exert myself to the utmost." He asked only that Audubon trust the extremity of his efforts to "give satisfaction."[8] Audubon did not pretend, before such humility, to have been other than harsh, but he begged Havell to appreciate the gravity of the situation. "Did you know how *I* am hurt when I write such letters," he replied, "you would next to pity me. . . . I am more low spirited than I ever experienced in my life about my Work, and as I said . . . I *must* do something to amend it, or give it up. . . . However, *perhaps* something will be done, and I must not trouble you any more at present."[9]

On their return to London early in July the Audubons were greeted with mixed news. Queen Adelaide had subscribed as a patron, but the question of her attentiveness to obligations, so steadfastly ignored by the late king, arose.[10] To a plea for candid criticism, Bonaparte had taken withering exception to the naming of certain birds and the careless spelling of Latin names. For the first and only time, Audubon addressed himself to the Prince like the knight errant of natural history that he was:

> To no one on earth have I spoke so openly. . . . I know you believe me when I say that I really and truly do all *in my power.* Yourself knows better than any man, being the best judge, that I am not a learned naturalist . . . only a *practical* one. What I have seen or found and concluded within myself was true, I have attempted to represent, and now attempt to diffuse, with the mere hope that some *one thing* in the work may be useful hereafter. This being the case, it is to you that I look for advices, and it is from yourself alone that I wish to receive them. In errors of nomenclature I doubtless will be much reprimanded, because the short notices in your *Synopsis* puzzle my poor brains. . . . I wish I could be near you for a year or so to study the mere alphabet of such matters. I would try to improve, although I am fast getting old. I have shewn your letter to Mr. Havell and he has began the amending of the plates of which you complain.[11]

The overthrow of Charles X ruled out a visit to the perplexing agent Pitois of Paris. Audubon went to Bristol while trying to decide whether to flee the apathy of England for the more favorable economy and the calm of Edinburgh. First, he broached the subject of scientific aid by Swainson for a consideration. He believed that at Swainson's farm he could finish a "pleasing, instructive" initial volume of text that autumn. He himself would draft his frontier "adventures and anecdotes" for leaven to the publication; the remainder would need a masterly editor such as Swainson. The Audubons would furnish their own "wines, porter or ale" as paying guests in a plan that he made sound like a *fait accompli.*[12]

Swainson answered curtly that such boarding was "never done in England." However, he might consider collaboration, as equal coauthor, after he finished his work for Richardson on *Fauna-Boreali Americana*.[13] His tone was far from that of his "little people" in their late enthusiasm for having "Mr. Audubon help celebrate all their birthdays."[14]

Audubon had no intention of sharing authorship or of paying the fee demanded, as his polite but abrupt letter made plain. Swainson let five weeks go by before he stormed back:

> Your friends would tell you, if you enquired . . . that even *my* name would *add* something to the value of "The Birds of America." You pay me compliments on my scientific knowledge, and wished you possessed a portion; & you liken the acquisition of such a portion to purchasing the sketch of an eminent painter—the simile is good, but allow me to ask you, whether, after procuring the sketch, you would mix it up with your own, and pass it off to your friends as your production? I cannot possibly suppose that such would be your duplicity and I therefore must not suppose that you intended that I should give all the scientific information I have laboured to acquire during twenty years on ornithology—conceal my name,—and transfer my fame to your pages & to your reputation.[15]

In addition Swainson accused Audubon of withholding certain data needed for his work with Richardson on the fauna, of talking nonsense about the "Downy Woodpecker," of rejecting good advice freely given, and of currying favor with the British Museum by presenting them with thirty rare skins before Swainson could "name, measure and describe them" in order to assure credit to Audubon. As matters stood, someone else could claim and name the species. He would not. For the *coup de grâce* Swainson admitted himself "rather glad" that Sir William Jardine had hired him to work on a miniature of the Alexander Wilson classic, a windfall that made Audubon's offer unacceptable in any case. Moreover, he would apply his unique Quinarian system to that work, to its profit.[16]

So Audubon was not to have the doubtful benefit of what Traill once called Swainson's "little grammatical confusions," or of his actually bogus "system."[17] Unaware that Bonaparte and Swainson were contemplating a joint work on the birds of the world (soon, however, to be scrapped in a disagreement over fees), Audubon asked the Prince to believe that he had not intended to "plume" himself on Swainson's erudition.[18]

A circuitous journey to Scotland had its compensations, including the patronage of Lord Ravensworth and the Marchioness of Hertford. The Honorable Thomas Liddell, Ravensworth's young son, saw in Audubon a kindred spirit, a "perfect specimen of 'the Child of Nature'" whose powerful "sense of duty" impelled the enlightenment of others "on the mysteries of living creation."[19] Thus an enduring friendship began; Audubon promised specimens of American shrubs and trees for the Ravensworth castle. As for the Marchioness of Hertford, she wisely refrained from disclosing her plan to let the first few dozen prints form a dado in her dining salon.

From Newcastle, Audubon sent Harlan on the first day of October a hastily written bulletin about several matters, some of pride and at least one dear to his heart. His election to the Royal Society had raised his stock in Philadelphia. He seemed to find a connection between that fact and his chances of reaching the Pacific:

"I am glad to see you say that my having raised to the Fellowship of the Royal Society of London is likely to bring on a reaction in my favour with the Philadelphians. I need the assistance and support of all, and it is always my desire to be at peace with everyone; yet it would be impossible for me to suffer being trampled upon without feeling a degree of displeasure if not of resentment. . . . Now between you and me and the post, do you think that I could rise a company of ten good fellows, each willing to pay 1,000 [dollars] to go to the Pacific mouth of the Columbia . . . for a couple of years? . . . I will lay down that [sum] at once, although you know I am poor enough, God knows, to assist in such an undertaking, and many want the privilege of *the Birds!* Feel the pulses and let me know—our country has not been ransacked . . . thousands of Praises [prizes] still lay on the wheel of knowledge."[20]

For a fortnight a rheumatic arm forced Lucy to bed and away from her appointed tasks as Audubon's secretary and copyist in Edinburgh. After that she was again in the thick of her labors. The scope of the bird biographies frightened Audubon as he drudged away, an admittedly poor writer in English and "not much better" at French. Nevertheless, he believed his journals and memorandum books made his knowledge of birds greater than that of many other ornithologists.

To overcome his deficiencies he engaged a thirty-four-year-old graduate of Kings College and university professor of comparative anatomy, William MacGillivray (1796–1852).[21] Recommended by the painter-zoologist James Wilson, brother of the *Blackwood's* editor, MacGillivray—a scientist, writer, and competent artist—welcomed the association and extra income. His fee, two guineas per galley of sixteen pages, was a fraction of Swainson's proposed charge of $3.78 for each printed page. Credit for the correction of "asperities," and for supplying technical data along with simple woodcuts of anatomical detail, was not discussed. Audubon considered his "standard of ornithology" his own conception from start to finish. Hired services, like gratuitous favors, would be acknowledged when the time came.

After New Year's 1831, vertigo, headache, and added weight made Audubon a casualty of his "scribbling."[22] From four o'clock until an hour before midnight, he and Lucy were "up to the eyes at writing." Except for mealtime and tea, interruptions were ruled out.[23] Among the rival works of the "natural history mad" were compilations by Jameson and Jardine of Wilson's *American Ornithology; Constable's Miscellany*, which helped itself to Audubon's art; and another piratical work, this one by Captain Thomas Brown, who affected Audubonesque botanical enchantments amid bits stolen from Bonaparte and Wilson.[24] None of these unoriginal, parasitic offerings worried Audubon. Indeed, he thought their limitations might bend the novelty-loving British in his favor.

However, a forthcoming work by Thomas Nuttall (1788–1859) of Boston was another matter, and kept Audubon's need of more birds starkly before him. Unless Audubon returned to America within a year, the engraving would very likely come to a standstill for want of drawings. He was about to appoint Dr. Richard Harlan of Philadelphia to handle the printing of an American edition in that city, albeit Harlan had responded not at all to the pleas for needed species.

The Edinburgh bookseller and politician Adam Black became nominal publisher of *Ornithological Biography*. Owner of the copyright of the *Encyclopaedia Britannica*, he enjoyed the respect of the Wernerians. How accurately Bewick had spoken of the book business Audubon found out when his text began to come off the presses on February 1, 1831. He had to call on Havell for help with distribution. Neither Black nor his associate and nephew nor indeed anyone in the trade would invest a penny in the work.

Lucy shipped the first proof sheets to Harlan. She told Victor to be ready to reimburse the doctor if his estimated $700 for the printing of the first volume proved insufficient. If Victor ran short, William Bakewell was to be called on to reimburse the Philadelphia agent. Audubon had instructed Harlan to offer the Philadelphia entomologist Henry McMurtrie (1793–1865), an Academy lecturer on vertebrates, an honorarium of fifty dollars to select paper and type, check punctuation, and reconnoiter for good reviews.[25] McMurtrie had just translated Cuvier's *Animal Kingdom*.

Audubon began to think much about some day beginning a work on the mammals of his country. The synopsis of the species in the *Birds*, to which he thought "posterity" was entitled, remained to be done.[26] Then, too, there was the traveling gallery of 400 oils by Kidd, in perfect imitation of the originals, that could not be forgotten. If the oils should go to some rich speculator or to an institution, instead of circling the globe, so much the better. For this tour de force—to last until "time immemorial"—he ordered Havell to forward millboard, canvas, and stretchers without delay.[27]

As *The Birds of America* became, from only just so many fine fragments, ready for binding into a first huge volume, the need for a title page arose. This in turn raised the delicate question of a copyright to protect the work from confiscation in the United States and the connivance of "cormorants" everywhere. Havell learned that provided there were no table of contents and no "flourishes" (to which Audubon was opposed, in any case) for the title page, no copyright would be required. Otherwise the Folio would have to be presented to every public library in Britain.[28]

To avoid having *Ornithological Biography* and its profits attached by old creditors Audubon considered using Victor's name instead of his own for the American edition. He had yet to learn that to copyright his work he had only to deposit the title page in a United States district court.

In Manchester in April he learned of Havell's collapse from the rigors of the first Folio volume. Audubon concealed his horror of death for him—or for himself—in a cool note of sympathy to Mrs. Havell. "The more he works . . . the more he will enjoy his older days when Industry herself becomes impotent and drowsy." In such a way would Havell "live to see his name raised sky high above that of all other engravers of birds."[29] But Audubon's request for the Havells to send Victor and John brushes and colors at once spoke volumes.

In Liverpool, the dying William Roscoe obligingly repeated the myth of Audubon's American birth in a letter of introduction to Lafayette.[30]

Rather than take the Red Rover stagecoach to London the Audubons chose a heady twenty-four miles an hour on the new railway.

XXII.
Eyes of the World

T HE ILLUMINATIONS for the coming coronation of William IV, and the sight of 400 elegant coaches bound for a levee, contrasted too sharply, for Audubon, with the poor beside the curb as he and Lucy rode toward their rooms at 121 Great Portland Street.[1]

A surprisingly friendly letter from Swainson awaited him. "I do not wish to read a lecture to you," Audubon ventured to reply as he sent him his latest, sympathetically reviewed writings, "but from my heart I am sorry you should be *à la joute* with anyone . . . [I am] hoping you will have no more of this sort of warfare." Swainson, on his steady way downward, had published an attack on certain French naturalists.[2]

Letters from America increased Audubon's eagerness for a voyage to America by September. Nicholas and Eliza had moved to New York City, Johnny was working on a New Orleans-Louisville steamer rather than compete with William's brother-in-law in the countinghouse. And, now that his sweetheart had married a rival, Victor wished to know what the future held for him and John; he declared

Frederick Cruickshank. Miniature portraits.
Private collection. John James Audubon,
1831. Lucy Bakewell Audubon, *1831.*

himself in favor not so much of what would bring wealth as, simply, the best for all.

Thomas Sully entreated Audubon not to avoid his country any longer: "I trust that the few opposers you have here will be silent when they learn that the learned individuals and societies in France and England commend your labors— be true to yourself, Audubon and never doubt success."[3] The "opposer" Ord was berating *The Birds of America* as "wretched," and, except for its wild turkey, no better than a six-penny pamphlet. "John Bull" had been humbugged, he said, and it was no wonder Lawson claimed he could have done better with *"a pitchfork!"*[4] In his satisfaction over the "eulogisms" in *Blackwood's* and Jameson's *Journal*, Audubon would not have cared, if he had known, that Ord was in York-shire with Waterton, busily drafting notes for a fresh attack. But neither Audubon nor Ord dreamed that on July 15 the American Philosophical Society, overcoming its storied indif-ference, had elected him a member.

In May Audubon composed a bold reminder to Cambridge University that its first Folio volume was complete and ready for a suitably fine binding.[5] He dropped the hint through Professor John Stevens Henslowe, whom he asked for advice about booksellers there. Henslowe was busy with projects of his own, not the least of which was that of obtaining a post for his favorite pupil, Charles Darwin, with the expedition of the *Beagle*. Audubon also wrote to Washington Irving for ad-vice on how to approach such publications as *Silliman's Jour-nal* and the *Transactions* of the Linnaean Society, London.[6]

The Paris visit included no journey to Couëron.

On his return Audubon received a long, fault-finding let-ter from Bonaparte, who declared the Columbia jay, which the Prince himself had given Audubon, a Mexican species. He called the coloring bad. "Compare it with the amazingly true plate of the Kingfisher," he urged. But he took care to balance criticism and praise neatly enough to keep peace: "I do not conceive why you should suppose a smile on my lips at the idea of your book. . . . I always advised you to write something, at least upon your own species. . . . Since you were so modest as to require assistance it would have been quite agreeable to me to help you myself, and I will feel proud if my writings have been of some assistance, even in the little interesting part of nomenclature and philosophy of the science. The really interesting part will be the habits of the feathered tribes which you have studied so successfully and in so original a manner." He considered Audubon lucky to have found MacGillivray, whose fine paper on the gulls he had read. "I approve also greatly your heroic determination to visit the unsearched part of your noble country. You will really have lived an ornithological life. . . ."[7]

Ord wished to help Waterton destroy *Ornithological Biography* for its introduction, so insulting to Philadelphia. He saw why Swainson had "very properly declined having anything to do with the affair." Then he got down to something more than slander for Waterton's inspiration:

> The members of the Academy would have had no objections to Mr. Audubon, provided they had thought him to be an honest man. But when they were informed that he had basely traduced the character of one of their deceased associates, the illustrious Alexander Wilson, by publicly reporting that when the latter visited Louisville he was hospitably entertained for *two weeks*, at Audubon's home, received a great variety of valuable information from him, with an account of some new species, all of which Wilson published to the world as his own without mention of Audubon—when the members of the Academy were thus informed they indignantly rejected the candidate, although the proposal of membership was backed by the Prince of Musignano, Lesueur and some more influential men.[8]

Ord had flourished the original Wilson diary before the members to prove that Wilson had tarried for only five days in Louisville, hunted but one afternoon with Audubon, found no new birds, and fled the place in utter disgust. "This is something like proof that the discoursing author of *American Ornithology* did not consider Monsieur Audubon either a man of science or literature." (Ord did not furnish Waterton with the original diary. Slightly differing versions were to appear in print under his auspices before its apparently premeditated destruction.)

Common traits and strangely similar experience bound

Long-billed Curlew. *Plate 231 of* The
Birds of America. *Engraved by Robert
Havell, Jr., in 1834 after the original study.
The background is based on* View of Charles-
ton, *a watercolor by George Lehman.*

the two misogynists, Waterton and Ord. Overweening self-esteem was the besetting sin of each. Both widowers had sons reared by maiden sisters. The fifty-two-year-old Waterton had lost his bride of seventeen, a granddaughter of Minda the Arawak princess, after the birth of his son, now approaching sixteen months. She had been promised to him, half in jest, since her christening, which he had attended. She was led to the altar straight from convent school, then to Europe on a honeymoon through the natural history galleries. After her death the squire gave his eccentricities free reign. His *Wanderings*, an account of a solo expedition to South America, and his militant Roman Catholicism became shibboleths. When not plotting to avenge insults and injuries he was meting out "justice." He slept on the floor, rose at times to pray, and by the light of dawn prowled his wild, high-walled grounds.

Audubon made up his mind to sail for America. But on balancing his accounts with Havell and depositing £600 for the engraver to draw upon, he sounded out Harlan as if in need of encouragement before recrossing the Atlantic. After granting Harlan and McMurtrie carte blanche with the first volume of text, he penned: "Sell or give away, choose agents, fix prices, &c, &c, as you like." But then he added uneasily: "I wish you could ascertain on *what grounds* the Philadelphians are so virulent towards me. I would like to bring these estimable folks to the Bull ring! . . . I have some hopes that affairs will turn rather more favourable to me in America and Philadelphia, more especially when I have written three more Volumes and *my Life!*—assisted by yourself, McMurtrie and Featherstonhaugh." He closed with an invitation to look at his honors, indicated by ten new sets of membership initials scribbled boldly beside his name. "Don't you think that I might, without *blinking*, been [sic] entitled to a seat in your own Academy?"[9]

His "133 subscribers"—a total smaller by ten than at his last sailing—Audubon took in stride. By losing fifty all told, he had been deprived of a possible $50,000; he trusted that this sum would be realized as soon as Victor, Havell, and new agents scoured the provinces for new subscribers. He congratulated himself on having disdained any burdensome favors—on having trusted to "providence" alone. "The whole business is really wonderful. . . . Forty thousand dollars have passed through my hands for the completion of the first volume." Who would believe that he had landed lonely and friendless in England with barely enough money to travel before actually accomplishing so much? Who would believe that once, in London, he had only one sovereign in his pocket? Indeed, he had "extricated himself by rising at 4 o'clock, working all day," and accepting for his oils prices that a day laborer would see as barely enough to live on.[10]

The taxidermist Henry Ward sailed with the Audubons on the *Columbia* in August, to serve on a cruise of the Atlantic seaboard with the artist. Audubon, counting on George Lehman to paint backgrounds for him again, hoped to reach the Pacific before returning to England.

The *Columbia* touched New York at 8:00 A.M., September 3, 1831. Fifteen minutes later, after passing through Customs without inspection, the Audubons went to see the Berthouds. The voyage had been long and rough. A week of "great comfort" was particularly welcome to Lucy.[11] They found Eliza as cordial and obliging as could be wished, Nicholas hardly less so.

The same could not be said of the Lyceum. William Cooper examined with studied indifference the bag of sixteen birds taken by Audubon at sea. He took pleasure in showing him some needed species but pretended not to hear hints. Nor did he offer any clues to possible subscribers. Later he wrote the Prince that Audubon was "much altered in some respects," and quite visibly "mortified" not to be permitted to borrow skins. "He seems to be looked up to by the Scotch and English as a great naturalist, which he himself says he is not. You, he says, are a great naturalist."[12]

The artist wondered what the moral temperature of Philadelphia would be as he neared that always intimidating city. He was relieved to pick up its *Literary Gazette* and find a piece that quoted *Blackwood's* paeans.[13] Like the New York press, it

John Woodhouse Audubon. Dr. John Bachman, 1837. Oil on canvas, 30 × 25 in. Courtesy Charleston Museum, Charleston, South Carolina.

hailed his arrival and achievements. The American Philosophical Society and the Academy of Natural Sciences subscribed; so did Harlan and a relative of Mill Grove's owner. To be able to show those who scoffed at his rattlesnake paper what an intrepid reporter he could be, he agreed to communicate from the Floridas with G. W. Featherstonhaugh's new scientific monthly. "If I do not go ahead through the wilderness," he wrote Harlan from Baltimore, "the Devil is a ram!" [14]

In Washington, Audubon went before the secretaries of the Navy and Treasury to ask for a cutter to cruise the waters of Florida, Mexico, and California, and north to the mouth of the Columbia River. Victor was taken aback to hear him declare that a two-year absence from his beloved family might be necessary in the cause of science. Colonel John James Abert of the Topographical Engineers gave a dinner in his honor, and volunteered to write what he knew of climbing rattlers for Featherstonhaugh. "*Such* snake stories I never heard before," Audubon wrote Harlan. General Gibson, for instance, had reportedly shot a rattlesnake coiled in an oak eight feet from the ground. [15]

Representative Edward Everett was the most helpful of Audubon's friends. The future Massachusetts governor and Harvard president-to-be had lately arranged to have the new aquatints exhibited in the Library of Congress and at the Boston Athenaeum. He had nominated Audubon for the American Academy of Arts and Letters, and his distribution of the prospectus was brought off with a competence worthy of this former editor of the *North American Review*. He was also working to have the *Birds* and *Ornithological Biography* admitted from England duty-free.

Audubon returned to Baltimore to see Lucy and Victor off to Kentucky, uneasy about his effortless success in Washington and the actual possibility of a long separation. As he sailed down Chesapeake Bay with Lehman he confessed his trepidation in lines to Lucy after a wakeful night: "So full was I of thy company that my eyes closed only at intervals, and at last the headache brought me to the deck again." [16]

The Governor of Virginia showed the party the sights of

Richmond and promised to jog the legislature for the *Birds*. By a mail coach that overturned in the night in knee-deep mud, then by ramshackle wagon, and finally by stage through the swamplands under waves of migrating robins and mocking-birds, Audubon and Lehman reached Charleston.

While Audubon and a clergyman named Gilman, to whom one of his 200 introductions was addressed, walked about in search of rooms, John Bachman, pastor of St. John's Lutheran Church, rode up on horseback.[17] The ministers exchanged greetings. When Audubon explained that he had come to Charleston to await a revenue cutter for a natural history expedition to the Floridas, Bachman insisted he come to his Rutledge Avenue mansion for a month or longer. The brilliant scientist did not intend to let the interesting and altogether charming Frenchman disappear without revealing much more about his plans.

Audubon could have imagined nothing better than this chance meeting with a great-hearted man of science, one not seeking personal glory, but only eager to be of assistance. Blue-eyed, affable, his weathered cheeks deeply dimpled as if by inveterate smiling, Bachman possessed a sense of humor, penetrating mind, and good but plain manners that made their encounter seem luck itself. The Lutheran minister looked the part of a descendant of one of Penn's Swiss-Rhineland agents. His account of a boyhood visit to the Oneidas was enthralling. The fact that he had once sent Alexander Wilson, a friend of his Philadelphia days, a Canada jay that the ornithologist never acknowledged helped put Audubon at ease. But Bachman's admission that in the course of correspondence with Ord about learned papers for the American Philosophical Society he had found him a tiresome pedant helped still more. Tuberculosis in young manhood had compelled the native of Rhinebeck, New York, to leave a post in Pennsylvania for milder Charleston in 1814.

The white mansion, set in brilliant gardens, faced the cooling sea breeze. The house stood among roses, jasmine, and mossy green islands bordered by verbena, sweet alyssum, mignonette, and snow-on-the-mountain. Orange wall flow-

ers, wisteria, patches of yucca, splashes of petunias and ar-
borvitae, camellias, and boughs of pomegranate abounded.
Trumpet vines, dear to the hummingbird, climbed the magnolias. A kitchen garden was fringed by mulberry and fig
trees. Beyond lay a duck pond, a chicken house, pigeon
cotes, beehives, an aviary, and, finally, slave quarters.

In the low-ceilinged rooms were formal fireplaces, deep
window seats, high wainscoting, Adam furniture, and bits of
Dresden China. The gracious Mrs. Bachman, granddaughter
of an American Revolutionary hero, seemed accustomed to a
flow of guests. Miss Maria Martin, her gifted sister, showed
Audubon drawings she had made for Bachman's scientific
papers. Although five Bachman children had died of their father's dormant affliction, six daughters and two sons remained, one an infant in his cradle.

"We removed to his house in a crack," Audubon wrote
Lucy, "found a room already arranged for Henry to skin our
birds—another for me and Lehman to draw, and a third for
thy husband to rest his bones in on an excellent bed! Mr.
Bachman!! Why Lucy, Mr. Bachman . . . would have us to
make free there as if we were at our encampment at the headwaters of some unknown river . . . as if his heart had been
purposely made of the most benevolent materials granted to
man by the Creator to render all about him most happy." [18] To
Harlan he was soon rejoicing, "Bachman takes us all over the
country, after specimens, in two carriages." [19]

Within a week, despite intense heat, he finished five drawings with Lehman's help.[20] Ward skinned 157 birds. Slaveboys
and Newfoundland dogs led forays on Sullivan's Island. At
night the two bosom companions, Bachman and Audubon,
wrote and studied in a library den amid stuffed owls and
monkeys, atlases, books, bottled reptiles and freaks of nature, caged wild birds, and lively pet rodents.

"I am convinced," wrote Harlan regarding so much good
fortune, "that your work is going down to Posterity and will
make a great impression on the present world. And *one, you
know, would not look ugly, when one's dead!*" For his part, he
had to hope that such a friend would show the works of Har-

lan—a "distinguished naturalist" and servant of science—to Londoners to help him win Zoological Society membership.[21]

When the children were absent the silence in the Bachman home was broken only by the Daniel Burlap steeple clock on the landing. Members of the Charleston Natural History Society joined in rapt discussions in the study. Invitations to dine out were numerous enough that the failure of people to subscribe puzzled Audubon. Bachman, who soon became his unsalaried adviser and agent, thought cost the deterrent. He himself was so convinced of his guest's genius that he fell in with the idea of a joint study of mammals, for later on. He pledged his constant assistance. To Harlan he shipped skins, to Lord Stanley three live deer. He made notes for episodes that Audubon was to furnish. The Folio volume used as a sample to show royalty in France went, on approval, to a Major James M. Glassell and to Columbia College. On its return it was to go to Bachman as thanks for favors.

A delay of more than one month in Charleston would positively mean missing out on the nesting of Florida water birds. Hopeful that the revenue cutter would soon follow, Audubon and his men caught the packet *Agnes* for St. Augustine.

Off Georgia, near St. Simon's island, a gale drove the schooner ashore. The seasick Audubon welcomed a walk on land. At the mansion of islander Thomas Butler King he presented his card, was shown in, and, before he knew it, was receiving a morning shave from King's manservant. He and his host strolled in the gardens until Ward came running to warn that their boat was sailing. King pressed a card into Audubon's hand for a bona fide but dilatory subscription which was to take a full decade for final collection.

St. Augustine was like "some old French village." Its narrow sandy streets, orange trees, small garrison, and decaying Spanish castle of shell stone burned beneath the sun. Pine, live-oak, myrtle, and magnolia trees relieved the bleak environs. "Hare, fish and venison" were the fare for breakfast and dinner at the boardinghouse at four and one-half dollars weekly.[22] On nearby St. Anastasia Island pelicans and herons nested. Audubon watched them by the hour with his spyglass. He waded past the nimble sandpipers while going after live shells, butterflies, and flowers. The noon heat did not slow his efforts to portray the marvelous softness and complexity of plumage before his prizes faded. The warier water birds were harder by far to observe and take than land birds. After watching flocks return at evening, he described their flight with utmost precision in his ledgers.

An illness of some days was the consequence of working "like a horse" until December. But with Lehman's help 16 water birds, represented as never before, and a new vulture were ready for Havell's burin. Lehman drew shells and crustaceans, as well as flowers, "beautifully," but birds less well.[23] Ward skinned more than 100 birds to add to those from Charleston, bringing the total to 383, and helped fill two chests with seashells. But what Lehman regarded as Ward's indolence caused friction between the two.

Lethargic St. Augustine began to pall. Audubon thought that if the cutter failed to arrive he might buy a barge and hire Indian guides, following the suggestion of Hugh Williams, a local explorer familiar with every inlet.

Lucy had been sending press notices to remind her husband that the world had its eyes upon him. She was tempted to send Johnny down to help and to learn.[24] Sitting in his window that overlooked the harbor filled with gulls and brown pelicans, which he called the "reverend Sirs," Audubon answered her questions. He could not have Johnny because of unexpected mounting expenses, although he said that he was thinking of sending Victor to London as business manager. Havell's long silence made him fear that he might be seriously ill, if not dead. Should anything happen to the engraver he believed that the assistant Blake could be trusted to finish the job. He made no mention of his own recent illness.[25]

"The scribblers about rattlesnake stories will now have to hang their ears and shut their invidious mouths," he told Lucy. He had the "certificate" of an observer who had seen a reptile that had "twisted around the top of a mahogany bed post."[26] Encouraged by Abert, he had already spoken out

boldly against his detractors in Featherstonhaugh's *Journal:*
"The good people . . . who pass their lives in stores and
countinghouses ought not to contradict these facts because
they do not meet rattlesnakes hissing and snapping at them
from the paper mulberries as they go home to their dinners."
(Here was a jibe against fortune seekers in the widespread
mulberry speculation.)

On Christmas morning the party ended a ten-day visit to
the vast plantation of General Hernandez below St. Anastasia by tramping fifteen miles to Bulowville. Young, Paris-
educated Bulow took them aboard his schooner for a forty-
mile cruise south to the Halifax River.[27] At Live-Oak Landing,
Audubon waded in fish-filled waters to observe the nesting
of brown pelicans and rarer water birds. The labors of two of
the black crewmen to free the boat, grounded in mud during
a night of bitter cold, would have cost their lives if his search
of the groves for dry firewood had failed. When the schooner
was finally dragged to a creek and floated forth, the crew set
the marsh on fire in their joy at escaping death. The blaze
sent "thousands" of rabbits scampering off in all directions.

Audubon and his men had had enough. They chose to
walk back through the loose sands against a sharp wind to
reach the Bulow plantation. A letter from Lucy awaited him,
one filled with dislike for the casual Bakewell domesticity,
their too commercial friends, and the coarseness of Kentucky. She doubted that anyone in America would lift a fin-
ger to help Audubon or his family. Unless he objected, she
intended to return to England with the Gordons in the autumn. The cold was so intense, as she wrote, that even her
basin and jugs had frozen over.

Audubon begged patience commensurate with his own
perseverance while he struggled for a goal of which "nothing
but an accident" could deprive him. "My name is now rang-
ing high, and . . . will stand still higher should I live through
my present travels. Therefore the name of our sons will be a
passport through the world. . . . Be gay—be happy. . . .
Urge our children to follow honest men's conduct. . . . I feel
fully decided that we should all go to Europe together and to

work as if an established partnership for life, consisting of husband, wife and children."[28]

After his hazardous journeys were over there would be nothing to fear; "current opinion" was in his favor. Hardship, the stuff of greatness, had not hurt him, any more than John's new job on a river steamer could harm the boy. Lucy's suspicion that Berthoud, now that he was Audubon's agent, might attach subscription dues in payment of Audubon's debt of $7,000 in the Henderson failure he did not take to heart. But he would not hear of her thought of returning to England without him. He insisted that she try to meet him in New Orleans in March, instead.

There was still no sign of the cutter by New Year's Day. Yet the uneasy Audubon managed a resolution to quit snuff forever. Because the 29 species and 550 skins he had collected represented nothing new, he spent the next fortnight in the fan grass and palmetto. He and two slaves returned with three new heath hens and a supposedly new ibis. He also had a fresh stock of lively episodes to publish.

Audubon was helping Henry skin a "tremendous large Alligator" when he was handed a newspaper account of Reform Bill riots in England.[29] His anxiety to finish in the South and return to London was greatly increased by what he read.

Piercy, a naval commander stationed near Bulowville, agreed to carry an expedition up the St. John's River for several weeks aboard the *Spark*. Audubon, jubilant, notified Lucy of his good fortune:

> What will my Philadelphia friends say or think when they read that Audubon is on board the U.S. schooner-of-war, the *Spark*, going around the Floridas after *Birds*? I assure thee, sweet girl, I begain to be proud of myself when I see that my industry, perseverance and honesty has thus brought me so high from so low as I was in 1820, when I could not even procure, through my relatives and former partners, the situation of a clerk on board an Ohio steamer. Now they prize me—nay, wish me well. Very good, I wish them the same, and may God grant them peace and plenty.[30]

Because of a hurricane the *Spark* returned to St. Augustine for a week of waiting.

In mid-February, 100 miles up the St. John's, Audubon began to feel he had been "deceived most shamefully about the
Floridas." Half the crew fell too ill from "the stink of the
river" to bring the ship to Lake George. "God knows if this
will ever reach thee," he wrote plaintively to Lucy. The *"wild
and dreary* and desolate" region had "scarcely a bird" to
offer—rare or common. "No one in the Eastern States has
any *true* idea of this peninsula."His own report would differ
radically from "the flowery sayings of Mr. Bartram":

> We are surrounded by thousands of Alligators, and I dare not suffer
> my beautiful and faithful and good Newfoundland dog *Plato* to go in
> the river, although I have seen him leap overboard and give chase to
> porpoises. Nothing but sand barrens are about and around us.
> When an *impenetrable* swamp is in sight it is hailed with the greatest
> of pleasure, for in them, only, game or birds of any sort can be pro-
> cured. . . . We are now living not "on the fat of the land," for of fat
> there is none, but on the poorest of "poor jobs," opossums, young
> alligators, &c., &c. Henry caught five alligators, at one grasp, the
> other morning and we have 25 or 30 on board.[31]

Piercy's sudden decision to turn back to Norfolk for repairs,
after having obligingly ignored orders to do so, brought a
clash. Audubon disembarked and left Henry to wait on shore
with the baggage while he and Lehman tramped back toward St. Augustine.

Near sundown a gust cleared the air. Evening showers
ended in torrential rain. At a divide in the Seminole traces
Plato became so confused that Audubon groped in the dark
for a trail on which to set him. Guided by lightning they
reached a swollen stream and open barren. Then the stars
came out over the salt marshes and the lights of St. Augustine twinkled in the distance. Plato raced through most of
the last of the eighteen miles. Steaming with sweat and "covered to the knees with mud," the painters startled the tavern
folk with their wild appearance.

In the morning, before sailing on the *Agnes*, Audubon sent
a wagon for Henry. He was amazed to have Piercy appear
alongside the schooner and come aboard with "a superb pair
of Swans" for him, and also to ask that the recent falling-
out be kept a secret from the Navy.[32] Gales drove the *Agnes*

back toward Savannah. The seasick Audubon was put ashore at Cockspur Island. He tramped fourteen solitary miles to reach the city. His battered leather hunting dress and full beard and mustachios as "gray as a badger's" drew wondering glances.

Among the guests at the hotel of the affable William Gaston was young Major John Le Conte, of the U.S. Topographical Engineers, whom Audubon regaled with sharp witticisms at the expense of Ord and Philadelphia. Gaston subscribed, produced two other signers, promised more patronage, and sent his bearded guest off by mail coach for Charleston in soaring spirits.[33] The chance meeting had enriched Audubon by a vitally necessary $1,000. It brought his list since landing in the United States to fifteen, a substantial showing.

To the amused and delighted Bachman, Audubon resembled nothing so much as a "grizzly bear, forty-seven years old."[34] A notice from Washington that the man-of-war *Marion* would reach Charleston in two weeks for "scientific researches" awaited him. So did a reminder from Lucy that a certain friend who had met Havell's wages expected prompt repayment. Her husband, she warned, was off at too many natural history tangents in the pursuit of fame. Moreover, the risks and expense of his expedition seemed to her reason enough for abandoning the cruise and all thought of pushing to the West. She also passed along word of Dr. Harlan's unreliability in business matters.

Audubon replied with exasperation that he must have "*so many drawings*" by September.[35] Only lack of funds compelled him to agree that the Pacific must be forgotten for a time. Her announcement that some carelessly colored portraits in the *Birds* sent to Jardine and Selby had angered them to the point of their canceling subscriptions shocked and injured him beyond words.

A late November message from Havell caught up with Audubon: "Mr. Gould has been very successful in his [book] of Birds which has caused him to think not a little of himself. He has just issued a prospectus and as soon as I have one I will send it you, announcing a work on English birds . . .

next June . . . first part, 25 plates, price 3/16/o. I regret much that he should have this field to himself, and more particularly as his conceit leads him beyond common sense, as I experienced at York."[36]

On his return six weeks later from a cruise of the Florida Keys on the Marion, Audubon was richer by four captive eaglets, which he presented to Bachman, and 1,000 birdskins. Some of the cache was for the guidance of Havell's artisans, the rest for the London market. *Ornithological Biography* would gain from his thrilling observations and episodes. He instructed Lucy and Victor to meet him in Philadelphia in June for a summer in New England.

He had yet to receive an account published by the London *Literary Gazette* on October 29, 1831. After reporting the death of Alexander Wilson—actually in his grave since 1813—the paper apologized with the assurance that it had meant to note Audubon's passing. Kidd, not to let the macabre joke go by, had Captain Brown communicate a denial that elicited this question from the watchful *Caledonian Mercury:* "What is the editor about—he first resuscitates a man who has been dead eighteen years, only to kill him again, and then, by way of correcting his error, kills another, who is now clearly proved to have been alive and well several days after the date of his obituary in London."[37]

Death had, however, been real enough in other quarters. On April 21, 1832, Sarah Palmer Pears died in Pittsburgh, six days after her husband Thomas. A spring flood of the Ohio had driven them and their children, the youngest of whom was seven, out of their house. An endless succession of troubles came to a close for the unlucky couple when they returned too soon to their dank rooms and died of pneumonia.[38]

XXIII. New England and Labrador

T HE BALTIMORE PRESS saluted Audubon for exploits "as great as his genius" and denounced "his own country's" neglect of *The Birds of America*.[1] Audubon was therefore "crazed and quite at a loss" to understand how Waterton could pen a diatribe like the one handed him in Philadelphia. Five years had elapsed since his paper on the buzzard made its appearance. To have it excoriated now passed understanding. On second thought, he was sure that Ord was the instigator. He would be facing him momentarily, he knew, at an American Philosophical Society meeting. "How he will stand mine eye is more than I can tell," he wrote Bachman.[2]

Audubon's suspicion of Ord was not unfounded. The Philadelphian and the crotchety squire of Walton Hall were often exchanging letters. They threatened his "exposure" by more attacks as violent as those in *Loudon's* for April. Ord contended that Alexander Wilson had done more for "natural history in one year than Audubon" in twenty. He was satisfied that the latter's bird biographies had been "manufactured" in Great Britain from "the bowels of Wilson" and the fatuous outpourings of Buffon. If Audubon was "so great a naturalist," why did he turn to Swainson, an "indoor naturalist" who had never set foot in America? "I wish you would gather up some authentic information regarding Audubon's life," Waterton proposed. "All our gaping John Bulls are convinced that he has spent his whole life in examining the haunts and economy of your birds." Again, wearisomely, he called for examination of "Audubon's hunting-rattlesnake adventures."[3]

The vulture and its "nose" had at least drawn Waterton from a barrage against Professor Rennie of King's College and the temptation to peck at Bonaparte's work—so "uncommonly dry and disgustingly crammed with nomenclature!" He admitted a shocking fact: he had not bothered to read Audubon's paper before drawing up his "pretty stiff account in favor of the Vulture's nose." He had "taken the liberty of chiding the immense naturalist" on still another count:

> By the by, I gave A. a shot . . . concerning his fiddle faddle story of the amours of the eagle owl. There seems to be nobody so high in favor with our indoor London and Edinburgh ornithologists . . . but I will touch him up now and then. It strikes me very forcibly that that man came to England solely to get his drawings engraved; and I cannot divest myself of the idea that he had no thoughts of becoming an author until he was put up to it by good people on this side of the water . . . How came it that when I was in Philadelphia not one of your scientific men mentioned his name to me? The only place I ever heard of him was at Dr. Mease's, who invited him to tea in order that I might see his drawings. . . .[4]

What Briton, Waterton yearned to know, was lending "ample polish" to the writings of "the Prince of Naturalists"? The bird biographies were actually no more than a transparent imitation of his *Wanderings*, he pointed out, despite their "poor composition and logic."[5]

Ord congratulated Waterton: "The lovers of romance may now felicitate themselves upon the ascendancy of an observer whose *credible* narratives may aspire to the honor of ranking with the tales of the *artless* John Dunn Hunter, or the wonders of that pink of *veracity*, the renowned Sir Mandeville. . . . His far-famed Rattlesnake story is a miserable fab-

rication—one of the clumsiest lies that ever was invented."
He himself was too confirmed a coward to risk more than a
tame jibe in his edition of Wilson at the British weakness for
"tales and novelty."[6] He defended his own revision of Wilson's "poor" description of the turkey vulture.

What in reality gnawed at Ord's vitals was the effrontery of
Audubon's vow during his first crusade in Philadelphia in
1824 to "convince the world of his superior knowledge."
Ord's "ignorance" had been his particular target during and
after the Bayou Sara buzzard experiments. Ord wished Waterton to believe that "for the sake of peace" he had passed up
repeated chances for personal revenge. He did not wish a
"swarm of hornets" about his head for exposing the "impudent pretender and his stupid book." His private opinion of
The Birds of America was that no one endowed with "the least
taste or knowledge in the fine arts" could abide anything "so
vile." Never did birds perch or move as Audubon showed
them, no matter how hard the enraptured connoisseurs might
try to "elevate" these caricatures by fine phrases. The *Bird of
Washington* would one day be discounted as an immature
bald eagle, and other blunders of "that individual," Audubon, would be exposed. "But the time for fully displaying all
this man's incompetency and mendacity is not yet come."[7]

Never more openly accused, Audubon asked himself
whether a man like Waterton, aided and abetted by one like
Ord, could do him serious harm. There was no time to wonder. As in the past, work would have to be the palliative for
shock, injury, and bewilderment about the behavior of men.

Sympathizers were few and far between. An epidemic that
threatened to spread across the border had drawn Harlan to
Canada as an observer with the cholera commission. Only
the rising Academy curator, Charles Pickering—grandson of
Colonel Timothy Pickering, a secretary of state, postmaster
general, and senator—took an active interest. He examined
the skins Audubon had collected in Florida, identified them,
and provided needed data. He had abandoned medicine for
botany and zoology; he would be appointed chief zoologist
of the Wilkes Expedition to the South Pacific (1838–42).

The delay of Lucy and Victor despite strict orders to hasten made Philadelphia all the more irksome. But John's pallor when he made an unexpected appearance with his mother and brother explained their procrastination. Lucy had taken it upon herself to bring him away from the uncertainties of Kentucky and a possible relapse. She proudly reported that "Uncle Bakewell" had sung Audubon's praises during her brief pause in Pittsburgh.

Lucy asked to be taken to Audubon's Camden boardinghouse rather than the far too expensive Philadelphia hotels. There the "little alliance" began to think and plan in unison as efficiently "as the Holy one."[8] Although they agreed that Havell was due for some criticism, the fact that his wages were fifty pounds in arrears made them think twice. Audubon served mild notice that the bite of the engraved line resembled lithography too closely, even though the effect of the *Whip-poor-will* and *Screech Owl* was superb.[9] Victor, not famous for diplomacy, sailed into Havell for his "blotting" and for printing wrong titles.[10]

In Boston the sacrosanct Athenaeum and its president, that richest of citizens, Colonel Perkins, subscribed along with Harvard. Audubon was pleased with a "gem" of a former Yorkshireman, ornithologist Thomas Nuttall, for saying that the eccentric Waterton was not to be taken seriously.[11]

From Boston to Eastport and Dennysville, and from Maine to New Brunswick the family traveled by steamer, stage, scow, and cart, in closer unison than since Henderson days. Everywhere a visit to Labrador was urged until Audubon, impressed, decided to winter in Boston with Lucy and John, and then by summer reach the far North. On October 16, 1832, with a red-tailed hawk for Lord Stanley, Victor sailed for England on the ship *South America*.

Among the interesting, genteel guests at Joshua Davis's boardinghouse was the noted phrenologist Kaspar Spurzheim. Scores of Bostonians, undeterred by a mild wave of cholera, called on the Audubons. But to John, in need of more social graces, his parents left the costly, time-consuming fashionable rounds. Senator Daniel Webster brought a fine

brace of ducks that John helped paint so ably he was promised "a good share in the labor" to come.[12]

Bachman resigned himself to awaiting the end of the cholera season for a visit from the Audubons. But he was impatient for their queries about southern birds and began to
send flowers drawn by Maria for the backgrounds.

Some domestic pigeons that John painted for the family
doctor, George Parkman, turned out so well that he was
given a tree sparrow to draw for the Folio. The results were
faithful to the model, and Audubon promised him full credit;
but Victor and Havell were to ignore the injunction passed
on by John himself with his father's blessing. His credit for
this and other work was to be buried unobtrusively in *Ornithological Biography*.

A superb golden eagle from the White Mountains, acquired from the New England Museum in Boston, nearly
proved Audubon's undoing. Rather than allow its plumage
to fade from the use of shot or blade, he tried to end its life
with charcoal gas in a well-sealed room. But while he and
John repeatedly fled to the fresh air, the valiant captive stood
erect and bright-eyed, refusing death. At last the dagger had
to bring the finish. But sixteen hours of the "severest labor"
ended in a "spasmodic affection," and Audubon required
the attendance of three physicians.[13] His brief, nearly fatal
illness was aggravated by remorse for the eagle's ordeal.
As soon as he was able he begged Victor and Havell to get
on with the task, now that the halfway mark of *The Birds of
America* had been reached.[14] His narrow escape and the news
of the death of Havell's father in November increased his
mindfulness of time and its vagaries.

At the Berthouds' home in March, Audubon read Victor's
complaint that there were actually forty subscribers fewer
than the supposed 200. Audubon dismissed the rebuke with
the assurance that a recount of the districts would boost the
total. His mind on Labrador, he rushed about New York and
Philadelphia to collect what little equipment he could. Between times he sat for a likeness by Henry Inman; he pronounced it the truest ever. Inman, sometimes accused of flat-

Great Black-Backed Gull. *Plate 241 of* The Birds of America. *Engraved by Robert Havell, Jr., after the original study drawn in Boston, December 1821.*

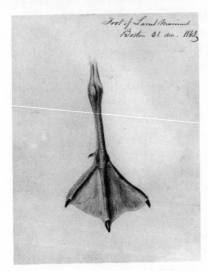

Foot of Great Black-Backed Gull, *1832. Pencil and watercolor drawing. Courtesy The New-York Historical Society, New York. The detail of the foot appears in plate 241 of* The Birds of America, *but not in the original study drawn for that plate.*

tering his subjects, saw before him and portrayed faithfully a man of great physical strength and sensitivity. Audubon was within a week or so of his forty-eighth birthday, graying slightly at the temples. His dark, lustrous hair hung to his shoulders. His nearly toothless gums gave his upper lip a firmer line. The proud head, on a broad pillar of neck, was more like that of a master of foils than of the arts. Behind the intense, far-gazing eyes lay a brain teeming with high aims.

There was ample reason for the earnest expression. The hapless American edition of the bird biographies, thanks to Harlan, was mired in debt. American subscribers were behind in their obligations. Bindings for the Folio, though optional, added to vexations. As Audubon soldered and insured tins of drawings for the uncommunicative Havell, he prayed for their safe crossing over wintry seas.[15]

Lucy continued to whisper her warning that Berthoud might impound deposits of $1,300. Audubon refused to think him capable of such deceit. He presented Nicholas with a bound volume of the *Birds*. His offer to let him have half the proceeds if he could collect Lieutenant Audubon's hoary debt from David Ross & Company—a bid as shrewd as it was generous—Nicholas accepted. But he said he would wait for the cholera wave to end before undertaking to settle a matter that dated back more than forty years.

The New York chronicler, mayor, and artist Philip Hone received Audubon and read his lines of introduction from Quincy, president of Harvard. Guessing his age by seven years too many, Hone characterized him more generously than had Dunlap:

> He is about setting out on one of his enterprising excursions, to the coast of Labrador . . . to illustrate his favorite science . . . with the ardor of a lover to his mistress. He is an interesting man of about fifty-five . . . modest . . . possessing general intelligence, an acute mind, and great enthusiasm. His work . . . is probably the most splendid book ever published . . . ; all the drawings are executed by himself or under his special superintendence. Wilson's book on the same subject is deservedly celebrated—beautiful, no doubt, but comparing with Audubon's as the Falls of Trenton to those of Niagara.[16]

Cooper gave Audubon to understand that Bonaparte objected to having been placed well down in the acknowledgments of his Prospectus. "A plain-sailing man" like himself would scarcely wish to "lower" the friend who helped introduce him to the world, he hastened to write.[17]

Audubon thanked fortune for Bachman's simplicity and fidelity. A letter from Charleston said to expect a shipment of birds believed new, to be claimed by Audubon before the local naturalist Ravenel did "what he has no right to do." Bachman offered to "claim" the birds if Audubon wished while repeating that his only real desire was to "know enough to enjoy" *The Birds of America* and help with a "little information" about Carolina birds. The credit would still be all Audubon's. As for Maria Martin, she was as willing as ever to attend to requests for backgrounds: "Drawing is an amusement to her and to gratify you will always afford her pleasure."[18]

Near the first of May, Audubon left for Boston with John, still uncertain how to raise $500 for his chartered schooner without touching funds left with Nicholas. Parkman lent him part of that sum at reasonable interest.

Fanny Kemble and her father, Charles, were playing their Shakespearean repertory in the city. Their host, Colonel Thomas H. Perkins of the Athenaeum, introduced Audubon to the actress. She seemed, as he presented her with a volume of his writings, to regard him "as an original Bear" of some sort. Her journal makes clear how, in fact, she saw him:

> [Audubon] called on us Sunday last. He is enchanting. I wish it had been my good fortune to see him oftener; one of the great men of his country; he would have been a first-rate man all the world over; and like all first-rate people, there is a simplicity, and a total want of pretension about him that is very delightful. He gave us a description of Niagara which did what he complained no description of it ever does—conveyed to us an exact idea of the natural position and circumstances which render these falls so wonderful; whereas, most describers launch forth into vague and untangible rhapsodies, which, after all, convey no express idea of anything but water in the abstract, he gave me, by his simple words, a more real impression of the stupendous cataract than all that was ever writ or spoken of waterfalls before, not excepting Byron's Terni.[19]

The impressions of young Joseph Coolidge of Eastport, a member of the expedition, add a dimension. He saw in Audubon a "magnificent gray-haired" gentleman, "childlike in his simplicity, kindhearted, noble souled, a lover of nature and lover of youth, a friend of humanity, and one whose religion was the golden rule."[20] Audubon, conscious of his magnetism, joked in his farewell to Lucy of "the Great, the Wonderful Audubon."[21]

The three-day voyage to Eastport had been an unpropitious start. Audubon had to sleep on the floor of the cabin that served all the passengers. The spectacle of boats capsizing in Eastport harbor and his seasickness on cruises of the nearby islands impelled him to beg Victor to see *The Birds of America* through, for Lucy's sake, if "the Author of all things" doomed him.[22] MacGillivray's wishes, arriving about now, had their poignancy: "When the cholera skimmed over the Atlantic I was afraid I should never see you again. I hope in God I shall. I have not seen so excellent a friend since I saw you."[23]

George Shattuck, Jr., and William Ingalls, sons of Audubon's Boston friends, joined the party. Thomas Lincoln, son of Audubon's Dennysville host of the previous summer, was one of those who donned "fearnoughts," oil jackets, over-trousers, and a white woolly cap with a jaunty neck flap.[24] Audubon doubted, and did not ask, whether these young men would help defray expenses. He had decided to leave the outcome to his chimerical partner, fate.

On June 6, 1833, under an escort of crying gulls and petrels, the *Ripley* headed a short way up the Little River, then crossed the Bay of Fundy, finally anchoring near the mouth of the Canso Straits. The steward turned out to be a former bodyguard of Vincent Nolte. The pilot was a onetime "egger," or Labrador nest raider.[25]

The violent motion of the ship made all but Lincoln seasick. At the first opportunity, Audubon, much baffled by the native patois, walked ashore. At first he admired the stark scenery of Magdalen Island and Great Bird Rock with its multitude of gannets; but the treeless, mossy land soon grew unbearably monotonous.

On wet, cold days—all too frequent—he sent the boys

ashore while he drew birds beneath the glass-covered hatch by the hour. He would rouse John at dawn and put him to skinning the quarry of the day before.

A British surveying ship, the *Gulnare,* kept within visiting distance of the *Ripley* for days as both sailed northward. Her medical officer freely shared his botanical knowledge of the region.

Day after day the *Ripley* cruised past the moss-clad granite cliffs toward Belle Isle Straits. Black flies and savage mosquitoes kept Audubon below decks at his drawing. Only five new species had rewarded the furious scouting of his helpers.

Sometimes he philosophized in his journal on the mysteries of nature. The cloudlike dipping and flowing of migratory waves under the command of instinct he thought "as wonderful as it is beautiful." The spectacle of "delicate, diminutive creatures" which, by divine command, desert latitudes "a thousand times more congenial" in order to fill the desolate North with song for two months of each year, seemed to him miraculous. But where, much longer, could man find the beauty of wilderness undisturbed? At one time the slaughter of birds had slight effect on their multitudes. But "cupidity and love of gold," which sent twenty or more ships among the "wonderful nurseries" to harvest thousands of eggs each nesting season, cried out for the intervention of "some kind government" before too late. Four robbers had lately been guilty of stealing 40,000 eggs on a single cruise. Sometimes, to make the birds lay again, they broke a few eggs only. (Audubon had not forgotten his own past excesses; as recently as the Floridas cruise he had called the day that yielded no more than 100 birds a poor one.)

The drawing continued until the summer's output reached twenty-three portraits, some of them due to be finished in the year ahead. At dawn, when his "spirits" roused him, Audubon's weary body begged the brain to rest. Whether close to illness from fatigue or not, he would rise and, once more, pore over his observations and episodes. Dusk, with its soft light toward midnight, was an ideal hour for examining "light and shade" on paper. One day he shouldered his much-neglected gun to go out and prove his aim as good as ever by dropping twenty-seven puffins in rapid succession. The sharpest fatigue he had ever known did not daunt him.

In mid-August the *Ripley* put about for the Canso Straits. She had spent but three nights at sea during the summer, for which Audubon thanked heaven. Much as he longed to visit Quebec before returning to Lucy he could not see how it was to be done, short of a miracle. As matters stood he faced the necessity either of tapping his savings or of borrowing, somewhere, to meet the balance of his charter in Eastport. Final costs totalled $2,000. Nonetheless, Quebec might, if he could manage, redeem the disappointments of the Labrador expedition.

At St. George's Bay he trilled a round or two on his flageolet for a fishermen's ball before retiring early. Johnny fiddled for the dancers, among whom were his comrades, until half-past seven in the morning.

At Roy's Island, Audubon, John, and two others of the party walked to Pictou, Nova Scotia, ahead of their heavy baggage, which followed in a haycart. Professor Thomas McCulloch, of whom Audubon had heard much while in Scotland, invited him to help himself to birdskins, shells, and minerals at the Academy. He sent him off with names of naturalists to see in Truro.

Halifax could provide but one room. The place seemed ripe for the mordant pen of the peripatetic Mrs. Trollope, whom Charles Waterton once called "a jaundiced old jade."[26] St. John, New Brunswick, afforded no better.

At Windsor the party "perambulated" the streets in search of rooms until the wee moonlit hours. Audubon was astounded next morning to have none other than Edward Harris, bound for Fredericton to hunt, walk up to him with letters from Lucy while he waited for the Eastport boat. Harris studied him as he read that two Kentucky newspapers had been devoting space to a debate fomented by remarks in *Ornithological Biography*. One said Audubon seemed "misinformed on the subject of his nativity," and unsure whether he was born in Kentucky or Louisiana. Harris, at Lucy's bidding, had communicated an explanation, saying that use of the word "native" had meant only to connote that he had lived there.[27]

Messages that awaited Audubon at the house of the postmaster in Eastport dimmed his hopes of visiting Quebec. Havell was demanding more pay for work on the ornate water bird portraits, and he asked to be allowed a special assistant. For presenting such "a reform bill" Audubon thought him a "knave, or a fool or a crazed man." He wondered whether Waterton might have put him up to this arbitrary mischief.[28] News that Victor and Lucy's cousin Robert Bakewell, well-known geologist of Hampstead, had answered Waterton's attacks in Loudon's magazine scarcely delighted him. Victor had charged that only a coward would have impugned the honor of a man who was busy in the wilds and unable to reply. Bakewell dared to point out that, unlike the solitary field naturalist Audubon, Waterton had been aided by slaves during his much mooted "wanderings" in South America.[29]

"I wonder if Waterton believes in my drawing the birds I publish?" Audubon wrote Lucy. "Poor beast, the cudgel is all that is fit for him, but depend on it, I shall not notice him."[30]

On August 25 he directed a bold hint to Parkman: "Should we give up the journey to Quebec . . . for want of cash—indeed I will have to ask of you to accept and pay a debt, to assist me, in the fitting out of our chartered schooner. I must acknowledge to you that I may take this liberty in preference to Drawing on my Brother at law at New York." In the end he paid Parkman what he already owed him with funds drawn on his account with Nicholas Berthoud.[31]

Having come to terms with Captain Emery, he departed with John for New York City, arriving at the Berthouds' on September 7, 1833.

XXIV. War of Words

THE ARRIVAL OF AUDUBON AND JOHN brought the Berthoud household to eighteen. Much had to be seen to, regardless of the confusion. Ward's mother was demanding birdskins and passage home for Henry. Audubon answered that her son had signed his release in Charleston, free to join his brother Frederick and work exclusively for William Cooper. As for skins, he asked her to believe that Henry would be given a perfectly fair allotment.

Victor had admitted, for the first time, that he no longer hoped to match his father's effectiveness in affairs of art and management.[1] He enumerated nineteen honorary societies to which Audubon belonged by way of stressing the discouragement of competing. "Suffer not your spirits to droop," Audubon replied. His own overseas indoctrination, he believed, had been much harder. Good books and companions and the study of old masters could make up the difference. The question of how to deal with Kidd he left entirely to Victor.

As for Havell, if he should throw down the gauntlet, the

assistant Blake could fill his shoes. And, Audubon emphasized, Blake had shown his skill surreptitiously with a sketch
of a sparrow—one good enough to entitle him to some pam-
pering and a "small present" just in case. (Victor had warned
him to speak of Blake as "Signor Screamerini" in letters, a
precaution that he evidently thought too ridiculous to follow.) It was reassuring to know that the Linnaean botanist
David Don was still helping to name the plants in habitats of
The Birds of America.[2]

John started ahead by steamer for Charleston with the im-
pedimenta. On September 25, Audubon and Lucy followed
by land. On reaching Philadelphia they were stunned when
the sheriff knocked on the door of Mrs. Newlin's boardinghouse on Walnut Street with a warrant for arrest.[3] Diehard
Indiana creditors Elias Ayres, Enos Woodruff, and Jacob
Deterly were responsible. Audubon's bailiff, William Norris,
kept him out of jail by taking immediate action while the
couple made off for Baltimore. Theodore Anderson, brother-
in-law of Lucy, was of utmost help. A respected citizen and
port officer, he directed the rounds of likely Baltimoreans.

In Washington the overtures to obtain a Government cutter for a cruise were handicapped by the loss of an important
letter of introduction.[4] The well-known writer Washington
Irving sympathized with Audubon and his predicament and
promised to approach the Treasury Department in his behalf. Whether his efforts would succeed the Audubons did
not know as they departed for Baltimore and the voyage
from there to Richmond.

From Richmond they, and a company of noisy musicians,
traveled by stagecoach to Petersburg. At Blakeley they rode
by train behind a spark-spouting locomotive to Raleigh at
twelve miles per hour. From there a flatboat that lighted
flares in the darkness brought them to Columbia College,
South Carolina, and the hospitality of Dr. Thomas Cooper
(1759–1840), college president. The venerable proselyte of
Joseph Priestley was delighted to learn that Lucy was the
niece of Benjamin Bakewell, friend of his late idol. He gave
Audubon a written testimonial about the rattlesnake which

George Peter Alexander Healy. John James
Audubon, *1837. Oil on canvas, 45 ×
36 in. Courtesy Boston Museum of Science.*

he had seen climb a five-rail fence.[5] But it was far from a substitute for the lost letter to Secretary of War Cass that said,
"The whole world knows and respects Audubon." Cooper
advanced $400 toward a college subscription. His generosity
enabled the Audubons to hire a carriage for the four-day
journey to Charleston.

The first thing they observed upon arriving at the Bachman mansion on October 4 was that their son John had fallen
in love with the eldest of the daughters, Maria. They were
taken aback. He was unready to admit as much to Victor,
however. "I am working that I may some day become a second Audubon—not to make a fortune," John wrote him. (He
and Miss Martin, for whom his Maria had been named, were
painting insects and flowers for habitats under his father's
watchful eye.) "My wish is that I may some day publish some
birds and quadrupeds, and that my name may stand as does
Father's. We were delighted to see that the Right Honorable
George Ord has at last been poked before the public by
Swainson [an allusion to what Swainson had written for
Loudon's after a friendly talk with Victor.] How he will relish
Mr. Swainson's and your reply to Waterton! I have drawn
several birds for publication that (at least) are well done; and
I hope to rattle them off as fast as my Father in another year."[6]

Although Swainson disliked Audubon, he fairly despised
Waterton, who had dared to ask him why he had refused to
work with Audubon. Waterton's chiding of Audubon for not
answering the *Mechanics Magazine* article about the rattlesnake antagonized Victor. In *Loudon's* for September, Swainson had replied with the help of Robert Bakewell.[7]

Victor canvassed France, Holland, and western Germany
to head off a similar subscription tour by the hugely successful bird painter John Gould. A shaky subscription from the
Dutch government was the sole result.[8] Introductions to
Lafayette, Talleyrand, and Prussian Prince Frederick were
mild compensation for so much effort.

Havell was glad to be left to his own devices. Never did he
accept criticism from anyone but Audubon without reluctance. William Cuthbertson of Kentucky and London, a fam-

ily friend, was asked to drop in for a look at the engravings. Once he even obligingly met Havell's wages. Far from suffering from lack of supervision, Havell surpassed himself; this even the always reluctant Victor had to admit.

The suspicion that Waterton had put Havell up to his complaining proved fully justified. Victor learned that their enemy had called on the engraver and insinuated that the bird biographies were written with hired professional assistance. What else Waterton may have said Havell declined to tell.

"As to Waterton and the other scribblers, the *Mechanics Magazine* is a dirty thing. . . . I never thought of noticing it," Victor wrote his father, "and I shall say no more to anyone. My reply to Waterton is enough for the present." But it was not enough, once Victor had talked to Swainson and been influenced to throw a final dart.

Audubon wanted no part of the recriminations. "I am sorry," he told Victor, "that you should trouble yourself about the attacks of Mr. Waterton."[9] He might have been less sanguine and detached if he had known what Ord wrote Waterton after querying Kentucky and the South—that in those districts Audubon was looked on as a "well meaning sort of man though a great liar."[10] Unaware, he penned this advice to the hypersensitive Victor:

> . . .—depend upon it, the World will judge for itself. . . . The world is well aware that it is not necessary for anyone inclined to publish falsehoods or form tales of Wonder, to travel as I constantly do. . . . I might with tenfold more ease settle myself in some corner of London and write *nolens volens* all such fables as might cross my brains and publish these without caring one jot about the consequences— but I feel greatly proud of my work . . . of a most excellent Wife and Two sons. . . . every word which I have published or shall publish is truth and nothing but the result of my own observations in fields and forests where neither of my enemies ever have or ever will tread with as firm a foot. . . . I have firmly attached to me . . . a large set of excellent and attached friends . . . unprecedented privileges at the hands of our Government as well as from that of England. I see our work progress well and steadily, in a word I feel happy within my heart. This is the palm I have always reached for, and it is the truest blessing on Earth![11]

Again, in December, he sought to comfort Victor: "That subscribers should die is a thing we cannot help . . . nothing more can be done than what we do."[12]

William Rathbone and others were advocating Audubon's swift return to England to "keep unreasonable people quiet."[13] Bachman could not resist having his say in the acrid debate, and so drew a bead on Waterton:

> Audubon has been rudely assailed about a 'snake story' but Water-
> ton has given us several stories that fairly fill us with wonder and
> dismay. Instead of a contemptible rattlesnake . . . he tells us of a
> great 'Boa' . . . he pierced with his lance, and tying up his mouth
> carried him as a trophy to the British Museum. The snake was so
> large that it took three men to carry it, and so heavy that they had to
> rest three times.
>
> He gives another snake story—a snake ten feet long. Waterton
> was alone. He seized him by the tail, the snake turned and came
> after him with open mouth, seeming to say, 'What business have
> you to meddle with my tail!' In this emergency, he put his fist in his
> hat and rammed it down the snake's throat. Suffering the snake
> to wind itself around his body, he walked home in triumph. . . .
> I am somewhat indifferent with regard to Mr. Waterton and his
> marvelous book. But it is well for the public to know who this cham-
> pion of truth is, that comes to accuse the American ornithologist of
> exaggeration.[14]

So saying, Bachman returned to his ministry, to tutoring Johnny—"Jostle"—in the mysteries of nomenclature, and to experiments with Audubon on the "nose" of the buzzard in order to send "the Demerara gent" downhill for good. He was also managing to help establish the South Carolina Horticultural Society.

Audubon took pride in letting Harlan hear of Bachman's paper on their experiments on the buzzard's olfactories. "I send it to you, my good friend," he said, "because I know you a party concerned with my warfare and welfare in this world. I wish you to hand it to the proper person [Ord] . . . and have the said read loudly, but without any flourish of trumpets or buggles, for after all Naked Truth is a Beautifull Demoiselle, which although madening is so very *respectable* that she will not even care about *The Happy & Most Learned Biographer of Alexander Wilson.*" [15]

The fifty new birds found in the Everglades by the German botanist Edward F. Leitner of Charleston gave Audubon an excuse to try to interest Harris in helping to finance an expedition. But Harris's asthma ruled out the swamps for him. The disappointed, overworked, much worried Audubon took to his bed the last ten days of November. Captain Robert Day, with whom he had cruised the Keys, was refused a cutter after ignoring orders to report to New York City. The total stranger who was to take Day's place could not arrive in time for the Florida nesting season. However, within a year Audubon was to count his 100 drawings of water birds and the eggs of many, drawn with John's help, a labor which would contribute greatly to ornithology. He could now describe nearly 100 birds of land and water omitted by Bonaparte and Wilson. "I doubt if any other family with pecuniary means ever will raise for themselves such a Monument . . . over their tomb!" [16] he rejoiced to Victor, as the second volume reached completion. About the poor supervision of shipments that had arrived saltwater damaged he refrained from speaking, lest Havell take offense. The speed of the engraver was not to be hampered by criticism. "The machine, methinks, is wearing out," he wrote him tactfully, "and it would indeed be a pleasure for me to see the last plate of the present publication." [17]

Victor thought that the bazaar which was about to rise on the site of the razed Pantheon would be a likely place for future showing of the Kidd oil copies. But the progress of that speculation was suddenly cut short. In October, Kidd informed Victor that he was at work on an ambitious *Miscellany of Natural History* with Captain Thomas Brown and Sir Thomas Dick Lauder. For this boldly piratical venture—one day to become a prize of collectors—Kidd had drafted a life of Audubon from the introduction to *Ornithological Biography*. Without permission he copied a portrait of the artist: "I do not know what you will say to all this, but it was chiefly done by me. I proposed that a portrait of your father, in place of any defunct naturalist, should embellish the work. . . . My opinion is that it will add much to the fame of the American ornithologist. . . . I wonder what your Papa will say when he sees his own *face* in a book. Few living authors have enjoyed this compliment, and sure I am none ever deserved it half so much." [18] The miserable prospectus gave the details of Kidd's oil copies of the *Birds* and of Audubon's proposed universal exhibition. *Blackwood's* blindly recommended the opportunistic *Miscellany* and asked for still more marvels of the kind.

Audubon's sole concern was that Victor should rescue the original studies from the copyist. The unpredictable Kidd might "borrow" and publish them before he himself could bring out a miniature edition. As for the expropriated portrait, he laughed about that, and ignored the rest.

Among Audubon's anxieties of the New Year, however, was the plight of the United States Bank and its effect on public confidence. Also, the failure of Havell and Victor to ship twenty more Folios for a potential $20,000 caused deep chagrin. But overshadowing these was the renewal of threats from Henderson, this time through a Charleston lawyer. Judge Benjamin Faneuil Dunkin of the High Court, after he and Bachman heard Audubon's explanation of the whole affair, advised him to post bond and settle out of court. Only the sixty drawings that John and Maria were helping to finish kept him from departing in humiliation.

When the Audubons departed in March, John was engaged to Maria Bachman, though without a formal agreement between the reticent families. Two vultures from the Bachman garden and four caged mockingbirds died after a day and night in their cages on top of the stagecoach. At Norfolk, Colonel Abert boarded the same boat as the Audubons and urged them to visit Washington. By refusing, Audubon was spared the painful discovery that the Library of Congress intended to suspend subscription, lest its first Folio volume wear out before the others arrived.

In Baltimore the "great stir about money matters" made

the ordinarily enthusiastic city as trying as any other, with one subscription gained for another lost. Philadelphia's response was wholly discouraging. Harlan could not even pay the twenty pounds he had borrowed from Victor in London.

Insects, not birds, occupied the scientists of New York. At prevailing prices, none could be sent to Children in addition to three cases shipped earlier as a reward. It was disconcerting to find Thomas Nuttall's work on water birds in the bookshops. Even more so was the report that Nuttall and the Philadelphia pharmacist John Kirk Townsend (1809–51) were westward bound with the Wyeth Expedition. The Philadelphia Academy was showing great interest in the rarities expected from the Columbia River region. At least Kidd's *Miscellany* held no terrors of competition: "I have seen my portrait, engraved by Kidd. The Devil himself could not wish better fun than to catch me in such trim as this fellow has represented me in. Like me? God bless you, not a bit of it!"

A piqued query from Bachman about whether it was true that he had dropped Judge Dunkin for another legal representative drew a denial of having told James L. Petigru, who had won the state's subscription, that he wanted him to represent him in the pending suit: "I went to gaol at Louisville after having given all up to my creditors. I wish friend Judge Dunkin to do all he can to put a *conclusive stop* to this matter, for it makes me sick at heart!" [19]

Harris came from Moorestown to say good-by, then went along to shop for theorem paper and models wanted by Charleston ladies. The lack of any such supplies seemed natural in a city with soul so dead as to starve its drawing masters. Among the new books for sale was one which drove its pen mercilessly into Audubon. Dunlap, in his *History of the Arts of Design in the United States*, touched points of utmost vulnerability:

> It was after his visit to Britain and before his return to that country . . . that I had a few interviews. . . . If I did not become attached to [Audubon], it was not because he failed in compliments to my work. I saw the plates . . . admired them generally—some of them much— and I admired the energy he had shown, in so far accomplishing his

purpose. . . . He tells us that he 'received life and light in the new world'; but this is little more definite than saying that he was born on the globe; he leaves us to fix the spot between the north and south poles; but I understand he gives New Orleans, or at least Louisiana, as the place of his birth, and the U.S.A. as his country.[20]

Dunlap did not mind saying that the boyhood "frenzy and ecstasy" over birds admitted by Audubon had for him a sickening effect.

Audubon managed to get off a fillip, in the letter to Miss Martin, about hoping to marry off Victor and John to Bachman daughters. Then, without reference to Dunlap, he capitulated to his gloom:

> For myself who have done next to nothing since I left you, I have had the horrors all around me. Dreams of sinking and burning ships at night—fears of lost drawings and failures of subscribers by day— have ever and anon been my companions. Not even the bustle of this large town can dissipate these unpleasant fancies. I walk the streets, it is true, but neither hear nor see anything but my fancies dancing through the atmosphere like so many winged imps, resembling in shapes, color, and capers all the *beau idéal* of the Infernal regions! . . . The wind blows a heavy gale. . . . How glad I shall be when no more of these voyages will be necessary—when I can retire from this busy world and rest amid—well—kind friends who can close my eyes and pray for me![21]

The unfailingly sympathetic Harris tried to console Audubon by paying his subscription in full. He had been performing many thankless tasks such as digging skins out of boxes stored with Berthoud and shipping them to Charleston, and he had made overtures to the jealous Peale for birds still needed. Yet apart from hoping to find rapport in his occasional tirades on "Jacksonism," Harris expected no return; a close correspondence concerning natural history he could take for granted. He had to content himself with this evasive explanation of Dunlap's indignity: "Only one or two besides yourself have *an Idea* of what I have undergone, but if God grants me life I shall publish that story, and send you the sheets thereof, as they are struck by the printer."[22] It was an idle promise, impossible of fulfillment.

How, in truth, did matters stand with Audubon when he,

John, and Lucy sailed for England on the *North America* in mid-April? His list of new signers totalled sixty. Before embarking he sent Victor £500. He had a balance of exactly thirty sovereigns in his pocket. Half a dozen years of unremitting labor lay ahead. He would have to return to the United States at least once more for the birds he lacked. He preferred not to anticipate the atmosphere of London since the unfortunate, acrimonious debate in *Loudon's*. He did not know that George Ord, vengeful as ever, had advised the magazine to print no further vindication of what, he said, was well known to Americans as impudent "quackery." Ord and Peale saw the latest slurs against Dr. Harlan (for proclaiming, among other inanities, "the common *house Rat*" a new species) as a blow sure to ricochet toward Audubon.[23] Harlan was constantly under fire for his plagiaristic writings and errors. One Judge Hall, the brother of an investor in a new edition of the late lamented and thoroughly exploited Alexander Wilson, was publishing in the *Western Monthly* of Cincinnati a harsh critique of Aubudon aimed at prejudicing the public against any, and all, rivals of "the father of ornithology."[24]

Audubon had left to John the task of impressing on Victor that, should the ship go down, the work must nonetheless go on. John, for his part, had a more personal concern. "Go to Charleston and become acquainted," he wrote to Victor, "and if you have not had an eye to any lady already," to marry his beloved Maria would be a mutual kindness. "But may the *Great Spirit* let us *all* live for the sake of each other, and may we all be settled in this our happy country. Amen. Should you never hear of us more, you will be alone in the world, and a friend will cheer your solitary stay. . . . So let me, though too young, beg you to fix yourself as soon as possible in case we never meet [again]. . . . The lady I call my Maria is Miss Bachman and is, some day, if we prosper, to be your sister."[25]

American Merganser. *Plate 331 of* The Birds of America. *Engraved by Robert Havell, Jr., in 1835. Audubon redrew his original study in Edinburgh in 1835 from earlier studies and selected skins.*

PART FIVE: HIGH TIDE

XXV. "Something Within Me"

G OOD WEATHER AND THE BEST CABIN on the ship made the voyage a pleasanter one than most. Audubon landed in Liverpool on May 7, 1834. He needed no reminders from Victor, such as he found waiting, to dun laggards along the way to London.

Still weak from influenza and suffering from eye strain, Victor was more than ready to surrender command. Word from Kidd just before his father returned made him all the more anxious. Fletcher, the Edinburgh framer, was about to sue for settlement of an account. Kidd had witnessed every meeting between Audubon and Fletcher and would have to testify against the defendant. In fact, he felt sure things would go against Audubon unless he settled quickly.[1] Before taking a much needed rest alone at the seashore, Victor moved from his rooms to a place near the Havells' and where the family settled.

Two weeks after landing, Audubon received a message of thanks from Kidd for a letter that afforded "more pleasure" than Kidd had known "for many, many months," and which

THE GREAT COHOE WATERFALL: ON THE MOHAWK RIVER.

Cohoes Falls, New York. *Published May 24, 1827, by R. H. Laurie of London. Courtesy The New-York Historical Society, New York. This view of the Cohoes Falls appears as the background of* American Merganser.

praised his employer extravagantly for his success abroad. "I have no doubt that your new collection of drawings and scientific information are both splendid and interesting, and I long exceedingly to have a peep. . . . I need hardly inform you how I have been led into the world of speculation. . . . I presume you are now aware, and I will not (till I see you) run the risk of boring you . . . with a subject which I cannot think or speak of without falling into fits of gloom and melancholy. Suffice it to say that our speculations or publications have *stopt,* and thus I am now busy with nothing whatever but your pictures, nor am I at all likely to embark into any such works again, never if I know myself. . . . In a day or two I will send you what pictures I have finished."[2]

Indifferent to the efforts of Swainson to depose MacGillivray, Audubon got back to his letterpress in earnest. Although his prose was still prolix, it had fluency and a charm due in part to its very excesses. He did not let the specter of money keep John from music or from studying portraiture with the painter Middleton.

In July, when Victor returned, he prepared for a long-delayed exploratory visit to Couëron. Such a journey had been talked of the year before, but because he lacked information he had hesitated. Indeed, Audubon himself felt sufficiently removed that he had recently spoken of Gabriel as "George" on letting Victor know that the Couëron relatives were looking for him any time.[3]

After a brief pause in Paris to request the government to return a volume of the *Birds* which the late Baron Cuvier had left unpaid-for, Victor was off on the thirty-four-hour ride by diligence coach to Nantes. From there he sailed nine miles down the Loire to Couëron. There was no danger of his learning more than his father or Gabriel and Rose wished him to know of the unsavory lawsuits against the estate of Lieutenant Audubon. Gleaning as much as his feeble grasp of French allowed, he reported that persons whose names he did not know were seeking to interfere with Madame Audubon's bequests. They demanded half of her real and personal property, plus their alleged share of 20,000 francs from the Haitian holdings still in the Audubon family.

Gabriel complained to him that the claims and the cost of litigation amounted to 50,000 francs, which ate up whatever rents there were from Couëron and Haiti. The strangers expected 4,000 francs from Gabriel, at once, for agreeing to claim no more than half of the 16,000 francs still due and payable. Victor stressed in his letter that it would be necessary to occupy *La Gerbetière* immediately if Audubon did not wish to lose his share. The run-down villa would bring but 1,600 francs annual rent at best.[4] When Victor had learned and done all he could, Rose drove him to Nantes in her carriage; and as they parted she gave him a miniature of herself for his father.[5] There the peculiar mission ended.

The completion of more than 100 new biographies for his "standard" overtaxed Audubon and reduced him to illness for a week or longer. But Victor's return with a full account of failure in Couëron spurred him to action.

August was no time to canvass nearly "empty" London. But he knew that the "great usurer" Baron de Rothschild could be counted on to shun the watering places. Finally, in the Baron's awesome presence, Audubon displayed some prints and said that £100 as down payment would suffice. The portly Baron "hitched his trousers" at the mere suggestion that any birds could be reckoned worth more than five pounds.[6] He was outraged to be asked for his signature as if his word were not enough to secure a subscription. Audubon held his tongue and left the aquatints on approval. Two weeks later he had Havell pick them up but without the hoped-for order. Eventually, however, the immovable obstacle—thrift—was to yield to the famous Rothschild love of art.

A few weeks after Victor's return, Gabriel answered a letter of thanks from Audubon for his kindness and an invitation to bring the family to Couëron. He said that Rose thought of returning the visit and had in fact written to speak of her yearning to see her brother. The letter had been returned to her at the border for want of a better address. "Bonnitte informed you of her project for a trip to England in order to see you. But now," said Gabriel, "she as well as myself impatiently await your coming. So come along, dear friends, to console us belatedly. . . . Let us know the time of your arrival in Nantes; Bonnitte wishes absolutely to go and meet you." Gabriel himself had "the greatest desire" to be on hand, if his new duties as mayor of the commune did not confine him. "My dear Audubon," he continued earnestly, "I invite you to see, on your way through Paris, Monsieur Bernard des Essarts, legal counsel to the royal court and chevalier of the Legion of Honor, No. 5 rue Godot-Demauroy, Paris, who is the lawyer in charge of our affairs for Saint Dominigue indemnities. There you could learn what has been determined, and, in fine . . . what we shall in reality be able to receive. For I have seen nothing of cash—see about it, and try to bring us news, good or bad."

Gabriel quoted a late news dispatch concerning a certain "Mr. Dorbigny" and his scientific studies in South America—so distinguished as to have earned the plaudits of leaders of state and the grand cordon of the Legion of Honor. "If," he suggested, "the gentleman is the same as the one of our acquaintance, try to find him and discover his attitude in our regard, relative to his debt—and you will bring me news on the score." His son, young Gabriel, was still talking of Victor and how he missed him since their separation. "He chooses to believe that there is sympathy between your own character, and his, and that of his cousin." In the fleeting time that Victor was with him he had given only pleasure by his presence, which served to cement the family relationship, making for the happiness of all in their old age. He also remarked that his brother Auguste Du Puigaudeau, Audubon's "former hunting companion among the sparrows &c., &c.," wished to be remembered to him and Victor. "My good mother, as well as my sister Madame Giraud, ask me, each time we meet, when you are coming . . . thousands of kisses from them and from Bonnitte and me . . . sent to you in friendship."

At the bottom of the letter in a bold, dignified, beautiful hand, Rose penned a greeting to her "dear friends." "You threaten me," she said, "with a sorrow for some days now, for it has been so long since we have seen you. I could wish

that the hurt experienced might be rewarded by a long sojourn which I desire with all my heart in order that I might
have the time to prove to you how keenly I feel about this."
She deplored Audubon's thought of perhaps bringing Lucy
without their sons, thus depriving her of the chance to meet
John as well as Victor, who, she emphasized, could not be
indifferent or ungrateful to her, and who knew it.

An extended stay would enable the Audubons to see her
daughter, Rose-Magdeleine, and her son-in-law, both of
whom wished to see Victor again and meet the rest of the
family. "In this hope . . . with all my heart, I am, your true
friend, sister, and aunt who wishes to kiss you and enfold
you in her arms." She signed, not "Rose," but "Madame
Puigaudeau the elder, né Audubon."[7] However, the reunion
was not to be, and for a host of reasons, some of them far
too delicate for explanation at the moment or, for that matter,
ever. ·

John George Children took nominal charge of Havell while
Audubon toured the North for a month, although actually he
himself was too occupied with the sale of his library (including *The Birds of America*) to help except when summoned.
Audubon's appearance in Manchester and Leeds had the unhappy effect of reminding several half-hearted subscribers of
their intention to cancel rather than clear their debts. Only
one new name was acquired on the way to Edinburgh.

MacGillivray was pleased with the new biographies which
Audubon had brought for his ministrations. If there was
bitterness in his tone it was rather for Havell, who, he fumed,
could "go to Jericho or elsewhere" for ignoring his request for
an estimate. MacGillivray had a work of his own, which was
dedicated to Audubon, under way. But he had no intention of
allowing his studies in craniology, his papers for the Wernerians, or even his project on British birds to interfere with the
Ornithological Biography. He thought the work might fare
better than the possibly "too aristocratic and exclusive" Folio,
if Audubon would consent to a smaller "post octavo" format
illustrated with inexpensive woodcuts from the famous *Birds
of America*.[8] Audubon declined to listen while the chance of
publishing a miniature edition of *Birds* still remained.

Kidd had been watching for news of Audubon's return. The copyist had not surrendered the original studies to Victor, a fact that made it all the more imperative for Audubon to see him. The *Miscellany*, an admittedly "foolish speculation," had plunged him into such "gloom and melancholy" that Audubon thought him more to be pitied than reproached. Besides, his copying was too satisfactory to be cast aside, especially now that he had "nothing whatever" and seemed quite harmless.[9] His brother had gone off to Jamaica and left him with six young children to support. He could barely manage this by taking pupils and by substitute teaching, along with art commissions from here and there.

Audubon gave Kidd his *Black-Throated Divers*—a pair of loons—to render in oil and also ordered him to copy his two canvasses of the Ohio River, not improved by their years in the Harris garret.[10]

Jameson, by now a competitor, kept his distance. Audubon took no notice of him or anybody else. From his pleasant rooms at 5 Lothian Road, he wrote Lucy to come at once and bring his notes, scripts, skins, inks, and colors along. This rankled Victor and John; they had counted on his bringing Kidd back to London as their painting teacher for the winter. They registered their disapproval by warning their father not to give away any more hard-gotten skins. "Most people are blameable for a *want* of generosity, you for too much,"[11] said John, recalling his dawn labors in Labrador. Victor, furious, refused to allow Lucy to manage the requested bulky paraphernalia, which he chose to send instead by van. Moreover, he ordered his father to change from the first to the third person in his episode, "Death of a Pirate." He told him that he should drop altogether the objectionable episode entitled, "The Lobster, Mayor and Constable."

Audubon as writer and Lucy as copyist "dashed away" at the second volume of biographies. They decided that in the future the work would be duplicated in Boston, under Parkman's direction, but not in Philadelphia. They lit their candles before daylight and kept on until time to light them again. "God preserve you and save you the trouble of ever publishing books on natural science," Audubon wrote Bachman. "For my part I would rather go without a shirt or any inexpressibles through the whole of Florida swamps in mosquito time than labor as I have hitherto done with the pen."

Only his dread of what the "monster" critics might say dimmed his satisfaction. "There is something within me that tells me that, should I be so fortunate as to see the close of my present publication, my name will be honorably handed to posterity."[12] In the name of the approaching union of the two families he implored Bachman to send birds in spirits, eggs, and nests, as well as descriptions and lively episodes. He promised that in his next volume his great aide and their "sweetheart," Miss Martin, would receive full recognition.

"You are right," replied Bachman with some difficulty, as the result of having smashed his right hand in a railway car door. "I will fight it out for you. Go on, friend—you will reap plenty of fame, but, I fear, less of money. I wish we both had *otium cum dignitate*. I am not quite sure that it would make us happier, but we seem to think so." He was reluctant to receive too much credit lest errors boomerang in his direction. "Men laugh at both of us," he candidly explained. "I have no objection to being referred to, with regard to the habits of some birds, but anything more will induce me to score you in fine style—and I will show the world how you have been caught napping in half a dozen birds."[13] The praise which Audubon had given him in Featherstonhaugh's *Journal* Bachman had heartily disliked. But Bachman was due for a shock in that Audubon had failed to credit him with the writing, virtually, of the biography of the vulture and his account of its olfactories.

Soon after Audubon happened across Lizars in Patrick Neill's shop, rumors began to fly that the artist was held "very cheap in Edinburgh." Lizars had told Waterton so and also reported that Audubon and Jameson were at odds.[14] (Lizars was out to even his score, it seemed, for the buffing away of his name by Robert Havell on the first ten plates.) Audubon was spared any knowledge of these words from Ord to Waterton the following April: "The notice of Audubon's second book in *Loudon's* is a miserable puff, and not entitled to the name of a review. . . . The brain of the poor wretch has been turned by injudicious applause, or he never would have fancied that he was the elect of God, to write the history of our birds."[15]

Ornithological Biography reached another milestone late in 1834. Bachman noted to his satisfaction that Audubon did not stoop to reply to the "blackguardism" of those "beetles of darkness," Waterton and Ord. Congratulations were in order:

> Never fear—you are safe in America, and intelligent men know it. Do not trouble yourself about opponents—never answer them. Your friends will do that for you. Go on with your work and prosper. It may leave you poor in purse but rich in fame. Men may talk of their Wilson (I mean the Philadelphians). Did they not neglect him while living, although they now wish to build him a monument when he is dead? I could give them an inscription. For I saw him dying by inches with poverty, neglect and mortification. They remind me of the wife that first broke her husband's heart, and then jumped into his grave, desiring to be buried with him.[16]

"Almost mad with the desire" to see both works through the third volume in the coming year of 1835, Audubon packed for London. Kidd and MacGillivray were so hard up, as he left, that he advanced their rent and felt pleased to have the means.

From London he kept up his needling of Bachman: "I must ask you to assist all you can and merely enable me to publish no trash, but pure clean truths, and nothing but— facts—which makes me so proud in my own estimation. . . . My work, I feel assured, will be a standard one for ages to come." A few lapses notwithstanding, accuracy of both words and drawings would greatly increase its importance. "I am growing old fast and must work at a double quick time now." But he was "as ardent" for the task as ever, "if not more so." "Buy, borrow, nay pocket," he begged, for science and also for the sake of *their children*. There was not an instant these days "to think of the blue devils."[17]

The death of Stewart, the chief colorer, soon after finishing the first plate of the new volume—a superlative *Mallard*— did not hold up the work for long. Another colorer, Dolphus, was elevated to the post after a pauper's burial was given Stewart, the plight of whose wife and children caused concern though there was only a pound or two to spare them.

While expenses were running to $450 weekly, Audubon took no notice of what his enemies might be saying. Waterton thundered on to please himself and the appreciative Ord, chiding Jameson for swallowing the snake story, a tale which after a decade still refused to die.[18] Audubon and Bachman would have been amused to know how far Ord had gone. Having begun to realize that Audubon's source for a spurious passage in the rattlesnake paper was the venerable university professor Benjamin Smith Barton, Ord asked Peale to sketch a fang and send it to him. He intended to prove that the two farm lads in the tale could not have died from wearing boots which still held the fangs that killed their father. When Ord broke the seal on what, he supposed, was only the requested sketch, he punctured his finger to the bone on an actual fang that Peale had enclosed. "Gentlemen," Ord managed to gasp, "should I die by this wound, you may place some reliance in Audubon's boot story."

Audubon dismissed as mere "rockets . . . dropped in the sea" such rantings of Waterton as penetrated the busy atmosphere of the shop. He had not heard—nor would he have cared—that the squire had just seen the Folio for the first time and castigated its "errors, caricatures and horrible distortions."[19] Only dyspepsia brought on by sedentary work troubled Audubon; to relieve it, he changed over to drawing. He was provoked to have to rely on prepared Zoological Society specimens for models. No more scintillating proof of his genius could be offered than the thirty-three portraits produced under this handicap by mid-April. Captain James Clark Ross, a nephew of the celebrated explorer Sir John Ross, contributed rare specimens. Captain George Back, author of the new *Narrative of the Arctic Land Expedition*, provided others. Swainson's colleague, Dr. John Richardson, of *Fauna-Boreali Americana* renown, could only suggest that Audubon consult his work, the sum of his knowledge.[20]

The aloofness of the British Museum became marked. The

officials to whom Audubon had sold some of his 3,000 skins of some 300 species were talking. They confided to Jardine, who in turn told Waterton, that one of the costliest items, a wild turkey skin, had been doctored with horsehair. Suspecting perfidy, Audubon condemned Jardine's latest compilation as the merest "trash." But when he learned the reason for the coolness around him, he was grieved. Many of his skins had come from professional hunters. The probable culprit, he believed, must have been the incorrigible Henry Ward. Audubon himself had recently been victimized while buying skins for Bachman and the Charleston Museum. A cunningly doctored skin was palmed off as a new species of warbler. The trick aroused fears that such goings on would "muddy the waters."[21] His own collection of skins was a matter of so much pride that he was thinking of presenting it to Congress eventually with his original paintings as a monument to the family name.

"Charley," or Bonaparte, had by no means dropped from sight. He sought Audubon's opinion of one volume of his work that he himself had not yet seen; it had yet to reach him from Philadelphia.[22] If Bonaparte's brother-in-law, Lord Dudley Stewart, had not neglected Folio payments for so long and consistently failed to send installments of prints to Italy, Audubon might have been more obliging. He pronounced the binding of Bonaparte's *American Ornithology* "bad," but at least better than at the start. If the Prince, he said, had availed himself of Havell's services, the engravings would cease to be too light to take color against the subtle aquatint shading. But such subtlety was not attainable by Lawson, as anyone could see. Bonaparte took no offense while his critic could still be useful to him. He hinted for certain skins as if he had entirely forgotten that he had intended to desert American birds for Italian fauna.

The Zoological Society was engaged in meetings that, because of violent differences of opinion, rocked it to its foundations. Its very existence seemed to be threatened by its pugnacious members locked in combat. Audubon was relieved to be outside it all. However, a message from Bachman seriously upset his equilibrium. He said to send cash at once for the settlement out of court. Audubon could only suggest that his friend collect what he could in the South to satisfy the judgment. Determined to erase all doubt of his innocence in the lawsuit, he philosophized to Bachman:

> It is reported that Napoleon . . . a wonderful man . . . never would suffer a debt to stand unpaid, *provided* the means were snug within his exchequer? You know that I am still a considerable admirer of that great man's deeds; there by I coincide with him in the matter now to be entered upon—namely, the paying of a most rascally debt, to a most infernal x x x x ! Ever since I was a lad, it has been my good fortune to be cheated by the *world* . . . I have become habituated to it. . . . Well then, my dear Bachman, all I have to say . . . in telling you that I am cheated, only, anew, and perhaps when the least expected, and also at a rather unwelcome time, is 'never you mind.' At the foot of this letter my son will give you an account of what is due me at Charleston . . . and at Savannah. This will enable you at once to collect . . . and God grant peace to the man who receives that amount![23]

Another gentle warning from Bachman elicited only: "Smoke from a dung hill!"[24] Audubon cared "not a fig" that the Boston art critic and editor John Neal had leveled charges to avenge suspension of his subscription as a poor risk. In *New England Galaxy* magazine Neal accused Audubon of having told Mason he was born in Haiti, although, in *Ornithological Biography*, he had made statements to the contrary. Mason reportedly painted legs, bills, and eyes, as well as habitats, leaving only the chalked body tints of many birds to Audubon.[25]

Economy drew Audubon to Edinburgh in June. To begin his biography of the white ibis he described the escape of one of the birds from an alligator: "Whilst in the company of Mr. Joseph Mason a young man who for some years was in my employ, and who could draw birds better than any man I am acquainted with, excepting always my valued and learned friend William MacGillivray of Edinburgh, we chanced one morning to be on the lookout for White Ibises. . . ." Before publication he eliminated the tribute to Mason and began anew.[26]

Weather ended a sketching tour of Wales for Victor and John. When they joined their parents at 5 India Street they were sorry to hear that Kidd, on whom they were counting for lessons in landscape painting, had quit without warning in order to join his brother in Jamaica. He had left his copying of birds for the universal exhibition no more than a quarter finished. Audubon gave him up for good.

Meanwhile, John was doing his best to prove his fitness to take a bride. Imitating the style of Raeburn, the "Scottish Van Dyck," he began to accept as many as five appointments daily. The mayor of Edinburgh and his lady were among his clients. He also found time to paint his own portrait for Maria.[27] It seemed to Audubon, as he watched John at his easel, that if he himself had enjoyed the same advantages he "might have become a great man" at portraiture, a medium he looked upon as higher art than the delineation of natural history.

The arrival in London of Daniel O'Connell—the Irish "Liberator" and darling of Lord Melbourne's Dublin clique— for more talks of union prompted Audubon to unburden himself of rancorous sentiments towards his "blood brothers," the Irish. What he wrote Bachman, a staunch Lutheran opposed to freedom for the tithe-impoverished Catholic peasant and the American slave alike, would fall on sympathetic ears. O'Connell had been refusing the contributions of slave-owning American planters for the cause of Irish freedom. Audubon's letter of September 15, 1835, surpasses anything else in the way of blind calumny ever to escape his pen:

Daniel O'Connell (I hope I pronounce his name right) has been here. A fine fat, tall, jolly man he is, I assure you—a perfect "Ladies Man" I take him to be. God bless us, what a fellow at scraping and bowing and dodging he is—especially when the whole rabble of auld Rickie is at his heels! Such hurrahs, such banners sending forth their voices toward the empty air. Such speeches, such toasts, such answers. But alas, alas! The Devil of Adrop of drink at the O'Connell's dinner; not a shillalagh admitted. Nay, although it poured rain not an umbrella was admitted to enter the *vaults* where the alligator alias agitator partook of the sumptuous repast. No, mind me, for I was not there—not I—who would dine with an Irish Beggar I should like to ask of you?

A man who after draining his *constituents* of something like 14,000 pounds sterling per annum, sings fol-de-rols to them and sends them to our shore to be there hereafter Hung and D D!—such a farce you never saw, and I hope you never will. If I was not a good man and a Christian I would have wished him under Way to the "sulphur Springs," and in the sulphur have been *upset*, yes upset and up to his lips in burning Lava! His race will be the *upsetting* of our country unless we dispose of them through the medium of sulphur or of good ropes, I do not know which, so that the one or other Method are employed and that very quickly too. Mrs. O'Connell I never have seen, but being an Irish lady I daresay that she like all her fair country women are fond of a drop—not a drop but an imperial measure of the "crattur" and her lasses and wee things all smell, *even at birth*, of the component inflamable substance of the parent stock. Basil Hall used to say to me—"Audubon, beware of Irishmen." He never added Irish ladies because he thought them most probably beyond the reaching of words. . . . I differ . . . I have known *a few* positively speaking, good noble-hearted and gentlemanly Irish men or women!—and I have seen (not known) thousands of blackguards among them. And when this extraordinary difference in men and ladies of all or any nation does not exist out of the pure-blooded Americans is a query which I now take pleasure in placing before you—and now I change the tune.[28]

In December, the third volume of *Ornithological Biography* was off the press. Elated, Audubon wrote Bonaparte to claim primacy and to enlist his aid in obtaining needed skins from Cooper.[29] He confided his new secret system of determining seabirds by formation of toe and claw, and intimated that Gray and the British Museum snobs should yet bow to his achievement. "I cannot expect *ever* to *clean* up the whole trash before the public, but merely live in hope that I may purge a portion of the matter."[30]

Bachman, above all, had encouraged this self-esteem. "Now for our friend Audubon," he had recently written to Richard Harlan, "in his Rattlesnake story, he was in some way deceived, but it is not part of his ornithology . . . Audubon may blunder among the reptiles and yet write a good book on ornithology." He admitted that he himself had studied birds since boyhood and knew "each one by his whistle blindfolded." He professed the ability to judge when a book such as his friend's was "full of truth and nature," apart perhaps from too much praise of human adherents. "I wish he had greased us less," he said; "it would have enabled us to be more open and bold in his cause and the public would have liked the book the better." Bachman invited Harlan to help "get up a bull fight" against "Charly Waterton" and divert the public while silencing every enemy.[31]

Bonaparte offered Audubon a loan of a few hundred dollars to enable him to buy skins on the market, but refused to wheedle skins from Cooper. Audubon soon let him know that he could accept money only for full value given.

From Green Bank at Christmastime, on the way to London, Audubon prodded Bachman and Maria Martin with facetious gusto:

> I think you extremely lazy! frightful—horrible—disgraceful . . . the older we become the more busy we ought to be *for the sake of our children* . . . fie, fie—stir up for the sake of yourself and an old friend. Climb up trees! Seek for the *rara avis* and then all will be right! Our sweetheart, too, and God bless her, though she may be becoming somewhat slack in ornithological delights or still worst on botanical ones, and may be forgiven, being one of the *slenderer* sex, but you a man, aye a D.D., to stand still—God help us—for if He does not, I greatly fear you will not in the least . . . to proceed is the maximum of all desiderata. Therefore, Mind Me, and keep up to it, or sure as fate the Devil will take the hindmost. . . . Your sincerest friend.[32]

Audubon resolved to reach the United States by June, before "some numbskull" published the Rockies fauna. Rumors of the western sojourn of Prince Maximilian of Neu-Wied increased his impatience to be off.[33] War between the settlers and the Seminoles, however, raised doubts about his chances of obtaining a revenue cutter for the Gulf. The war clouds which hung over France and England worried him far less. He believed his former friend the Duke of Orléans, now King of France, would assure his safe conduct over the Atlantic. It seemed best to take a short lease in Wimpole Street after New Year's and await developments.

At the end of January, Alexander Gordon arrived from New York with the news that a great fire had swept the city from Wall Street to the Battery, destroying the Forrestal, Gordon and Berthoud warehouse. Audubon's books, bedding, drawing kits, and—most essential of all at the moment—his guns were lost. In addition, a shipment of aquatints for Baltimore had been destroyed during riots; for these, at least, Berthoud seemed sure of partial indemnity. The Manchester gunsmith Conway could not promise delivery of new guns for many weeks; but, by his firm stand on the vitally important question, Conway created an ideal opportunity for John and Victor.[34]

In March they set out for the Continent with a note from their father to Bonaparte asking for introductions. Actually, Victor had had correspondence with the Prince the year before and felt no hesitation. Gabriel, delighted that he might see them and perhaps Audubon in July in Couëron, wrote that the possibility of a full reunion, while his own children and their partners were guests at Les Tourterelles, had become a regular topic of conversation in the villa. His son, son-in-law Pivert, and Bonnitte (as "the elder Mrs. Puigaudeau") signed the invitation with their "hearty embraces." But somehow a trace of cautious austerity crept in.[35]

The Wimpole Street house became a magnet for distinguished callers, among them Sir Edward Hamilton, descendant of the circumnavigator Anson; Hamilton held the rank of admiral. Dr. George Thackeray, retired King's College provost and subscriber, lived opposite. Benjamin Phillips, a physician, zoologist, and Royal Society member subscribed and became the family doctor and close neighbor. The Chorley brothers, harking back to Liverpool days, dropped by often to see John and Victor before their departure. Henry, a critic, had Mendelssohn, Rachel, and De Vigny for intimates. John, a poet, enjoyed equally brilliant associations. The Duke of Sussex invited Victor to his soirées. Lord Stanley brought his protégé Edward Lear, a bird painter of extraordinary gifts who was painting some of the collection at Knowsley. With Victor, Lear shared a preference for landscape art. Lear's classic, *The Book of Nonsense*, had begun to take shape as rhymes at random for a patron's son. But it was yet far removed from publication and the fame in store for it.

John Gould, rich and renowned, called with his wife, a skillful lithographer of his birds. The Honorable Thomas Liddell, more often in London than Durham, reported one day that he had tried to persuade the Duke of Northumberland to forget Waterton's caustic advice and acquire *The Birds of America* for his private library. But the father of the bastard Smithson—the future donor of the Smithsonian Institution—was biding his time.

Robert Bell (1800–67), editor of the weekly *Atlas*, drew attention to Audubon's activities. He and his kinsman Thomas Bell (1792–1880), a dental surgeon at work on a *History of British Quadrupeds*, had Louisville relatives whose friendship for the Audubons forged a link. Both Bells belonged to the Royal Society. Charles Wentworth Dilke (1810–69) was far from unwelcome among the Audubons because of his father's well-known aversion to George Keats of Louisville. The *Athenaeum*, founded by his father but which Dilke was gradually taking over, regularly took notice of Audubon's work. He was to refuse knighthood in 1853, an honor that he later accepted.

Vincent Nolte, again shorn of a fortune, yet ready as ever to take a gamble, was in London for the promotion of a money-getting scheme. He was arranging for the making of medallions of famous personalities by the European inventor of the method. Princess Victoria headed his list of English nominees for the honor. He kept the Audubons abreast of his vicissitudes as he went along.

Lieutenant Bowen of the *Gulnare*, which had trailed the *Ripley* in Labrador, called to say that his godfather, the Duke of Sussex, wished Parliament to acquire the original studies of the birds for the British Museum. But the institution had fallen so far behind with its subscription that Audubon was threatening suspension. He refused to let himself be taken in by the lieutenant's flattery.

Swainson shunned Wimpole Street. A widower now and hard up as always, and under withering fire for his "Quinarian system," he had let the public hear his contemptuous

White Pelican. *Plate 311 of* The Birds of America. *Engraved by Robert Havell, Jr., in 1836 after the original study redrawn in London in 1836 from earlier sketches and purchased skins.*

opinion of the first two volumes of *Ornithological Biography*. His endless feuding with enemies and rivals was, to Audubon, a classic example of the folly of recrimination.

On his way to post-graduate studies in Paris, George Shattuck, a veteran of the Labrador expedition, stopped off in London. He brought the shattering, not to say incomprehensible, news that most of the Boston edition of *Ornithological Biography* had been destroyed by fire. Audubon was at a loss to understand why Parkman had failed to notify him of the holocaust of nearly a year before, which wrote finish to the American edition. Yet he managed, after much schooling by every kind of adversity, to down his disappointment.

In April, Harlan's bitterness over their enemies, and the rapacity of their zeal to harm Audubon, evoked the calmest of advice. (Audubon had passed over his recent invitation to "vindicate" the true worth of Harlan's writings, in print.) Rumor and scandal notwithstanding, he pointed out that "to have enemies is no uncommon thing." "Let our enemies, such as *they are*, go for what *they are worth*. Trust in God, do all the good you can, and as little harm as you can, even by word, (which is my motto), and depend upon a spot in Heaven being kept for ourselves," he advised. No one would vote against Harlan in the London Zoological Society; this he promised. As for Waterton, now "rarely in London," he added: "Every one looks upon him as a crazed one, and no one cares about his paragraphs against others or puffs in his favour (written of course by himself)."[36]

John's and Victor's letters from France and Italy told of much sightseeing but little about commercial progress. Bonaparte had taken them to the opera and the natural history cabinet in Rome and to the Duke of Tuscany's camel farm. But he had discouraged hopes of patronage in Italy beyond the fine Folio already in the ducal library. The Prince's efforts to interest the Holy Pontiff, for the Vatican Library, had been bogged down by a hunting accident in which Bonaparte's younger brother had shot a relative of the Pope.

Audubon and Lucy agreed it was time their sons came home. Audubon wished to sail with John on the *Gladiator* for

Portsmouth on August 2. All thought of visiting Couëron in July had to be abandoned.

The London *Courier, Athenaeum*, and *Times* noted the departure. The French press copied the report, which prompted the long-suffering Gabriel Du Puigaudeau to send belated *bon voyage* greetings.[37] Captain Thomas Britton of Pittsfield, Massachusetts, had probably never taken on more colorful cargo. In addition to 400 skins from India, the Dutch East Indies, South America, and Europe for the Charleston Natural History Society, Audubon carried much more: 260 live birds in cages, 2 manx cats, and 3 hunting dogs for Bachman and his friend Dr. Samuel Wilson of Charleston from their grateful correspondent the Earl of Derby.

John went off assuring his mother that he would return a married man. Lucy and Victor planned to keep the Wimpole Street house unless economy compelled a move. That Victor might also become a bridegroom, meanwhile, appeared not unlikely. He was seeing much, since his return from abroad, of actress Fanny Kemble's younger sister, Adelaide. A promising singer hailed by the critics at her recent debut, Adelaide had qualities that pleased the Audubons. But Lucy, whose word was final, advised against haste which could only increase already heavy burdens. The Kembles themselves hoped the romance would soon fade. Adelaide was destined to marry Edward John Sartoris and, in middle age, to write a successful book, *A Week in a French Country House* (1867, 1902).

XXVI. Great Naturalist

F AST-GRAYING, LONG-HAIRED, ALMOST TOOTHLESS, but still
lithe and erect, Audubon peered through the drizzle toward Sandy Hook on September 4, 1836. He and John prepared themselves, their fifteen surviving British birds, four
captive petrels, and three dogs with a litter of seven born at
sea to go ashore. They sailed with the medical examiner for
Staten Island and quarantine, then on to Customs in New
York harbor.

What Audubon was eager to find out was whether the
Academy of Natural Sciences had received duplicate skins of
Rockies birds from Nuttall and Townsend. Harris would
know. If these were available through the Academy, which
had advanced cash for the promise of Western species, *The
Birds of America* would profit.[1] More than that, the "fatigues"
of an expedition, at a weary fifty-one, could be avoided.

The Academy had indeed received the treasure. Among
the 100 skins, 40 were believed to be of birds as yet un-
described. The announcement sprang Audubon out of the
hearty confusion at the Berthouds'. John set aside the portrait

that he had begun of his cousin Mary Berthoud Grimshaw to accompany his father. To the family's disapproval of the likeness he had written a joking defense.[2]

Learning that he could inspect the Nuttall treasure only with the consent of the naturalist, Audubon had no choice but to go to Boston. There, while he awaited the naturalist's return, Audubon signed a dozen Folio subscribers with the help of Everett, Webster, and others, and also collected $3,000. Thomas Mayo Brewer of neighboring Roxbury, a youthful ornithologist, promised skins.

Nuttall presented Audubon with several rare birds and with some butterflies for Bachman, but said the Academy must decide the fate of the remainder. He did not mind saying that he felt sure there were more new species to be found beyond the Rockies.

Berthoud, meanwhile, had garnered fifteen more New York subscribers. At the Lyceum, William Cooper did an about face and let several skins go to Audubon. In Philadelphia it was baffling to find even Titian Peale suddenly friendly, and ready to part with a family of rails that were to form a most engaging "domestic" portrait.[3]

That friend of friends, Harris, had succeeded in breaking down the Academy's resistance with the promise that Nuttall would be allowed to name the birds and be credited in full for his discoveries. Spokesman for the institution was the craniologist Samuel George Morton (1799–1851). Overwhelmed by so much good fortune, Audubon announced ecstatically to Bachman:

> Now good friend, open your eyes! Aye, open them right!! Nay, place specks on your proboscis if you choose! Read aloud!!—quite aloud!!! I have purchased ninety-three bird skins! . . . nought less than 93 bird skins sent from the Rocky Mountains and the Columbia River by Nuttall and Townsend! Cheap as dirt, too—only $184 for the whole of these, and hang me if you do not echo my saying so when *you see them!* Such beauties! Such rarities! Such novelties! Ah my worthy friend, how we will laugh and talk over them! Have you counted the points of exclamation? No, very well. Good then.[4]

He looked on the windfall as proof that even in Philadelphia he was at last regarded as "a—a—a— Great Naturalist!!!"

His toiling "like a cart horse for thirty years" was having its reward.

Bachman took the announcement calmly. The sorry state of the South occupied his thoughts, along with the near impossibility of collecting Folio dues in such "awful times."[5] As for the cutter, he feared that even if one should be acquired, the Indian fighting in the Floridas and Texas would keep Audubon out of those waters. He himself could not go along in any case. Maria, he indicated, was pining to see John.

While cholera in the Carolinas discouraged travel, John was hunting with a former Louisianan, Dr. James De Berty Trudeau, and drawing eggs in Philadelphia, true to a promise to Lucy to remain near Audubon. His discovery that Henry Inman was averaging $12,000 a year at portrait painting was food for thought.

In October the Audubons started south, glad in Baltimore of the goodly sum that city yielded. While waiting to see Jackson in Washington, Audubon chatted with his nephew-in-law Ralph Earl, at work on one of his many likenesses of the lank, leonine President. Earl may or may not have recalled the impoverished Audubon, whom he met many years earlier in New Orleans.

Between puffs on his corncob pipe, Jackson promised that a committee would weigh the cutter question. Audubon took care not to betray his belief that this rival of his friend Henry Clay had "done much good and much evil" to the land.[6] The next day the Chief Executive received John, and that evening when the Audubons dined at the White House politics was avoided. Jackson only sampled the wild turkey from nearby woods and waived dessert for a bowl of bread and milk. Earl showed the guests the Stuart portrait of Washington which Dolley Madison had found and rescued during the War of 1812.

Asked by the Navy Secretary for names of worthy recruits for the Charles Wilkes South Seas Expedition (1838–42), Audubon suggested George Lehman; the Boston entomologist Reynolds; and the son of his erstwhile Philadelphia friend McMurtrie. He "wished to God" that he himself might volunteer.

The Treasury Department gave Audubon a written endorsement to pass along to Napoleon Costé if his old friend could leave Florida duty and come to Charleston with his cutter, and on November 17 the famished and rather weary travelers embraced the tearful Bachman ladies.

"The old gentleman has rather overworked himself and is not quite well, and forced to give up his work for a few days," Bachman wrote Dr. Morton after Christmas.[7] There had been a frenzy of labor. John and Maria Martin helped finish the birds and plants—seventy-six drawings—of Nuttall and Townsend.

It was at about this time that Victor gave his father more advice. He wanted no more indiscreet remarks from him in letters or conversation, sure to be published some day. As for John, he suggested that he seek commissions to purchase paintings in Europe upon his return, these to form an American art gallery, of value to aspiring young artists. He intended to do so himself, within a year or two if he had the time. There the scheme ended.[8]

Before leaving for the Gulf on February 17, 1837, with John and Harris, Audubon sent Victor memoranda on how to carry on if death cheated him of the task. Besides the $600 in his wallet, he had about $3,000 cash deposited in Boston, New York, and Charleston. Harris was investing $900 in the expedition. They went to Augusta by rail, and on to Columbus and Montgomery by stage over wretched roads in bitter cold. They saw hundreds—then thousands—of Creek Indians in irons under military escort, exiled to the West. At Pensacola they were taken aboard the "superb" frigate *Constellation* for wine and snuff.[9] But Commander Dallas could promise no help during the Indian wars.

A report that Costé might arrive in New Orleans at any moment was enough for Audubon. He let Harris search for a needed ibis while he and John traveled to Mary Berthoud Grimshaw's in hopes of finding the cutter. Costé had left word that he would return after rescuing a ship off the Floridas.

Familiar faces were few in New Orleans. But one day when Audubon was not hunting mammals for Bachman, he came across that champion of his lost Philadelphia cause of 1824, Charles-Alexandre Lesueur. The disillusionment of Owen's "paradise" colony behind him, he was on a sketching tour of the South before returning to France for good.

If the city's social attentions secretly amused Audubon, his accounts of the kind had the opposite effect on Victor. "Every day," his son cautioned him, "we find such things as 'private correspondence' published here by the trade."[10] Audubon trusted Lucy to catch the humor between such lines as these: "I dined at Governor Roman's in a large company. He is a fine man, and has written a few kind things in the papers here—my 'Natal City!'"[11] The New Orleans *Courrier* had hailed Audubon as "a native of Louisiana."[12]

On his return, Costé treated Audubon and John to an alligator hunt before they all set out from New Orleans on the cutter *Campbell*.

Beyond Barataria Island—once the stronghold of the pirate Lafitte but by now the resort of pelicans, tringas, terns, and gulls—all was quiet. There was little besides the wretchedness of the Mexican prisoners in the Galveston garrison to remind the party of hostilities, but volatile sentiments for an infant republic of Texas made Galveston no place in which to linger. While hunting deer in the vicinity, Audubon saw "myriads of birds" beat their northbound way against the gales.

Off Houston, a rowboat drew him, with John and Harris, across the burning Gulf. They approached the half-finished capitol of the water-logged settlement, passed squalid shanties and partly built houses; and found their way to the tiny, littered quarters of Sam Houston. The six-foot "President," a hero since the Battle of San Jacinto, emerged from a saloon where he had been resisting the sale of spirits to already tipsy Indians. Before receiving his callers he changed to a velvet coat, gold-lace-trimmed trousers, and lacy cravat. Although cordial, he did not encourage Audubon to tarry.

After one last look at the liberty pole put up by the town for the anniversary of San Jacinto, the visitors were glad to flee the "melee of Indians and blackguards." The cruise that had yielded nothing new and cost far too much ended at Houston. Not a new bird had been seen, much less shot, among the countless migrating snipes, curlews, blackbirds, mockingbirds, hawks, and herons.

Audubon returned to New Orleans twelve pounds lighter than on his departure. Before he, John, and Harris breakfasted with former governor André Roman, they parted with their shaggy beards. Harris caught the next northbound steamer, on which Audubon put his hunting dog for William Bakewell and boxes of skins for New York. Before he himself set out for Charleston he shipped skins, crabs, and a muskrat to Bachman, and sent their friend Dr. Edward Holbrook (1794–1871) a rattlesnake for his emerging comprehensive study of North American reptiles, *Herepetology of the United States*. Maria Martin drew an overpowering blacksnake for Holbrook's third volume.

Audubon found Bachman worried about the times. But at least, according to Victor, Havell was coming on famously with the job. His brother Henry, back in London after failure in New York, was sometimes directing the colorers to help his brother out in a shop close by. Thanks to their doctor, Phillips, Henry narrowly escaped death by influenza; quite well again, he was urging Robert to join him for another try in America, once *The Birds of America* was finished. (Though Victor discreetly refrained from saying so, Havell thought the end of the work near enough that he had risked a three-week sojourn in Holland and the Rhineland.) All manner of natural history specimens were wanted by Bell, Liddell, Dilke, and the rest, should Audubon be coming.

Amid the pleasant excitement of wedding preparations John regretted that his brother's romance with Adelaide Kemble had come to nothing. Victor avoided the subject. He spoke instead of such preoccupations as the oil of *Black Cocks* that he had painted and its purchaser, Henry de Rham, Jr., son of the founder of the first French mercantile house in New York City. His father, a former Swiss consul, was a friend of Nolte's. Victor had done an oil portrait of the wealthy scion and ornithological collector while Frederick Cruickshank painted a miniature version. Dr. Rham promised to subscribe the moment he reached New York and obtained his father's draft.

Bachman had been having a slight altercation with Ord about a certain paper on color changes in birds and mammals submitted to the American Philosophical Society. Ord, whom Bachman had taken to task for his theories, at first pronounced it a "valuable contribution," and called his own lapses "trifling" and "silly," but then showed his true colors. He suggested that Bachman delete his "panegyric" to Richardson, Bonaparte, Wilson, and also to Audubon if he wished to see his paper in print.[13]

Neither Bachman nor Audubon knew—nor were they ever to discover—that Ord had once visited the region of "Audubon's adventures" to do some spying for Waterton's satisfaction.[14] Audubon did learn, however, that Waterton had alienated even his own York Philosophical Society, whose kindly officer Thomas Allis had subtly conveyed his sympathy with Audubon's right to free opinion.[15] No one cared a whit on either side of the Atlantic that Waterton was saying England was "at a loss for another lion," now that Audubon was "weak and old." Waterton had found a new scapegoat in Thomas Nuttall, "a most superlative ass and blockhead," in his opinion.[16]

Somewhat dispirited but far from weak and old, Audubon left Charleston late in June with John and Maria. Maria's excitement and wonder at the changing landscape refreshed her weary father-in-law. John and Maria were to honeymoon at Niagara for a fortnight before the voyage to England. Times "hard past reckoning" made collections difficult along the way.[17]

The one satisfaction in Washington was an interview with President Van Buren. Baltimore surrendered a reluctant $500 in dues, Philadelphia a paltry $165. Tightened credit had Berthoud fighting bankruptcy in New York. Thomas Bakewell had already failed in Cincinnati. Even with the aid of the rich George Keats, William Bakewell was having all he could do to keep his bank going. Forrestal, Gordon and Berthoud's dilemma had changed Nicholas's outlook. He regarded Audubon as "the happiest of men—free of debts and having *available funds and talents!*"[18] Yet he made no move to claim any part of the money in his hands as agent. Assets of $8,000, plus payments due and £1,100 Victor had insisted be converted into gold, inspired something other than the contempt and pity of the past. The greater part was entrusted to Nicholas for the day of the family's return to America for good.

When Audubon joined twenty-two passengers on the *England* on July 17 he looked forward to the day when he could close his "pinions" and "be pestered" no more by old cares. "What a strange realization of a dream, this finishing of a work that has cost me so many years of enjoyment, of labor, and of vexation," he mused.[19] A vexation, indeed, would be the discovery that the Townsend and Nuttall skins were not quite the rarities he supposed.

XXVII. Realization

CALM SEAS, a "very decent" ship's library, and a fine bathing room made the voyage an agreeable one. Not until the morning of August 5—the landing day— did seasickness trouble Audubon. Although only a few of the eighteen wild passenger pigeons intended for his friend Heppenstall of Sheffield survived, all fourteen of the live terrapins thrived at sea.[1]

Eager to know how a large alligator shipped from New Orleans might be faring, he went at once to the vessel that held it, only to learn the reptile had died at sea. But Maria's pet grosbeak, which had also come by the southern route, was alert; and a cage of four flying squirrels for Havell was intact and waiting.

The landing of the "American woodsman" was observed in all of its colorful details within the astonished Customs. A rumor began in Liverpool, then spread to Yorkshire and London, that Audubon appeared to have "turned regular trader in silk goods," when, in actuality, he was carrying only a silk shawl that Lucy had asked him to select for the wife of their faithful and deserving physician, Phillips.[2]

In April, Waterton gloated over the rumor. He informed Ord that Audubon was "very little heard of" any longer. "His manifest falsehoods seem at last to have opened the lead-lined eyelids of old Mr. Bull, who will swallow anything in the form of novelty, especially when offered to him by a foreigner. Three years ago it was all Audubon: lecturers, writers, bookmakers, professors, all were lost in admiration at Audubon's knowledge and the hardships he had undergone in quest of birds. A gentleman told me that A.'s family is living in one of the most fashionable parts of London. From whence comes the money?"[3]

London, the same "vast artificial area" he had left behind, seemed to him as overgrown with humbug as some prairie with broom grass. New productions by ornithologists Gould and Yarrell were the topic of the hour. Poor Swainson was still "rattling away as wild as ever" in defense of his "lunatic systematical rhapsodies." The rival ornithological systems Audubon dismissed with, "Memorials!" Swainson, Vigors, Temminck, and D'Orbigny could compete to their heart's content. His own innocence of academic pride and intellectual snobbery excused him; but he intended, all the same, to make the most of their cerebrations in his coming synopsis of The Birds of America. Indeed, he would do so if and whenever it served his dedicated purpose.

Charles Lucien Bonaparte happened to be in town to forward his particular system. He had not credited the wild turkey notes to Audubon on their publication. His renewed "pumping" vexed and wearied, after he and Audubon had exchanged greetings (on both cheeks, French fashion). Audubon helped find simple quarters for Bonaparte an agreeable distance from the country hall of his Uncle Joseph. The artist did not intend to play "green horn" any longer to the outwardly "mild, pleasant-speaking" puppet.[4] Completion of The Birds of America and the exacerbating matter of the Townsend and Nuttall skins came first.

The Prince would not be ignored. Once, when extreme fatigue had driven Audubon early to bed, the unabashed egoist woke him up and insisted on attention. For hours after his departure sleep refused to come. Yet the six or seven birds that the man might come through with in the end called for patience. Bonaparte persisted with endless queries. One day he persuaded Audubon to allow him to copy a list of new species, then walked out with both list and copy.

Antagonism toward the Prince deepened with the passing weeks. Bonaparte's failure to come to terms with Havell for services—his chief reason for visiting London—turned his tongue mordant. He spared Audubon his private revised opinion that the Folio was a "poor thing," but did not hesitate to say that some of its species, called "new," were actually discovered in the eighteenth century by others. Granting that eight of the skins from Nuttall were new, he challenged the genera and species of several. Thus he evened the score for Audubon's good-natured jibe that they both—as well as Wilson—had erred in mistaking immature birds for new species. At least the artist was getting at the real "character of Charley," but he also had to admit, to Bachman, that "poor Townsend did only obtain eight species" previously unknown. A telling stroke remained to be added to the realistic portrait of "Charley," one Audubon would not have to face until around New Year's after the Prince had faded from the scene.[5]

Tormented by the need of specimens for the anatomical descriptions still to be written by MacGillivray, Audubon got off a long list of desiderata to William Bakewell. It seemed that Colonel Webb had promised but failed to provide the needed species for shipment by James Grimshaw from New Orleans. The gravity of the American economic crisis, and what it was doing to the interests of his brother-in-law, was not yet borne in upon him in his own frenzy to get on with and end his endeavors.[6]

Townsend gave Audubon more than enough to think about, meanwhile. The naturalist, "poor fellow," returned from the West, and, to keep creditors from seizing his collection, entrusted the lot to the Academy in Philadelphia. He asked Harris to tell Audubon that fifty dollars down would do.[7] The final payment would come to what Nuttall had

Gyrfalcon, *1837. Pencil and watercolor drawing. Audubon drew the gyrfalcon in London for plate 366 of* The Birds of America. *John Heppenstall of Sheffield, England, provided the specimen. In a letter of October 10, 1837, to Thomas Allis of York, Heppenstall stated that Audubon had hoped to show a male and a female rather than two females. Heppenstall had had the bird for more than five years when it died. "Audubon and his wife were on a visit at my house while it remained in health. . . . He had cut his forefinger and was unable to [draw] it at the time. . . . Audubon's work is a faithful representation." Heppenstall thought the tongue too red in the first of the colored engravings.*

asked. Audubon was expected to choose for his own needs, then sell the rest in London to oblige Townsend. Harris had dropped supervision of the building of a new Episcopal church in Moorestown to go and seek agreement with the Philadelphian. Townsend was planning nothing more than a cheap, small book as his contribution to American ornithology. Even that little was painfully beyond his means.

Audubon pitied Townsend to the extent of getting off an opinion to Morton. He damned the "wealthy gents" who failed to come to the naturalist's rescue—in contrast with the way that Harris had helped *him* in days gone by.[8] How a second plea to Peale for a list of Pennsylvania birds for a paper on geographical distribution of the species would be received he had no idea.

Townsend was receiving far more moral support, if of a warped variety, than Audubon supposed. Ord took exception to his cooperation and had begun to sow dissension about whether Audubon should be granted such wholesale advantage. Townsend, Harlan, and Morton bickered among themselves about it. Meanwhile, Havell, already resentful over the prospect of more work than he had bargained for, idled along while the needed skins failed to appear.

Audubon got off a desperate representation to Harris: "If I do not figure the new species of Townsend, no one else will, for it would not pay anyone but me, and the skins would be suffered to rot in the public institutions of Philadelphia. . . . Wonderful friends of science, the Messrs. Ord & Company! *If I cannot have the skins*, pray send me Townsend's close descriptions of all those which you both consider new, that I may at least publish this in my last volume.[9] As for Morton, he asked him to believe that he was "not quite so *black*" as painted by some. And he promised that Townsend, like Nuttall, would be fully credited in *Ornithological Biography*.[10]

Before his words had traveled far, the skins were in his hands. Their arrival brought its share of disappointments because of the usual carelessness of Townsend, who had neglected to mark the value of the fishes, birds, and mammals. Audubon began to doubt the reliability of the descriptions that accompanied them. He recalled Bonaparte's warning that he—not Townsend or Nuttall—would be responsible for errors. Already some of the Western birds had appeared in *Ornithological Biography* with names that would have to be corrected in a later volume.

Before Christmas, during the latest vicissitudes, Thomas Sully and his daughter Blanche arrived in London. They were with his brother Robert, not far from Wimpole Street. The portraitist had come to England on the chance that he would be granted the honor of painting the future queen, Victoria. She was already installed in Buckingham Palace with her mother and awaited the coronation. Audubon had doubts of Sully's luck; Victoria seemed besieged by favor seekers.

Victor began to squire Blanche about, with Ann Gordon as chaperone. But one did not venture far at night that bitter winter while all London was on the lookout for "Jack the Ripper." The Thames froze solid, and pedestrians could cross on foot without danger. Day after day the Sullys were welcomed by the Audubons. "All adjourned to the dining room," the warm, mercurial Blanche wrote home, "where we spent the evening most merrily. I don't think I laughed so much as I did last night since we left home. At 10 P.M. Father called for me." Lucy was soon teaching her to knit. Before an evening at the Gordons' they were "dressed by the maids." Blanche confided that the music of the performing Audubons was only "tolerable." There were "plenty of pictures" to look at. "I cannot enough praise the kindness of Mr. Audubon and family; all that the most careful attention and delicacy can do has been shown us." She would never forget November 11 when Victor enabled her to watch, from a friend's window, a "Procession" at such close range as to permit her to see the Queen's dress."[11]

One day Sully called with a student artist, G. P. A. Healy, an American who was anxious to get on fast enough to marry his English fiancée and return home. He gave Audubon no peace until he agreed to pose. Because night was the only time that could be spared, Healy proceeded by gaslight while his sweetheart watched. Seated between Lucy and Maria, who were busily sewing, the girl squirmed while Audubon, in an open-necked hunting shirt, discoursed on marriage. "The only real happiness," he proclaimed it, gun in hand, chin well forward.[12]

In March, Sully had his wish. He arrived one evening from his first session with Victoria. The regal little personage had been charming—not at all formal. She had suggested that Blanche pose for the figure in full queenly regalia when the head was finished. Vincent Nolte, just out of gaol (partly for debt, but more as a consequence of having obtained an appointment with Victoria before his jealous creditor, the Duke of Brunswick, managed to do so) gave a contrasting slant. While Victoria listened to his petition to have her features reproduced in a medallion series, Nolte gained an impression not of a regal personality, but of a pretty, if silent and waddling, rather too plump young woman.

Weeks passed before Audubon mustered the courage to tell Bachman about Bonaparte's betrayal of trust. Joseph Edward Gray, the British Museum entomologist and official who was more than indifferent to Audubon, willingly served as an alibi for the Prince's duplicity. The appearance in January of Bonaparte's *A Geographical and Comparative List of the Birds of Europe and North America* had struck like a whip lash: "Bonaparte has treated me shockingly, published the whole of *our* secrets . . . after giving me his word of honor that he would not do so."[13] The work listed twenty more birds than Audubon could offer. His attempts to jest about his "hypochondriacal" spirits failed miserably. Overwhelming grief goaded him into a marathon of labor which Havell's determination to finish by June would, in any case, have necessitated.

In mid-April, Audubon finished 100 new drawings. Many of the figures had to be crowded together on copper without heed for the mixing of species and minus the usual botanical refinements. Although well drawn, they were closer to the prosaic compositions of a past era—a style that Audubon had always belittled. His former plan to devote a few final plates to eggs had to be abandoned, because those of Western birds were lacking.

The first eastbound crossing of Brunel's historic steam-powered *Great Western* gave Edward Harris the fever. A widower since 1830, he began to think also about a Rockies expedition with Audubon, Bachman, and Townsend for autumn. This idea sparked no enthusiasm in London or Charleston. Audubon said such a scheme must be contemplated for his "miniature" edition, but not yet. Such an edition had been talked of since 1833, if not before. A clapper rail by Audubon had been lithographed, octavo size, in Philadelphia in 1932.

Harris landed on May 25, 1838, agog from the rapid crossing by steam. Only Lucy had time to listen to his excited account of the voyage. He proceeded to Binfield to see his cousin Lady Vansittart, then he was off for France to buy Percherons—the first ever for American export. He planned to join the Audubons later in London or Edinburgh.

The Birds of America neared the end of its long, tortuous, sometimes almost hopelessly beleaguered way on June 20, 1838. On that day, amid the gay precoronation tumult, Havell pulled an impression of the final copper plate, a portrait of a pair of little dippers hopping on cliffs above the cascading Columbia River. But the silver loving cup which Audubon had long since given to Havell in proper gratitude still had to stand empty, until the last set was colored and delivered.

Before Audubon could rejoin MacGillivray, he had to set the wheels in motion for his last year in London. Henry Havell was entrusted with the mounting of the original studies on durable gray pasteboard for shipment to New York. (What should become of them after that remained to be decided.) Audubon told Havell to accept subscriptions only and to refuse to sell single prints and numbers, although he himself sold single prints to his agent William Coleman. Furthermore, no careless subscriber whining for replacements was to be accommodated. Between the refusal of the colorers to do more than the contract called for and the reluctance of Havell to placate them until concessions were assured, Audubon by no means exaggerated the rarity of his masterpiece. No more copies would be struck; that much was certain.

Audubon found MacGillivray discouraged with trying to shape the sparse observations of Nuttall and Townsend into readable bird biographies. Indeed, he walked in on the professor on a day of bitter disappointment that critics should have belittled the initial volume of his *History of British Birds*, undertaken only after Audubon had abandoned the idea of such a study. Not even a *succès d'estime* appeared possible in the face of the charge that the episodic style was too like Audubon's. As far back as May 1831, MacGillivray had hinted for credit as editor. "Nothing that has happened here for ten years," he had then written his employer, "has surprised me more than Jameson's having said to you that I did not deserve to be mentioned in your book." [14] He was insisting that in the fourth volume Audubon acknowledge his debt or else dispense with more aid. Once the embarrassed author agreed, the two set to work again side by side, only pausing at nightfall to walk out and see the rockets sent up in honor of Victoria. On June 13, two days after the coronation, the first Audubon grandchild, Lucy, was born in Wimpole Street.

John Bachman, in poor health and acutely lonesome for Maria, needed only an invitation to address the naturalists and physicians of a September anniversary congress, at Freiburg in Baden-Württemberg, to leave Charleston on June 5. He and young Christopher Happoldt, his science protégé, landed in Liverpool on July 2 after a voyage made memorable, for the crew, by his regular sabbath sermons in every kind of weather on the *Chicora*. Bachman spent a stimulating day or two in Liverpool in the company of Audubon's friend Melly, to whom he brought a box of insects. The mandate had been less bother than the live mockingbirds and the one anhinga that survived the voyage. Bachman also stopped at Oxford before going on to London, where he spent a day and a half in Wimpole Street, then left hurriedly for Edinburgh. There three weeks flew by, instead of an intended ten days of absorbing sessions with Audubon and Victor. The miniature edition of the *Birds* and a folio of quadrupeds were earnestly discussed. Bachman left with the stern injunction not to come to Charleston without plenty of American mammals from English collections. Victor followed him to London for the christening of little Lucy.

Phillips scotched Bachman's fears of spinal trouble, diagnosed his ailment as faulty digestion, and prescribed an occasional ounce or two of good whiskey. There was, and would continue to be, much joking about the mixture of "Johnny Crapeau" and "John Bull" and the Rhineland in the new family member.

At a moment when the Audubons were rejoicing over the finish of *The Birds of America,* Ord was finally letting Waterton in on the dismal, hoary affair of the so-called "Great Crow Blackbird." He himself was in England and the house guest of his old crony even as he wrote for him:

> As one of the Plates of the C. Bonaparte's continuation of Wilson's Ornithology (Vol. 1, plate V) bears the name of Audubon and Rider, some explanation of this circumstance may be necessary.
> When Bonaparte first beheld Audubon's drawings, he pronounced them far superior to any which had been produced by the pencil of Wilson, and he signified his intention of employing the former to make all the drawings necessary for his work. The drawing for the plate above mentioned, the male and female purple Jackdaw of Georgia [here Ord's memory of the species betrayed him] was completed by Audubon, who charged for it the sum of twenty-five dollars. When Bonaparte brought the drawing to his engraver Mr. Lawson the latter pronounced it unfit for the work, inasmuch as it did not possess those characters which are requisite in all natural history designs, intended to be engraved. However, as Bonaparte was urgent, Lawson dropped his objections, and declared his intention of commencing the plate. When the copper was prepared for the etching, the difficulty of transferring the outline was so great that the engraver lost his patience, and informed his employer in the most positive terms that unless better and more characteristic drawings were furnished him he would abandon the work. Bonaparte now perceived that he had got into a difficulty. Audubon's drawing was condemned, and Alexander Rider, a Swiss artist, was employed to draw the figures of the Jackdaws which are represented in the plate above named. The drawing was made from specimens in the Philadelphia Museum; which specimens had been shot in the Sea Islands of Georgia by Mr. T. Peale and myself. Audubon's drawing had an egg in it, and this egg is the only part which was either

copied or imitated by Rider. But Bonaparte's plate bears the name of Audubon as one of the artists engaged in producing the drawing! This name was put by order of Bonaparte himself who, in justification of the trick, declared that he did so, lest his friend A. should be hurt by the rejection of his drawing. Although the enormous sum of 25 dollars had been paid for this drawing, yet so vexed was Bonaparte at his disappointment in it that he told Rider he might do with it what he pleased. It is necessary to add that he never more employed the "Great Ornithologist" to produce drawings for the continuation of Wilson's Ornithology. The former drawing was given to me by Alexander Rider himself, and I preserve it for the purpose of proving the correctness of Mr. Lawson's assertion that Audubon's drawings could not be engraved.

This very drawing I showed, a few days ago, to Mr. Lizars, engraver of Edinburgh, Mr. Nichols, bookseller of Wakefield, and Mr. Waterton. Let these gentlemen say what they think of it.

Walton Hall, June 29th, 1838.   George Ord.

The letter of Ord (in the American Philosophical Society) deals the coup de grace to the representation of the pencil drawing by Alexander Rider (in the Lawson Papers at the Academy of Natural Sciences, Philadelphia) as the work of Audubon. The signature, "J. Audubon," is an obvious forgery; it bears no resemblance to the thousands available for comparison. The pencil drawing is uncolored, although in 1825 Bonaparte wrote to Audubon that Rider was to color the engraving when Lawson completed it. The admirable pencil and watercolor drawing of grackles by Audubon, sold at auction by Sotheby's on May 28, 1987, and long believed lost, made its first published appearance in the Sotheby catalog. The grackles of the Bonaparte work, long accepted as by Audubon in part, were neither by his hand nor were they his first published art.

On August 8 the Audubons gave up the Wimpole Street house. Bachman and Happoldt took rooms in Leicester Street. The family, including Elizabeth the maid, started for Scotland and 2 Alva Street, Edinburgh.

Another week of study at the British Museum and Zoological Garden, where his learning and friendly criticism were well received, did not suffice for the avid Bachman. Not until mid-August did he continue on his way to the congress.

With MacGillivray as courier the family toured the Trossachs, Loch Lomond, Tarbet, and Glasgow by stage and steamer. The week benefited the wan Maria and the extremely weary Lucy. Victor returned to London to help Havell and prepare for his departure for the United States to pave the way for the miniature *Birds*. Audubon returned to work, much relieved that Bachman intended to say nothing in Freiburg about their contemplated *Quadrupeds,* or admit more to the Germans than that American mammalogy was lagging. When Harris returned from Paris he found everyone too absorbed for grouse shooting and went back to France.

Audubon was deep in his *Synopsis* by late October. "I intend," he wrote Bachman, "to work with extreme care, without being influenced by anyone, and without in the least attempting systematization." He would offer no more than genus, species, sex, brood, and a note on scarcity or abundance. As for crediting the help of "that dirty mean fellow, the Bangs of Rome," that was unthinkable.[15] Bonaparte's name was dropped from the Folio.

Some ally of "poor devil" Ord had supposedly found a powerful olfactory nerve in the buzzard. Audubon declined the chance to debate the question further. But in his reaction to Gould's preparations for a family expedition to Australia he showed less restraint, and chose to see as absurd this move by one who had never so much as learned to "salt steaks with gunpowder." Gould's rumored annual income of $10,000 had made him no more attentive to obligations, including his Folio subscription. Indeed, his name had been dropped from the list. The family had scant admiration for the art of this man whom Victor, for one, rated a scamp for having aped *The Birds of America,* with a work of his own "so bad" it was "quite a pity to take it." To his father, some months before, he had written: "Gould's last Number is abominable. Mr. Lear is drawing for him as usual. He is not, however, fond of drawing birds."[16]

Actually, far more than Gould's plans left Audubon envious. As he sat writing the second to the last volume of the

biographies, the one on the sharp-tailed grouse led his pen—
by the mood it created—so far afield that a whole passage
had to be deleted by MacGillivray. He was faced with closing
both Folio and text without having seen living birds in the
Rockies—he who, for years, had so longed to reach the
Pacific:

> What opportunities, good Reader, have been lost in making the
> most valuable observations on the habits of our birds by scientific
> men being attached to what may well be called Galloping Parties? I
> could enumerate some hundred instances all of which would have
> proved of the greatest interest to both you and I but alas neither of
> us, I fear, can persuade the heads of mercantile men that to tarry for
> a few days on their march would be beneficial to Science, or prove to
> any Government that a ship, with orders to sail around the world
> and anchor for, at most, not more than one month during the great
> circuitous voyage, would at all be unavailing. What opportunities I
> must repeat are constantly lost through this method of proceding.
> For my part nothing in the world could ever induce me to join a cara-
> van of fur traders moving with all possible expedition from St.
> Louis—near the mouth of the Missouri bound for the Rocky Moun-
> tains at the rate of a fast trading vessel, when the country can afford
> that swiftness of movement, and far less indeed would I be caged on
> board of the finest Man-of-War if commanded by a more seafaring
> Gentleman whose whole desires are to sail and sail!—No Reader,
> give me youth and strength enough to ramble on foot over the Rocky
> Mountains, and thus be enabled to tarry when I choose, to diverge
> from the tract far and wide and to watch for weeks if necessary the
> habits of a single bird!—or suffer me to be landed on that cape, or
> that island, or any portion of any continent whenever it is my de-
> sires so to do, for then, and not until then, neither myself or any
> other man or set of men will succeed in producing the hundred por-
> tion of the benefits to science which would be attained under the
> state of traveling or of voyaging which I have attempted here to pro-
> pose to every true and ardent student of nature.[17]

Audubon's last winter and spring in England were marked
by weariness and confusion. He dared not lose his temper
with Havell at this critical stage, even if prints happened to
be going to persons long dropped from the list and dupli-
cates to others. (A certain peer had indignantly dropped out
on discovering a scrap of beef—the vestiges of some careless
packer's lunch—among his otherwise lovely aquatints.) An

invitation from Townsend to collaborate with him seemed more than preposterous at such a time.

In May 1839, Audubon and Havell differed sharply over payment for the few extra Folios engraved for sale in America. Havell objected that he had been put off far too long for these and other arrears and that he could not hope to meet his bills before autumn, by which time he hoped to be sailing with the Audubons. He could hardly be expected to come to terms for work on the *Quadrupeds* at this rate. However, Audubon could not see his way to pay passage for six adults and to insure the shipment of the copper plates and stock and, at the same time, settle in full with Havell. Instead, he persuaded the engraver that it would be wiser to take payment in the United States in gold rather than in sterling in London. The disappointed and disgruntled Havell extracted what he could of what was due him before leaving for Reading to rest. And then he thought better of leaving on the same ship with one who put new undertakings before outstanding obligations. Audubon joked that the *Quadrupeds* would be launched before the Havells got around to ferrying the Atlantic.

The *Synopsis of the Birds of America* came out in July. Its reception by the critics meant much to the chances of a miniature edition of the classic. On its emergence the fifth and last volume of *Ornithological Biography* drew a merciful review from Sir William Jardine, of all unlikely critics.

John and the expectant Maria left for Paris with their child and her nursemaid before sailing for home. His own departure with Lucy not far off, Audubon summed up and looked ahead, ostensibly for the benefit of Harlan, just then in Paris. "*The Birds of America* being now positively finished, I find myself very little the better in point of recompense for the vast amount of expedition I have been at to accomplish the task." But that fact could not alter his course. "I find that unless I do labor more—or as Madame G. would say, '*Je me tue pour vivre*,' why, I will in fact die perhaps still poorer than I was when I began, which, God knows, was in all respects poor enough indeed." But he repeated what he had often said, "The die is cast." He must publish the quadrupeds of

America—"*Conte qui conte*," come what may. "For should I not be better recompensed at the end of this second enterprise than I have been at the expiration of the first, I will yet trust to Providence to find me a place in some of the *Philadelphia* asylums wherein I may yet *rest* in comfort." To Harlan, as "sore and vexed" as anyone over finances, Audubon spoke freely: "I know of the furrows that now disfigure my once smooth features, but what of that? And what does it signify to me whether I stand more or less upright than I used to do some twenty years ago, when I knew that to seek the retreat of a mole, a black rat, or a striped squirrel I must land still lower and use my fingernail to come at the objects which I never will fail earnestly to examine, to portray and to describe. Then look upon the Quadrupeds of America as if already finished—and now, change the subject."[18]

But he had not said his last to this friend who had done him the favor of jogging the "old and lazy" agent Pitois. Three weeks later came word from Victor that "all Harlan's anatomical specimens were *burnt* up at John P. Wetherill's manufactory," and that Audubon must break the news. Break it he did, in nostalgic fashion:

> It being the bounden duty of any man who is the true friend of another to speak to him freely, even when what he has to relate is most highly painful to the heart of both parties, I cannot refrain from giving you sad melancholy news. But bear up, my good friend; for the will of God is undoubtedly to be, under any circumstances whatever, looked upon with quietude and the highest regard due to that Being from whom all on Earth have received light and life and support. . . . In the great fire at New York in 1835 I had effects and books destroyed to the value of about $7,000 . . . a heavy stroke to a poor man like me, and exceedingly painful to my dear wife. But through her own, always material, religious principles I did become reconciled, seeking by my labors to alleviate that loss, and I have done so. You are yet a young man and have a brave heart. Return to our country, recommence to collect as I did after the Norway rats had destroyed some hundred of my drawings, and all will still go well. In a word, do as I always have done, and never will cease to do. Rely upon the righteousness of the Almighty Will![19]

Thirteen years almost to the month had passed since Audubon's arrival in England. The congeries of emotion experienced upon his departure with Lucy on the *George Washington* on July 25, 1839, can only be imagined.[20] Bona fide subscriptions to *The Birds of America*, now 165 in all, fell far short of his onetime chimerical predictions.[21] A few weeks earlier that first faithful subscriber and good angel, the "Queen Bee" of Green Bank, had died of old age. For some time she had detached herself from the role of civic and cultural leader. But there can be no doubt that, with Audubon, she believed his vision fulfilled and his work a world classic, heroically realized.

The signs were entering new phases. In his pocket Audubon carried Bachman's most recent letter. It took for granted, quite obliviously, that there would be time before sailing to stir about for a raid on the rich English collections that could enrich the *Quadrupeds of North America:*

> It would be wise for you to study the skulls and teeth a little. You take these things by intuition. Although I would not go so far as others in the determination of species from skulls, you will find that they go very far towards it. . . . You must keep a book as you did of the birds, leaving room for a hundred species. I doubt whether we will go beyond that unless we include the whales and mammalia of that character. . . . Leave nothing in England that you may be obliged to send for hereafter. I promised Harris and others that I would give a full synopsis of American quadrupeds. I have done no more than make pretty full notes. These and all the information I have to give are at your service. But the book must be original and creditable—no compilation and no humbug. I am not often far out of the way in predictions, and I assure you it will, if managed with your usual zeal and the boys' industry and attention to the commercial part, be the most profitable speculation into which you have ever entered. It will amuse and occupy you in your old days and keep you from snuff and grog. The figures may, I think, be given without reference to any scale, those the size of a skunk full size, those above as taste or space will dictate. . . . Your range should be from the farthest North and on the West, the Pacific, south Texas and California.[22]

If Bachman seriously expected so much, so soon, he was doomed to disappointment. Audubon had had all he could do to finish old business.

Why he did not have John go down to Couëron from Paris can be explained by more than Maria's delicate condition. Maximum tact, patience, and practical judgment were not among this son's virtues. The fraying promise to visit Les Tourterelles had to be abandoned. A strained, embarrassing liaison with the French relations had two years to run before the death of Gabriel, four until that of Rose Bonnitte. Once more, and once only, would they importune.[23]

Leach's Petrel. *Plate 260 of* The Birds of America. *Engraved by Robert Havell, Jr., in 1835 after the original study, "Fork-tailed Petrel, male and female," drawn in August 1831 on the deck of the ship* Columbia.

XXVIII.
Homecoming

WHERE TO "PITCH CAMP" was the question—New York, Philadelphia, or Boston? The answer was no matter of indifference to Victor. Early in the year he had visited Charleston and fallen in love with Eliza, Maria's younger sister. Tired out before he left London and more so in Charleston, he had taken a rest cure at White Sulphur Springs before returning to New York. Eliza's delicate health left both the date and the wedding itself uncertain.

In July, Bachman came north to discuss the coming miniature edition, and again he and Victor saw eye to eye. The arrival of the family in the United States made Bachman exceedingly eager to see Maria as well as his grandchild. "I am told little Lucy has a will of her own," he wrote. "A pity that the grumbling Englishman and the excitable Frenchman should spoil the blood of so many good children."[1]

Audubon was in no mood for procrastination and at once chose New York City and a house at 86 White Street for home and office. Immediately, while John began to reduce the Folio birds with his camera lucida, he himself scoured

New York and Philadelphia for a lithographer and a printer. Dr. Morton was among the first to hear of Audubon's plans: "I am induced to publish our Quadrupeds because it appears that, unless I do, no one else will for years to come, and I think it much wanted. . . . The re-publication of *The Birds of America* will secure me the copyright and put an end to all spurious undertakings. . . . The more public you make this in Philadelphia . . . the better."[2]

Audubon's ulterior motive—to acquire the Townsend skins of Rockies mammals—was plain enough. Direct questions put to the "lazy and careless" Townsend met with disappointing answers marked by ingratitude for past favors.[3] Audubon began to fire requests in every direction for the skins of rodents.

With dispatch he signed a lithographer, J. T. Bowen of Philadelphia, to execute the miniature copies. Unwise investments had ended the prosperity of this English settler; he showed eagerness to begin.

Amid feverish activity in White Street a daughter, Harriet, was born to Maria.

On October 8, the *Commercial Advertiser* carried an invitation to the public to inspect "Audubon's Original Drawings." From 9:00 A.M. to dark at the Lyceum on Broadway they could be seen for twenty-five cents admission: "Every bird is represented as in a mirror with the exact dimensions of reality, and with admirable preservation of character. Such a collection has never been seen at any time or place; or so comprehensive, so complete, or so admirably executed, and, we may add, so beautiful."[4]

Asked in Philadelphia a month later why he did not repeat the show in that city, Audubon replied that he lacked the courage after taking a loss of fifty-five dollars in New York. "If I had an extra hog to show," he continued sarcastically, "and should place him in a large room on an elevated pedestal, with a comfortable bed of straw, I could draw thousands from far and near. But painting, however beautiful . . . will not attract enough people to cover the expense. In London I should be sure of constant visitors to my gallery, but not here." Samuel Breck, the English-born Philadelphian whom he was addressing, demurred that at least panorama painting seemed to be doing well enough in his city. He thought Audubon's "bold and eaglelike" face that of a "disappointed man."[5]

There was every reason for lugubriousness that November day. Victor had left in haste to be with Eliza in her illness. Audubon and John were saddled with his share of the work until the uncertain date of his return. Money was critically short. The unsold Folios had thus far attracted only John Jacob Astor; the King of Sardinia was temporizing. There was far too little time to push its sale during the birth pains of the new undertaking.

At the most trying of moments there came an appeal from Gabriel Du Puigaudeau. "Sixty-nine, bed-ridden, ready for death," yet unwilling to go until he could leave his children "exempt from every claim" and "die more peacefully" in the knowledge, he begged advice, help, or both. If it were not at once forthcoming and effective, he wanted power of attorney to settle a mutual "ruinous debt" by sale of part of the estate:

> For a long interval we have been paying interst on money borrowed to pay costs of a suit that we lost in a contest with the heirs of the deceased dame Bouffard of St. Domingue, for whose heirs the late Monsieur Jean Audubon had received securities to keep track of along with interest. From our savings we have paid interest and part of the sum borrowed, and we still owe £20,000, an enormous amount that we cannot repay, and the interest goes on ruining us. . . . I await your answer impatiently. And I pray you to embrace your dear wife and children for us. Your sister and my children join in my wishes for you: all the happiness that you deserve. I beg you to believe me, always, your brother and friend.[6]

Audubon saw that the time had come to close the door on the dreary affair and be left in peace, even if to do so meant renouncing all rights of inheritance in favor of Rose Bonnitte.

Two weeks after Victor reached Charleston, Eliza left her bed, and, over her father's worried objections, spoke her wedding vows in the briefest of ceremonies. Victor, on virtual orders from Audubon, brought her away at once.

The industrious pace of Bowen made the immediate hiring of a printer for the letterpress mandatory. Townsend had recommended J. B. Chevalier, whose name was to appear on the title page as copublisher.[7]

Bachman opposed the printing of a prospectus for the *Quadrupeds* until the wolves and foxes were described. The deer and squirrels, sent "by the Old Boy himself to puzzle naturalists," would be no joke either.[8]

Audubon took a sampling of the first lithographs of birds to Boston. Not yet having felicitated Bachman on the closer union of their families by the marriage of Victor and Eliza, he seized a moment to exclaim:

> I wish to congratulate you, as I congratulate myself on the happy event . . . when you acquired a second son and valuable friend, and myself a beloved and most welcome second daughter to my heart's wishes. Our children though poor will, I feel assured, be forever happy, inasmuch as they are the possessors of most excellent hearts and those honorable principles which ever tend to augment the felicities of a married life, unconnected with the pomp and grandeur of the world, according to the common acceptance of these words.[9]

Bachman replied on Christmas Eve, but not in kind. The haste, possible unwisdom, and lonely aftereffects of the wedding had caused deep grief, not to be concealed:

> Your congratulations about this double union in our families are all right and proper, no doubt—nor ought I to be so selfish as to wish to retain my children around me when their happiness requires a removal. But somehow the event which gives you so much pleasure has had a contrary effect on me, and I have on these two occasions looked forward to these happy events very much as a man to a funeral. I was glad, when Eliza left, that I was compelled to be absent and obliged to be preaching incessantly, twice a day, for a fortnight. . . . When I came home, however, the holidays had scattered the rest of my little flock, and Jane and Catherine only were left. I was so lonely that my dyspepsia has give me strong warning of another social visit. So it is, and I cannot help it. The girls have good husbands, who, I am sure, will take care of them, but to me I feel it to be a very great loss. However, I will try to put up with it as well as I can, and not complain about it, unless others wish me a joy which I do not feel and which I would be a hypocrite to acknowledge. But let us talk of other matters.[10]

Audubon did not, and could not, take offense. Mellower, aging, more patient, he accepted the candor of his friend who of late had been saying, "You cannot do without me in this business, I know well enough."

The New England tour was rewarding. So many orders for the new small work came of it, as well as much interest in the unborn but heralded *Quadrupeds*, that the pace appeared likely to continue, even gain momentum. An accident in the bindery to prints that would have yielded $1,500 did not dim the promise of the illustrious potboiler. Setbacks of this kind tormented Audubon far less now that thorny academic questions about birds seldom if ever arose. Nowadays customers were rarely naturalists; they cast no ornithological barbs. Audubon's striking looks and personal magnetism interested the public more than could learned airs. His eight teeth—the same number as his granddaughter "Lulu" had cut—did not cause him to bear himself less proudly.[11] The scientific grind he left wholly to Bachman.

"In the quadrupeds I will show you trap, my boy," the minister wrote. "Just bring along with you Harlan, Peale, Ord and the other bipeds . . . I will row you all up Salt River together . . . show the whole concern of you. . . . I am not ashamed to let my name stand along with yours. . . . The expenses and profits will be yours . . . and if the boys with their good points and industry cannot be independent . . . they deserve to starve." Seldom did his messages wander from the problem of the hour—the elusive, chiefly nocturnal mammals. "Don't flatter yourself that this Book is child's play—the birds are a mere trifle compared to this. I have been at it all my life and do not fear the bugs of Europe—but we have all much to learn. The skulls and teeth must be studied—color is as variable as the wind. Down—down into the earth they grovel, and in digging and studying we grow giddy and cross."[12]

It was for his daughter Maria, more than for Eliza, that Bachman might have worried. Her health had declined since the birth of Harriet to the point where John saw he must take her to Charleston, out of the northern winter. In February he set out with her and their infant, leaving "Lulu" to his mother. John intended to continue copying the Folio for Bowen while Maria gained strength.

Audubon accompanied them as far as Baltimore, where, however, he found Theodore Anderson too ill to receive or help him as in the past. He registered at the Eutaw House, then called on the banker Meekles, who went about the city with him. Fifty-two orders for the miniature during the first week or so multiplied to 162 before March began. The total for the nation exceeded five hundred in a month, so that Audubon began to foresee two thousand "good and true" clients for one hundred parts at one dollar each. He thought a fortune might well be in sight. Dr. Gideon Smith agreed to insure collections for each shipment received—and for only one-half percent over the ten asked by other agents.

The news that New York City civic leader James Lenox had taken the last remaining full-bound Folio, and that only two or three loose Folios and odds and ends remained, further encouraged Audubon. He tried his first social dancing since his Paris trip of 1828. But in a fall on his way to an interview he barked his shin; this hobbled his famous stride and ended all thought of cotillions. His dining at the Latrobe residence proved more painful than a dance would have been. No matter how unmistakably the widow and son of the late engineer-architect tried to show their respect for him and for his Pittsburgh family connections, he could not overcome his sense of inadequacy before them and their intellectuality.

Two bulletins marred the sweetness of spring. A piratical version of his still uncopyrighted miniature *Birds* was rumored to be coming out at fifty cents a copy or less. Bowen, his informant, was in trouble and faced a judgment of an impossible $322 for debt.[13] The printer faced jail if he failed to pay. Henry Havell had refused Bowen's offer of work with the bitter comment that the Havells had had their fill of Audubon for failure to pay $1,000 he still owed them.

Audubon's protest to Victor that he knew nothing of owing Havell any such amount drew quick confirmation. His intention to pay from dues that he looked for from England (even though his London friends Phillips and Yarrell were insisting that booksellers there wanted sixty percent to handle the miniature) would have to bow to prudence.[14] "I shall have to give him a check for it," wrote the disgruntled Victor.[15]

Luckily, Audubon obtained eighty-three orders in Washington and Richmond. This enabled him to send Chevalier money enough to keep Bowen free. But the plight of the lithographer, the dinning from Havell, and the painful fall—mingling as they did with the opening anticlimactic struggle of the miniature *Birds*—told on him. What he needed was the peace that Charleston had so often brought him in the past. He was eager to see Johnny's portrait of Bachman and his landscape with deer, both of the canvases as good, he hoped, as those the boys would show in New York in an important April exhibition.

It was not that the portrait disappointed Audubon as much as it did Bachman.[16] The "surprisingly fine" deer more than compensated for the portrait by its excellence.[17] But to find Maria dying, and the mansion as if already in mourning at the moment when he had been counting on cheer and good news, broke his spirit entirely. In past crises his pencil and colors were his armor and panacea. His resort to escape of another kind during his month in Charleston strained his welcome to the breaking point.

After his return to New York with the news that the end was near for Maria, and that John and the child would soon be coming without her, he remained strangely silent on the subject of Bachman. To try and find out the cause of the apparent differences between them, Victor decided to write and ask his father-in-law point-blank.

Never had Bachman had to perform a more painful duty. Happily for Audubon and his future, the lecture that the minister read him, in the "sincere wish to render him benefit," proved more than efficacious. It was a case of his having behaved in a "garrulous, dictatorial and profane" manner on several occasions, "while under the influence." The ladies had taken his part to the extent of begging the minister to "let him have his way" because of his condition, caused by ill-concealed anxiety. Friends who ventured to call at the mansion voiced concern that unhappiness could so overmaster Audubon. Everyone had been unprepared for the display. In vain John had tried to reason with his father. Finally, Bachman's "perfect abhorrence of intemperance" had caused him to withdraw to his study alone and lock the door.

But the question of his right to say that he set no store by what Audubon and John thought of Maria's state was the real and more serious cause of the break. He had declared Audubon "too sanguine," and John "too desponding" as well as "too positive, but a good fellow." John had taken refuge beside Maria, who, it was true, "shed many a tear" for the fault of one as beloved as a father.

"I saw one whom I esteemed beyond almost any other living man ruining his health and his intellect, setting a bad example to my children and rendering me perfectly miserable. I wished the infernal whisky jug at the bottom of the sea," Bachman continued. He admitted that in rebuking his friend for something, the seriousness of which Audubon seemed unaware, he had been too hasty. Nevertheless, he wished Victor to show his father the letter whenever he thought it "seasonable and proper" to do so. "Your father's name and memory are very dear to me. . . . I pray God to direct us in the right way."[18] The letter made clear that Audubon would be welcome only if he conducted himself as in years gone by.

Audubon was moved by a letter that awaited him from a lad in Carlisle, Pennsylvania. "You see, Sir, that I have taken— after much hesitation—the liberty of writing you. I am but a boy and very inexperienced," wrote Spencer Fullerton Baird, future secretary of the Smithsonian Institution, who had found *Ornithological Biography* as exciting as his "favorite novels." He wanted Audubon to name and publish a new bird he had discovered, and to do so in honor of his preceptor, Dr. Alfred Foster. Audubon agreed and invited the boy to contribute needed mammals.

Almost immediately he was off to New England on business that could not be postponed. He took with him the latest lithographs and two remaining Folios. Victor was to send fifty-three oil copies—whether by Kidd or John or both is uncertain—of *Birds of America* portraits to sell if buyers could be found.[19]

Parkman, Audubon's Boston representative, came to his aid with an advance of $1,000 at a modest rate. (The doctor had generously refused interest on a recent loan of $163.50.) Then the artist, "thin as a snake" by his own description, was on his seasick way to Nantucket. There a wealthy islander purchased both Folios and twenty-two odd aquatints to sell "on 'spec.'"

In Providence, Audubon came across the brother of his former skinner, Henry. The beggared, drunken degradation of Frederick Ward made his own cares seem light.

Often, in stagecoaches along the coast, he found himself beside whaling captains and their sea chests. He saw seals basking in an inlet before a storm which he fled by stage one day. Pauses allowed him to "botanize," or to gather shells for Lucy and the children. At the Pilgrim burial ground he received a chip of the landing rock. "Poor I," he wrote in August, "took my snuff and gazed on the Nature spread before me."[20]

Unexpectedly, in Hingham, Massachusetts, he saw some "truly wonderful drawings" by one Isaac Sprague (1811–95). Sprague himself was not present to hear his visitor declare his technique the equal of Alexander Wilson's or better. Audubon left a note of congratulation that may have made Sprague wonder whether, indeed, he had heard the last of his admirer. The former carriage-painter's apprentice would one day illustrate the standard *Manual of Botany* by the distinguished Asa Gray. He would also paint views of the White Mountains, lithographed by Bufford & Thayer.

Havell was waiting in Boston to tour New England with him and sketch the landscape, their differences forgotten. Late in September they continued south together. En route, Audubon found Philadelphia's Academy far from ready to meet its balance and in the most precarious financial state ever. His appearance was ill-timed. Ord had just delivered a formal attack on him before the American Philosophical Society because of certain remarks in the bird biographies. The statement that Wilson never acknowledged the "Small-headed Flycatcher,"[21] which, Audubon had said, he lent him to copy, Ord called a bald-faced lie. He swore that he himself was present when Wilson shot the species in the East. That a friend of Nuttall's also reported having seen the controversial flycatcher, near Salem, brought naturalists no nearer the phantom bird. It remained for posterity and tradition to classify it as an immature hooded warbler, or perhaps a female of that species. Actually, a letter of December 6, 1837, in the Tyler collection shows Audubon asking Swainson for a female. He wrote in the margin of Bonaparte's *American Ornithology:* "I consider this species as the same given as new by Swainson in the *Fauna borealis America* [sic] under the name of M[usicapa]. It is a true species very abundant in New Foundland in the month of August where it doubtless breeds. J. J. A." At the end of a quotation from Wilson on the birds he added: "Wilson thought on the above subject most erroneously, because it is well known that every species of Bird, of whatever denomination or sorts they may be, have a Natural propensity to move eastward and norwardly with the advancement of Spring and Summer, and no further proof of this fact is necessary than the enumeration of the bird he gives in the above paragraph, which migrate from south to north or East as far as possible by them to do at the seasons I have mentioned. The same is the fact all over the world." Little though these words add to the controversy, they prove his belief in the existence of the species.[22]

Ord brandished Wilson's diary, which was to be seen no more once he had published a freely edited version of its contents. He denounced Audubon as the author of other alleged lies beyond "the vocabulary of reprehension."

On the question of the *Mississippi Kite,* Ord was on firmer ground in claiming that Havell must have traced the lower of two plates from Lawson's engraving of the Wilson example. At any rate, the tracing—if tracing it was—robbed the kite of one toe; and the bird, a male, was marked "female." The upper figure, a magnificent drawing in Audubon's best style, puts its stiff mate to shame with an *élan* that somehow mitigates the artist's evident sin of expediency. He was absent in 1831 when Havell's engraving was finished, although the idea may have been his. Ord saw to it that Waterton received a copy of his "Oral Communication" about the flycatcher and kite for *Loudon's* magazine to copy, but he wished it sent back to him if publication were refused.[23]

All things considered, the malicious Philadelphian had shown remarkable restraint. He had just received confidential news from Waterton that could, had he chosen to betray it, have been severely damaging to their enemy. Bonaparte, then in Rome, was the source. Waterton had recently visited the Prince and his disappointing museum, and had been much annoyed by his host's bad manners. At least their talks had released a secret, hidden from the world:

> I asked Charles if it were true that Audubon had studied drawing under David. 'No,' he said emphatically, 'Audubon never studied under David.' I asked him how he knew that. He answered that he had asked David and that David had told him so. On saying this, he desired me not to mention the fact publickly, as he did not wish to have anything more to do with Audubon. Thus, you see, it is a kind of secret. I confide it to you but request you not to divulge it, as Charles seemed to wish me to consider it a secret. I see that he is no friend of Audubon's. What a pretty fellow Audubon is. If, on my return to England, I find that either he or his gulled friends have made any remarks on me, I will take up the pen and produce a pamphlet in which I will flay him alive.[24]

David, portraitist to the court of Napoleon, had died in exile in Brussels in 1825. The Prince revisited Europe the following year—too late for him to have interrogated David, unless he had already done so through an intermediary, by letter. John Stokoe, peripatetic agent of Joseph Bonaparte, may well have put the question to David at the request of Charles Lucien Bonaparte.

Bonaparte was not so eager to break with Audubon as he led Waterton to believe. He had been asking Gray of the British Museum only recently to keep him informed of the doings of Audubon and Swainson. "What do you think," he asked, "of my not having seen, as yet, Audubon's *Synopsis!!!* On what plan is it? Why is he angry against me to such an extent as to deprive me of my copy of his plates?"[25]

Swainson had gone over to the enemy for good. "Mr. Audubon is, confessedly, only a field naturalist, not a scientific one," he wrote in the new *Cabinet Cyclopaedia*. "He can shoot a bird, preserve it, and make it live again . . . but he cannot describe it in scientific . . . perfectly intelligible terms. . . . A want of precision . . . a general ignorance of modern ornithology sadly disappoint the scientific reader." Both the published "episodes" and the bird biographies were colored "somewhat too highly" for Swainson's taste. "It is singular," he concluded as he harked back to Audubon's skylarking in Paris while he himself studied, "how two minds, possessing the same tastes, can be so diversified, as to differ *in toto* respecting the very same objects."[26]

Eliza, ill since Maria's death, began to cough alarmingly. Dr. Morton of Philadelphia prescribed a winter in Cuba but could not predict a cure. Miss Martin came from Charleston to accompany her niece. They sailed with Victor by way of New Orleans.

The voyage to Louisiana so fatigued Eliza that she was put to bed at once at the home of her cousin Mary Berthoud Grimshaw. Victor pressed for subscribers, placed two sets of *Ornithological Biography* with the State of Louisiana, and obtained eleven orders for the miniature *Birds*, including one from the mayor of New Orleans. The sale of one of his oils, a landscape, for $150 rounded out his efforts.

The responsibilities left behind by Victor were divided between Audubon and John. The painful bereavement which caused John to disappear with his dogs into the Hudson River woods at every opportunity finally found consolation. John met a Brooklyn merchant's daughter, the mannerly Caroline Hall, of whom his mother heartily approved.

Audubon's latest tour of New England brought the miniature subscription to nearly 1,000 fairly dependable orders.

Most signers would turn out to be more punctual than the desultory Daniel Webster.

"We are what we make ourselves," Audubon chronicled after bringing the "famous and learned" blacksmith Elihu Burritt around.[27] Then he hurried to New York for Christmas, more determined than ever that *The Viviparous Quadrupeds of North America* (a title later to be relieved of its awesome adjective) should begin to appear by 1841.

An interesting company gathered in White Street on Christmas Day. George Burgess, a "fine young gent" sent by Robert Bakewell of Hampstead, chronicled the occasion.[28] As innocent as Eve, in Audubon's estimation, Burgess hoped to become a thread-miller owner. Not so naive as he seemed, Burgess thought his host's promise of introductions to manufacturers in Lowell, Massachusetts, rather too ready and his spirit far too sanguine. Yet the lad did not question the jovial reminiscences about King Louis Philippe and the monarch's promise—after ordering ten Folios—to place 100, if Audubon would publish the *Birds* in France. Nor did he wonder, apparently, whether Charles X had really said, on signing, "Yes, I know nothing of it, but subscribe to everything."

American Hare, *summer pelage. General Research Division, The New York Public Library, Astor, Lenox and Tilden Foundations. Drawn on stone by William E. Hitchcock for J. T. Bowen, after the watercolor study by Audubon for plate 12 of* The Viviparous Quadrupeds of North America.

XXIX. Minnie's Land

"**B**EGAINING THE NEW YEAR BY drawing the Beaver," Audubon wrote to Victor.[1] He did not let the merrymakers along Broadway disturb either his sketching or his letter-writing, including frantic appeals to friends for mammals.

Brief, inconclusive letters from Cuba suggested inactivity and downright laziness to the heavily burdened family head. He felt constrained to tell Victor to "get to work," sell the Folio and oils that he had with him, and not leave the family "in the lurch" about what went on in Cuba. He did not like it that the Bachmans should be hearing regularly while New York went without news. "Is that o.k.?" he wished to know.[2] He had no idea that Eliza was actually dying. Intuitively, however, he said nothing about John's approaching marriage, the end of mourning for Maria.

John had begun to think of devoting himself to portraiture for a living, if and when he could be spared. He was taking full-length likenesses of three of the Trudeau family.[3] But he thought his best effort, "by fifty percent," a portrait of his "'old dad' sitting in the wilds of America admiring the nature around him."[4] Lucy also posed for a seated, full-length portrait. In it she gazed wistfully, over sliding spectacles, at John.[5]

Before five months of work with Bowen were over Audubon saw that the lithographer must learn who held the reins. The distance between them had encouraged Bowen to take undue initiative in Philadelphia. Sometimes he simplified backgrounds to save time and expense. He had already received $1,200 for the first forty-five miniature prints when he threatened to take his seventy men off the job unless Audubon promised to meet the payroll each Saturday night. He complained of having lost $800 through the task. Audubon refused his proof impressions after summoning him to White Street. He warned that unless Bowen listened to reason, the pay he handed him would be his last. He would send John to England for fifty skilled finishers to speed up the job. He refrained from mentioning that Henry Havell was ready to turn out lithographs for two dollars less per hundred. There was no need to do so. Bowen mellowed "like an apple" in an oven. Audubon joked that he would preserve Bowen's rude ultimatum for *"Auld Lang Syne."*[6] He further demonstrated his command on March 8 by hiring a New York City artist, J. W. Childs, to color all plates for numbers 28–30 within a fortnight of their arrival from George Endicott, lithographer, for "$1,900 for every 100 Numbers of five plates each."

Hard though the times, Audubon paid Robert Havell the $500 due him. He felt "sick of him" and wished to "have done with him *in toto*," he told the family.[7] The settlement had the added advantage of pleasing Henry Havell, whom he could not yet afford to disillusion.

Rather than abandon his objectives, Audubon declined a bid from Secretary Joel Poinsett to lecture for the National Institution. He was counting on the administration of the newly elected President Benjamin Harrison to restore prosperity. All three of his lost Charleston agents he regarded as replaceable. The inability of his relatives, Grimshaw and Gordon, to make New Orleans collections he viewed as temporary. He overlooked the "impudence" of Harlan, who had proved "a real curiosity" by dint of a request for a loan of $700, with his Folio of the *Birds* as security.[8]

Audubon renewed his lease at $800 a year, sold his Boston and Providence securities before they declined further, and considered buying land on mortgage and bond as Victor had been urging.[9] But until John remarried, a move might, he concluded, better be put off.

On February 7 he wrote Victor to avoid accepting subscriptions in Cuba for the octavo *Birds* without demanding an advance of $100. "It is perfect nonsense for us to push the work abroad whilst we are unable, *actually,* to supply subscribers at *Home,* and we now have about 300 of them to supply, none of whom have as yet received a single number." He was sure that it needed "no pushing abroad," and hoped never to receive any more subscriptions from England, "as, to this day, we have not received one dollar, on account," for numbers sent to "that country."[10]

On April 19, 1841, possibly spurred to the action by the imminence of bereavement, Audubon made a will. He bequeathed his furniture, silver, and plate to Lucy, and real and other personal property to her, Victor, and John for them to share equally.

Victor was bringing Eliza home, but without hope. When the forlorn couple reached Charleston, Jane Bachman took Miss Martin's place before they fled the heat by boat.

Eliza went to bed immediately on reaching White Street. Two weeks later, on May 25, Audubon wrote on the margin of a drawing of a cottontail rabbit: "I drew this Hare during one of the days of deepest sorrow I have felt in my life, and my only solace was derived from my Labours. This morning our beloved Daughter Eliza died at 2 o'clock. She is now in Heaven, and may our God forever bless her soul!"[11]

Through the spring and the heat of summer Audubon drew mammals as if the very existence of the family depended on his industry, as indeed it did. He was as keen for the "completion of this department of natural science," he gave Baird to understand, as ever he had been for "our Birds."[12] His pleas to every recruit to the cause he could think of for wood rats, mice, moles, shrews, and squirrels brought enough for him to draw "about a hundred figures of thirty-six species" by mid-August. Bachman predicted that fully 200 more required "proper elucidation"; descriptions by Richardson, De Kay, Harlan, Godman, and others had not done them justice.[13]

On the same day, August 5, a letter quite different from that of Bachman was written to Audubon on behalf of the Emperor of all the Russias: "Dear Sir: I am happy to inform you that your admirable work has been presented to His Imperial Majesty a few weeks after my arrival, and that as a token of favour with which it was accepted, you are presented with a superb diamond snuff box, which, with the letter accompanying it, I shall have the pleasure of delivering into your own hands, as I am charged to do on my arrival, that is, on my return to New York, which will be early in the spring. I have the honor to be, dear Sir, Your most obedient svt. and sincere admirer, ALEXIS."

Audubon wrote to ask Dr. Phillips how much the box might bring. Phillips replied: " . . . with reference to the snuff box. I now find that from £45 to £50 is the amount which may probably be obtained for it. Supposing the diamonds to be taken out and paste substituted for them, the cost of the substitutes would not be above £4 or £5. The cost of mounting the diamonds, supposing them to be removed, would depend upon the manner in which it is done. I shall hold the box for your orders. If there be any point on which you desire information please let me know. I am, my dear Sir, Most faithfully yours." Audubon sold the box in New York City; what became of it remains a mystery.[14]

Bachman called for less talk and more listening from Audubon, and for some frankly calculated fraternizing with Cooper and the rest. Bachman had been tempted to abandon the *Quadrupeds* and the miniature *Birds* by an offer of the presidency of South Carolina College at $3,000 yearly. He preferred his congregation and irresistible hobby. "Nature, truth and no humbug," he preached to the Audubons, as he sent directions for skinning the ermines, hares, squirrels,

William Rickaby Miller. Minnie's Land, the Audubon Residence on the Hudson. *Print from* Valentine's Manual, *1865. Museum of the City of New York.*

and rats he was sending.[15] If Gray of London, or somebody, would not "diddle" him out of already published articles on half a dozen mammals, he would be content.

The mayor of New York City permitted the Audubons to shoot rats on the Battery at dawn provided they exercised due care.[16] Audubon thought the Norway brown rat might not be the only species haunting the wharves.

He may have been but half in earnest when he let Daniel Webster, the Secretary of State, know that he would not mind being appointed director of a new national museum of natural history. Indeed, on September 8 he proposed such an establishment with himself as its head.[17]

When he presented a paper before the assembled Academy in Philadelphia on previously unknown North American quadrupeds, he sensed how little harm Ord had managed to do him. The bankrupt American Philosophical Society and the teetering Academy had, by their weakened condition, extinguished some of the fire of Audubon's "Infernal City."

After the wedding of John to Caroline Hall on October 2, 1841, a larger house became indispensable for the family. Two years before his marriage, Audubon had admired the Benjamin Bakewell summer place north of Manhattan island on Bloomingdale Road. In Carmansville, up that way, he found twenty-four wooded acres that sloped gracefully down to the Hudson. The dread mortgage that had made him hesitate to acquire land was avoided when Mechanics Bank accepted his note for $1,200. The Audubons named their estate Minnie's Land, suggested by the Caledonian term of endearment they often used for Lucy. Builders began work at once on a roomy flat-topped wooden mansion with an impressive view of the Jersey palisades and the river. It rose on the site of a Revolutionary battle for New York City.

Young Baird paid Audubon a visit in January 1842. New York so far surpassed his boyish expectations that he frankly found Philadelphia dull and Carlisle "death itself" after "the bustle of Broadway."[18] Audubon acknowledged his thanks in patriarchal style: "That beautiful Carlisle, within the bosom of quiet nature, should appear to you as a small affair when compared to our largest city in the Union is not at all remarkable. . . . Would you not after all prefer little Carlisle than Great New York with all its humbug, rascality, and immorality? Surely, or I mistake your nature sadly, you do!" He reminisced on the Pennsylvania of his own youth: "It is a good long time since I was young and resided near Norristown . . . but still my heart and mind oftentime dwell in the pleasure I felt there. . . . Within a few miles of that village my [father] did live, and it was there also that my good fortune led me to know and to marry the excellent wife I have." He wished Baird to price clings, yellows or red, or blood-red peaches for Minnie's Land.[19] John was up there supervising the building of pens, clearing woods, plotting orchards, and readying the soil for planting. The move from White Street was already set for April.

On March 30, a fine spring day, Lucy, in mourning for her sister Sarah, arrived with Caroline, Harriet, and "Lulu" in a handsome barouche paid for by a loan of $225 from Carman of Carmansville. Audubon and John were waiting. Cartload after cartload of caged rats, weasels, and other rodents; furniture; and personal belongings had already braked down the rough lane that wound among the tulip and chestnut trees, the century-old pines and flowering dogwood. For the second time in a fortnight the artist was so "drained" of funds that he had been obliged to ask John's father-in-law, James Hall, for twenty-five dollars.[20] Yet, as Victor left for New England to "push" for business, his father managed to joke about trusting to a Providence higher than the capital of Rhode Island.

Despite a deep attachment for home, Audubon had to bow to other considerations. If he seriously hoped for government support of a Rockies expedition, he knew he must brave the heat of July for the cause.

In Washington he began a stream of homesick letters from his room in the Fuller Hotel: "Methinks I see the grass growing along the wall, but methinks also that it is too soon, and only a dreamlike Dream. . . . Trumpet flower, *remember; Rats do remember. . . .* Oh, when will I again be at home?"[21] By morning he was in the throes of cholera morbus, the victim of green apples. He lay in furnace-like heat for a day or two, barely able to open his ledgers. Then, to his sorrow, he found that Victor had again been making errors, in addition to several perpetrated in Havell's favor earlier in the year.

New laws prohibited federal departments from subscribing to works which the copyright law obtained for the Library of Congress. President Taylor was too busy to see Audubon. Webster made the usual excuses. "The great Webster is indebted to everybody, and everybody says I never will have a dollar from him," he complained.[22] To make amends Daniel Webster offered him a "fat" post that he promptly scorned as so much "humbug." Webster, amazed, came through with $100. He saw to it that President John Tyler wrote an open letter of introduction, in which he, like Webster, called Audubon "a native of the USA."

Commander Charles Wilkes, whose South Seas Expedition materials were on exhibition, did not mind Audubon's intimations that the drawings of Peale, the official expedition artist, were mediocre.[23] Wilkes was still some years removed from his eventual suppression of Peale's work in sensational proceedings. He merely asked whether Audubon could recommend George Lehman to finish some delineations. "No go!" came the reply. Lehman had fallen in his esteem, for undisclosed reasons.[24]

Another hotel guest, Colonel Pierre Chouteau, scion of the trading founders of St. Louis, promised to arrange Audubon's passage to the Yellowstone in spring. Chouteau had news of Rozier. " *'Dit-donc'* Rozier has repudiated his wife and she has gone some distance from him—that is news for you!" Lucy was soon to read.[25] Constance Rozier had dared to speed the elopement of the eldest of her ten children with their German clerk.

"Nothing can be worse for anyone than to be thought a Great Man," mused Audubon, "perambulating the streets" on the trail of debtors and signers. "What a strange world we do live in, to be sure."[26] He was visiting the dawn markets daily. One morning he proudly showed his first beautiful lithographed plates of the *Quadrupeds* to Congress. The more innocent members mistook the squirrels for rats, the muskrats for beavers.

Russian Minister Krüdener appeared to have forgotten his old pledge. Unctuously he told Audubon to expect the snuffbox that the Emperor had already sent to him. Lord Ashburton, in Washington to negotiate a treaty between his country and the United States through Secretary Webster, had to be convinced that he was not already a subscriber. The much embarrassed peer signed up and promised to call at Minnie's Land.

In shirt sleeves while at his window to catch a breath of air, Audubon chided his "dearest friend" for neglecting "her poor old man":

> You cannot conceive, hardly, how I long to be at home, to see you all, to kiss you all, and to watch the progress of the wall, the filling in and the sodding by Johnny, to see how the potatoes grow in the field, the cabbage, chickens, dogs and so forth. I dreamt last night that I was throwing in earth from a cart to help, and also protecting a tree from being cut down. Do take good care of Dearest Mother. I wish I was by her side at this moment, half past ten o'clock, to give her lunchun and her grog. I would have no objection to join in a mouthful of *Wine* and *Water* and a ginger cake or so. But here I am, scribbling away with a miserable iron pen and will not eat until half past three. I have not lunched once since I left you, and my ginger cakes are quite out. . . . I have seen no spot that I like as well as our own, and when I came down the Chesapeake Bay it looked dry, barren, and shockingly poor. *Minniesland* forever, say I! And now Dearest friends, one and all, God bless you. Kiss all the Darlings for me, talk to them, and believe me for life your husband, your father and friend.[27]

In Richmond, where Audubon spent a day, his one reward was to be soundly kissed by fluttering young autograph-seekers at a female seminary. He stopped in Washington again, but only for long enough to collect introductions from the President, General Scott, and Webster.[28] Frantic that there should still be no word from home, he hastened northward to discover why he had been neglected. (Demands of the miniature *Birds* and of house guests explained the remissness.) Al-

Young Raccoon, *1841. Pencil, ink, and watercolor draw-*
ing, 18 × 30 in. Courtesy Department of Library Services,
American Museum of Natural History. Original study,
lithographed for plate 61 of the octavo edition of The Viviparous Quadrupeds of North America.

most immediately he was on board the *Kosciusko* for Boston. His harried thoughts were all of matters close at hand—of paintings perhaps big enough to cover a possible English demand, in accordance with Victor's wishes—thoughts all far from Couëron. But on that day, August 3, 1842, Rose Du Puigaudeau died at Les Tourterelles.

Audubon was shocked to notice, while in Boston, that for some unaccountable reason Victor had deleted an acknowledgment to Miss Martin in the miniature *Birds*.[29]

He had hardly returned, to admire the strawberry beds and floral borders and inspect his caged rodents, when he was off again, and with good reason. They would all remain "poor as rats," in Victor's words, unless Canada, still untapped, took to the miniature—now in its fifth volume—and samples of the *Quadrupeds*.[30]

Audubon caught the *Swallow* at the Battery one day in September. As he steamed past Minnie's Land, Victor and John waved to him from their sailboat. They were out to surpass their summer record of a 200-pound sturgeon.

That night Audubon preferred stretching his "old bones on a bench" to enduring the bedbugs in his cabin.[31] Bells clanged at each of more than fifty stops. Before morning a cloudburst drove him inside. He changed to the superb *White Hall* for St. John's, New Brunswick, and from there went by train to Montreal.

The Canadian press reported Audubon's distinguished presence, but the response was mild. When someone advised him not to be "out of heart," he fumed at the suggestion. "Now I should like to know when, notwithstanding the thousand and one disappointments I meet in this life, I have felt cast down for more than a few moments. When the rats destroyed my drawings at Henderson is an exception, and the losing of my own two sweet little daughters and daughters-in-law are exceptions."[32]

Someone else predicted that Audubon "never would live to finish the *Quadrupeds*." A phrenologist remarked that he had no "coloring" about him. "Poor fool!" Audubon exploded. "Would to God that he had drawn and colored and composed as many *Pictures* as I have accomplished these forty-five years past, and then methinks he would have found out that . . . my practical knowledge surpasses his quackery!" News of Caroline's loss of her first-born made Montreal's "humbug" harder to endure.

Quebec proved no better, but Audubon forced himself to appear delighted with his surroundings. At the Governor's dinner in his honor he pleased the company with a dramatic recitation of "The Prairie," one of his frontier episodes. His host's daughter, for one, thought him "a darling gentleman." But neither his social success nor the fact that he shook hands one day with every member of the Assembly compensated for a glaring reality—that, by mid-October, he had won but one order each for his two superb Folios and only a paltry few for the miniature *Birds*. The $3,000 these would bring fell stunningly short of expectations.[33]

Eager to be back at Minnie's Land for the last days of Indian summer, he stowed some souvenir stones from the monument to Wolfe in a box of mammal skins bought in the market, and departed. In his eagerness to be off, he forgot the young bloodhound a peer had given him. In his pocket was a letter from Victor, who said that the want of cash was dire.

While Lucy nursed "little Lucy" past danger from scarlet fever, contracted from the servants who had been exposed to the epidemic at church one Sunday, Audubon feigned cheer to Bachman. On November 7 he said that he was "highly pleased" with his "fruitful journey" and with all that he had "done and seen." Determined to be sanguine he changed the subject to the pleasures of Minnie's Land. "We have fish whenever we draw the seine, and this summer we have caught one sturgeon that measured upward of eight feet." As for "the boys," they often went sailing, but without him. "Although I have crossed the Atlantic pretty frequently I have an inward dislike to the water after it is more that 2 or 3 fathoms deep!" The turning leaves that would not be seen again, once gone, unless the "Almighty" willed, spoke to him of old age, and he seemed to say so.[34]

In December, at the start of an early and severe winter, Audubon again prepared to canvass Boston. He regretted that he could not promise his "beloved sweetheart" any easing off of his killing rounds, which were worrying Lucy to the point of illness.[35]

But the recession in New England balked his efforts. It seemed to him that the "slim and flimsy" paper selected by Victor and Chevalier for the *Quadrupeds* might well hurt his chances. All in all, he did not feel justified, before starting home for Christmas, in spending even eighteen dollars for a sleigh that caught his eye in a shop window.[36]

During his absence Audubon had had two important callers—Colonel Webb, a Mexican War veteran, and Sir William Drummond Stewart, a big game hunter, who left word for Audubon to meet them in St. Louis for an expedition to the "mountains of the wind."[37] Audubon had other ideas, but refrained from confiding them. To follow in the footsteps of Alfred Miller, the artist for Stewart on an American Fur Trading expedition of 1837, would be to surrender the initiative of which he felt doggedly jealous.

Those invited to dine at Minnie's Land on Christmas Day included the Bowens; young George Burgess; the lawyer I. H. W. Page of New Bedford; Caroline's parents, the Halls; Mr. and Mrs. Pierre Chouteau, Jr., of St. Louis; Chouteau's brother Charles of New York; the latter's daughter Julie and her suitor, Major John F. A. Sanford; and their cousin Brigadier General Charles Gratiot of Washington, D.C. Gratiot was the grandson of the founder of St. Louis, Pierre Chouteau. Burgess recorded in his diary his impressions of the company. Bowen he saw as "an intelligent, sturdy English artisan who, like many others, had made money by his profession but lost all by speculating in stocks." Charles Chouteau played the piano beautifully. Pierre, still a mysteriously rich prince of the trade despite the bankruptcy of the North American Fur Company, told of watching Clay win a huge fortune in a wager with British Minister Fox in Washington. The smitten Sanford, a former subagent to the Mandan Indians but now the New York representative of the American

Fur Company, was seeking a Papal dispensation to wed the "reserved, sensible" Miss Chouteau, said to be "pretty good for $250,000."[38] The close friend of Caroline, Georgianna Mallory—to whom Victor had just become engaged—was spending a last Christmas at home.

Preparations for the expedition to the Upper Missouri sped along. The ever-practical Harris, before becoming its secretary, was renting his farm to help defray a fifth of the expeditionary costs. Spencer Baird's walking record for 1842—a redoubtable 2,100 miles—and his precocious corresponding memberships in the Philadelphia Academy and the National Institution won him an invitation. Baird hesitated to join, yet he predicted that "the general sum of knowledge in every department of science" would be increased by the undertaking.[39] Audubon, not so sure, demurred: "I have no very particular desire to embark as deep in the Cause of Science as the great Humboldt . . . simply because I am both too poor . . . and too incompetent. But I wish nevertheless *to attempt* to open the Eyes of naturalists to *Riches untold*, and *facts hitherto untold.*" He hoped to go where no "white Man" had been before. "Oh, my dear young friend, that I did possess the wealth of the Emperor of Russia, or of the King of the French; then indeed I would address the Congress." He would ask all imaginable help, and in return give away to the country's deserving scientific institutions the fruit of his labors. Family reverses, fears for her son's weak heart, and the dangers of "the Great Wilderness" compelled Mrs. Baird to oppose her son's joining. The determined Audubon promised Baird half of whatever birds he skinned, as well as one-fourth of the mammals except those "exceedingly rare" and new.[40] The boy was not to fear that Audubon would be "hard on the trigger" with him. No matter, Baird was not to be recruited.

Bachman proposed for taxidermist "a good practical naturalist," John G. Bell of Spark Hill, New York, who had won prizes for his skill.[41] His partner had been Frederick Ward until the latter's penchant for drink had led him to his death in the Philadelphia Almshouse. But Harris objected to Bell's

appointment on the grounds that he would expect unre-
stricted choice of the western skins. Harris's talk of resigning
as secretary and contributor to the fund forced Audubon to
come to swift terms for a fee of $500 for Bell, with no unusual
concessions.[42] Isaac Sprague, the former coach painter whose
art had so favorably impressed Audubon in Hingham, Massachusetts, signed as his assistant. An exuberant neighbor of
the Audubons, "tough, active, and very willing" young Lewis
M. Squires, joined as general helper. Victor and John were
left in charge in New York.

On March 11, when Audubon left for the West in "dark
frock coat, velvet vest and blue hunting shirt," he was almost
as lithe, slight, and erect as ever.[43] His features were sharper,
his burning eyes more deeply set. His nearly toothless mouth
wore a more determined line. His long hair was nearer white
but no less crestlike. He was not, as he staunchly notified
Prince Charles Lucien Bonaparte, too old to return "loaded
with knowledge." To please the younger De Rham and the
family doctor Van Rensselaer, who had been relaying Bonaparte's pleas for the balance of the Folio, he broke a long
silence and put a gentlemanly finish to the business. "That I
was displeased with your conduct towards me when in London is the truth. And I acknowledge that I said to some of
your remarkable friends there that I would not deliver you any
more of my work unless you did pay me the balance then
standing. . . . I have put up all the plates you want . . . and
to prove you further that I feel no enmity toward you, I send
you a copy of the first number of a work on the Quadrupeds
of North America." He admitted to "being no scholar," and
hence to grasping not "a word" of Bonaparte's latest publication; he would cherish it as a memento of one he once *"did
love as a Brother."*[44] An ultimate reserve was unmistakable.

Bonaparte still fancied himself admired by the hypocritical
Waterton and Ord. All three remained in fair agreement about
Audubon. Although the Prince had rescued Waterton from a
distressed ship in the Mediterranean, the squire was confiding to Ord, almost immediately afterward, that Bonaparte's
new *Fauna Italiana* would hardly offer "much original and cor-

rect information," considering its hothouse sources. Ord, no more of an admirer of Bonaparte's attainments, nevertheless sycophantically agreed that Audubon's failure to acknowledge his help in the *Synopsis* again proved him to be the barefaced forger "who duped Cuvier." Waterton's admittedly growing "disinclination" to play at verbal darts was the direct result not of sudden charity, but of the world's manifest indifference to his opinion. For a year and a half he had been, by his own description, "something like Rip Van Winkle." [45]

Victor had married Georgianna Mallory on March 2. He accompanied his father as far as Philadelphia, where Edward Harris and the rest of the party were waiting at the Sanderson Hotel.

Harris had bought a small journal for his expedition records. In a few months, when the adventure was over, he was to enter this memorandum: "Mr. Audubon's father was an officer in the French Navy during the revolutionary war. Came over with Count Rochambeau, quitted the Navy and entered the Army and fought at Valley Forge and several of the Revolutionary battles, afterwards receiving a new commission in the Navy and died an admiral at upwards of 90 years, an active man to an extreme age; his wife died upwards of 80 years old." [46] The credulous Harris, Audubon's friend of nineteen years' standing, fully believed these uneasy exaggerations. While in Alabama that autumn he jotted them in his journal.

XXX. Upper Missouri

H ARRIS HAD PROMISED the Philadelphia Academy to report on the geology of the Upper Missouri. Audubon
went with him on Sunday morning to pick up a list of queries
on the Yellowstone River region from Dr. Morton.[1]

The following day Audubon said good-by to Victor and
Bowen before joining his party in the "steam car." Gratiot
and Pierre Chouteau, Jr., were among those chuckling, as
the train pulled out, at the doomsday prophecies of the
charlatan visionary William Miller in the daily papers. Audubon had his sights on more realistic questions, such as the
date when his boat, the *Omega*, would be ready. He was
counting on Nicholas Berthoud, newly established with his
son in St. Louis, to help in many ways.

In the stagecoach, out of Baltimore, Gratiot fell ill and had
to be left behind at Cumberland. A heavy snowfall over the
Gap and the Alleghenies hampered progress. At Wheeling
the party boarded a steamer that labored toward Cincinnati
through fast-freezing waters. There they changed to the mail
steamer *Pike* for Louisville after Audubon let his struggling

brother-in-law Thomas see how well retributive justice had served him.

William Bakewell, "the Nimrod of the West," whom Audubon would have liked to take with him, turned down a place but parted with his gun.[2] He and his wife and their guests, the Alexander Gordons, took Audubon to a ball, where he danced past midnight among "the elite of Louisville." Most were strangers, but Dr. Galt and Gwathmey of the Indian Queen Hotel were on hand to greet him. He heard that Mrs. Rankin of Henderson was now a poor widow, supported by her son Adam.[3] William implied that Thomas Bakewell's dependence on George Keats had helped bring the latter to his death, but not until after William's involvement in their affairs made his own ruin certain. Georgiana Keats titillated the gossips with her hasty marriage to John Jeffrey, a Scottish engineer and philanderer sixteen years her junior. They and her eight children continued to occupy the mansion from which George had virtually ruled the cultural life of Louisville. (Her daughter Isabel shot herself in October.)

The steamer *Gallant*, "filthiest of all filthy rat-traps," received the party for the run to St. Louis. Henderson and the old mill stirred bitter memories along the way. There was but one bar of soap for the melee of settlers, gamblers, and drunkards who shared the leaky cabin—a hole "better fitted for the smoking of hams than the smoking of Christians."[4] Corn shucks served as pillows. The river water froze in the basins. Now and then the miserable craft struck a sawyer. Once during a more abrupt grounding than most, the women screamed, infants wailed, dogs howled, and livestock took alarm. Surveying the scene, Audubon quipped that Miller's prophecy might after all be coming true. In a race the *Cicero* and the *Gallant* locked bows. They remained so for half a mile downstream. Sixty miles above St. Louis the roof sprang a leak, and passengers and belongings were inundated.

Berthoud and his son James, general mercantile commissioners on a much less ambitious scale than in New York days, put themselves out to oblige Audubon and invited him to stay with them until the rising of the waters. Harris and the others registered at the Planter's, then at the Glasgow, but finally went out to Edwardsville to hunt while waiting.

Audubon bought claret, staples, and ammunition in the dawn market, as well as beads, rings, knives, combs, and trinkets for barter with the Indians of the frontier. One day he drew a pair of handsome squirrels.[5] The captain of the *Omega*, Joseph A. Sire, a native of La Rochelle, drove Audubon out to the Chouteau place. Ninety-year-old Pierre Chouteau, uncle-in-law of Sire, had founded the trading post of St. Louis with his brother Auguste in 1764. The legendary trader, still a good shot and raconteur, was amused to watch Audubon trap four pouched rats in his garden and draw them life-size for the *Quadrupeds*.[6]

Chouteau gave his son Pierre permission for their famous hunter, Étienne Provost, discoverer of the South Pass, to join Audubon at a monthly wage of fifty dollars. The *Omega*, under Chouteau's nephew, John Sarpy, was also to carry 100 of Chouteau's trappers. For his personal scout Audubon engaged a handsome, powerful half-blood, Alexis la Bombarde.

During the four weeks that "the old man with silver locks and weight of years upon him" restlessly watched the swans, geese, ducks, and cranes overhead, local reporters interviewed him. "Mr. Audubon is quite an aged man, but his active and hardy life has given a vigor and strength to his constitution which renders him far more active than the generality of men of his years," said one account. Audubon assured the journalist he could still tramp thirty-five miles day after day in any weather, on soaked biscuit and molasses that suited his toothless gums (soon to be parted from their last molar). His interviewers found him a bit "severe on Buffon," the coiner of the marvelous in nature. For comfort and convenience Audubon got a haircut, but he stored the shorn locks with a box of skins in Berthoud's warehouse.[7]

The "rather tall, very slender, lisping" Sir William Drummond Stewart appeared in a blue and scarlet cavalier uniform. An accident on the river had cost him his expedition boat. He prepared to start overland, but failed to tempt Audubon to join him for the Southwest with an offer of a wagon and five mules. One of his clerks—either Adolphus or Theodore Heermann—happened to be the son of a notoriously flirtatious pupil of Audubon's New Orleans days. Young Heermann, blissfully unaware that his father had once fired the artist, showed particular disappointment over his refusal of Stewart's bid. Mrs. Heermann might have been amused by these lines sent by the inveterate admirer of pulchritude to Lucy: "We have not seen a genteel-looking woman in the streets thus far, and I cannot crow to the beauty of the ladies without *seeing* some of them."[8]

Audubon drew up some last-minute reminders for Minnie's Land to send skins to Bachman, to keep the drawings safe upstairs, to take the "greatest care" of Lucy and the "sweet little ones." He imagined John setting potatoes, or shad fishing, or putting down eighty more apple trees, or having the new dock driven. He hoped that the poultry were laying, that the new road down the hill would soon be open, that the hotbed was flourishing, and that the outdoor garden was almost ready. Johnny had done well to clear 100 stumps away for another grazing pasture. To each one at home he sent a kiss "with all possible affection" and asked to be remembered to the servants and the gardener.[9]

On the bright, balmy morning of April 25, 1843, the day before his fifty-eighth birthday, Audubon boarded the *Omega* with relief. Bell could be kicked by no more horses for a while, and Sprague would not, hopefully, drop his gun again in the river water. Now, with the aid of a "good and kind Providence"—and the support of two extra bulkheads—all would go well.[10] An old, old ambition seemed about to be fulfilled. It would be, if men willing to venture into the Blackfoot country could be found.

The tipsy trappers—Creoles, French Canadians, Italians, and half-bloods—triggered a deafening salute on the hurricane deck as the boat slipped her moorings. After roll call some of the Indians sang and yelled eerily; others squatted silently in their blankets. In fine quarters (ordinarily the ladies cabin), which he shared with Harris, Audubon dashed off a few more lines below decks: "When I see you again I will tell you many a strange fact differing *in toto* from what has been printed in great books."[11]

Sarpy brought some Indian chiefs to inspect the animal pictures by the "Great Divine." The lifelike rodents brought smiles to the ordinarily saturnine faces and won invitations for the "great man" to visit their nations as honored guest. Audubon applied salve to the sore eyes of one chief and became, forthwith, "ancient and medicine man."[12]

The excitement of the day sent Audubon to bed early. But an onslaught of vermin soon drove him on deck with his blanket.

His early fascination with the western Indians rapidly dwindled. Tribes along the route, in their poor, disease-ridden, unregenerate state—whether Sac, Iowa, Fox, Potawatomi, Omaha, Ponca, Arikara, Mandan, Assiniboin, or Gros Ventres—only repelled him. They possessed none of the grandeur that George Catlin's writings and paintings had led Audubon to expect.[13] Once, when Indians on shore began to shoot at the *Omega* to satisfy what Audubon rated as arrogant and stupid curiosity, the boat slipped out of range.

Only when overnight stops ended the vibration could drawing be attempted. Audubon would then work by candlelight at a big table in his stateroom. From morning till night he and Harris scanned shore and skies for deer, wolves, buffalo, teals, thrushes, cormorants, partridges, woodpeckers, warblers, rare peregrine falcons, and snowy white pelicans. At fueling stops they hunted with their men, never venturing far.

Snags and a stubborn current balked the *Omega*. She was grounded for three days on a sandbar.

Beyond Fort Leavenworth, gateway to the Indian country, a thunderstorm washed away the last traces of winter. Through the May sunshine, land and water birds sailed in marvelous variety. At Independence, starting point of the Santa Fe caravan route, the boat entered far wilder frontier country. Mackinaw barges loaded with buffalo meat called out for news as they moved toward St. Louis.

At Fort Croghan, Audubon was given a horse for a canter

but told to stay close by. Near Decatur, he watched stags lock horns in a mating contest. At the mouth of the Big Sioux, near present-day Sioux City, the future prairie states of Nebraska, Iowa, and South Dakota met. Buffalo were becoming a common sight in the river, sometimes swimming across the *Omega's* path.[14] The dead animals of herds that had been trapped by winter snows drifted with the current.

At Fort George it became clear that murderous tension between trappers and Indians was no mere rumor. Nor did the prevalence of Indian women among white officials mitigate the hatred. How all this might affect their plans, which called for an absence of six months or more, remained to be seen. Audubon had time to draw a buffalo calf at the fort.[15] His sketch went well, but when he examined Sprague's, he was so caustic that the assistant said he would turn back home with the *Omega* at Fort Union. Audubon talked him out of any such idea.

The country around Fort Pierre was peaceful enough for hunting. The June landscape and brilliant sunsets made Audubon wish that Victor could paint them. But he wrote the family that the scenery was not so remarkable that they were missing much. His sense of the dramatic was as powerful as ever. One might have thought that he was truly realizing his old dream of "ransacking" the West, and not too sadly late for primacy as a discoverer. "I have not once pulled off my breeches when I have tumbled down at night to go to sleep," he wrote. Somehow the excitement was that of a grand tour, and likely to remain so. Victor could expect an Indian tipi, which he must put up "in the sweet spot that overlooks the river," where he and Caroline's brother James could enjoy their cigars each evening.[16]

At Fort Clark, Audubon visited a Mandan village of 100 mud lodges set among fields of corn, beans, and pumpkins. In one hut he met the survivor of a smallpox epidemic that had been more devastating to the tribe than a famous Arikara battle. He was treated to pemmican and corn steamed in a hanging cauldron, but his escort warned that no such hospitality awaited visitors to the treacherous Blackfoot country.

Toward the journey's end flying cinders set the *Omega's* stern on fire. The blaze was put out before it could ignite 1,000 pounds of gunpowder in the hold. The boat moved on at her usual speed. Indians, watching on shore, thought her under the power of whisky and the devil.

On June 12 the expedition neared Fort Union, six miles below the mouth of the Yellowstone River. Flags were flying on the east bluff of this the most important American Fur Trading Company post on the upper Missouri. The fort's salute reverberated up and down the waters. The *Omega's* six guns thundered a reply. Down the bluff rode a cavalcade headed by the post agent, thirty-four-year-old Alexander Culbertson (1809–78), to greet the arrivals. Audubon and Harris were promptly treated to a fast, rough wagon ride over the prairie. Far hills lay dark against the cloudy sunset. A black-headed grosbeak caroled in a thicket. The party rode back in the dusk for a last night aboard the *Omega*.

For his safe conduct of the party on the 1,400-mile voyage, Audubon presented Captain Sire with a pistol and fully signed testimonial. He also handed him a letter to post in St. Louis; it explained to Minnie's Land that the Blackfoot and Rockies country would have to be forgotten. The lively account of grizzlies, wolves, and mountain sheep to be seen near Fort Union could not mask his disappointment.

The next morning the *Omega* put about under a boisterous cannonade that sent dogs scurrying. Indian women and children ran for cover. Owen McKenzie, half-blooded son of the Scottish builder of Fort Union, was among those to greet Audubon at the entrance of the two-story cottonwood stockade. Outside the huge double gate hung a treaty scene for the benefit of Indians passing through. Huge whitewashed stone bastions supported high indoor balconies, lookouts, cannon, and a store of muskets. Sixty-foot flagpoles flew the Eagle and the Stars and Stripes. A weather vane of buffalo and eagle silhouettes moved with the wind.

The office, living apartments, mess, saddlery, and tailor shop were papered and hung with pictures. There were also a retail store, warehouse, and skin press within the walls of

Ackermann. Fort Union on the Missouri,
*1841. Aquatint, after pencil sketches by Karl
Bodmer, 1833. Joslyn Art Museum, Omaha,
Nebraska.*

the fort. One building housed the clerks, another trappers and hunters. Beside the mess hall were kitchen, icehouse, henhouse, dairy, and copper shop. The trading room, entered by a separate gate at certain hours, was sealed from the fort proper. Beyond the Indian camp was a hay enclosure and vegetable gardens. The immense prairie stretched toward the bluffs and wooded bottomlands beside the Missouri.

The big chamber set aside for the party had been occupied ten years earlier by the naturalist Prince Maximilian of Neu-Wied. The Prussian's Swiss artist, Karl Bodmer, had portrayed the Indians and the West with sympathetic brilliance.

The noise of reels and cotillions to fiddle, drum, and clarinet lured the newcomers from bed to join the trappers and Indians below. To interest the hunters in bringing him rare species, Audubon passed his lithographs around.

Very soon a gray wolf, a fawn, an antelope, and a bighorn were brought for the cause of the *Quadrupeds*. Eager to try a practical joke on Bachman, Audubon forged a letter, supposedly from "110 miles above Fort Union." He hoped that the newspapers would copy his description of a fabulous creature, the "Ke-ko-ka-ki" or "Jumper." Although domesticated by the Indians, it was his official discovery and likely to put him well above his "compeers" by its "use*less*ness and value." Except for its pouchless belly, antlers, gargantuan 600 pounds, and formidable nine feet, four inches from head to tail, it resembled the kangaroo.[17]

Culbertson staged a sham buffalo hunt. Audubon, watching from a balcony, had never seen the equal of the horsemanship of the agent and his beautiful Blackfoot princess, Natawista. Nothing would do but that they should pose for portraits. For want of canvas, Audubon used mattress ticking.[18] Natawista, who was then eighteen, became Culbertson's wife sixteen years later in Peoria, where they again posed for portraits by another artist.

Another account, this one more unlikely, relates that one day while the restless Culbertson was posing, a sentinel in the tower reported the approach of a band of a dozen Assiniboins in war paint. They brandished lances, rifles, and knife-studded clubs. Their scout, with her face painted black to signify peace, came to tell of their victory over the Blackfoot murderers of their high-ranking tribesmen. She borrowed a drum and soon a war dance began. Out of patience with their whooping and yelling, Culbertson sent them off.[19]

Harris, Squires, Bell, and Culbertson were constantly in the saddle after buffalo. Audubon and Sprague were left to their drawing. Now and then curiosity made the artist ride along to watch the fray. Audubon had promised Lucy to take no foolish risks. But the buffalo-hunting fever became a mania. He was infected enough that he rode to the edge of one particularly wild skirmish in which Harris rode herd so zestfully that no one would have guessed he had never before ridden "straddle," or that he had never dropped so much as a buck deer in the way of big game until seven years before. An angry bull passed Audubon's horse, then charged. Bell saw what was happening and swiftly took aim, in time.

The diaries of both Audubon and Harris paint a nearly orgiastic picture of buffalo hunting. Squires was so avid for the sport that he begged Audubon to let him spend the winter at Fort Union. A fall from his horse in July that nearly put an end to his earthly adventures settled the question.

By August, Audubon, not himself guilty of wanton killing at Fort Union, was expressing genuine sorrow over the murder of "immense numbers" of bison by both savage and civilized hunters. This, with the ravages of snow and flood, pointed toward the extinction of the animals. Harris felt "almost ashamed" of the number of bulls that he and Squires and Bell left to the wolves after butchering them for their tongues. A novice at murder, he owned to feeling "more depressed than exalted" in the beginning. But his excesses began to inure him to the tragedy and to inspire in him no more remorse than would the shooting of "a Towhee Bunting."[20] His hard riding cut his weight by twenty-four pounds. Audubon, less active, gained twenty-four.

Turning leaves and cooler mornings were not the only reminders that it was time to leave Fort Union. An anticlimactic trip with the trapper François Detaille into the Bad Lands

Swift Fox, *1844. Pencil, ink, and watercolor drawing. Courtesy Department of Library Services, American Museum of Natural History, New York. Drawn from a fox brought live from Fort Union, for plate 51 of* The Viviparous Quadrupeds of North America.

Pennant's Marten, *1841. Pencil, ink, and watercolor drawing. Wadsworth Atheneum, Hartford, Connecticut; Gift of Henry Schnakenberg. Drawn from a live marten brought to Audubon by Spencer Fullerton Baird; never lithographed.*

for bighorn convinced Audubon of the advisability of starting home by mid-August. A forty-foot Mackinaw barge, the *Union*, had just been built on the banks. On August 16 the expedition party, the hunter Detaille, and the Culbertsons and their infant left for the lower Missouri. Besides his drawings, skins, and Indian trophies, Audubon started out with a caged swift fox, a pet badger, and a timid Rocky Mountain deer for his Minnie's Land menagerie. He had obtained birdskins for plates 484–489, 492, 494, and 600. Lewis and Clark had reported one of these species; the finch for another, *Harris's Titmouse*, was the one contribution of that avid sportsman.

The company cooked on campfires beside the river. On September 24, at Ponce Island, the expedition boarded a steamer for St. Louis and there disbanded. At the Berthouds', Audubon found news from home. June and July drought had been followed by torrential rains with much damage to the vegetables and berries. Distressing was word that Georgianna had suffered a miscarriage. Caroline was soon to be confined. As for business, it was slow, although Prince Albert had ordered a set of the *Quadrupeds*.

Audubon caught the *Nautilus* for Pittsburgh, where he boarded an Erie Canal barge for Philadelphia. His gray beard and hawklike "noble Roman countenance," as he lay curled beneath skins and blankets, caught the eye of a young passenger. But when Audubon rose to be introduced as the famous naturalist, the boy recognized him without more from the captain. While they walked beside the plodding barge, Audubon scanned the horizon with "Indian's eye." Once he was taken for an elder of the bearded Dunkers.

On the afternoon of November 6, 1843, he leaped from the hired wagon that turned in at Minnie's Land and bounded down the hill to Lucy, who stood waiting on the veranda. Victor and John had seen the wagonload of boxes and cages approach and raced up the road. The little girls ran after. John, struck by his father's patriarchal look, insisted that he pose in full beard, long hair, and richly furred, double-breasted green blanket coat before submitting to a barber.[21]

XXXI.
And Now, Adieu

BACHMAN WAS ON TENTERHOOKS for particulars, totals, and facts. A vague message from Fort Leavenworth with an invitation to visit New York was all he had received. He was also on the lookout for a report from Harris, who had paused in Louisville to juggle expedition accounts and rest a bit.[1]

Audubon had been at home but a few days when a letter arrived from Bachman:

> Tell me all your news. We had in the newspapers a letter addressed to me from you which did not come to hand, in which you were bringing on some kangaroo kind of animal as big as a camel. But anyhow, you must have many things rare, some things new. Oh, how I long to tumble over your skins. Talk of turtle soup and all other delicacies—they are trifles compared to such a treat. How can I come to you, friend? Your animals require an examination of three months. I cannot be spared from home for a single Sunday. . . . I am quite sure that you will soon be here with all your treasures, and we will discuss these matters as men ought to do who are in earnest. . . . Write on foolscap—fully—fearlessly. . . . Out with your deeds and let us have an overhauling.[2]

"Your treasures"—Bachman was in for a surprise and disappointment. Unwilling to confess just yet that his journal
teemed with buffalo hunts but little else, Audubon stressed
the fourteen supposedly new birds and a new antelope and
sketches of flowers and scenery.[3] Work on these necessitated
postponement of a trip to Charleston.

The ailing Bachman aired his disillusionment. He com-
mended Audubon for the "grand haul" of birds but sensed
that the buffalo forays were out of all proportion to the expedition's purpose. As for the antelope, he hoped it a bona fide
claim but had his doubts because of Audubon's suscepti-
bility. (He was to find that Ord had long since described the
species from Lewis and Clark discoveries.) Bachman cited
the instance of the northern hare, a common rabbit which he
himself had erroneously described years earlier. But eager to
give the benefit of the doubt, he changed the subject to Audubon's amusing resemblance to the Pennsylvania Dunkers:
"I think the nearest to the Old Boy I ever saw you was at the
time you came from Florida in the stage—with a beard two
months old, gray as a badger, and not over-clean. I think a
Buffalo bull, after having wallowed in the mud, or a grizzly
bear forty-seven-years-old, must have claimed you as *par
nobile frater.*"[4]

Bachman's sarcasm on the subject of snuff and a mutual
resolve to quit it forever stung Audubon. He answered, in
kind, that if he had kept his beard, his neck would be warmer
these mornings, and that if "teetotaller" Bachman liked ab-
stinence, he himself would take "good wine" and "a good
deal of snuff" whenever he pleased. So much for the "science
of teetotallism," but Audubon dared not deny the charge that
he had grown too obese on "bison's humps" to bestir himself
for "new quadrupeds."[5] He could only try to keep the telltale journal out of Bachman's hands.

In another year the miniature *Birds of America* was to be
complete in seven volumes. The prospect raised the question
of a future living for the Audubons. Thus far the energies
and talents of Victor and John had been sheared off, all but
devoured, by the demands and necessities of Audubon and

his masterpieces. Yet they still counted on their own independent chance. At Christmas time, when Thomas Sully came to nearby Fanwood to paint a portrait of Colonel Monroe's wife, they made a point of observing his technique.

By the spring of 1844, John Bachman was hailing the latest *Quadrupeds* lithographs as "beautiful and perfect specimens of the art," probably unique "in the world of natural history."[6] His opinion of the scientific work being done at Minnie's Land was something else. He cited errors made by the Audubons and Bowen, while continuing to belittle the upper Missouri expedition. Nevertheless, his loyalty to his colleague remained unimpeachable. If anyone challenged Audubon's position, he lashed out in his defense. Cooper, for instance, in his newly issued *Birds of Long Island*, was guilty of errors, omissions, and false assumptions, as Bachman openly advised him: "In your preface you allude favorably to preceding authors but make no allusion to the *Synopsis* of Audubon."[7] Although the *Synopsis* had been Cooper's guide, he had failed to grant its author "a single line."

Other enemies of Audubon had resumed their mischief. Waterton and Ord were reviling the "lies and misrepresentations" of *Ornithological Biography*, a "voluminous romance."[8] Waterton began to think of bringing out a pamphlet full of "strictures" suggested by Ord. But Ord hesitated because of Bachman's skill at retaliation. Moreover, Waterton's pen had run dry temporarily: to beat a dead horse was idle, and besides, he believed Audubon in poor enough "odour" in England to need no more flogging. He could gloat over Ord's report of talks with Havell, who "often cursed the day" that he met Audubon. It was good to hear also that when Audubon asked the respected Temminck to subscribe, the zoologist had hurled this insult, "Sir, I cannot subscribe to your work, for I find it quite ridiculous."[9] The best consolation of all for Waterton and Ord was Audubon's refusal to challenge the discovery, by a London surgeon, of olfactory organs in the buzzard. Yarrell, the author of a new study of British birds which they denounced as wretched, was the only English friend Audubon had left, so they said.

In blossom and planting time Audubon turned his back wistfully on Minnie's Land to "keep hammering at the Yankees" of New England. Because their minds were on "new churches, asylums," and civic improvement, he found canvassing hard going. Their procrastination left him with more leisure than he wanted. Sprague was not in Hingham when Audubon went to pass some time in his company; the assistant had been invited to China by a wealthy kinsman. The galleries of Boston offered not very palatable diversion. Audubon thought the much discussed *Belshazzar's Feast* by the painter Washington Allston "very so-so indeed." Crawford's sculpture he found downright absurd.[10]

Throughout the summer, bulletins reached Audubon from Minnie's Land. The frolicsome deer from the West was continually escaping to the woods. Finally, it was penned in an enclosure beside the river. John had painted an oil of the piano tuner's wife. The garden produce was sufficient for some neighborhood sales and profit.

In mid-August Audubon visited Rochester. The modern beehive of 25,000 inhabitants, with its banal social life that left no room for appreciation of the arts, was not at all to his liking. Furthermore, Rochester failed to take an interest in either of his current publications. West of Utica his train jumped the track and plunged into a ditch, injuring several passengers. Shocked but unhurt, he "trudged and trudged" along the dozen miles back into town.[11]

In Troy a friend presented him with a live raccoon and 100 live crayfish for his brook. The boat that brought him down the Hudson obligingly put him ashore at Minnie's Land with his peculiar cargo.

Orders for the *Quadrupeds* were nearing the 200 mark. Victor had told Bowen to print 300. All the same, it was distressing to receive cancellations from such particular friends as Dr. Van Rensselaer, Pierre Chouteau, Jr., and the baronet Stewart.

The completion of the miniature *Birds* was not all that made the close of 1844 memorable. Audubon and Bachman had had their differences in the past, but none so serious as now. A major rift threatened. The minister reported having heard that Audubon did not plan to credit his assistance. This was the signal for a sweeping denial at New Year's: "Why you should have taken such a report or saying as truth is actually beyond my most remote thought. I could well prove by upwards of one hundred of our last subscribers I always mentioned your name to each . . . and many that know you were glad that I had so good and so learned a man at my elbow." [12] The lying confidante deserved a rough "lesson on propriety." With characteristic insouciance, and as though the charge were only a tiresome interruption, Audubon asked Bachman to send a wolf and black bear from the Carolinas. He had already posted ten new papers on mammals for him to examine. As for Bachman's criticism of his drawing of a Texas skunk, he staunchly defended its correctness.

Baird followed a gift of a live marten with a visit to Minnie's Land. Audubon let him choose from among duplicate skins from the upper Missouri and elsewhere. His own remarkable collection was enriched by forty or more.

Still the American Philosophical Society neglected its unpaid balance. Audubon and Victor advanced on the formidable institution for another try. They knew that Peale, now a half-hearted civil servant in Washington, would not be around to cause discomfort. Imagine their astonishment, however, to be received by Ord. Indeed it was he who spoke for the Society on all three of their visits. No one would have guessed that there had ever been trouble between them. When Ord described his experience to Waterton, he even permitted the word "great" to slip into his reference to *The Birds of America*. He described Audubon as "very venerable" but still "robust" and "agile," and determined to see the completion of *The Quadrupeds of North America*. He predicted failure for the latter; however, at last, he conceded that if the "fidelity of his narratives had corresponded with his perseverance," Audubon's fame would endure. "But what will the decision of posterity on the merits of one who has wantonly violated the dignity of Truth by rendering her subordinate to fiction?" he asked.[13] Waterton said he would have given much to see Ord's expression when the Audubons walked in. He thought the upstart naturalist's books ought to meet the same fate as Don Quixote.[14]

On July 19, 1845, "Providence" made an inscrutable move to insure the rarity of the Folio edition of the *Birds*. Many copper plates were damaged, others utterly destroyed, by a fire that swept lower Manhattan. Audubon accepted the loss and declined to brood on it. Other, more consequential worries crowded upon him; above all, the need of mammals that must be bagged, begged, or borrowed.

Bachman came to Minnie's Land to confer with the Audubons in the fall. Again the Missouri journal was kept out of his hands. Plans for the expedition to Texas fully occupied them. Bachman promised to call on Townsend in Philadelphia, and Peale in Washington, to plead for mammals. He departed without any real awareness of the cause of the "sad mistakes" which Audubon continued to make. Perhaps only Lucy saw that a creeping inexorable weariness of mind and body were to blame.

Bachman's hectoring continued unabated from Charleston. Surely, he wrote heatedly, the brush that still created "the very best drawings in the world" must not be thrown in the shade because of Audubon's laxity on scientific data. "Wake up and work as you used to do when we banged at the Herons and roared at the fresh-water Marsh hens." Reputations were at stake, and Victor and John must, he threatened, see that scientific nomenclature was not approached the way "man works at making Jews harps by the dozen," or the way the "children of Israel" tried to make bricks without straw. In short, unless all three Audubons managed to round up needed reference works to help him avoid damning errors, the work would founder and disgrace them all.

In desperation Bachman had set his daughter Lynch to translating the work of an unassailable German authority. Not even a certain fallible wilderness witness could be ignored; of his work Bachman told Victor: "I received your notes and extracts from old Rafinesque. . . . The old fellow was very rambling, careless and, the world says, dishonest. I wish we could do without quoting him, but so it is. I will kick him off in almost every case." Bachman boasted that he could list fifteen species of rodents to the Greek's four. "The white-footed mouse will, however, claim him as a father. I doubt whether we will be able to get along without copying all he has said about the quadrupeds. There is one advantage in his descriptions; if they were very bad, they were very short, so they won't take long to copy." Bachman added that he "must say a word to the Daddy" before he closed.[15]

A beautiful drawing of the "hind foot of a muskrat obtained at Aiken," done in pencil by Maria on the border of a subsequent letter, more than proves her fitness to assist with the *Quadrupeds*. For fully twenty years she had been drawing mammals for Bachman. But there is no evidence that she served as more than an amanuensis to him, by way of forwarding the final classic effort in which drawing honors were to be about equally divided between Audubon and John. Victor was to draw some backgrounds; how many, and which, would be hard to determine in later years.

On Christmas Eve, when no reform was in prospect, Bachman turned to Edward Harris. "Four years of remonstrance, mortification, and disappointment" had about convinced him that the Audubons and their "blunders" were a hopeless case. Yet he was as willing as ever to go on for "the cause of science" without remuneration if authoritative references could be provided. He thought that perhaps Audubon ought to send a qualified explorer on a tour of collection and not rely on the dubious efforts of amateurs like John, although he refrained from mentioning his son-in-law by name:

> I find the Audubons are not aware of what is wanted in the publication of *Quadrupeds*. All they care about is to get out a Number of engravings in two months. They have not sent me one single book out of a list of a hundred I gave them, and only six lines copied from a book after my having written for them for four years. When he published his birds he collected hundreds of thousands of specimens. In his *Quadrupeds*—tell it not in Gath—he never collected or sent me one skin. . . . Now he is clamorous for the letterpress. . . . I know nothing of what he did in the West. . . . I am to write a book without

the information he promised to give—without books of reference, and above all what is a *sine-qua non* to me without specimens. In the meantime my name is attached to the book.[16]

Harris sent the letter on to Audubon that he might make amends—as he promptly did—and avert the loss of Bachman's friendship and assistance.

The Texas expedition turned out to be little more than a costly adventure. The outlining of routes, choice of Indian guides and professional hunters, and seasoned advice of Colonel Jack Hayes of the Texas Rangers could not redeem it.

In April, John Woodhouse Audubon and the former gardener of Minnie's Land returned. To handle the southwestern skins, which, unluckily for John, had been stripped before measurement and without system, they brought back an Indian named Henry Clay. Bachman was soon hectoring his son-in-law for his negligence: "Victor tells me I am growing quite savage. True my boy, I am schoolmaster just now, and have some rascally, large scholars. I am trying to lash them up to the work. When they get out their ABC's, and behave like good boys I will pat them on the head and give them sugar plums."[17]

Victor tried a mild counterthrust, questioning the naming of a certain squirrel. The redoubtable Bachman referred him to one of his own papers published in London.

More than the transgressions of those at Minnie's Land weighed on their collaborator. His wife was dying of *tic douloureux*. Three slaves had succumbed of colds and fever. His chronic eyestrain was compelling him to rely more and more on Maria Martin.

Audubon remained impervious to attack. On the margin of a beautiful, faithful drawing of a "Pennsylvania meadow mouse" that he sent down to Bachman he wrote, "Know nothing." An explosion followed. "If you know nothing then I pity you all, for it is the most abundant species you have beneath your noses," came the reaction from Charleston. A marginal comment on an exquisite rendering of a beaver elicited the assurance that "it would require a Philadelphia lawyer to make out the meaning."

When at last the Missouri journal was surrendered to his scrutiny Bachman scoffed: "I am afraid the broad shadows of the elk, buffalo and big-horn hid all the little marmot squirrels, jumping mice, rats and shrews. Why man, what poor trappers you proved yourselves to be. . . . Do you know what I should have done? . . . make a brush fence a foot or eighteen inches high . . . and I would have had a couple every night . . . in they go, and by the neck they hang." He would have "given up three buffalo hunts and dug out the red fox." Not that he thought those hunting accounts less than "first rate," but only costly in the light of the expedition's showing. One good skunk from Culbertson would have been more welcome in Charleston than the "buffalo-brain-eating, horse-straddling" princess Natawista.

A remark from Victor should have served to warn Bachman: "If you have Leconte's pine-vole John can make a better drawing of them, perhaps, than those my father has done, as these animals are very small. And my father's eyes are not quite so good as they have been." [18] The "old gentleman" was drawing far less and confining himself to acknowledgments for the *Quadrupeds* and lighter tasks.

In the spring, Captain Cummings came down from Pittsfield, Massachusetts, to visit Audubon. He had been responding to pleas for skins from time to time, beginning in 1840 [19] with a "polecat" shipped in a keg of rum. They did much reminiscing while they fished together on the Hudson. Lucy baked her Sally Lunn tea cake for their breakfasts.

In New York a strange answer arose for an even stranger dilemma. On June 10, 1846, barely two months after he returned from Texas, John sailed with his family for England. His plan was to draw from preserved specimens of American mammals in foreign collections. Victor became virtual editor of the text of the *Quadrupeds*. Bachman asked for as few alterations of his own writing as possible; but Victor, under constant pressure from Bowen and the parlous state of funds, punctuated, emended, and condensed at will to speed the work through. He refused to be intimidated by advice that too many styles would mar the whole. [20] Seldom did he consult Harris, a bridegroom for the second time, at forty-seven. Harris found no time or perhaps felt disinclined to report on his visit to Maximilian of Neu-Wied during his wedding trip.

During the summer of 1846, Mrs. Bachman died in Charleston. Soon afterward, Bachman brought Jane for treatment by a New York doctor. He thought Audubon infirm but otherwise much like his old self. Apparently he and Bachman were not present on the day "the American Leonardo da Vinci," Samuel F. B. Morse, conducted an experiment from the laundry room of Minnie's Land. Morse came with a telegraphic company expert to string wire to the Jersey shore, paid twenty dollars for the inconvenience, and went his way.[21]

One or two other callers, however, recorded their impressions. A writer who came down through the woods past gabbling geese, scolding turkeys, and staring elk and deer to spend an hour in the "noble and commanding presence," thought Audubon a remarkably agile seventy (nine years older than the artist actually was). His hazel eyes, although still piercing, had faded to gray. The white-maned patriarch spoke with gentleness; his accent had lost none of its Gallic piquancy when declaring his visitor wise to flee the "crazy city"—even for a glimpse of "a poor old man!"[22]

That autumn, as the first volume of writings for the *Quadrupeds* emerged, Victor yearned for the end of the grueling task, despite growing uneasiness about the future. He turned to William Bakewell for advice on how best to find a livelihood for the family. Letting an invitation to Minnie's Land be his excuse for writing, he lamented that, although he was "one of the National Academicians," he might have to give up painting, except for "amusement."

> It is always with affection that I think of you, and I shall never forget your kindness to me. We are now at a period in our business here which makes me feel uncertain what John and I may have to do, hereafter, to keep the old folks comfortable. I have sometimes thought of going into business in New York as a commission merchant. . . . Anything that would be a more *permanent* occupation than our present one I should prefer, for it is *very difficult* in America to make a *comfortable and respectable* living by Painting.[23]

A severe infection from dog bite shortened Bachman's already much frayed temper. The critical illness of his daughter Harriet Bachman Haskell added to his tribulations. Ten days before Christmas—again at his wit's end—he berated Victor, whose onetime vindictiveness had finally given way to fairly saintly patience: "Is it not a shame—a disgrace—a sin that John should be so miserably careless as not to send us the names of the species? All my writing and scolding do no good. Say to him I am as mad as Thunder at being treated so much like either a witch or a jackass. I cannot know things without books, by intuition, and am not so stupid as to hazard names that may already have been given half a dozen times for aught I know." He was "grieved, ashamed and almost maddened" by this show of scant regard for "anything but the painted figures."[24] Little, certainly, had been coming from the frustrated John in London.

Just before Christmas Eve, Bachman apologized to his old friend for directing tirades to Victor only: "I say to him do, and he doeth it (not always, it is true, as quickly as I wish). I can scold him for neglect and he is too respectful or too goodnatured to scold back."[25]

The real reason was, of course, that by this time Audubon was counted as outside the range of responsibility in most matters. However, he had the heart, will, and clarity for a rare kind of service to the future of American science. One of the last important acts of his life took the form of a sovereign favor. Spencer Fullerton Baird, married and teaching at Dickinson College, aspired to a Smithsonian Institution curatorship. In his application he stressed the importance of his collection, "probably the richest in North American species of any in the world," some of the species being "unknown even to John James Audubon." Audubon's endorsement of Baird was a model of dignity, loyalty, and good taste, not to say penmanship of a noticeably smaller, more restrained but still beautiful kind.

On February 11, 1847, Audubon answered, and spiritedly, still another message from Baird. Eleven days later he declined an invitation to Moorestown in a hand smaller and more refined than ever, quite conspicuously neater and far

less bold than in the past. He regretted that he could not undertake travel, but said he hoped to see the Harrises at Minnie's Land soon. He said Victor was painting the river near
Manhattanville. He himself was watching Lucy give little
Harriet and "Lulu" their lessons. "And now," he closed,
with none of the old ebullience, "adieu, and with kind remembrance to you."[26]

Baird stopped by Minnie's Land in July on his way north,
to ask if a live red fox that he had sent in April was ever delivered. If so, the usual grateful, graceful line of thanks had not
arrived. But a glimpse of Audubon, whom he found "much
changed," was answer enough.

XXXII. Long Pond

DURING THE WINTER of 1847 the New York Central prepared to lay tracks along the Hudson shore. The actual havoc had not begun but was only months away. Trains were due to clatter across the foot of Minnie's Land. At 152nd Street a station began to rise. Mercifully, the blow did not penetrate to Audubon, "lost in his little fancies."

Between the shocking change in his father and the railroad's encroachment, John's homecoming was a dreary one. He wanted to seek an injunction without delay, but Victor spoke of other things that were crying to be done. For one, Bachman was still waiting for descriptions and data. John would have the unhappy task of explaining that Joseph Edward Gray of the British Museum had declined to help, and, in a curtly brief letter, had said to consult Richardson's *Fauna*.[1]

Bachman, in mourning for his daughter Julia, wanted John to come to Charleston and bring the children. But John could no more think of deserting Victor than of letting the children go south without him.

Protests throughout the spring and summer to the New

York Central were of no avail.[2] If the city granted the railroad right of way, as began to seem likely, litigation in a court of chancery might follow.[3] The lawyers saw no possibility of restitution except for claims of damage to health by the operations. In December, the Audubons capitulated. A settlement of $2,500 was offered and accepted.

John went on painting mammals, Victor backgrounds. While Bachman tried to keep pace with the second volume of the *Quadrupeds*, his sight rebelled. Also, he had to pause for a Lutheran Synod in Georgia. In December, on his return, he all but lost his eyesight in an accident. A mixture of gunpowder, sulphur, and lard for treating dog mange caught fire. The explosion singed Bachman's eyelids and damaged his eyes so severely that for days he was confined to bed in darkness. The prospect of a visit from the scientist Agassiz and an indomitable will abruptly ended his convalescence. It was disappointing to find Agassiz none too interested in mammals.[4]

Bachman persisted in the belief that bats, seals, and a whale or two belonged in the *Quadrupeds*. Audubon had drawn a few bats in fine style a few years back, and John several less prepossessing studies; but they were not numerous enough to warrant inclusion of the species. To bring Bachman away from this dubious preoccupation, Victor overwhelmed him with rough biographies of other mammals, using his father's journals and notes for substance. Little by little the stratagem worked, and the impossible was relinquished.[5]

Under the rain of half-joking, half-serious maledictions from Charleston, John maintained surprising patience. "You suppose me to have far more knowledge of the smaller animals than I can boast of myself," he answered reasonably. "For until I went to Texas I never thought I should have to become in any degree naturalist as well as artist. As for the notes to be made in Europe, I did make all I could get at, but the publications of those societies are so voluminous that for as poor a reader as I am to have to read up (even if there was anything worth knowing, *which I doubt*) would have taken me months. And in Germany my ignorance of the language would be a bar." He had not, for that very reason, braved Germany.

But John could turn with impunity to a subject dear to them both—their "angel Maria."[6] He invited Bachman to help Harriet and "Lulu" (to whom their Grandmother Audubon had so gladly been a mother), if he were able, but not if it increased his worries.

It was too soon after the Texas fiasco and the failure of the English mission for John to be caught up by the wild, sudden gold rush excitement. He felt the urge, but for the time being kept silent about a possible journey to California.

In February, vexed by the mails, Bachman rejoiced that "talk by telegraph" was about to be possible throughout the South.[7] But by May he decided that firsthand talk was indispensable. When he arrived in New York with Jane to have her treated for threatened blindness, he found Victor and John frantically busy. Audubon took no part. It grieved Bachman to see the "poor old gentleman . . . his mind all in ruins."[8] He had become "crabbed, uncontrollable," childishly given to pranks about the house—hiding hens' eggs, ringing the dinner bell at all hours, ordering John to feed the dogs, and pestering the weary Lucy for "dry shirts." Never until night did the "worrying and bothering," the incessant chatter, the nerve-wracking pleas for food leave off. Then he would call for "his little songs in French," ask a kiss from each of the ladies and children, and let himself be hustled off to bed.

Ann Gordon arrived after Bachman's departure. She thought Audubon's bodily strength fast giving way, his voice feebler, and his steps less light. "It is indeed melancholy to see him," she wrote William.[9]

Poor Bowen was not without his troubles. In June he complained to Victor: I have made a Nother attempt at the pattern of the Sea Otter . . . 4th attempt, so you see I am not more or better pleased with the plate than yourself. . . . If I color it heavier I shall be obliged to distroy the forms of shadow, the indication of hairing etc., as it was drawn from a brown in place of a black animal. I think I may improve on this one in the lot. Don't you think it would be better to take the long hairs out—on the top of the back. Please let me have the name, etc., for Black Bear. Yrs always faithfully.[10]

Bachman's eyes failed him once more, and once more Maria Martin became his amanuensis. This and the "derangement of the mails" lowered his spirits until the arrival of two beautifully bound Folio volumes of the *Quadrupeds*. Before Christmas he blithely announced his approaching marriage to Miss Martin: "Maria has been weak enough to consent to take the old man with all his infirmities of mind and eyes, for better or for worse, and thus lawfully become his nurse and scribe December 28." He asked the Audubons to admit that he had chosen "a first-rate old girl . . . so good-tempered that she will not scratch out the poor remnant of eyes that are left."[11]

The Audubons took the news in stride—perhaps even with relief. It had been disconcerting to hear Bachman plead, "I will aid you all I can, but I cannot consent to endanger sight and life to oblige even you, for whom I will do more than for any other human being. When I begin again I know I cannot stop—but you must have pity on me. Whilst you are thinking of yourself, think also of me." However, Maria was to receive no particular recognition from Bachman's collaborators or from the world. "We shall try," Victor wrote her concerning her bridegroom, "to make him some return one way or another."[12] The woman who for sixteen years had drawn flowers and insects on demand; kept track of Audubon's cash at times in Charleston; and served Bachman as artist, copyist, editorial helper, secretary, and now life partner was to be forgotten.

A year had gone by since an American mill hand ran through the streets of San Francisco shouting "Gold!" It was a year of growing uneasiness for John and Victor. The time when returns from their father's classic would somehow have to be supplemented drew near.

On February 8, 1849, John Woodhouse Audubon set out with a profit-sharing company of eighty for California. Cash for the venture was put up by Daniel and Ambrose Kingsland and Cornelius Sutton. John believed their stake of $27,000 would not only handsomely reward the investors, but bring his family "at least $20,000." Into his pack went introductions Victor had obtained in Washington. Edward Harris admitted to Victor when approached that although the "gold rash" had "broken out" on him at the outset, it had so far receded as to enable him to pass up "the golden prospect and leave it to some more fortunate adventurer to build his castles."[13]

None of the excitement got through to Audubon, completely detached from reality. His morning walks continued but he could no longer roam about unaccompanied. "My poor father is apparently comfortable, and enjoys his little notions, but has no longer any feeling of interest in any of us, and requires the care and attendance of a man," Victor wrote Bachman. "This is the hardest of all to bear among trials in store for us."[14]

Ord heard of Audubon's decline and let Waterton know. "Your account is a melancholy one," the squire replied. "Poor fellow! Had he merely stuck to the painting of birds he might have jogged on pretty fairly. But when he borrowed the character of an ornithologist, it bore him too high up, and then let him fall, to rise no more."[15]

The quest for gold was a tragic fiasco. From Cairo, Illinois, the Mexican war veteran and explorer Colonel H. L. Webb led the company south to the mouth of the Rio Grande. Ten men, among them John Howard Bakewell, son of Lucy's brother Thomas, died of cholera in March. Webb deserted. Twenty men, including Jacob Henry Bachman, the minister's nephew, turned back. The entire fund was stolen and only part of it recovered.

John assumed leadership of the pitiful little band. Twice he was stricken with cholera as they moved from northern Mexico to Colorado. In the parched Gila Valley desert supplies ran low. Mules dropped from lack of forage. Paper, intended for preserving plants, went instead to wad guns. John became doctor, nurse, and confidant to the dying. The survivors trudged into San Diego in shoes fashioned from saddle skirts, only to find the mines depleted. With $400, all that was left, they moved on to San Francisco 600 miles north, then scattered.

John returned after an absence of a year and a half without money, gold dust, or western mammals. A few landscapes and a sketchy journal he meant to publish were all he had to show. Bachman sent him word that he must not despond while "youth and health" remained.[16] He was sure that his son-in-law was "a wise and better man" for all he had been through. The Audubons scraped enough money together for reparations to the disappointed investors. Lucy was often ill and apprehensive during these trials.

By December 1850, Victor was finding "a great deal more excitement over the fugitive slave bill than about the Quad-rupeds" in Massachusetts. His siege of that state had won only one order for the work. "Tell the dear old Critter to keep up her spirits," he wrote John, meaning "Minnie." "I hope she is well now."[17] From Boston he spoke sympathetically of the growing care that Audubon had become: "It is a great pity that you have to apply to be guardian to the poor old man. Would to God it were not so. I hope at all events that it will not be the occasion of making his melancholy case known more than it is at present. Do the best you can to keep it quiet." Audubon's enviable public image remained a precious asset. Victor added that if "Mr. Harris" showed no inclination to give the family a note in their dilemma, there was still Caroline's father to turn to.[18]

After Christmas, Victor notified John, from Philadelphia, that there was no use trying, no matter what the season, to conceal the fact of their present straits. "I have had one of my old tormenting pains over the right eye," he wrote. He had been resorting to the blue pills and an antibilious nostrum unknown to others of the family. "I shall take quinine this afternoon and hope to be all right tomorrow."[19]

Some months earlier the brothers had ventured to acquire a foundry, which, after the turn of the year, they tried to pass (along with its precarious future) on to their neighbor Stafford. Of this contretemps, Bachman took no notice. He had turned to a search for the middle path between theology and science and was reporting the results in *The Unity of the Human Race.*

William Bakewell had recently visited Minnie's Land. When he surprised the old painter in one of his reveries, Audubon, at first bewildered and then delighted, gazed up for an instant and—to everyone's astonishment—exclaimed, "Yes, yes, Billy! You go down that side of Long Pond, and I'll go this side, and we'll get the ducks."[20] Those words were his last.

One Sunday morning in January, Audubon declined breakfast and a morning saunter, and returned to bed. Twenty-four hours later, extreme pain and paralysis were evident. Drawn features, a deepening pallor, and a fainter heartbeat gave warning. At five o'clock on the evening of January 27, 1851, John James Audubon, the old "wistful and clear" expression on his face, turned to look once more at Lucy, Victor, and John, then fell asleep.[21] The suffering was over. At a quarter past ten Lucy closed his eyes.

In the morning John made a hasty sketch of his father's head before he and Victor undertook a death mask.[22]

Only a few old friends gathered in the parlor on the blustery morning of January 29. More might have been present had the *Evening Post* not mistakenly printed the name Anderson instead of Audubon.[23] The cortege filed up the hill to Trinity Church and a spot that the painter had chosen some years earlier. Before long the cemetery was to be moved many yards eastward for the widening of Broadway. Near the turn of the century a tall runic cross, the gift of rich and famous men who were strangers to Audubon, would rise above the family crypt on a day of eulogies and wreaths. The one who for so long had been a fugitive from his shadow would have been the last to protest the mistaken digit in his birth date.[24] *The Birds of America* was his monument and memorial.

Henry Inman. John James Audubon,
1833. Oil on canvas, 24⅛ × 20 in. Private
collection.

NOTES

Key to Abbreviations

AHJ	Maria R. Audubon, ed. *Audubon and His Journals.* 2 vols. New York, 1897. Includes "Myself," which was originally published in *Scribner's* in 1893.
AMNH	American Museum of Natural History, New York.
APS	American Philosophical Society, Philadelphia.
BMHN	Bibliothèque du Muséum d'Histoire Naturelle, Paris.
CMBC	Charleston Museum, Bachman Collection.
DBP	Donald Bakewell Papers, estate of Mrs. Donald Bakewell.
FHH	Francis Hobart Herrick. *Audubon the Naturalist.* 2 vols. New York, 1917; revised 1938.
HLHU	Houghton Library, Harvard University.
Howland	Howland Papers, Buffalo Museum of Science.
HSP	Historical Society of Pennsylvania.
Lavigne	Estate of Henri Lavigne.
Letters	*Letters of John James Audubon, 1826–40.* 2 vols. Cambridge, Mass., 1930.
MFOM	Ministère de la France d'Outre-Mer, Paris.
Moore	Estate of Sir Alan Hilary Moore, Waterton Collection.
NYPL	New York Public Library.
OB	John James Audubon. *Ornithological Biography.* 5 vols. London, 1831–39.
Pears	Papers of Thomas Clinton Pears III.
PUL	Princeton University Library: Firestone Library, Rare Books and Manuscripts.
Shaffer	Estate of Susan Lewis Shaffer, Cincinnati.
Tyler	Morris Tyler Collection, New Haven, Conn. Many of the documents formerly in the Tyler Collection have been donated to Yale University; those cited as Tyler remain in the Tyler Collection.
Yale	Yale University: Beinecke Library of Rare Books and Manuscripts.

I. Three Worlds *(pages 13–43)*

1   See Audubon family chart in Appendices (Archives de la Roche-sur-Yon).

2   Service record of Jean Audubon (Service Historique de la Marine, Paris. See Appendices).

3   Marriage record of Jean Audubon and Anne Moynet (Les Archives Départementales de Loire-Atlantique, Nantes).

4   Marriage record of George Ricordel and Anne Moynet, May 8, 1764 (Parish records of the Church of St. Opportune, Paimboeuf, in Les Archives Départementales de Loire-Atlantique, Nantes). Dossier of Coiron Frères (Archives Départementales, Nantes: *Les Fonds Marines et les Fonds du Commerce*).

5   Dossier of the Bouffard family (Archives de la Charente-Maritime, La Rochelle). Gabriel sailed for Les Cayes on the *Le Don de Dieu* on May 16, 1755.

6   Dossier of the Bouffard family.

7   Dealings of David Ross and Jean Audubon (Lavigne). See Appendices.

8   Purchase of La Gerbetière (Archives Départementales, Nantes). The Audubons sold a ruined chapel and grounds, just west, to Rivière de Héros of Couëron.

9   Gabrielle-Louise-Rosalie Beauchêne de la Morinière married Le Jeune, "gentleman of Vaugeon, lawyer of *Parlement* and Superintendent of Waters, Woods and Forests of the Duchy of Rohan and the Earldom of Porthoët," on August 21, 1775, in Nantes. They had three children (Archives Départementales, Nantes). Audubon and Le Jeune had dealings in 1778 (Lavigne).

10   Marriage of Jean-Baptiste Le Jeune de Vaugeon and Marie-Anne-Claire Audubon, September 16, 1783, at the Church of St. Clément, Nantes (Archives Départementales, Nantes). She was born in Les Sables d'Olonne in 1750 and died in 1815 (Archives Départementales, Nantes).

11   Passenger list of *Le Conquérant* (Archives Départementales, Nantes, and Les Archives Nationales, Paris).

12   See family chart in Appendices (Archives Départementales, Nantes). Les Touches was a familiar source of domestics for Nantes and the landed gentry. Cebron could have recommended Jeanne Rabine of Les Mazures, a hamlet near his tannery. He had witnessed the marriage of her parents, as well as both marriages of Anne Moynet Audubon. Jean Loire, Cebron's nephew-in-law, married Marie Rabine, Jeanne's sister. Jeanne Rabine herself was the godmother of one of Cebron's nephews. Her mother was related to Cebron's close friend, the lawyer Charles Le Comte.

13   Dossier of Jacques Pallon de la Bouverie and his notaries (MFOM).

14   Accounts of Sanson (Lavigne); facsimile of crucial entries (FHH, I, 54ff).

15   Les Touches Parish record: April 13, 1767, "*Marie Tessier, femme de Pierre Rabine, présente au baptême un enfant né ce jour du villages des Mazures, enfant de Pélagie Douet et de père inconnu.*" April 28, 1767, "*mariage de la dite Pélagie Douet et de Guillaume Le Ray qui reconnaissent le dit Guillaume comme leur enfant.*"

16   Receipt of the surgeon Guerin after the birth of Rose "Bonitte" (Lavigne): "*J'ai reçu de Monsieur Audubon la somme de cent livres . . . qu'il me devoit pour salve, et cette de Deux cent livres pour [——?] sur deux tête de négres qu'il m'avait envoi, nomme [——?] et Sans Pareil, et cette de cent livres pour les couches de Sanitte, sa ménagère. 24 juillet 1787.*" Guerin (Services of 1785 and 1786: £2,100).

17   Baptism of Jeanne Rabine (Les Touches Parish Record): *le 14 jour du mois de mars mil sept cent cinquante huit est née et a été baptissée Jeanne, fille de Guillaume Rabine et de Marie Le Conte . . . On été paraîn: H. G. Pierre Tiger et marraine Marie Tiger qui a declare ne savoir signer.* [Jeanne Rabine's grandmother was variously named as Thessier and Texier.]

Burial of Jeanne Rabine (MFOM): 1785 Sépulture *L'onze novembre mil sept cent quatre vint-cinq a été inhumé dans le cimetière de cette paroisse le corps de demoiselle Rabin, native de Nort, diocèse de Nantes, décédée la veille, agée de 24 ans. Eglise de Notre-Dame de l'Assomption. La paroisse des Cayes du Fond de l'Ile à Vache, Saint-Domingue.* [Parish register, 1698–1788: R]

18   Lavigne.

19   Ibid.

20   Ibid.

21   Ibid.

22   Passenger list of the ship *Le Duguesclin* (Archives Départementales, Nantes).

23   Archives Départementales, Nantes, for all references to Maisonneuve.

24   Parish record of Paimboeuf, 1780 (Archives Départementales, Nantes): marriage of Charles Garet and Jacquette Croizet, November 1, 1780. Her father was a dealer in block pulleys. Garet was born in Gratz, 1749, and died in Nantes, 1823.

25   Lavigne. Previous wills appear in FHH. Marie-Gabrielle was evidently the daughter of the late Sebastien Turpin, merchant, and the late Marie-Gabrielle Moinereau of St. Clément parish, Nantes (Archives Départementales, Nantes).

26   Historical Society of Pennsylvania, Philadelphia, MSS. Day book, David Evans, July 19, 1781.

27   Montgomery County Historical Society publications. Montgomery County Court House deeds. (See Appendices for transfers, et al., of Mill Grove.) Prevost had known General George Croghan (d. 1782) at Fort Pitt. Croghan was a forebear of Audubon's Kentucky friend George Croghan.

28   Lavigne.

29   "To David & Francis Clark. Mr. Odeboung. For a new sulke with falle Back tope and steel springs wooden apron Boady painted a fine sky Bleu with a hansom boarder around all the Pannels with mantlings and your Coat of armes on the front & hind pannels gilded mouldings and Boady high Varnished harnes for one horse platted. 75.0.0

Extra charges for the Boady being linned with morrocka 2.0.0

2 platted boses for the sadle   1.0.0

1 platted front to the bridle   0.15.0

a pair of new phaiton wheels   7.10.0_____

86.5.0

Received 25 April of Mr. Odebon eighty-two pounds twelve shillings and six pence for a sulke harnes for one horse" (Lavigne).

30   *Marine 2321 Régistre Désarmaments 1790.* (Archives Départementales, Nantes): "The schooner Victoire, 70 tons, left Les Cayes on October 26, 1789 . . . left isle of La Pierre à Joseph off Saint-Domingue on June 14, 1790. Called at Cap Français, base of owners Lessene & Sicard. Arrived Philadelphia on July 6; at Belle Isle off Brittany on September 8." Captain Pinson paid his crew in Nantes on September 14, with Captains Audubon and Jacques Hardy as witnesses. Coiron Frères endorsed payment. Captain M. Susselle of Bordeaux had abandoned his command of the disabled schooner on December 7, 1789. A letter from Prevost dated March 25, 1791, proves that he lent Audubon his passage money. Another letter, also in the Lavigne Collection, places Audubon in Philadelphia as late as August 2.

31   *"Louise-Françoise-Josephine, née le onze mai 1790, fille naturelle de Marguerite Bouffard demeurant aux Cayes, présente à l'Etat-Civil pour sonstater son état en présence de Joseph Fougas, propriétaire cultivateur, et de Sophie Roux. Signature de Roze Bouffard, tante de l'enfant"* (MFOM: Répertoire des Naissances).

32   See Appendices (Mill Grove).

33   Lavigne.

34   Ibid.

35   Ibid.

36   Passenger list of the ship *Le Tancrède* (MFOM and Archives Départementales, Nantes). See Appendices.

37   Passenger list of the ship *Les Bons Amis,* May 1, 1776 (F⁵B, Vol. 23: Nantes 1776, Archives Nationales, Paris).

38 Death of Jean Audubon's mother (Archives Municipales, Nantes).
39 Archives Départementales, Nantes.
40 Ibid., #L-621, 628.
41 FHH, I, 74; Journal (Archives Départementales, Nantes).
42 Death of Madame Le Jeune de Vaugeon, née Audubon. Le Jeune *sépultures:* G. 40, 563, 587 (Archives Départementales, Nantes). See Appendices.
43 Yale.
44 For *Le Cerbère* (petitions and letters concerning the battle) see Audubon dossier, Les Services Historiques (Archives de la Marine, Paris).
45 Bouffard dossier (Archives de la Charente-Maritime, La Rochelle). *"Marie Magdelaine, agée de seize ans, native de cette paroisse, fille de la citoyenne Catherine ditte Bouffard est décédée en plaine et a été enterré dans le cimetière de cette paroisse ce jourd'hui vingt quatre aôut mil sept cent quatre vingt treize, l'an deuxième de la République française. Joullan, curé."* Evidently, she was living at no. 5 Perches with her mother, Sanitte, and her sisters. The word *plaine* refers to the Plain of Jacob (MFOM: *Sépultures*).
46 Rose Victorine (MFOM: Répertoire des Naissances). *"Née le 4 septembre mil an cent quatre vingt treize aux Cayes, fille naturelle de Marguerite Bouffard, présente à l'Etat-Civil pour constater son etat en présence de Joseph Martin, capitaine des navire de commerce, et de Rose Bouffard."* [Sanitte and Rose signed; child born September 4, 1793.]
47 Bouffard dossier (Archives de la Charente-Maritime, La Rochelle).
48 FHH, II, Appendices.
49 Archives de la Marine, Rochefort-sur-Mer.
50 Letters of Miers Fisher (Yale). City Hall Records (Philadelphia): Appearance docket for 1793, p. 260 (Office of the Prothonotary, Supreme Court): "Mary Wert and children Susannah and Mary vs. John Audubon." Audubon, through attorney Hallowell, pleaded not guilty of nonpayment of debts dating from December 5, 1791. Docket for 1794, p. 207: A special jury found Audubon guilty; a judgment of £220 and 6 pence was granted on April 7, 1794 (on December 30, 1794, Fisher borrowed in order to pay that sum and to meet interest due Prevost). Fisher tried but failed to collect from David Ross. He leased Mill Grove to William Thomas for $400 a year for five years (Yale). Power of attorney to Fisher, July 31, 1790 (Lavigne).
51 "Myself," an autobiographical sketch edited by Maria R. Audubon; first published in *Scribner's*, Vol. XII (1893): 267–87; hereafter referred to as "Myself."
52 Les Archives de la Marine, Rochefort-sur-Mer.
53 Ibid.
54 *Registre . . . Article #D²6*, Municipal Administration, 1797–1800, Rochefort-sur-Mer. Applications for 2nd Class grade by "mousses." Mousse Audubon: F3P¹45. Arsenal records show young Audubon present February 20–April 20; May 29–September 22, 1798; September 21, 1799; and February 20–March 21, 1800.
55 Initial proposal for new rank: *Côte* 1A 92, year 1795; action deferred. Archives de la Marine, Rochefort-sur-Mer. Request for transfer: ibid., Vol. 1A, 101–3. Service record, record of battle wounds, appeal for help toward colonial settlement, et al.: Dossier of Jean Audubon, Service Historique de la Marine, Paris. Service journal, January 19–September 10, 1797. Archives Départementales, Nantes.
56 Archives of the Archdiocese of Nantes.
57 Bibliothèque Nationale, Paris; Ecole des Beaux-Arts, Paris.
58 Yale.
59 Lavigne.

II. Mill Grove *(pages 45–56)*

1 Secondary sources mistake Greenwich, mentioned in "Myself," for a town in Connecticut, and Norristown, Pennsylvania, for Morristown, New Jersey.

2   Miers Fisher (1748–1819), "profound lawyer and man of solid sense" (Du Ponceau).

3   Jones was licensed by Philadelphia Presbytery in 1801 and ordained 1807. He taught English, Latin, and Greek.

4   The village, nameless until 1823, became Shannonville. It was named Audubon in 1899.

5   William Bakewell's manuscript journal proves Audubon's memory in "Myself" faulty concerning his first meetings with the Bakewells. The journal also disproves January 1805 as the time of a Bakewell loan of $150 (FHH, I, 336).

6   Jean de Colmesnil was born July 31, 1787, in St. Marc Parish, Saint-Domingue. He and his father, Louis-Gabriel de Colmesnil, escaped Haiti, with the help of a slave, for Philadelphia, Trenton, and in 1800, the Savannah area. After his father's death, Jean came north and visited Audubon.

7   Dr. Benjamin Rush (1745–1813), the first American "psychiatrist" and a friend of Franklin, was an author and a signer of the Declaration of Independence.

8   Neither baptism nor adoption records justify Audubon's use of "Laforest," which he affected before and just after his visit to France in 1805 and which Madame Audubon used throughout her life in letters to him. It appears on his sister's marriage certificate, on a number of 1805–06 drawings, on the missing souvenir gun of Madame André, on a London presentation drawing of the 1820s, and in Lucy's letters over a long period. Perhaps he imagined himself related to the equerry marshall de la Forest of La Garenne, not far from Couëron.

9   In "My Style of Drawing Birds," *AHJ*, II, 522–27; first published in *Edinburgh Journal of Science*, Vol. VII, No. 1 (1828): 48–54 (Kingfisher). First drawing, a stuffed dove (*OB*, II, 354); banding experiment (*OB*, I, 122).

10   For the Dacosta–Lieutenant Audubon exchange, see FHH, I, 113–26. Fisher advised against the grant of land to Thomas. Mortgage agreement, August 1804, and settlement of April 5, 1807, signed by Fisher (Montgomery County Court House). Rozier arrived in Nantes in 1805, aboard the frigate *President* (FHH, I, 245).

11   Norristown (Pennsylvania) *Register*.

III. A Mission *(pages 57–64)*

1   Fisher manuscript journal, January 2 and 5, 1805 (Friends Historical Library, Swarthmore, Pennsylvania).

2   William Bakewell manuscript diary (Shaffer).

3   Dr. James Mease (1771–1846) was a physician, merchant, and historian.

4   "Mr. Prentice, the artist of these threshing machines is . . . excellent mechanical philosopher . . . and a millwright by trade . . . a great acquisition to his country." Mease to William Young, Wilmington, Delaware, February 28, 1805 (HSP). The two-horse machine threshed three dozen wheat sheaves in eleven minutes. Mease, founder of the Pennsylvania Horticultural Society and of the Philadelphia Athenaeum, wrote to Baron Cuvier (BMHN) on September 17, 1801: "The persecutions of England have secured the retreat of the immortal Priestley among us, and though placed in the retired corner of Northumberland, he prosecutes his experiments with unceasing assiduity." Pierce Butler, Mease's son, married Frances Anne Kemble, the Shakespearean actress.

5   "Myself."

6   FHH, I, 336, dated loan January 1805 (Bakewell manuscript journal, March).

7   Manuscript diary of Thomas Bakewell in re *Hope* (DBP).

8   *The Observer*, August 4, 1805, noted the closing of the Cabinet.

9   Dacosta–Lieutenant Audubon exchange (FHH, I, 113–26).

10   U.S. National Archives, Washington, D.C.: brig *Hope*, master John Williams. April 12, 1805: Williams protested the voyage of the *Hope* as unsafe when it left Bor-

deaux for New Orleans. June 30, 1805: *Hope* described as unfit at time of sale (Marine Notes of Protest, 1804–05, pp. 193ff. Consulate, Bordeaux).

11   John James Audubon to William Bakewell, May 20, 1805.

12   Le Jeune de Vaugeon died July 27, 1806 (Archives Départementales, Nantes).

13   Audubon boarded *L'Eveille* on November 22, 1794; André Du Puigaudeau, December; Joseph Du Puigaudeau, June 15, 1795. Claude Audubon signed off April 19, 1795. Audubon boarded the *Cerbère* on May 3, 1794, to escort lugger St. Jean from Ile de Yeu to Vannes (Archives, Rochefort-sur-Mer).

14   Audubon-Rozier partnership Articles (FHH, I, 146; and II, 345–49). Rozier senior was said to have put up 16,000 francs.

IV. Preludes *(pages 65–74)*

1   Rebecca Smith, daughter of realtor Robert Smith of Philadelphia, married William Bakewell at the Second Presbyterian Church in Philadelphia on December 10, 1805 (Presbyterian Historical Society, Philadelphia).

2   William Bakewell, in his journal, entered a shorthand symbol after "did not bring" that is taken to mean "permission to marry," then mentioned the loan.

3   Earliest extant signed and dated American drawing is of false foxglove. Dated July 15, 1806; privately owned. (PUL is believed to have the earliest extant American bird study, dated July 21, 1806; a nighthawk identified by Audubon as a whip-poor-will.) On March 4, 1807, the Botanical Society changed its name to the Philadelphia Linnaean Society, with Dr. Benjamin Smith Barton as president. Not until fifteen years later did America have its first handy grammar of botany.

4   Book of Arrivals, 1798–1807: Landing Reports, U.S. District Court, Philadelphia.

5   Guardianship Acts & Articles (*tutelles*), 1788–89, of the Sénéchausée of Nantes (Archives Départementales, Nantes). Evidence against Jean Audubon's having, by proxy, appointed a guardian of Jean Rabine in 1788 is the necessity of obtaining a legal declaration of the appointee's intention to surrender the appointment on demand. (Before the Revolution, acts of guardianship had to be drawn up in the presence of a legal council to protect the ward's rights.) He wanted delay tactics and secrecy instead. A child without property was naturally not involved in such acts of law; and, then, there were no allocations, no obligatory vaccinations, and nothing in the statutes to require bringing the ward into the light.

The *tutelle* of July 2, 1806 (evidently withdrawn from the official records) is in the Lavigne collection. Ferrière remains unidentified save for this action and his alleged part in it. Also among these papers is this memo: *"Doit, Audubon. Des éritiers Bouffard dont je suis chargé 140,000 intéret de deux années"* [sic].

6   Montgomery County Court House, Montgomery, Alabama.

7   Pears Papers.

8   Dr. Samuel Latham Mitchill (1764–1831) was a founder and coeditor of *Medical Repository*, United States senator, charter member of the New-York Historical Society, and founder and first president of the Lyceum of Natural History.

9   John James Audubon to Lieutenant Jean Audubon, April 24, 1807 (FHH, I, 159–60).

10   Letters of John James Audubon to Claude-François Rozier, May 6 and 30, 1807, and to Lieutenant Jean Audubon, May 6, 1807 (FHH, I, 159–65).

11   John James Audubon to Claude-François Rozier, July 19, 1807 (FHH, I, 165–66).

12   FHH, II, 354–55.

13   George Rogers Clark (1752–1818) was a noted frontier leader and Indian fighter. William Clark (1770–1838) is known for his participation in the Lewis and Clark Expedition to the mouth of the Columbia River (1804–06). Major George

Croghan (1791–1849), hero of British siege of Ft. Stephenson on the Ohio, 1813, became postmaster of New Orleans in 1824. For encounters with Audubon, see latter's 1820–21 *Journal*, p. 44; "The Swift" in *OB*.

14 James Berthoud, born in the Neuchatel, Switzerland, before its accession, sailed on the *Birmingham* from Frankfurt, Germany, for Philadelphia with his wife, Marie-Ann-Julia Tarascon, and their son, Nicholas, on August 25, 1794.

15 Louis-Anastase Tarascon left Marseille in 1794. A faithful Republican, he called himself "Citizen Tarascon" but never returned to France. In 1806 he and his brother John settled in Shippingport (*The History of Ohio Falls Cities* [1882], I, 488). He was naturalized on December 20, 1797, in Philadelphia (Department of Records, City Hall; witness, John Tarascon).

V. A Wilder Range *(pages 75–82)*

1 "Married on Tues., the 5th inst., by the Reverend Wm. Latta, Mr. J. Audubon, of Louisville, to Miss Lucy Bakewell, eldest daughter of Mr. Bakewell, of Fatland Ford, in this county." (Norristown *Weekly Register*, April 6, 1808.) In *Life of John James Audubon*, Latta is called "Latimer"; in "Myself," the date April 8 is erroneous. William Latta (1768–1847), a native of Bucks County, headed various Chester County churches for more than forty-seven years (Presbyterian Historical Society, Philadelphia).

Miers Fisher almanac diary describes weather (Friends Historical Library, Swarthmore, Pennsylvania).

2 *OB*, I, 29, 290, 437.

3 Victor Gifford Audubon (1809–60) was named in honor of cousins in Derbyshire, England: Richard Gifford and his daughter, Euphemia (the husband and the daughter of Elizabeth Woodhouse).

4 John Gwathmey, the nephew of George Rogers Clark, married Ann Buchanan Booth.

5 *OB* makes frequent reference to Alexander Wilson; he had published the first two volumes of his work by 1808. The Wilson manuscript diary is missing. See *Pennsylvania Monthly*, Vol. X, 433–58.

6 The report of the journey in Audubon's "Journey up the Mississippi," in *Winter's Wreath for 1829*, differs somewhat from the version in *Life of John James Audubon*.

7 Jules-Louis-René de Mun was born in Port-au-Prince in 1782, the son of a chevalier of the royal bodyguard. Educated in France, he came to the United States by way of England as a refugee in 1803. In 1812 he left Ste Geneviève for St. Louis (Missouri Historical Society *Collections*, Vol. V [1928]). In "Myself," Audubon calls him "Count de Mun," but as only a grandson of a marquis, De Mun had no title.

VI. Cross Currents *(pages 83–94)*

1 "A Wild Horse," *OB*, III, 270. See also *OB*, I, 2.

2 "We take the liberty to inform you that we have established a house in this city [New Orleans] under the firm name of Audubon & Bakewell." Audubon to William Clark, October 19, 1811; includes a list of business references in Boston, New York City, Philadelphia, Baltimore, and Pittsburgh (Missouri Historical Society).

3 "A Wild Horse," *OB*, III, 270. Lucy to cousin, January 5, 1812; Benjamin Bakewell to same, December 9, 1811 (PUL).

4 John James Audubon to Rozier, November 2, 1811 (FHH, I, 243).

5 William Bakewell to William Thomas, December 1809, about debt of August 18, 1804 (DBP).

6 *Memoirs of Vincent Nolte* (London, 1854; reprinted 1934). *OB*, III, 270.

7 "The Earthquake," *OB*, I, 239.

8 Audubon to Rozier, January 29, 1812, *Cardinal*, Vol. IV, No. 7 (1938).

9 "House Wren," *OB*, I, 427.

10 "Broad-winged Hawk," *OB*, I, 461.

11 Audubon to Rozier, January 29, 1812 (Christy, "Four Audubon Letters").

12 Audubon to Rozier, August 10, 1812 (FHH, I, 243–44).

13 *OB*, I, xiii. Many drawings survived, however. Audubon said the 200 drawings represented "nearly a thousand inhabitants of the air" (FHH, I, 320). In 1836 he wrote to Bachman, "Yet after all, who can say that it was not a material advantage . . . that the Norway rats destroyed those drawings?" It is hinted that the 1835 fire destroyed other drawings (AHJ, I, 40). In 1839 Audubon told Harlan "one hundred."

14 This watercolor is missing. It was often repeated in oil between 1822 and 1828. J. T. Bowen reproduced it by lithograph in *Quadrupeds* Folio, plate LI.

15 Shrike (HLHU). Reproduced in *Bird Biographies of John James Audubon*, ed. by Alice Ford (New York, 1957).

16 Boone to Audubon, St. Charles, July 11, 1813 (private collection).

17 "The Prairie," *OB*, I, 290. The time of this half-mythical journey is hinted at (*AHJ*, I, 230n.) as the spring of 1812; however, it was not possible then.

18 *AHJ*, I, 32. See Joseph B. Lockey, "The Florida Intrigues of José Alvarez de Toledo," Florida Historical Society *Quarterly*, Vol. XII, No. 4 (1934).

19 Norristown *Herald*, sale ad, 1813, cited by H. S. Dotterer, "The Perkiomen Region," Montgomery Historical Society *Papers*, Vol. III (1900): 88. Only parcels of land were sold before 1823, the date of the final sale of Fatland Ford.

20 Pears Papers.

21 Ibid.

22 Thomas W. Bakewell manuscript autobiography (DBP).

23 "Myself" mentions the Holly "burying ground." *Henderson, A Guide* (Northport, L.I., 1941) mentions a Hopkins farm burial.

VII. Aftermath *(pages 95–100)*

1 A précis by L. Lavigne of a John James Audubon letter shown to him in 1930 by Morris Tyler is the source of this information.

2 Power of attorney to Gabriel Du Puigaudeau, July 26, 1817 (Records Office, Henderson, Kentucky, in FHH, I, 64).

3 Catherine Françoise, born 1785, godchild of Jean Audubon. Anne-Elizabeth, born 1787. Dominica, born 1789 (Bayonne Archives).

4 Vincennes land tract: abstract, August 13, 1817 (U.S. Archives, General Land Office, Washington, D.C.).

5 Death registry, February 19, 1818 (Archives de la Préfecture, Nantes). These archives show Le Pellerin, St. Etienne de Montluc, and Les Sables d'Olonne land transfers to his wife (under "Mutations").

6 Deed of land to Anonyme Le Jeune II, 1815 (Lavigne). Marriage to Cécile Anne Vilmain (Archives Départementales, Nantes).

7 Gabriel Du Puigaudeau to John James Audubon, August 15, 1819 (FHH, I, 266). In his letter of June 24, 1820, Du Puigaudeau alluded to Audubon's letter of July 22, 1818, and listed letters sent September 15, October 30, and December 19, 1818, and February 1, April 15, May 15, and August 3, 1819 (FHH, I, 268).

8 Rafinesque, born Schmaltz, to a Greek mother. (Smithsonian Institution, Washington, D.C.: MS. notebooks).

9 *OB*, III, 568: brief mention of George Keats.

VIII. Windward *(pages 101–9)*

1   Action of January 6, 1819 *(extrait)*, and decree of February 12, 1819 (Lavigne). Madame Audubon–Le Jeune de Vaugeon did not live to see the defeat of her son and nieces. She died January 16, 1815 (Archives Départementales, Nantes).
2   Gabriel Du Puigaudeau to Audubon, August 15, 1819 (FHH, I, 266).
3   Subpoena, November 30, 1813 (Lavigne).
4   Samuel Wetherill purchased Mill Grove on February 5, 1813. Wetherill was a druggist and paint manufacturer in Philadelphia; the War of 1812 had barred importation of pig lead, hence the buy. The lead, however, was of poor quality and never sold well. Wetherill gave up mining, but the farm remained in the family for generations *(Sketches,* IV, 222–24, 1910; Montgomery Historical Society).
5   Du Puigaudeau to Audubon, August 15, 1819 (FHH, I, 266).
6   Du Puigaudeau to Audubon, no date (Lavigne).
7   FHH, I, 130.
8   Madame Supiot (née Bouffard) died August 11, 1840 (FHH, I, 56–57n).
9   Thomas Bakewell to his father, March 24, 1819 (DBP).
10   *Letters of John Keats,* ed. by John G. Speed (New York, 1883), I, 79, 103.
11   FHH, I, 257–58. Court House, Henderson, Kentucky.
12   Circuit Court of Louisville (not Owensboro) held a claim of $1,169.64 plus $200 damages filed by Bowen. Suit dropped.
13   Henderson Court House record indicates balance of $1,300 due Berthoud.
14   *OB,* III, 1: "Canada Goose."
15   Mittenberger had issued a warrant for his arrest in Henderson. Berthoud paid the balance due on Vincennes land, $1,186.09, in March 1820 (Louisville Circuit Court Order 13727). On August 6, 1819, Audubon gave John H. Clark a promissory note for $493.91, due in sixty days. The note was sold for $110.
16   *OB,* IV, 584: "Sand Swallow."
17   H. B. Forman, *The Keats Circle* (London, 1914), 89, 175, 207.
18   Ibid. (1931 ed.), 492.
19   *AHJ,* I, "Myself."
20   Cincinnati Historical Society, Lytle Papers: Box XII, No. 203.1.
21   Lucretia Y. Farmer, "Audubon in Vanderburgh County" (Audubon Memorial Museum, Henderson, Kentucky: MS.).
22   On August 3, 1819, Gabriel wrote to John James Audubon: "Mlle Ferret torments me still but up to now I am maintaining my rights, and have no intention of becoming involved in her affairs." On May 5 he had written: "La Dame Ferret wrote to me through a Nantes lawyer. I did not wish to answer in writing but have declared verbally that I do not wish to hear the matter discussed, as I was not in a position to settle debts contracted by others, and especially when I do not know the heir in question" (Lavigne). That this woman was Marie-Elizabeth Ferré, widow of a certain Pierre Lejeune (Liquidations de Colons de Saint-Domingue), seems unlikely, although Pierre was related to Le Jeune de Vaugeon.

IX. Down the Mississippi *(pages 111–32)*

1   Daniel Drake (1785–1852) was a physician with mercantile and scientific interests. His pamphlet *Flora* and his *Cincinnati* (1810) are now collector's items.
2   *OB,* II, 353.
3   "Myself" errs about Rose. She was born in Shippingport in the autumn of 1819 and died in Louisville in the winter of the same year or early 1820.
4   Note by Rebecca on face of Thomas receipt dated November 8, 1819 (DBP).
5   Pears Papers.
6   Daniel Drake, "An Anniversary Discourse on the State and Prospects of the Western Museum Society," delivered at the opening of the museum, June 10, 1820

(Cincinnati College). See Dorothy Gillespie, "Relations of Audubon with the Western Museum" (Cincinnati, 1937; pamphlet).

7   Gabriel Du Puigaudeau to Audubon, June 24, 1820 (FHH, I, 267–68; Lavigne).

8   Dash figured in a shocking parrot experiment before whelping to test the theory of early American explorers that the birds were poisonous to mammals (*Journal*, 1820). Bachman once scored Audubon's dislike of "hounds."

9   The autobiographical sketch in his 1820 *Journal* is fallible but on the whole more ingenuous and less self-conscious than "Myself" and his introduction to *OB*. In the *Journal* an unknown hand changed "younger" to "older" before the word "brothers" and wrote "remarried" before his reference to Jean Audubon's only wife, Anne Moynet. Someone effaced the lines presumably about Jeanne Rabine.

10   *AHJ*, I, 37, implied that Audubon met Long on his way west, rather than, as it happened, east. See *Mississippi Historical Review*, Vol. XLI (1947): 147–63, 266–84, for the journal of T. R. Peale (1799–1885), youngest son of C. W. Peale, and Ord's artist in Georgia and Florida in 1818; later artist for C. Bonaparte.

11   Thomas Bakewell wrote to his brother William on March 26, 1834: "I have yours of the 22nd . . . which I believe closes all matters . . . for Prentice & Bakewell. There was no better man to plan than D. Prentice but he either would not or could not execute his plans to make them work well—when we were together I was the merchant, he the mechanic, and I did not presume to put my then crude ideas of machinery against his—and there has been too much just cause for complaint with his [engineering]" (Shaffer).

12   The episode was enclosed in a letter begun May 24 and ended on June 1, 1821, which ends this chapter. The 1821 *Journal*, February 21, states: "I had a likeness spoken of in very rude terms by the fair lady it was Made for and perhaps will Loose My Time and the reward expected for My Labour,—Mrs. André I here mention the name as I May Speak More of the Likeness as the occasion Will require."

13   HSP.

14   William Bakewell's will, April 16, 1812, recorded April–May 1822, Montgomery County Court House, disproves that Lucy had patrimony at marriage, apart from furniture, etc. In 1810 he and Rebecca had Arthur Kinder request that Lucy renounce all claims of dower in writing (FHH, I, 200).

15   Thomas W. Bakewell to Rebecca Bakewell, April 8, 1821 (DBP).

16   Lease from Rebecca Bakewell to George Reader, April 1, 1822 (DBP).

17   First portion of letter of May 24, 1821 (Winterthur). Remainder, beginning "sake of the actresses" (APS) passed from Maria Rebecca Audubon as, mistakenly, "Odd leaves from Grandfather's Journal."

X. On a Desperate Rock *(pages 133–44)*

1   St. Francisville was disfranchised in 1926.

2   Oakley has been made into an Audubon memorial by the State of Louisiana. It is five miles from Bayou Sara, according to Audubon's 1821 *Journal*, which is the source for all uncited quotations in this chapter.

3   The portrait is said to hang in the cathedral in Havana, Cuba.

4   See Appendices (Wills).

5   Last will of Rebecca Smith Bakewell, May 2, 1821, recorded May 22, 1822, as given in Genealogical Society of Pennsylvania *Publications*, Vol. V, No. 3, 286.

6   From Gabriel Du Puigaudeau to "Mr. John Garnier, Merchant at New Orleans," December 24, 1821: "Under the auspices of . . . merchants of Nantes, I . . . ask you to make possible inquiries as to what perhaps became of Mr. John Audubon who should be dwelling in Henderson, Kentucky, if it possible for you, by correspondence, to find out . . . what he is doing. I shall need this information for family business that I am about to settle and in which he has a part for something"

(Lavigne). Garnier appears in Audubon's 1820–21 *Journal:* "The Natchez . . . is a good house . . . kept by Mr. John Garnier. . . . Mr. Garnier . . . told me that he had given Liberty to a Mocking Bird after several years and that for several years the Bird came daily . . . as if to thank him . . . for Past Kind Attentions" (December 27, 1820). On the ark on December 28, 1820, Audubon wrote, "Mr. Garnier, a French gentleman of agreeable manners . . . kindly procured me Willson's Folio."

7 For kinsmen of Garnier of Point Coupée, see *Les Annales de Nantes*, Vol. XIX, No. 116 (1960): 10.

8 One aspect of this "family business" was a debt owed to Du Puigaudeau and his wife, Rose, by the tanner Jean-Michel Cebron, of the family long close to Jean Audubon and his wife, Anne. The Du Puigaudeaux won the suit and received payment of the money owed the estate of Jean Audubon as well as court costs and damages, totaling over 252 francs (July 4, 1823; Archives Départementales, Nantes).

9 Audubon's 1826 manuscript journal proves that this painting went abroad. Its subsequent fate is unknown.

10 The name of the itinerant John Steen is not found in lexicons, nor does the Historical Society of Washington, Pennsylvania, know of him. According to Edward Dwight, he had tutored the landscapist Thomas Cole.

11 *AHJ*, I, 52.

12 Beech Woods burned in 1916; Oakley and Greenwood survive.

13 The watercolor is not extant; the oil is illustrated in *Audubon's America*, by Donald Culross Peattie.

14 Audubon to Rozier, October 14, 1823 (Yale). *OB*, III, 371.

15 *Life of John James Audubon*, 97.

16 *AHJ*, I, 54.

XI. Adrift Again *(pages 145–56)*

1 See *Life of John James Audubon*, 105–06, for Sully's introductions for Audubon to Gilbert Stuart, Washington Allston, and John Trumbull.

2 Audubon, in his earliest autobiography (1820 *Journal*), does not claim David as a teacher, a significant omission. David visited Nantes when Audubon was five.

3 George Ord (1781–1866) edited the eighth volume of Wilson's *American Ornithology*. The ninth volume, with a short biography of Wilson, was wholly by Ord, who brought Wilson's total of 278 drawn and described species to 320, all but one of which were later approved, although 23 were mistakenly believed common to Europe. See *Cassinia*, 1908–09; *Pennsylvania Magazine*, Vol. IV (1880).

4 Thomas Say (1797–1834). *American Entomology*, Pt. I, 1817; Vol. I, 1824; Vol. II, 1825; Vol. III, 1828.

5 Charles-Alexandre Lesueur (1778–1846) arrived in Philadelphia in 1816, and returned to France in 1839 and headed the natural history museum in Le Havre. He undertook the first study of Great Lakes fishes toward an ichthyology of North American species. His great drawings and watercolors of marine life, which are at Le Havre, were photocopied for the APS; transparencies and photographs may also be seen at the Worcester Museum, Worcester, Massachusetts.

6 Alexander Lawson (1772–1846) was a nearly self-taught etcher and mezzotintist. He was an engraver for Wilson, Lewis and Clark, and Bonaparte. The Academy of Natural Sciences owns his engravings.

7 *Diary of William Dunlap*, III, 705–08. New York, 1930 edition.

8 *American Ornithology, or the Natural History of the Birds of the United States, not Given by Wilson*. 4 vols., Quarto, with 27 colored engravings by Alexander Lawson from drawings by T. R. Peale and A. Rider. Philadelphia, 1825–33, p. 36.

9 The 1826 manuscript journal entry for September 8 indicates that the bank note engraving with the figure of the "grous" was actually made. However, no copy

is known to exist. See PUL *Chronicle*, XXI, Nos. 1–2, 1959/60, item 44: "Bank notes with engraving of a pair of quail."

10   Edward Harris (1799–1863). His papers are in the Alabama State Archives, Montgomery. Audubon told him his father had traveled down the Ohio "shortly after Braddock's defeat." Braddock was defeated in 1755, when Captain Audubon was eleven.

11   Reuben Haines (1785–1831) was corresponding secretary of the Academy of Natural Sciences, Philadelphia. See W. W. Hinshaw, "American Quaker Genealogy," *Pennsylvania Magazine*, Vol. XV, 475.

12   "Swallows," Lyceum of Natural History *Annals*, Vol. I (1824): 166–68. Presented August 11, 1824. De Kay (1792–1851): *Natural History of New York* (1842).

13   "Niagara," *OB*, I, 362.

14   "Meadville," *OB*, I, 182. Several copies exist; one is in the NYPL.

15   James Reid Lambdin opened a gallery in his native Pittsburgh in 1828. He returned to Philadelphia in 1837, later becoming director of the Pennsylvania Academy of Fine Arts. He painted the presidents from John Quincy Adams to Garfield.

16   Basham memoirs and Audubon's sketchbook. See also *Audubon's Butterflies*, edited by Alice Ford (New York, 1952).

XII. Immense Ocean *(pages 157–76)*

1   The peddler "lithograph" (*Life of John James Audubon*, 113) was a wood engraving by George Gilbert of Philadelphia. The example formerly in the collection of A. E. Lownes of Providence, Rhode Island, has a list of Gilbert's services and a calling card autographed "Mr. Audubon" attached.

2   *Life of John James Audubon*, 114. The same source gives an erroneous total of $3,000 as Lucy's loan to Audubon.

3   Audubon to De Kay, May 24, 1825 (BMHN). See also FHH, I, 344.

4   Audubon to Bonaparte, April 14, 1825 (BMHN).

5   Audubon to Haines, January 25, 1825 (Haverford College Library).

6   Bonaparte to Audubon, March 15, 1825 (Yale).

7   Pears Papers.

8   Audubon, "Alligator," *Edinburgh New Philosophical Journal*, Vol. II (1826–27): 270–80.

9   Audubon, "Turkey Buzzard," *Edinburgh New Philosophical Journal*, Vol. II (1826–27): 172–84; VI: 156–61; "Carrion Crow" (1826–27).

10   Bonaparte to Audubon, July 28, 1825 (Yale).

11   Audubon to Bonaparte, October 1, 1825 (Yale). This is his letter copy; the original is in the BMHN with numerous other letters from Audubon to Bonaparte. All are on microfilm at the APS.

12   Bonaparte to Cooper, February 9, 1826 (BMHN).

13   On April 26, Audubon wrote, "If not sadly disappointed, my return to these happy shores will be the brightest birthday I shall ever have enjoyed" (1826 manuscript journal).

14   Audubon's 1826 manuscript journal contains a copy of the governor's letter.

15   Nolte's letter of introduction to Rathbone is copied in Audubon's 1826 manuscript journal.

16   The "Equator" passage date in Audubon's manuscript journal differs from that given in Alice Jaynes Tyler, *I Who Should Command All* (New Haven, 1937), which neglects to state that many lines are heavily blacked out, possibly to protect the "dauphin" myth.

17   Audubon's 1826 manuscript journal (*AHJ*, II, 301–09). Audubon's 1826 *Journal*, as first published in 1898, was heavily bowdlerized. Allusions to birth: *OB*, I, *v*; *OB*, IV, 37; *Letters*, II, 152–54; *AHJ*, I: "Myself"; reminiscences of Mrs. Pope, in S. C. Arthur (Biblio.); Bachman letter, November 29, 1843 (Charleston Museum).

XIII. First Flight *(pages 177–87)*

1   All quotations in this chapter, unless otherwise indicated, are from Audubon's 1826 manuscript journal or its letter copies.

2   Audubon to Roscoe, August 9, 1826 (Liverpool Public Library): "I called on my friend A. Gordon, Esqr., last evening . . . and having shewn him the draft you made to announce the re-exhibition of some of my 100 drawings, I also beg.d his answer.—'Mr. A., no persons in my opinion can advise you better than Mr. Roscoe and his polite attention to you proves the great desire he has that you should succeed, and I think that all different advises than those he gives ought to Fall before his' . . . so that . . . I hesitate no longer and will now exhibit my Drawings if I receive permission . . . at the Royal Institution with a feeling entirely cleared of the clouds that I dreaded before now might have thickened and put a stop to my career."

3   Jane Roscoe's sonnet in honor of Audubon, from *The Winter's Wreath*, 1832 (FHH, II, opposite p. 1):

To J. J. Audubon, Esq. on Beholding his Drawings

Is there delight in Nature's solitudes,
    Her dark green woods, and fragrant wilderness,
In scenes, where seldom human step intrudes,
    And she is in her wildest, loveliest dress?
Is there delight in her uncultured flowers,
    Each ripened bloom or bright unfolding dye,
Or in the tribes which animate her bowers,
    And through her groves in living beauty fly?
Then, on thy canvas as they move and live,
    While taste and genius guide the fair design,
And all the charms which Nature's works can give
    With equal radiance in thy colours shine;
Amidst the praise thy country's sons extend,
    The stranger's voice its warm applause shall blend.

4   *Letters*, I, 54; APS.

5   *Poetry of the Birds* by Mrs. R. Rathbone, 1833. One of Mrs. Roscoe's studies appears in plate 266 of Gordon Dunthorne's *Flower and Fruit Prints of the 18th and 19th Centuries* (Washington, D.C., 1938), a standard reference on floral art.

XIV. Manchester *(pages 189–96)*

1   Audubon to Sully, September 16, 1826; Audubon to Traill, October 28, 1826; Audubon to Lucy, October 1, 1826; Audubon to Bonaparte, October 22, 1826; Audubon to William Rathbone, November 24, 1826. All quotations in this chapter, unless otherwise indicated, are from Audubon's 1826 manuscript journal.

2   Samuel Greg's name is misspelled "Gregg" in *AHJ*. He was born in Belfast, c. 1758, and opened Quarry Bank mills in 1784. This son of Irish Presbyterian Samuel Greg I joined the Unitarians, led by Joseph Priestley.

3   Henry G. Bohn's first name is mistakenly given as John in *AHJ*. The bowdlerized *AHJ* reads: "[Bohn] strongly advised me to have the work printed and finished in Paris, bring over to England say 250 copies . . . to be issued to the world of England as an English publication. This I will not do; no work of mine shall be other than true metal—if copper, copper, if gold, gold, but not copper gilded." Audubon's manuscript version reads: "He strongly advised me to have the work all published and finished in Paris, where he thinks it is best for me to undertake it. But he said to bring over to England, say 250 copies to receive its form and to have its title page printed, to be issued to the world of England as genuine English production, an astonishing advantage in matters of this kind. . . . I will follow this plan and no

other until I find it impossible to succeed." Bohn (1796–1884), son of a German bookbinder, emigrated to England, dealing in rare and remaindered books. He became a noted rose grower, and better known than when he and Audubon met.

4   The turkey seal with Audubon's motto is in the Audubon Memorial Museum, Henderson, Kentucky. The thumbnail sketch is in the Reynolds Rathbone Collection. The seal arrived in Edinburgh in November 1826, engraved by "Mr. Gifford" of Roskell's firm in Liverpool.

XV. False Start (pages 197–213)

1   Audubon's 1826 Journal, 136. All quotations in this chapter, unless otherwise indicated, are from Audubon's 1826 manuscript journal or its letter copies.

2   Traill to Knox, August 9, 1826: "I shall make no apology for making you acquainted with . . . Mr. Audubon . . . whose portfolio will astonish you no less than his manner will interest you. Any manner in which you can bring his merits before competent judges . . . will gratify me. Mr. A. means to publish a splendid work on ornithology, and naturally courts the acquaintance of those . . . capable of judging his labours."

3   Robert Jameson founded his Edinburgh New Philosophical Journal in 1819 with Sir David Brewster. See Vol. II, 210–11, for "Mr. Audubon's Great Work," and Vol. X, 317–22, under Jameson's pseudonym "Ornithophilus." Jameson wrote on mineralogy and geology; his collection is in the Royal Scottish Museum, Edinburgh.

4   Prideaux John Selby (1788–1867) and Sir William Jardine (1800–74) had been at work on a folio, Illustrations of British Ornithology, since 1819, finished in 1835.

5   In AHJ, I, "venerable" was changed to "venerated," perhaps to support the noble birth legend.

6   OB, III, 305.

7   Syme's portrait of Audubon, November 1826 (The White House, Washington, D.C.). It was never engraved by Lizars, but rather by Charles Wands for Lizars, November 1827 (reproduced in S. C. Arthur, Audubon the American Woodsman, 366). J. B. Kidd engraved it for Miscellany of Natural History, by Brown and Lauder.

8   A sketch of Cats Fighting is in Audubon's 1826 manuscript journal. The oil, exhibited at the Royal Scottish Academy in 1827, was acquired a few years ago by Edward Dwight for the Munson-Williams-Proctor Institute, Utica, New York.

9   Greg to Mrs. Rathbone, December 14, 1826 (University of Liverpool Library).

10   Much later Audubon named a bird and plate "Rathbone's Warbler."

11   Bonaparte to Cooper, October 6, 1826 (BMHN).

12   This brooch is in the Audubon Memorial Museum, Henderson, Kentucky.

13   For the wild pigeon, see Edinburgh Journal of Science, Vol. VI (November–April 1826–27): 256–65. For the alligator paper, see the Edinburgh New Philosophical Journal, Vol. II (October–April 1826): 270–80. For the rattlesnake paper, see the Edinburgh New Philosophical Journal, Vol. III (April–October 1827): 21–30.

14   Letter 156, Roscoe Papers (Liverpool Public Library).

XVI. The Monster, London (pages 215–28)

1   On this occasion Audubon requested "a few lines from your own hand . . . with the hope that my efforts to advance ornithological studies . . . may be thought worthy of your kind attentions." The author replied: "I am sure you will find many persons better qualified than myself . . . and my ignorance does not permit me to say anything on the branches of natural history of which you are so well possessed. But I can easily and truly say, that what I have had the pleasure of seeing, touching your talents and manners, corresponds with all I have heard in your favor . . .

though I have not the knowledge necessary to form an accurate judgment." *Life of John James Audubon*, 143. See also *AHJ*, I, 211–12.

2 "College, 13 January, 1827: . . . Mr. Audubon read an interesting memoir on . . . alligator . . . much new information. . . ." "27 January . . . Mr. Audubon's paper on rattlesnake was at his request delayed till next spring." "10 February . . . Mr. Audubon requested that his paper on the rattlesnake might be further delayed. He laid before the Society several specimens of the coloured plates for his great work on the American ornithology, and they were much approved." "24 February . . . Mr. Audubon of Louisiana . . . read an account . . . of the rattlesnake, illustrated by a very beautiful drawing of the animal suffering the attack of Mockingbirds" (Minutes of the Wernerian Society, University of Edinburgh Library).

3 Audubon to Lucy, March 12, 1827 (FHH, I, 370; *Letters*, I, 17, 20, 22, 31; APS). Audubon to Victor G. Audubon (*Letters*, I, 37; APS).

4 Victor G. Audubon to Audubon, April 17, 1827 (Tyler). See *OB*, I, 130.

5 Sir Walthen Waller was mistakenly called Sir Matthew Waller in Audubon's 1826 manuscript journal.

6 W. H. Lizars to Audubon, June 16, 1827 (Yale).

7 Audubon to Lucy, June 20, 1827 (PUL).

8 Nicholas Aylward Vigors (1785–1840) was secretary of the Zoological Society of London and editor of the Society's journal.

9 Bonaparte to Cooper, September 24, 1827 (BMHN).

XVII. Against the Wind *(pages 229–40)*

1 Pope's Villa, Twickenham, Sunday, August 26, 1827. My Dear Sir [Thomas Lawrence], It was not until yesterday that I was enabled to lay before His Majesty the wishes of Mr. Audubon . . . yesterday he was pleased to honor me with an audience of nearly two hours alone, and I took that opportunity of shewing [the prints] to his Majesty, and requesting the Honor of his Patronage of the Work, and I am delighted to add that he seemed much pleased with the Prints, and ordered me to leave them with him, and at the same time gave me his commands, to inform Mr. Audubon that he was at Liberty to publish the Work under his Majesty's particular Patronage, Protection and Approbation. I lose no time in forwarding this intelligence to you and assuring you how much satisfaction it has afforded *me*, to promote any wish of the Husband of one of my earliest Friends, to whom as well as to yourself I beg my kindest regards and remain ever my dear Sir,
W. W. Waller [Sir Walthen Waller, Bart.]
May I also request you to desire that Mr. Audubon would insert *my* name in the List of his subscribers for one copy of the Work (Yale).

2 *Letters*, I, 53; APS.

3 Audubon to Lucy, December 5, 1827 (APS). In his letter of September 17, 1826, Audubon suggested that Lucy bring John (*Letters*, I, 53).

4 Audubon to Victor G. Audubon, September 21, 1827 (APS).

5 Audubon to Lucy, December 5, 1827 (APS).

6 Audubon to Lucy, December 7 and 24, 1827 (APS).

7 Audubon's 1826 manuscript journal; *Letters*, I, 57; APS.

8 FHH, II, 69–70.

9 Cooper to Bonaparte, October 12, 1827, and November 2, 1828 (BMHN).

10 From Liverpool, December 12, 1827: "My Dear Sir, I was born in Santo Domingo fourty three years ago . . . reared in Europe untill nearly half grown—am an anthusiastic admirer of Nature's varried Works and have more than once crossed the United States of America in search of the beauteous Feathered Tribes. . . . Two

thirds of my life have been spent to accomplish a work on Ornithology of that Country, that now only *needs the support* of the Learned and Wealthy, but without which, like an Ephamara must fall and die! . . . John J. Audubon, who is with great respect your humble servant. . . . A citizen of the United States" (John Rylands Library, Manchester). Audubon also listed his honorary fellowships.

11 *Winter Wren*, signed and dated 1827. For the platypus, see *AHJ*, I, 270.

12 *Letters*, I, 55; APS.

13 Audubon to Daniel Lizars, January 21, 1828 (FHH, I, 385–86).

14 Kidd to Audubon, April 2, 1828 (Yale).

15 Audubon gave Lansdowne the first proof impression of the *White-Headed Eagle*. Both studies are at the New-York Historical Society.

16 Howland.

17 Hay to Eubank (Yale).

18 Hay to Vernon (Yale).

19 *Letters*, I, 64; APS.

20 Audubon to Swainson, April 9, 1828 (FHH, I, 400–401, 405).

21 Bonaparte to William Cooper, April 4, 1828 (BMHN).

22 Audubon to Bonaparte, April 18 and 29, June 2, and November 3, 1828 (BMHN).

23 Audubon to Bonaparte, May 10, 1828 (BMHN).

24 Audubon to Bonaparte, May 29, 1828 (BMHN).

25 Audubon to Swainson, May 1, 1828 (Linnaean Society, London).

26 Audubon to Swainson, April 18, 1828 (Linnaean Society, London).

27 Audubon to Swainson, June 1828 (Linnaean Society, London).

28 Vigors to Audubon, August 23, 1828 (FHH, I, 407–408; Howland).

29 *Blackwood's* for June 16, 1828, praised James Wilson's *Illustrations of Zoology* and called Audubon a "man of wonderful genius, and destined ere long to be illustrious." Audubon was irked by the phrase "ere long," as well as the remark that Wilson was not inferior to himself as a delineator.

30 *Letters*, I, 53; APS.

31 FHH, I, 400–401.

32 Audubon left this portrait with W. H. Bentley of Manchester; it later became part of the Tyler Collection. "August 25, 1828: Mr. Parker has nearly finished my portrait, which he considers a good one, and *so do I*" (*AHJ*, I, 303). In 1826 Parker's posthumous portraits of Washington, Jefferson, Lafayette, and Franklin had been unveiled at the Louisiana State Legislative Hall.

33 Bonaparte to Cooper, August 26, 1828 (BMHN).

34 Audubon to Bonaparte, November 3, 1828 (BMHN).

35 Bonaparte to Cooper, August 26, 1828 (BMHN).

XVIII. Paris *(pages 241–49)*

1 Audubon to Mrs. Swainson, August 27, 1828: "Should we ever have to *bivouac* at Dover, *Three* as good hearted Centinels as ever watched, will guard you, and *two, two*, I can promise will lay down their cloaks for you, if not with as much grace as Rowley [Raleigh] did to your English queen, at least with as much will as to preserve you from Dampness" (Linnaean Society, London).

2 P.C.R. Constant Duménil, who excelled at natural history prints, on seeing the *Birds* exclaimed, "Oh, mon Dieu! quel ouvrage!" (*Life of John James Audubon*, 176).

3 *AHJ*, I, 313. Also *Life of John James Audubon*, 175–79.

4 Notes in the University of Liège mention Audubon's meeting with Redouté.

5 Audubon implied, deceitfully, to his son Victor that he and Gerard were classmates under David (*Letters*, I, 72; APS).

6 FHH, I, 128–30. "October 8 . . . had the great pleasure of meeting my god-

son, Charles D'Orbigny. Oh what past times were brought to my mind!" (*Life of John James Audubon,* 179). In actuality, his godson was Gaston Edouard.

7   Will of G. G. Bouffard; notary Herard, act dated September 13, 1817. Minutes of Leroux (Archives de la Charente-Maritime, La Rochelle). Letter of Rose (ibid.). Correspondence with mayor of La Rochelle, dated September 26, 1817, mentions "Mlle. Bouffard, age 26, quadroon born in Les Cayes." She had to return to Haiti within two years in order to share in profits from salt marshes worth an estimated 6,000 francs. There is no evidence that "Laize" collected her inheritance.

8   Maria R. Audubon's famous "little black notebook," a transcript of the burned diary, says that the "elder brother of Jean Audubon" was an "active politician in Nantes, La Rochelle and Paris from 1711 to 1796" and lived "in great affluence and *piety*" (Audubon Memorial Museum, Tyler loan). However, Nantes and La Rochelle archives list every prominent citizen of the period; no such brother is listed. Lieutenant Audubon's brother Claude lived in Bayonne. An alleged rift between "Admiral" Audubon (as Maria and her grandfather referred to Jean Audubon) and the mysterious uncle is wholly without basis in fact. The present biographer agrees with Herrick, who rejects the story (FHH, I, 270).

9   Maria R. Audubon's transcript of Audubon's diary (Audubon Memorial Museum, Tyler loan).

10   Audubon wrote to Baron de la Brouillerie on September 13, 1828, concerning a subscription of the Royal Library for the Folio: "Being a Creole of Louisiana by birth I do hope, Sir, that you will excuse the faulty French which perhaps fills this letter" (Archives Nationales, Paris).

XIX. Strange Ultimatum *(pages 251–57)*

1   Audubon to Swainson, November 7, 1828 (Linnaean Society, London).

2   Swainson to Audubon, [January 18, 1829] (FHH, I, 415).

3   Audubon to Bonaparte, November 3, 1828, and February 10, 1829; Bonaparte to Audubon, January 10, 1829 (BMHN).

4   Audubon to Lucy, November 10, 1828 (Yale), and November 17 and 28, 1828 (*Letters,* I, 83; APS).

5   Audubon to Victor G. Audubon, November 10, 1828 (*Letters,* I, 70–73).

6   Audubon to Lucy, December 23, 1828 (APS).

7   Audubon to Swainson, December 20, 1828 (Linnaean Society, London).

8   *Life of John James Audubon,* 181.

9   Ibid., 182. Audubon mistakenly called Burlington House "Somerset House."

10   Oudanel to Audubon from the Palais Royal, "le 7 février" (Howland). The Duke sent £23/2/0 toward the Folio but later declined two pictures offered in "hommage" to his lady.

11   *Letters,* I, 78, 80–82.

12   The original study (Folio Pl. LXIV) is inscribed as quoted. George Bird Grinnell, a friend of Lucy, later expressed doubt that she drew it. The Audubon Memorial Museum has a sketch attributed to her that could have been drawn by her granddaughter Lucy. HLHU has a drawing marked "Penna., March 12, 1812."

13   *Letters,* I, 81–82.

14   Mrs. William Rathbone, Sr., to her son William, March 13, 1829 (Tyler).

15   Yale.

XX. Wander Year *(pages 259–70)*

1   Audubon to Lucy, May 4 and 6, June 15, and July 15, 1829 (APS).

2   Thomas P. Jones, "The Romance of the Rattlesnake," *Journal of the Franklin Institute and American Mechanics' Magazine,* Vol. II, n.s. (1828): 144.

3 Cooper to Bonaparte, November 2, 1828 (BMHN).

4 Bonaparte to Swainson, July 30, 1829 (Linnaean Society, London).

5 "Report . . . to examine splendid work of Mr. Audubon," *Silliman's Journal*, Vol. XVI (1829): 353–54.

6 *Letters*, I, 81.

7 Audubon to Cooper, June 5, 1828 (APS).

8 *OB*, II, 114.

9 *OB*, III, 606.

10 A line drawing of a "Red-breasted Snipe" is heavily annotated and dated "July 15, 1811, Great Egg Harbor," New Jersey. Audubon was in Kentucky on that date and did not visit that area until June 1829 (Haverford College Library).

11 Anne Hudson to Audubon, spring, April 14, and June 23, 1829 (Tyler).

12 FHH, I, 424.

13 FHH, I, 425–26n. lists sixteen birds for which Lehman drew the habitats, and to these may be added the blue grosbeak. "I have found here a young gentleman of the name of Lehman, a German whom I knew at Pittsburgh 5 years since, who is helping me in my plants," Audubon to Lucy, July 15, 1820 (APS). " . . . a young Swiss . . . whom I have known about 6 years, having found him at Pittsburgh when on my way back from the Northern Lakes" (*Letters*, I, 97). Lehman is presumed to be the itinerant painter in the "Meadville" episode (*OB*, I, 182). The New-York Historical Society has a number of Folio originals whose backgrounds should be attributed to Lehman and Mason rather than Audubon.

14 Audubon to Lucy, July 15, 1829 (APS).

15 *Letters*, I, 88–92; APS.

16 Audubon to Lucy, August 25 and 28, 1829 (Linnaean Society, London). Audubon to Victor G. Audubon, August 28, 1829 (*Letters*, I, 93, 96; APS).

17 *OB*, I, 447.

18 Audubon to Swainson, September 14, 1829 (Linnaean Society, London).

19 On May 11, 1828, John Le Conte wrote to Swainson: "I am very sorry to say that Dr. Harlan is a very rash and inconsiderate young man, who is continually publishing things which at some future period he will blush to think of" (Linnaean Society, London). Le Conte was the father of naturalist John Lawrence Le Conte.

20 Harlan to Swainson, October 20, 1829 (Linnaean Society, London). Harlan's letter was occasioned by Swainson's impatience to receive an honorary diploma from Philadelphia. Harlan blamed Haines for the failure of the diploma to arrive.

21 *OB*, I, 52.

22 *AHJ*, I, 62–63.

23 Anne Hudson to Audubon, August 2, 1829 (Tyler).

24 Audubon to Havell, December 16, 1829 (FHH, I, 433–34).

25 Audubon to Harlan, November 18, 1829 (FHH, I, 427–29). The hawk is the Red-tailed hawk, *Buteo borealis*.

26 Mrs. Havell, Jr., to Audubon, November 29, 1829: "Mr. Swainson . . . has desired us to stitch 125 of your prospectus in his next number of *Zoological Illustrations*" (HLHU).

27 Audubon to Harlan, January 29, 1830 (Tyler).

28 *Life of John James Audubon*, 203.

29 See Edward Everett to Dr. Wainright, March 18, 1830 (Howland).

30 See R. C. Watters, "Audubon and His Baltimore Patrons," *Maryland History Magazine*, Vol. XXXIV (1939): 138–43. Audubon named a larkspur for his Baltimore agent, Gideon B. Smith, founder of the Horticultural Society, 1832.

31 D'Orbigny to Audubon, September 6, 1829 (Tyler).

XXI. A Return *(pages 271–80)*

1   *Letters*, I, 105, mentions the mask, destroyed in a fire in April 1875. A later cast by D. Baird is in the Museum of Comparative Zoology, Cambridge, Massachusetts. The location of the cast of Audubon's head by P. Neill is unknown. (*AHJ*, I, 205.)

2   Havell, Jr., to Audubon, January 20, 1830 (HLHU).

3   Swainson to Audubon, May 1 [10?], 1830 (FHH, II, 97–98).

4   Ord to Peale, January 8, 1830 (HSP).

5   Hall to Audubon, August 3, 1828 (Tyler).

6   Hall to Audubon, July 12, 1830 (Tyler).

7   *Letters*, I, 111.

8   Havell, Jr., to Audubon, June 30, 1830 (HLHU).

9   *Letters*, I, 113 (HLHU).

10   Audubon to Sir Walthen Waller, July 26, 1830 (APS).

11   Audubon to Bonaparte, July 14, 1830 (BMHN).

12   Audubon to Swainson, August 22, 1830 (FHH, II, 101–103). He planned to include lives of great Americans.

13   Swainson to Audubon [between August 24 and 28, 1830] (FHH, II, 103–105).

14   Mrs. Swainson regarding the children, December 22, 1828 (Yale).

15   Swainson to Audubon, October 2, 1830 (FHH, II, 106–108).

16   Ibid.

17   Traill to Swainson, January 27, 1833 (Linnaean Society, London).

18   Audubon to Bonaparte, January 2, 1831 (BMHN).

19   Liddell to Audubon, November 17, 1832 (Tyler).

20   Audubon to Harlan, October 1, 1830 (Tyler).

21   For their agreement, see Audubon to Bonaparte, January 2, 1831 (BMHN).

22   *AHJ*, I, 63.

23   Lucy to the Havells, December 2, 1830, and February 27, 1831 (HLHU).

24   FHH, I, 442–44. Brown pirated the hibiscus of Plate XX.

25   *Letters*, I, 127 (HLHU). Also FHH, I, 338.

26   Audubon, in his letter of January 2, 1831, to Bonaparte (BMHN), forecast the synopsis, which was to rely heavily on the Prince's nomenclature. He also forecast the *Quadrupeds*, "a work which, if I do not live to see finished will, I hope . . . be completed by one of my sons."

27   Audubon to Havell, Jr., November 28, 1830 (HLHU).

28   See Edward Everett to Audubon, May 19, 1831 (FHH, I, 448–51), for American copyright and free entry.

29   Audubon to Mrs. Havell, Jr., April 13, 1831 (HLHU).

30   April 13, 1831 (Roscoe Collection, Liverpool City Library).

XXII. Eyes of the World *(pages 281–98)*

1   *Life of John James Audubon*, 207–208.

2   Audubon to Swainson, April 28, 1831 (FHH, II, 112).

3   Sully to Audubon, May 27, 1831 (HLHU).

4   Ord to Waterton, dated "Walton Hall, July 20, 1831" (APS).

5   Audubon to Henslowe, April 28, 1831, *Three Letters . . .* (Roxburghe Club, San Francisco, 1943).

6   Audubon to Irving, May 9, 1831 (Yale).

7   Bonaparte to Audubon, April 10, 1831 (Yale).

8   Ord to Waterton, dated "Walton Hall, July 20, 1831" (APS).

9   Audubon to Harlan, June 10, 1831 (Tyler).

10   *Life of John James Audubon*, 207. Also *Letters*, I, 136, 205.

11   Audubon to Havell, Jr., September 20, 1831 (BMHN).
12   Cooper to Bonaparte, September 21, 1831 (BMHN).
13   For the review, see *Edinburgh New Philosophical Journal*, Vol. X (1830–31): 317–32; reprinted in *Philadelphia National Gazette and Literary Register*, June 10, 1831.
14   Audubon to Harlan, October 6, 1831 (Tyler).
15   Ibid.
16   Audubon to Lucy, October 9, 1831 (*Letters*, I, 137; APS).
17   Audubon to Lucy, October 23, 1831 (*Letters*, I, 142; APS).
18   *Letters*, I, 142; APS.
19   Audubon to Harlan, October 30, 1831 (Tyler).
20   *Letters*, I, 145; APS.
21   Harlan to Audubon, November 17, 1831 (Yale).
22   Audubon to Lucy, November 23, 1831 (HLHU).
23   Audubon to Havell, Jr., December 7, 1831 (HLHU).
24   Lucy to Audubon, October 12, 1831 (Yale).
25   *Letters*, I, 166; APS.
26   Ibid., 165.
27   FHH, II, 15–19. The Seminoles burned the Bulow house in 1836. On its 6,000 acres, 300 slaves had produced cotton, indigo, rice, and sugarcane. The Bulows came from Charleston in 1820 to tame and cultivate the tract.
28   *Letters*, I, 160–61; APS.
29   Ibid., 170.
30   Ibid., 175.
31   Ibid., 183.
32   Ibid., 184.
33   Gaston, a jurist, statesman, and later Supreme Court Justice of North Carolina, took a continuing interest in Audubon. See *OB*, II, 549.
34   Bachman to Audubon, November 29, 1843 (in reminiscence) (CMBC).
35   Audubon to Lucy, March 29, 1832 (*Letters*, I, 189; APS).
36   Havell, Jr., to Audubon, November 30, 1831 (Tyler).
37   For the rumor of Audubon's death, see FHH, II, 3.
38   Pears Papers.

XXIII. New England and Labrador *(pages 299–310)*

1   The Baltimore *Patriot* copied a Charleston *Courier* report of the arrival of the "distinguished Naturalist" with "more than 550" plants, seeds, shells, and skins, including the "largest Eagle in the world" with its four eaglets. The story also said the labors of the "genius" were not "adequately patronized" in the United States.
2   Audubon to Bachman, July 1, 1832 (*Letters*, I, 195; APS).
3   Waterton to Ord, December 1, 1831 (Moore).
4   Waterton to Ord, February 16, 1832 (Moore).
5   Waterton to Ord, February 14, June 4, and October 1, 1832 (Moore).
6   Ord to Waterton, April 23, 1832 (APS).
7   Ibid.
8   *Letters*, I, 276.
9   Audubon to Havell, Jr., August 13, 1832 (HLHU). He referred to nos. 24–25 of the Folio.
10   Victor G. Audubon to Havell, Jr., July 21, 1832 (HLHU).
11   Audubon to Harlan, August 14, 1832: "Nuttall is a gem . . . quite after our own heart" (HSP). Audubon mentions Nuttall in his 1820 journal, p. 70.
12   Folio Plates 322 and 333 were drawn with John W. Audubon's help from the skins Webster supplied.

13   Audubon to Victor G. Audubon, March 5 (not February 5), 1833 (FHH, II, 35). Also January 17, 1833 (Howland). Backgrounds of plate and study differ.

14   Audubon to Victor G. Audubon, March 19, 1833 (APS).

15   For the insurance, see FHH, II, 37–40.

16   Philip Hone, *Diary of Philip Hone, 1828–51*, 2 vols. (New York, 1889), I, 73.

17   Audubon to Bonaparte, May 1, 1833 (FHH, II, 119). Cooper to Bonaparte, August 25, 1832 (BMHN).

18   Bachman to Audubon, March 4 and April 1, 1833; reply April 7, 1833 (Tyler).

19   Frances Anne Kemble, *Journal*, 2 vols. (Philadelphia, 1835), II, 151–52.

20   Coolidge to Maria R. Audubon, 1896 (*AHJ*, I, 68).

21   Audubon to Lucy, May 4, 1833 (PUL). On May 2 the *Philadelphia National Gazette* noted his departure, as did other papers (*Letters*, I, 238; PUL).

22   Audubon to Victor, May 31, 1833 (PUL).

23   MacGillivray to Audubon, March 7, 1833 (Yale).

24   Young Lincoln was the source of "A Moose Hunt" (*OB*, II).

25   Labrador Journal (*AHJ*, I, 344–449).

26   Moore.

27   Correspondence of Lucy and Harris (Tyler).

28   Audubon to Lucy, August 31, 1833 (Howland).

29   Robert Bakewell, "Mr. Waterton's Attacks on Mr. Audubon," *Loudon's*, Vol. VI (1833): 369–72, 550–53. Waterton denied to Ord in July 1833 that he had owned slaves or a plantation (Moore).

30   Audubon to Lucy, August 31, 1833 (Howland).

31   From *The Month at Goodspeed's*, February–March 1950. Fourteen years after this, Parkman was murdered by Professor J. W. Webster.

XXIV. War of Words *(pages 311–21)*

1   *Letters*, I, 209 (PUL); 256 (APS).

2   Audubon to Victor G. Audubon, February 24, 1833 (*Letters*, I, 198).

3   Appearance docket, December 1833: District Court, p. 75, no. 148 (Philadelphia, City Hall). Debit bail, $900.

4   Letter from Dr. McKenney to Cass (*Life of John James Audubon*, 377).

5   Cooper testimonial letter, October 21, 1833 (FHH, II, 78).

6   John W. Audubon to Victor G. Audubon, November 5, December 7, 1833 (APS).

7   *Loudon's*, Vol. VI (1833): 550.

8   A receipt for Volume I from Teyler's Museum, Holland (where the volume remains) is in the collection at Yale.

9   Audubon to Victor G. Audubon, November 4, 1833 (*Letters*, I, 263; APS).

10   Ord to Waterton, April 28, 1833: "If I possessed any important information about this man, I certainly should give it to you; but all my inquiries have one result, *viz*. that 'he is a well meaning sort of man, though a great liar'" (APS).

11   Audubon to Victor G. Audubon, November 4, 1833 (*Letters*, I, 263; APS).

12   December 22–23, 1833 (*Letters*, I, 272; APS).

13   Rathbone to Swainson, February 26, 1834 (Linnaean Society, London).

14   John Bachman, "In Defense of Audubon," *Loudon's*, Vol. VII (1834): 164–75.

15   Audubon to Harlan, January 20, 1834 (College of Physicians and Surgeons, Philadelphia).

16   *Letters*, I, 272; APS.

17   *Letters*, I, 267.

18   Kidd to Victor G. Audubon, October 4, 1833 (APS).

19 Audubon to Bachman, April 5, 1834 (*Letters*, II, 15; APS).
20 William Dunlap, *History of the Arts of Design in the United States* (1834), II, 402–8.
21 Audubon to Maria Martin (*Letters*, II, 21; HLHU).
22 Harris to Audubon, April 11, 1834 (Yale); Audubon to Harris, April 16, 1834 (FHH, II, 66).
23 Waterton to Ord, August 1834 (Moore); Ord to Waterton, November 15, 1834 (APS).
24 James Hall, "American Ornithologist," *Western Monthly*, Vol. II (July 1834): 337–50. His kinsman Harrison Hall issued the ornithology of Wilson in three volumes, edited by Ord, 1825–29.
25 John W. Audubon to Victor G. Audubon, New York, April 6, 1834 (Yale).

XXV. "Something Within Me" *(pages 323–42)*

1 Kidd to Victor G. Audubon, May 5, 1834 (Tyler).
2 Kidd to Audubon, May 22, 1834 (NYPL: MSS.).
3 Audubon to Victor G. Audubon, February 24, 1833 (*Letters*, I, 200; HLHU).
4 Contrary to Herrick's statement (FHH, I, 269n.), Rose was still bound by Anne Moynet Audubon's will to share with Audubon the colonial indemnity which was paid by the French government about a year after Victor's visit to Couëron. Letters from the Tyler Collection show Victor's ignorance of the identity of the litigants. The following names the Haitian litigants: "*Hearing*, April 26, 1824: Jean-Baptiste Nelson LEMERLE, without profession, husband of Marie-Catherine AU-POIX-AUPOIX, living in Cayes, southern Haiti. And Olivier LOWINSKY-AUPOIX, emancipated miner, under authority of Monsieur Guillaume CHEYDREY of Cayes. Heirs of the late dame Marguerite Bouffard. *Against:* Monsieur Gabriel Loyen DU PUIGAUDEAU, property owner, and dame Rose AUDUBON, heir of the late Jean AUDUBON, her father, living at the place called *Les Tourterelles* in Couëron. And AUDUBON junior, landlord and property owner, heir of Jean AUDUBON" (Hearing no. 6U341, Civil Tribunal, Archives Départementales, Nantes). The Haitian litigants could be Sanitte Bouffard's children by Jean Audubon's successor.
5 This portrait of Rose is in the Audubon Memorial Museum, Henderson, Kentucky, on loan from the Tyler Collection.
6 *Life of John James Audubon*, 381–83.
7 Gabriel and Rose Du Puigaudeau to Audubon, August 30, 1834 (Yale).
8 MacGillivray to Audubon, May 28, 1834 (FHH, II, 126), and July 18, 1834 (*Auk*, 1901).
9 Kidd to Audubon, May 22, 1834 (NYPL: MSS.). Audubon to Lucy, October 7, 1834: "Kidd . . . paints and draws so well that I wish we could have him with us to teach the Dear boys, and finish a collection of Birds in Oil" (APS).
10 Audubon to Victor G. Audubon, October 31, 1834: "Kidd has painted two beautiful Black-throated Divers in an elegant style" (Yale). Reply of Victor, November 3, 1834: "Brother thinks it would be well not to have any painting done on the old pictures [sent by Dr. John J. Spencer from the Harris garret at Audubon's request], but let them be traced on new canvas [by Kidd] and repainted" (Yale).
11 John W. Audubon to Audubon, late 1834 (Yale).
12 Audubon to Bachman, December 10, 1834 (*Letters*, II, 50, 58: HLHU).
13 Bachman to Audubon, December 16, 1834 (CMBC). Victor had scored Audubon's omission of credit to Bachman.
14 Waterton to Ord, November 2, 1834, and May 6, 1835 (Moore).
15 Ord to Waterton, April 17, 1835 (APS).
16 Bachman to Audubon, March 25, 1835 (CMBC).
17 Audubon to Bachman, January 16, 1835 (*Letters*, II, 60–62; HLHU).

18 Waterton to Jameson, January 27, 1835 (Waterton, *Essays on Natural History*, ed. by N. Moore [London, 1870], 585–90).

19 Waterton to Ord, May 6, 1835 (Moore).

20 Richardson to Audubon, June 25, 1835 (Howland).

21 Audubon to Bonaparte, July 25, 1835 (BMHN), mentions trickery in regard to skins.

22 Bonaparte to Audubon, September 9, 1834 (National Audubon Society).

23 Audubon to Bachman, May 8, 1835 (*Letters*, II, 71; HLHU).

24 Audubon to Bachman, July 20, 1835 (*Letters*, II, 77; HLHU).

25 John Neal, "Audubon, the Ornithologist," *New England Galaxy* (Boston), January 3, February 7, and April 18, 1835. *Letters*, II, 20, 75.

26 "White Ibis" for *OB*, (Yale: MS.).

27 Audubon to Bachman, May 8, 1835 (*Letters*, II, 73): "John has sent *you* a few Skins, and his Portrait painted by himself [for Maria] after 4 months study" (APS). The portrait was long attributed to John James Audubon.

28 Audubon to Bachman, September 15, 1835 (*Letters*, II, 87–88; HLHU).

29 A memorandum in the Edinburgh Royal Museum indicates Robert Jameson's decision to lend no more skins to anyone. Audubon had returned to him a pair of scarlet ibises, mounted on stands, that were "covered with dust, the stands so much soiled that it was necessary to repaint them."

30 Audubon to Bonaparte, October 14, 1835, and January 6, 1836 (BMHN).

31 Bachman to Harlan, June 29, 1835 (College of Physicians and Surgeons, Philadelphia).

32 Audubon to Bachman, December 27, 1835 (*Letters*, II, 108; APS).

33 Audubon to Bachman, December 10, 1834 (*Letters*, II, 57; APS). The reference is to Prince Maximilian's *Travels in the Interior of North America* (1833–34).

34 The gun made by Conway is owned by Princeton University. Three other guns are known to exist; they are owned by descendents of Victor Gifford Audubon and William Gifford Bakewell. The gun given to Audubon by Madame André is believed to have been destroyed in a Manhattan fire in 1835.

35 Gabriel Du Puigaudeau to Audubon and Victor G. Audubon, April 4, 1836 (Yale). Aimable A. Pivert married Rose Magdeleine Du Puigaudeau (no issue); Gabriel-Jean-André Du Puigaudeau, had a daughter, Rose, mother of Henri Lavigne.

36 Harlan to Audubon, March 29, 1836; Audubon to Harlan, April 28, 1836 (Yale).

37 Du Puigaudeau to Audubon, September 12, 1836 (Yale).

XXVI. Great Naturalist *(pages 343–50)*

1 Audubon to Harris, September 12, 1836 (FHH, II, 147–48).

2 February 17, 1836 (Yale).

3 Folio plate CCXIX.

4 Audubon to Bachman, October 23, 1836 (*Letters*; APS).

5 C. L. Bachman, ed., *John Bachman* (Charleston, 1888). Containing mostly letters, much bowdlerized and altered, this is a precarious source.

6 *Life of John James Audubon*, 399.

7 Bachman to S. G. Morton, December 30, 1836 (APS).

8 Victor G. Audubon to Audubon, November 9, 1836 (Yale).

9 Audubon to Bachman, March 3, 1837 (*Letters*, II, 148; APS).

10 Victor G. Audubon to Audubon, November 9, 1836 (Yale).

11 Audubon to Lucy, March 23, 1837 (*Letters*, II, 154; APS).

12 New Orleans *Courier*, March 11, 1837, quoted Cuvier on Audubon's "birth in Louisiana." Afterwards, Audubon dared to write in *OB*, IV, 37, "Would that I were once more extended on some grassy couch, in my native Louisiana."

13 Ord to Bachman, May 26, 1837 (HLHU), refers to Bachman's paper on color mutations.

14 Waterton to Ord, January 6, 1836 (Moore).

15 Allis to Waterton, November 11, 1836: "I consider Natural History a kind of Freemasonry . . . to see Truth promulgated . . . error should be corrected by all in a spirit of kindness and conciliation. . . . I have ascertained indirectly that thy resignation was received, and that it was not noticed, from a hope that thou wouldst reconsider the subject" (York Public Library, York, England).

16 Waterton to Ord, July 4, 1836 (Moore).

17 Audubon to Havell, Jr., July 8, 1837 (*Letters*, II, 167; APS).

18 Audubon to Bachman, July 16, 1837 (*Letters*, II, 169; HLHU).

19 *Auk*, Vol. XX (1903): 382–88.

XXVII. Realization *(pages 351–67)*

1 Heppenstall to Allis, October 30, 1837 (York Public Library, York, England).

2 Waterton to Ord, January 14 and February 14, 1838 (Moore).

3 Ibid.

4 Audubon to Bachman, August 14, 1837 (*Letters*, II, 174–78; HLHU).

5 Ibid.

6 Audubon to Bakewell, September 19, 1837 (Los Angeles Athletic Association).

7 Harris to Audubon, December 4, 1837 (Yale).

8 Audubon to Morton, December 26, 1837 (APS). Refers to Townsend's *Manual*.

9 Audubon to Harris, October 1837 (FHH, II, 170).

10 Audubon to Morton, January 19, 1838 (APS).

11 Sully letters, I, 20, 22, 24, 113 (Winterthur: MSS.).

12 Harris to Victor G. Audubon, December 1, 1851 (Yale). Harris offered Victor £20 for the Healy oil, whereupon Healy offered to copy it for £40. Victor asked $100, but Harris came back with an offer of his miniature *Birds* plus his *OB* bound in morocco gilt, his *Quadrupeds* Folio, and $400 cash. It was copied thirteen years later by Healy, and this copy came to be known as the original. The copy was given to the Boston Society of Natural History (now the Museum of Science) by a patron, Mr. Bradlee. Records show that William Stone presented a copy thought to be by William Brewster to the Museum of Comparative Zoology in Cambridge, Massachusetts; but if so, where is the original? It is more likely that Colonel John E. Thayer was the donor to the museum. He purchased the oil from the Harris estate.

13 Audubon to Bachman, August 14, 1837 (HLHU).

14 MacGillivray to Audubon, May 7, 1831 (Tyler).

15 Audubon to Bachman, October 22, 1838 (*Letters*, II, 206–209).

16 Victor G. Audubon to Audubon, January 6 and March 14, 1837 (Tyler).

17 *OB* MS. (Yale). Audubon omitted the Sharp-shinned grouse passage from the published *OB*.

18 Audubon to Harlan, June 30, 1839 (Yale).

19 Audubon to Harlan, July 23, 1839 (Yale).

20 They arrived in New York September 2, 1839 (National Archives).

21 Forty copies of the Folio had been sold in Britain and France, seventy-five in the United States, or so he informed subscriber Jonathan Prescott in the 1840s (Howland). The memorandum by Hall was discovered years later in his presentation copy of *OB*; it recorded the claim that Audubon's costs were "27,000 pounds sterling," and losses $25,000.

22 Bachman to Audubon, September 13, 1839 (CMBC).

23 Gabriel had informed Audubon of the marriage of his son to Josephine Ambroise in August 1837. Gabriel directed a letter to London in September, too late. (Gabriel died in 1840, Rose in 1842.)

XXVIII. Homecoming *(pages 369–81)*

1 Bachman to Audubon, September 9 and 13, 1839 (CMBC).
2 Audubon to Morton, September 9, 1839, and October 12, 1840 (APS).
3 Audubon to Bachman, December 8, 1839 (*Letters*, II, 225–26; HLHU).
4 New York *Commercial Advertiser*, October 8, 1839 (New-York Historical Society).
5 H. E. Scudder, ed., *Recollections of Samuel Breck, with Passages from His Notebooks (1771–1862)* (London, 1877), 260 (November 16, 1839).
6 Du Puigaudeau to Audubon, September 1839 (Lavigne MSS.). Settlement of Les Cayes estate appears in *Etat Détaille des Liquidations . . . Loi de 1826* (Paris, 1834), Vol. I, 692. Manuscripts of all such settlements were destroyed by a fire at Versailles in the late nineteenth century.
7 Bachman to Audubon, September 13, 1839: J. B. Chevalier, "a French gentleman" of Philadelphia, was getting up a "sort of ornithology, with short descriptions and a small figure of each species" for J. K. Townsend, who was to be editor on stipend, the whole to be brought off in Paris "in the event of sufficient subscribers" (CMBC). The scheme fell through; so Chevalier was free to work for Audubon.
8 Bachman to Audubon, September 13, 1839 (CMBC).
9 Audubon to Bachman, December 8, 1839 (*Letters*, II, 225; HLHU).
10 Bachman to Audubon, December 24, 1839 (CMBC).
11 Audubon to Bachman, January 2, 1840 (*Letters*, II, 229; HLHU); Audubon to Lucy, March 1, 1840 (*Letters*, II, 239; APS).
12 Bachman to Audubon, January 13, 1840 (CMBC).
13 Audubon to family, March 24, 1840 (APS).
14 Yarrell to Audubon, March 10, 1841, and December 17, 1842 (FHH, II, 223, 246). Yarrell showed the first lithographs of the *Quadrupeds* to the Linnaean Society and Zoological Society, London, in December 1839. They were admired but not ordered. Yarrell resented making private efforts to spare Audubon an agent's fee.
15 Victor G. Audubon to John W. Audubon, April 23, 1840 (Yale).
16 Victor G. Audubon to his family, April 15, 1840 (*Letters*, II, 257; APS).
17 The deer painting, *Last Resort*, is in the AMNH. See *Letters*, II, 259.
18 Bachman to Victor G. Audubon, June 25, 1840 (Yale).
19 Audubon to Victor G. Audubon, July 24 and 30, 1840 (*Letters*, II, 274, 277).
20 Audubon to his family, August 10, 1840 (*Auk*, April 1935).
21 Folio plate 434, fig. 2.
22 *American Ornithology*, VI, 62–63; partial set in the Audubon Memorial Museum, Henderson, Kentucky, on loan from the Tyler Collection.
23 George Ord, "Oral Communication," American Philosophical Society *Proceedings* I (1840): 272–73. For flycatcher debate, see F. Burns in *Wilson Bulletin* (Oberlin, 1908–10), Vols. XX, XXI. See also Audubon's 1820 journal, pp. 161, 183.
24 Waterton to Ord, August 4, 1840 (Moore).
25 Bonaparte to Gray, May 8, 1838, and June 19, 1840 (British Museum).
26 William Swainson, "J. J. Audubon, Animal Painter," in *Taxidermy, Bibliography and Biography* (London, 1840), 116–17.
27 Audubon to his family, August 10, 1840 (*Auk*, April 1935).
28 George Burgess manuscript diary (NYPL, Burgess Papers).

XXIX. Minnie's Land *(pages 383–98)*

1 Audubon to Victor G. Audubon, December 30, 1840 (APS).
2 Ibid.
3 Audubon to Victor G. Audubon, February 11, 1841 (APS).
4 Ibid. This portrait of Audubon is in the AMNH.
5 John W. Audubon's portrait of Lucy is in the Audubon Memorial Museum.

6 Audubon to Victor G. Audubon, January 25, 1841 (*Auk*, April 1935).

7 Audubon to Victor G. Audubon, January 30, 1841 (APS).

8 Audubon to his family, January 9, 1841 (APS).

9 Audubon to Victor G. Audubon, January 9, 1841 (APS).

10 Audubon to Victor G. Audubon, February 7, 1841 (Yale).

11 Original study for *Quadrupeds* volume, Pierpont Morgan Library, New York.

12 Audubon to Baird, [Spring] 1842 (Tyler).

13 Bachman to Audubon, August 5, 1841 (CMBC).

14 Snuff box letters (Yale).

15 Bachman to Audubon, December 7, 1841 (CMBC).

16 Permission from Robert H. Morris, August 20, 1841, "to shoot rats at the Battery early in the morning, so as not to expose the inhabitants in the vicinity to danger" (HLHU; copy at Yale).

17 Audubon to Webster, September 8, 1841 (HLHU).

18 Baird to Audubon, February 8, 1842 (FHH, II, 231–32).

19 Audubon to Baird, February 10, 1842 (FHH, I, 103; II, 231–32).

20 Audubon to Victor G. Audubon, March 23, 1842 (APS).

21 Audubon to his family, July 17, 1842 (APS).

22 Audubon to his family, July 19, 1842 (APS).

23 Ibid.

24 Yet in 1836, when Wilkes had asked, Audubon proposed Lehman. Since their meeting in 1824, Lehman had earned himself a certain reputation. In the considerable competition among engravers and lithographers of the time, Lehman, under the firm name of Lehman & Duval, attained some measure of success.

25 Audubon to his family, July 19, 1842 (APS).

26 Ibid.

27 Ibid.

28 For the letters of introduction see FHH, II, 242–43, and *Auk*, 1902.

29 Audubon to Victor G. Audubon, August 20, 1842 (APS).

30 Victor G. Audubon to Audubon, August 1842 (Tyler).

31 Audubon to his family, September 13, 1842 (APS).

32 Quotations from Audubon's Canadian tour are from his 1842 *Journal*.

33 The Folio was supposedly sold out before October 1842. Perhaps this sale involved a returned Folio.

34 Audubon to Bachman, November 7, 1842 (University of Kentucky Library, Lexington).

35 Audubon to his family, December 18, 1842.

36 Audubon to Baird, November 29, 1842 (FHH, II, 248).

37 Audubon to Sir William D. Stewart, n.d. (Yale). In a cautious query about the expedition, Audubon calls himself a man of "60 years," but young in enthusiasm. (He was 57).

38 Burgess Papers, NYPL. She was his sister-in-law, and chose instead to marry Dr. William Maffitt, U.S. Army surgeon, late in 1843.

39 William Healy Dall, *Spencer Fullerton Baird* (Philadelphia, 1915), 77.

40 Ibid.

41 Bachman to G. P. Giraud, Jr., February 1, 1842 (H. B. Martin Collection).

42 Harris to Audubon, January 31, 1843 (FHH, II, 251).

43 Middletown (Connecticut) *Sentinel and Witness*, September 6, 1843.

44 Audubon to Bonaparte, February 26, 1843 (BMHN).

45 Waterton to Ord, June 7, 1841; Ord to Waterton, January 5, 1843 (Moore).

46 Edward Harris, *Up the Missouri with Audubon: The Journal of Edward Harris*, edited by J. F. McDermott.

XXX. Upper Missouri *(pages 399–410)*

1 For Harris report see *Proceedings* of the Academy of Natural Sciences, Vol. I (1845): 235–38. See also *Wilson Bulletin*, Vol. LX (1948): 167–84.
2 Audubon to Harris, February 10 and March 4, 1843 (HLHU).
3 Audubon to his family, March 23, 1843 (National Audubon Society).
4 Audubon to James Hall, March 29, 1843 (*AHJ*, I, 459); Audubon to his family, March 2, 1843 (National Audubon Society) and April 2, 1843 (PUL).
5 *Quadrupeds*, Folio Pl. LXVIII.
6 Ibid., Pl. XLIV.
7 Audubon to reporters (*Auk*, April 1917).
8 Audubon to Victor G. Audubon, April 2, 1843 (PUL).
9 Audubon to his family, April 1843 (National Audubon Society).
10 Audubon to his family, April 25, 1843 (National Audubon Society).
11 Ibid.
12 *Audubon's Animals*, edited by Alice Ford, p. 31.
13 Audubon to J. B. Hyde, September 25, 1842 (HLHU); *Auk*, April 1935. Catlin visited Fort Union in 1831.
14 The term "buffalo" refers to the American bison.
15 This drawing, long in the Shaffer Collection, has often been reproduced.
16 Audubon to his family, May 8, 1843 (National Audubon Society).
17 Ord to Waterton, August 23, 1843 (APS), says of Audubon's letter on the "jumper" that the government had nothing to do with Audubon's trip or his "catch-penny" mammals.
18 Three years later a Jesuit, Nicholas Point, painted their portraits at Fort Lewis (published in color in his *Flowering Wilderness*, reissued 1967). Although the Audubon likenesses existed in a Boise attic in 1955, their fate is now unknown.
19 *AHJ*, II, 429.
20 Harris to Dr. Spencer, his brother-in-law, December 1, 1843, admits shame for his murderous sport as a "Buffalo debutante" (Alabama Archives, Montgomery).
21 The portrait is in the AMNH.

XXXI. And Now, Adieu *(pages 411–22)*

1 The cost of the expedition was $1,994.86. Audubon paid four-fifths of the expense, Harris, one-fifth (Harris Collection, Alabama Archives, Montgomery).
2 Bachman to Audubon, November 1, 1843 (CMBC).
3 Audubon to Bachman, November 12, 1843 (HLHU).
4 Bachman to Audubon, November 29, 1843 (CMBC).
5 Audubon to Bachman, December 10, 1843 (HLHU).
6 Bachman to Audubon, February 8 and March 14, 1844 (CMBC).
7 Bachman to Cooper, May 4, 1844 (CMBC). Three Cooper notebooks on birds of Long Island (December 1826–May 1832) are in the AMNH.
8 Ord to Waterton, February 24, 1844 (APS).
9 Waterton to Ord, April 19, 1844 (Moore).
10 Audubon to his family, May 12 and 29, 1844 (APS).
11 Audubon to his family, August 11, 1844 (APS).
12 Audubon to Bachman, January 8, 1845 (FHH, II, 264–67).
13 Ord to Waterton, June 25, 1845 (APS).
14 Waterton to Ord, July 24, 1845 (Moore).
15 Bachman to John W. Audubon, December 5, 1845 (CMBC); December 10, 1845 (Yale); and February 7, 1846 (Yale).
16 Bachman to Harris, December 24, 1845 (FHH, II, 269).
17 This and following uncited quotations are taken from Bachman's 1846 letters to the Audubons (CMBC).

18 Victor G. Audubon to Bachman, March 27, 1846 (HLHU).

19 Audubon to Cummings, January 17, 1840; November 28, 1844; June 26, 1846; and August 25, 1846 (Los Angeles Athletic Association).

20 Victor G. Audubon to Bachman, May 13, 1846 (HLHU). Victor's share of the work has been unfairly minimized.

21 C. Mabee, *The American Leonardo, Samuel F. B. Morse* (New York, 1943), 291.

22 FHH, II, 237, 238.

23 Victor G. Audubon to William Bakewell, February 2, 1846 (Shaffer).

24 Bachman to Victor G. Audubon, December 14, 1846 (CMBC).

25 Bachman to Audubon, December 23, 1846 (Tyler).

26 Audubon to Harris, February 22, 1847 (HLHU).

XXXII. Long Pond *(pages 423–29)*

1 See Victor G. Audubon to Bachman, May 31, 1847 (HLHU). John W. Audubon to Bachman, May 4, 1847 (HLHU) refers to Gray as a "closet naturalist."

2 Victor G. Audubon to Bachman, October 14, 1847 (HLHU). Victor to W. G. Bakewell, December 10, 1847 (Shaffer).

3 Victor G. Audubon to W. G. Bakewell, December 10, 1847 (Shaffer).

4 Bachman to Victor G. Audubon, January 6, 1848 (CMBC).

5 For bats, see Victor G. Audubon to Bachman, January 10, February 2, March 10, April 4, June 17, and August 1, 1848 (*Letters*, II, 155–56; HLHU).

6 John W. Audubon to Bachman, February 20, 1848 (CMBC).

7 Bachman to Victor, February 3, 1848 (CMBC).

8 Bachman to Maria Martin, May 18, 1848 (CMBC).

9 Ann Gordon to William Bakewell, June 25, 1848 (Shaffer).

10 Bowen to Victor G. Audubon, June 8, 1848 (Yale).

11 Bachman to the Audubons, September 16 and December 18, 1848 (CMBC).

12 Victor G. Audubon to Maria Martin, January 8, 1848 (Tyler).

13 Harris to Victor G. Audubon, February 14, 1849 (Yale).

14 Victor G. Audubon to Bachman, December 15, 1849 (CMBC).

15 Waterton to Ord, July 27, 1849 (Moore).

16 Bachman to John W. Audubon, July 13, 1850 (CMBC).

17 Victor G. Audubon to John W. Audubon, December 3, 1850 (Tyler).

18 Ibid., December 14, 1850.

19 Ibid., January 5, 1851.

20 Note by Maria Dillingham Bakewell, January 30, 1912 (Shaffer).

21 Victor G. Audubon to Morton, February 3, 1851 (Library Company, Philadelphia).

22 The death mask possibly burned in the 1875 fire, Shelbyville, Kentucky.

23 New York *Evening Post*, January 29, 1851: "Died: on Monday, 27th inst., John James Anderson [*sic*], aged 76. The funeral will take place on Wednesday next, 28th inst., at 3 o'clock, P.M., from his late residence, 155th Street, North River. The remains will be interred in Trinity Cemetery. The attendance of his friends is invited" (New-York Historical Society). Last will, Surrogate's Court, New York.

24 *The Life of John James Audubon*, which gives the fictitious birth date of May 4, 1780, accounts for the erroneous date on the monument. The mistake is repeated in *AHJ*. In July 1905 *Auk* reported on the 150th anniversary exercises of May 5, 1905, at the Church of the Intercession, Broadway and 158 Street. For the Audubon Monument Fund, the De Rham family donated $300; John D. Rockefeller, $200; William H. Vanderbilt, $200; and Cornelius Vanderbilt, Andrew Carnegie, J. P. Morgan, Thomas Edison, and William E. Dodge, $100 each. Of the $10,525.21 total, only $2,600 was spent on the monument, the rest on committee endeavor, save for a balance of $1,700.86. Sexton records present a detailed yet baffling arrangement of coffins in the vault, including family and at least two favored friends.

APPENDICES

Chronology

1785	April 26	John James Audubon (born Jean Rabine) is born in Les Cayes, Saint-Domingue.
	November 10	Audubon's mother, Jeanne Rabine, dies in Les Cayes.
1787	April 29	Rose Bouffard, Audubon's half-sister, is born in Les Cayes.
1788	August 26	Jean Rabine (the future Audubon) arrives in Nantes.
1789	March 28	Captain Audubon buys Mill Grove farm, near Norristown, Pennsylvania.
1790	August	Captain Audubon's final return to France, on the ship *Le Victoire*.
1791	June 24	Rose Bouffard arrives in Nantes, on the ship *Le Tancrède*.
1794	March 7	Jean Rabine and Rose are adopted by their natural father, Jean Audubon, and his wife, Anne Moynet.
1796–1800		Audubon receives naval training at Rochefort-sur-Mer.
1800	October 23	Audubon is baptised under the name given upon adoption: Jean-Jacques-Fougère Audubon.
1801–02		At La Gerbetière, family villa near Nantes.
1803	Summer	Arrives in New York. Illness.
	Autumn	Convalescence in Norristown and near Philadelphia; work in Norristown.
1804	Winter	Romance with Lucy Bakewell of nearby Fatland Ford.
	December 15	Partial sale of Mill Grove to Francis Dacosta.
	November to February 1805	Grave illness at Fatland Ford.
1805	March	Return visit to France, around March 15.
	December 16	Half-sister Rose marries in Couëron.
1806	May 28	Arrives in New York City with Ferdinand Rozier as partner in Mill Grove.
	June 4	Reunion with Lucy at Fatland Ford.
	July	Captain Audubon sues for guardian-

		ship, in absentia, of the children of the late Sanitte Bouffard.
	September 5	Applies for American citizenship (see 1812). Apprenticeship in Manhattan.
	December	Return visit to Fatland Ford and to Lucy, his fiancée.
1807	August 31	Departure for Louisville with Rozier for joint venture in commerce.
1808	April 5	Marries Lucy; they depart for Louisville.
1809	June 12	Victor Gifford is born in Louisville.
1810	March	Visit from ornithologist Alexander Wilson; Audubon vows to surpass him.
	March 19	William Bakewell, as agent for Audubon, sells remaining land at Mill Grove to Dacosta and partners.
	Summer	Audubon and Lucy settle in Henderson, Kentucky.
	December	Audubon and Rozier depart for Ste. Genevieve.
1811	April 6	Audubon returns to Lucy; they lodge on the Rankin farm.
	Summer	Audubon & Bakewell firm established, with Thomas Woodhouse Bakewell, Lucy's brother, in charge of New Orleans branch headquarters.
	November	The Audubons and infant ride from Kentucky to borrow from Bakewell. Audubon returns home alone in December.
1812	February	Audubon returns to Pennsylvania before start of War of 1812.
	July 3	Citizenship granted in Philadelphia.
	July	Second and last meeting with Wilson, unwitting catalyst of Audubon's ambition. The Audubons return to Kentucky.
	August	T. W. Bakewell returns to announce failure of the New Orleans concern.
	November 30	Second son, John Woodhouse, is born.
1813		T. W. Bakewell plans for building of mill.
	December	Audubons withdraw from Rankin farm to log house and tract in Henderson.
1814		More lots purchased in Henderson.
1815		Daughter, Lucy, is born.
1816	Spring	Mill erected after delays.
	By December	Pears, then Bakewell, withdraw from partnership, effective July 1817.
1817		Daughter Lucy dies. The Bakewells depart. Timber tract bought in Vincennes.
1818	February 19	Jean Audubon dies in Nantes. Long litigation begins over his estate.
	Summer	Rafinesque visits Audubon in Hender-

		son. George Keats and his wife are paying guests. Trouble over the sale of boats.
1819	July	Henderson enterprises collapse, followed by Audubon's departure alone for Louisville, his arrest, and his declaration of bankruptcy.
	Autumn	Daughter, Rose, is born to the reunited Audubons. Audubon teaches art and pursues chalk portrait commissions.
1820	Winter	Infant Rose dies. Audubon departs for temporary job as a taxidermist at the Western Museum, Cincinnati, a month before summoning Lucy.
	Autumn	Audubon departs by barge with Joseph Robert Mason for work on a growing portfolio of North American birds.
	December	Fails to gain assurance of appointment to the Red River survey expedition at Port of Arkansas.
1821		Teaching and portrait commissions in New Orleans. New virtuosity as painter of birds attained while tutor at Oakley.
	December	Audubon rejoined by family in New Orleans.
1822	March 16	Audubon and Mason depart for Natchez.
	July 23	Mason withdraws as assistant artist. Lucy and sons arrive in Natchez.
	Autumn	Audubon receives his first instruction in the use of oils from John Steen.
1823	Spring–Summer	Unsuccessful tour with Steen and Victor.
	Autumn	Audubon and Victor leave for Shippingport. Sign painting and steamboat murals. Victor apprentices with Berthoud.
1824	March	Audubon arrives in Philadelphia to seek support for publication of a folio of birds.
	July	Commission to draw for engraving on a New Jersey bank note—Audubon's first published art. Two papers in the *Annals* of the Lyceum of Natural History—Audubon's first publications.
	Autumn	Visits to Albany, Niagara Falls, and Pittsburgh; a chance meeting with a future assistant, George Lehman.
	November 24	Reunion with Lucy at Beech Woods in Louisiana.
1825		Saves toward journey abroad.
1826	April 26	Departs for New Orleans; brief return.
	May 27	Sails on *Delos*.

	July 21	Arrives in Liverpool; swift social conquests.
	Autumn	Exhibition of bird drawings in Liverpool, Manchester, and Edinburgh.
	November 1	Trial agreement with the engraver W. H. Lizars of Edinburgh.
	November 26	First proofs (three birds) result in contract for a folio, *The Birds of America.*
	December	Prepares papers for the Wernerian Society and publication in England.
1827	February 3	Exhibition at Royal Institution, Edinburgh; continuing public adulation.
	March 17	Publication of the *Prospectus.*
	April 5	Departs for London via the North; arrives on May 21.
	June	Lizars resigns, and is soon succeeded by the London firm R. Havell & Son.
1828	March	Audubon tours England for subscribers. Writes for *Loudon's.* Meets Swainson.
	September	Visits Paris with the Swainsons. R. Havell, Jr., in command of the Folio; Havell, Sr., withdraws. More papers published in Edinburgh, Liverpool, and Philadelphia.
1829	April 1	Departs for America; arrives on May 5.
	Mid-May to September 12	Painting in Camden and Great Egg Harbor and in Great Pine Forest.
	To October 28	Painting in Philadelphia, with Lehman.
	November 17	Arrives at Beech Grove, location of Lucy's new teaching post, for a reunion.
1830	January 7	Departs with Lucy for Kentucky, New York, Washington, and New York harbor.
	April 1	Audubon and Lucy sail for England.
	October	Works on *Ornithological Biography,* the text for the Folio, with Lucy as aide and copyist, MacGillivray as scientific editor.
	November 26	Contract between Audubon and Kidd for oils to be shown in a projected "perpetual" exhibition.
1831	February to March	Publication of first volume of text, and arrangement for American edition.
	April 15	Returns to London.
	May 7	Audubons depart for a month in Paris.
	July 15	Audubon elected to the American Philosophical Society.
	September 3	Audubons arrive in New York.
	September to October	Audubon, his taxidermist Henry Ward,

		and his assistant artist George Lehman form an expedition to the South. In Charleston Audubon's host, John Bachman, becomes a collaborator.
	November to December	Hunting, drawing, and writing in the Floridas.
1832	April 15	Aboard the cutter *Marion* for a cruise of the Keys, after a cruise up the St. John on the *Spark*.
	June	Audubon meets Lucy and sons in Philadelphia after revisiting Bachman in Charleston. Via New York and Boston, family visits Maine and New Brunswick.
	August	Audubon, Lucy, and John in Boston for the winter; Victor prepares to sail for England in October to represent his father.
	November 21	Robert Havell, Sr., dies.
1833	March	Audubon arrives in New York with Lucy and John to forward new expedition plans and seek subscribers.
	June 6	Labrador cruise from Eastport, Maine; returns August 31.
	September 7	Returns to Lucy in New York.
	September 25	Arrested in Philadelphia for Kentucky debts; bailed without detention.
	October 24	Arrives in Charleston with Lucy.
1834	March 1	Audubon, Lucy, and John depart from Charleston to sail for England via New York on April 1.
	May 7	Audubons arrive in Liverpool; Audubon canvasses the North for subscribers.
	December	Departs for London.
1835	June	Returns to Edinburgh with Lucy for more work on *Ornithological Biography*. Arrival of announcement of the burning of the American edition in a Boston fire.
1836	January	News of a New York fire and the burning of drawing kits and valuable guns needed for coming expedition.
	August 2	Audubon sails with John, who had just toured the continent with Victor.
	September 13	Travels to Philadelphia for Western skins, which are acquired in October only after Edward Harris negotiates purchase of Nuttall-Townsend collection.
	November 17	Arrives in Charleston to draw the skins and await a revenue cutter requisitioned in Washington.
1837	February 17	Audubon departs with John and Harris

		for Pensacola, then for spring cruise from New Orleans to Houston.
	May	Audubon and John return to Charleston.
	July 17	Audubon, John, and his bride, Maria Bachman, depart for Liverpool and London.
1838	Mid-April	Completes the last of 100 new drawings.
	June 20	Completion of the aquatint engraving of the fourth and last Folio volume of *The Birds of America*, with only some coloring of final plates still to be done.
	August 7	Lucy departs from London for Edinburgh to join Audubon; a family tour of the Trossachs.
	October	Initial work on a *Synopsis* for *The Birds of America*.
	December	Victor departs for America to prepare for the return of the Audubons for good.
1839	May	Publication of the fifth and final volume of *Ornithological Biography*.
	July	Publication of the *Synopsis*.
	September	Audubon and Lucy depart, John and Maria having sailed earlier. They lease a house at 86 White Street, New York.
1840	October	Plans for *The Viviparous Quadrupeds of North America*. Work commences on an octavo *Birds of America*, lithographed by J. T. Bowen of Philadelphia, with John Bachman as "junior author" of the text, and J. B. Chevalier as copublisher with Audubon, assisted by Victor and John.
	Autumn	Victor marries Eliza Bachman in Charleston. Incessant canvassing by Audubon for the *Quadrupeds*.
	September 23	Maria Bachman Audubon dies in Charleston.
1841	Spring	Land purchased for the estate Minnie's Land.
	May 25	Eliza Bachman Audubon dies in New York, after journey to Cuba with Victor.
	October 2	John marries Caroline Hall.
	October 5	Audubon presents paper on mammals for publication before Academy of Natural Sciences, Philadelphia.
1842	April	Entire Audubon family removes to Minnie's Land.
	August	Rose, Audubon's half-sister, dies in Couëron.
	September 12	Audubon departs for a month-long tour to Canada in search of subscribers.

	October 20	*Prospectus* of the *Quadrupeds* published.
	December	Audubon returns from canvassing tour of New England to plan for Western expedition.
1843	March 2	Victor Audubon marries Georgianna Mallory.
	March 11	Audubon departs for St. Louis.
	April 25	Audubon, Harris, and party depart for the Upper Missouri and Fort Union.
	June 12 to August 16	At Fort Union for drawing and hunting.
	November 6	Audubon arrives at Minnie's Land.
1844		Octavo edition of *The Birds of America* in seven volumes completed.
1845		First Imperial Folio volume of the *Quadrupeds* published.
1846		Publication of second Folio volume of the *Quadrupeds*. Audubon abandons work as his sight fails.
	June 10	John W. Audubon goes to London in search of mammal skins stored in the collections.
1847	February	Audubon writes his last letters.
	Spring	Audubon suffers a light stroke. New York Central Railroad claim of estate frontage.
1848		Third and last Folio volume of the *Quadrupeds* published.
1849	February 8	John W. Audubon, hoping to rescue the family from insufficiency, departs as leader of a California gold rush expedition.
1850		Foundry, acquired by Audubon's sons to rescue fading resources of the family, opens but swiftly fails.
1851	January 27	John James Audubon dies at Minnie's Land.
1851–54		Octavo *Quadrupeds* published in three volumes.
1863		Original studies for *The Birds of America* sold to the New-York Historical Society.
1886		First Audubon Society organized by George Bird Grinnell.
1893		Runic cross dedicated as a monument above Audubon's burial crypt in Trinity Church cemetery.
1913		Audubon's "infernal mill" burned in Henderson.
1931		Audubon mansion at Minnie's Land razed.

Genealogical Chart

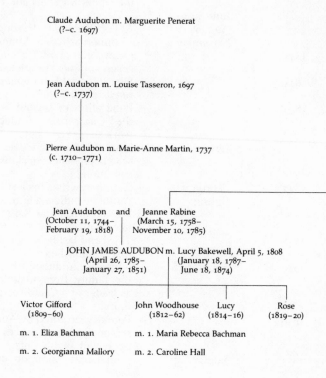

Claude Audubon m. Marguerite Penerat
(?–c. 1697)

Jean Audubon m. Louise Tasseron, 1697
(?–c. 1737)

Pierre Audubon m. Marie-Anne Martin, 1737
(c. 1710–1771)

Jean Audubon   and   Jeanne Rabine
(October 11, 1744–   (March 15, 1758–
February 19, 1818)   November 10, 1785)

JOHN JAMES AUDUBON m. Lucy Bakewell, April 5, 1808
(April 26, 1785–   (January 18, 1787–
January 27, 1851)   June 18, 1874)

Victor Gifford   John Woodhouse   Lucy   Rose
(1809–60)   (1812–62)   (1814–16)   (1819–20)

m. 1. Eliza Bachman   m. 1. Maria Rebecca Bachman

m. 2. Georgianna Mallory   m. 2. Caroline Hall

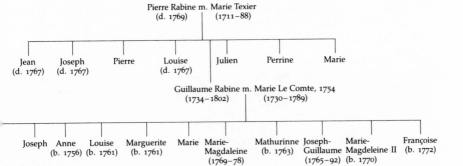

Family Documents

Service Record of Jean Audubon, 1757 to 1801 (Archives du Service Historique de la Marine, Paris)

1757: Cabin boy on *La Marianne;* Captain Pierre Audubon (father). From Les Sables d'Olonne to Louisburg, Cape Breton, Canada. "Seized by the English; wounded in the left leg in sea battle and imprisoned until peace of 1763." Merchant marine.

1763: Novice on *La Caille;* Captain Pigeon. From Sables to Miquelon; returned 1765. Merchant marine.

1766: Seaman on *Le Printemps;* Captain André Ferret. From La Rochelle to the New World, for two months.

1767: Lieutenant on *La Marianne;* Captain Jean Orceau. From La Rochelle to the New World, for six months.

1768: Lieutenant on *La Marianne;* Captain Bouron. From Sables to the New World, for six months.

1768: Seaman on *Le Propre;* Captain Pierre Martin (uncle). From Sables for coastal trade in August.

1770: First lieutenant on *La Dauphine;* Captain Jean Pallueau. From Nantes to Saint-Domingue, for eleven months.

1771: Second lieutenant on *La Dauphine;* Captain Pallueau. For ten months.

1772: The same, for eleven months.

1774: Captain of *Le Marquis de Levy.* From Nantes to Saint-Domingue, for seven months.

1775: Captain of *Les Bons Amis.* From Nantes to Saint-Domingue, for six months.

1776: The same, for five months.

1777: Captain of *Le Comte d'Artois.* From Nantes to Saint Domingue, for eight months.

1778: The same, for nearly eleven months. An interest in this ship had been sold by Coiron Frères of Nantes to Audubon. Lacroix, Formon de Boisclair, and Jacques of Cayes bought his share on February 21, 1779 (FHH, I, 33). "Audubon was seized on the return voyage after having jumped ship. He was taken prisoner, jailed in New York City by the English for 13 months. Next he was in command of the corvette *La Reine Charlotte* at the Surrender of Yorktown, after the agreement of M. de la Luzerne, Ambassador to the U.S.A., obtained his release. He then made a voyage to Brest and engaged in battle after leaving the base at Sainte, and held this command until peace time, when the Coiron Brothers of Nantes engaged him to handle their affairs in Saint-Domingue. [In 1790] he returned to France and entered the National Guard. He was a member of the Conseil de Marine and also of the Department of Nantes until June 25, 1793."

The following entries appear under the heading "Government Service."

1768:   Seaman on *Le Cerf-Volant;* Captain Segueran. From Rochefort-sur-Mer and return, for six months.

1769:   Seaman on *L'Expérience;* Captain Ravenel. Rochefort, for three months.

1793:   Commissioned ensign on *Le Cerbère.* Rochefort. "Wounded in the left leg on July 2, in a three-hour battle with *Le Brillant,* English corsair of 14 canons, which tried to seize him and a load of American flour destined for La Rochelle."

An III: Ensign on *l'Eveillé.* Rochefort, naval station; also on port duty.

An V: Lieutenant Commander on training ship *l'Instituteur.* Rochefort to Brest. [His son Jean Rabine was with him.] In *An VI* he was assigned to the watch at Les Sables d'Olonne.

Recapitulation: For the Government, eight years, two months, seventeen days; for the Merchant Marine, eleven years, six months, twenty-five days. Total: nineteen years, nine months, twelve days; compiled at Rochefort-sur-Mer, *le 7 Ventose, An IX.* Jean Audubon retired on January 1, 1801, as Lieutenant de Vaisseau, his rank since October 11, 1797, one grade lower than full captain, and equal to frigate lieutenant or merchant marine mate. The record at Rochefort-sur-Mer praises his "zeal and activity" as worthy of the promotion (Côte 1 A 92, Archives de la Marine). It also lists him as Enseign de Vaisseau in command of the frigate *Chouteau* at the Ile de Ré off Rochelle and of that station, and subsequently in charge of gunners at the adjacent island of Aux in December 1796 (Côte 1 D³5).

"The Lt. de V. Audubon, attached by the [Ministère de la Marine, Rochefort] to the Dept. of Brest, having represented to me, Citizens, that his health requires that he receive particular care from his family, and that he would be more inclined to obtain this by remaining in Rochefort where he is now employed, I authorize you to have him placed on the lists of this port. I give orders to remove him from that of Brest." Signed for the Minister, Aug. 17, 1799, Rochefort-sur-Mer. (Archives de la Marine, Vol. I, A101, 102, Rochefort-sur-Mer.)

His pension was granted, upon his request at age 57, because of a "pulmonary affection."

He is described as of medium height, full-faced, ruddy, gray-eyed, and with straight chestnut-colored hair when a cabin boy (Folio 92, Les Sables d'Olonne). At forty-eight his certificate of residence dated June 13, 1793, describes him as five feet five inches tall, oval-faced, blue-eyed, and graying, with chestnut-colored eyebrows, large mouth, and prominent nose.

Contract of Captain Jean Audubon with David Ross & Company

(In English only. Missing words make the document, which is in the Lavigne Collection, a parlous one.)

It is agreed upon between Captain John Audubon, part owner, and David Ross & Co., for themselves, and on behalf of the other owners of the ship Annette, now loaded, and bound for Nantes, that the owners of the vessel and cargo shall be to the said Audubon, on his order, but on Mr. Ezekiel Edwards, the friend and partner of the said David Ross & Co. is settled in Nantes, and fully informed in regard to the whole of their business, and whose experience in the trade of this country makes him well acquainted with the kind of goods most suitable to the American market. It is farther agreed upon and understood between the partners that neither the sale of the tobacco, or the purchase of any goods in return shall be made but with the consent, had in writing, and that he, and the said Captain Audubon, shall concur in whatever may be done in regard to the dispatch of the said vessel and that the said Audubon having the address of the vessel shall also, of right, have the whole of the customary commissions, on the sale of the cargo, the expenses upon the vessel, and, if he does not lay in the goods, upon the money paid unto Mr. Edwards. In witness whereof the parties have hereunto set their hands and seals this 9th day of April 1782.

Test. Will Hunter   Signed: Jean Audubon, David Ross & Co.

In a receipt for £1,165 drawn on Saint-Domingue, dated September 4, 1780, Jean Audubon mentions Virginia (Lavigne). Edwards, Nantes agent, died in London before autumn 1782 per Audubon to Dacosta (FHH, I, June 14, 1805. Audubon's visit to Virginia was 1788, not 1789 as he says in this letter). Mary Berthoud Grimshaw wrote, in spring 1840, "Uncle Victor Audubon is in Virginia," in pursuit of the supposed $17,000 owed by Ross (Life of John James Audubon). Lucy Audubon to Victor, July 7 and August 25, 1833, touches on the Ross collection problem (Letters of John James Audubon, I, 215, Ross). Events prove that Audubon did not fully understand what he was signing when it came to the power vested in Edwards.

Appeal by Jean Audubon for Saint-Domingue Settlement with Aid of Navy

(The following is a translation of the document in the Ministère de la Marine, Paris.)

Aug. 25, 1799, to Citizen Minister of the Navy and Colonies, Paris:

Your letter of 15 Therm. which you had the kindness to send to Nantes just reached Rochefort. I have filed no residence certificate since June 19, 1798. My service did not permit me, because of absence on duty, to send particulars [until] three months ago [paper torn].

In the service of my country without interruption since 1790, I had dared to flatter myself that I could have restrictions lifted on my Saint-Domingue property in the district of Cayes-St. Louis, Fond de l'Ile à Vache, where I have a sugar plantation which was burned, a sugar warehouse which was burned, and a warehouse in town worth upwards of 10,000 francs a year—still under sequestration despite my being in the service uninterruptedly, and in spite of my having sent my certificate of residence successively.

Allow me, Citizen Minister, I pray you, to have regard for the request of a longstanding servant of the State who has shed blood for his country. [Citizen B?] the younger, from my district, actually a public representative, promises me that he would be glad to undertake the necessary steps (subject to your approval) to put me in touch with his nephew Mr. Poudet toward removal of restrictions on my property.

Good health . . . and respectfully yours, Citizen Audubon.

The restrictions referred to barred Audubon from collecting income through rents from his island holdings.

Colonial Settlement

Record of claim and settlement of the Saint-Domingue holdings of the late *Lieutenant de Vaisseau* Audubon as published in *Etat Détaillé des Liquidations . . . des Colons de Saint-Domingue . . . loi de 1826* (Paris, Imprimérie Royale, Ministère des Finances, 1834, Vol. I, p. 692, No. 100–187, for payment of Claim No. 7369):

AUDUBON, Jean (former proprietor). Claimant:

Bouffard (Rose), wife of Loyen-Dupuigaudeau, sole legatee of Audubon

Kind of Property: moiety of land.

Name of Rural District: Fraisse. (According to the preceding letter of appeal for aid by Jean Audubon, his warehouse "in town" was all he had left. "Rural," here, was part of the settlement form, and inapplicable.)

City: Cayes

Date of Settlement: November 6, 1832.

Date of Forwarding of Cash: January 1, 1833.

Total indemnity: 3,333.33 francs.

The original documents published by the *Ministère des Finances* were destroyed by fire in the nineteenth century. Lieutenant Audubon reckoned his estate losses, through the Insurrection, as 1,500,000 francs (FHH, I, 83).

Victor G. Audubon to his parents in London:

Paris, July 26, 1834:

My dear Parents: I have just arrived from Nantes and while waiting Mr. Pitois's [agent for Audubon] arrival I write to let you know I am well. . . . I found after further insight into the Nantes business that we have *one half of all the property . . .* but this will not prove much, owing to claims which have been paid by Pigodeau [*sic*] to the amt. of about 30,000 francs and his bills for other expenses about 20,000 francs. We have, as offset to these sums, the rents which have been received on the St. Domingo claims and 4,000 francs are now payable, but a claim for this has been started by some persons unknown to me, and I am told that Pigaudeaux [*sic*] has offered to take half of that payment of 4,000 f., if the other party will relinquish all claims on the balance, which they say will be about 16,000 f., but as I cannot enter into particulars now, I merely say that there will be something for us in time. I did not proceed to anything like a settlement because the affairs are complicated, and if you do not intend to go and live at *La Gerbetière* you will have to sell your half of the estate, which is not to be done in a few days. The income is not above 1,600 or 1,800 f. on the whole estate, as I am told, but I leave all this until we meet, when you will form your plans and write to an agent at Nantes if you think it proper. I have your sister's portrait. They were all well when I left, and my *aunt* was very kind to me and came to Nantes to see me off.

Five days later Victor repeated by letter: "St. Domingo claims amounting to 20,000 francs . . . in dispute between our side and some strangers whose names I do not know" (Yale).

Petition of Jean Audubon for Guardianship of his Children, Nantes, July 2, 1806

The guardianship action, or *tutelle* of Jean Audubon for legal custody of his "five minor children of Sanitte Bouffard," declared that, except for his adoptive daughter Rose, their names were unknown to him. The last will of Sanitte had appointed a certain Monsieur Ferrière as guardian effective on her death. On April 25, 1805, Ferrière had obtained control of her children in the courts of "New Jersey or New York," according to his Nantes lawyer, who, however, lost the case when he failed to produce the will. Audubon made his son-in-law Gabriel Du Puigaudeau his deputy. The lawyer Brumande de la Souchais won for Audubon the right to "govern the persons" of the minors and to control their means in a spirit of "friendship." The witnesses were Pierre Denis, former ship captain; Joseph Raimbaud, "gentleman"; François Gillets, grocer and refugee of Saint-Domingue; Matthew C. Gaudrais, watch merchant; and Julien Beuscher, merchant of the Rue Soufflot. (Beuscher had witnessed the adoption and baptism of Jean Rabine. A son of Gillets visited Mill Grove.) (Lavigne.)

The inference is that Sanitte fled Haiti with Ferrière, but without the children, one of whom married a certain Aupoix who was to sue the estate of Jean Audubon years later. In 1808 Audubon recorded that the Bouffard heirs had dunned him for "140,000 interest for two years." There being no trace of the action in the Nantes or St. Etienne de Montluc records, the supposition is that the judgment was discreetly withdrawn by Jean Audubon (Lavigne).

The orphans court records of New York and New Jersey have yielded no clues about the appointment of Ferrière or the will of Sanitte. One Pierre Ferrier (var. Ferriere?) was a neighbor of Augustin Bouffard in Cavaillon (MFOM: *Etat Détaillé*).

Mill Grove Plantation, a Précis

James Morgan bought 153 acres from Thomas and Richard Penn, Governors-in-Chief of Province of Pennsylvania and counties of Newcastle,

Kent, and Sussex on the Delaware River. Parchment patent dated April 7, 1758 (Lavigne).

Between 1722 and 1786 Rowland Evans took over sundry Mill Grove tracts by deed and indenture, some of which form part of the Lavigne Collection. In 1722 Edward Farmer bought 203 acres from three Londoners: Tobias Collett, Daniel Quare, and Henry Goldney, which he in turn sold to Thomas Morgan in 1738, who sold to James Morgan in 1746, who in 1758 bought more pieces from the Penns (Montgomery County Mortgage Books H or A, Vol. 5, p. 108; Vol. 20, p. 182). In 1761 James Morgan sold land, a sawmill, and two water-, corn-, or gristmills to Rowland Evans. In 1771 Morgan bought some land from Evans, who in 1770 had also sold a portion to the Pennsylvania Land Company (John Fothergill, Jacob Cooper, Samuel Shoemaker, and Joshua Howell). Between 1771 and May 22, 1784, the date when Henry Augustin Prevost bought Mill Grove from Samuel Morris, there were several intervening indentures. On February 8, 1786, Prevost bought more of the acreage.

On March 28, 1789, Prevost sold Mill Grove to Jean Audubon by mortgage indenture; first payment, May 1, 1790, £915; second, July 27, 1790, £430; third, 1792, £1,215, "satisfied and cancelled." On April 1, 1793, Miers Fisher, agent, made another payment. On July 10, 1790, Audubon leased "about 280 acres" to Prevost for £170 per annum, assuming the two-year-old mortgage for £1,200 held by Dr. Samuel Stringer of Albany; Prevost had reduced the mortgage to £500, however (Lavigne). Prevost "secured" Audubon against foreclosure. If Audubon were to "default," the indemnification of Prevost was not to extend beyond January 1, 1790, the date set for the sixth of seven installments for payment of a total of $3,500 (Mortgage Book I, 275). Audubon subsequently rented the land to a tenant farmer already farming for Prevost, William Thomas.

On December 15, 1804, Jean Audubon sold half the land to Francis Dacosta, by an indenture lost en route from France but replaced in Couëron on June 3, 1805. He sold half of his own half-interest to the Roziers of Nantes. On September 15, 1806, John James Audubon and Ferdinand Rozier sold 113½ acres to Dacosta, retaining 171¾ acres. On March 19, 1810, they sold the latter to Joseph Williams, per William Bakewell, agent.

F. Dacosta and associates sold to F. Beates on December 31, 1812. Beates sold entire plantation to Samuel Wetherill, Jr., on February 5, 1813. In 1833 Wetherill partitioned part in favor of S. P. Wetherill; and from that time until 1876, when Emily Wetherill sold all to Israel Wood, there were various Wetherill family transfers. In 1877, Wood sold to Eliza Jane Reed. High Sheriff Clinton Rorer sold to William H. Wetherill. The Wetherills sold to Montgomery County in 1951, for creation of an Audubon memorial monument and park called Mill Grove.

John James Audubon spent less than a year in the Mill Grove house. From December 5, 1804, to February 5, 1805, he was the guest of Fatland Ford (William Bakewell diary), after which he was the lodger of William Thomas, the tenant farmer, two miles or so away (Pears Papers).

When Jean Audubon leased Mill Grove to Prevost on July 10, 1790, for £170 and one ear of corn "each April" on demand, and for "600 pannels of fence of sawed and framed posts and rails such as are used by James Vaux,

Esq., on the adjoining plantation . . . in good workmanlike manner, and the repair of the mill dam, and a new water wheel," he asked Prevost to notify Miers Fisher "within two days in the event of a major catastrophe." On April 1, 1796, Audubon made a final payment of £38.04/11/3 (Lavigne).

(Mortgager Index, Montgomery County Court House, Norristown, Pennsylvania, for transfers involving Prevost and Audubon, and by Dacosta to Beates.)

Promissory Note of William Bakewell

> I promise to pay to William Thomas [tenant and keeper of Mill Grove] on order the sum of two hundred dollars as soon as the said sum becomes due according to a certain article of agreement between the said William Thomas and [Jean] Audubon dated the eighteenth day of August in the year of our Lord, one thousand eight hundred and four (and which sum is his, the said [Jean] Audubon's, moiety of half of the four hundred dollars payment mentioned in the said article) and according to the interpretation put upon the said article by Cadwalader Evans, Job Roberts and Mathias Holstein in their report made in the Prothonotaries office in a suit between William Thomas and Francis Dacosta as witness my hand this 25th day of December in the year of our Lord, 1809.
> Witness S. Chapman   (Signed) William Bakewell

Overleaf: "Received November 8th, 1819, of [Rebecca] Bakewell $200 in full, of J. Audubon's moiety or share of the sum to be paid to said William Thomas for the discovery of a lead mine, in full of all demands. Witness present: Jos. Crawford." Beneath this is pencilled (by Rebecca?): "to be taken from Mr. Audubon's share of estate" [of William Bakewell]. The latter was added before Bakewell's death and refers not to Jean Audubon (who was deceased) but to John James Audubon (DBP).

Deeds of John Audubon and Francis Dacosta (Montgomery County Court House, Norristown, Pennsylvania)

DEED I: JOHN AUDUBON to FRANCIS DACOSTA. This *indenture* made the [3rd] day of [June] in the year [1805] Between JOHN AUDUBON late of the city of Philadelphia in the Commonwealth of Pennsylvania, gentleman, at present being in the City of Nantes in France and Ann Moynette his wife of the One Part and FRANCIS DACOSTA of the said city of Philadelphia, gentleman, of the other part. WITNESSETH that he paid John Audubon and Ann Moynette . . . 31,000 franks lawful money of France . . . 2 water, corn or grist mills under one roof with 2 pair of stone and saw mill plantation and 2 tracts of land situate on both sides of *Perkioming* Creek in New Providence township in the County of Montgomery. [Here follow neighbor boundaries: James Vaux, Barney Pawling, Valentine Sailor, Jacob Vanderslice, Peter Stump.]

"Same premises" as those sold by Henri and Susannah Prevost, and sold to John Audubon on March 28, 1789. The deed gives Dacosta "one full and undivided moiety of, and in, the said above described," namely, of the whole plantation. It was signed and sealed in the presence of "G. Vallin, Mayor of Couëron village, France; and G. Loyen Puigaudeau," and signed by Audubon and wife. On the opposite page of the Deed Book is a supplement making Madame Audubon the knowing and willing partner of her husband in his decision to sell half; in accordance with Pennsylvania law. (See also FHH, I, 113.)

DEED II: Deed of Release: JOHN AUDUBON et al to FRANCIS DACOSTA. This *indenture* of 4 parts made in the *15th day of September in . . . 1806* Between John Audubon the elder . . . now residing in . . . Nantes . . . and Anne Moynette his wife by John Audubon the younger and Ferdinand Rozier, their attorneys for this special purpose . . . by letters dated October 22, 1805 . . . *and* Claude Francis Rozier of . . . Nantes aforesaid merchant by the name of F. Rozier and J. Audubon . . . and F. Dacosta of . . . Philadelphia. WITNESSETH that [for] $9,640.30, John Audubon the elder, his wife, Claude Francis Rozier, Ferdinand Rozier and John Audubon, Jr. . . . quit claim unto the said F. Dacosta and his heirs and assigns:

All the said John Audubon the elder's, Anne Moynette his wife's, Claude F. Rozier's and John Audubon the younger's and each and every of their estate rights title interest use possession claim and demand in law and equity whatsoever of into and out of

All that certain Messuage or Tenement, 2 water corn or grist mills under one roof with two pair of stones and saw mill plantation and tract of land situate on the south east side of the Perkioming Creek in New Providence Township [boundaries follow] . . . containing 113 acres and 74 perches of land. Also Perkioming Creek bed and waters on both sides premises, part of shore and stones needed for purposes of the dam and mills plus all . . . other buildings, improvements, ways, woods, waters, water courses, mines veines ores, minerals (and especially a certain *led* mine therein recently discovered) rights liberties privileges, hereditaments and appurtenances whatsoever. . . . The said herein . . . being part of those premises [sold by Prevost to the elder Audubon].

Recorded October 27, 1806 in Book 22.

The deed states that the Audubons and Roziers cannot claim or challenge "any estate right title or interest in law or equity" in regard to the land, and that they shall have to guarantee that the land is unencumbered. On September 19, 1806, Audubon, Jr., and Rozier, Jr., appeared as guarantors of the deed and its contents before Mayor Inskeep of Philadelphia, which granted Dacosta the right to occupy the mansion if he wished, "from time to time."

The Henderson Mill

The following chronology supersedes all previous published accounts. It is based on the Pears Papers (MS. Book 4), by Thomas C. Pears III (PUL):

1813–14		Scheme for a steam mill is proposed by Thomas W. Bakewell.
1814	June	Thomas Pears visits Henderson to discuss partnership.
	July	Pears helps to engage the Philadelphia mechanic David Prentice as builder of an engine.
	August	Prentice is appointed.
	September	Pears visits Pittsburgh for collections.
	November	Prentice arrives in Henderson.
1815		Pears brings his family to Henderson.
1816		Mill erected (before May) following delays, but Pears withdraws and returns to Pittsburgh. By December 1 Bakewell has dissolved his partnership with Audubon. He agrees to stay on until July 1, 1817.
1817		Bakewell and his brother William withdraw, taking Prentice along to Louisville, where they establish a foundry.
1819		By July the enterprise has collapsed for Audubon and his shareholders.
1913		The mill burns to the ground.

David Prentice to Thomas Pears, July [1814], Philadelphia:
I received a letter from Bakewell & Audubon . . . about the expenses and power of a steam engine. I am willing . . . but being in a pretty decent way here I did not chuse to leave a certainty for an uncertainty. . . . I think the erecting of a steam engine for you will bring me into notice and I am therefore willing to . . . for very little compensation. I have told [T. W. Bakewell] that I am willing to superintend the works while putting up for $3 a day and expenses of traveling paid, or that I would furnish and fit up at Henderson a 16-horse engine for $400 . . . castings, blacksmith's work and wages to get the engine in motion as far as the fly wheel inclusive. The hauling, the time and the masonry to be at your expense, as also my personal boarding . . . these prices are about half what is commonly got for them. . . . The wages I have asked are only those of journeymen. I wish it to be understood that I am willing to lose my time for a while so as to get known in the country. . . . I am willing to superintend . . . as far as driving the stones, but would rather you got a mill wright . . .

to who, however, I would give the necessary instructions to make his work meet mine. If the business should go no farther I would wish you not to state to anyone the offers I have made you, because I would not chuse to make them to others, and it is not easy to raise a price when once down.

David Prentice

Thomas Woodhouse Bakewell to William Gifford Bakewell (Shaffer):

Cincinnati 26 March 1834
I have yours of 22nd and informing of the results of [Ward's] suit—which I believe closes all the matters and things for Prentice & Bakewell. There was no better man to plan than David Prentice but he either would not or could not execute his plans to make them work well—when we were together I was the merchant, he the mechanic, and I did not presume to put my (then crude) ideas of machinery against his—and there has been too much just cause for complaint with his [engineering].

Passenger List of the Merchant Vessel **Le Conquérant** *(Archives Nationales, Paris; translation)*

Le Conquérant of Nantes, 248 tons, belonging to Coiron Frères, equipped in Nantes to sail for Les Cayes, St. Louis. Sailed September 26, 1783, returned April 27, 1784. Captain Jean Louis le Febvre. Passengers (for Les Cayes):
[Jacques] Pallon de la [Bouverie], former official residing in the colonies, age 56
Demoiselle Rose Génerèse, his wife, age 40, and their children:
Dlle. Magdeleine Marie Rose Pallon, age 19
Dlle. Marie Louis, her sister, age 15
Dlle. Catherine, her other sister, age 12
Jeanne Rabin, of Les Touches parish, diocese of Nantes, age 25, their *fille de chambre* . . .
Jean Audubon (boarded at Paimboeuf), of Paimboeuf, age 38, former ship captain, going to Les Cayes on business. . . .
All passengers disembarked November 26, 1783.

Arrival of Jean Rabine (Audubon) from Saint-Domingue: Passenger List of the Vessel **Le Duguesclin** *(Archives Nationales, Paris)*

Le Navire Le Duguesclin, de 400 tx., armé de 2 canons, appartenant au sieur Vilmain, armé à Nantes par le dit sieur sous le commandement du sieur Charles Garet. Allant aux Cayes St. Louis. Parti de Nantes le 9 avril 1788, retour le 26 août 1788.
Captaine Charles Garet, de Nantes, 37 ans.

Pilotin: Charles Garet, de Nantes, 15 ans.
Remplacement, le 7 juillet 1788: Jacques Le Floc, d'Auray, matelot
Passagers:
Maison neuve, agé de trois ans, fils du sieur Audubon
Le sieur J. Bte Massé.
Aux frais des armateurs de la goélette Le Lokro, de Nantes:
Francois Bardet, charpentier de la goélette Le Lokro.
    Vu aux Cayes le 12 juillet 1788
signé: Caissier d'Outremer, Offier d'Administration chargé du détail des classes.
Vu par nous, Commissaire des Colonies chargé du Service de la Partie du Sud.

Arrival of Rose Bouffard (Audubon) from Saint-Domingue: Passenger List of the Vessel Le Tancrède *(Archives Nationales, Paris; translation)*

Colonies, July 1791: . . . *Le Tancrède,* Captain Mathurin Gautreau, coming from Les Cayes. Passengers for Nantes:
    Mr. Victor Grandier, living at Cavaillon
    Demoiselle Roze Bonite, age 4, natural daughter and orphan of Dlle. Robin [Rabin], white
    Mr. Esmanyard, Lieutenant de Vaisseaux of the king
    Two children of Mr. Moutou, ages 10 and 7 . . .
    The bonded servant named Nanette, belonging to Mr. Marineau and the said Jean Philippe, belonging to the same.
In the duplicate record in the Archives Départementales, Nantes, the first sailing date is indicated as April 22–24, 1791, because the bonded mulatto servants lacked proper papers. The actual sailing date was June 24, 1791.

Passenger List of the Schooner La Victoire *(Archives Départementales, Nantes; translation)*

The Schooner *La Victoire* . . . left La Pierre à Joseph Island [near Cap Dame Marie, above Les Cayes] June 14, bound for Cap Français and arrived . . . in Philadelphia July 6, 1790. . . . Passengers for Belle Ile: Messrs. Vinches, inhabitant of Saint-Domingue; Audubon, merchant of Les Cayes; Major Prevost, inhabitant of Philadelphia.

Two disembarked at Belle Ile on September 8, 1790. The schooner, originally bound for Bordeaux, proceeded to Nantes for *"désarmement,"* and for payment of the crew, witnessed by Jean Audubon on September 14 and endorsed by Coiron Frères.

    Disagreements between the captain and owners at Cap Français (*La Victoire's* home port when in Saint-Domingue) over the seaworthiness of the vessel led to the captain's resignation. His replacement took months before the June departure.

Jean Audubon agreed to join *La Victoire* at Cap Français after buying more sugar. A letter in the Lavigne Collection places him in Philadelphia as late as August 2, 1790. Sugar bills place him in Les Cayes in January, February, and April 1790 (Lavigne). A letter from Prevost (dated Dover, March 25, 1791) proves that he paid Audubon's passage, which he politely asked him to return (Lavigne).

Marriage of Gabriel Du Puigaudeau and Rose Bouffard Audubon

The civil ceremony was held in the Town Hall, Couëron, on December 16, 1805. The next day the Bishop of Nantes published the banns for the church wedding held in Couëron on December 17.

"Gabriel Loyen Du Puigaudeau and Rose Bouffard, daughter of the late Catherine Bouffard, Creole of Saint-Domingue, adopted by Mr. Jean Audubon, ship captain and his legitimate wife Anne Moynet by an Act of 17 *ventose, An X* [March 7, 1794] . . . born in Saint-Domingue on April 26 [29], 1787, age 18, younger daughter of Catherine Bouffard; the adoptive father is present and consents to the marriage" (Translation).

The witnesses who signed were J. L. J. Audubon, "son and brother"; Ferdinand Rozier, Nantes; Louise Moynet, aunt of the bride; Madame Giraud of Port Launay, sister of the groom; André Loyen Du Puigaudeau, ship captain, brother of the groom; Georges Beaudry Martin; Madame André Du Puigaudeau, née Chauveau, Nantes; Jean Perchais, justice of the peace, age 56; mother of the bridegroom; and Jean Audubon and wife.

Rose makes her birth date conform with her erroneous adoption record.

A daughter, Rose Magdeleine Du Puigaudeau, was baptized in Couëron on February 20, 1811; born in Port Launay near La Gerbetière on February 16. Her mother is called "Rose Bouffard," and Madame Audubon her "adoptive grandmother." She married a *capetane de long course* (ocean-going), Aimable-Auguste Pivert; no issue. She died on October 20, 1881.

A son, Gabriel-Jean-André Loyen Du Puigaudeau, was born on November 13, 1813. He registered in the navy as a *novice*, 1832, and died at his villa, Les Tourterelles, on June 23, 1892. His daughter Rose married notary Louis Lavigne, whose grandson, Jean-Louis Lavigne, and granddaughters, Françoise and Anne, continue the line. There are no living male descendants of the family Du Puigaudeau since the death of the impressionist painter Ferdinand Loyen Du Puigaudeau in Paris in 1930.

Marriage Act of the Parents of Jeanne Rabine (Les Touches Parish Register, Archives Départementales, Nantes; translation)

On January 22, 1754, after publication of the banns on three consecutive Sundays without opposition . . . I, the undersigned pastor, have admitted to the nuptial blessing William, son of the well-known Peter Rabinne, and Marie Texier, his father and mother, with Marie the daughter of the honorable Sebastian Le Comte and of Jeanne Tertrin, also her father and mother, both from the village of Mazures; in the presence of Peter Rabinne, the father of the groom, of John Sebron, Sebastian Le Comte, the father of the bride, and of Julian Bourgeois, [all of whom] signed except Peter Rabinne, who cannot write.

Marriage of Georges Ricordel and Anne Moynet (Archives de la Préfecture, Nantes; translation)

On May 8, 1764, have been received by me, choir priest of the Church of St. Vincent, the undersigned, with the consent of the Reverend Rector, the merchant Georges Ricordel, widower of the late Marguerite Guichant of the parish of Paimboeuf in this diocese—on the one hand—and Demoiselle Anne Moynet, elder daughter of the merchant François Moynet and his wife Julienne Richard, her parents of this parish—on the other hand—after publication of the banns without opposition either in this parish or that of the aforesaid Paimboeuf, considering the certificate of Mr. Juvenot, vicar of Paimboeuf, dated April 30, considering also the dispensation from the two other bans granted by Mr. de Regnon, vicar-general, on April 23, duly authorized and enforced on the same date as the above signed Le Beau du Bignon and Giron. [Witnesses]: François Moynet, father of the bride; Pierre François Bouvier; Louis Thélot; Jean Cebron; Mathurin Thélot; and several others who have signed: [bride and groom, and parents of same]; Louis Moynet [sister of the bride]; Bonnier; Ledain; Jean and Jan Cebron; J. Pichot; Madame Verrier; Madame Caille and daughter Marie Anne; Loyseau Ollive; Marie Ricordel [sister of the groom]; François Cochard, [uncle or cousin of the groom]; J. F. Racault, priest.

The presence of the Cebrons of Les Touches parish is the first documentary clue to the eventual liaison between Jean Audubon and Jeanne Rabine. Jean Cebron had also witnessed the marriage of the parents of Jeanne Rabine ten years earlier; their other ties are indicated elsewhere in this book. The Cebrons were linked by marriage to the Thélots, also of Les Touches Parish, and the Thélots to the Rabines.

According to the Lavigne MSS., Ricordel was a ship carpenter originally of Prinquiau parish, Nantes diocese; he was the son of Guillaume Ricordel and Jeanne Cochard.

Act of Marriage, Parish Register, Paimboeuf: Jean Audubon and Anne Moynet, Widow of Georges Ricordel: August 24, 1772 (Archives de la Préfecture, Nantes; translation)

No 191: August 24, 1772. Considering the certificate of the age of the husband, legalized August 17 by Monseigneur the Bishop of

Luçon, and considering also the consent of the mother of the bridegroom, reported on August 8 by Bréchard, the notary of the Crown, and made legal on August 11, and considering likewise the announcement of the banns two times and of permission for the betrothal postponed until today, granted, by Msgr. Serin de la Cordinière, venerable Vicar-General of the diocese of Luçon, as of August 8, and by Msgr. de La Tullaye, Vicar-General of this diocese, as of August 22, registered and validated at Luçon on August 8, and at Nantes on August 22, after publication of a bann of marriage last Sunday at high Mass in that parish, and on August 9 in that of Les Sables d'Olonne according to the certificate of Msgr. Le Marchand, rector of the aforesaid parish, without opposition from any of those acquainted with the affianced; also by consent Msgr. the rector of Paimbouef, Jean Audubon, [*noble homme*, or esquire], aged 28, ship captain born at Les Sables d'Olonne his domicile, son of the late Mr. Pierre Audubon, ship captain, and of Marie Anne Martin his wife—on the one hand—and, on the other, Anne Moynet, aged about 42, native of St. Léonard parish in Nantes, and domiciled in this parish [Paimbouef], widow of Mr. Georges Ricordel. Those present: Demoiselle Marie-Anne Audubon, sister of the bridegroom, Mr. Louis Papineau his cousin—both domiciled at Les Sables d'Olonne; Mr. François Moynet, the father of the bride, from St. Vincent parish, Nantes; D.elle Louise Moynet of the parish of Ste. Croix, Nantes, sister of the bride. [The family, the vicar, and the rector signed.]

Alliance of the Families Audubon and Le Jeune de Vaugeon

The marriage contract of Jean-Baptiste Le Jeune de Vaugeon and Marie-Anne-Claire Audubon is so rich in detail that it sheds light on both families and their circumstances. It describes the bridegroom as "a Parliamentary lawyer, Master of Waters, Woods and Forests of the County of Porhoët in the Duchy of Rohan." His mother was Marie-Madeleine Cadoret. His bride lived in the residence of Jean Audubon, "the quarter La Fosse, the Bourse, St. Nicholas parish."

The contract lists eight conventions, or agreements, about common property; payment of all debts before the ceremony; a dowry of £1,000, as well as a fortune of "£6,000 sterling in safekeeping" with Captain Audubon and wife; separate inventories of property; renunciation of rights by each party in case of death whether or not they were without issue; and indemnities. The bridegroom listed his library, jewels, clothing, linens, and arms at tedious length (Archives Départementales, Nantes).

Two pallbearers of the first wife of the bridegroom (François and Louis Bouré) were apparently kinsmen-in-law of Jeanne Rabine. On February 21, 1775, her aunt Anne Rabine married Joseph Bouré and her uncle Pierre married Marie Bouré in a double wedding ceremony. Jeanne, then nineteen, no doubt attended.

Le Jeune de Vaugeon was related to the family Le Jeune de la Martinais of Chateaubriant in the Duchy of Condé, owners of plantations on the islands of Saint-Domingue and Bourbon (*Les Annales de Nantes*, I, 16, 1961).

Le Jeune de Vaugeon died on July 27, 1806, at No. 1 Rue Démosthène, Nantes. His gardener and an "associate" were witnesses. After his own chattels were auctioned, his widow moved with hers to the Rue Killev.

A *Declaration de Mutations* (Les Archives Départementales, Nantes) after his death noted a debt of £300 on the part of Captain Audubon. After the death of Marie-Anne-Claire Audubon, her brother, the Captain, conveyed his share of their joint inheritance of Les Sables Property—at least in part—to her second son Anonyme Le Jeune II (Lavigne).

Anonyme I was born and baptized October 10, 1784; Anonyme II, December 6, 1786. After his birth Anonyme I disappears from the records.

Death of Marie-Anne-Claire Audubon, widow of Le Jeune de Vaugeon (Archives Départementales, Nantes; translation)

> At noon on January 16, 1815, have appeared before us, the under-signed deputies and officers of the Civil Government delegated by the Mayor of Nantes, officer of the Legion of Honor: Messrs. Pierre Tertrin, Bureau Chief of the office of the mayor, and Sebas-tien Mathurin Humbert . . . who have declared to us that at 4 P.M. Marie-Anne-Claire Audubon, property owner, aged 64, native of Les Sables d'Olonne . . . widow of Le Jeune, died in her dwelling at 11 rue [Killev], 5th Canton.

Record of Marriage of the Son of Madame Marie-Anne-Claire de Vaugeon (Archives Départementales, Nantes; translation)

> Act of marriage of Monsieur Anonyme le jeune De Vaugeon, mer-chant, [younger] son of the late Jean-Baptiste lejeune [*sic*] de Vaugeon and of the late Madame Marie-Anne Audubon, born December 6, 1786, in Les Touches . . . and residing in Nantes . . . and of Mademoiselle Cecile Anne Vilmain, the younger daughter of the late Monsieur Augustin-Toussaint Vilmain and of Madame Desirée Rocher, the wife of Joseph-Pierre-Marie Delgusé by her second marriage, and born on Prairial 3, in the year 1800 at Nantes, where she has been living at the residence of her grandfather [Vilmain].

The grandfather of the bride was the owner of the ship *Le Duguesclin*, which had carried Jean Rabine to Nantes from Les Cayes. The marriage act was witnessed by, among others, Mélanie, Anonyme's sister; Louis Ro-main de Bray, Receiver of Lottery; and the grandfather, Vilmain. Monsieur de la Tullaye signed for the mayor as his deputy. The record mistakenly calls the bridegroom "elder" son.

Second and Last Will of Lieutenant de Vaisseau Jean Audubon

(The following is a translation of the document in the Lavigne Collection; for the French version, see FHH, II, 360–62.)

I, the undersigned, Jean Audubon, living at *La Gerbetière* in the commune of Couëron, department of la Loire-Inférieure.

Herewith, my testament.

I give and bequeathe to Dame Anne MOINETTE, my wife, the available part and portion, in use according to what I shall have in general, of all property movable and immovable, which will belong to me at the moment of my death, and for her lifetime.

I give and bequeathe to Monsieur Jean RABAIN, creole of Saint-Domingue, whom I believe to be actually in the United States without, nevertheless, being sure of it, husband of Mademoiselle Lucy BACKWELL [sic], half of all property in general, all goods movable and immovable, which will belong to me at the moment of death to be treated and disposed of according to his will, according to the constant trust of his allowing Dame Anne Moinette, my wife, to take possession of her legacy herein designated, for her lifetime.

I give and bequeathe to Dame Rose Bouffard, creole of Saint-Domingue, wife of M. Gabriel Loyen du Puigaudeau, actually living at Port Launay, Couëron, half likewise, in general, all movable goods which will belong to me at the moment of my death, for her to do with and dispose of entirely according to her will, according to the constant trust of her allowing Dame Anne Moinette, my wife, to enjoy her legacy . . . for her lifetime.

I wish and intend that in case of the death of M. RABAIN or Madame Puigaudeau, my last two heirs here designated, or even of both, their immediate heirs should come into the inheritance. That is to say, let the heirs of M. RABAIN inherit what is left to him and let those of Dame Puigaudeau do likewise in case the said *sieur* Rabain and dame Puigaudeau do not inherit because of preceding me, the maker of this will, in death; or in case of some attack on my bequests which I have made in favor of Jean Rabain and Rose Bouffard . . . for an annulment, I declare that I give all my property movable and immovable, unconditionally and without exception, to my wife Anne Moinette.

Made in my dwelling . . . La Gerbetière in Couëron, March 15, 1816. Long live the King! [Signed: AUDUBON]

In the archival registers at the Préfecture, Nantes, are *mutations,* or declarations, transferring the property of Jean Audubon in the communes of Le Pellerin, St. Etienne-de-Montluc, and Les Sables d'Olonne. Mme. Audubon is declared his sole legatee *en universalité.*

Last Will of Madame Anne Moynet Audubon, September 8, 1821

The following, given in translation, does not appear in FHH, which calls the fourth will, dated July 16, 1821, the "last." This one differs from previous wills (Lavigne).

Madame Anne Moynet, landlord, gentlewoman, widow and sole legatee of Mr. Jean Audubon late captain and *lieutenant de vaisseau,* the said lady now residing at the villa *Les Tourterelles*, near Couëron in this canton.

That person being in good health and of sound mind and judgment. . . .

Wishing to avoid all formalities and court procedures which might occur after my death I give and bequeathe to Madame Rose Bouffard, wife of Mr. G. L. Du Puigaudeau . . . and in case they precede me in death, to the children of their lawful marriage, the generality of both my movable and immovable property upon my decease, without exception or reservation, naming the said Dame Rose Bouffard and her children as my sole heirs and general beneficiaries, keeping exact and faithful account of my half of my net assets, and to Mr. Jean Rabain, otherwise known as Jean Audubon, Créole of Saint-Domingue whose present address I know not, or in any case, if he should be dead, to his children; wishing that my said estate be divided equally between the said . . . Rose . . . and her brother Jean Rabain called Jean Audubon, or their lawful heirs; and according to regulations, should either one happen to claim to have received legally established benefits from their late common father, my husband Jean Audubon.

I know the inclination [of the] above to avoid all difficulties after my death. . . . I wish that no seals be affixed, or other formalities whether judicial or extrajudicial. In consideration of the absence of Mr. Jean Rabin called Jean Audubon. . . . I charge the notary Mr. Maigret to take what measures he deems fitting to establish the record of my succession which will be divided as I have said above, revoking herewith all previous wills.

I wish also to have the right to live at *Les Tourterelles* and to occupy two rooms, above the salon, where I shall be allowed to arrange my belongings as I please. I wish the right also to go and come to the salon when I feel like it. As for my board, I shall continue to live with M. and Mme. Puigaudeau as in the past, praying them to have the regard and consideration to which my position and age entitle me.

Such is the testament of Madame Anne Moynet, widow of Mr. Jean Audubon, which she has dictated word for word in the presence of the Messrs. M. Gaudin, Jean-Etienne Babin, François and Etienne Turpin, and which has been executed and written entirely by M. Noël-Etienne Maigret, notary, in the presence of four witnesses. . . . [Signed by Mme. Audubon, J. E. Babin, F. Babin, and Maigret.]

The inventory of the property of Anne Moynet, widow of Jean Audubon (Lavigne, Document No. 142; dated November 14, 15, and 17, 1821, signed by Antoine Barbet, Notary, Couëron) indicates that litigation had eaten away her once respectable personal fortune. She owned La Gerbetière and some furnishings. Property in adjacent communities and in Les Sables d'Olonne had evidently been sold after probate of the will of Jean Audubon. To have claimed his share of the estate John James Audubon would have had to take up residence at La Gerbetière.

Last Will and Testament of William Bakewell
(Montgomery County Court House, Norristown, Pa., dated April 16, 1812,
recorded 1822.)

Abstract

I. Fatland Ford farm ("upwards of 200 acres," according to an ad of 1813), to be sold and proceeds invested in "U.S. funds" or other "real securities" and paid thus:
Interest from one-third, to wife Rebecca till her death, then to children.
Interest from two-thirds, to the 6 children, equally, when each turns 21, and their "heirs and assigns forever."

II. "All my land near Northumberland purchased from Joseph Priestley," or if title be "not substantial" the money paid, with all interest due on it, to Thomas Woodhouse Bakewell, eldest son.

III. 400 acres, "near the Alleghanny" River, formerly owned by wife Rebecca, to William Gifford Bakewell, younger son.

IV. All plate and furniture bought since marriage, and one-quarter of other furniture (including Rawlinson portrait of her husband and one-sixth of the books till death, then to Thomas Woodhouse Bakewell), to wife Rebecca who was to relinquish all claims on the estate "in right of dower," even as her husband renounced any claim on her late father Robert Smith's estate as executor.

V. Books, five-sixths to two sons. "Guns, globes, medicine and chemical chests, watch, and philosophical instruments," to two sons.

VI. Furniture, three-fourths in equal shares to "Eliza, Sarah and Ann." (Lucy received a portion on marriage.)

VII. Stock and farm utensils; Canal shares; house and lot in New Haven, Connecticut, to be sold at once; proceeds, after debt payments: one-third to be lent to son Thomas "on his bond" at 6 percent payable to Rebecca, and on her death to be divided equally among the 6 children; two-thirds to be divided among the 6.

(Executrix, daughter Sarah; she, brothers, Eliza, and Ann made Nicholas Berthoud absolute administrator of will in spring 1822. Lucy did not sign.)

Last Will and Testament of John James Audubon

First, I order and direct that all my just debts and funeral expenses be paid as soon after my decease as conveniently *can* be done.

Second, [to my wife and sons] . . . all my real and personal property of whatever nature or kind soever (excepting my household furniture, articles of silver plate) share and share alike.

Third . . . all my household furniture, articles of silver and silver plate . . . [to my wife].

This revokes and annuls all other and former wills.

John James Audubon

Written on April 19, 1841. Proved in New York City where made, July 15, 1851. On file in the Hall of Records, Surrogate's Court, New York (Book 102, page 106).

The Naturalization of John James Audubon (Landing Report, U.S. District Court, Philadelphia; Book of Arrivals, 1798–1807)

On . . . 5th Sept. 1806, John Audubon a free white person . . . age 23. . . arrived in the United States after the passing of . . . an act [of April 14, 1892] to establish an Uniform Rule of Naturalization. . . ⟋ John Audubon was born at Aux Cayes . . . St. Domingo sometime in the Year 1783 and is . . . a member of the French Nation . . . arrived at the Port of N.Y. on or about Aug. 27, 1802 . . . about the 21st March, 1805 he returned to France from whence he again migrated to the U.S. on or about April 12, 1806 and arrived N.Y. . . . about May 27, and . . . it is his intention to settle in the State of Pennsylvania [Signed] J. Audubon. Recorded . . . by me D. Caldwell, Clk. Dist. Ct.

Audubon was in fact 18, and arrived in 1803. He was born April 26, 1785. Rozier recorded their joint arrival from France on May 28, 1806. William Taylor, Jr., of Philadelphia, vouched for Audubon as "a man of good Moral Character, attached to the principles of the Constitution . . . and well disposed to the good order and happiness of the same." In the oath of allegiance Audubon renounced "allegiance and fidelity to every foreign prince . . . and particularly Napoleon I." He was sworn on July 15, 1812, before the eventual president of the American Philosophical Society, Peter Stephen Du Ponceau, a distinguished French-born philologist and lawyer.

According to Francis J. Dallet, discoverer of the above, the National Archives has a State Department record showing that a passport dated March 19, 1830, describes Audubon as "46, 5' 8½", common forehead, hazel eyes, prominent nose, common mouth, pointed chin, greyish hair, brown complexion, oval face." He reached 45 one month later. Clothing at the AMNH tallies with this height.

Honorary Memberships of John James Audubon

Academy of Natural Sciences, Philadelphia
American Academy of Arts & Sciences, Massachusetts
American Philosophical Society, Philadelphia
Antiquarian Society, New Castle-on-Tyne
Linnaean Society, London
Literary & Historical Society, Quebec
Literary & Philosophical Society of Liverpool
Literary & Philosophical Society of New Castle
Lyceum of New York
Manchester Society for Promoting Natural History
National Academy of Design, New York City

Natural History Society, Boston
Natural History Society, Montreal
Ornithological Society, London
Royal Jennerian Society, London
Scottish Antiquaries Society, Edinburgh
Société d'Histoire Naturelle de Paris
Société Linnenne de Paris
Society for Promoting the Useful Arts, Edinburgh
Wernerian Natural History Society, Edinburgh
Zoological Society, London

Recognition of Audubon in France in 1828

Recognition of Audubon in England, before his mission to Paris, had been generated by letters of introduction, personal hospitality in Liverpool and Manchester, Royal Society favors, and reviews, few but valuable, as *The Birds of America* began to emerge. He was armed with some of his original paintings and matching engravings when the Baron Cuvier received him. It was the public praise accorded by Cuvier that represented a kind of universal sanction. His initial but much briefer and more cautious fiat appeared in the *Mémoires de l'Académie Royale des Sciences,* given here, and followed by the much longer tribute that appeared in the journal *Le Moniteur Universel,* Paris:

> Among the magnificent works which have been devoted in various countries to represent the productions of nature, none surpasses for finish of engraving and coloring that which Monsieur Audubon has published on the birds of North America, and it has no equal for natural grandeur; and when the bird is large enough to fill the print, it is repeated in an attitude common to it. The Academy has taken cognizance of it with interest, and it is a great pleasure for it, as for all friends of the sciences, to see, today, the naturalization of the New World render, with interest to Europe, the equivalent of instruction that they have received.

Le Moniteur Universel, Paris, October 1, 1828
> Oral Report delivered before the Royal Academy of Sciences by Monsieur Cuvier, on the Natural History of the Birds of North America of Mr. Audubon:
> The Academy has requested me to deliver a report on the work . . . by Monsieur Audubon, whose subject was the birds of North America.
> The work can be characterized briefly by the statement that it is the most magnificent monument which has yet been raised to ornithology.
> The author, born in Louisiana, and who has devoted himself from his youth to painting, came to perfect himself in the art at the school of David. Upon returning to his country he thought himself able to put his talent to more useful service, that of dedi-

cating himself to the most brilliant representation [of the birds] of this hemisphere. The scrupulous observation necessary to such images as he wished to make soon turned him into a naturalist: various English collections include interesting written accounts from his pen and assure that there exist, in England and America, oil paintings equal to those of Oudry and Desportes. In his double capacity of artist and savant he has produced the work which has been brought before the Academy for inspection. You have been struck by a format equal or superior to the greatest that have been published. . . . This extraordinary size has permitted him to delineate the various eagles and vultures in their natural size, and to multiply the smaller species in such a manner as to show them in various attitudes.

He has also been able to depict, on the same plates, and in their natural grandeur, the plants which are their natural habits, and to include their nests and eggs in minute detail.

The execution of these plates, so remarkable for their grandeur, appears to us to have been equally successful as to harmony of design and engraving. [Easel] painting is not, strictly speaking, a medium for works of natural history; naturalists prefer the actual color of their subjects to the accidental hues that are the result of varying reflections of light necessary to arrive at pictorial truth, but limited and even detrimental to scientific truth. . . .

These forty-five prints are no more than a modest sampling of the work. Mr. Audubon has already prepared 400 drawings which contain nearly 2,000 figures, and he proposes to publish them successively if encouraged by collectors.

A work conceived and executed according to so vast a plan has but one fault, one that my listeners have already foreseen. Its cost renders it nearly inaccessible to most of those to whom it would be the most necessary. Nevertheless, one cannot say that its price is exorbitant. One Number consisting of five plates costs 2 guineas; each plate comes, then, to 10 or 11 francs; and since only five Numbers are to appear each year, the annual outlay for its purchase would not be enormous. It is desirable at least as much in the interest of art, as in that of science, that the great public repositories and their heads who like to enrich their libraries with rich works should wish to procure it.

He has attained 165 subscribers in England, and King George IV has permitted him to place his name at the head of the list. One must hope that the Continent will be no less eager to favor this magnificent enterprise. Heretofore it was the European naturalists who were obliged to make known to America the riches which it possessed. Now the Mitchills, the Harlans, the Wilsons, share with us in Europe what America has received. The story of the birds of the United States of Wilson already equalled our finest ornithological works in elegance. If that of Mr. Audubon is completed, it will be America which, for magnificence of execution, will have surpassed all efforts of the old world.

The Family Vault

To all but their descendants, it may come as a surprise that the Audubons and three friends and neighbors are buried beneath the Runic cross erected just before the turn of the century at Broadway and 155th Street, a few yards from Trinity Church. They sleep quite near their last homes, and not far from what was once Audubon Park. In 1888, when Broadway was widened, the following were moved from across the street to a newly made family vault, approached by a stairway seven feet deep and nearly six feet wide: John James Audubon, his wife, and sons; Georgianna Mallory Audubon (died October 13, 1882); Rosa Audubon (died October 9, 1879); May Eliza Bachman Audubon; Jane Audubon; Anton Heinrich, indigent musician. But Addison G. Gerome, neighbor, was reburied in lot 1069 after removal. (Other death dates are given in the text.)

Later these were buried in the sixteen-by-eighteen-foot vault: Anne Gordon Audubon (died August 7, 1907); Victor G. Audubon, Jr. (died September 19, 1914); Maria Eliza Audubon (died November 23, 1917); Joseph Whitley, neighbor (died January 12, 1891); John James Audubon II (died March 6, 1893); Lucy B. Audubon, granddaughter of Lucy, wife of the painter (died April 2, 1898).

Sexton records also show that Audubon was placed in a tomb just north until spring, then placed in the vault. They show further that John James Audubon II, son of Victor (he was first of two to be II), was brought from a grave of 1842 to be buried at Lucy's interment.

The Audubon Classics

The Prospectus of The Birds of America *Folio*

The first prospectus, issued March 17, 1827, was a paper pamphlet. The 1831 prospectus, which was owned by Edward Harris, is in the Houghton Library. The 1826 MS. journal mentions a draft of one by William Rathbone; however, it is not among his papers at the University of Liverpool. Audubon mentioned one in a letter to William Roscoe (Liverpool City Library), evidently discarded: "My Prospectus is a very humble one and I sent it you now in its nakedness that you may clothe it (if you please) as you may best think fit." Audubon wrote to William Rathbone that the prospectus is "not so fully represented as I intend to have one become, but sufficiently so, I hope, to obtain subscribers" (letter copy in 1826 journal).

All but two unaccounted-for drawings mentioned in the prospectus, and all other original studies finished later for the Folio, are owned by the New-York Historical Society. They were acquired from Lucy Audubon in 1863 by public subscription, after her unsuccessful efforts to sell them to the "National Museum" (or the British Museum, as a near last resort). She informed the Society on February 23, 1863, that her inventory of drawings came to "469 sheets." Drawings of eggs (unpublished) by John W. Audubon, James D. Trudeau, and possibly others are in the New Orleans Historical Society. Intended for the final pages of the Folio, they had to be abandoned because of incompleteness of species and for reasons of cost. See JJA to Havell, February 12, 1837; JJA to Morton, December 26, 1837; Thomas Brewer in *Harper's* magazine, October 1880 (Letters, I, 272–77; II, 182 and 196).

The Birds of America *Folio*

Eighty-seven numbers of five hand-colored copper plate engravings each. Total: 435 double-elephant aquatints—small, medium, and large—on paper by J. Whatman, size to 39½" by 29½". Four volumes, with title page, but without table of contents or text. Published in London, 1827–38. Original cost: $1,000, or £182/40/0 sterling.

The first ten plates, engraved and colored by William Home Lizars in Edinburgh late in 1826 and early in 1827, were retouched in part or entirely recolored by Robert Havell of London. Probably none were re-engraved by Robert Havell, Jr., who was responsible for the balance of the work, together with his artisan engraver assistants and colorers, who numbered up to fifty in the workroom. For a study of the successive stages and techniques, see Howard C. Rice, Jr., Princeton University Library *Chronicle*, Vol. XXI, Nos. 1–2 (1959–60), 42–49. See also *Audubon Magazine*, September 1958 and February 1960, for articles by Waldemar H. Fries, and his census of existing Folios.

"A few" copper sheets measuring up to six square feet were ruined by fire in New York City on July 19, 1845. On August 7, Audubon wrote to Baird that he was attempting repairs. The 350 remaining plates were not sold in 1865, as stated, but in 1869 to Phelps Dodge and Company of New York City. Besides those privately owned, there are copper plates in the following institutions: American Museum of Natural History, New York City; Smithsonian Institution; Princeton University; Wesleyan University; Groton School; New York Botanical Garden; Pratt Memorial Library, Cohasset; Carnegie Library, Pittsburgh; Wadsworth Atheneum, Hartford; and Pleasant Valley Bird Sanctuary, Lenox, Massachusetts. For the fate of others see FHH, 295, 306ff. Mrs. Audubon's offer to sell the copper plates at market value, $3,000, was refused by the Smithsonian and by the New-York Historical Society. Joseph Henry, Secretary of the Smithsonian, agreed to follow her suggestion that he offer them to the King of Portugal, a lover of birds; there it ended. Meanwhile her friend George Burgess, merchant, stored them in his Manhattan establishment for a year while Putnam, publisher, advertised them for Lucy in the *American Literary Gazette & Publishers Circular* on September 1, 1869, in vain. In March 1869 *The New York Times* printed this footnote to a shocking history: "THE AUDUBON PLATES SOLD FOR OLD COPPER. There is something almost sad that the original plates of the . . . *Birds of America* were recently sold for their value as old copper, after having sought a purchaser upon their artistic merits. But the new owners, who are well-known merchants, have agreed to wait a reasonable time for any proposition to redeem the plates from destruction, which otherwise awaits them." Earlier they were called "dated in style" or too costly to print, or both, by various printers whom Lucy approached.

In 1832, Audubon hired Childs & Inman of Philadelphia to lithograph his "Marsh Hen" *Rallus crepitans* (not the one in the Folio) (FHH, II, 26).

Memorandum from Lucy Audubon to George Burgess, ca. 1862: Inventory of the Original Water Color Drawings for **The Birds of America** *(NYPL)*

Mr. J. J. Audubon's Original Drawings

Portfolio No. 3	100 Land Birds
Portfolio No. 4	100 Water Birds
Portfolio No. 5	100 Land Birds
Portfolio No. 6	100 Water Birds
Portfolio No. 7	69 Land Birds

These port folios I looked over October 18, 1862. They were carefully placed and put away all in as good preservation as the day the drawings were made.

Mr. Robert Havell the 'Engraver of the Birds of America' in London assures me there are 436 plates of copper of different sizes, all of the best and purest metal. The weight can only be ascertained by having them weighed.

Havell probably said 435 rather than 436, unless he included the engraved title page. What the unmentioned Portfolios 1 and 2 may have contained is not stated. The ones numbered 3–7 total 469, or 10 more than the total of 459 sheets mentioned by Lucy in a letter dated February 23, 1863, to the New-York Historical Society, four months before their purchase (NYPL). The Society thus acquired many drawings beyond those published in 1827–38 in the great Folio of Audubon. Apart from one or two missing studies, those which served as models for *The Birds of America* were published in two volumes (in far less than natural size for the most part) in 1966, and as a group for the first time.

On April 9, 1863, Lucy wrote Burgess: "I this morning received a note from Mr. De Peyster which I intended sending to you for advice as to what I should do next. I perceive from your very friendly note to me that we both take the same view of the Historical Society." On April 12, Lucy wrote: "Last evening Mr. Knapp called upon me with a message from the gentlemen of the Historical Society, begging that I would not for a short time send the Drawings to Europe as 15 of the Committee had resolved to try and raise the money." (NYPL).

The New-York Historical Society has other letters on the subject of the purchase.

The Binding of **The Birds of America** *Folio*

On December 2, 1830, Lucy Audubon wrote from Edinburgh to Robert Havell, Jr., in London: "Enquire from several book binders for what sum they would bind ten copies of [*The Birds of America*] in the neatest, best manner in *Calf skin* binding. . . . Mr. A. wishes a *rolling back*. . . . and also the lettering on the back in gilt characters" (HLHU). Many subscribers eventually chose their own binders.

On December 23, 1830, Havell, Jr., wrote to Audubon: "Dear Sir, I have sent to Mr. Hill the 10 sets of No. 20, and one for yourself with the five drawings of No. 20. . . . The lowest estimate I can get to have the Work well done is as follows for Binding in Half Russian will be 3/10/0 if uncut around the Edges, and somewhat plainer 3/3/0. Every Binder I have consulted respecting the Open back informs me that it would not do as the weight of the book is so great they would soon break out and the binding come undone. . . . Other Binders have asked 4/4/0 and five guineas" (Yale).

From Edinburgh on November 8, 1834, Audubon wrote to C. L. Bonaparte that "Hering of London" was his binder (BMHN). A week earlier Audubon had mentioned to Havell a stock of half-bound Folio volumes (*Letters*, II). On November 23, 1839, he wrote to Samuel G. Morton of Philadelphia that he had a "full bound @ $1,075," a "half-bound @ $950," and unbound fascicules @ $850 (APS).

The Birds of America *Octavo or Miniature*

One hundred parts of five colored lithographs each by J. T. Bowen and assistants from camera-lucida copies of the Havell aquatints made by John

Woodhouse Audubon, plus sixty-five plates lithographed from drawings by John J. and John W. Audubon, assisted by Maria Martin on the background accessories. The habitat details were occasionally modified by Bowen in an arbitrary fashion for economy and his convenience. Some of the added plates were based on the final overcrowded Folio plates, with figures separated and set in their own grounds. Imprint of volumes one through five: J. J. Audubon, New York, and J. B. Chevalier, Philadelphia; of six and seven: J. J. Audubon, New York and Philadelphia. It was issued in paper covers for binding by subscribers, 1840–44. For minor differences in text of the miniature and *Ornithological Biography,* see the foreword, *Bird Biographies of John James Audubon.* Various editions—supposedly eight or more—the final ones minus plates, were published by George R. Lockwood through 1870 or 1871. Original Cost: $100 complete.

Variation in credits is partly explained by a letter of Audubon to Bachman, March 4, 1841 (Yale), in which he mentioned that trouble with Bowen had led him to give lithographer George Endicott of New York Numbers 28–30 for printing. Audubon also signed an agreement with J. W. Childs of New York City to color "1,500 Numbers, each of Numbers 28, 29 and 30 consisting of 5 plates," for delivery by Endicott to Childs who asked $1,900 for coloring "every 100 numbers, each of them of five plates," with payment on delivery.

"A Summary of Editions," by George Lockwood (a rare four-page publication of 1862), offered some of the Audubon classics at stated prices.

The Birds of America *Chromolithographic Folio*

A single volume of 106 double-elephant folio plates, chromolithographed by Julius Bien and issued by John W. Audubon in New York in 1860 under the imprint of Roe Lockwood and Son, with plates dated 1858 and 1859. (Bien [1826–1909] was a political refugee who came from Germany about 1849, rather than a printer brought to the United States by John Woodhouse Audubon, as Maria Rebecca told Henry Howland.) Some of the plates differ in background detail from their model, the original Folio. The Civil War brought this inferior but nevertheless imposing—and at points beautiful—work to a halt. The stone plates, stored in a New Orleans warehouse, were destroyed when the warehouse was shelled. The artisans were "W. Hitchcock, I.C., A.V. and C.P.," per plate marks. The first (30 plates) printing was finished by December 5, 1839. The text could be ordered separately; 200 copies were run off (FHH, II, 211, 219).

This excessively rare Audubon folio volume is owned by, among others, Yale University, Harvard University, the Brooklyn Museum, the Flint (Michigan) Public Library, and the New York Public Library. Single prints, also rare, are owned by Berea College; Colonial Williamsburg; Audubon Memorial Museum, Henderson, Kentucky; Shaffer Collection, Cincinnati; and others. By 1973, W. H. Fries had located forty-nine copies, publicly and privately owned. For Prospectus see FHH, II, 389.

Uncolored Proof Impressions of the Folio Aquatints

Mrs. Audubon owned 840 in December 1862. Two years later she gave her friend and adviser George Burgess many for his children to "color" or keep. His son Thomas sold 37 in 1902 to a dealer and to W. W. Grant of Summit, N.J.; in 1905 he sold an unknown number to P. F. Madigan, a New York dealer (NYPL: MSS: Burgess). The American Museum of Natural History still owned 167 (of a much larger number presented earlier by Maria R. Audubon) in 1964. Besides random private holdings are those of Princeton, Yale, and Harvard universities; and one in the Stark Museum, Orange, Texas.

Ornithological Biography

All five volumes were published in Edinburgh, 1831–39. Volume I was published simultaneously in Philadelphia, Volume II, in Boston. Audubon, as author, had assistance from his wife, Lucy, and from Professor William MacGillivray of the University of Edinburgh as scientific and general editor. Unillustrated except for ninety-eight anatomical drawings by MacGillivray, engraved on wood, presumably by Alexander Slater for the printer of the whole, Patrick Neill of Old Fish Market, Edinburgh, the work was bound by Thomson of Edinburgh. For imprint variations, see FHH, II, 402–404, 439n. The text underwent minor emendations and some new matter was added and deletions made for the text of the miniature *Birds of America*.

A Synopsis of the Birds of North America

An index to the Folio and *Ornithological Biography*, listing American birds of 491 recognized species, 139 genera, and 45 families. Published in July 1839 under the imprint of Adam and Charles Black, Edinburgh, primarily for Folio subscribers.

The Viviparous Quadrupeds of North America *Folio and Miniature*

Thirty parts of five imperial folio plates each, lithographed and colored by J. T. Bowen of Philadelphia, for binding in two volumes of 150 plates, at $10 per part, or $300 complete, 1845–48. Bowen asked $30 to $40 per drawing on stone; 18¢ to 25¢ each for coloring by hand (Victor to Webber, February 28, 1849) (HLHU). About half of the illustrations were drawn by John Woodhouse Audubon, despite engraved credit on plate margin of many of these to Audubon.

Three accompanying octavo volumes of text, the third of which dropped *Viviparous* from its title and included five additional octavo lithographed plates, were issued to subscribers in 1846, 1851, and 1854. The last two volumes gave the name of Victor G. Audubon as publisher.

An octavo or miniature edition, *The Quadrupeds of North America*, combining all 155 plates (150 folio plates plus the five in the third volume of text) by John J. and John W. Audubon, was published 1851–54 in three volumes. Some backgrounds—exactly which ones is uncertain—were painted by Victor G. Audubon. Again Bowen was lithographer, assisted by Ralph Trimbly and DeWitt Hitchcock, whose names appear on some plates. Bisbaugh printed the drawings, Henry Ludwig, the letterpress.

The New York Public Library (Burgess Papers) has a prospectus dated October 20, 1842:

Prospectus of The Viviparous Quadrupeds of North America

The plates will be Lithographed in a style superior to any thing hitherto executed in this country, and will be printed on the best Imperial folio paper, (22 × 28 inches), and carefully colored from Mr. Audubon's original drawings. . . . [They] will be delivered . . . in numbers of 5 plates each, at intervals of 2 months from the publication of each number, making 6 numbers annually, and the whole work will be completed in about 30 numbers.

The price . . . $10 each number. . . . The first number will appear in December next.

The Birdskins Originally Owned by Audubon

Audubon wrote to Bachman on August 25, 1834, that he had sold skins to the British Museum for £52 and again for £25, and that his own "double collection" he had "in drawers at home" (*Letters*, II, 28). The latter he took with others to the United States in 1839. (In *Bird Lore*, July 1912, George Grinnell, a neighbor, said the boxes reached to the roof of the barn of John Woodhouse Audubon.) Some had been sold to the Philosophical Society, York, England; Havell sold others in London. Audubon gave skins to the Charleston Natural History Society. The Museum of Comparative Zoology, Cambridge, Massachusetts, has two of the skins. The family of Edward Harris, who had acquired some of them, presented them to the Academy of Natural Sciences, Philadelphia. Those given by Audubon to S. F. Baird for his collection went to the Smithsonian Institution.

A letter of August 3, 1882, at the American Museum of Natural History, written by Henry A. Ward, son of Audubon's taxidermist Henry Ward, states that he and two helpers had sorted and cleaned and discarded from among "about 600." Audubon had given them to Ward as part of their contract. Henry A. Ward of Ward's Museum, Rochester, New York, proposed to sell them and his own collection. (*Ward's Natural Science Bulletin*, No. 1 (1882): 16, states that Maria R. Audubon had lately offered to sell Audubon's collection, long in the care of George N. Lawrence.) Ward sold the skins to E. E. Farman, who presented them to Amherst College, as reported in the *Amherst Graduates Quarterly*, November 1932.

On May 16, 1839, the Museum of the Royal College of Surgeons acknowledged a gift from Audubon of the organs of the Turkey Vulture, Florida Cormorant, Coot, Northern Diver, Great-Eared Grebe, Carolina Dobchick, Night Heron, Eider Duck, and Ivory-Billed Woodpecker. On December 13, 1838, it added thanks for organs of the Pelican and Anhinga.

Original Studies for Imperial Folio Quadrupeds

The locations of the original studies for *The Quadrupeds* are listed in *Audubon's Animals*, 215–16, to which the following may be added:

Red Texas Wolf. Unsigned, undated oil on canvas, reported by Kennedy Galleries, Inc., New York. Probably the study for Pl. 82, lithographed as by J. J. Audubon, but actually by J. W. Audubon, who seldom if ever signed his studies of mammals and birds.

Yellow-Bellied Marmot. Unsigned and undated oil on canvas. Probably the study for Pl. 172. By John Woodhouse Audubon. (Mrs. Benjamin M. Rice, Peterborough, New Hampshire.)

Otter in a Trap. The original watercolor (fate unknown) was painted in Henderson, Kentucky, in 1812, then executed in oil in New Orleans in 1822 (fate also unknown). In early autumn, 1826, Audubon painted an oil for Mrs. Richard Rathbone; it is now in the University of Liverpool. Late in 1826 another otter, identical with the others and with the one eventually lithographed by Bowen for Pl. 51, was painted in Edinburgh. It may be one of several now owned in the United States. Still others were painted in London as potboilers in 1827. Audubon wrote that this brought the total to seven (*Life of John James Audubon*). One dated Oxford, 1827, was sold to Edward Harris by Mrs. Audubon after the artist's death; it is now in the Corning Collection, Mentor, Ohio. An unsigned, undated oil of an otter was presented by John Hill Morgan to the Museum of the City of New York. The Milwaukee Art Center has an undated version, *ca.* 1826.

Common Mouse, Pl. 123; *American Hare*, Pl. 12; and *Pouched Rat*, Pl. 110, were shown in a benefit exhibition of Audubon's work in 1954 at the Kennedy Galleries, Inc., New York. Privately owned watercolor and pencil studies of *Brown or Norway Rat*, Pl. 154, and *Woodchuck*, Pl. 2, were on loan.

R. Havell & Son (NYPL, Genealogy Room)

Robert Havell, founder of R. Havell & Son, was born in Reading, England, on December 29, 1769. He died in London on November 21, 1832. He was the son of Daniel Havell, first engraver of the family and founder of the firm of Daniel & Robert Havell. Their progenitor, Luke Havell, born in Ashampstead in 1641, was Yeoman Warder of the Tower of London. In 1810 that firm engraved the drawings of William Havell (1782–1857), *A Series of Picturesque Views of the River Thames*. The work of William and Luke Havell, brothers of Robert, Sr., are in the South Kensington Museum, London.

Robert Havell, Sr., opened his shop at 79 Newman Street, London, before his son Robert joined him. He retired in 1828, leaving completion of the Folio of *The Birds of America* to Robert, Jr. His wife, Lydia M. Phillips, died in 1834, two years after her husband. Their other sons were George (born 1797), an animal painter who died in India in 1823, and Henry Augustus (born 1803), an artist and engraver.

Robert Havell, Jr., was born in Reading in 1793, and died in Tarrytown, New York, in 1878. He is buried in Sleepy Hollow Cemetery. Before the famous house of Colnaghi discovered his genius he worked as an engraver for Smith, Elder & Co. of London. He himself aquatinted many of the Audubon plates and supervised the engraving of all but the first ten (which were engraved by W. H. Lizars of Edinburgh). His father supervised the coloring of the plates until his retirement, and occasionally helped supervise the artisans. Robert Havell, Jr., engraved *Alexandrian Plants* of the noted botanical painter Mrs. Bury; a version of *The Birds of Paradise* by Le Vaillant; *Floral Illustrations of the Seasons* by Mrs. Edward Roscoe; and more. To him and Amelia Jane Edington were born Amelia Jane (1825–70), Robert Audubon (1827–29), Robert N. (1828–30), and Marianne E. (1847–1915). The family emigrated to the United States shortly before the Audubons returned home in 1839. A number of Havell's engravings made in America are in the Stokes Collection of the New York Public Library. His brother Henry also emigrated with his wife, Eliza Sims, and their line continues in America.

Marginalia

Marginalia written by Audubon on *American Ornithology; or, the Natural History of the Birds of the United States*, by Alexander Wilson (Philadelphia, 1808–14).
Volume I
> *Wood Thrush.* Wilson quoted a witness as to its scarcity. Audubon penciled beside it: "Whoever composed this letter never took a step toward procuring a specimen. I have killed as many as I pleased to destroy of a day." (This species he once declared his favorite.)

Volume III
> *Head of a Pileated Woodpecker, size of life.* "The neck is about double the size of nature, J.J.A."

Volume IV
> *Sparrow Hawk.* Under Figure 2; "Shew me a hawk carrying prey on the wing and exhibiting the claws and I will cry out, Nature is at fault."
> *Snow Owl.* Under Figure 1: "These legs are quite out of proportion."

Volume V
> *Barn Swallow.* "This bird can scarcely be considered as specifically different from ours. . . . The affection of our swallow for chimnies may be in the greater cold of our climate."

Volume VI
> *Small-Headed Flycatcher.* " . . . It is a true species very abundant in New Foundland in the month of August where it doubtless breeds." Also: "Wilson thought on the above subject most erroneously, because it is well known that every species of Bird, of whatever de-

nomination or sorts they may be, have a *Natural propensity* to move eastward and norwardly with the advancement of Spring and Summer, and no further proof of this fact is necessary than the [enumeration] of the bird he gives in the above paragraph, which migrate from south to north or East as far as possible for them to do at the seasons I have mentioned. The same is the fact all over the world."

Hawk Owl. Audubon agrees that many owls, including the "short earred, the Snowy, and the other cineria," may also hunt by day.

Whooping Crane. Wilson: "I met with several . . . in South Carolina. I also saw a flock at the ponds near Louisville, Ky." Audubon: "This wonderful sight was granted to Mr. Wilson at the request of *I.* Mr. Wilson then did not believe in the *existence* of *Blue Winged Teal.*"

Wood Ibis. Wilson: "solitary." Audubon: "All my eye and Betty Martin."

Scarlet Ibis. Wilson: found in "most southern parts of Carolina." Audubon: "There never was one procured in either of the Carolinas. I much doubt if they are ever even seen in any section of the Floridas!" Wilson: "Build on the ground." Audubon: "Build on trees."

Golden Eye. Audubon approved: "Capital talk. Good, Wilson!!! Second you in this!" Here he filled a space with a skillful pencil sketch of barnyard fowl.

Shoveller. "When approached by the Wood Duck the Shoveller swells its neck and curving it high gives chase, and utters the while a whistle, a low rough gutteral sound, and again returns to its female or companion."

Marginalia written by Audubon on *American Ornithology* as extended by Charles Lucien Bonaparte (Philadelphia, 1825–33).
Volume I

Preface, iv. Beside a claim that the illustrator Titian Ramsay Peale drew "from the recent bird, and not from the preserved specimen," Audubon wrote: "John J. knows better, for he has seen Mr. Peale at work from skins brought 2,000 miles and not in the very least best order." Next to praise of the engraver Lawson he wrote: "This wonderful hero of the Graver, for ever and in defiance of all that can be said to him on the subject, alters the Drawings and regularly represents Both *thighs* and consequently both Legs as if belonging to one side. J.J.A., who knows a little of neighbor Lawson."

Fork-tailed Flycatcher. Bonaparte: " . . . a great rarity . . ." Audubon: "Had my good friend C—— B—— rambled with me along the flats of the mouth of the Mississippi Valley he would not call it so very rare a bird."

Female Golden-Crowned Gold-Crest. "No bird of this kind will ever eat dead food. J.J.A." Bonaparte: "moves in small bands." Audubon: "Quite the contrary. I have seen upwards of 50 collected at once in Louisiana."

Yellow-Headed Troopial. Bonaparte: "Eats no fruits; insects only, and worms, grains and small seeds." Audubon: "What an error."

Cape May Warbler. Female. Bonaparte: It can be mistaken for "an imperfect *Sylvia coronata.*" Audubon: "I cannot conceive how Charles B.

can for a moment have thought so. This observation must belong to the illustrious Say." Near the admission of Bonaparte that neither he nor Wilson had obtained a supply, nor heard its song, Audubon wrote: "Can any naturalist be satisfied with this?"

Great Crow Blackbird. For the enraged comments of Audubon see pages 162 and 165.

Burrowing Owl. "Owls do not fly heavily nor do they confine their hunting times to the alternative twilights, but lightly . . . with great swiftness, pouncing on their prey as valiantly as most expert falcons. J.J.A."

Cliff Swallow. Bonaparte: "It is probable that they rear two broods in that region [Rockies], though in Kentucky and Ohio, agreeably to Mr. Audubon, they have but one in the year." Audubon: "Why is it *probable?* When the summers are positively shorter than in either Kentucky or Ohio."

Wild Turkey. Audubon furnished a lengthy description for this biography, which, at points, he faulted. As for the allegedly "remarkable voice of their wooing," he wrote: "Must acknowledge this to be beyond anything *I* ever heard or saw." Also: "I would prefer saying that the young males are distinguished when very small from the females by the great length of neck and legs and more stately appearance that is never lost." After describing "two males fighting," he concluded: "The most singular remarks and yet a very common occurrence is that the moment the vanquished is dead the conqueror treads it under foot with all the movements usually employed to caress a female." Where Bonaparte wrote that the young rarely survive a complete wetting, Audubon noted: "Against this inconvenience or misfortune the mother, like a good Phisician, plucks the buds of the Spice Wood Bush and gives it to her young, thus saving the lives of many." He denied that old turkeys cease to moult regularly: "Wild Turkeys owned by myself that I knew to be more than 10 years of age never exhibited such appearance when the freedom of the forests was granted them every day."

Volume IV (Annotations written in Boston in 1833)

Condor. Audubon: "A splendid figure after all." Also: "Bring me the vulture that can call with a 'shrill' note and I, poor I, will pay £1000." The assertion that the bird goes "through the belly" in order to "extract all the bones," elicited: "Wont do. Shocking story." "Fudge! . . . all fudge," as to method of discovering carrion. He denied that alligators' eggs are eaten: "Our alligators form nests of such strength as all vultures in the creation could not perforate." Bonaparte: "They swallow bones and flesh together." Audubon: "Never!"

Glossy Ibis. Audubon: "The body stands at an angle of nearly 45 degrees while the bird is walking" and it is *not* "kept almost horizontal." To the remark, "Nothing is yet ascertained of their mode of propagation," he retorted: "How does any Bird propagate?"

Sandpiper. "Humbug," Audubon wrote at one point; but he thought the description "excellent" on the whole, while considering the figure drawn by Swainson "much better."

Peale's Egret Heron. At one point Audubon remonstrated, "This will not hold, my learned friend!" He disagreed with the idea that their flesh is "quite unpalatable." Down, at one point, came his pencil with: "Damn Mr. Lawson!—" And: "I do not see how the formation of their feet goes to enable them to watch their prey." That the bird would strike at almost any fish drew: "Who is *he* that ever saw it strike a whale?" (To Audubon the latter was apparently not a mammal.)

Esquimaux Curlew. Bonaparte: "mute." Audubon: "When are they mute? Fudge!"

Yellow-Breasted Rail. Bonaparte: "nocturnal disposition, hide closely by day." Audubon: "This is wrong. It is a well ascertain [*sic*] fact that they are diurnal as well as nocturnal, having seen them in the Floridas at meridian."

Compiled by Alice Ford at the Audubon Memorial Museum, Henderson, Kentucky, in 1951.

SELECTED BIBLIOGRAPHY

Manuscript and Archival Materials: Private Collections

Bakewell, Mrs. Donald, Estate of. Sewickley, Pa. Documents, letters; diary and autobiographical sketch of Thomas Woodhouse Bakewell.
Lavigne, Madame Henri. Couëron, France. Papers of Jean Audubon.
Martin, Henry Bradley. New York. The 1826 journal.
Moore, Sir Alan Hilary, Estate of. Battle, Sussex, England. Waterton letter collection.
Pears, Thomas Clinton III. Pittsburgh. Papers of Thomas Pears. Sara White Pears, and laterals. Presented to Princeton University, 1985.
Shaffer, Susan Lewis, Estate of. Cincinnati, Ohio. Letters, papers, reminiscences of William Gifford Bakewell and family; MS. journal of William Bakewell, his father.
Tyler, Morris. New Haven, Conn. Documents, letters, papers, memorabilia, including collection of Victor Morris Tyler. Presented in part to Yale University, 1985.

Manuscript and Archival Materials: Other Collections

American Museum of Natural History, New York. MSS. of *Ornithological Biography;* selected MSS. dealing with Cooper, Peale, and Ward.
American Philosophical Society, Philadelphia. Notable letter collection, published in part in *Letters of John James Audubon.* Microfilm of Bonaparte collection of Audubon letters in the library of the Muséum Nationale d'Histoire Naturelle, Paris. Ord-Waterton letters from the collection of Mrs. Yvonne Waterton.
Archives de Bayonne, France. Claude Audubon family records.
Archives de la Charente Maritime, La Rochelle, France. Bouffard papers.
Archives Départementales de Loire-Atlantique, Nantes, France. Jean Audubon report as Republican civil commissioner; marriage record of his sister; miscellaneous parish records; passenger lists.
Archives de la Marine, Rochefort-sur-Mer, France. Service record of Audubon and related records of his father, Jean Audubon.
Archives Municipales, Nantes, France. Birth and death registers.
Archives Nationales, Paris. Letter of Audubon to Baron de la Brouillerie; Louis A. Tarascon file. Passenger lists.
Archives de la Roche-sur-Yon, France. Birth and marriage records.

Audubon Memorial Museum, Henderson, Ky. Letters, ledgers, documents, deeds; notarized "transcript" of banished 1828 Audubon diary.
British Museum, London. Bewick-Donovan letters.
Buffalo Museum of Science. Howland MSS., letters and papers.
Charleston Museum, Charleston, S.C. Bachman collection.
Filson Club, Louisville, Ky. Miscellaneous files.
Friends Library, London. Rathbone Collection.
Harvard University, Cambridge, Mass. 8 vols. of accounts of Audubon and sons; notable letter collection, published in part in *Letters of John James Audubon;* account books; MS. journals, 1820–21, 1840–43.
Henderson Records Office, Henderson, Ky. Land transfers and litigation records.
Historical Society of Pennsylvania, Philadelphia. Letters and papers.
Jefferson County Court House, Louisville, Ky. Records.
Linnaean Society, London. Swainson collection.
Liverpool City Library. Rathbone and Roscoe collections.
Ministère de la France d'Outre-Mer, Paris. Registers, files.
Missouri Historical Society, St. Louis. Chouteau, Walsh, Moffitt collections.
Montgomery County Court House, Norristown, Pa. Records, deeds, wills.
Nantes Archbishropic, France. Baptismal record of Audubon.
National Archives, Washington, D.C. Land tracts; ship landings and registries; subscription records.
National Audubon Society, New York. Letters; *Ornithological Biography* MSS.
New-York Historical Society, New York. "Stock purchase," MS.
New York Public Library, New York. Sully MS. journal, Burgess diary, letters. Berg Room, letter.
New York Surrogate's Court, New York. Audubon family wills.
Philadelphia Academy of Natural Sciences. Lawson Collection, letters.
Philadelphia City Hall. Records.
Presbyterian Historical Society, Philadelphia. Records.
Princeton University Library, Princeton, N.J. Notable letter collection, published in part in *Letters of John James Audubon;* two *Ornithological Biography* MSS.
Royal Society of Arts Library, London. Mease letters.
Service Historique de la Marine, Paris. Jean Audubon service record.
Tulane University Library (Howard-Tilton Memorial Library), New Orleans. Six letters in French, Audubon to Rozier.
University of Edinburgh. Wernerian Society minutes.
University of Wisconsin, Madison. Victor Gifford Audubon papers.
Yale University (Beinecke Library), New Haven. 118 MSS. of *Ornithological Biography;* letters.
York Public Library, York, England. Letters.
Winterthur Museum, Library, Wilmington, Del. Sully family letters.

Biographies, Memoirs, Letters, and Journals

Aldington, Richard. *Charles Waterton.* London, 1944.
Arthur, Stanley Clisby. *Audubon: An Intimate Life of the American Woodsman,* New Orleans, 1937.

[Atkins, Anna]. *Memoirs of J. G. Children, Esq.* Westminster, 1853.
Audubon, John James. *Audubon and His Journals.* Edited by Maria R. Audubon, with notes by Elliott Coues. 2 vols. New York, 1897; reprint, 1962. MS. journal of 1826 proves this compilation of 1826–28, 1833, and 1843 MSS. to be bowdlerized and heavily edited. First edition includes most of the episodes published in *Ornithological Biography.*
———. [Four letters to Rozier, originals now at Tulane University], *The Cardinal* (Sewickley, Pa.), Vol. IV, No. 7 (1938).
———. Introduction to *Ornithological Biography.* 5 vols. Edinburgh, 1831–39. Includes a brief, imprecise autobiography.
———. *Journal . . . Made During His Trip to New Orleans in 1820–1821.* Edited by Howard Corning. Cambridge, 1929.
———. "Letter to the Editor," *Monthly American Journal of Geology and Natural Science,* Vol. I (December 1831): 7, 31; *ibid.* (June 1832): 358–63.
———. "Letter . . . to William MacGillivray," *Edinburgh Journal of Natural History,* Vol. I (December 1838): 171. Dated April 18, 1837.
———. *Letters of John James Audubon, 1826–40.* Edited by Howard Corning. 2 vols. Cambridge, 1930. Limited to 220 copies.
———. "Letters . . . to Harlan, Townsend; letters of Bachman to Harlan," *The College of Physicians of Philadelphia: Fugitive Leaves from the Library,* n.s. 64–65 (October–November 1963). Twelve mimeographed pages, edited by W. B. McDaniel II, curator.
———. [Letters to and from MacGillivray], *Bulletin, Nuttall Ornithological Club,* Vol. V (1880): 193–204. Quoted in F. H. Herrick.
———. [Letters to and from MacGillivray, Baird, Harris, Swainson, *et al.*], *The Auk,* Vols. XXI– (1894 to present; old and new series). Scores of letters and pertinent articles, many since quoted in F. H. Herrick and others.
———. [Letters to and from William Swainson], *The Osprey,* Vols. IV–V (Washington, 1900), reprinted from *The Auk,* Vol. XV, 11–13. Quoted in F. H. Herrick.
Audubon, John Woodhouse. *Western Journal: 1849–1850.* Cleveland, 1906; Grabhorn Press, 1957, with additional plates. Reissued from *Illustrated Notes of an Expedition through Mexico and California* (New York, 1852), which appeared in *The Magazine of History, with Notes and Queries,* No. 41, pp. 1–83, with 4 col. plates (Tarrytown, 1915).
Audubon, Lucy, ed. *The Life of John James Audubon, the Naturalist.* Introduction by James Wilson. New York, 1869. Revised American edition of the Buchanan version (see below). Erroneous at many points.
Audubon, Maria Rebecca. "Audubon's Story of His Youth," *Scribner's* Vol. XIII (1876): 267–87. Included as journal sketch, "Myself," in her edition of *Audubon and His Journals* (New York, 1897).
Bachman, C. L. *John Bachman.* Charleston, 1888. Based on Charleston Museum letters, heavily edited.
Bakewell, Thomas W. "Audubon and Bakewell, Partners; Sketches of the Life of Thomas Woodhouse Bakewell . . . by Himself," *The Cardinal,* Vol. IV, No. 2 (1935).
Biographical Encyclopedia of Kentucky. Cincinnati, 1878. On Daniel Boone, John Colmesnil, Tarascons, *et al.*
Bölön, Alexander Farkas de. *Travels in North America,* 1834. The "Russian general" referred to in *Life of Audubon.*

Brannon, Peter A. *Edward Harris, Friend of Audubon.* New York, 1947.

Brewer, Thomas M. "Reminiscences . . ," *Harper's New Monthly Magazine,* Vol. LXI (1880): 666–75. Numerous Audubon letters.

Buchanan, Robert, ed. *The Life and Adventures of John James Audubon, the Naturalist.* London, 1868. Edited from the MS. arranged by Lucy Audubon and the Reverend Charles Coffin Adams in New York. Bowdlerized, revised. The Buchanan edition was publicly renounced by Lucy Audubon, although many imprecisions are apparently her own.

Call, Richard E. *The Life and Writings of Rafinesque.* Louisville, 1895. Indictment of Audubon for his practical joke.

Cap, P.-A. *Audubon, naturaliste américain.* Paris, 1862.

Cassinia. 1908–1909. George Ord biographical sketch.

Delecluze, E. J. *Louis David, son école et son temps.* Paris, 1855. No mention of Audubon, who by 1855 was famous enough even in Paris to have been singled out if there were reason.

Dictionary of American Biography. New York, 1921–24. Vols. I–XXI.

Dictionary of Artists. Edited by D. H. Wallace and G. C. Groce. New Haven, 1957.

Dictionary of National Biography. London and New York, 1885–1901. Vols. I–LXIII.

Dunlap, William. *Diary.* . . . 3 vols. New York, 1930.

Godwin, Parke. "John James Audubon," in *Homes of American Authors, by Various Writers.* New York, 1896.

Gosse, P. *The Squire of Walton Hall* [Waterton]. London, 1940.

Greg, Mrs. Eustace, ed., *Reynolds-Rathbone Diaries & Letters, 1753–1839.* University of Edinburgh, 1905.

Griswold, Rufus W. *The Prose Writers of America.* Philadelphia, 1847.

Günther, Albert. " . . . Unpublished Correspondence of William Swainson. . . ," *Proceedings* of the Linnaean Society, 112th session. London, 1900. Twenty-four Audubon letters.

Hall, C. R. *Samuel Latham Mitchell.* New York: Columbia University Press, 1934.

Harris, Edward. *Up the Missouri with Audubon: The Journal of Edward Harris.* Edited by John Francis McDermott. Norman, 1951. 1843 journal; with introduction and notes by the editor.

Herrick, Frances Hobart. *Audubon the Naturalist.* New York, 1917; 1938 revised, with Foreword and Postscript: "Audubon and the Dauphin." Indispensable but by now fallible and incomplete source; for nearly half a century the standard.

Irwin, R. A., ed. *Letters of Charles Waterton.* London, 1944.

MacGillivray, William. *A Memorial Tribute to . . . MacGillivray.* Edinburgh, 1901.

Pennsylvania Monthly, Vol. X (1879): 443–55. "Private Letters of Wilson, Ord and Bonaparte."

Rathbone, Eleanor. *William Rathbone, a Memoir.* London, 1905.

Scott, Sir Walter. *Journal.* Edited by J. G. Tait. Edinburgh and London, 1950. First faithful edition of MS. journal in Pierpont Morgan Library, New York City.

Simon, Charlie May. *Joseph Mason, Apprentice to Audubon.* New York, 1946. Interpretative rather than factual portrait.

Speed, John E., ed. *Letters of John Keats.* New York, 1883. Includes notes on boat deal.

Stoke, Edith S. *With Napoleon at St. Helena . . . the Memoirs of Dr. John Stokes.* London and New York, 1902. From the French by Paul Frémeaux.

Towles, Susan Starling. *John James Audubon in Henderson, Kentucky, a Sketch.* Louisville, 1925.

Tyler, Alice Jaynes. *I Who Should Command All.* New Haven, 1937.

Waterton, Charles. *Wanderings in South America.* London, 1825.

Wilson, Alexander. Lost (or missing?) diary. Passages quoted by F. H. Herrick, I, 224–25, differ at points from MS. of "Oral Communication," delivered by George Ord before the American Philosophical Society, September 18, 1840 (*Proceedings*, I, 1840). Read in Yvonne Waterton collection before its acquisition by the Society.

General Histories

Barker, Virgil. *American Painting.* New York, 1950. On George Cooke *et al.*

Chittenden, H. M. *The American Fur Trade of the Far West.* New York, 1935. On the Chouteau family.

Cuming, Fortescue. *A Tour of the Western Country.* Philadelphia, 1807. For Shippingport, Ky.

Edwards, Bryan. *An Historical Survey.* London, 1797. On Saint-Domingue.

Fréville. *L'Intendance de Bretagne.* 3 vols. Rennes, 1935. Includes plan of Nantes in the 1790s, and local history.

Moreau de St. Méry, Médéric-Louis-Elié. *La Partie Française de l'Isle de Saint-Domingue.* Paris, 1958 ed. Vol. III, 1302–23.

Stanislaus, F. A. (Baron de Wimpffen). *A Voyage to St. Domingo . . . 1788–90.* London, c. 1797.

Trollope, Mrs. *Domestic Manners of the Americans.* London, 1832. On Cincinnati art schools.

U.S. Work Projects Administration. *Henderson, a Guide.* Northport, L.I., c. 1941.

Newspapers

Baltimore Patriot [Winter, 1832]. Copied from *Charleston Courier.* Clipping in letter from Lucy Audubon to R. Havell, Jr., June 24, 1832, in Bonaparte Collection, Muséum Nationale d'Histoire Naturelle, Paris.

Edinburgh *Caledonian Mercury,* September 8, November 3, 1831. Corrects a false death notice.

Lexington, Ky., *The Reporter,* July 28, 1819. Obituary of James Berthoud, d. July 14 at Henderson.

London *Observer,* August 4, 1805: "A Cabinet established in New York for . . . natural history . . . has been given up . . . from want of public support."

New Orleans *Times-Picayune,* August 16, 1916: "Audubon in West Feliciana," by S. C. Arthur.

New York *Home News,* November 7, 1917: ". . . Minniesland."

New York *Mirror,* April 20, 1833: "Mr. Audubon."
New York Times (Sunday), April 27, 1958: "Audubon Estate Erased by Time."
Norristown, Pa., *Register,* April 6, 1808, notice of Audubon-Bakewell marriage on April 5.
Norristown *Times,* April 3, 1935. Reminiscences of Audubon's teaching days in Norristown.
Philadelphia *Aurora,* December 17, 1811. Manifesto of Don Alvarez de Toledo.
St. Louis *Daily Evening Gazette,* March 11, 14, 16, 1843. Impressions of and interviews with Audubon.
St. Louis *Missouri Reporter,* January 4, 1843. Berthoud partnership.

Periodicals and Learned Society Publications

Abert, John. "Habits of Climbing of the Rattlesnake," *Monthly American Journal of Geology and Natural Science,* Vol. I (1832): 221–23.
Allen, Elsa Guerdrum. "History of Ornithology before Audubon," *Transactions,* American Philosophical Society, n.s., Vol. XLI, Part 3 (1951): 387–591.
Audubon, John James. "Account of the Carrion Crow . . ." *Edinburgh Journal of Science,* Vol. VI (1826–27): 156–61.
——. ". . . the American Goshawk . . . ," *Edinburgh Journal of Natural and Geographical Science,* Vol. III (1831): 145–47. Reissued.
——. [Article on alligator; episodes on cougar, hurricane, and the Ohio reissued in *Ornithological Biography*], *Edinburgh New Philosophical Journal,* Vol. II (1826–27): 270–80; Vol. XI (1831): 103–15; Vol. XII (1831–32): 278–81.
——. "Facts and Observations Connected with the . . . Swallows . . . ," *Annals of the Lyceum of Natural History of New York,* Vol. I (1824): 166–68.
——. "The Fair Incognito," *The Collector,* March, 1948. Privately printed by Walter R. Benjamin, New York.
——. ". . . Habits of the Turkey Buzzard . . . ," *Edinburgh New Philosophical Journal,* Vol. II (1826–27): 172–84. Written to stress the importance of sight above that of smell in its quest.
——. "Journey up the Mississippi," *The Winter's Wreath,* for 1829 (1828): 104–27.
——. ". . . the Method of Drawing Birds . . . ," *Edinburgh Journal of Science,* Vol. VII (1828): 48–54. Reissued.
——. ". . . the Mississippi . . . ," *Edinburgh Literary Journal,* February–March 1831, pp. 140–42, 194–95. Reissued.
——. ". . . New Species of Quadrupeds . . ."; ". . . New North American Fox . . . ," *Proceedings* of the Academy of Natural Sciences, Philadelphia, Vol. I (1843): 92–103; Vol. VI (1852–53): 114–16.
——. "Notes on the Bird of Washington" [bald eagle], *Loudon's,* Vol. I (1828–29): 115–20. Reissued.
——. "Notes on the Rattlesnake . . . ," *Edinburgh New Philosophical Journal,* Vol. III (1827): 21–30.
——. "Notes on . . . Wild Pigeon," *Edinburgh Journal of Science,* Vol. VI (1826–27): 256–65. Reissued.

Audubon, Maria Rebecca. "Reminiscences of Audubon by a Granddaughter," *Scribner's*, Vol. XIII (1876): 333–36. (Daughter of John and Caroline.)

Audubon, Victor Gifford. ". . . Reply to Mr. Waterton's Remarks . . . ," ". . . in reply to Mr. Waterton," *Loudon's*, Vol. VI (1833): 369, 550–53.

Bachman, John. "An Account of Some Experiments Made on the Habits of the Vultures Inhabiting Carolina . . . ," *Journal of the Boston Society of Natural History*, Vol. I (1834): 15–31.

Bakewell, Rev. Gordon. "Reminiscences," *Publications* of the Louisiana Historical Society, Vol. V (1911): 31–41. In support of Louisiana birth legend.

[Bland, D. S.] "Audubon in Liverpool," *Outlook* (*Bulletin* of the Department of Extra-Mural Studies, University of Liverpool), No. 4 (1962): 3–6.

Brewster, David. "Mr. Audubon's Ornithology . . . ," *Edinburgh Journal of Science*, Vol. VI (1826–27): 184. First such recognition of work by a learned journal.

Colles, George W. "A Defense of Audubon," *Scientific American*, Vol. XCVIII (1908): 311.

Cosnil, M-L. "Audubon," *Informations et Documents* (Paris), October 1960.

Cuvier, Baron Georges. "*Rapport verbal à l'Académie Royale des Sciences . . . sur l'histoire naturelle des Oiseaux d'Audubon,*" *Mémoires* . . . , Vol. XI (1832); and *Le Moniteur* (Paris), October 1, 1828.

Dallet, F. J. "Citizen Audubon, a Documentary Discovery," Princeton University Library *Chronicle*, Vol. XXI (1959–60): 89–93. Naturalization papers.

Deane, Ruthven. "The Copper Plates of the Folio," *The Auk*, October 1908.

Dubois de Patellière, H. "Notes sur Couëron," *Revue Historique de l'Ouest*, Série Notices et Memoires, 1887.

Dwight, Edward H. "The Autobiographical Writings of J. J. Audubon," *Bulletin* of the Missouri Historical Society, Vol. 19, No. 1 (1962): 26–35. Unedited version of introduction to *Ornithological Biography*.

Elliott, Daniel G. "The Life and Services of J. J. Audubon," address before the New York Academy of Sciences, April 26, 1893, published in *Transactions*, Vol. XIII (1893): 43–57. For "Report" of grave monument committee, see Vol. XIII (1893): 23–69.

Eudel, P. "*Naintes en 1792,*" *Mémoires de la Société Archéologique de Nantes*, Vol. XLIX (1908): 207.

Ford, Alice. "An Early Audubon Drawing," Princeton University Library *Chronicle*, Vol. XV (1954): 169–78.

Fries, Waldemar H. "The Elephant Hunter," *Audubon Magazine*, Vol. LX (1958): 222–23, 244–45; Vol. LXII (1960): 6–8, 36, 42, 48. Search towards a census of existing folios of the *Birds*.

———. "Some Remarks on Audubon's Writings," address before Friends of Princeton Library, May 15, 1959, Princeton University Library *Chronicle*, Vol. XXI (1959–60): 1–7.

Gardner, Albert Teneyck. "John James Audubon . . . ," The Metropolitan Museum of Art *Bulletin*, May 1963, pp. 309–16. Publication of notice of certification of Kidd copy of Ivory-billed Woodpecker as by Audubon.

Gifford, Dr. G. E., Jr. "Audubon's Baltimore Physician Patrons," *Bulletin* of the University of Maryland School of Medicine, Vol. 49, No. 1 (1964): 14–20.

Goodwin, Parke. "John James Audubon," *U.S. Magazine & Democratic Review*, Vol. X (1842): 436–50.

Graustein, J. R. "Audubon and Nuttall," *Science Monthly*, Vol. LXXIV (1952): 84–90.

Griswold, Rufus W. "John James Audubon," *International Monthly Magazine*, Vol. II (1850–51): 469–74.

Guérin. *"Mort de Jean-Jacques Audubon, célèbre naturaliste américain,"* Journal *Universel*, Vol. III (1851): 70–71.

Harris, Edward [Articles on geology and species of the Upper Missouri], *Proceedings* of the Academy of Natural Sciences, Philadelphia, Vol. II (1845), 235–38, 300–301. For articles of interest on Harris's scientific work, see P. B. Street, "The E. Harris Collection of Birds," *Wilson Bulletin*, Vol. LX (1948): 167–84.

Harris, H. "Uncolored Prints from Havell's Engravings," *The Auk*, January 1918.

Herrick, F. H. "Audubon and the Dauphin," *The Auk*, Vol. LIV (1937).

Hutt, W. N. "Audubon the Original Nature Fakir," *Scientific American*, Vol. XCVIII (1908): 59.

Lallié, Alfred. "Diocèse de Nantes Pendant la Révolution," *Notices Biographiques*, 1893. Vol. 2 mentions Tardiveau, who baptized Audubon.

Lewis, H. F. "Some Canadian Auduboniana," *Canadian Field-Naturalist*, December 1933.

Minerva, The. Vol. I, n.s. (1824): 312–13. First published comment (anonymous) on Audubon's ornithological bent.

New York Lyceum of Natural History. "Report of a committee . . . the splendid work of Mr. Audubon . . . ," *Silliman's American Journal of Science and Arts*, Vol. XVI (1829): 353–54.

"North, Christopher" [John Wilson]. ". . . 'Ornithological Biography,'" *Blackwood's Magazine*, Vol. XXX (1831): 1–16; Vol. XXX (1831): 247–80.

Parker, Kenneth C. "Audubon's Mystery Birds," *Natural History*, Vol. 90, No. 4 (April 1985): 88ff.

Pennsylvania Magazine of History and Biography, Vols. I–LXXV (1877–1951). Various biographical references.

Perkins, S. E. "Episodes in the Life of Audubon in Indiana," *Wilson Bulletin*, Vol. 48, No. 1 (1936): 17–22.

Rice, Howard C., Jr. "Mr. Audubon's Lucy," Princeton University Library *Chronicle*, Vol. XXIV (1963): 128–34.

Richards, I. T. "Audubon, Joseph Robert Mason, and John Neal," *American Literature* (Durham, N.C.), Vol. VI (1934): 122–40.

St. Jordan, David. "Rafinesque," *Popular Science Monthly*, Vol. XXIX (1886): 212–21.

Stevens, G. A. "Audubon's Journey up the Missouri River, 1843," *North Dakota Historical Society Quarterly*, Vol. X, No. 2 (April 1943). Issued also as a leaflet.

Swainson, William. ". . . the Work . . . by Mr. Audubon," *Loudon's*, Vol. I (1828–29): 43–52.

Waterton, Charles. [Attacks on Audubon's published paper on the rattlesnake], *Loudon's Magazine of Natural History*, Vol. VI (1833): 464–65; Vol. VII (1835): 663–68.

———. [Attacks the Audubon theory on the vulture's olfactories], *Loudon's*, Vol. V (1832): 233–41; Vol. VI (1833): 162–71, 465–68; Vol. VII (1834): 276–83.

———. "Audubon's . . . Birds of America," *Loudon's*, Vol. VIII (1835): 236–38. Not reprinted with other articles in his *Essays*.

Williams, George A. "Robert Havell, Junior, Engraver of Audubon's 'The Birds of America,'" *Print-Collector's Quarterly*, Vol. VI (1916): 225–57. Serious, but often in error.

Winterfield, Charles. "About Birds and Audubon," *American Review: A Whig Journal*, Vol. I (1845): 371–83. Recalls 1843 introduction.

Special Exhibitions

New York. National Audubon Society. *Audubon as an Animal Painter*, October 16–November 30, 1951. Catalog of the Third Audubon Centennial Exhibition. Introduction by Alice Ford.

Paris, France. Centre Culturel Américain. *John James Audubon, 1785–1851*, October–November 1960. Introduction by Dr. Howard C. Rice, Jr. First formal tribute outside America in this century.

Philadelphia, Pa. The Academy of Natural Sciences. *A National Exhibition of the Works of John J. Audubon, Commemorating the Hundredth Anniversary of the Publication of the Elephant Folio, "The Birds of America,"* April 26–June 1, 1938. First outstanding retrospective.

Princeton, New Jersey. Princeton University Library. *The World of John James Audubon*, May 15–September 30, 1959. Introduction by Dr. Howard C. Rice, Jr. Detailed record published in special "Audubon" issue of the Princeton University Library *Chronicle*, Vol. XXI, Nos. 1–2 (1959–60): 1–93. Preceded by a notable exhibition in 1951 commemorating the centennial of Audubon's death; no catalog.

Miscellaneous Sources

Beinecke, Frederick W. *The Birds of America*. New York, 1960. "A pictorial description of the original Folio in the library of Beinecke [Yale]."

Brown, Captain Thomas. *Ornithology of Alexander Wilson and Charles Lucien Bonaparte*. Folio. Edinburgh, Dublin, London, 1835. Plate XLI contains Wild Althea plant pirated from Audubon's Folio Plate XX. For piracies by Brown, refer to *Austral Avian Record*, Vol. IV, No. 7, pp. 176–94.

Bruet, E., ed. *Les Oiseaux d'Amerique* [d'Audubon]. 2 vols. Paris, 1945.

Coffin, Annie Roulhac. "Maria Martin (1796–1863)," reprinted from *The Art Quarterly*, Autumn, 1960, pp. 281–300.

Ford, Alice. *Audubon's Animals*. New York, 1951. Quadrupeds plates with unpublished mammal paintings and drawings; checklist.

———. *Audubon's Butterflies, Moths and Other Studies*. New York, 1952. An unknown sketchbook; first such illustrated tribute to Maria Martin's share.

———, ed. *Bird Biographies of John James Audubon*. New York, 1957. Abridged text of *Birds of America* octavo; twelve early drawings; foreword concerning differences between *Ornithological Biography* and octavo.

Fries, Waldemar H. *The Double Elephant Folio*. Chicago: American Libraries Association, 1974.

Graves, Algernon. *The Royal Academy of Arts . . . Dictionary . . . 1769–1904*. London, 1905–1906. Only Victor Gifford Audubon exhibited.

Holbrook, John E. *Herpetology*. 5 vols. Charleston, 1835–37; discontinued, 1842. Maria Martin, Plate 11 (Vol. III); George Lehman, Plates 8–12 (Vol. I).

Iredale, Thomas. "Audubon in Australia," *Australian Zoologist*, Vol. 11, Pt. 4 (1951): 318–21.

Peters, Harry T. *America on Stone*. New York, 1931.

Prideaux, S. T. *Aquatint Engraving*. 1909. On Havell *et al.*

Swainson, William. "J. J. Audubon, Animal Painter." In *Taxidermy, Bibliography and Biography. The Cabinet Cyclopedia*. Compiled by D. Lardner. London, 1840. A caustic pen.

Welker, R. H. *Birds and Men*. Cambridge: Belknap Press, 1955.

Zabriskie, George A. *The Story of a Priceless Art Treasure: The Original Water Colors of John James Audubon*. Ormond Beach, Fla., 1950.

A brief compendium, compiled by Alice Ford, of errata in works by Arthur, Dwight, Fries, and Herrick is available for reference at the Frick Art Reference Library, New York.

INDEX